ASP.NET 2.0
All-in-One Desk Refe...
For Dummies®

D1398709

Standard Controls

Control	Description
Label	Displays text on the page.
Textbox	Lets the user enter text.
Button	Lets the user submit a page.
LinkButton	Same as a Button, but resembles a hyperlink.
ImageButton	Same as a Button, but displays an image.
CheckBox	Lets the user select an option.
CheckBoxList	Displays a list of check boxes.
RadioButton	Lets the user select one of several options.
RadioButtonList	Displays a list of radio buttons.
Image	Displays an image.
ListBox	Displays a list of items.
DropDownList	Displays a drop-down list of items.
MultiView	Creates multiple views, each of which contains a group of controls. Only one view is visible at a time.
Wizard	Creates a wizard that consists of multiple steps.
Calendar	Displays a calendar.
FileUpload	Lets the user upload a file.

Page Directives

Directive	Description
Page	Marks the start of a page.
Master	Marks the start of a master page.

Master Page Controls

Control	Description
ContentPlaceHolder	Indicates the location of content in a master page. Used in master pages only.
Content	Indicates content that should be placed in a ContentPlaceHolder control. Used only in content pages.

Validation Controls

Control	Description
RequiredFieldValidator	Ensures that the user enters data.
CompareValidator	Compares the entered data with a constant, the value of another control, or a data type.
RangeValidator	Ensures that the entered data falls within a given range.
RegularExpressionValidator	Ensures that the entered data conforms to a specified pattern.
CustomValidator	Lets you perform custom validation.
ValidationSummary	Displays a summary of validation errors.

For Dummies: Bestselling Book Series for Beginners

ASP.NET 2.0
All-in-One Desk Reference
For Dummies®

Cheat Sheet

Data Source Controls

Control	Description
SqlDataSource	Connects to a SQL database.
AccessDataSource	Connects to an Access database.
ObjectDataSource	Connects to a custom object.
XmlDataSource	Connects to XML data.
SiteMapDataSource	Connects to a sitemap file. (Used with navigation controls.)

Data Controls

Control	Description
GridView	Displays database data in a grid format.
DataList	Displays database data as a list.
DetailsView	Displays details for a single database record.
FormView	Displays a form for database data.
Repeater	Displays repeating data.

Navigation Controls

Control	Description
Menu	Displays a menu.
TreeView	Displays a tree derived from XML data or a SiteMapDataSource control.
SiteMapPath	Displays the user's location in the Web site.

Login Controls

Control	Description
Login	Lets the user log in to the application.
LoginStatus	Displays the user's login status.
LoginName	Displays the user's login name.
LoginView	Lets you display custom content based on the user's login status.
CreateUserWizard	Lets the user create an account.
ChangePassword	Lets the user change his or her password.
PasswordRecovery	Lets the user recover a lost password.

Copyright © 2006 Wiley Publishing, Inc.
All rights reserved.

Item 8598-9.

For more information about Wiley Publishing, call 1-800-762-2974.

For Dummies: Bestselling Book Series for Beginners

ASP.NET 2.0
ALL-IN-ONE DESK REFERENCE
FOR
DUMMIES®

by Doug Lowe, Jeff Cogswell, and Ken Cox, Microsoft MVP

WILEY

Wiley Publishing, Inc.

ASP.NET 2.0 All-in-One Desk Reference For Dummies®

Published by
Wiley Publishing, Inc.
111 River Street
Hoboken, NJ 07030-5774

www.wiley.com

For general information on our other products and services, please contact our Customer Care Department within the U.S. at 800-762-2974, outside the U.S. at 317-572-3993, or fax 317-572-4002.

For technical support, please visit www.wiley.com/techsupport.

Wiley also publishes its books in a variety of electronic formats. Some content that appears in print may not be available in electronic books.

Library of Congress Control Number: 2006922516

ISBN-13: 978-0-471-78598-9

ISBN-10: 0-471-78598-9

Manufactured in the United States of America

10 9 8 7 6 5 4 3 2

1B/SQ/QW/QW/IN

WILEY

About the Author

Doug Lowe has written a bevy of computer books, including more than 35 For Dummies books. Among his most recent are ASP.NET Everyday Applications For Dummies, Java All-In-One Desk Reference For Dummies, Networking For Dummies, 7th Edition, Networking For Dummies All-In-One Desk Reference, Second Edition, PowerPoint 2003 For Dummies, and Word 2003 All-In-One Desk Reference For Dummies. He lives in sunny Fresno, California, where the weather is always bad for half of the farmers, with his wife, the youngest of three daughters, and a couple of crazy dogs. He is the Information Technology Director for Blair, Church & Flynn Consulting Engineers, an engineering firm in nearby Clovis, CA.

Jeff Cogswell is a software engineer and trainer living in the Cincinnati area. He has written several books, including two previous Dummies books, one on C++ and one on LAMP. When not programming or writing about computers, he enjoys traveling and writing fiction and screenplays. Jeff also conducts ASP.NET training sessions; contact him at training@jcogs.com or visit www.jcogs.com for more information.

Ken Cox is a Canadian writer and programmer whose claim to fame is that he has chatted in English and French with Queen Elizabeth II of England. His degree in Radio and Television Arts from Ryerson University led to a 25-year career as a broadcast journalist in Toronto and Quebec City. Waving his college certificate in Technical Communication, he launched a second career as a technical writer for companies including Nortel (yes, before it wilted).

Somehow, he parlayed zero/zilch formal training in computers into a third career as a programming writer, technical editor, and Web developer. Microsoft has repeatedly honoured him as a Most Valuable Professional (MVP) for ASP.NET in recognition of his contributions to the .NET developer community.

Ken, his wife Vilia, and their dog Goldie (a GoldenDoodle) spend spring, summer, and fall at a peaceful lakefront home in a forest in Nipissing Township, Ontario. They winter in Victoria, British Columbia.

Dedication

To Debbie, who wondered where I was.

— Doug Lowe

To my wife, Vilia, for encouraging me to pursue my dreams.

— Ken Cox

Author's Acknowledgments

I'd like to thank everyone who helped make this book happen, starting with project editor Blair Pottenger, who did a great job guiding this project through from start to finish. I'd also like to thank my co-authors Ken Cox and Jeff Cogswell, and copy editor Barry Childs-Helton who dotted my t's and crossed my eyes, or something like that, and managed to turn my strange ramblings into readable English. And, as always, thanks to all the behind-the-scenes people who chipped in with help whenever help was needed.

— Doug Lowe

Thanks to Scott Guthrie, Nikhil Kothari, Rich Ersek and the the rest of Microsoft's Web Platform & Tools team for creating the fascinating ASP.NET technologies.Thanks also to Katie Feltman, Blair Pottenger, and Doug Lowe for giving me the opportunity to contribute to this book.

— Ken Cox

Publisher's Acknowledgments

We're proud of this book; please send us your comments through our online registration form located at www.dummies.com/register/.

Some of the people who helped bring this book to market include the following:

Acquisitions, Editorial, and Media Development

Project Editor: Blair J. Pottenger

Acquisitions Editor: Katie Feltman

Copy Editor: Barry Childs-Helton

Technical Editor: Ken Cox

Editorial Manager: Kevin Kirschner

Media Development Specialists: Angela Denny, Kate Jenkins, Steven Kudirka, Kit Malone, Travis Silvers

Media Development Coordinator: Laura Atkinson

Media Project Supervisor: Laura Moss

Media Development Manager: Laura VanWinkle

Media Development Associate Producer: Richard Graves

Editorial Assistant: Amanda Foxworth

Sr. Editorial Assistant: Cherie Case

Cartoons: Rich Tennant (www.the5thwave.com)

Composition Services

Project Coordinator: Jennifer Theriot

Layout and Graphics: Claudia Bell, Carl Byers, Andrea Dahl, Denny Hager, Joyce Haughey, Stephanie D. Jumper, Barry Offringa, Melanee Prendergast, Julia Trippetti

Proofreaders: John Greenough, Leeann Harney, Christy Pingleton, Linda Quigley

Indexer: Kevin Broccoli

Publishing and Editorial for Technology Dummies

Richard Swadley, Vice President and Executive Group Publisher

Andy Cummings, Vice President and Publisher

Mary Bednarek, Executive Acquisitions Director

Mary C. Corder, Editorial Director

Publishing for Consumer Dummies

Diane Graves Steele, Vice President and Publisher

Joyce Pepple, Acquisitions Director

Composition Services

Gerry Fahey, Vice President of Production Services

Debbie Stailey, Director of Composition Services

Table of Contents

Chapter 2: Using Profiles 715

Chapter 3: Site Navigation 739

Introduction

*W*elcome to *ASP.NET 2.0 All-in-One Desk Reference For Dummies,* the one ASP.NET programming book that's designed to replace an entire shelf full of the dull and tedious ASP.NET books you'd otherwise have to buy. This book contains all the basic and not-so-basic information you need to know to get going with ASP.NET Web programming, including the basics of working with Visual Studio or Visual Web Developer Express, using Web controls, working with databases, and learning the basics of both C# and Visual Basic .NET.

Of course, you can — and probably should — eventually buy separate books on each of these topics. It won't take long before your bookshelf is bulging with 10,000 or more pages of detailed information about every imaginable nuance of ASP.NET programming. But before you're ready to tackle each of those topics in depth, you need a birds-eye picture. That's what this book is about.

And if you already own 10,000 pages or more of ASP.NET information, you may be overwhelmed by the amount of detail and wonder, do I really need to read 1,200 pages about the .NET Framework classes just to create a simple Web page? And do I really need a five pound book on ADO.NET?

Truth is, most 1,200 page programming books have about 200 pages of really useful information — the kind you use every day — and about 1,000 pages of excruciating details that apply mostly if you're writing guidance-control programs for nuclear missiles or trading systems for the New York Stock Exchange.

The basic idea here is that we've tried to wring out the 100 or so most useful pages of information on eight different ASP.NET programming topics: basic programming, Web controls, HTML, C#, Visual Basic, database programming, the .NET Framework, and advanced programming topics. Thus, here's a nice, trim 900-or-so-page book that's really eight 100-page books. (Well, they didn't *all* come out to 100 pages each. But close!)

So whether you're just getting started with ASP.NET programming or you're a seasoned pro, you've found the right book.

About This Book

ASP.NET 2.0 All-in-One Desk Reference For Dummies is intended to be a reference for all the great things (and maybe a few not-so-great things) that you may need to know when you're writing ASP.NET programs. You can, of course, buy a huge 1,200-page book on each of the programming topics covered in this book. But then, who would carry them home from the bookstore for you? And where would you find the shelf space to store them? In this book, you get the information you need all conveniently packaged for you in between one set of covers.

This book doesn't pretend to be a comprehensive reference for every detail on these topics. Instead, it shows you how to get up and running fast so you have more time to do the things you *really* want to do. Designed using the easy-to-follow *For Dummies* format, this book helps you get the information you need without laboring to find it.

ASP.NET 2.0 All-in-One Desk Reference For Dummies is a big book made up of several smaller books — mini-books, if you will. Each of these mini-books covers the basics of one key element of programming, such as installing ASP.NET and compiling and running programs, or using basic ASP.NET statements, or using ADO.NET to write database programs.

Whenever one big thing is made up of several smaller things, confusion is always a possibility. That's why this book is designed to have multiple access points to help you find what you want. At the beginning of the book is a detailed table of contents that covers the entire book. Then, each mini-book begins with its own mini-table of contents that shows you at a mini-glance what chapters are included in that mini-book. Useful running heads appear at the top of each page to point out the topic discussed on that page. And handy thumbtabs run down the side of the pages to help you quickly find each mini-book. Finally, a comprehensive index lets you find information anywhere in the entire book.

This isn't the kind of book you pick up and read from start to finish, as if it were a cheap novel. If we ever see you reading it at the beach, we'll kick sand in your face or toss you an inflatable shark in a Hawaiian shirt. This book is more like a reference, the kind of book you can pick up, turn to just about any page, and start reading. You don't have to memorize anything in this book. It's a "need-to-know" book: You pick it up when you need to know something. Need a reminder on the properties for the ListBox control? Pick up the book. Can't remember the goofy syntax for C# `foreach` loops? Pick up the book. After you find what you need, put the book down and get on with your life.

All code listings used in this book are available for download at `www.dummies.com/go/aspnetaiofd`.

How to Use This Book

This book works like a reference. Start with the topic you want to find out about. Look for it in the table of contents or in the index to get going. The table of contents is detailed enough that you can find most of the topics you're looking for. If not, turn to the index, where you can find even more details — and (just as important) what pages they're on.

Of course, the book is loaded with information, so if you want to take a brief excursion into your topic, you're more than welcome. If you want to know (for example) the big picture on database programming, read all of Book 6. But if you just want the details on using the GridView control, go straight to Book 6, Chapter 3.

How This Book Is Organized

Each of the eight mini-books contained in *ASP.NET 2.0 All-in-One Desk Reference For Dummies* can stand alone. Here is a brief description of what you find in each mini-book.

Book 1: ASP.NET Basics

This mini-book contains the information you need to get started with ASP.NET. It includes a brief introduction to what ASP.NET is and why it's so popular, provides instructions on how to install Visual Studio .NET, and serves up the basics you need to know to create simple applications.

Book II: Web Controls

This mini-book covers all the basic server controls you'll use in your ASP.NET Web pages. You get familiar with basic controls such as labels and text boxes, and get the word on how to use validation controls to make sure the users of your application don't enter bad data. You'll also learn about more advanced controls such as list boxes, calendars, and wizards.

Book III: HTML

You can't do any serious ASP.NET programming without diving into the guts of HTML. The chapters in this mini-book show you how to code correct standards-based HTML markup and how to use advanced features such as CSS and client-side scripting.

Book IV: C#

This mini-book focuses on the C# programming language. You'll get a handle on data types, basic statements, and how to create classes that include features such as inheritance and polymorphism.

Book V: Visual Basic

If you don't want to use C#, you can turn to this mini-book to learn the alternative: Visual Basic. Here you find all the important details about how to code Visual Basic statements, how to work with classes, how to use arrays, and so on.

Book VI: Database Programming

Database programming is the heart of most ASP.NET applications. In this mini-book, you'll learn how to work with ASP.NET's powerful data sources and database controls, including the `GridView`, `FormView`, `DetailsView`, and `Repeater` controls. You also sneak up on a bit of XML in its native habitat, just for good measure.

Book VII: Using the .NET Framework

ASP.NET is a part of the .NET Framework, which provides thousands of classes that you can use as you develop your programs. The books in this part cover the .NET classes that are most useful for ASP.NET programming. You'll learn how to use classes that manipulate strings, dates, and collections. In addition, you'll learn how to use the new generic collection classes that were added for version 2.0 of ASP.NET and the .NET Framework.

Book VIII: Advanced ASP.NET Programming

This last mini-book gets into some of the more interesting aspects of ASP.NET programming, many of them new with version 2.0. Specifically, you get a shot at working with login controls, site navigation, themes, portals, and much more.

Icons Used in This Book

Like any *For Dummies* book, this book is chock-full of helpful icons that draw your attention to items of particular importance. You find the following icons throughout this book:

Pay special attention to this icon; it lets you know that some particularly useful tidbit is at hand.

Danger, Will Robinson! This icon highlights information that may help you avert disaster.

Did we tell you about the memory course we took?

Hold it — overly technical stuff is just around the corner. Obviously, because this is a programming book, almost every paragraph of the next 900 or so pages could get this icon. So we reserve it for those paragraphs that go into detail explaining how something works under the hood — probably deeper than you really need to know to use a feature, but often enlightening.

You also sometimes find this icon when we want to illustrate a point with an example that uses some ASP.NET feature that hasn't been covered so far in the book, but that is covered later. In those cases, the icon is just a reminder that you shouldn't get bogged down in the details of the illustration, and instead focus on the larger point.

Where to Go from Here

Yes, you can get there from here. With this book in hand, you're ready to plow right through the rugged ASP.NET terrain. Browse through the table of contents and decide where you want to start. Be bold! Be courageous! Be adventurous! And above all, have fun!

Book I

ASP.NET Basics

Contents at a Glance

Chapter 1: Welcome to ASP.NET Programming

In This Chapter

✔ Zeroing in on the advantages of ASP.NET

✔ Getting the hang of Web servers and Web browsers

✔ Comparing static and dynamic Web pages

✔ Dissecting a typical ASP.NET application

This chapter is a gentle introduction to the world of ASP.NET programming. In the next few pages, you'll learn what ASP.NET is and how it can be used to create Web applications. You'll also learn about the various versions of Visual Studio 2005 used to create ASP.NET applications. And, you'll also discover some features unique to the newest version of ASP.NET, known as ASP.NET 2.0.

Throughout this chapter, you'll find little snippets of ASP.NET program code. Some of this code will be in C# and some will be in Visual Basic. These are the two most commonly used programming languages for ASP.NET. If you aren't experienced with either of these languages, don't worry. The code shown here is pretty simple and straight forward, and you can always turn to Book 4 for more information about C# or Book 5 for more information about Visual Basic.

All code listings used in this book are available for download at www.dummies.com/go/aspnetaiofd.

What Is ASP.NET, and Why Is It So Great?

ASP.NET is a platform for developing Web-based applications. It lets you create sophisticated Web applications that can interact with users. For example, ASP.NET applications can use data-entry controls (such as text boxes and buttons) to accept input data from a user; process, retrieve, or update database data; and send the results of these operations back to the user.

ASP.NET isn't the only platform available for creating Web applications. Popular alternatives to ASP.NET include PHP, ColdFusion, and several Java-based tools such as Java Server Pages and Java Servlets. ASP.NET differs from these alternatives in several significant ways. The following sections describe the most important distinguishing features of ASP.NET.

Windows and IIS dependence

Unlike most alternatives, ASP.NET will only work on Microsoft Windows–based Web servers. That means the operating system must be a recent version of Windows, and the HTTP server software must be Microsoft's *Internet Information Services,* also known as IIS.

Specifically, ASP.NET 2.0 requires the following support software:

✦ Windows 2000 Server (with Service Pack 3) or Windows Server 2003. (For development systems, Windows 2000 with SP3 or Windows XP Professional is required.)

✦ Internet Information Services 5.0 or later. (IIS 6.0 is recommended.)

✦ Microsoft .NET Framework 2.0.

One practical advantage of ASP.NET is that it works entirely on Microsoft software — you don't have to fuss with installing and configuring software from multiple suppliers. However, the flipside of that advantage is that ASP.NET locks you into using the Microsoft platform. (Most of ASP.NET's alternatives will run on Linux, which is available from a variety of sources.) But if yours is already a Microsoft shop, you should be in good shape.

Note that although ASP.NET is tied to Windows and IIS, you do have alternatives to the Microsoft platform in two areas:

✦ **You don't have to use Microsoft's SQL Server as your database engine.** ASP.NET works well with Oracle and other database servers. (For more information, refer to Book 6.)

✦ **Your users don't have to use Internet Explorer as the default browser.** Users can access ASP.NET applications using other browsers such as Netscape and Mozilla's Firefox.

There is an open-source effort to run ASP.NET applications on Apache and other Web servers. For more information, refer to www.mono-project.com.

Object orientation

ASP.NET is inherently object-oriented. If you're new to programming, that probably doesn't mean much. But if you're familiar with programming and have worked with object-oriented programming languages such as C++ or Java, you'll appreciate the benefits immediately.

ASP.NET applications are made up from self-contained programming elements called *objects*. Simply put (don't you love it when you read that in a computer book?), an *object* is a programming entity that represents either some real-world object or an abstract concept. In ASP.NET, the most common type of object is a Page, which represents (you guessed it) an HTML page that can be displayed in a Web browser. Each ASP.NET page is derived from a class called `System.Web.Page`. (The term *class* refers to the code you write to define an object such as a page. For more information about what this means, refer to Chapter 3 of this mini-book.)

A major attraction of ASP.NET's object orientation is that it allows you to take advantage of a vast library of predefined classes known as the *.NET Framework*. (The part with the extra period is pronounced "DOT-net.") Many .NET Framework classes are designed specifically for working with ASP.NET — for example, those that represent controls such as text boxes, radio buttons, and drop-down lists. You'll also find classes that simplify the task of accessing data in a database. Plus, you'll find a host of useful, general-purpose classes that aren't specifically related to Web applications. (For more information about such classes, refer to Book 7.)

Choice of languages

Most Web-development platforms tie you to a specific language. For example, Java-based tools such as Java Server Pages tie you to the Java language; other tools, such as ColdFusion, use their own proprietary languages. But ASP.NET gives you the choice of two languages to use for your Web pages:

✦ **Visual Basic .NET:** Visual Basic .NET (VB.NET) is a modern version of the venerable Basic programming language. Basic was originally intended as a limited language designed for beginners, but the current version of Visual Basic is as powerful a language as you'll find.

✦ **C#:** C# (pronounced *C-Sharp*) is a relatively new language designed by Microsoft specifically for .NET. Its syntax is similar to Java, so if you're an experienced Java programmer, you won't have much trouble learning C#.

✦ **J#:** Microsoft's version of Java. This language isn't covered in this book, as it isn't used much for ASP.NET development.

Visual Studio

One of the best features of ASP.NET is Visual Studio, the integrated development environment that combines a Web-page editor, a code editor, a debugger, and several other development tools into one easy-to-use program. The more you work with Visual Studio, the more you come to appreciate the many ways it simplifies the job of creating ASP.NET Web applications.

Figure 1-1 shows an ASP.NET Web application being developed in Visual Studio, using a what-you-see-is-what-you-get Web-page editor. This approach is especially useful for designing Web pages by dragging and dropping controls such as labels, text boxes, and buttons onto the page. If you prefer to work directly with code, you can switch to Source view, call up the HTML that defines the application's pages, and edit it directly.

Figure 1-1:
Visual Studio makes it easy to create ASP.NET Web applications.

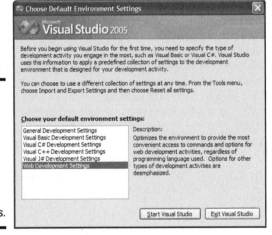

For more about how Visual Studio works, dig into Chapter 3 of this minibook; no need to obsess over it just now.

Understanding Web Servers and Browsers

One crucial point to understand about Web applications is that they work by using both client and server software:

✦ The *client* is a Web browser that runs on the end-user's computer. In most cases, the Web browser is Microsoft Internet Explorer, but other programs such as Mozilla Firefox can be used as the client.

✦ The *server* is software that runs on the server computer that hosts the Web application. For ASP.NET applications, the server software is always Microsoft Internet Information Services (also known as IIS). The server computer must also have Microsoft .NET Framework software installed, as ASP.NET is a part of the .NET Framework.

The server computer also typically has *database server* software (such as Microsoft SQL Server) installed. In some cases, the database server may run on a separate computer to improve the main server machine's performance.

You'll run into these two other alphabet-soup buzzwords constantly as you develop ASP.NET applications:

✦ *HTML* (short for *Hypertext Markup Language*) is a standardized set of markup tags used to format the Web pages displayed by a Web browser.

✦ *HTTP* (short for *Hypertext Transfer Protocol*) is the standardized protocol that Web browsers and Web servers use to communicate with each other. You'll learn more about how HTTP works in the next section.

Understanding Static Web Pages

The World Wide Web was originally designed to display *static pages* — that is, pages that are the same every time they are displayed. In fact, many pages available on the Internet today are still static pages.

A typical way to initiate display of a static Web page is for a user to enter the Web address of the page in a browser's address bar, or for a user to click a link that leads to the page. Either way, the browser sends an HTTP message called an *HTTP request* to the server specified by the Web address. This request message includes the name of the HTML file that defines the page being requested by the user. In addition, the request message includes the address of the browser that's requesting the file.

When the server machine receives the request, it locates the HTML file on its disk and sends the HTML back to the browser by way of an *HTTP Response* message. Then, when the browser receives the response, it decodes the HTML file and displays the Web page. Figure 1-2 shows how static pages work.

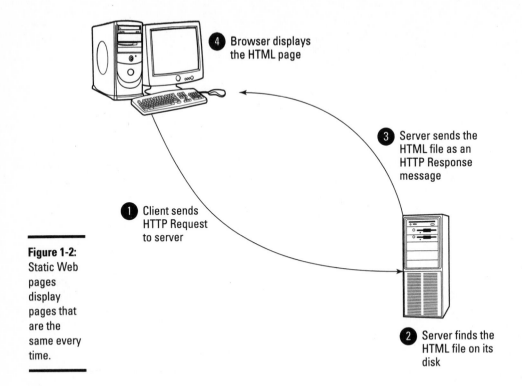

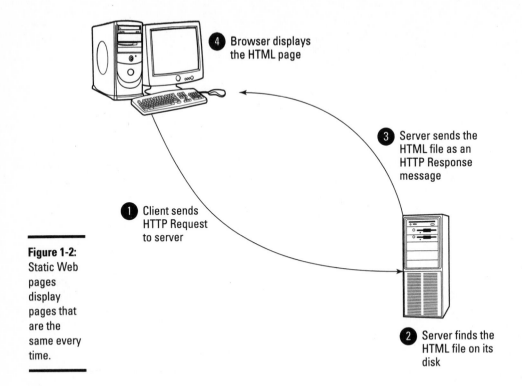4 Browser displays
the HTML page

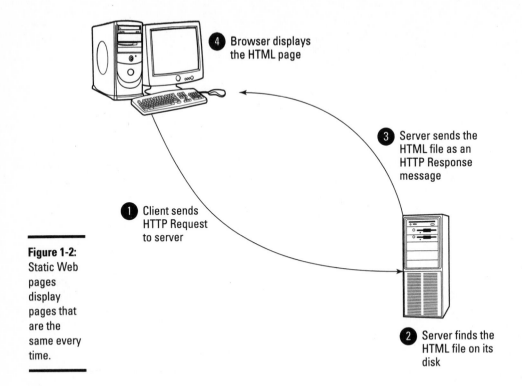3 Server sends the
HTML file as an
HTTP Response
message

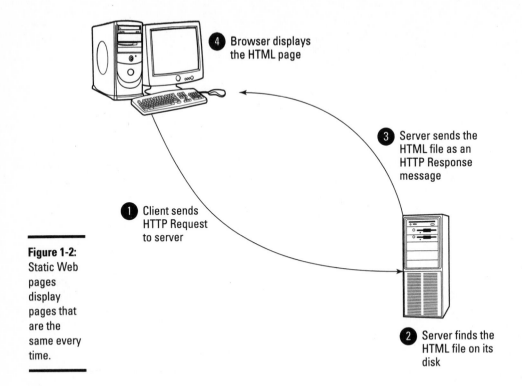1 Client sends
HTTP Request
to server

Figure 1-2:
Static Web
pages
display
pages that
are the
same every
time.

2 Server finds the
HTML file on its
disk

Understanding Dynamic Web Pages

Although the World Wide Web was originally designed for static Web pages, most Web pages these days display *dynamic content* — that is, content that changes each time the page is retrieved. Instead of retrieving HTML data from a file, dynamic Web pages work by running a program that *generates* the HTML sent back to the browser. The program can generate different HTML each time the page is requested.

Figure 1-3 shows how dynamic HTML pages work. As you can see, the first and last steps are the same as for static Web pages: The browser sends an HTTP request to the server to request the page, and when the browser receives the HTTP response, it displays the page. However, what goes on at the server is different: Instead of locating an HTML file on the disk, the server runs a program to generate the HTML for the requested page — and that's what returns to the user via an HTTP response.

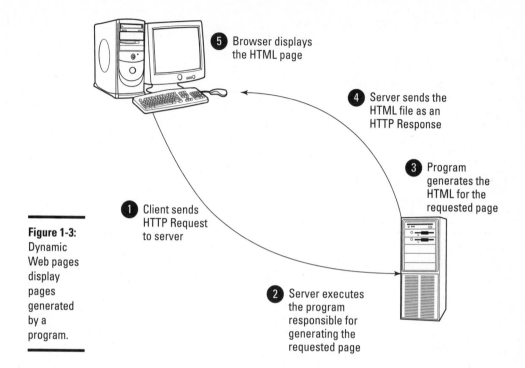

Figure 1-3:
Dynamic
Web pages
display
pages
generated
by a
program.

The usefulness of dynamic Web pages is that the program that generates
them can do just about anything necessary to generate the requested page.
In some cases, this might be simple. For example, the requested page might
consist mostly of static data, but might include the current date in a header
or footer. Then, the program that generates the page simply reads the static
part of the page from an HTML file, adds the current date, and sends the
page on to the user.

Sometimes the page consists almost entirely of dynamic data. For example,
the result page displayed by a search engine is mostly a set of search results
generated to show data retrieved from a database.

Looking at a Simple ASP.NET Application

To help you understand how a typical ASP.NET application works, Figure 1-4
presents a simple calculator application: It lets the user enter two numbers,
and when the user then clicks the Add button, the application adds up the
two numbers and displays the result.

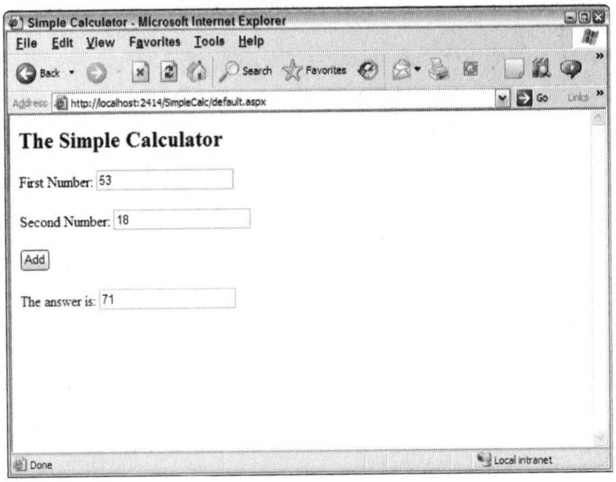

Figure 1-4:
A simple
calculator
application.

Although this application is simple enough, it illustrates many basic notions that underlie ASP.NET programming. Most importantly, the Simple Calculator application demonstrates how you can use ASP.NET *controls* on a Web page to retrieve data entered by a user, write code that processes the data, and modify the page that's sent back to the user so it shows the results of the page processing.

The Simple Calculator page includes four controls:

+ A text box that lets the user enter the first number to be added.

+ Another text box that lets the user enter the second number to be added.

+ A button the user can click to submit the page and calculate the sum of the two numbers.

+ A label that displays the result of the addition.

Of course, this sample ASP.NET application is trivial. More realistic ASP.NET applications consist of more than one page and usually retrieve information from a database. Still, this simple application is a good place to start learning about ASP.NET.

To develop a single-page ASP.NET application such as the Simple Calculator application, you create two source files:

+ **The markup file (or the** `.aspx` **file)** defines the appearance of the Web page.

+ **The code-behind file** provides the code that's executed when the user submits the page.

Separating the code that defines the appearance of the page from the code that defines the processing performed for the page is called *code separation*, and is considered by most programming gurus to be a good idea.

Although it's possible to write ASP.NET applications that combine the two types of code into a single file, Visual Studio uses a separate code-behind by default. Chapter 4 of this mini-book tells you more about how code separation works in ASP.NET.

The .aspx (Markup) File for the Simple Calculator Application

Listing 1-1 shows the file that defines the appearance of the Simple Calculator page in the previous section. (Note that this file assumes that the application is written using C#. If you're using Visual Basic, you'll see a few minor differences.)

Listing 1-1:   The appearance of the Simple Calculator (C#)

```
<%@ Page Language="C#" AutoEventWireup="true"
   CodeFile="Default.aspx.cs" Inherits="_Default" %>
<!DOCTYPE html PUBLIC "-//W3C//DTD XHTML 1.0
   Transitional//EN" "http://www.w3.org/TR/xhtml1/DTD/xhtml1-
   transitional.dtd">
<html xmlns="http://www.w3.org/1999/xhtml" >
<head runat="server">
    <title>Simple Calculator</title>
</head>
<body>
    <form id="form1" runat="server">
    <div>
        <h1>The Simple Calculator</h1>
        First number:
        <asp:TextBox ID="txtFirst" runat="server" />         →1
        <br /><br />
        Second number:
        <asp:TextBox ID="txtSecond" runat="server" />        →2
        <br /><br />
        <asp:Button ID="btnAdd" runat="server"               →3
           OnClick="btnAdd_Click" Text="Add" />
        <br /><br />
        The answer is:
        <asp:Label ID="lblAnswer" runat="server" />          →4
    </div>
    </form>
</body>
</html>
```

I don't expect you to leap to instant mastery of all (or even any) details of this file at this early stage, but take a look at this code now so you'll have an idea of what ASP.NET coding looks like. You'll be writing a lot of code that looks like this as you develop ASP.NET applications.

I would like to draw your attention to a few sections of this listing:

+ →**1:** This line defines the text box for the first number to be entered by the user. This text box is named `txtFirst`.

+ →**2:** This line defines the text box for the second number. This text box is named `txtSecond`.

+ →**3:** This line and the next line define the button the user clicks to add the number. The name of the button is `btnAdd`, the text displayed on the button is `"Add"` and the C# code that's run when the user clicks the button is called `btnAdd_Click`.

+ →**4:** This line defines the label that displays the result of the addition. The label is named `lblAnswer`.

The Code-Behind File of the Simple Calculator Application

After a look at the markup file for the Simple Calculator application, check out Listing 1-2: It shows the C# code-behind file. Don't be concerned if the details of this listing seem arcane at the moment; it's an early glimpse of what C# coding looks like for a simple ASP.NET Web page.

Listing 1-2:   The code-behind file of the Simple Calculator (C#)

```
using System;
using System.Data;
using System.Configuration;
using System.Web;
using System.Web.Security;
using System.Web.UI;
using System.Web.UI.WebControls;
using System.Web.UI.WebControls.WebParts;
using System.Web.UI.HtmlControls;
public partial class _Default : System.Web.UI.Page
{
    protected void btnAdd_Click(object sender,              →1
        EventArgs e)
```

```
    {
        decimal a = decimal.Parse(txtFirst.Text);
        decimal b = decimal.Parse(txtSecond.Text);
        decimal c = a + b;
        lblAnswer.Text = c.ToString();
    }
}
```

The part of this code you should focus on is identified with the `btnAdd_Click` routine (properly called a *method* in C#), marked by the →1 in the listing. This code converts the values entered by the user in the two text boxes to decimal values, adds the two values together, and displays the result in the label.

If you have done some C# (or perhaps Java) programming, you may be alarmed to notice that this code doesn't do any error checking. As a result, if the user doesn't enter a valid number in both text boxes, the program will crash with what's called an *unhandled exception* in .NET lingo.

Don't be concerned — this time. I didn't fall asleep while I was writing this program; I left out the error checkout on purpose, for two reasons. First, it keeps the example program simple; second, it provides a natural way to introduce the basic concepts of debugging in Chapter 4 of this mini-book.

That's enough of a quick look to provide a simple introduction to ASP.NET. Of course, there's a lot about ASP.NET that goes way beyond the basics of this chapter. If you're itching to get at it, okay — all in good time — but first things first: Make sure you've successfully installed Visual Studio on your computer (covered in the next chapter) and have taken a crack at developing simple ASP.NET applications (described in Chapter 3 of this mini-book).

Chapter 2: Installing Visual Studio Web Developer 2005 Express Edition or Visual Studio 2005

In This Chapter

✔ Comparing the editions of Visual Studio

✔ Registering and test-driving Visual Web Developer Express

✔ Installing Visual Studio successfully

*B*efore you can use Visual Studio to develop ASP.NET 2.0 applications, you must install the Visual Studio software. This chapter introduces you to the various versions of Visual Studio available for you to choose from, and then walks you through the process of installing the most popular version for ASP.NET Web development — Visual Studio Web Developer Express Edition. (The setup process for other versions of Visual Studio is similar.)

Looking at Visual Studio 2005 Editions

Like most Microsoft software, Visual Studio 2005 comes in several different versions. Here's the rundown on each one:

✦ **Visual Studio 2005 Standard Edition:** This is the basic version of Visual Studio 2005. It includes everything you need to develop Windows applications using Visual Basic, C#, or C++, or ASP.NET 2.0 Web applications using Visual Basic or C#. It also comes with SQL Server Express Edition, a scaled-back version of SQL Server that's designed to use while you're developing applications that access a database.

✦ **Visual Studio 2005 Professional Edition:** This is a beefed-up version of the Standard Edition, with added features that are useful for professional developers — in particular, advanced debugging features and the capability to create complex Setup projects for deploying your applications.

✦ **Visual Studio 2005 Team Edition:** This is the top-of-the-line Visual Studio edition. It includes all the features of the Professional Edition, plus advanced features designed specifically for large development projects, such as built-in code profiling, unit testing, and project management features.

✦ **Visual Studio Web Developer 2005 Express Edition:** This is a low-cost version of Visual Studio that's designed for beginning and casual ASP.NET

Web developers. This edition of Visual Studio is sometimes referred to as *VWD Express* or even just *VWD*. VWD is described in greater detail in the next section.

Considering Visual Web Developer 2005 Express Edition

For most people getting started with ASP.NET 2.0, Visual Web Developer 2005 Express Edition (VWD) is the tool of choice. It includes everything you need to create basic Web applications in Visual Basic or C#. We recommend using this version while you're learning ASP.NET Web programming, for two reasons. First, it's simpler to use because it isn't cluttered up with features that aren't related to ASP.NET Web development. Second, it's cheap. In fact, you can download it for free from Microsoft until November 7, 2006. After that, it will cost a mere $49. That means major savings over the other editions, as summarized in Table 2-1.

Table 2-1	Pricing for Visual Studio 2005 Editions
Edition	*Price*
Visual Web Developer 2005 Express Edition	Free download until November 7, 2006. After that, $49.
Visual Studio 2005 Standard Edition	$299
Visual Studio 2005 Professional Edition	$799
Visual Studio 2005 Team Edition	$5,469

The following are some important things you need to know about VWD:

✦ VWD supports Web applications developed in either Visual Basic or C#.

✦ VWD includes SQL Server Express Edition, so you can use it to develop sophisticated database applications.

✦ Microsoft does not place any limits on how you can use VWD. Thus you can use VWD to develop commercial applications.

✦ VWD provides most of the same features as other editions of Visual Studio 2005 for Web development. However, there are a few features missing, such as advanced deployment tools.

Installing Visual Web Developer 2005 Express Edition

The following procedure shows you how to download and install the free version of Visual Web Developer 2005 Express Edition (VWD):

1. **Go to Microsoft's Web site and locate the Visual Web Developer 2005 Express Edition download page.**

At the time we wrote this, the download page was located at

`http://msdn.microsoft.com/vstudio/express/vwd/download/`

Microsoft has been known to change things around on its Web site, so if this address doesn't get you there, poke around a bit until you find it.

2. **Click the Download link.**

Opening the link begins the download. If a Security Warning dialog box appears, click Run to allow the download.

The initial download may take a minute or two, so please be patient. Eventually the Setup program shown in Figure 2-1 appears.

You can download Visual Web Developer 2005 Express Edition for free from Microsoft until November 7, 2006. After that, it will cost $49.

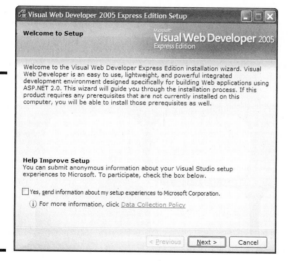

Figure 2-1:
The Visual
Web
Developer
2005
Express
Edition
Setup
program
comes
to life.

3. **Click Next.**

A screen displaying the license agreement appears. The license agreement was written by and for lawyers. Read it if you enjoy such things.

4. **Check the "I accept the terms of the License Agreement" check box, then click Next.**

The next dialog box asks whether you want to install two optional components: the product documentation and SQL Server 2005 Express Edition, as shown in Figure 2-2.

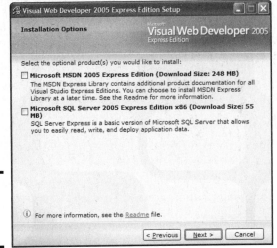

Figure 2-2:
What do
you want to
install?

5. Check both options, then click Next.

Doing so indicates that you want to install both the product documentation and SQL Server 2005 Express Edition.

The next dialog box, shown in Figure 2-3, lets you specify where you want the software installed on your hard drive. We suggest you accept the default.

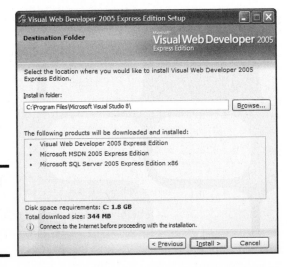

Figure 2-3:
Choose
where to
install the
software.

6. Click Next.

Now comes the l-o-n-g download and installation process, as shown in Figure 2-4. The download is well over 300 MB, so it will take awhile, even with a high-speed Internet connection.

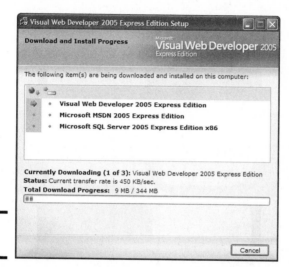

Figure 2-4:
Zzz.

After everything has been downloaded and installed, the screen shown in Figure 2-5 appears and congratulates you on your success, if a little prematurely. You're not really done yet.

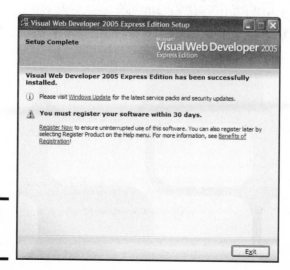

Figure 2-5:
Almost
done!

Although the screen shown in Figure 2-5 has a Register Now link that lets you register the product, don't click it just yet. If you do, you'll have to follow a somewhat awkward registration procedure. Instead, follow the steps listed in the next section ("Registering Visual Web Developer 2005 Express Edition) to register the software.

7. Click the Windows Update link.

This action takes you to the Windows Update Web site, where you can download any late-breaking updates to VWD, the .NET Framework, or Windows itself.

8. Follow the steps at the Windows Update Web site to update your computer.

This process takes a few minutes to complete, but the safety of having the latest security updates applied to your system is well worth the wait. Figure 2-6 shows the Windows Update Web site in action. Here, Windows Update has detected a few updates that need to be applied to our system.

If you use Internet Explorer and have blocked pop-up advertising, you'll need to watch for the yellow bar at the top of the window and enable any pop-ups that might try to open from the Windows Update site. Otherwise Windows Update won't work properly.

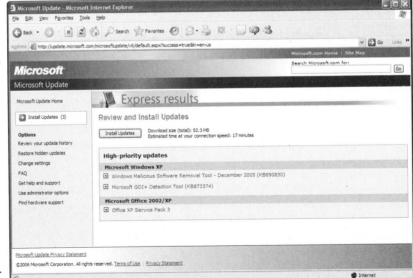

Figure 2-6: Windows Update automatically updates your system with the latest improvements to Windows and other components.

9. **Continue with the next step in the installation, and** *then* **register VWD by following the procedure described in the next section.**

10. **Click Exit.**

The Setup program graciously allows you to exit.

Registering Visual Web Developer 2005 Express Edition

After you've installed Visual Web Developer 2005 Express Edition (VWD), you have 30 days to register it. We suggest you don't put that off, especially since it takes only a few minutes. Here are the steps:

1. **Start Visual Web Developer 2005 Express Edition.**

To do so, click the Windows Start button, and then choose All Programs⇨ Microsoft Visual Web Developer 2005 Express Edition. Visual Web Developer springs to life, as shown in Figure 2-7.

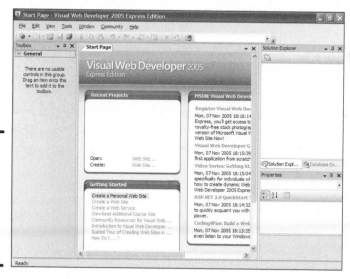

Figure 2-7:
Visual Web
Developer
2005
Express
Edition
comes
to life!

The first time you start Visual Web Developer, it spends a few minutes setting up its initial configuration. Don't worry: VWD will start much faster after this initial configuration is done.

2. Choose Help⇨Register Product.

This brings up the dialog box shown in Figure 2-8.

Figure 2-8:
This dialog box lets you register VWD.

3. Click the Register Now link.

This takes you to a Web page where you can register your copy of VWD.

4. Follow the steps at the registration Web site to register your copy of VWD; the following procedures get you started:

a. The VWD registration page requires you to create a Microsoft Passport account if you don't already have one.

b. After you sign in with Passport, the registration Web site asks for your name, e-mail address, and Zip code. You can also complete a little survey about the programming and technology topics you're interested in.

c. Eventually the registration Web site displays a page similar to the one shown in Figure 2-9. This page includes a 14-character registration key that you should copy and paste into the Registration dialog box in Visual Studio.

5. Highlight the registration key in the Registration Web page, press Ctrl+C to copy it to the clipboard, and then close the browser window.

You're returned to the VWD, where the Registration dialog box is still open, awaiting your registration key.

6. Click in the Registration Key text box, and then press Ctrl+V.

This pastes your registration key into the text box.

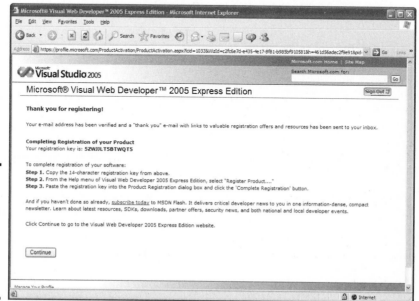

Figure 2-9:
The
Registration
Web site
displays
your
registration
key.

7. Click Complete Registration.

The dialog box shown in Figure 2-10 appears, thanking you for registering the product.

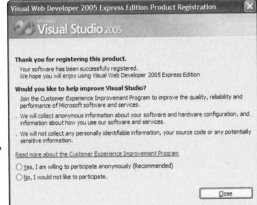

Figure 2-10: Registration is complete!

8. **Indicate whether you want to participate in the Customer Experience Improvement Program by selecting an option button.**

The Customer Experience Improvement Program is a fancy name that means Microsoft spies on you while you work with their products. That sounds a lot worse than it is — it's really just an effort Microsoft is making to find out how users actually work with their products so they can try to focus development efforts on the most commonly performed tasks. If you're paranoid or think that Bill Gates is trying to take over the world, feel free to opt out of this program.

It's not paranoia if they really are out to get you. Your call.

9. **Click Close.**

That's it. VWD is now registered.

Installing Visual Studio 2005

The installation procedure for other editions of Visual Studio 2005 is similar, except that you install the software from a disk rather than downloading it from the Web. Here are the steps:

1. **Insert the Visual Studio 2005 disk in your CD-ROM or DVD-ROM drive.**

The Setup program comes to life automatically, as shown in Figure 2-11. As you can see, the Setup program allows you to install Visual Studio 2005 — along with its documentation — and to check for updates.

Figure 2-11:
The Visual
Studio 2005
Setup
program.

2. Click the Install Visual Studio 2005 link.

Setup grinds and whirs for a moment, and then displays the dialog box
shown in Figure 2-12.

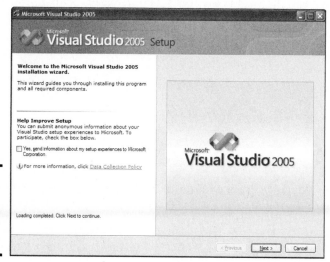

Figure 2-12:
Visual
Studio 2005
installation
begins.

3. Click Next.

The screen shown in Figure 2-13 appears.

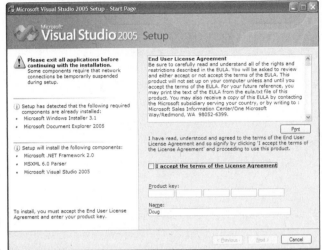

Figure 2-13:
Entering
your product
key.

4. **Check the box that indicates you agree to the license agreement; then enter your product key and name in the text boxes and click Next.**

You'll find the *product key* number printed on the package that the installation disc comes in. Be sure to enter it exactly as it appears on the package.

When you click Next, the screen shown in Figure 2-14 appears.

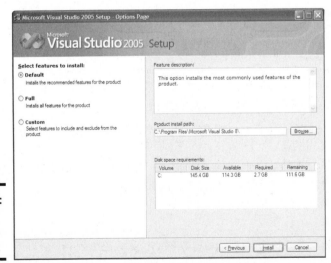

Figure 2-14:
Choosing
the instal-
lation type.

5. **Select the type of installation you want.**

You have three choices:

- **Default:** Installs Visual Studio 2005 with the most commonly used features.

- **Complete:** Installs all Visual Studio 2005 features. Unless you're short on disk space, this is the option I recommend.

- **Custom:** Lets you choose which features you want to install.

6. **Click Install.**

The installation begins.

7. **Take a nap.**

Hey, why not? The installation takes half an hour or so, even on a fast computer.

8. **Click the** `http://windowsupdate.microsoft.com` **link to update your computer.**

This takes you to the Windows Update site, where you can download the latest updates for your computer.

9. **Click Finish.**

You return to the Setup screen (refer to Figure 2-11).

10. **Click Install Product Documentation.**

This launches a Setup Wizard that installs the Visual Studio 2005 documentation.

11. **Follow the steps of the Wizard to install the documentation.**

There's a lot of documentation, so this will take a few minutes. When the documentation has been installed, you're again returned to the Setup screen that was shown in Figure 2-11.

12. **Click Check for Service Releases.**

This takes you to Microsoft's update site and checks for any updates that must be applied to Visual Studio.

13. **After you've installed any necessary updates, click Exit to close the Setup program.**

That's all there is to it!

After you install both Visual Studio 2005 and Visual Web Develop 2005 Express Edition, your tools are in place; you're ready to get into building your first Web application. For that, you are cordially invited to proceed to the next chapter. Good luck!

Chapter 3: Creating Your First ASP.NET 2.0 Application

In This Chapter

✔ Planning a Visual Studio project

✔ Building a Web site from scratch

✔ Using Solution Explorer, controls, properties, and titles

✔ Coding and running your application

*I*n this chapter, you get a crack at creating a simple, one-page Web application using Visual Studio 2005 Standard Edition. We walk you through the entire process step-by-step, so you'll get a good idea for how Visual Studio works and how ASP.NET applications are built.

Note that although this chapter uses a particular version of Visual Studio 2005 — the Standard Edition — to build a Web site, the procedure is nearly identical for other editions of Visual Studio. That includes Visual Web Developer 2005 Express Edition; you shouldn't have any trouble adapting the information in this chapter to other versions of Visual Studio.

All code listings used in this book are available for download at www.dummies. com/go/aspnetaiofd.

Understanding Visual Studio Projects

Visual Studio organizes the files of an ASP.NET application by using logical containers called *projects* and *solutions*. Here's a summary of the most important details you need to know concerning projects and solutions:

✦ A *project* is a container that holds all files related to a single ASP.NET application — including the .aspx files that define the application's Web pages, the code-behind files that provide the code executed when the application runs, and other files used by the application.

✦ A *solution* is a container that can hold one or more projects. Solutions let you group related applications.

✦ Most solutions contain just a single project. In fact, when you create a new Web application, Visual Studio creates two containers: a project to hold the application's files and a solution to hold the project.

✦ Visual Studio includes a window called the *Solution Explorer* within which you work with the files in a project. The Solution Explorer lists all projects that make up a solution, as well as all files that make up each project in the solution. You can double-click a file in the Solution Explorer to open the file, or you can right-click a file to reveal a shortcut menu that provides quick access to common tasks. (For more about how all this works, see the section "Using the Solution Explorer" later in this chapter.)

Previous versions of Visual Studio used separate project files (.prj) to store settings related to projects. In Visual Studio 2005, the project files have been eliminated.

Creating a New Web Site

To create a new Web site in Visual Studio 2005, follow these steps:

1. **Choose the File⇨New⇨Web Site command.**

Alternatively, you can click the New Web Site button shown in the margin. (Note that this button has a drop-down menu that lets you choose whether to display the New Web Site, New Project, Open Web Site, or Open Project buttons. If one of the other three buttons is visible instead of the New Web Site button, click the down arrow next to the icon and choose New Web Site from the menu that appears.)

When you choose File⇨New⇨Web Site or click the New Web Site button, the New Web Site dialog box appears, as shown in Figure 3-1. This dialog box lets you select the language you want to use for the Web site, the name of the Web site, and the location where you want to create the Web site.

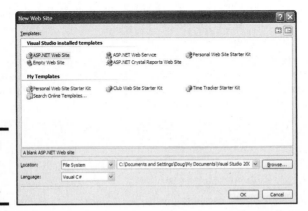

Figure 3-1:
The New
Web Site
dialog box.

2. Choose ASP.NET Web Site from the list of available templates.

In all likelihood, this template is already selected.

3. Choose File System, HTTP, or FTP from the Location drop-down list.

The Location drop-down list in the New Web Site dialog box offers you various ways to access the Web site:

- **File System:** The simplest way to access a Web site in Visual Studio is to create a *file-system Web site* — a folder on your hard disk that contains all the files that the Web site needs — `.aspx` files that define the pages displayed by the application, `.vb` (Visual Basic) or `.cs` (C#) files that define the code that's executed when the application runs, and other files that define the Web site's configuration, provide it with data, or implement its other features. The Web site shown in this chapter is a file-system Web site.

You can run a file-system Web site directly from within Visual Studio by using Visual Studio's built-in Web server. However, you can't run a file-system Web site directly from Internet Information Services (IIS) without first configuring the Web site from within IIS (which Chapter 5 of this mini-book shows you how to do).

- **HTTP:** Another way to access a Web site from within Visual Studio is to use the HTTP protocol to access a Web site that's under the control of an IIS server. When you use this option to create a Web site, Visual Studio uses HTTP to connect to an IIS server and create a Web application. The benefit of creating an HTTP Web site is that you don't have to later configure IIS to run the application as you do with a file-system Web site. The disadvantage is that you must have access to an IIS server to create this type of Web site.

Note that to create an HTTP Web site on a remote IIS server, the server must have the FrontPage 2002 Server Extensions installed. If the IIS server doesn't have the extensions installed, you'll have to create an FTP site instead, as described next.

- **FTP:** The third way to create a Web site is to use the almost-ancient FTP protocol to access a remote server. This option is best when you're creating a Web site on a remote server that doesn't have FrontPage 2002 Server Extensions installed.

4. Enter the location for the Web site in the combo box that's to the right of the Location drop-down list.

How you specify the location depends on which option you choose for the Location drop-down, as follows:

- **File System:** Enter the path to the main folder for the application. The path defaults to

```
My Documents\Visual Studio 2005\Websites\WebSite1
```

You should change `WebSite1` to the name you want to use for your Web site.

- **HTTP:** Enter the Web address of the Web site you want to create. For example, to create a Web site named `SimpleCalc` at an IIS server named `www.myserver.com`, enter

    `http://www.myserver.com/SimpleCalc`

    If you're using a local IIS server (that is, a server running on your own computer rather than on a remote computer), use `localhost` as the hostname. For example: `http://localhost/SimpleCalc`.

- **FTP:** Enter the FTP address for the application — for example, `ftp://ftp.myhost.com`.

5. **Choose the language you want to use to create the site.**

    The options are Visual Basic, Visual C#, and Visual J#.

    To create the Simple Calculator application (described in Chapter 2 of this mini-book), choose File System for the Location drop-down list, replace `WebSite1` with `SimpleCalc` as the file location, and choose Visual C# for the language.

6. **Click OK.**

    Visual Studio creates the project and awaits your command, as shown in Figure 3-2.

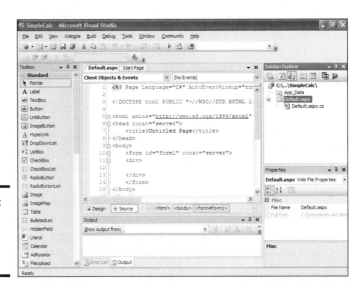

Figure 3-2:
A new project in Visual Studio.

Here are a few other pointers about creating Web sites in Visual Studio:

✦ Visual Studio creates a default page for the application named `default.aspx` and opens that page in the editor window. If you select Visual C# for the application's language, the `default.aspx` file is opened in Source view as shown in Figure 3-2. That way, you can directly edit the markup code for the page. However, if you select Visual Basic as the language, the page is initially opened in Design view, which shows a what-you-see-is-what-you-get view of the page. As you'll learn later in this chapter, you can switch between Design and Source view simply by clicking the Design and Source buttons at the bottom of the editor window.

✦ Although Visual Studio 2005 doesn't create a Project file for each project, it does create a Solution file for each solution. The Solution file is created in `My Documents\Visual Studio 2005\Projects`.

Using the Solution Explorer

The *Solution Explorer* is a window — normally located on the right side of the Visual Studio 2005 screen — in which you work with the files and subfolders that make up a project. In Figure 3-2, the Solution Explorer indicates that the `SimpleCalc` project has just one subfolder (named `App_Data`) and two files (named `Default.aspx` and `Default.aspx.cs`).

ASP.NET applications can have any of several standard subfolders; here's the rundown on what they do:

✦ **App_Data:** This folder holds database files used by the application. For applications that use large databases managed by a database-server program (such as Microsoft SQL Server), you may prefer to forego the `App_Data` folder and store the database files in a separate location. (For more information, refer to Book 6, Chapter 1.) But for most applications, the `App_Data` folder is the preferred place to store database files. Visual Studio 2005 always creates this folder when you create a new Web project.

✦ **App_Code:** If an application uses any program-code files other than the code-behind files associated with Web pages, those files are stored in the `App_Code` folder. Visual Studio 2005 creates this folder automatically whenever you add a new code file to a project.

✦ **App_Themes:** This folder contains the files needed for applying themes to influence the appearance of the application — and it's created automatically if you add a theme to a project. (For details, refer to Book 8, Chapter 4.)

Note that a project can also contain other folders of your own choosing. For example, we like to create a folder named Images to store the images displayed by the application. You can add a folder to a project by right-clicking the project name in the Solution Explorer window and then choosing New Folder from the shortcut menu that appears.

The Solution Explorer also has a nice row of buttons at the top — but they're more than just decorative. Table 3-1 describes their functions.

Table 3-1		Solution Explorer Buttons
Button	*Name*	*What It Does*
	Properties	Displays the Properties window for the selected item.
	Refresh	Refreshes the Solution Explorer — sometimes useful if you've added files to the project from outside Visual Studio.
	Nest Related Files	Indicates whether related files (such as Default.aspx and Default.aspx.cs) should be nested in the Solution Explorer window.
	View Code	Opens the file in the code editor.
	View Designer	Opens the file in a Designer window.
	Copy Web Site	Copies the entire Web site to another location.
	ASP.NET Configuration	Calls up the ASP.NET Web-based configuration tool, in which you set various options for the Web site (as detailed in Book 8, Chapter 1).

Working with Controls

When you create an ASP.NET Web site, Visual Studio adds a blank Web page named Default.aspx to the project. The first step in developing the application is to add some controls to this blank page.

ASP.NET comes with dozens of controls you can add to your Web pages. Table 3-2 lists the eight ASP.NET controls used most commonly — and outlines their basic functions. (There's much more about them in Book 2.)

Table 3-2	Eight Commonly Used ASP.NET Controls	
Toolbox Icon	*Control Name*	*What It Does*
A	Label	Displays text on the page.
abl	TextBox	Creates a text box in which the user can enter data.
ab	Button	Creates a button the user can click to submit the page.
	DropDownList	Creates a drop-down list.
	ListBox	Creates a list box.
	CheckBox	Creates a check box.
	RadioButton	Creates a radio button.
	Image	Displays an image.

The Simple Calculator application created in this chapter uses several of these controls, as shown in Figure 3-3. As you can see, this page uses four labels, two text boxes, and one button control. The first two text boxes let the user enter the two numbers to be added. (Actually, there's a third text box that isn't visible in the figure. It displays the the result of the calculation after the user clicks the button. This particular text box is set to read-only so it can display a text value, but the user can't enter a text value into it. More about why in a moment.)

Labels   Text boxes

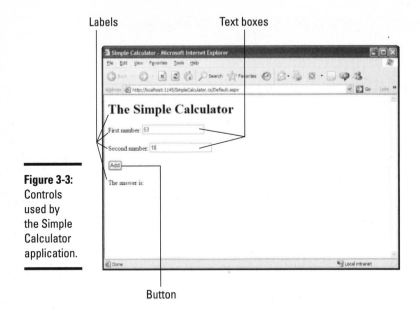

Figure 3-3:
Controls
used by
the Simple
Calculator
application.

Button

The easiest way to add controls to a Web page is in Design view:

✦ If you're using C# as your application's language, you switch to Design view by clicking the Design button at the bottom of the code editor's window.

✦ If you chose Visual Basic as the application's language rather than C#, you're already in Design view.

Figure 3-4 shows the `SimpleCalc` project with the `Default.aspx` page open in Design view. As you can see, Design view gives you a blank slate on which you can create a usable Web page.

In Design view, you can add a control to a page simply by dragging the icon for the control from the Toolbox (the narrow strip of controls that appears at the left of the Visual Studio window) onto the editor window. Alternatively, you can position the cursor in the window where you want a control to appear, and then double-click the control in the Toolbox to add the control at the current location.

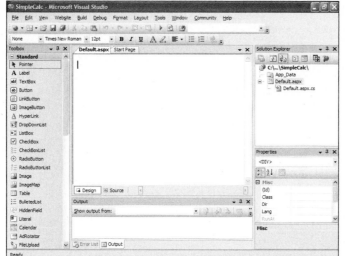

Figure 3-4:
The
Default.aspx
page in
Design view.

Figure 3-5 shows how the Default.aspx page looks after we've dragged controls onto it. To create this page, follow these steps:

1. **Double-click the Label tool in the Toolbox to create a label.**

2. **Click End, and then press Enter twice.**

3. **Double-click the Label tool to create another label.**

4. **Double-click the TextBox control to create a text box on the same line.**

5. **Repeat Steps 2, 3, and 4 to create another line with a label and a text box.**

6. **Click End, then press Enter twice.**

7. **Double-click the Button control to create a button.**

8. **Repeat Steps 2, 3, and 4 to create a third line with a label and a text box.**

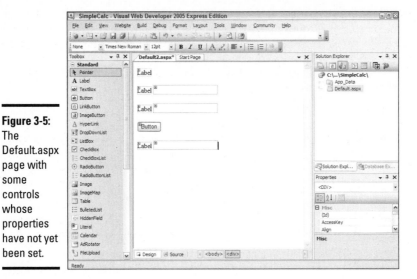

Figure 3-5:
The
Default.aspx
page with
some
controls
whose
properties
have not yet
been set.

Although the Web page now has the controls it needs, those controls don't look anything like the controls on the page shown in Figure 3-2. To get the look of those controls, you have to set *properties* for each control, as described in the next section.

Setting Properties

Properties are what give a control its distinctive look and behavior. Without properties, all labels will look alike — as will all text boxes, buttons, and other controls. If you want to create a really useful (and easy-to-use) Web page, you have to set the properties of each control on the page.

To set the properties of a control, first select the control by clicking it. Then, use the Properties window located at the bottom-right corner of the Visual Studio screen to set the various properties that are available for the control.

Each different type of control has its own collection of properties you can set, but some properties are common to most controls. These include

✦ **ID:** This property specifies the name of the control. Visual Studio picks a generic name for each control you create, such as `Label1` or `TextBox2`. You can leave these default values as they are, but if you plan on writing C# or Visual Basic code that will refer to the control, it's a good idea to give the control an ID that has a clearer functional meaning.

When you set the `ID` property of a control, a common practice is to begin the ID with a two- or three-character prefix that indicates the control's type. In the Simple Calculator application, for example, you might use `txtNumber1` and `txtNumber2` for the two input text boxes, and `txtAnswer` for the text box that displays the answer. (The `txt` will remind you that the control is a text box.)

✦ **Text:** Most controls that display a text value have a `Text` property you can use to set the value to display. Depending on the type of control, you'll often want to set this value to something other than the default. For example, Visual Studio sets the `Text` property of `Label` and `Button` controls to the `ID` of the control. As a result, you'll almost always have to set the `Text` property for `Label` and `Button` controls. The text property for `TextBox` controls is blank by default, which is usually what you want.

✦ **Font:** Controls that display text also have a set of `Font` properties you can use to specify how the text should be displayed. In the Properties window, you can click the + sign next to the Font property to reveal a whole list of font-related properties you can set — font name, size, and bold or italic formatting.

✦ **TabIndex:** The `TabIndex` property determines the order that controls are activated when the user presses the Tab key. You can use this property to make sure the Tab key moves the cursor as expected among the controls on your page.

Besides these common properties, most controls have their own unique properties as well. For example, `TextBox` controls have a `ReadOnly` property you can use to prevent the user from entering data in the text box. (Book 2 delves deeper into these.)

To get the SimpleCalc application closer to its final form, set the properties for its controls, as indicated in Table 3-3.

Table 3-3	Control Properties for the SimpleCalc Application	
Original ID of Control	*Property*	*Value*
Label1	Text	The Simple Calculator
	Font-Size	X-Large
	Font-Bold	True
Label2	Text	First Number:
TextBox1	ID	txtNumber1
Label3	Text	Second Number:
TextBox2	ID	txtNumber2
Button1	ID	btnAdd
	Text	Add

(continued)

Table 3-3 *(continued)*

Original ID of Control	Property	Value
Label4	Text	The answer is:
TextBox3	ID	txtAnswer
	ReadOnly	True

After you set the control properties as indicated in the table, the page should look like the page shown in Figure 3-6.

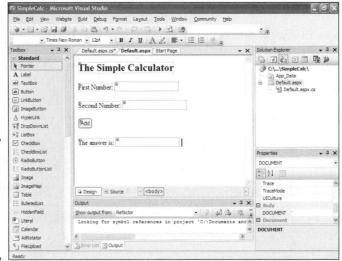

Figure 3-6: The Default.aspx page with its control properties set.

Setting the Page Title

In addition to setting property values for the individual controls on a page, you can also set property values for the page itself. To do so, click somewhere on the page away from any of the controls; doing so selects the page. Then you use the Properties window to set the page-property values.

The property you're most likely to set for the page itself is the `Title` property, which specifies the text that appears in the title bar when the page is displayed in a browser window. For the Simple Calculator application, set the `Title` property to `Simple Calculator`.

Looking at the Source Code

When you've added some controls and set their property values, click the Source button at the bottom of the Designer window to see the actual HTML source code for the page you've created. It should resemble the C# code shown in Listing 3-1.

Listing 3-1:   The Default.aspx file (C#)

```
<%@ Page Language="C#" AutoEventWireup="true" CodeFile="Default.aspx.cs"
    Inherits="_Default" %>
<!DOCTYPE html PUBLIC "-//W3C//DTD XHTML 1.0 Transitional//EN"
    "http://www.w3.org/TR/xhtml1/DTD/xhtml1-transitional.dtd">
<html xmlns="http://www.w3.org/1999/xhtml" >
<head runat="server">
    <title>Simple Calculator</title>
</head>
<body>
    <form id="form1" runat="server">
        <asp:Label ID="Label1" runat="server" Font-Bold="True" Font-Size="X-
    Large" Text="The Simple Calculator"></asp:Label><br />
        <br />
        <asp:Label ID="Label2" runat="server" Text="First Number:"></asp:Label>
        <asp:TextBox ID="txtNumber1" runat="server"></asp:TextBox><br />
        <br />
        <asp:Label ID="Label3" runat="server" Text="Second Number:"></asp:Label>
        <asp:TextBox ID="txtNumber2" runat="server"></asp:TextBox><br />
        <br />
        <asp:Button ID="btnAdd" runat="server" Text="Add" /><br />
        <br />
        <asp:Label ID="Label4" runat="server" Text="The answer is:"></asp:Label>
        <asp:TextBox ID="txtAnswer" runat="server" ReadOnly="True"></asp:TextBox>
    </form>
</body>
</html>
```

If you'll look through this listing, you'll see that Visual Studio has generated a set of lines that begin with asp:*control* for each control you create. These lines contain the property settings you specified for each control.

For example, here's the code for the first label:

```
<asp:Label ID="Label1" runat="server"
    Font-Bold="True"
    Font-Size="X-Large"
    Text="The Simple Calculator">
</asp:Label>
```

Note that we formatted it a little differently by putting each property on its own line, but the code is the same as in the listing.

Because the `.aspx` file is actually coded in HTML, the term *attribute* is usually used when referring to property names as they appear in the `.aspx` file. Throughout this book, we use those terms somewhat interchangeably. Thus if we say "Text attribute" or "Text property" we're referring to the same thing. You'll encounter both terms in software development.

Notice also that each control includes a `runat` attribute that specifies `server` as its value. This is a required attribute setting for all ASP.NET Web controls. It simply indicates that the control is to be processed by the Web server after the user submits the page.

All code shown in Listing 3-1 is generated automatically by Visual Studio, in response to the editing done in Design view. As a result, you don't have to worry too much about the nuances of this code — at least for now. After you get a handle on the basics of creating simple ASP.NET applications, you can turn your attention to directly editing the `.aspx` code. Until then, there's not too much shame (kidding!) in letting Visual Studio generate the code for you.

Adding Some Code

At this point, you could run the Simple Calculator application — sorta. It wouldn't actually do anything: If you entered numbers in both text boxes and clicked the Add button, nothing would happen; it doesn't know how to add the numbers yet. (D'oh!) To make the application add the two numbers together and display the result, you have to write some C# (or Visual Basic) code.

The easiest way to write code for an ASP.NET application is to double-click one of the controls while in Design view. This creates a routine (called a *method* in programmer-speak) that's executed when the user performs the default action for the control. For a `Button` control, the default action is clicking the control. As a result, you can write code that's executed when the user clicks a button by doing no more than double-clicking the appropriate button in Design view.

Figure 3-7 shows the Code Editor window that's displayed when you double-click the Add button for the Simple Calculator application. As you can see, Visual Studio has created a method named `btnAdd_Click` and positioned the insertion point right in the middle of this method. So you can start typing the code you want to execute when the user clicks the Add button.

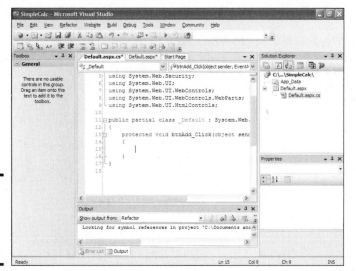

Figure 3-7:
Adding
code to an
ASP.NET
application.

When the user clicks the Add button, we want to add the values that the
user has entered into the first two text boxes and display the result in the
third text box. At first glance, you might expect that the code would look
something like this:

```
txtAnswer.Text = txtNumber1.Text + txtNumber2.Text;
```

If you're new to C# programming, there's a lot going on here that needs
explaining. First, every statement must end with a semicolon. And second,
the periods are used to separate object names from property names. Thus
txtAnswer.Text refers to the Text property of the txtAnswer control.

Okay, maybe all this seems straightforward enough — but (unfortunately) it
doesn't work at all the way you'd expect it to. If you were to run the application with this code and enter (say) 12 for the first number and 2 for the second
number, you'd expect the answer to be 14. Instead, the answer displayed is
122. That's because the Text property represents string values, not numeric
values. And in C# (as well as in Visual Basic), the + symbol when applied to
strings simply means to combine the strings.

So what we need to do is first convert the Text property values to numbers
so we can add them and display the result. Here's the code that will do that:

```
decimal num1 = Decimal.Parse(txtNumber1.Text);
decimal num2 = Decimal.Parse(txtNumber2.Text);
decimal ans = num1 + num2;
txtAnswer.Text = ans.ToString();
```

Here's what's going on in the code:

✦ The first line begins by creating a *variable* named num1. The decimal keyword allows this variable to store decimal numbers. Then, it uses a built-in routine called Decimal.Parse to convert the string value of the Text property for txtNumber1 to a decimal value. Finally, the converted value is assigned to the num1 variable.

✦ The second line does the same thing for the second text box.

✦ The third line creates a variable named ans, adds num1 and num2 together, and sets the ans variable to the result.

✦ Finally, the fourth line sets the Text property of the third text box to the ans variable after converting its value to a string.

Note that the code you write to handle button clicks and other similar occurrences isn't stored in the same file with the .aspx tags that define the page. Instead, the code is stored in a separate file called the *code-behind* file — and that's where the application looks for it. This file has the same name as the .aspx file for the page, but adds the extension .cs (for C#) or .vb (for Visual Basic). Thus, the C# code-behind file for the Default.aspx page is named Default.aspx.cs.

The next chapter of this mini-book delves into how all this works. For now, have a look at Listing 3-2 — the complete C# code-behind file for the Simple Calculator program — and notice that the btnAdd_Click method contains the code that's executed when the user clicks the btnAdd button.

If all this talk of variables and conversion and built-in routines is giving you a serious headache, take heart: You can find help for C# in Book 4 and Visual Basic in Book 5.

Listing 3-2:   The code-behind file for the Simple Calculator application (C#)

```
using System;
using System.Data;
using System.Configuration;
using System.Web;
using System.Web.Security;
using System.Web.UI;
using System.Web.UI.WebControls;
using System.Web.UI.WebControls.WebParts;
using System.Web.UI.HtmlControls;
public partial class _Default : System.Web.UI.Page
```

```
{
    protected void btnAdd_Click(object sender, EventArgs e)
    {
        decimal num1 = Decimal.Parse(txtNumber1.Text);
        decimal num2 = Decimal.Parse(txtNumber2.Text);
        decimal ans = num1 + num2;
        txtAnswer.Text = ans.ToString();
    }
}
```

Running the Application

 Aha, the moment of truth: When you've created the `Default.aspx` page and the code-behind file, you can run the application to see how it works — and still be able to tinker with it if it doesn't. To do so, click the Start Debugging button (shown in the margin), choose Debug➪Start Debugging, or press F5. Whichever way you go about it, Visual Studio builds the application, starts the built-in Web server, runs the application, and opens a browser window to display the page.

The first time you run an application from Visual Studio, you'll see the dialog box shown in Figure 3-8. This dialog box is simply informing you that debugging has not yet been enabled for the application. Debugging must be enabled via a configuration file named `web.config`. The first option in this dialog box automatically generates a `web.config` file so you can run the application with the debugger enabled. Select this option and then click OK.

Figure 3-8:
Enabling
debugging
for a new
ASP.NET
application.

Note that this dialog box only appears the first time you run the application.

 If you made a mistake when you entered the code for the code-behind file, Visual Studio will display a message indicating that the build failed and the application can't be run. In that case, Visual Studio will display an Error List window that lists each error. You can then examine each error message and correct your code accordingly.

Assuming your code doesn't contain any errors that prevent it from building successfully, the application will appear in a browser window as shown in Figure 3-9. Then, when you enter a number in each text box and follow each entry with a click of the Add button, the numbers are added and the result is displayed in the third text box.

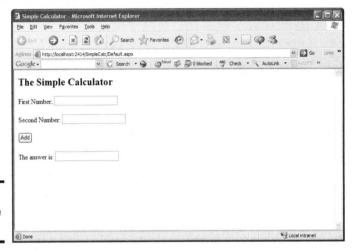

Figure 3-9: Running the application.

Of course, just because the application builds successfully and runs doesn't mean the application is free from errors. Try clicking the Add button without entering any numbers in the text boxes. The result will be a cryptic error message such as `Input string not in the correct format`. That's because this program doesn't do any checking to make sure the user actually enters a value number as a value before it attempts to add the numbers. The user might have entered a word, or dropped something on a random key. Fortunately, Chapter 6 of this mini-book gives you the lowdown about finding and correcting problems like this in your ASP.NET applications. (And Book 2, Chapter 2 shows you how to add validation controls to ensure that the user does enter correct values.)

Chapter 4: Understanding Postback, Events, and Code-Behind

In This Chapter

✓ Posting pages to the server

✓ Working with events in Visual Basic

✓ Working with events in C#

✓ Getting behind the scenes of code-behind

*T*hree of the most important concepts in ASP.NET programming are the ideas of (1) posting pages to the server, (2) handling events, and (3) code-behind. *Postback* refers to what happens when the user clicks a button or performs some other action that sends the page displayed in the browser window to the server so whatever data the user entered on the page can be processed. *Events* are the processes that ASP.NET uses to deal with user interaction when a page has been posted. And *code-behind* is how ASP.NET lets you separate the code that's executed when events occur from the markup code that defines how pages appear.

This chapter introduces you to these three all-important ASP.NET concepts.

All code listings used in this book are available for download at www.dummies. com/go/aspnetaiofd.

Understanding Postback

You're probably familiar with Web pages that include a Submit button. For example, consider a typical search-engine Web page that has a text box and a Submit button. When you click the Submit button, the text you entered into the text box is sent to the search-engine's server, which looks up the results of your search and sends the results back to the browser. The process of sending the page to the server is called a *postback*.

Note that the term *postback* implies that the ASP.NET page has already been displayed in the browser. When the user clicks a button, the page along with any data entered by the user is sent to the server. The server then runs the code associated with the page to process the data entered by the user.

When a page is posted, ASP.NET gets busy with the following tasks:

1. **ASP.NET receives the data sent back to the server, including any data that the user entered into controls such as text boxes.**

2. **ASP.NET determines which page in the application was displayed in the browser window and loads that page into memory on the server.**

3. **The properties of any controls that appear on that page are set based on the data entered by the user.** For example, if the page contains a text box and the user entered data into that text box, the Text property of the text box is set to the data value entered by the user.

4. **A special variable named** IsPostBack **is set to** True. **This enables the application to determine if a postback is occurring.** (The next section digs into how to make this process happen, and explains why it's significant.)

5. **The code that handles events generated for the page is executed.** (For more about what that means, flip ahead to the later parts of this chapter, and look for the section "Understanding Events.")

6. **After all of the event code has been executed, the page is sent back to the browser in the form of HTML so the user can see whatever updates have been applied to the page.**

One important thing to know about the way ASP.NET applications work is to realize that not every type of control causes the page to be posted back to the server. For example, when a user selects an item from a drop-down list, the page isn't normally posted. Nor is the page posted when the user selects a check box or radio button or enters a value into a text box. The user has to click a button to post the page. (As described in Book 2, you can change the behavior of controls such as drop-down lists and check boxes so they do post back when the user selects them — but don't post the page by default.)

Using the IsPostBack Variable

A *postback* occurs only when the user clicks a button or performs some other action that causes the page currently displayed by the browser to be sent back to the server. The first time a page is retrieved by a user, a postback doesn't occur. For instance, when the user starts the Simple Calculator application (our example from the previous chapter of this mini-book) by browsing to the application's Default.aspx page, the page is loaded into server memory and events are processed, but a postback doesn't occur. (In the case of the Simple Calculator application, a postback doesn't occur until the user clicks the Add button.)

As you'll see throughout this book, you'll often write code that checks to see if a postback has occurred. For example, suppose you want to initialize the

`Text` property of a label to `"Good Morning!"` the first time a page is posted, but to change the label whenever the user posts back to the page by clicking a button; then the label should display `"Hello Again!"` instead of `"Good Morning!"` In that case, you might write Visual Basic code that looks like the following:

```
If IsPostBack Then
    lblGreeting.Text = "Hello Again!"
Else
    lblGreeting.Text = "Good Morning!"
End If
```

If you're working in C#, the code would look more like this:

```
if (IsPostBack)
    lblGreeting.Text = "Hello Again!";
else
    lblGreeting.Text = "Good Morning!";
```

Either way, the `IsPostBack` variable is used to determine whether a postback has occurred — if it has, the label's `Text` property is set accordingly.

Careful how you use this one. Using `IsPostBack` incorrectly can lead to all sorts of programming problems. If you find that a variable or field is incorrectly reset to the same value each time the page is posted, you may need to add an `if` statement to set the variable or field only when `IsPostBack` is false.

You'll see many more examples of the `IsPostBack` variable in use throughout this book.

Understanding Events

Events are the key to ASP.NET programming because most of the code you write for an ASP.NET application is executed in response to events that are raised as a page is processed. In essence, an ASP.NET application consists of two things:

+ **A set of Web pages that contain controls that users can interact with.** When a user interacts with one or more of the controls on a page, an event is generated to record the interaction.

+ **Code executed in response to the events generated when the user interacts with the controls on the Web pages.**

For example, consider the Simple Calculator application presented in the previous chapter of this mini-book. In practical terms, it's a Web page that displays some labels, text boxes, a button, and some code that's executed when the user clicks the button.

Button-click events are among the most common types of events — but by no means the only events — that ASP.NET pages encounter. Every time a page is posted to a Web server, a series of events are processed — or *raised* — by the ASP.NET server. In particular, the following events are always raised every time a page is posted:

✦ `Preinit`: This is the first event raised as a part of page initialization. It occurs before ASP.NET initializes the page. It allows you to change properties that may affect the way the page is initialized.

✦ `Init`: This event occurs after ASP.NET has initialized the page; it allows you to add additional initialization code.

✦ `Load`: This event kicks in after the controls have been initialized with their correct values.

✦ **Control events:** Any events that result from the user interacting with controls, such as when the user clicks a button or selects an item from a drop-down list, are raised after the Load event. For example, if the user clicks a button, the Click event will be raised after the Load event.

Note that it's entirely possible (and quite common) for more than one control event to occur each time a page is posted. For example, if a user selects an item from a drop-down list, clicks a check box to select it, then clicks a button, the page is posted when the button is clicked. Then three events are raised after the Load event: one to indicate that the user has selected an item from the drop-down list, a second to indicate that the user has clicked the check box, and a third to indicate that the user has clicked the button.

✦ `PreRender`: This event is raised after all of the control events have been raised but before the HTML that will be sent back to the browser is generated.

✦ `Unload`: This event is raised when the page has been sent back to the browser.

The process of connecting a method (or, as it's called in VB.NET, a `Sub` procedure) to an event is called *wiring*. There are two ways to wire events, depending on whether you're working in Visual Basic or C#. The next two sections describe the two techniques. (Hint: No screwdriver required.)

Using the Handles Clause in Visual Basic

The `Handles` clause is it a piece of classical Christmas music (say, what Handel wrote right after he finished *Messiah*)? Nope. It actually refers to a clause you can add to a `Sub` procedure in Visual Basic. Its job is to designate that the procedure should be invoked when a particular event is raised. In short, the Handles clause is what links controls in an .aspx file to procedures in a Visual Basic code-behind file. (The Handles clause only applies to VB.NET programs. For a look at how events are handled in C#, refer to the next section.)

The format of the Sub statement with a Handles clause is as follows:

```
Protected Sub name(parameters) Handles control.event
End Sub
```

For example, here's a Sub procedure that handles a button-click event:

```
Protected Sub Button1_Click(ByVal sender As Object, _
        ByVal e As System.EventArgs) Handles Button1.Click
    Button1.Text = "Got me!"
End Sub
```

Here, the Text property of the button named Button1 is changed to "Got me!" when the button is clicked.

The Sub procedure has two parameters, named sender and e. The sender parameter refers to the control that generated the event, in this case, Button1. The e parameter provides additional arguments that might be useful to the event handler. (For more information on event handler arguments, you can look up System.EventArgs in the Visual Studio help.)

Fortunately, you don't have to worry about coding the Handles clause — or the parameters — if you don't want to. Instead, you can simply double-click a form control in the Web Designer view. Then Visual Studio automatically creates an event handler with the proper Handles clause and parameters.

Note that it's possible for a single Sub procedure to handle an event for two or more controls. Here's an interesting, if not very practical, example:

```
Protected Sub Button1_Click(ByVal sender As Object, _
        ByVal e As System.EventArgs) _
        Handles Button1.Click, Button2.Click
    If sender Is Button1 Then
        Button1.Text = ""
        Button2.Text = "Click me!"
    Else
        Button1.Text = "Click me!"
        Button2.Text = ""
    End If
End Sub
```

In this example, the text "Click me!" jumps from button to button when the user clicks either Button1 or Button2.

Designating an Event Handler in C#

C# doesn't have an equivalent to Visual Basic's `Handles` clause. Instead, C# programs take a different approach to designating the code that is executed in response to events. Instead of specifying the event handling in the code-behind file, you specify it in the `.aspx` file by adding an `OnEvent` attribute to the tag for the control. For example, here's the code for a button that specifies an event handler:

```
<asp:Button ID="btnAdd" runat="server" Text="Add"
    OnClick="btnAdd_Click" />
```

Here the `OnClick` attribute indicates that the method named `btnAdd_Click` should be executed when the user clicks the button. In the code-behind file, the `btnAdd_Click` method makes no reference to the `btnAdd` control or the `Click` event. Like Visual Basic event handlers, however, C# event handlers must specify the `sender` and `e` parameters. Here's an example:

```
protected void btnAdd_Click(object sender, EventArgs e)
{
}
```

Once again, you don't have to worry about coding these parameters or the On*Event* attributes yourself. Simply double-click a control in the Web Designer and Visual Studio will automatically create an event handler for you with the correct On*Event* attribute and the correct parameters.

Note that Visual Basic also lets you use the On*Event* technique to handle events. However, the `Handles` clause is more common in VB.NET because Visual Studio uses it for generated code.

Using C#'s Auto Event Wireup

In addition to the On*Event* technique described in the previous section, C# uses a technique called *auto event wireup* to automatically call the methods that handle page-level events such as `Init` and `Load`. Then all you have to do to handle these events is create a method with the appropriate name in the code-behind file. The following methods are automatically wired:

✦ `Page_Init`: Wired to the `Init` method for the page. This method executes after the page is initialized.

✦ `Page_Load`: This method executes when the page is loaded.

✦ `Page_PreRender`: This method executes after all control events for the page have been executed, but before any HTML has been generated for the page.

✦ `Page_Unload`: This event is typically where you put any cleanup tasks required by the application, such as closing files or terminating database connections.

Auto-event wireup is controlled (no surprise) by the `AutoEventWireup` attribute on the `Page` directive that appears at the top of every `.aspx` file. For example:

```
<%@ Page Language="C#" AutoEventWireup="true"
    CodeFile="Default.aspx.cs" Inherits="_Default" %>
```

When you use Visual Basic, `AutoEventWireup` is set to `False`. Then the methods that handle page-level events must specify a `Handles` clause, as in this example:

```
Protected Sub Page_Load(ByVal sender As Object, _
        ByVal e As System.EventArgs) Handles Me.Load
End Sub
```

Understanding Code-Behind

Code-behind is one of the most important concepts (and techniques) in ASP.NET programming. It uses a separate file to contain the VB.NET or C# code that's executed in response to events — and only that code — rather than intermingling the VB.NET or C# code with the `.aspx` code that defines the Web page.

The main benefit of code-behind is to separate the code that defines the appearance of a Web page from the code that defines the behavior of the page. Result: code that is easier to write, debug, and maintain. And it lets you direct your focus while you're developing your applications. You can begin by creating a basic page that has the controls you need, without worrying too much about how the page looks. Then you can focus on getting the code to work so the page does its job correctly. After you have the code working, you can return to the `.aspx` file to refine the appearance of the page.

In the real world, there isn't always a clean separation between the appearance of a page and its behavior. Often, as a result, you end up alternating between tweaking the `.aspx` file and tinkering with the code-behind file; changes in one file inevitably affect code in the other file. Even so, separating the appearance-making code from the behavioral code is a big step forward.

To understand how code-behind works, you need to understand two things: partial classes and code generation.

✦ **A *partial class* is a VB.NET or C# class defined by two or more files.** Partial classes are integral to code-behind because a Web page must be defined by a single class that represents the *controls* on the page (that is, the appearance of the page) as well as the *event handlers* for the page (that is, the behavior of the page). The code-behind file is a partial class that supplies the methods that handle events. The other part of the class is what the .aspx file provides.

✦ *Code generation* **(that is, the automatic creation of code) is a required step because the** .aspx **file is not written in either C# or Visual Basic.** Instead, it consists of a mixture of HTML and ASP.NET markup tags. When ASP.NET processes a page, it reads this markup and then generates C# or VB.NET code — which represents the page, its HTML, and all its controls. This code is a partial class that matches the partial class represented by the code-behind file.

Thus the complete processing for an ASP.NET page consists of the following events:

1. **The** .aspx **file is processed by ASP.NET, which generates a source file that defines a partial class that represents the HTML and controls for the page.** This source file is generated in C# or VB.NET, depending on the language specified for the page.

2. **The source file generated in Step 1 is compiled by the C# or VB.NET compiler to create a partial class.**

3. **The code-behind file is compiled by the C# or VB.NET compiler to create a partial class.**

4. **The partial classes created in Steps 2 and 3 are combined to create the complete class that represents the page.**

5. **The resulting class is loaded into memory and executed.**

Using Single-File Pages

Code-behind isn't the only code model supported by ASP.NET. If you prefer, you can also mix code directly in the .aspx file, eliminating the need for a code-behind file. To do so, you simply uncheck the "Place code in separate file" option when you create a new Web page. Then, Visual Studio inserts special <script> tags that contain the code that would otherwise be placed in the code-behind file.

Note that the Web Designer works pretty much the same whether you use code-behind or the single-file model. Either way, you can double-click a control to call up the Code Editor to write event-handler code. However, the resulting .aspx file looks very different if you use the single-file model. For example, Listing 4-1 shows the complete .aspx file for the Simple Calculator application implemented as a single page. As you can see, the btnAdd_Click method is contained within a <script> element rather than in a separate file.

Listing 4-1: The Simple Calculator application using the single-page model (C#)

```
<%@ Page Language="C#" %>
<!DOCTYPE html PUBLIC "-//W3C//DTD XHTML 1.0 Transitional//EN"
    "http://www.w3.org/TR/xhtml1/DTD/xhtml1-transitional.dtd">
<script runat="server">
    protected void btnAdd_Click(object sender, EventArgs e)
    {
        decimal num1 = Decimal.Parse(txtNumber1.Text);
        decimal num2 = Decimal.Parse(txtNumber2.Text);
        decimal ans = num1 + num2;
        txtAnswer.Text = ans.ToString();
    }
</script>
<html xmlns="http://www.w3.org/1999/xhtml" >
<head runat="server">
    <title>Untitled Page</title>
</head>
<body>
    <form id="form1" runat="server">
    <div>
        <asp:Label ID="Label1" runat="server" Font-Bold="True" Font-Size=
        "X-Large" Text="The Simple Calculator"></asp:Label><br />
        <br />
        <asp:Label ID="Label2" runat="server" Text="First Number:"></asp:Label>
        <asp:TextBox ID="txtNumber1" runat="server"></asp:TextBox>
        <br />
        <br />
        <asp:Label ID="Label3" runat="server" Text="Second Number:"></asp:Label>
        <asp:TextBox ID="txtNumber2" runat="server"></asp:TextBox>
        <br />
        <br />
        <asp:Button ID="btnAdd" runat="server" OnClick="btnAdd_Click" Text="Add" />
        <br />
        <br />
        <asp:Label ID="Label4" runat="server" Text="The answer is:"></asp:Label>
        <asp:TextBox ID="txtAnswer" runat="server" ReadOnly="True"></asp:TextBox>
    </div>
    </form>
</body>
</html>
```

Chapter 5: Creating Multipage Applications

In This Chapter

✔ Learning the basics of a multipage application

✔ Adding pages to a Web project

✔ Getting from one page to another

✔ Keeping track of an application's state

✔ Dipping your toe into data binding

✔ Using Master Pages to create a consistent look among your pages

*O*nly the most trivial and boring of Web sites have just one page. Most Web sites go way beyond one page — perhaps to dozens or even hundreds of pages. Pervasive as they are, these *multipage* Web sites present several interesting challenges. This chapter shows how to add pages to your Web applications — and deal with the complications that result from having multiple pages. Those include such issues as how your users can get from one page to another, how to create pages that have a consistent appearance, and how to manage the "state" of an application so the application knows where it's been and where it's going.

All code listings used in this book are available for download at www. dummies.com/go/aspnetaiofd.

Understanding the Basics of a Multipage Application

To illustrate the programming techniques you'll learn in this chapter, we'll take a close look at a simple shopping cart application, similar to many similar applications you've undoubtedly encountered on the Web. Of course, this application is dramatically simplified so we can focus on a few basic programming techniques. For example, this online store (which sells Halloween costumes) has only a few products for sale. And the shopping cart doesn't mention the price of the products you buy — just the description and quantity of each product. (Hey, why not? Imaginary stores can afford to be simplistic.)

Figure 5-1 shows the first page of the Shopping Cart application, `Default.aspx`. Here you can see that the page consists of three controls: a list box from which you can select a product, a text box in which you can enter a quantity, and a button you can click to add the selected product to your shopping cart.

Figure 5-1:
The first page of the Shopping Cart application.

When the user selects a product, enters a quantity, and clicks the button, the application adds the selected product to the user's shopping cart. Then the application displays the second page of the application — `Cart.aspx` — as shown in Figure 5-2, where a list box displays the contents of the user's shopping cart.

Figure 5-2:
The second page of the Shopping Cart application.

The second page of the Shopping Cart application has two buttons. The first simply returns to the first page so the user can change what's in the shopping cart by adding or removing items. The second button is a Check Out button that . . . okay . . . doesn't do anything in this particular application. It's there only because in a realistic Shopping Cart application, you'd see a button that lets the user complete the order.

Although this application is simple, it utilizes some important ASP.NET programming techniques — in particular, these:

+ **The application uses two pages, so it must provide a way for one page to lead to the other.** For example, when the user clicks the Add To Cart button on the `Default.aspx` page, the application displays the `Cart.aspx` page. And when the user clicks the Continue Shopping button on the `Cart.aspx` page, the application displays the `Default.aspx` page. (For more about adding pages to your Web site and navigating between them, see the "Adding Pages" section later in this chapter.)

+ **In addition to the classes that represent the** `Default.aspx` **and** `Cart.aspx` **pages, the application uses a custom class called** `ShoppingCartItem` **to represent the items in the shopping cart.** (Books 3 and 4 get into the fine details of classes).

+ **The application uses an ASP.NET programming feature called** *session state* **to store the actual shopping cart data.** A .NET Framework class called `ArrayList` — which is designed to store collections of repeating data — stores the data and keeps track of the session state. (For more about how that works, see the "Using Session State" section later in this chapter.)

+ **The application uses another ASP.NET programming feature called** *data binding* **for automatic display of the data stored in the shopping cart's** `ArrayList` **object.** The data shows up on-screen in the list box that appears in the `Cart.aspx` page. (This chapter gives you a glimpse of data binding, but the best in-depth look is in Book 6.)

+ **Notice how both pages in this application have the same graphic displayed at the top?** You could simply copy and paste this graphic on each page. But there's a better way: *Master Pages*. The Master Page feature makes it easy to create applications whose pages have common elements such as banners, navigation menus, and so on. (For the masterful details, see the "Using Master Pages" section later in this chapter.)

The rest of this chapter takes a closer look at each of these programming techniques. Then I present the code for the Shopping Cart application so you can see how everything works together.

Adding Pages

When you first create an ASP.NET Web application, the application consists of a single Web page named `Default.aspx`. Few applications use just a single page, so one of the first things you have to get Visual Studio to do is add a new page to your Web site. Fortunately, the procedure is relatively simple. Just follow these steps:

1. **Choose Website⇨Add New Item.**

If you prefer, you can use one of the following shortcuts:

- **Ctrl+Shift+A.**

- **The Add New Item button in the Standard toolbar (shown in the margin).**

- **Right-click the project in the Solution Explorer, then choose Add New Item.**

Either way, the Add New Item dialog box appears, as shown in Figure 5-3.

Figure 5-3:
The Add
New Item
dialog box.

2. **Make sure Web Form is selected in the Templates box.**

Usually this item is already selected. But check to make sure.

3. **Enter a name for the page in the Name text box.**

The default name is — *ahem* — `Defaultx.aspx`. Now, I'm guessing you don't want to create a Web site full of pages named `Default1.aspx`, `Default2.aspx`, and so on. So give your page a more meaningful name.

4. **Select the programming language.**

The default is the language you chose when you created the Web site. Sure, you *can* mix languages within a single Web site, but it's seldom a good idea to do so. Normally it's best to leave this option untouched.

5. **Make sure the Place Code in Separate File option is checked.**

   This option, which is checked by default, creates a code-behind file for the page's event handlers. If you don't want to use a code-behind file, uncheck this option.

6. **If you're using Master Pages, check the Select Master Page option.**

   For more about how Master Pages work, see the "Using Master Pages" section later in this chapter.

7. **Click Add.**

   Visual Studio grinds and whirs for a moment, and then adds the page. You'll see an icon for the new page in the Solution Explorer, and the .aspx file opens in the Web Designer window. (If you selected C# as your language, the page opens in Source view; if you selected Visual Basic, the page opens in Design view.)

You can, of course, add as many pages as you want to an ASP.NET project. If a project requires a lot of pages, you may want to use subfolders to organize the pages. To create a subfolder, right-click the project in the Solution Explorer and choose New Folder. Then type a name for the new folder and press Enter.

Redirecting to Another Page

When your Web site has more than one page in it, you need a way to take the user from one page to another. ASP.NET provides several ways to do this. The most common is to call Response.Redirect in the Click event handler for a button. For example, if you want the page Default.aspx to be displayed when the user clicks a button named btnContinue, you would code the following C# event handler for the btnContinue button:

```
protected void btnContinue_Click(object sender,
    EventArgs e)
{
    Response.Redirect("Default.aspx");
}
```

The VB.NET version of this event handler would look like this:

```
Protected Sub btnContinue_Click( _
        ByVal sender As Object, _
```

```
        ByVal e As System.EventArgs) _
        Handles btnContinue.Click
    Response.Redirect("Default.aspx")
End Sub
```

An alternative to the `Response.Redirect` method is another method, `Server.Transfer`. The difference between `Response.Redirect` and `Server.Transfer` is pretty straightforward:

✦ `Response.Redirect` **actually sends a message to the user's browser, instructing it to post a request for a different page back to the user.** As a result, this technique requires an additional round-trip between the server and the browser.

✦ **In contrast, the** `Server.Transfer` **method simply transfers the server directly to the other page, so an additional round-trip isn't needed.**

You might think that `Server.Transfer` would be preferred because it avoids the extra round-trip over the Internet, but it turns out that `Server.Transfer` has a serious limitation: The user's browser continues to display the original page in its Address bar. So if you want to display a page other than the one posted by the user, and you want the user to see the address of the new page, you should use `Response.Redirect` instead.

A new technique that's available in ASP.NET 2.0 is called *cross-page posting:* You create a button control that automatically posts back to a different page. To use cross-page posting, you use the `PostBackURL` attribute to specify the page you want to post to. For example, here's the markup that creates a button that posts to a page named `Default.aspx`:

```
<asp:Button ID="btnContinue" runat="server"
    Text="Continue Shopping"
    PostBackURL="~/Default.aspx" />
```

Whenever you find yourself coding a `Click` event handler for a button, and it consists of nothing other than a call to `Response.Redirect`, consider using cross-page posting instead.

Adding Classes

In addition to other Web pages, you can also add classes to an ASP.NET application. The Shopping Cart application uses a class to represent each item in the shopping cart. This class, called `ShoppingCartItem`, defines three properties:

Description, Quantity, and ItemLine. The Description property provides a text description of the item, while the Quantity property provides the quantity of the item requested by the user. The ItemLine property provides a simple text string that's displayed in the shopping cart.

To add a class to a Web site, follow these steps:

1. **Choose Website⇨Add New Item.**

If you prefer, you can use one of the following shortcuts:

- **Ctrl+Shift+A.**

- **The Add New Item button in the Standard toolbar (shown in the margin).**

- **Right-click the project in the Solution Explorer, then choose Add New Item.**

One way or another, the Add New Item dialog box that was shown back in Figure 5-3 appears.

2. **Select Class in the Templates box.**

Usually this item is already selected. But check to make sure.

3. **Enter a name for the class in the Name text box.**

The default name is Class1. You can do better than that.

4. **Select the programming language.**

Once again, this defaults to the language you selected for the project. You'd best not change it.

5. **Click Add.**

The class file is added to the App_Code folder, a special folder designated for holding your class files.

If this is the first class you are adding to a project, Visual Studio will display a dialog box asking if you want to create the App_Code folder. Click Yes to create the folder.

After the class has been created, it's displayed in the Code Editor, as shown in Figure 5-4.

6. **Edit the class any way you like.**

For the Shopping Cart application, you'll want to add code that implements the shopping cart functionality the application needs, as described in the following paragraphs.

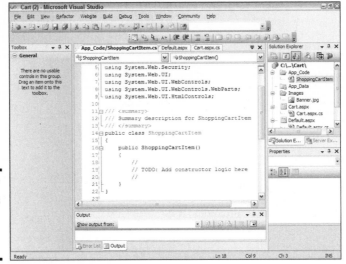

As you can see in Figure 5-4, the class file created when you add a class to a project contains some skeleton programming elements — such as `using` statements (known as `Imports` in VB.NET), comments, a class declaration, and an empty constructor.

Here is the complete C# code for the `ShoppingCartItem` class after I finished editing it:

```csharp
public class ShoppingCartItem
{
    public string Description;
    public int Quantity;
    public ShoppingCartItem(string description,
        int quantity)
    {
        Description = description;
        Quantity = quantity;
    }
    public string ItemLine
    {
        get
        {
            string line = Quantity.ToString() + " "
                    + Description;
            if (Quantity == 1)
                line += " costume";
            else
                line += " costumes";
```

```
                   return line;
           }
       }
}
```

As you can see, I removed the using statements that aren't required for this class, added two public fields (Description and Quantity), a constructor, and a property named ItemLine.

The VB.NET version of this class looks like this:

```
Public Class ShoppingCartItem
    Public Description As String
    Public Quantity As Integer
    Public Sub New(Description As String, _
            Quantity As Integer)
        Me.Description = Description
        Me.Quantity = Quantity
        End Sub
    Public ReadOnly Property ItemLine As String
        Get
            Dim Line As String
            Line = Quantity.ToString() & " " _
                    & Description
            If Quantity = 1 Then
                Line = Line & " costume"
            Else
                Line = Line & " costumes"
            End If
            Return line
        End Get
    End Property
End Class
```

If you find yourself staring confusedly at "The C# Version of the Shopping Cart Application" (later in this chapter) and the code shown in Listings 5-1 or 5-2 seems no less dense, you may want to skip ahead to Book 4 or Book 5 for a refresher on the basics of C# or VB.NET programming. They should clear up that headache right away.

Using Session State

One of the most important things to know about ASP.NET application programming is that whenever a page is sent to the user's browser, the program that created the page no longer exists in the server's memory. As a result, the typical ASP.NET program has a very short actual lifetime — which goes like this:

1. **The user clicks a button or takes some other action that causes a page to be posted to the server.**

2. **The server determines which page was posted by the user, locates the program that corresponds to that page, and starts the program.**

3. **The program retrieves any data entered by the user, generates HTML for the page, and sends it back to the user.**

4. **The generated page is sent back to the user's browser.**

5. **The program ends.**

When a user works with an ASP.NET application, he or she repeats this sequence of steps many times. Collectively, this is referred to as the user's *session.*

A critical aspect of any ASP.NET application is keeping track of the application's status during each user's session. For example, the Shopping Cart application must keep track of what's in the user's shopping cart. The shopping cart can't simply be stored as a program variable because the program ends when a page is sent back to the user. As a result, the program must find some other way to store the contents of the shopping cart.

There are several ways to store this kind of information during a user's session. One of the most common ways is the ASP.NET *session state* feature: ASP.NET creates and maintains an object called the *Session object* for each user who accesses an application. The application can use this object to store and retrieve data between pages.

The `Session` object can be accessed as a property of the `Page` class, from which all ASP.NET pages are derived. The `Session` object maintains a collection of data items. Each item has both a name and a value. The value can be any type of object, from a simple string or number to a complex object created from a .NET Framework class. For example, the Shopping Cart application uses an object created from the .NET `ArrayList` class to store the user's shopping cart.

Here's a C# example of code that creates an `ArrayList` object and adds it to session state using the name `cart`:

```
ArrayList cart = new ArrayList();
Session["cart"] = cart;
```

Here's the equivalent in VB.NET:

```
Dim cart As New ArrayList()
Session("cart") = cart
```

Here's an example (in C#) of how to retrieve an item from session state:

```
ArrayList cart = (ArrayList)Session["cart"];
```

Note that you must cast the item to an `ArrayList` type. And here's the VB.NET version:

```
Dim cart As ArrayList = CType(Session("cart"), ArrayList)
```

In many applications, you need to test whether an item exists in session state. If so, you simply retrieve the item. If not, you create a new item and add it. Here's C# code that does just that:

```
ArrayList cart;
if (Session["cart"] == null)
{
    cart = new ArrayList();
    Session["cart"] = cart;
}
else
{
    cart = (ArrayList)Session["cart"];
}
```

Here's VB.NET code that does the same thing:

```
Dim cart As ArrayList
If Session("cart") Is Nothing Then
    cart = New ArrayList()
    Session("cart") = cart
Else
    cart = CType(Session("cart"), ArrayList)
End If
```

Here are a few additional details you need to know about session state:

✦ **ASP.NET automatically keeps track of user sessions.** When a user hasn't posted a page after a certain amount of time (typically 20 minutes), the session is closed and any objects stored in session state are deleted.

✦ **A single user can have two sessions open at the same time.** This can happen if the user visits your application using two separate browser windows. Don't worry, ASP.NET is able to keep these browser sessions separate.

✦ **Normally** Session **objects are stored in memory on the server.** That works well for small applications, but it creates problems when more than one server is required to support the application. In that case, ASP.NET lets you move the session state from server memory to somewhere else — either a database or a special server designated for holding session-state data. Fortunately, changing where the session-state data is stored doesn't affect the way you write the code that accesses session state.

Looking into Data Binding

The Shopping Cart application uses *data binding,* a technique designed to simplify the task of getting data out of databases and into controls that can be displayed on a Web page. Data binding lets you point a *control* (such as a drop-down list or a list box) at a *data source* (such as a database or some other object that contains a collection of data items). Then the control automatically extracts specific data from the data source and displays it.

The Shopping Cart application doesn't use a database. However, it does use data binding to display the contents of the user's shopping cart in a list box on the Cart.aspx page (refer to Figure 5-2). The shopping cart itself is stored as an ArrayList object, which is just a collection of individual objects. Each object stored in this ArrayList is a ShoppingCartItem object created from the ShoppingCartItem class.

The magic code that makes all this work is found in the Page_Load method of the Cart.aspx page. Here's the C# version:

```
ArrayList cart = (ArrayList)Session["cart"];
lstCart.DataSource = cart;
lstCart.DataTextField = "ItemLine";
lstCart.DataBind();
```

Here's what's going on in this code, step by step:

1. **The first line retrieves the** ArrayList **object from session state.**

2. **The next line sets the** DataSource **property of the list box (named** lstCart**) so it points to the shopping cart object.**

3. **The** DataTextField **property of the list box is set to** ItemLine**, the property of the individual** ShoppingCartItem **objects that provides the text to be displayed.**

4. **The** DataBind **method of the list box is called to actually bind the data.**

Here's the VB.NET version of the same code:

```
Dim Cart As ArrayList
Cart = CType(Session("cart"), ArrayList)
lstCart.DataSource = Cart
lstCart.DataTextField = "ItemLine"
lstCart.DataBind()
```

If none of this makes sense to you, don't worry. You'll find more information about list boxes in Book 2, Chapter 3, and you'll find more about data binding in Book 6.

Using Master Pages

ASP.NET's Master Pages feature makes it easy to create pages that have a consistent appearance. A *Master Page* is simply a template — a page that provides elements that appear consistently on each page, as well as *content placeholders* that specify where the variable content for each page should appear. A page that actually holds the content that a Master Page displays in its content area is called (wait for it) a *content page*.

Master Pages are such a useful feature that I recommend you use them in all your ASP.NET applications. Unfortunately, the Default.aspx page generated when you first create an ASP.NET application *doesn't* use Master Pages. Well, then, to the dungeon with it. Here's how:

1. **Delete the** Default.aspx **page immediately after starting a new Web site.**

2. **Create a Master Page you can use for the project.**

3. **Use the Add New Item command to add a new** Default.aspx **page to the project, selecting the Master Page for the page.**

When you've added a Master Page to the project, all remaining pages in the project should be content pages rather than regular Web pages. You'll learn how to create master pages and content pages in the following sections.

Creating a Master Page

To create a Master Page, you simply choose Website⇨Add New Item, and then select Master Page from the Templates box. This creates a basic Master Page that has a content placeholder and nothing more, as shown in Figure 5-5.

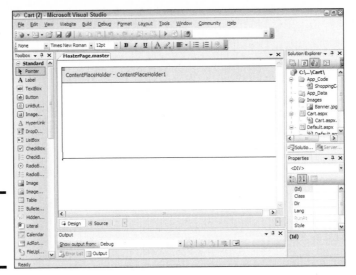

Figure 5-5:
A blank
Master
Page.

You can add any elements you want to the Master Page. For example, you may want to add a banner graphic that appears at the top of each page. To do that, follow these steps:

1. **Add the graphic to your project by using the Website⇨Add Existing Item command.**

2. **Browse to the image file you want to use as the banner, and then click Add.**

3. **This adds the image file to the project.**

4. **Drag the image file from the Solution Explorer window to the Designer window and drop it at the location in the Master Page where you want it to appear.**

Figure 5-6 shows how the Master Page for the Shopping Cart application appears after a banner graphic has been added.

If you look at the `.aspx` code for a Master Page, you'll find that it is different from a regular ASP.NET page in several respects. Here's the code for the Master Page used in the Shopping Cart application:

```
<%@ Master Language="C#" AutoEventWireup="true"
    CodeFile="MasterPage.master.cs"
    Inherits="MasterPage" %>
<!DOCTYPE html PUBLIC "-//W3C//DTD XHTML 1.0 Transitional//EN"
```

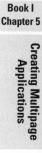

```
        "http://www.w3.org/TR/xhtml1/DTD/xhtml1-transitional.dtd">
<html xmlns="http://www.w3.org/1999/xhtml" >
<head runat="server">
    <title>Acme Pirate Store</title>
</head>
<body>
    <form id="form1" runat="server">
    <div>
        <img src="Banner.jpg" /><br>
        <asp:contentplaceholder id="ContentPlaceholder1"
            runat="server">
        </asp:contentplaceholder>
    </div>
    </form>
</body>
</html>
```

Figure 5-6:
A Master
Page with
a banner
graphic.

There are several noteworthy items in this code:

✦ **Instead of the** `Page` **directive found at the start of most** `.aspx` **files, a Master Page starts with a** `Master` **directive.**

✦ **The** `<img>` **tag identifies the image that's displayed at the top of each page.**

✦ **The** `<asp:contentplaceholder>` **tag identifies the area of the page where the content of each page will be displayed.**

Creating a content page

After you've created a Master Page, you can create *content pages* that display information in the content placeholder of the Master Page.

There are two ways to create a content page:

✦ **Use the Website⇨Add New Item command, select Web Page as the template, check the Select Master Page option, and then choose the Master Page you want the content page applied to.**

✦ **Select a Master Page either in the Solution Explorer or the Web Designer window, then choose the Website⇨Add Content Page command.**

When you create a content page in this manner, initially the page contains just the following markup:

```
<%@ Page Language="C#"
    MasterPageFile="~/MasterPage.master"
    AutoEventWireup="true" CodeFile="Default.aspx.cs"
    Inherits="_Default" Title="Untitled Page" %>
<asp:Content ID="Content1"
    ContentPlaceHolderID="ContentPlaceholder1"
    Runat="Server">
</asp:Content>
```

As you can see, a content page is much simpler than a regular Web page. The `Page` directive uses a `MasterPageFile` attribute to indicate that the page should use the Master Page file named `MasterPage.master`. Then the `Content` element provides the content to be displayed on the page.

All markup for the page's content — that is, text, HTML tags, and ASP.NET server controls — should appear between the `<asp:Content>` and `</asp:Content>` tags. For example, here's the markup for the `Cart` page:

```
<%@ Page Language="C#"
    MasterPageFile="~/MasterPage.master"
    AutoEventWireup="true"
    CodeFile="Cart.aspx.cs" Inherits="Cart"
    Title="Shopping Cart" %>
<asp:Content ID="Content1"
        ContentPlaceHolderID="MainPage"
        Runat="Server">
    <br />
    <asp:ListBox ID="lstCart" runat="server" />
    <br /><br />
    <asp:Button ID="btnContinue" runat="server"
        Text="Continue Shopping"
```

```
        OnClick="btnContinue_Click"/>
       
      <asp:Button ID="btnCheckOut" runat="server"
        Text="Check Out" />
</asp:Content>
```

As you can see, tags that define a list box and two buttons appear between
the `<asp:Content>` and `</asp:Content>` tags.

The C# Version of the Shopping Cart Application

This section presents the C# version of the Shopping Cart application for
your perusal and edification. Peruse the listings at will, and return to the
following list to review the highlights of each one:

✦ **Listing 5-1 is the Master Page.** It displays the banner image (`banner.jpg`)
and provides a single content placeholder named `ContentPlaceholder1`.

✦ **Listing 5-2 is the** `Default.aspx` **file, the markup file for the first content page.** It displays a drop-down list that's preloaded with four costumes: `Pirate`, `Frankenstein`, `Dracula`, and `Clown`.

✦ **Listing 5-3 is the** `Default.aspx.cs` **file, the code-behind file for the
first content page.** Its `Page_Load` method retrieves the shopping cart
from session state if it exists; otherwise the shopping cart is created
and added to session state — and its `btnAdd_Click` method adds the
selected item to the shopping cart.

✦ **Listing 5-4 is the** `Cart.aspx` **file, the markup file for the second content page.** It displays a list box that shows the user's shopping cart and
two buttons.

✦ **Listing 5-5 is the** `Cart.aspx.cs` **file, the code-behind file for the
second page.** Its `Page_Load` method retrieves the shopping cart from
session state, and then sets up the data binding for the list box. The
`btnContinue_Click` method simply redirects the user back to the
`Default.aspx` page.

✦ **Listing 5-6 is the C# version of the** `ShoppingCartItem` **class file.**

Listing 5-1:   The MasterPage.master file (C#)

```
<%@ Master Language="C#" AutoEventWireup="true"
   CodeFile="MasterPage.master.cs"
   Inherits="MasterPage" %>
<!DOCTYPE html PUBLIC
   "-//W3C//DTD XHTML 1.0 Transitional//EN"
```

(continued)

Listing 5-1 *(continued)*

```
    "http://www.w3.org/TR/xhtml1/DTD/xhtml1-transitional.dtd">
<html xmlns="http://www.w3.org/1999/xhtml" >
<head runat="server">
    <title>Acme Pirate Store</title>
</head>
<body>
    <form id="form1" runat="server">
    <div>
        <img src="Banner.jpg" /><br />
        <asp:contentplaceholder id="ContentPlaceholder1"
            runat="server">
        </asp:contentplaceholder>
    </div>
    </form>
</body>
</html>
```

Listing 5-2: The Default.aspx file (C#)

```
<%@ Page Language="C#"
    MasterPageFile="~/MasterPage.master"
    AutoEventWireup="true"
    CodeFile="Default.aspx.cs"
    Inherits="_Default"
    Title="Product Page" %>
<asp:Content ID="Content1"
    ContentPlaceHolderID="ContentPlaceholder1"
    Runat="Server">
    <br />
    Product:
    <asp:DropDownList ID="ddlItem" runat="server"
        Width="140px">
        <asp:ListItem Text="Pirate"></asp:ListItem>
        <asp:ListItem>Frankenstein</asp:ListItem>
        <asp:ListItem>Dracula</asp:ListItem>
        <asp:ListItem>Clown</asp:ListItem>
    </asp:DropDownList><br />
    <br />
    Quantity:
    <asp:TextBox ID="txtQuantity" runat="server"
        Width="82px" />
    <br /><br />
    <asp:Button ID="btnAdd" runat="server"
        Text="Add to Cart"
        OnClick="btnAdd_Click" />
</asp:Content>
```

Listing 5-3:   The Default.aspx.cs file (C#)

```csharp
using System;
using System.Data;
using System.Configuration;
using System.Collections;
using System.Web;
using System.Web.Security;
using System.Web.UI;
using System.Web.UI.WebControls;
using System.Web.UI.WebControls.WebParts;
using System.Web.UI.HtmlControls;
public partial class _Default : System.Web.UI.Page
{
    ArrayList cart;
    protected void Page_Load(object sender,
        EventArgs e)
    {
        if (Session["cart"] == null)
        {
            cart = new ArrayList();
            Session["cart"] = cart;
        }
        else
            cart = (ArrayList)Session["cart"];
    }
    protected void btnAdd_Click(object sender,
        EventArgs e)
    {
        ShoppingCartItem item;
        string description = ddlItem.Text;
        int quantity = Int16.Parse(txtQuantity.Text);
        item = new ShoppingCartItem(description,
            quantity);
        cart.Add(item);
        Response.Redirect("Cart.aspx");
    }
}
```

Listing 5-4:   The Cart.aspx file (C#)

```
<%@ Page Language="C#" MasterPageFile="~/MasterPage.master"
    AutoEventWireup="true"
    CodeFile="Cart.aspx.cs" Inherits="Cart"
    Title="Shopping Cart" %>
<asp:Content ID="Content1"
    ContentPlaceHolderID="ContentPlaceholder1"
    Runat="Server">
```

(continued)

Listing 5-4 *(continued)*

```
        <br />
        <asp:ListBox ID="lstCart" runat="server" />
        <br /><br />
        <asp:Button ID="btnContinue" runat="server"
            Text="Continue Shopping"
            OnClick="btnContinue_Click"/>
         
        <asp:Button ID="btnCheckOut" runat="server"
            Text="Check Out" />
</asp:Content>
```

Listing 5-5:   The Cart.aspx.cs file (C#)

```csharp
using System;
using System.Data;
using System.Configuration;
using System.Collections;
using System.Web;
using System.Web.Security;
using System.Web.UI;
using System.Web.UI.WebControls;
using System.Web.UI.WebControls.WebParts;
using System.Web.UI.HtmlControls;
public partial class Cart : System.Web.UI.Page
{
    protected void Page_Init(object sender,
        EventArgs e)
    {
        ArrayList cart = (ArrayList)Session["cart"];
        lstCart.DataSource = cart;
        lstCart.DataTextField = "ItemLine";
        lstCart.DataBind();
    }
    protected void btnContinue_Click(object sender,
        EventArgs e)
    {
        Response.Redirect("Default.aspx");
    }
}
```

Listing 5-6:   The ShoppingCartItem.cs file (C#)

```csharp
public class ShoppingCartItem
{
    public string Description;
    public int Quantity;
    public ShoppingCartItem(string description,
```

```
        int quantity)
{

    Description = description;
    Quantity = quantity;
}
public string ItemLine
{
    get
    {
        string line = Quantity.ToString() + " "
                    + Description;
        if (Quantity == 1)
            line += " costume";
        else
            line += " costumes";
        return line;
    }
}
}
```

The VB.NET Version of the Shopping Cart Application

This section presents the Visual Basic version of the Shopping Cart application. Here's the list of what's what, followed by the code listings:

 ✦ **Listing 5-7 is the Master Page.**

 ✦ **Listing 5-8 is the** Default.aspx **file.**

 ✦ **Listing 5-9 is the** Default.aspx.vb **file.**

 ✦ **Listing 5-10 is the** Cart.aspx **file.**

 ✦ **Listing 5-11 is the** Cart.aspx.vb **file.**

 ✦ **Listing 5-12 is the VB.NET version of the** ShoppingCartItem **class file.**

Listing 5-7:   The MasterPage.master file (VB)

```
<%@ Master Language="VB"
    CodeFile="MasterPage.master.vb"
    Inherits="MasterPage" %>
<!DOCTYPE html PUBLIC
    "-//W3C//DTD XHTML 1.0 Transitional//EN"
    "http://www.w3.org/TR/xhtml1/DTD/xhtml1-transitional.dtd">
<html xmlns="http://www.w3.org/1999/xhtml" >
<head runat="server">
    <title>Acme Costume Store</title>
</head>
<body>
```

(continued)

Listing 5-7 *(continued)*

```
    <form id="form1" runat="server">
    <div>
        <img src="Banner.jpg" />
        <asp:contentplaceholder
            id="ContentPlaceHolder1"
            runat="server">
        </asp:contentplaceholder>
    </div>
    </form>
</body>
</html>
```

Listing 5-8:   The Default.aspx file (VB)

```
<%@ Page Language="VB"
    MasterPageFile="~/MasterPage.master"
    AutoEventWireup="false"
    CodeFile="Default.aspx.vb"
    Inherits="_Default" %>
<asp:Content ID="Content1"
    ContentPlaceHolderID="ContentPlaceHolder1"
    Runat="Server">
    <br />
    Product:
    <asp:DropDownList ID="ddlItem" runat="server" Width="160px">
        <asp:ListItem Text="Pirate"></asp:ListItem>
        <asp:ListItem>Frankenstein</asp:ListItem>
        <asp:ListItem>Dracula</asp:ListItem>
        <asp:ListItem>Clown</asp:ListItem>
    </asp:DropDownList>
    <br /><br />
    Quantity:
    <asp:TextBox ID="txtQuantity" runat="server"
        Width="81px" />
    <br /><br />
    <asp:Button ID="btnAdd" runat="server"
        Text="Add to Cart" />
</asp:Content>
```

Listing 5-9:   The Default.aspx.vb file (VB)

```
Partial Class _Default
    Inherits System.Web.UI.Page
    Private Cart As ArrayList
    Protected Sub Page_Load( _
            ByVal sender As Object, _
            ByVal e As System.EventArgs) _
            Handles Me.Load
        If Session("cart") Is Nothing Then
            Cart = New ArrayList()
            Session("cart") = Cart
        Else
```

```
                            Cart = CType(Session("cart"), ArrayList)
                End If
            End Sub
            Protected Sub btnAdd_Click( _
                    ByVal sender As Object, _
                    ByVal e As System.EventArgs) _
                    Handles btnAdd.Click
                Dim Item As ShoppingCartItem
                Dim Description As String = ddlItem.Text
                Dim Quantity As Integer
                Quantity = Integer.Parse(txtQuantity.Text)
                Item = New ShoppingCartItem( _
                    Description, Quantity)
                Cart.Add(Item)
                Response.Redirect("Cart.aspx")
            End Sub
        End Class
```

Listing 5-10:   The Cart.aspx file (VB)

```
<%@ Page Language="VB"
    MasterPageFile="~/MasterPage.master"
    AutoEventWireup="false"
    CodeFile="Cart.aspx.vb"
    Inherits="Cart"%>
<asp:Content ID="Content1"
    ContentPlaceHolderID="ContentPlaceHolder1"
    Runat="Server">
    <br /><br />
    <asp:ListBox ID="lstCart" runat="server" />
    <br /><br />
    <asp:Button ID="btnContinue" runat="server"
        Text="Continue Shopping"
        OnClick="btnContinue_Click" />
     
    <asp:Button ID="btnCheckOut" runat="server"
        Text="Check Out" />
</asp:Content>
```

Listing 5-11:   The Cart.aspx.vb file (VB)

```
Partial Class Cart
    Inherits System.Web.UI.Page
    Protected Sub Page_Load( _
            ByVal sender As Object, _
            ByVal e As System.EventArgs) _
            Handles Me.Load
```

(continued)

Listing 5-11 *(continued)*

```
        Dim Cart As ArrayList
        Cart = CType(Session("cart"), ArrayList)
        lstCart.DataSource = Cart
        lstCart.DataTextField = "ItemLine"
        lstCart.DataBind()
    End Sub
    Protected Sub btnContinue_Click( _
            ByVal sender As Object, _
            ByVal e As System.EventArgs) _
            Handles btnContinue.Click
        Response.Redirect("Default.aspx")
    End Sub
End Class
```

Listing 5-12:   The ShoppingCartItem.vb file (VB)

```
Public Class ShoppingCartItem
    Public Description As String
    Public Quantity As Integer
    Public Sub New(ByVal Description As String, _
    ByVal Quantity As Integer)
        Me.Description = Description
        Me.Quantity = Quantity
    End Sub
    Public ReadOnly Property ItemLine() As String
        Get
            Dim Line As String
            Line = Quantity.ToString() & " " _
                        & Description
            If Quantity = 1 Then
                Line = Line & " costume"
            Else
                Line = Line & " costumes"
            End If
            Return Line
        End Get
    End Property
End Class
```

Chapter 6: Testing and Debugging Your ASP.NET Applications

In This Chapter

✔ Dealing with errors

✔ Using the debugger

✔ Stepping through your code

✔ Using breakpoints

✔ Working with Response.Write

*V*isual Web Developer includes a variety of built-in debugging features that can help you track down the nasty bugs that are sure to creep into your application. With the applications we've presented so far, it's hard for anything to go wrong because the applications don't really do any significant work. So, this section starts by presenting a simple calculator application that we can use to explore Visual Web Developer's debugging features.

All code listings used in this book are available for download at `www.dummies.com/go/aspnetaiofd`.

Creating a Simple Calculator Application

Figure 6-1 shows a simple Web page that accepts two numbers as input and displays the sum of the numbers when the user clicks the button. I'll use this simple program as an example for the debugging features presented in this chapter.

The `.aspx` file for this page is shown in Listing 6-1. Listing 6-2 shows the version of the code-behind file for this page. Note that although this program is shown in C#, the same debugging skills apply just as easily to Visual Basic.

Listing 6-1: The Default.aspx page for the Simple Calculator application (C#)

```
<%@ Page Language="C#"
    AutoEventWireup="true"
    CodeFile="Default.aspx.cs"
    Inherits="_Default" %>
<!DOCTYPE html PUBLIC
    "-//W3C//DTD XHTML 1.0 Transitional//EN"
    "http://www.w3.org/TR/xhtml1/DTD/xhtml1-transitional.dtd">
<html xmlns="http://www.w3.org/1999/xhtml" >
<head runat="server">
    <title>Simple Calculator</title>
</head>
<body>
    <form id="form1" runat="server">
        <asp:Label ID="Label1" runat="server" Font-Bold="True" Font-Size="X-
    Large" Text="The Simple Calculator"></asp:Label><br />
        <br />
        <asp:Label ID="Label2" runat="server" Text="First Number:"></asp:Label>
        <asp:TextBox ID="txtNumber1" runat="server" />
        <br /><br />
        <asp:Label ID="Label3" runat="server"
            Text="Second Number:" />
        <asp:TextBox ID="txtNumber2" runat="server" />
        <br /><br />
        <asp:Button ID="btnAdd" runat="server"
            Text="Add" OnClick="btnAdd_Click" />
        <br />
        <br />
        <asp:Label ID="Label4" runat="server"
            Text="The answer is:" />
        <asp:TextBox ID="txtAnswer" runat="server"
            ReadOnly="True" />
    </form>
</body>
</html>
```

Book I
Chapter 6

Testing and
Debugging Your
ASP.NET
Applications

Listing 6-2: **The code-behind file for the Simple Calculator application (Default.aspx.cs) (C#)**

```csharp
using System;
using System.Data;
using System.Configuration;
using System.Web;
using System.Web.Security;
using System.Web.UI;
using System.Web.UI.WebControls;
using System.Web.UI.WebControls.WebParts;
using System.Web.UI.HtmlControls;
public partial class _Default : System.Web.UI.Page
{
    protected void btnAdd_Click(object sender,
        EventArgs e)
    {
        decimal num1 = Decimal.Parse(txtNumber1.Text);
        decimal num2 = Decimal.Parse(txtNumber2.Text);
        decimal ans = num1 + num2;
        txtAnswer.Text = ans.ToString();
    }
}
```

You can see right away the problem waiting to happen with this application. It parses whatever the user enters into the two text boxes to decimal types, and then adds the numbers and displays the result. The application will work fine as long as the user enters valid numbers in both text boxes. But if the user leaves one or both boxes blank, or enters something other than a valid number, the program will fail.

In this case, the problem is easy enough to find. However, this simple program is adequate to demonstrate most of Visual Web Developer's debugging features.

Running an ASP.NET Application

Once you've entered the code for your application, you should run the application to make sure it works. There are several ways to do that. Here are the most common:

✦ **Click the Start Debugging button (shown in the margin), choose Debug➪Start Debugging, or press F5.** This builds the application and runs it in a separate Web server using the built-in Web server and Visual Studio's debugger.

✦ **Choose the Debug⇨Start Without Debugging command, or press Ctrl+F5.** This runs the application in a browser window without starting the debugger.

✦ **Right-click the page in the Solution Explorer window and choose View in Browser.** This also starts the application without running the debugger.

The first time you run an application from Visual Studio, the dialog box shown in Figure 6-2 is displayed. This dialog box indicates that debugging hasn't been configured for the application. Select the first option, which automatically generates a `web.config` file that enables debugging, then click OK to run the application.

Figure 6-2:
You must enable debugging before you can run the debugger.

You can also run an application directly within Visual Studio. To do so, follow these steps:

1. **Right-click the page in the Solution Explorer and choose Browse With.**

This brings up the dialog box shown in Figure 6-3.

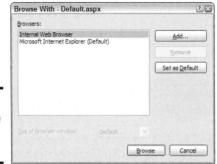

Figure 6-3:
The Browse With dialog box.

2. **Choose Internal Web Browser.**

Book I
Chapter 6

Testing and
Debugging Your
ASP.NET
Applications

3. Click Browse.

This displays the application within Visual Studio, as shown in Figure 6-4.

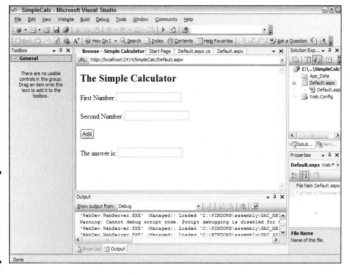

Figure 6-4:
Running an
application
within Visual
Studio.

Dealing with Errors

If your application builds successfully, you can test it to make sure it functions properly. During this testing, you're likely to encounter errors that prevent the application from executing properly. When that happens, an *exception* is thrown. The exception indicates the specific type of error that was encountered and provides useful information that can help you correct the error.

In most cases, your application should anticipate exceptions and provide special code to handle them. You'll learn how to do that in C# in Book 4 and in Visual Basic in Book 5. If you don't provide code to handle an exception, and if the Visual Studio debugger isn't running, a Server Error page such as the one shown in Figure 6-5 is displayed in the browser window.

Although the Server Error page isn't as useful for debugging as the Visual Studio debugger, it does provide information that may help you track down a problem. In particular, here's what the error page in Figure 6-5 shows:

✦ **The name of the application that was running** (`"SimpleCalc"`).

✦ **A descriptive error message** (`"Input string was not in a correct format."`).

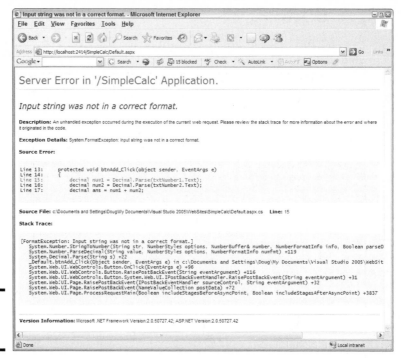

Figure 6-5:
A Server
Error page.

✦ **The code line that was executing when the exception happened (Line 15).**

✦ **The name of the source file (`Default.aspx.cs`).**

In many cases, this information is enough to figure out what went wrong. For example, consider that the line 15 calls the `Decimal.Parse` method to parse the contents of `txtNumber1.Text.` to a decimal value — and the error message is `"Input string was not in a correct format"` — you can pretty much figure out that the value of `txtNumber1.Text` could not be converted to a decimal value. Therefore it's safe to assume that the user didn't enter a value that could be converted to a decimal number — and that the program didn't provide error-checking code to catch the error (if it had, it would have displayed an appropriate error message).

If the information shown in the Server Error page isn't enough to solve the problem, run the application again with the debugger enabled. Then you can use the debugging techniques presented in the rest of this chapter to find and correct the problem.

Working in Break Mode

**Book I
Chapter 6**

**Testing and
Debugging Your
ASP.NET
Applications**

If an unhandled exception (an exception that hasn't been anticipated in your code and handled by a `Try/Catch` statement, as described in Books 4 and 5) occurs while the application is running with the debugger active, the Server Error page isn't displayed. Instead, the application is placed in Break mode, and the debugger takes over as shown in Figure 6-6.

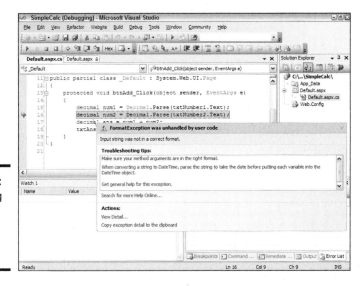

Figure 6-6:
Debugging
an appli-
cation in
Visual
Studio.

In Break mode, Visual Studio highlights the statement that threw the exception, and displays a balloon with helpful information about the exception. Here you can see the same error message that was displayed in the Server Error page in Figure 6-5: `"Input string was not in correct format."` The balloon also displays some helpful debugging tips.

Displaying Variable Data

One of the most useful debugging features in Visual Web Developer is the *DataTips* feature, which displays the value of a variable when you point at it while the system is in Break mode. For example, if you point at the `Text` property for the `txtNumber2` text box in Figure 6-6, a tip balloon appears and shows the current value of this property, as in Figure 6-7.

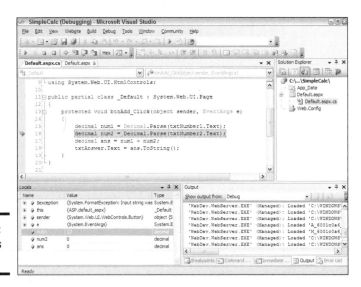

Figure 6-7:
Displaying
a DataTip.

You can even use a DataTip to change the actual value of a variable while the program is running. Just click the value in the DataTip, and then type a new value.

Another way to determine the values of variables is to use the Locals window. Figure 6-8 shows the Locals window in the lower-left corner of the screen. As you can see, the value of the num1 variable has been properly parsed to the value 12, but the num2 variable remains at its default value, 0 (zero).

Figure 6-8:
The Locals
window.

If the Locals window isn't visible, you can summon it by choosing Debug➪ Windows➪Locals.

**Book I
Chapter 6**

Testing and
Debugging Your
ASP.NET
Applications

To find the value of the `Text` property of a control in the Locals window, first expand the `this` node, which is located near the top of the Locals window. (If you're working in Visual Basic, use the `Me` node instead.) This lists all the controls on the current page. Locate and expand the control you're looking for, then locate and select its `Text` property.

Stepping Through a Program

One of the best ways to find stubborn program bugs is to execute the program one statement at a time. This can help you track the flow of the program, and can also help you study the effect that each statement has on the program's variables.

Table 6-1 lists the buttons that appear on the Debug toolbar to help you control the program's execution. (The Debug toolbar usually appears near the top of the screen, just beneath the Standard toolbar.)

Table 6-1		The Debug Toolbar Buttons
Button	*Name*	*Function*
▶	**Continue**	Continues execution with the next statement.
❚❚	**Break**	Interrupts the application and puts Visual Web Developer in Break mode.
■	**Stop Debugging**	Stops the application.
⤶	**Restart**	Restarts the application.
⇨	**Show Next Statement**	Highlights the next statement to be executed.
⤸≣	**Step Into**	Executes the next statement and then breaks. If the statement calls a method, then execution stops with the first statement in the method.
⤵≣	**Step Over**	Executes the next statement, and then breaks. If the statement calls a method, then the entire method is executed without breaking.
⤴≣	**Step Out**	Finishes the current method and then breaks.

Setting Breakpoints

A *breakpoint* is a statement in the program that you've marked so that the program will temporarily stop its execution when it the statement is reached. When the application reaches a statement that's been marked as a breakpoint, the application suspends execution and enters Break mode. Breakpoints are useful when you know you have a problem area in your program that you want to make the focus of your debugging efforts. For example, suppose a particular statement is throwing an exception and you can't figure out why. You might set a breakpoint a few statements ahead of the problem statement, then step into the program just before the problem statement, moving one statement at a time. This can give you an idea of what actions are leading up to the problem.

To set a breakpoint, click in the gray bar that runs down the left side of the Code window, next to the statement where you want the breakpoint to be set. A big red dot will appear to let you know you've set the breakpoint, as shown in Figure 6-9.

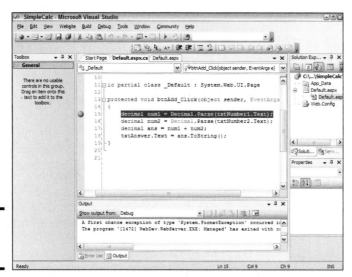

Figure 6-9:
Setting a
breakpoint.

Here are a few other interesting things you can do with breakpoints:

✦ **You can see a list of all the breakpoints you have set for the entire application in the Breakpoints window.** To display this window, choose Debug➪Windows➪Breakpoints.

Book I
Chapter 6

Testing and
Debugging Your
ASP.NET
Applications

✦ **To remove a breakpoint, click the big red dot that represents the breakpoint and press the Delete key.** Or, click the breakpoint in the Breakpoints window to select it and then hit the Delete key.

✦ **To remove all breakpoints, choose Debug⇨Delete All Breakpoints.**

✦ **You can disable a breakpoint by right-clicking its big red dot and choosing Disable Breakpoint.** Or you can uncheck the breakpoint in the Breakpoints window.

✦ **To disable all breakpoints, choose Debug⇨Disable All Breakpoints.**

Using Response.Write for Debugging

One more debugging technique I want to mention before putting a breakpoint (so to speak) on this chapter is the `Response.Write` method. `Response.Write` lets you write any text you want to the output page. For example, if you're not sure of the value of a variable or property, you can use `Response.Write` to display the variable or property value on the page, like this:

```
Response.Write(txtNumber1.Text);
```

Note that any text you write via the `Response.Write` command will appear at the top of the page, before the HTML for any controls.

Also, the `Response.Write` method doesn't automatically force output to appear on a separate line. To force a line break, add an HTML <br> tag to the output, like this:

```
Response.Write(txtNumber1.Text + "<br>");
```

Although this way of doing the job may be crude compared to the power of Visual Studio's debugger, there are still many situations where a judiciously placed `Response.Write` call can help solve tough debugging problems.

Book II

Web Controls

The 5th Wave   By Rich Tennant

WANDA HAD THE DISTINCT FEELING HER HUSBAND'S NEW WEB SITE WAS ABOUT TO BECOME INTERACTIVE.

Contents at a Glance

Chapter 1: Using Basic Web Server Controls

C ontrols are the building blocks of ASP.NET pages. In fact, about half of ASP.NET programming consists of dragging controls from the toolbox onto the page and tweaking the properties of the controls to get them just right.

This chapter presents a basic subset of ASP.NET controls that you'll use in many, if not most, of the applications you work on. In particular, you get a look at six different controls and how to use them: Label, TextBox, Button, CheckBox, RadioButton, and Image. In addition, this chapter introduces an important feature called View State that's available for all ASP.NET controls.

All code listings used in this book are available for download at www.dummies. com/go/aspnetaiofd. In addition, although the code listing in this chapter is written in C#, the VB.NET version is available for download too.

Using Label Controls

A Label control displays text to identify a feature on a Web page. For example, the page in Figure 1-1 shows four Label controls. The first provides instructions for the user. The next two identify input fields the user should enter data into. The fourth label displays the result of a calculation.

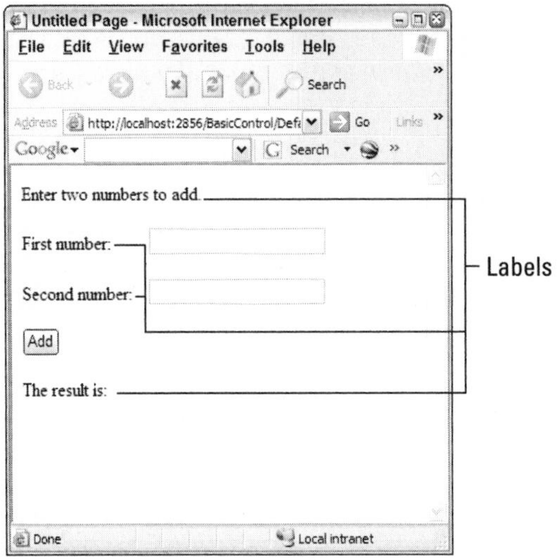

Figure 1-1:
A page
with labels.

The .aspx markup looks like this for the four labels shown in Figure 1-1:

```
<asp:Label ID="Label1" runat="server"
    Text="Enter two numbers to add." />
<asp:Label ID="Label2" runat="server"
    Text="First number:" Width="110px" />
<asp:Label ID="Label3" runat="server"
    Text="Second number:" Width="110px" />
<asp:Label ID="lblResult" runat="server"
    Text="The result is: " />
```

The first two properties specified for these label controls are found in all ASP.NET controls. ID provides a name for the control that you can use to refer to the control from your code. If you don't plan on referring to a control in your code, you'll probably leave the ID set to the default generated by Visual Studio when you drag the control from the toolbox to the page. But if you do plan on referring to the control in your code, you should change the ID property to something more meaningful. In this example, I left the first three labels at their generated values (Label1, Label2, and Label3) but changed the ID of the fourth label to lblResult.

The `runat` attribute is also required for all ASP.NET controls. It indicates that the control will run at the server rather than at the browser. Note that `server` is the only value you can code for the `runat` attribute.

To set the text that's displayed by a label, you use the `Text` property. You can set the `Text` property in the `.aspx` markup file by using the `Text` attribute, as each of the four controls in this example do. You can also set the `Text` property in code. Here's what that looks like:

```
lblResult.Text = "The result is: " + answer.ToString();
```

The `Label` control also includes many other properties that let you control the way the label and its text will appear. For example, you can change the color, font, or size of the label. You can also specify the width of the label by using the `Width` property. This property is useful because it lets you line up text boxes or other controls that are associated with labels. For example, the two text boxes shown in Figure 1-1 line up because the `Width` property of the labels next to them are both set to 110.

The `Text` property of a `Label` control can include HTML tags. Then, the HTML tags are used to format the text displayed by the label. For example, you can display text in bold by using the `<b>` tag, like this:

```
Label1.Text = "Have a <b>great</b> day!";
```

Here the word **great** is displayed in boldface.

Using TextBox Controls

A `TextBox` control provides a way for users to enter text data. For example, Figure 1-2 shows a page that features two text box controls. The user can use these text boxes to enter a username and password. Notice that when the user enters data into the second text box, the data isn't displayed; instead, dots are displayed to hide the data entered by the user (a common requirement for password-entry fields).

The `.aspx` markup for these two text boxes is as follows:

```
<asp:TextBox ID="txtName" runat="server" />
<asp:TextBox ID="txtPassword" runat="server"
    TextMode="Password" />
```

Here, you can see that `TextMode` has been set to `Password` for the second text box.

Text boxes

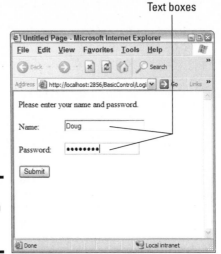

Figure 1-2:
A page with
two text
boxes.

The following table lists the properties you're most likely to use with a
`TextBox` control:

Property	Description
ID	The ID of the control.
Runat	Must specify `Runat="Server"`.
Text	The text displayed by the control.
TextMode	`SingleLine` (the default), `MultiLine`, or `Password`.
Wrap	`True` to automatically wrap long lines.
Columns	Sets the width of the text box.
Rows	Sets the height of the text box.
MaxLength	Sets the maximum number of characters the text box will accept.
ReadOnly	If true, the text box is read-only.

To create a multiline text box, set the `TextMode` property to `MultiLine`.
Then, the text box will accept more than one line of input. Then you can use
the `Rows` property to specify the height of the text box. You may also want
to set the `Wrap` property to `True` so text that goes beyond the width of the
text box will wrap automatically. Here is markup that's typical for a multiline
text box:

```
<asp:TextBox ID="txtDescription" runat="server"
    TextMode="MultiLine"
    Rows="5" Wrap="True" />
```

Understanding view state

All ASP.NET server controls have a feature called *view state* that maintains the state of the control's properties between round trips to and from the server. By default, view state is maintained for all controls.

Whenever a program changes the value of a control property, the property value is written to a special hidden field called `ViewState`. This field is sent to the browser. Then, when the user posts the page back to the server, the `ViewState` field is sent back to the server and used to set property values to their previous settings.

For example, suppose you change the `Text` property of a `Label` control. Then the value

you set the `Text` property to will be included in the `ViewState` field. That way, when the page is sent back to the server, the value you set will be restored.

View state is enabled by default, but you can disable it for a control by specifying `Enable ViewState="False"` for the control. You should disable view state in two situations:

✦ When you have changed the value of a property, but you want the property to be restored to its default value (or the value you specified in the `.aspx` file) at the next round trip.

✦ When the page will not be posted back to itself.

You can also use the `Text` property to retrieve data entered by the user. The `Text` property is a string value, so you'll need to convert it to an appropriate type if the value represents a number. For example, here's how to convert text input to a decimal value in C#:

```
decimal amount = Decimal.Parse(txtAmount.Text);
```

In VB.NET, the code would look like this:

```
Dim Amount As Decimal
Amount = Decimal.Parse(txtAmount.Text)
```

In both cases, the conversion will throw an exception if the user doesn't enter a valid number. So you'll need to put the conversion inside a `try` statement. For more on exceptions, see Book 4 for C# and Book 5 for Visual Basic. (Note that you can also avoid the exception by using a validation control as described in the next chapter.)

Using Button Controls

ASP.NET provides three distinct types of `Button` controls: `Button`, `Link Button`, and `ImageButton`. These three types of buttons have the same behavior, but they each have a different appearance. A standard `Button` control looks like a regular button that the user can click. A `LinkButton` looks like a hyperlink, and an `ImageButton` displays an image file, so its appearance depends entirely on the content of the image file. Figure 1-3 shows a Web page with a button of each type.

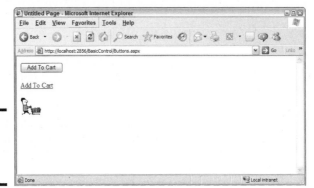

Figure 1-3:
A page
with three
buttons.

Here is the markup for the three buttons shown in Figure 1-3:

```
<asp:Button ID="Button1" runat="server"
    Text="Add To Cart" />
<asp:LinkButton ID="LinkButton1" runat="server"
    Text="Add To Cart" />
<asp:ImageButton ID="ImageButton1" runat="server"
    ImageUrl="~/cart.gif" />
```

Note that the `Text` property for a `LinkButton` control can also be specified as content that appears between the start and end tags, like this:

```
<asp:LinkButton ID="LinkButton1" runat="server" >
    Add To Cart
</asp:LinkButton>
```

Either method is an acceptable way to code a `LinkButton`.

Because the purpose of a button is to allow the user to click it, normally a button control has an event handler for the `Click` event associated with it. In C#, you use the `OnClick` attribute to specify the event handler, like this:

```
<asp:Button ID="Button1" runat="server"
    Text="Add To Cart" OnClick="Button1_Click" />
```

Here the method named `Button1_Click` will be called when the button is clicked.

In Visual Basic, you specify a `Handles` clause on the `Sub` statement for the procedure that handles the event. Here's an example:

```
Protected Sub Button1_Click (sender As Object, _
        e As EventArgs) Handles Button1.Click
```

Then, you don't need to specify the `OnClick` attribute in the `.aspx` file. (You can use `OnClick` in VB.NET if you prefer, but it's more common to use `Handles`.)

Here are a few other things you should know about button controls:

✦ **The page is automatically posted back to the server when the user clicks a button.**

✦ **For an `ImageButton` control, the `e` argument that's passed to the event handler includes the X and Y coordinates of the point within the button image where the user clicked.** In some cases, you may need to use this information to determine what part of the button image the user clicked.

✦ **In addition to the `Click` event, buttons also raise a `Command` event if the `CommandName` property has been set for the button.** Then the `e` argument includes the `CommandName` property of the button that was clicked. This feature of button controls can come in handy when you want to use a single event handler for several buttons.

Book II
Chapter 1

Using Basic Web
Server Controls

Using CheckBox Controls

A *check box* is a control that the user can click to either check or uncheck. Normally check boxes are used to let the user specify Yes or No to an option. Figure 1-4 shows a page with three check boxes.

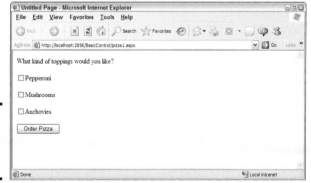

Figure 1-4:
A page with three check boxes.

Here's the markup I used to create these three check boxes:

```
<asp:CheckBox ID="chkPepperoni" runat="server"
    Text="Pepperoni" />
```

```
<asp:CheckBox ID="chkMushrooms" runat="server"
    Text="Mushrooms" />
<asp:CheckBox ID="chkAnchovies" runat="server"
    Text="Anchovies" />
```

By default, a check box is initially unchecked. To make a check box checked when it's initially displayed, set its Checked property to True. For example, here's how you can suggest Anchovies to your customers:

```
<asp:CheckBox ID="chkAnchovies" runat="server"
    Text="Anchovies" Checked="True" />
```

Checking the Checked property

Usually check box controls do not cause a postback when they are clicked. The most common way to deal with check boxes in your code is to check their status in the Page_Load method or in another event handler, such as the handler for the Click event of a button. Here's a Page_Load method that uses the Checked property of the three check boxes on the page, and then sets the Text property of a label to indicate which toppings were ordered:

```
protected void Page_Load(object sender, EventArgs e)
{
    String order = "";
    if (chkPepperoni.Checked)
        order += "Pepperoni<br>";
    if (chkMushrooms.Checked)
        order += "Mushrooms<br>";
    if (chkAnchovies.Checked)
        order += "Anchovies<br>";
    lblOrder.Text = order;
}
```

Figure 1-5 shows how the page appears after the user has selected two of the check boxes and clicked the Order Pizza button.

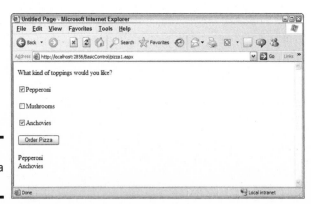

Figure 1-5:
Confirming a pizza order.

For you Visual Basic programmers, here's the equivalent code in VB.NET:

```
Protected Sub Page_Load(ByVal sender As Object, _
        ByVal e As System.EventArgs) _
        Handles Me.Load
    Dim Order As String = ""
    If chkPepperoni.Checked Then
        Order &= "Pepperoni<br>"
    End If
    If chkMushrooms.Checked Then
        Order &= "Mushrooms<br>"
    End If
    If (chkAnchovies.Checked) Then
        Order &= "Anchovies<br>"
    End If
    lblOrder.Text = Order
End Sub
```

Another way to check the Checked property

If you prefer, you can provide an event handler for the CheckChanged event method of a check box, which is raised when the user clicks the check box. Note, however, that clicking a check box doesn't usually cause a postback. As a result, the page won't actually be submitted to the server until the user clicks a button or other control that *does* cause a postback. Then the CheckChanged event handler can be called — after the Page_Load method but before the handler for the event that caused the page to be posted.

Listing 1-1 shows a C# version of a code-behind file that handles the CheckChanged events for the pizza-order check boxes. As you can see, the CheckChanged event for each check box sets a boolean variable that indicates whether the item has been ordered. Then, the Click event for the btnOrder Pizza button uses these boolean variables to determine which items have been ordered. (The VB.NET version of this code would be very similar.)

For this listing, you can assume that the .aspx markup file includes the necessary onCheckChanged and onClick clauses to call the event handler methods in the code-behind file. For example, the markup for the check boxes look like this:

```
<asp:checkbox id="chkPepperoni" runat="server"
    oncheckedchanged="chkPepperoni_CheckedChanged"
    text="Pepperoni" />
<asp:checkbox id="chkMushrooms" runat="server"
    oncheckedchanged="chkMushrooms_CheckedChanged"
    text="Mushrooms" />
<asp:checkbox id="chkAnchovies" runat="server"
    oncheckedchanged="chkAnchovies_CheckedChanged"
    text="Anchovies" />
```

Book II
Chapter 1

Using Basic Web
Server Controls

And the markup for the `btnOrderPizza` button looks like this:

```
<asp:button id="btnOrderPizza" runat="server"
    onclick="btnOrderPizza_Click" text="Button" />
```

Listing 1-1:   The code-behind file for a pizza order page (C#)

```csharp
using System;
using System.Data;
using System.Configuration;
using System.Collections;
using System.Web;
using System.Web.Security;
using System.Web.UI;
using System.Web.UI.WebControls;
using System.Web.UI.WebControls.WebParts;
using System.Web.UI.HtmlControls;
public partial class Pizza2 : System.Web.UI.Page
{
    boolean boolPepperoni = false;
    boolean boolMushrooms = false;
    boolean boolAnchovies = false;
    protected void chkPepperoni_CheckedChanged(
        object sender, EventArgs e)
    {
        boolPepperoni = chkPepperoni.Checked;
    }
    protected void chkMushrooms_CheckedChanged(
        object sender, EventArgs e)
    {
        boolMushrooms = chkMushrooms.Checked;
    }
    protected void chkAnchovies_CheckedChanged(
        object sender, EventArgs e)
    {
        boolAnchovies = chkAnchovies.Checked;
    }
    protected void btnOrderPizza_Click(object sender,
        EventArgs e)
    {
        String order = "";
        if (boolPepperoni)
            order += "Pepperoni<br>";
        if (boolMushrooms)
            order += "Mushrooms<br>";
        if (boolAnchovies)
            order += "Anchovies<br>";
        lblOrder.Text = order;
    }
}
```

Using RadioButton Controls

Radio buttons are similar to check boxes, but with a crucial difference: Radio buttons travel in groups, and a user can select only one radio button in each group at a time. When you click a radio button to select it, whatever radio button in the group was previously selected is automatically deselected.

Figure 1-6 shows a page with two groups of radio buttons. The first group lets the user select the size of a pizza to be ordered. The second group lets the user select the crust style.

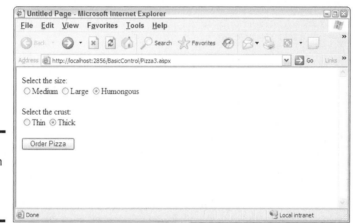

Figure 1-6:
A page with
two groups
of radio
buttons.

The markup used to create these radio buttons is as follows:

```
<asp:RadioButton ID="rdoSizeMedium" runat="server"
    GroupName="Size" Text="Medium" />
<asp:RadioButton ID="rdoSizeLarge" runat="server"
    GroupName="Size" Text="Large" />
<asp:RadioButton ID="rdoSizeHumongous" runat="server"
    GroupName="Size" Text="Humongous" />
<asp:RadioButton ID="rdoCrustThin" runat="server"
    GroupName="Crust" Text="Thin" />
<asp:RadioButton ID="rdoCrustThick" runat="server"
    GroupName="Crust" Text="Thick" />
```

As you can see, the GroupName attribute specifies the group to which each radio button belongs. The first three buttons specify Size as the GroupName, while the last two specify Crust.

As with check boxes, you use the `Checked` property to determine whether a radio button has been selected. For example, here's a snippet of C# code that sets a label's `Text` property to indicate the size and crust style of a pizza:

```
string pizza = "";
if (rdoSizeMedium.Checked)
    pizza += "Medium ";
else if (rdoSizeLarge.Checked)
    pizza += "Large ";
else if (rdoSizeHumongous.Checked)
    pizza += "Humongous ";
if (rdoCrustThin.Checked)
    pizza += "Thin Crust";
else if (rdoCrustThick.Checked)
    pizza += "Thick Crust";
lblPizza.Text = pizza;
```

Here's the equivalent in VB.NET:

```
Dim pizza As String = ""
If rdoSizeMedium.Checked Then
    pizza &= "Medium "
Else If rdoSizeLarge.Checked
    pizza &= "Large "
Else If rdoSizeHumongous.Checked
    pizza &= "Humongous "
End If
If rdoCrustThin.Checked Then
    pizza &= "Thin Crust"
Else If rdoCrustThick.Checked
    pizza &= "Thick Crust"
End If
lblPizza.Text = pizza
```

Using Image Controls

An *image control* is simply a control that displays an image file; the user clicks the image to use the control. The two most common types of image files used in Web applications are JPEG and GIF files. JPEG files are used typically for larger, more detailed images; while GIF files are the standard choice for small icons or images on buttons.

Figure 1-7 shows an ASP.NET page with an image control. The markup used to create this control is as follows:

```
<asp:Image ID="Image1" runat="server"
    ImageUrl="~/Odie.JPG"
    Height="200px" Width="285px"
    AlternateText="This is Odie." />
```

Figure 1-7:
A page with
an image
control.

As you can see, the ImageUrl property provides the URL of the image to be displayed. In this case, the file Odie.JPG within the project's root folder (that's what the ~ indicates) is displayed. The Height and Width properties indicate the size of the image, and the AlternateText property provides text that's displayed if the user's browser can't display the image.

Chapter 2: Using Validation Controls

In This Chapter

✔ Using validation controls to validate user input

✔ Working with advanced validation controls

✔ Adding a validation summary to a page

✔ Validating more than one group of input fields

*V*alidation is one of the most important parts of any type of computer programming. The moment you expose your program to the outside world by asking a user to input some data, the possibility arises that the user will enter the wrong data, or that the user will forget to enter any data at all. To get any real work done, ASP.NET programs need to protect themselves from such errors and omissions.

You won't be able to catch all the errors a user might make. For example, a user might spell his or her name wrong (due to a bad day, lack of coffee, or whatever). But you can detect and prevent common types of errors. For example, you can require that the user enter some data into a text box — and, if the text box is supposed to contain a number, you can require that the user enter a valid number. This chapter shows how to do that and more.

All code listings used in this book are available for download at `www.dummies.com/go/aspnetaiofd`.

Validating the Hard Way

In Book 1, I present a simple calculator program that added two numbers entered by the user. In real-world terms, that program is a little too simple; it didn't include any validation code. It would crash if the user failed to enter correct numeric data.

One way — okay, the hard way — to add validation code to that program (or to any other program) is to type in some code that checks the validity of each input field before the program acts on the data. The program will display an error message if any incorrect data is detected.

For a glimpse of what this approach would look like, consider the following
`.aspx` file:

```
<%@ Page Language="C#"
    AutoEventWireup="true"
    CodeFile="Default.aspx.cs"
    Inherits="_Default" %>
<!DOCTYPE html PUBLIC
    "-//W3C//DTD XHTML 1.0 Transitional//EN"
    "http://www.w3.org/TR/xhtml1/DTD/xhtml1-transitional.dtd">
<html xmlns="http://www.w3.org/1999/xhtml" >
<head runat="server">
    <title>Simple Calculator</title>
</head>
<body>
    <form id="form1" runat="server">
        <asp:Label ID="Label1" runat="server"
            Text="First name:" />
        <asp:TextBox ID="txtFirstName" runat="server" />
        <asp:Label ID="lblErrorFirstName" runat="server"
            ForeColor="Red" EnableViewState="False" />
        <br />
        <asp:Label ID="Label2" runat="server"
            Text="Last name:" />
        <asp:TextBox ID="txtLastName" runat="server" />
        <asp:Label ID="lblErrorLastName" runat="server"
            ForeColor="Red" EnableViewState="False" />
        <br /><br />
        <asp:Button ID="btnSubmit" runat="server"
            Text="Submit" OnClick="btnAdd_Click" />
        <br /><br />
        <asp:Label ID="lblValid" runat="server" />
    </form>
</body>
</html>
```

This page displays two text boxes, named `txtFirstName` and `txtLastName`.
Next to the text boxes are labels named `lblErrorFirstName` and `lblError`
`LastName`. A button named `btnSubmit` lets the user submit the first and last
name he or she entered, and a final label named `lblValid` is used to display
a message that indicates whether the user entered valid data.

The validation requirements for this page are simple: The user must enter
something in both of the text boxes. Here's the `Click` event handler for the
`Submit` button:

```
protected void btnAdd_Click(object sender, EventArgs e)
{
    if (validData())
        lblValid.Text = "You entered valid data.";
    else
        lblValid.Text = "You did not enter valid data.";
}
```

As you can see, the `Click` event handler calls a method named `validData` to determine if the user entered correct data. This method is defined as follows:

```
private boolean validData()
{
    boolean valid = true;
    if (txtFirstName.Text == "")
    {
        lblErrorFirstName.Text
            = "Required field.";
        valid = false;
    }
    if (txtLastName.Text == "")
    {
        lblErrorLastName.Text
            = "Required field.";
        valid = false;
    }
    return valid;
}
```

Figure 2-1 shows this page in action. Here you can see an error message displayed for the `LastName` text box because the user didn't enter a last name.

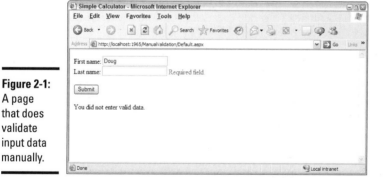

Figure 2-1:
A page
that does
validate
input data
manually.

That's a lot of work just to make sure the user has entered some data. As the next section reveals, however, this type of code is rarely necessary in ASP.NET applications.

Validation Controls to the Rescue!

The good folks at Microsoft realized that most ASP.NET applications would need to validate input data, and that programmers like to write as little code as possible. To meet both criteria, they created a collection of handy *valida-tion controls* that can automatically validate input data, with little or no code required.

These validation controls live in the Validation section of the toolbox. (The Validation section is the third section of the toolbox, beneath the Standard controls and the Data controls.) There are six different validation controls you can use:

✦ `RequiredFieldValidator`: This is most popular of the validation con-trols. It requires the user to enter some value in a field. Any value will do, but the user must enter something.

✦ `CompareValidator`: This validator compares the value entered by the user with some predetermined value. One of the most common uses of this validator is to ensure that the user enters data of the correct type. For example, if a text box requires numeric input, you can use a `CompareValidator` to make sure the user enters a valid number.

✦ `RangeValidator`: This validator makes sure that the value entered by the user falls within a given range.

✦ `RegularExpressionValidator`: This validator makes sure that the user enters a value that matches a pattern. For example, you can use this validator for Zip codes, telephone numbers, and so on.

✦ `CustomValidator`: This validator lets you write your own code to deter-mine whether the user entered correct input data.

✦ `ValidationSummary`: This control is used along with other validation controls to display a summary message that lists all errors discovered on the page.

As with any other ASP.NET control, you can add a validator to a page by dragging it from the toolbox onto the page. If you're working in Design view, you can use the Properties window to set the properties of the validator con-trol. If you prefer to work in Source view, you can edit the markup directly to set the validator's properties.

Using the RequiredFieldValidator Control

The most basic type of ASP.NET validation control is the *required field valida-tor*. As its name implies, it requires the user to enter some value — any value will do — into an input field. `RequiredFieldValidator` controls are used most often with `TextBox` controls, but you can use them with other types of input controls as well.

Besides the ubiquitous ID and Runat attributes, a RequiredFieldValidator control has two important attributes you should always set:

✦ ControlToValidate: Provides the ID of the input control that the required field validator should be associated with.

✦ ErrorMessage: Provides the text that the validator control will display if the user doesn't enter any data into the associated input control.

For example, here's a typical RequiredFieldValidator control:

```
<asp:RequiredFieldValidator ID="RequiredFieldValidator2"
    runat="server"
    ControlToValidate="txtLastName"
    ErrorMessage="Required field." />
```

**Book II
Chapter 2**

Here the required field validator is associated with the control named txtLastName and the error message is "Required field."

You should place the RequiredFieldValidator control where you want the error message to be displayed if the user fails to enter a value. Listing 2-1 provides the complete .aspx file that creates a page similar to the one shown in Figure 2-1:

**Using Validation
Controls**

Listing 2-1: A complete .aspx file for validating input data (C#)

```
<%@ Page Language="C#"
    AutoEventWireup="true"
    CodeFile="Default.aspx.cs"
    Inherits="_Default" %>
<!DOCTYPE html PUBLIC
    "-//W3C//DTD XHTML 1.0 Transitional//EN"
    "http://www.w3.org/TR/xhtml1/DTD/xhtml1-transitional.dtd">
<html xmlns="http://www.w3.org/1999/xhtml" >
<head runat="server">
    <title>Simple Calculator</title>
</head>
<body>
    <form id="form1" runat="server">
        <asp:Label ID="Label1" runat="server"
            Text="First name:" />
        <asp:TextBox ID="txtFirstName" runat="server" /> 
        <asp:RequiredFieldValidator ID="RequiredFieldValidator1"
            runat="server"
            ControlToValidate="txtFirstName"
            ErrorMessage="Required field." />
        <br />
        <asp:Label ID="Label2" runat="server"
            Text="Last name:" />
        <asp:TextBox ID="txtLastName" runat="server" /> 
```

(continued)

Listing 2-1 (continued)

```
        <asp:RequiredFieldValidator ID="RequiredFieldValidator2"
            runat="server"
            ControlToValidate="txtLastName"
            ErrorMessage="Required field." />
        <br /><br />
        <asp:Button ID="btnSubmit" runat="server"
            Text="Submit" OnClick="btnAdd_Click" /><br /><br />
    </form>
</body>
</html>
```

Here the two labels named `lblErrorFirstName` and `lblErrorLastName` have been replaced by required field validators that automatically validate the text boxes. No server-side code is required to validate the input data.

It's important to understand that ASP.NET validators use client-side code to perform their validation. Thus, if the user clicks a Submit button and the validators determine that at least one of the input fields on the page contains invalid data, the page won't be posted to the server. (The validation controls also use server-side code to check the data's validity. That's necessary because it's possible for the user to disable or bypass the client-side code.)

Using the CompareValidator Control

Next to the `RequiredFieldValidator` control, the `CompareValidator` control is probably the validator you'll use most. It performs several basic types of comparison checks on an input field. It can perform the following basic types of comparisons:

✦ **Constant comparisons, in which the value entered by the user is compared with a constant value.** For example, you can ensure that a numeric value is greater than zero.

✦ **Comparisons with other controls, in which the value entered by the user is compared with the value entered for another control.** For example, if a page has fields that let the user enter a start date and an end date, you can use a `CompareValidator` control to make sure that the end date does not occur before the start date.

✦ **Type comparisons, which let you verify that the user has entered the correct type of data.** This is one of the most useful types of comparisons performed by the `CompareValidator` control.

The following table lists the properties you're most likely to set for the `CompareValidator` control:

Property	Description
ControlToValidate	The ID of the input control you want to validate.
ErrorMessage	The error message displayed if the control fails the validation.
ValueToCompare	The value that the control should be compared to.
ControlToCompare	The ID of another control that will supply the value to compare.
Operator	The comparison operation to perform. You can specify Equal, NotEqual, LessThan, LessThanEqual, GreaterThan, GreaterThanEqual, or DataTypeCheck.
Type	The data type. You can specify String, Integer, Double, Date, or Currency.

If the user doesn't enter any data into a control, the validator doesn't do the comparison. Accordingly, you should always include a RequiredField Validator control if you want to require the user to enter a value.

When you use more than one validator for a single control, you'll usually want to set the validator's Display property to Dynamic. This property sets the width of the control to zero if the validation succeeds. If you leave the Display property set to its default (Static), the validator takes up space on the page even if no error message is displayed.

Here's an example of a text box that has a RequiredFieldValidator control and a CompareValidator control that makes sure the value is an integer:

```
<asp:TextBox ID="txtQuantity" runat="server" />
<asp:RequiredFieldValidator ID="RequiredFieldValidator1"
    runat="server"
    ControlToValidate="txtQuantity"
    Display="Dynamic"
    ErrorMessage="Required field." />
<asp:CompareValidator ID="CompareValidator1"
    runat="server"
    ControlToValidate="txtQuantity"
    Display="Dynamic"
    ErrorMessage="Must be a number."
    Operator="DataTypeCheck"
    Type="Integer" />
```

Note that if you use an operator other than DataTypeCheck, a data-type check happens automatically. That means you don't need to use a separate CompareValidator control to test the data type before you do a comparison.

For example, suppose you want to make sure a field is entered, is a valid number, and is greater than zero. In that case, the following validators will do the job:

```
<asp:TextBox ID="txtQuantity" runat="server" />
<asp:RequiredFieldValidator ID="RequiredFieldValidator1"
    runat="server"
    ControlToValidate="txtQuantity"
    Display="Dynamic"
    ErrorMessage="Required field." />
<asp:CompareValidator ID="CompareValidator2"
    runat="server"
    ControlToValidate="txtQuantity"
    ErrorMessage="Must be greater than zero."
    Type="Integer"
    Operator="GreaterThan"
    ValueToCompare="0" />
```

Using the RangeValidator Control

The RangeValidator control is similar to the CompareValidator control, but instead of doing a single comparison check, it does two checks to make sure the value entered by the user falls within a particular range of values. Here's a table that sums up the properties you can use with the RangeValidator control:

Property	Description
ControlToValidate	The ID of the input control to validate.
ErrorMessage	The error message displayed if the control fails the validation.
MinimumValue	The smallest acceptable value.
MaximumValue	The largest acceptable value.
Type	The data type. You can specify String, Integer, Double, Date, or Currency.

Here's an example of a RangeValidator control that makes sure a value falls between 0 and 100:

```
<asp:RangeValidator ID="RangeValidator1" runat="server"
    ControlToValidate="TextBox1"
    Display="Dynamic"
    ErrorMessage="Must be between 0 and 100. "
    MinimumValue="0"
    MaximumValue="100"
    Type="Integer" />
```

Using the RegularExpressionValidator

Many types of data-entry fields follow standard patterns. For example, U.S. phone numbers follow the pattern (nnn) nnn-nnnn, and U.S. Zip codes are either nnnnn or nnnnn-nnnn.

The RegularExpressionValidator control is designed to let you validate data against patterns like this. The term *regular expression* refers to a somewhat standardized language used to define these patterns. Regular expressions can be extremely powerful, and also extremely confusing. A complete discussion of regular expressions would fill an entire chapter, but you'll find a description of the basics in this chapter's sidebar, "Using Regular Expressions."

You use the ValidationExpression property to specify the regular expression you want to use for the validation. For example, here's an example of a RegularExpressionValidator control that validates a U.S. Social Security number:

```
<asp:RegularExpressionValidator
    ID="RegularExpressionValidator1"
    runat="server"
    ControlToValidate="txtSSN"
    ErrorMessage="Invalid entry."
    ValidationExpression="\d{3}-\d{2}-\d{4}" />
```

Fortunately, Visual Studio provides several predefined regular expressions you can use with the RegularExpressionValidator control. The pre-defined expressions are listed in Table 2-1. To use one of these expressions, select a RegularExpressionValidator control in the Web designer, and then double-click the ellipses that appear next to the ValidationExpression property in the Properties window. Doing so brings up the dialog box shown in Figure 2-2, from which you can choose the expression you want to use.

**Book II
Chapter 2**

Using Validation
Controls

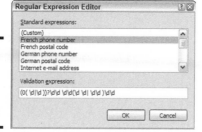

Figure 2-2:
Choosing a predefined regular expression.

Table 2-1	Predefined Regular Expressions
Name	*Expression*
French phone number	`(0( \d|\d ))?\d\d \d\d(\d \d| \d\d )\d\d`
French postal code	`\d{5}`
German phone number	`((\(0\d\d\) |(\(0\d{3}\) )?\d )?\d\d \d\d \d\d|\(0\d{4}\) \d \d\d-\d\d?)`
German postal code	`(D-)?\d{5}`
Internet e-mail address	`\w+([-+.']\w+)*@\w+([-.]\w+)*\.\w+([-.]\w+)*`
Internet URL	`http(s)?://([\w-]+\.)+[\w-]+(/[\w- ./?%&=]*)?`
Japanese phone number	`(0\d{1,4}-|\(0\d{1,4}\) ?)?\d{1,4}-\d{4}`
Japanese postal code	`\d{3}(-(\d{4}|\d{2}))?`
P.R.C. phone number	`(\(\d{3}\)|\d{3}-)?\d{8}`
P.R.C. postal code	`\d{6}`
P.R.C. Social Security number	`\d{17}[\d|X]|\d{15}`
U.S. phone number	`((\(\d{3}\) ?)|(\d{3}-))?\d{3}-\d{4}`
U.S. Social Security number	`\d{3}-\d{2}-\d{4}`
U.S. Zip code	`\d{5}(-\d{4})?`

Using regular expressions

Most regular expressions simply match characters to see if a string complies with a simple pattern. For example, you can check a string to see whether it matches the format for Social Security numbers, phone numbers, or more complicated patterns such as e-mail addresses.

You can match a specific character in a regular expression by including the character directly in the expression. For example, the expression abc will match only the string abc.

More useful expressions use *character classes* that represent a particular type of character rather than a specific character. There are two types of character classes: predefined classes and custom classes. The predefined character classes are as follows:

. : Any character

\d: Any digit (0–9)

\D: Any non-digit (anything other than 0–9)

\s: Any white-space character (such as spaces, tabs, newlines, returns, and backspaces)

\S: Any character other than a white space character

\w: Any word character (a–z, A–Z, 0–9, or an underscore)

\w: Any character other than a word character

The period is like a wildcard that matches any single character. For example, the expression c.t matches strings such as cat and cot but not cart.

The \d class represents a digit. Here's the expression \d\d\d-\d\d-\d\d\d\d that validates U.S. Social Security numbers. The \d class has a counterpart — \D — which matches any character that is *not* a digit.

The \s class matches white-space characters including spaces, tabs, newlines, returns, and backspaces. This class is useful when you want to allow the user to separate parts of a string in various ways.

The last set of predefined classes are \w and \W. The \w class identifies any character that's normally used in words. Such characters include upper- and lowercase letters, digits, and the underscore.

You can add the following *quantifiers* to an expression to create patterns that match a variable number of characters at a certain position in the string:

?: Zero or one times

*: Zero or more times

+: One or more times

{n}: Exactly *n* times

{n, }: At least *n* times

{n,m}: At least *n* times but no more than *m* times

To use a quantifier, you code it immediately after the element you want it to apply to. For example, here's an alternative way to write the Social Security number expression:

    \d{3}-\d{2}-\d{4}

The ? quantifier lets you create an optional element that may or may not be present in the string. For example, suppose you want to allow the user to enter Social Security numbers without the hyphens. Then, you could use this pattern: \d{3}-?\d{2}-?\d{4}. The question marks indicate that the hyphens are optional.

There's much, much more you can do with regular expressions. Search the Web for "Regular Expression" and you'll find many helpful Web sites with information about how to create your own expressions.

**Book II
Chapter 2**

**Using Validation
Controls**

Using a CustomValidator Control

If ASP.NET doesn't provide a validator control that offers the type of validation you need, you can tool up your own by using a CustomValidator control. For example, suppose you're validating a product-code field and the validation requirement is that the value entered by the user must exist in a database table that holds valid product codes. You can do that fairly easily with a CustomValidator control.

The .aspx markup for a CustomValidator control is similar to the markup for other validator controls. For example, here's the markup for the custom product-code validator:

```
<asp:CustomValidator ID="CustomValidator1"
    runat="server"
    ControlToValidate="txtProductCode"
    ErrorMessage="Incorrect product code."
    OnServerValidate="CustomValidator1_ServerValidate" />
```

Notice that the `CustomValidator` control includes an `OnServerValidate` attribute that specifies the name of the method to execute when the custom validator is called upon to validate the data. This method is passed a parameter named `args`, which contains two properties you can use to perform your own validation routine:

✦ `IsValid`: Your routine should set this property to indicate whether the value entered by the user is valid.

✦ `Value`: This is the value entered by the user.

For example, here's a simple `ServerValidate` routine:

```
protected void CustomValidator1_ServerValidate(
    object source, ServerValidateEventArgs args)
{
    args.IsValid = IsValidCode(args.Value);
}
```

Here a private method named `IsValidCode` is called to determine whether the value entered by the user (available as `args.Value`) is indeed a valid product code. This method, which isn't shown here, looks up the product code in a database and then returns `True` (if the code exists) or `False` (if the code doesn't exist).

If you're working in Visual Basic, you don't use the `OnServerValidate` on the markup for the `CustomValidator` control. Instead, you use a `Handles` clause on the `Sub` procedure that performs the validation, like this:

```
Protected Sub CustomValidator1_ServerValidate( _
        ByVal source As Object, _
        ByVal args As System.Web.UI.WebControls. _
                ServerValidateEventArgs) _
        Handles CustomValidator1.ServerValidate
    args.IsValid = IsValidCode(args.Value)
End Sub
```

Using the ValidationSummary Control

The `ValidationSummary` control is designed to let you display validation-error messages at the top or bottom of the page, rather than intermixed with the input controls. The ValidationSummary control can also display a simple message to indicate that at least one validation error has occurred on the page. Or, if you prefer, it can show the individual error messages for each validation error as a list, a bullet list, or a single paragraph. It can even display a pop-up message box that lists the errors.

When you use a ValidationSummary control on a page, you usually want the individual validation error messages to appear in the validation summary at the top or bottom of the page, rather than intermixed with the input controls. It's common practice simply to highlight each control that has a validation error with an asterisk, as shown in Figure 2-3.

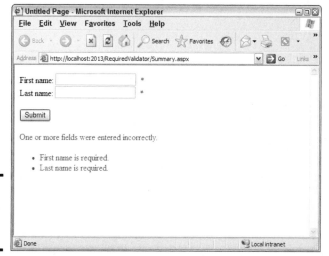

Figure 2-3:
A page with a validation summary.

You use the Text property to provide the asterisk that's displayed next to the invalid field, like this:

```
<asp:RequiredFieldValidator ID="RequiredFieldValidator1"
    runat="server"
    ControlToValidate="txtFirstName"
    ErrorMessage="First name is required."
    Text="*" />
```

This code specifies that the ErrorMessage property is to be displayed by the ValidationSummary control rather than the RequiredFieldValidator control.

Here's the markup for the `ValidationSummary` control shown in Figure 2-3:

```
<asp:ValidationSummary ID="ValidationSummary1"
    runat="server"
    HeaderText="One or more fields were entered incorrectly." />
```

The following table lists a few additional properties you can specify for the `ValidationSummary` control:

Property	Description
ShowSummary	Specifies whether the error messages for each invalid validator should be displayed. The default is `True`.
DisplayMode	Specifies how the error messages should be displayed. The options are `List`, `BulletList`, or `SingleParagraph`.
HeaderText	Specifies a text message to be displayed above the summary.
ShowMessageBox	Specifies whether a pop-up message box should be displayed.

If you specify `ShowMessageBox="True"`, a pop-up message box will be displayed if there is a validation error, as shown in Figure 2-4. The user must close this dialog box before correcting the entry error.

Figure 2-4:
A pop-up message box indicating a validation error.

Using the CausesValidation and ValidationGroup Properties

Some Web pages have two or more buttons that can post data to the server. In such a case, you may need to specify which controls should be validated when the user clicks one of the buttons. For example, have a look at Figure 2-5. This page has two text boxes and three buttons. When the user clicks the first button, the first text box is submitted. When the user clicks the second button, the second text box is submitted. If the user clicks the third button, neither text box is submitted.

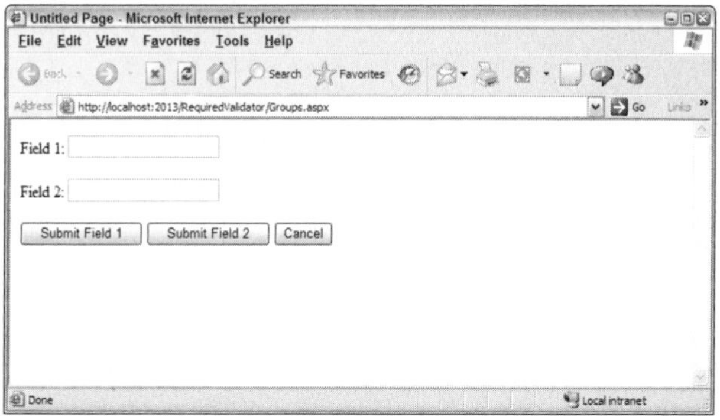

Book II
Chapter 2

Using Validation
Controls

Figure 2-5:
A page that
has three
buttons,
each with
different
validation
require-
ments.

To set the validation controls for this page, you must use two new properties:

✦ CausesValidation: You can use this property on a button control to
indicate whether the control causes validators to be executed. The
default is True. If you specify False, no data is validated when the
button is clicked.

✦ ValidationGroup: You can use this property on button controls and on
validators. If you specify this property on a button control, only those
validators that specify the same value will be validated when the user
clicks the button. In addition, you can use this property to segregate
your validators into groups that are processed only when a certain
button is clicked.

Listing 2-2 provides the complete markup for this page:

**Listing 2-2:   A sample page specifying which controls to validate when a button
is clicked (C#)**

```
<%@ Page Language="C#" AutoEventWireup="true"
    CodeFile="Groups.aspx.cs"
    Inherits="Groups" %>
<!DOCTYPE html PUBLIC
    "-//W3C//DTD XHTML 1.0 Transitional//EN"
    "http://www.w3.org/TR/xhtml1/DTD/xhtml1-transitional.dtd">
<html xmlns="http://www.w3.org/1999/xhtml" >
<head runat="server">
    <title>Untitled Page</title>
</head>
<body>
    <form id="form1" runat="server">
    <div>
        Field 1:
        <asp:TextBox ID="txtField1" runat="server" />
```

(continued)

Listing 2-2 (continued)

```
        <asp:RequiredFieldValidator ID="RequiredFieldValidator1" runat="server"
            ControlToValidate="txtField1"
            ErrorMessage="Required field."
            ValidationGroup="Group1" />
        <br /><br />
        Field 2:
        <asp:TextBox ID="txtField2" runat="server" />
        <asp:RequiredFieldValidator ID="RequiredFieldValidator2"
            runat="server"
            ControlToValidate="txtField2"
            ErrorMessage="Required field."
            ValidationGroup="Group2" />
        <br /><br />
        <asp:Button ID="btnSubmit1" runat="server"
            Text="Submit Field 1"
            ValidationGroup="Group1" />
        <asp:Button ID="btnSubmit2" runat="server"
            Text="Submit Field 2"
            ValidationGroup="Group2" />
        <asp:Button ID="btnCancel" runat="server"
            CausesValidation="False"
            Text="Cancel" />
    </div>
    </form>
</body>
</html>
```

Chapter 3: Using List Controls

In This Chapter

✔ **Working with CheckBoxList controls**

✔ **Toiling with ListItem elements**

✔ **Utilizing RadioButtonList controls**

✔ **Employing ListBox controls**

✔ **Making use of DropDownList controls**

✔ **Doing more with ListItem elements**

The controls I present in Chapter 1 of this mini-book work with individual items of data. In this chapter, you get a look at four server controls that work with lists of data. First are the CheckBoxList and RadioButtonList controls, which display lists of check boxes and radio buttons. Finally, the ListBox control and DropDownList controls are presented. These controls let the user select an item from a list of options.

Using the CheckBoxList Control

The CheckBoxList control displays a list of check boxes. It provides a simple way to present a set of options to the user without requiring you to code each check box individually.

Figure 3-1 shows a page that displays a CheckBoxList control. Here, the CheckBoxList control lists several toppings that can be ordered on a pizza. When the user clicks the Order Pizza button, the program displays the items selected by the user in a label that appears beneath the button.

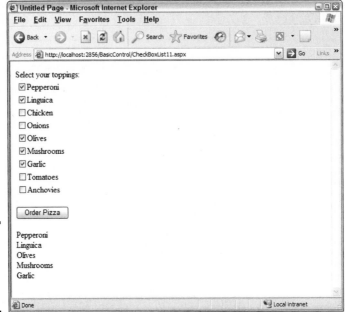

Figure 3-1:
A page with
a Check
BoxList
control.

Here's the C# markup used to create the CheckBoxList control shown in Figure 3-1:

```
<asp:CheckBoxList ID="cblToppings" runat="server">
    <asp:ListItem>Pepperoni</asp:ListItem>
    <asp:ListItem>Linguica</asp:ListItem>
    <asp:ListItem>Chicken</asp:ListItem>
    <asp:ListItem>Onions</asp:ListItem>
    <asp:ListItem>Olives</asp:ListItem>
    <asp:ListItem>Mushrooms</asp:ListItem>
    <asp:ListItem>Garlic</asp:ListItem>
    <asp:ListItem>Tomatoes</asp:ListItem>
    <asp:ListItem>Anchovies</asp:ListItem>
</asp:CheckBoxList>
```

The CheckBoxList control has several properties that let you control the way list items are formatted. In particular, you'll run across these:

Property	Description
TextAlign	Specifies whether the text appears to the right or left of the check boxes. You can specify Right or Left. The default is Right.
RepeatColumns	The number of columns to display. The default is 1.

Property	Description
RepeatDirection	Vertical or Horizontal to indicate whether the check boxes are repeated vertically or horizontally.
RepeatLayout	Table or Flow. Table (the default) indicates that an HTML table should be used to control the column layout.
CellPadding	When Table layout is used, sets the size of the gap between the contents of a cell and the cell's border.
CellSpacing	When Table layout is used, sets the amount of space that appears between the table cells.

Creating columns

The most common use of the CheckBoxList control properties is to break the list of check boxes into multiple columns. For example, Figure 3-2 shows two ways to break the list of toppings into three columns. The first way specifies Vertical for the RepeatDirection property, and the second way specifies Horizontal.

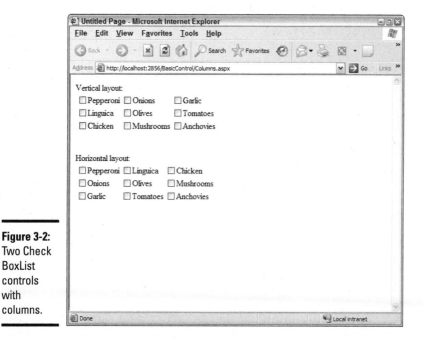

Figure 3-2:
Two Check
BoxList
controls
with
columns.

Here's the markup used to create this page:

```
Vertical layout:<br />
<asp:CheckBoxList ID="cblToppings" runat="server"
    RepeatColumns="3" RepeatDirection="Vertical">
    <asp:ListItem>Pepperoni</asp:ListItem>
    <asp:ListItem>Linguica</asp:ListItem>
    <asp:ListItem>Chicken</asp:ListItem>
    <asp:ListItem>Onions</asp:ListItem>
    <asp:ListItem>Olives</asp:ListItem>
    <asp:ListItem>Mushrooms</asp:ListItem>
    <asp:ListItem>Garlic</asp:ListItem>
    <asp:ListItem>Tomatoes</asp:ListItem>
    <asp:ListItem>Anchovies</asp:ListItem>
</asp:CheckBoxList>
<br /><br />
Horizontal layout:<br />
<asp:CheckBoxList ID="CheckBoxList1" runat="server"
    RepeatColumns="3" RepeatDirection="Horizontal">
    <asp:ListItem>Pepperoni</asp:ListItem>
    <asp:ListItem>Linguica</asp:ListItem>
    <asp:ListItem>Chicken</asp:ListItem>
    <asp:ListItem>Onions</asp:ListItem>
    <asp:ListItem>Olives</asp:ListItem>
    <asp:ListItem>Mushrooms</asp:ListItem>
    <asp:ListItem>Garlic</asp:ListItem>
    <asp:ListItem>Tomatoes</asp:ListItem>
    <asp:ListItem>Anchovies</asp:ListItem>
</asp:CheckBoxList>
```

Aligning text with check boxes

By default, the check boxes in a CheckBoxList control appear to the left of
the text that describes each text box. You can change that orientation by
including the TextAlign property when you create the CheckBoxList. For
example, the following markup places the check boxes to the right of the
text that describes them:

```
<asp:CheckBoxList ID="cblToppings" runat="server"
    TextAlign="Left">
    <asp:ListItem>Pepperoni</asp:ListItem>
    <asp:ListItem>Linguica</asp:ListItem>
    <asp:ListItem>Chicken</asp:ListItem>
    <asp:ListItem>Onions</asp:ListItem>
    <asp:ListItem>Olives</asp:ListItem>
    <asp:ListItem>Mushrooms</asp:ListItem>
    <asp:ListItem>Garlic</asp:ListItem>
    <asp:ListItem>Tomatoes</asp:ListItem>
    <asp:ListItem>Anchovies</asp:ListItem>
</asp:CheckBoxList>
```

Figure 3-3 shows how the pizza-toppings check box list appears to the right of the text rather than to the left.

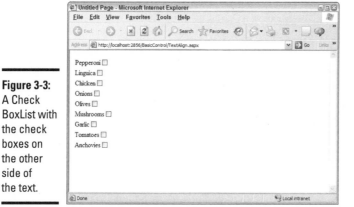

Figure 3-3:
A Check
BoxList with
the check
boxes on
the other
side of
the text.

Spacing things out

If the items in a `CheckBoxList` control seem crowded, you can space them out by using the `CellPadding` and `CellSpacing` properties. Note that these properties work only when you specify `Table` for the `RepeatLayout` property (or let it default to `Table`). Then, the `CellPadding` property lets you add extra space within each cell of the HTML table that's used to display the check box list, and the `CellSpacing` property adds extra space between the cells. Together, these properties let you add extra space so the items in the list don't seem so crowded. You usually have to experiment with these settings to get the list to look the way you want it to.

Working with ListItem Elements

The items displayed by the `CheckBoxList` control — and any other type of list control, for that matter — are defined by `ListItem` elements that appear between the start and end tags for the `CheckBoxList` control.

`ListItem` elements are the same for all four types of list controls presented in this chapter. So heads up — you can use what you get from this section throughout the chapter.

Using the Text property

You can supply the `Text` property for a list item in one of two ways: By listing the text value between the start and end tags for each list item, or by using the Text attribute. For example, the following markup can also be used to create the CheckBoxList that was shown in Figure 3-1:

```
<asp:CheckBoxList ID="cblToppings" runat="server">
    <asp:ListItem Text="Pepperoni" />
    <asp:ListItem Text="Linguica" />
    <asp:ListItem Text="Chicken" />
    <asp:ListItem Text="Onions" />
    <asp:ListItem Text="Olives" />
    <asp:ListItem Text="Mushrooms" />
    <asp:ListItem Text="Garlic" />
    <asp:ListItem Text="Tomatoes" />
    <asp:ListItem Text="Anchovies" />
</asp:CheckBoxList>
```

Using the Value property

If you don't provide a Value property for a list item, the Value property is given the same value as the Text property. In some cases, that's what you want. But you may want the value of a selected item to be different from the text displayed for the item. For example, suppose you want the value for each topping to be a short code rather than the full name of the topping. Then you could use markup like this to create the CheckBoxList:

```
<asp:CheckBoxList ID="cblToppings" runat="server">
    <asp:ListItem Text="Pepperoni" Value="PEP" />
    <asp:ListItem Text="Linguica" Value="LIN" />
    <asp:ListItem Text="Chicken" Value="CHK" />
    <asp:ListItem Text="Onions" Value="ONI" />
    <asp:ListItem Text="Olives" Value="OLI" />
    <asp:ListItem Text="Mushrooms" Value="MUS" />
    <asp:ListItem Text="Garlic" Value="GAR" />
    <asp:ListItem Text="Tomatoes" Value="TOM" />
    <asp:ListItem Text="Anchovies" Value="ANC" />
</asp:CheckBoxList>
```

Then, if the user checks the Pepperoni, Olives, and Mushrooms items, the label displays the following text:

```
PEP
OLI
MUS
```

Determining which items are selected

The code that determines which items are selected — and sets the label's Text property accordingly — looks like this:

```
string items = "";
foreach (ListItem l in cblToppings.Items)
{
```

```
        if (l.Selected)
            items += l.Value + "<br>";
    }
    lblOrder.Text = items;
```

Here a `foreach` statement is used to loop through all items in the `Items` collection of the `CheckBoxList` control. Each of these items is an object of the `ListItem` type, which has the following properties you can use:

Property	Description
Text	The text displayed for the item.
Value	The value associated with the list item.
Selected	A `boolean` value that indicates whether or not the user selected the item.

Here's the equivalent code in VB.NET:

```
Dim Items As String
For Each l As ListItem In cblToppings.Items
    If l.Selected Then
        items &= l.Value & "<br>"
    End If
Next
lblOrder.Text = items
```

Using the Collection Editor dialog box

If you don't want to hand-code the ListItem elements for a list control, you can use the ListItem Collection Editor dialog box to create the list items, as shown in Figure 3-4. To summon this dialog box in Design view, click the Smart Tag icon at the top right of a CheckBoxList (or other list) control, and then chose Edit Items. Or you can click the ellipses that appear next to the Items property in the Properties window for the list control.

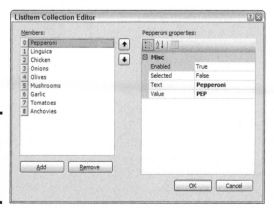

Figure 3-4:
The ListItem Collection Editor dialog box.

With the Collection Editor dialog box open, you can add an item to the collection by clicking the Add button. Then you can change the `Enabled`, `Selected`, `Text`, or `Value` properties for each item. You can also remove items or change the order in which items appear.

Don't forget that the `ListItem` elements that make up the list of items for a list control are the same no matter which type of list control you're using.

Toiling with the RadioButtonList Control

The `RadioButtonList` control is similar to the `CheckBoxList` control, with the exception that — you guessed it — it creates a list of radio buttons rather than check boxes. Here's an example of the markup for a `RadioButtonList` control:

```
<asp:RadioButtonList ID="RadioButtonList1" runat="server">
    <asp:ListItem>Individual</asp:ListItem>
    <asp:ListItem>Small</asp:ListItem>
    <asp:ListItem>Medium</asp:ListItem>
    <asp:ListItem Selected="True">Large</asp:ListItem>
    <asp:ListItem>Extra Large</asp:ListItem>
    <asp:ListItem>Humongous</asp:ListItem>
</asp:RadioButtonList>
```

Figure 3-5 shows a page that includes this radio-button list. As you can see, this page also includes a label that displays the size of pizza ordered after the user clicks the `Order Pizza` button.

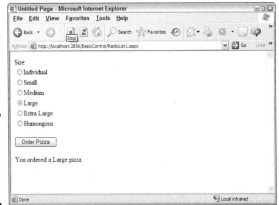

Figure 3-5:
A page that uses a RadioButton List control.

You should always set the `Selected` property of one of the list items in a radio button list to `True`. If you don't, the user might forget to select an item.

Most of what the previous sections tell you about the `CheckBoxList` control applies to the `RadioButtonList` control as well. However, there are a few important variations:

✦ **The** `RadioButtonList` **has a** `SelectedValue` **property you can use to get the** `Value` **property of the selected item.** This is possible because, unlike a `CheckBoxList`, a `RadioButtonList` can have only one item selected at a time.

✦ **The code that displays a specific value — such as the size of the pizza the user ordered — uses the** `SelectedValue` **property:**

```
lblSize.Text = "You ordered a "
    + rblSize.SelectedValue
    + " pizza.";
```

Here's the Visual Basic equivalent:

```
lblSize.Text = "You ordered a " _
    & rblSize.SelectedValue _
    & " pizza."
```

**Book II
Chapter 3**

Using List Controls

✦ **If you prefer, you can use the** `SelectedIndex` **property to get the index value of the selected item.** Then, you can use this index value to access the selected list item based on its position in the list. In most cases, however, `SelectedIndex` isn't as useful as `SelectedValue`.

If you do use `SelectedIndex`, remember that index values begin with 0, so the item with index 1 is actually the *second* item in the list.

Utilizing ListBox Controls

A `ListBox` control is similar to a `CheckBoxList` or `RadioButtonList` control, but it displays simple text lines rather than check boxes or radio buttons. A list box can be configured to limit the user to a single selection, or it can allow the user to select more than one item from the list. And — unlike a check-box list or radio-button list — a list box can include scroll bars.

Figure 3-6 shows a page that uses a list box to let the user choose one or more toppings for a pizza order. Once again, the label beneath the button lists the toppings that the user selected. The markup used to create this list box is as follows:

```
<asp:ListBox ID="lbToppings" runat="server"
    SelectionMode="Multiple">
    <asp:ListItem>Pepperoni</asp:ListItem>
    <asp:ListItem>Sausage</asp:ListItem>
    <asp:ListItem>Chicken</asp:ListItem>
    <asp:ListItem>Linguica</asp:ListItem>
```

```
      <asp:ListItem>Salami</asp:ListItem>
      <asp:ListItem>Canadian Bacon</asp:ListItem>
      <asp:ListItem>Olives</asp:ListItem>
      <asp:ListItem>Mushrooms</asp:ListItem>
      <asp:ListItem>Tomatoes</asp:ListItem>
      <asp:ListItem>Pickles</asp:ListItem>
      <asp:ListItem>Anchovies</asp:ListItem>
      <asp:ListItem>Garlic</asp:ListItem>
</asp:ListBox>
```

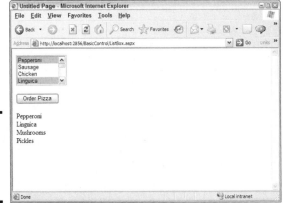

Figure 3-6:
A page that
uses a
ListBox
control.

Notice that the tag for the `ListBox` control specifies `SelectionMode=`
`"Multiple"`. This lets the user select more than one item from the list by
holding down the Shift or Ctrl key while selecting items. If you want to limit
the user to a single selection, specify `SelectionMode="Single"` instead.

If you want, you can set the number of rows displayed in the list box by
using the `Rows` property. The default setting is 4. Note that a scroll bar will
appear automatically if the number of list items exceeds the setting for the
`Rows` property.

Here's the C# code that lists the selected items when the user clicks the
`Order Pizza` button:

```
String toppings = "";
foreach (ListItem l in lbToppings.Items)
{
    if (l.Selected)
        toppings += l.Value + "<br>";
    }
lblOrder.Text = toppings;
```

And here's the VB.NET version of the code:

```
Dim Toppings As String
For Each l As ListItem In lbToppings.Items
    If l.Selected Then
        Toppings &= l.Value & "<br>"
    End If
Next
lblOrder.Text = Toppings
```

Employing DropDownList Controls

A `DropDownList` control combines the features of a text box with the features of a list box. Unlike a list box, the list of items in a drop-down list doesn't appear until the user clicks the drop-down arrow that appears as part of the control. Also, unlike a list box, a drop-down list limits the user to a single selection.

Figure 3-7 shows a page that uses a drop-down list to let the user select the size of a pizza to order. Notice that this page includes a label that displays the size selected by the user — but it doesn't include a button that lets the user submit the form. Instead, the page is posted automatically whenever the user changes the selection in the drop-down list. This happens because the markup for the drop-down list specifies `AutoPostBack="True"`.

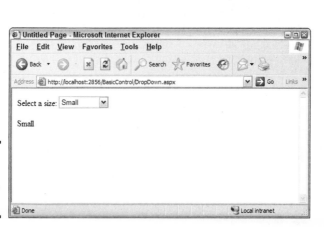

Figure 3-7:
A page that uses a drop-down list.

Here's the markup for this drop-down list:

```
<asp:DropDownList ID="ddlSize" runat="server"
    AutoPostBack="True"
    OnSelectedIndexChanged="ddlSize_SelectedIndexChanged">
    <asp:ListItem>Individual</asp:ListItem>
```

```
      <asp:ListItem>Small</asp:ListItem>
      <asp:ListItem>Medium</asp:ListItem>
      <asp:ListItem Selected="True">Large</asp:ListItem>
      <asp:ListItem>Extra Large</asp:ListItem>
      <asp:ListItem>Humongous</asp:ListItem>
</asp:DropDownList>
```

Note that the `AutoPostBack` property is set to `True`, which causes the page to be posted whenever the user changes the selection. In addition, the `OnSelectedIndexChanged` attribute specifies the name of the method to be called when the user changes the selection. (If you're working in VB.NET, you probably won't specify this attribute. Instead, you'll specify a `Handles` clause on the `Sub` procedure that handles this event.)

Here's the C# version of the `ddlSize_SelectedIndexChanged` method:

```
protected void ddlSize_SelectedIndexChanged(
    object sender, EventArgs e)
{
    lblSize.Text = ddlSize.SelectedValue;
}
```

As you can see, this method sets the label's `Text` property to the `SelectedValue` property of the drop-down list.

The `SelectedIndexChanged` event is raised whenever the user changes the selection for a drop-down list. That lets the program change the value of the `lblSize` label when the user changes the size — but how can the label display the initial setting? You could simply hard-code the label's `Text` property to `Large`, but a better way is to set the label in the `Page_Load` event. You'll need to use the `IsPostBack` property to make sure this code is executed only when the page is first posted, and not for a postback. Here's an example:

```
protected void Page_Load(object sender, EventArgs e)
{
    if (!IsPostBack)
        lblSize.Text = ddlSize.SelectedValue;
}
```

Here are the VB.NET versions of both the `Page_Load` and the `ddlSize_SelectedIndexChanged` methods:

```
Protected Sub Page_Load( _
        ByVal sender As Object, _
        ByVal e As System.EventArgs) _
        Handles Me.Load
    If Not IsPostBack Then
        lblSize.Text = ddlSize.SelectedValue
    End If
End Sub
```

```
Protected Sub ddlSize_SelectedIndexChanged( _
      ByVal sender As Object, _
      ByVal e As System.EventArgs) _
      Handles ddlSize.SelectedIndexChanged
   lblSize.Text = ddlSize.SelectedValue
End Sub
```

Accomplishing More with List Items in Code

When you've had a chance to inspect the various types of list controls you can use in ASP.NET applications, there are a few additional techniques you need to know before you have all you need for working with list items. These techniques are summarized in the following sections.

Adding an item to a list

In many cases, you can specify all items in a list control by using `<ListItem>` tags in the `.aspx` file for the page. However, in some cases you won't know what items need to be added until the page is run. Then, you can add the items by calling the `Add` method of the `Items` collection.

For example, forms that let the user enter credit-card information usually have a drop-down list for the expiration year. It makes no sense to let the user use a card that's already expired, so this list is usually filled with numbers that start with the current year. Here's some C# code that does that:

```
int year = DateTime.Now.Year;
for (int y = year; y < year + 5; y++)
    ddlYear.Items.Add(y.ToString());
```

If the current year is 2006, this code adds 2006, 2007, 2008, 2009, and 2010 to the list. Here's the equivalent code in VB.NET:

```
Dim Year As Integer
Year = DateTime.Now.Year
For y As Integer = Year To Year + 4
    ddlYear.Items.Add(y.ToString())
Next y
```

Clearing the list

You can remove all items from a list by calling the `Items.Clear` method, as in this C# example:

```
ddlToppings.Items.Clear();
```

If you find that the number of items in a list control grows each time you post a page, it's probably due to one of two errors: Either you aren't checking `IsPostBack`, or you aren't calling `Items.Clear` before adding new items to the list control.

The VB.NET version is almost identical, without the semicolon:

```
ddlToppings.Items.Clear()
```

Selecting and deselecting items

You can select an item in code by setting the item's `Selected` property to `True`. Here's a little C# routine that selects all of the items in a list box:

```
foreach (ListItem l in lbToppings.Items)
    l.Selected = true;
```

Here's the VB.NET version:

```
For Each l As ListItem In lbToppings.Items
    l.Selected = True
Next
```

(Of course, this will work only if the list box allows multiple selections.)

To deselect all items, just set `Selected` to `False` instead of `True`.

You can also select a specific item by using an index value. Here's an example:

```
lbToppings.Items[2].Selected = true;
```

This code selects the third item in the list box. (Remember that items are numbered starting from zero.) Here's the equivalent VB.NET code:

```
lbToppings.Items(2).Selected = True
```

Finding an item

Suppose you want to write code that selects a particular item according to its `Text` or `Value` property. For example, say you want to select `Pepperoni`, using its value (`PEP`). One way to do that would be with a `foreach` loop, like this:

```
foreach (ListItem l in lbToppings.Items)
    if (l.Value == "PEP")
        l.Selected = true;
```

Here's a VB.NET version:

```
Dim l As ListItem
For Each l In lbToppings.Items
    If l.Value = "PEP" Then
        l.Selected = true
    End If
Next
```

A better way is to use the `Items.FindByValue` method to search for the item on the basis of its value. The `FindByValue` method returns the item whose `Value` matches the value you pass as an argument. If there is no item with that value, `FindByValue` returns null.

Here's a C# code snippet that selects the `Pepperoni` item using the `FindByValue` method:

```
ListItem l = lbToppings.Items.FindByValue("PEP");
if (l != null)
    l.Selected = true;
```

In VB.NET, the code would look more like this:

```
Dim l As ListItem
l = lbToppings.Items.FindByValue("PEP")
If l Is Not Nothing Then
    l.Selected = True
End If
```

You can use the similar `FindByText` value to search for items based on the `Text` property rather than the `Value` property.

Chapter 4: Using Advanced Web Server Controls

In This Chapter

✔ Working with the MultiView control

✔ Making use of the Wizard control

✔ Using the Calendar control

✔ Utilizing the FileUpload control

This chapter presents four interesting ASP.NET server controls. The `MultiView` and `Wizard` controls both let you create controls that have multiple groups of controls inside them — although only one group at a time is displayed. The `Calendar` control displays calendars. And the `FileUpload` control lets your users upload files (for example, completed pizza orders) to your Web site.

All code listings used in this book are available for download at www.dummies. com/go/aspnetaiofd. Note that you'll find both C# and VB.NET versions of all the listings in this chapter available for download from the Web site.

Enjoy!

Using the MultiView Control

A `MultiView` control is a control that contains one or more *views*, each of which can display a different set of controls. `MultiView` controls are typically used to create pages that require a lot of input from the user. Rather than throw all the input controls at the user at once, a `MultiView` control lets you break the input controls into sections and display only one group of controls at a time. The result is a less confusing page that's easier to use.

To illustrate, Figure 4-1 shows a Web page that steps the user through the process of ordering a pizza. First, the user selects the pizza size and clicks Next. Then the user selects the toppings and clicks Next. Finally, the user enters his or her name and clicks Finish. In response, the application displays a summary of the pizza order in a label that appears beneath the `MultiView` control — and it's chowtime.

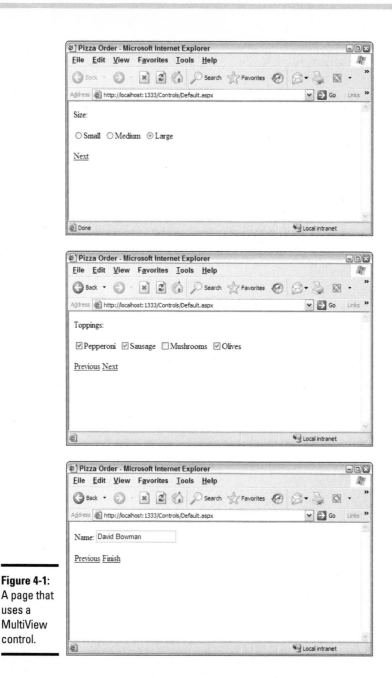

Figure 4-1:
A page that
uses a
MultiView
control.

The MultiView control is actually a container that holds a collection of individual View controls. In turn, each of those View controls is a container that

can hold still other controls such as labels, text boxes, and so on. Only one of the `View` controls in the `MultiView` control is active at any given time, and only the controls in the active `View` control are shown on the page.

The markup for a `MultiView` control can look pretty complicated, but it follows a pretty simple structure:

```
<asp:MultiView ID="MultiView1" runat="server"
    ActiveViewIndex="0">
    <asp:View ID="View1" runat="server">
        Controls for first view go here
    </asp:View>
    <asp:View ID="View2" runat="server">
        Controls for second view go here
    </asp:View>
    <asp:View ID="View2" runat="server">
        Controls for third view go here
    </asp:View>
</asp:MultiView>
```

To create a `MultiView` control in Design view, first drag the `MultiView` control from the toolbox onto the page. Then you just drag one or more `View` controls into the `MultiView` control. The `View` controls will appear on-screen one beneath the other, as shown in Figure 4-2. Rest assured that even though all the views are visible in the Web Designer, only one of the views will be shown on the page when the application runs.

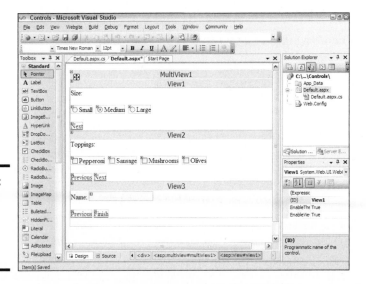

Figure 4-2: Creating a MultiView control in Visual Studio.

You can specify the initial view by setting the `ActiveViewIndex` attribute in the markup for the `MultiView` control. And you can change to a different view by setting the `ActiveViewIndex` property in your code. For example, you can move to the next view by providing a button whose `Click` event handler includes C# code like this:

```
MultiView1.ActiveViewIndex += 1;
```

(The VB.NET version of this code is the same, but without the semicolon.)

Fortunately, you can avoid writing code for simple view navigation by providing button controls within the `View` control that specify one of the following values for the `CommandName` property:

CommandName	Description
NextView	Displays the next view in the sequence.
PrevView	Displays the previous view in the sequence.
SwitchViewByID	Displays the view whose `ID` is specified by the `CommandArgument` property.
SwitchViewByIndex	Displays the view whose `Index` is specified by the `CommandArgument` property.

For example, here's a button that displays the next view:

```
<asp:Button ID="Button1" runat="server"
    CommandName="NextView" Text="Next" />
```

And here's a button that returns to the first view:

```
<asp:Button ID="Button1" runat="server"
    CommandName="SwitchViewByID"
    CommandArgument="0"
    Text="First" />
```

The complete markup for the page shown in Figure 4-1 makes its appearance in Listing 4.1. Note that this is the C# version of the markup; the VB.NET version will vary slightly due to the settings in the Page directive and the way events are handled. (The VB.NET version is available for download from the book's Web site.) The following list describes the highlights:

✦ →**1:** The start tag for the `MultiView` control. The `ActiveViewIndex` attribute specifies that the first view should be displayed by default.

✦ →**2:** The start tag for the first view in the `MultiView` control, named `View1`. This `View` control contains radio buttons that let the user select the pizza size.

✦ →**3:** This link button specifies NextView for the CommandName attribute. Then the second view is displayed when the user clicks this button.

✦ →**4:** The second view contains check boxes that let the user select the pizza toppings.

✦ →**5:** This link button specifies PrevView for the CommandName attribute, so the first view is displayed when the user clicks this button.

✦ →**6:** This link button specifies NextView for the CommandName attribute, so the third view is displayed when the user clicks this button.

✦ →**7:** The third view contains a text box that lets the user enter his or her name.

✦ →**8:** This link button specifies PrevView for the CommandName attribute, so the second view is displayed when the user clicks this button.

✦ →**9:** Unlike the other link buttons, this one doesn't use the CommandName attribute. Instead, it specifies a Click event handler that displays the user's name, the pizza size, and the toppings.

✦ →**10:** This line marks the end of the MultiView control.

Listing 4-1:   A page with a MultiView control (C#)

```
<%@ Page Language="C#" AutoEventWireup="true"  CodeFile="Default.aspx.cs"
    Inherits="_Default" %>
<!DOCTYPE html PUBLIC
    "-//W3C//DTD XHTML 1.0 Transitional//EN"
    "http://www.w3.org/TR/xhtml1/DTD/xhtml1-transitional.dtd">
<html xmlns="http://www.w3.org/1999/xhtml" >
<head runat="server">
    <title>Pizza Order</title>
</head>
<body>
  <form id="form1" runat="server">
  <div>
    <asp:MultiView ID="MultiView1" runat="server"                    →1
        ActiveViewIndex="0">
     <asp:View ID="View1" runat="server">                            →2
        Size:<br /><br />
        <asp:RadioButton ID="rdoSmall" runat="server"
           Text="Small" GroupName="Size" /> 
        <asp:RadioButton ID="rdoMedium" runat="server"
           Text="Medium" GroupName="Size"
           Checked="True" /> 
        <asp:RadioButton ID="rdoLarge" runat="server"
           Text="Large" GroupName="Size" />
        <br /><br />
        <asp:LinkButton ID="LinkButton1" runat="server"              →3
           CommandName="NextView" Text="Next" />
     </asp:View>
```

(continued)

Listing 4-1 *(continued)*

```
        <asp:View ID="View2" runat="server">                    →4
            Toppings:<br /><br />
          <asp:CheckBox ID="chkPepperoni" runat="server"
              Text="Pepperoni" /> 
          <asp:CheckBox ID="chkSausage" runat="server"
              Text="Sausage" /> 
          <asp:CheckBox ID="chkMushrooms" runat="server"
              Text="Mushrooms" /> 
          <asp:CheckBox ID="chkOlives" runat="server"
              Text="Olives" />
          <br /><br />
          <asp:LinkButton ID="LinkButton3" runat="server"      →5
              CommandName="PrevView" Text="Previous" />
          <asp:LinkButton ID="LinkButton2" runat="server"      →6
              CommandName="NextView" Text="Next" />
        </asp:View>
        <asp:View ID="View3" runat="server">                    →7
          Name:
          <asp:TextBox ID="txtName" runat="server" />
          <br /><br />
          <asp:LinkButton ID="LinkButton4" runat="server"      →8
              CommandName="PrevView" Text="Previous" />
          <asp:LinkButton ID="btnFinish" runat="server"        →9
              Text="Finish"
              OnClick="btnFinish_Click" />
        </asp:View>
      </asp:MultiView>                                          →10
      <br /><br />
      <asp:Label ID="lblOrder" runat="server" />
      </div>
      </form>
  </body>
</html>
```

Utilizing the Wizard Control

The `Wizard` control is like the `MutliView` control on steroids. It's designed to create sequences of steps, such as the check-out page for an on-line store or the sign-up page for a members-only Web site. Figure 4-3 shows a typical example, a four-step wizard for ordering a pizza. The first three steps are like the three views used by the `MultiView` control shown in the previous section. The fourth step is a final confirmation step that summarizes what the user has selected before completing the wizard.

Like the `MultiView` control, the `Wizard` control is a container for groups of other controls that are displayed one at a time. Instead of *views*, however, these groups of controls are called *steps*. Unlike the `MultiView` control, the `Wizard` control has automatic features built in that let the user move from step to step.

Figure 4-3:
A page with
a Wizard
control.

The basic structure of the tags for a `Wizard` control is as follows:

```
<asp:Wizard ID="Wizard1" runat="server" >
    <WizardSteps>
        <asp:WizardStep runat="server" Title="Step 1">
            Controls for first step go here
        </asp:WizardStep>
        <asp:WizardStep runat="server" Title="Step 2">
            Controls for first step go here
        </asp:WizardStep>
        <asp:WizardStep runat="server" Title="Finish" >
            Controls for final step go here
        </asp:WizardStep>
    </WizardSteps>
</asp:Wizard>
```

There are a few properties you may want to specify on the `Wizard` element
itself. These properties are listed in Table 4-1, and here's an example that
includes several of these properties:

```
<asp:Wizard ID="Wizard1" runat="server"
        ActiveStepIndex="0"
        HeaderText="Sample Wizard"
        DisplayCancelWizard="False" >
```

Table 4-1	Wizard Element Properties
Property	*Description*
DisplaySideBar	True if a sidebar with navigation controls should be displayed.
DisplayCancelButton	True if the wizard should display a Cancel button to allow the user to cancel the wizard.
CancelButtonText	The text that should be displayed in the Cancel button.
CancelButtonDestinationPageURL	The URL of the page that should be displayed if the user clicks the Cancel button.
HeaderText	The text to display at the top of the wizard.
StartNextButtonText	The text to display in the Next button on the Start step.
StepNextButtonText	The text to display in the Next button on a regular step.
StepPrevButtonText	The text to display in the Previous button on a regular step.
FinishPrevButtonText	The text to display in the Previous button on the final step.
FinishCompleteButtonText	The text to display in the Finish button.
FinishCompleteButtonPageURL	The URL of the page that should be displayed if the user clicks the Finish button.

Creating steps in Visual Studio

✦ Wizard

To create a Wizard control in Visual Studio, first drag the Wizard control icon (shown in the margin) from the toolbox onto the page. This creates a basic Wizard with two steps, as shown in Figure 4-4.

You can switch to a particular step by clicking the step's name in the sidebar area that appears on the left side of the Wizard control. Or you can use the drop-down list in the Smart Tag menu to choose the step you want to view.

To add controls or other content to a step, just click the center of the Wizard control and start adding controls and content. If you add any controls or other content, what you add becomes part of the currently selected step.

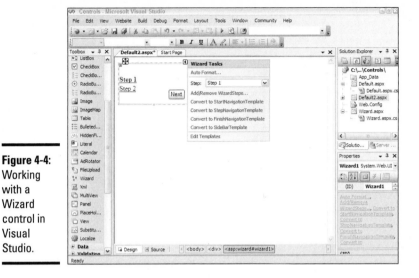

Figure 4-4:
Working
with a
Wizard
control in
Visual
Studio.

To add a step, choose "Add/Remove WizardSteps..." from the Smart Tag menu. This brings up the dialog box shown in Figure 4-5.

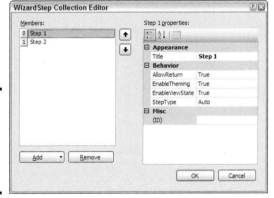

Figure 4-5:
The
WizardStep
Collection
Editor
dialog box.

You can use this dialog box to add steps (just click the Add button), remove a step (click the Remove button), or change the order of the steps (use the up and down arrow buttons). You can also set the properties of each step. At the least, you'll want to change the `Title` property to provide a meaningful title for each step.

You may also want to change the `StepType` property. There are five different types of steps:

✦ `Auto`: This is the default step type. ASP.NET determines the role of the step based on its position within the `<WizardSteps>` element.

✦ `Start`: The first step in the wizard. It features a Next button that the user can click to move to the next step.

✦ `Step`: Any step other than a Start, Finish, or Complete step. This type of step displays both a Previous and a Next button so the user can move to the previous or next step.

✦ `Final`: The last data collection step. It features a Previous and a Finish button.

✦ `Complete`: This is the last step of the wizard. It is often used as a confirmation step to indicate that the data collected by the other steps has been processed.

In most cases, you can omit the `StepType` property and let ASP.NET figure out the role of each step based on its position within the `WizardSteps` element.

One other property you might want to change is `AllowReturn`. If you set this property to `False`, the user will not be allowed to return to the step once the step has been completed.

Using Wizard events

When the user clicks the various buttons that appear in a wizard, the `Wizard` control raises the following events:

Event	Description
`ActiveStepChanged`	Raised whenever the active step changes.
`FinishButtonClick`	Raised when the user clicks the Finish button.
`CancelButtonClick`	Raised when the user clicks the Cancel button.
`NextButtonClick`	Raised when the user clicks the Next button.
`PreviousButtonClick`	Raised when the user clicks the Previous button.
`SideBarButtonClick`	Raised when the user clicks one of the buttons in the navigation sidebar.

With several of these buttons, your code needs to determine which wizard step is active. You can find that out via the `ActiveStepIndex` property of the `Wizard` control itself. Here's an example:

```
if (Wizard1.ActiveStepIndex == 2)
    // Step 3 is active
```

Looking at the code for a Wizard control

Now that you've seen the basics of working with the `Wizard` control, Listing 4-2 presents the complete markup for the page shown in Figure 4-3. Note that this is the C# version of the markup; the VB.NET version will vary slightly due to the settings in the `Page` directive and the way events are handled. (The VB.NET version is available for download at the Web site for this book.)

The following list describes the key lines of this listing:

✦ **→1:** The `Wizard` element provides the initial step (`"0"`), the header text, the height and width of the `Wizard` control, and an event handler for the `OnActiveStepChanged` button.

For VB.NET, you should omit the `OnActiveStepChanged` attribute.

✦ **→2:** The `WizardSteps` element is a container for the individual wizard steps.

✦ **→3:** The first wizard step gets the pizza size.

✦ **→4:** The second wizard step gets the toppings.

✦ **→5:** The third wizard step gets the user's name.

✦ **→6:** The fourth wizard step provides a label that's used to display a summary of the user's order. The handler for the `ActiveStepChanged` event sets the `Text` property of this label when this step is displayed.

**Book II
Chapter 4**

**Using Advanced
Web Server
Controls**

Listing 4-2: The Wizard.aspx file (C#)

```
<%@ Page Language="C#" AutoEventWireup="true"
    CodeFile="Wizard.aspx.cs" Inherits="Wizard" %>
<!DOCTYPE html PUBLIC
    "-//W3C//DTD XHTML 1.0 Transitional//EN"
    "http://www.w3.org/TR/xhtml1/DTD/xhtml1-transitional.dtd">
<html xmlns="http://www.w3.org/1999/xhtml" >
<head runat="server">
    <title>Pizza Wizardry</title>
</head>
<body>
  <form id="form1" runat="server">
  <div>
    <asp:Wizard ID="Wizard1" runat="server"                      →1
        ActiveStepIndex="0"
        HeaderText="Pizza Order Wizard"
        Height="131px" Width="338px"
        OnActiveStepChanged="Wizard1_ActiveStepChanged">
        <WizardSteps>                                            →2
          <asp:WizardStep runat="server" Title="Size">          →3
            What size pizza do you want?<br />
            <br />
            <asp:RadioButton ID="rdoSmall"
                runat="server"
                GroupName="Size" Text="Small" />
```

(continued)

Listing 4-2 *(continued)*

```
                <br />
                <asp:RadioButton ID="rdoMedium"
                    runat="server"
                    GroupName="Size" Text="Medium"
                    Checked="True" />
                <br />
                <asp:RadioButton ID="rdoLarge"
                    runat="server"
                    GroupName="Size" Text="Large" />
                <br />
            </asp:WizardStep>
            <asp:WizardStep runat="server"                                →4
                Title="Toppings">
                What toppings do you want?<br />
                <br />
                <asp:CheckBox ID="chkPepperoni"
                    runat="server"
                    Text="Pepperoni" />
                <br />
                <asp:CheckBox ID="chkSausage" runat="server"
                    Text="Sausage" />
                <br />
                <asp:CheckBox ID="chkMushrooms"
                    runat="server"
                    Text="Mushrooms" />
                <br />
            <asp:CheckBox ID="chkOlives" runat="server"
                Text="Olives" />
        </asp:WizardStep>
        <asp:WizardStep runat="server" Title="Name">          →5
            Please enter your name:<br />
            <br />
            <asp:TextBox ID="txtName" runat="server" />
        </asp:WizardStep>
        <asp:WizardStep runat="server"                       →6
            Title="Finish">
            <br />
            <asp:Label ID="lblOrder" runat="server" />
            <br />
        </asp:WizardStep>
    </WizardSteps>
  </asp:Wizard>
 </div>
 </form>
</body>
</html>
```

The C# code-behind file, shown in Listing 4-3, responds to the ActiveStep Changed event. It has a single method that checks the ActiveStepIndex property of the Wizard control. If this value is 3 (indicating that the final step has been reached), the Text property of the lblOrder label is set to display a summary of the order.

Listing 4-3:   The Wizard.aspx.cs file (C#)

```
using System;
using System.Data;
```

```
using System.Configuration;
using System.Collections;
using System.Web;
using System.Web.Security;
using System.Web.UI;
using System.Web.UI.WebControls;
using System.Web.UI.WebControls.WebParts;
using System.Web.UI.HtmlControls;
public partial class Wizard : System.Web.UI.Page
{
    protected void Wizard1_ActiveStepChanged(
        object sender, EventArgs e)
    {
        if (Wizard1.ActiveStepIndex == 3)
        {
            String order = "Thank you, ";
            order += txtName.Text + "<br><br>";
            order += "You have ordered a ";
            if (rdoSmall.Checked)
                order += "small ";
            else if (rdoMedium.Checked)
                order += "medium ";
            else if (rdoLarge.Checked)
                order += "large ";
            order += "pizza with the "
                + "following toppings:<br><br>";
            if (chkPepperoni.Checked)
                order += "Pepperoni<br>";
            if (chkSausage.Checked)
                order += "Sausage<br>";
            if (chkMushrooms.Checked)
                order += "Mushrooms<br>";
            if (chkOlives.Checked)
                order += "Olives<br>";
            lblOrder.Text = order;
        }
    }
}
```

Listing 4-4 shows the VB.NET version of the code-behind file.

Listing 4-4:   The Wizardvb.aspx.vb file (VB)

```
Partial Class Wizardvb
    Inherits System.Web.UI.Page
    Protected Sub Wizard1_ActiveStepChanged( _
            ByVal sender As Object, _
            ByVal e As System.EventArgs) _
            Handles Wizard1.ActiveStepChanged
        If Wizard1.ActiveStepIndex = 3 Then
            Dim order As String = "Thank you, "
```

(continued)

Listing 4-4 *(continued)*

```
            order &= txtName.Text + "<br><br>"
            order &= "You have ordered a "
            If rdoSmall.Checked Then
                order &= "small "
            ElseIf rdoMedium.Checked Then
                order &= "medium "
            ElseIf rdoLarge.Checked Then
                order += "large "
            End If
            order &= "pizza with the "
            order &= "following toppings:<br><br>"
            If chkPepperoni.Checked Then
                order += "Pepperoni<br>"
            End If
            If chkSausage.Checked Then
                order += "Sausage<br>"
            End If
            If chkMushrooms.Checked Then
                order += "Mushrooms<br>"
            End If
            If chkOlives.Checked Then
                order += "Olives<br>"
            End If
            lblOrder.Text = order
        End If
    End Sub
End Class
```

Working with the Calendar Control

Many applications require that users enter a date. One way to do that is simply to provide a text box, and then use a `CompareValidator` control to ensure that the user has entered data in a correct date format. However, ASP.NET provides a more interesting (and less haphazard) alternative: the `Calendar` control, which displays a calendar that lets the user select a date. Figure 4-6 shows a page with a `Calendar` control.

With this simple control, the user can select a date by clicking it. The user can also change the month by clicking either button at the top of the control.

The markup for the `Calendar` control shown in Figure 4-6 is embarrassingly simple:

```
<asp:Calendar ID="Calendar1" runat="server" />
```

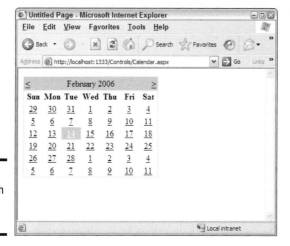

Figure 4-6:
A page with
a Calendar
control.

In other words, Figure 4-6 shows the default appearance and operation of the `Calendar` control. You can modify the `Calendar` control's appearance and behavior by setting various properties. Table 4-2 lists the properties you're most likely to change:

Table 4-2	Common Calendar Control Properties
Property	*Description*
`Caption`	Provides a caption displayed at the top of the calendar.
`DayNameFormat`	The format used to display the day names. Options are `Full`, `Short`, `FirstLetter`, `FirstTwoLetters`, and `Shortest`.
`FirstDayOfWeek`	Lets you pick the starting day for the weeks. The default is `Sunday`.
`NextPrevFormat`	Indicates how the buttons that move to the next and previous month are displayed. Options are `CustomText`, `ShortMonth`, or `FullMonth`.
`NextMonthText`	The custom text displayed for the button that leads to the next month. The default is a `&gt`, a greater-than sign.
`PrevMonthText`	The custom text displayed for the button that leads to the previous month. The default is a `&lt`, a less-than sign.
`SelectedDate`	The selected date.
`SelectionMode`	Controls what the user can select. Options are `Day` (the user can select a single day), `DayWeek` (the user can select a single day or an entire week), and `DayWeek Month` (the user can select a single day, an entire week, or an entire month).

(continued)

Table 4-2 *(continued)*

Property	Description
ShowGridLines	Controls whether grid lines are displayed for the calendar.
ShowNextPrevMonth	Controls whether the next and previous month buttons are visible.
ShowTitle	Controls whether the title is displayed.
TitleFormat	Controls the title format. Options are Month (just the month) and MonthYear (the month and year).
VisibleDate	Specifies the date that should be visible when the calendar is displayed. If you don't set this property, the current date will be displayed.

You can also apply an autoformat to a Calendar control to give it a more attractive appearance. To do that, choose AutoFormat from the Smart Tag menu, then select the format you want to apply. Figure 4-7 shows a Calendar control with the Professional 2 autoformat applied.

The Calendar control has a plethora of properties — you can set the style for the many elements that make up the control. If you want to create a custom style, I suggest you start by applying an autoformat that's close to what you want. Then you can adjust the formatting properties set by the autoformat to suit your tastes.

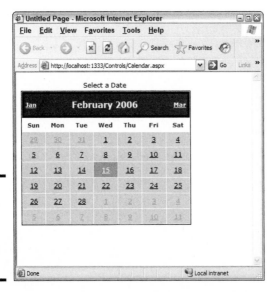

Figure 4-7:
A Calendar control with an autoformat applied.

By default, the `Calendar` control will display the current date even if a different date is selected. This can be a problem if the selected date is not in the same month as the current date. For example, suppose you set the `SelectedDate` property to `December 1, 2006`, then display the page. If the current date is March 28, 2006, the selected date will not be visible because the calendar will display March, not December. The solution is to set the `VisibleDate` property to the value of the `SelectedDate` property, as in this C# example:

```
Calendar1.VisibleDate = Calendar1.SelectedDate;
```

(The VB.NET code would be the same but without the semicolon.)

Making Use of the FileUpload Control

The `FileUpload` control lets users upload a file to your Web site. It displays a text box in which the user can enter a filename and path. In addition, a Browse button displays a dialog box the user can access to browse to the file. Figure 4-8 shows a page with a `FileUpload` control.

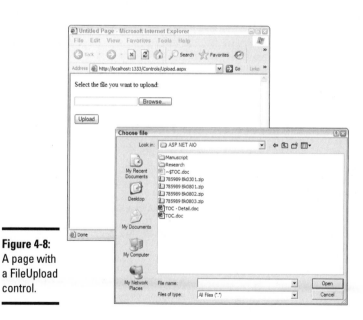

Figure 4-8:
A page with
a FileUpload
control.

The markup for the `FileUpload` control shown in Figure 4-8 is as follows:

```
Select the file you want to upload:
<br /><br />
<asp:FileUpload ID="FileUpload1" runat="server" />
<br /><br />
<asp:Button ID="btnUpload" runat="server" Text="Upload" />
```

Notice that the Upload button displayed in Figure 4-8 *isn't* provided by the `FileUpload` control. Instead, a separate button is required to actually upload the file selected by the user. The `Click` event handler for this button must call the `PostedFile.SaveAs` method of the `FileUpload` control, as shown in this C# example:

```
protected void btnUpload_Click(Object sender,
    System.EventArgs e)
{  _
    String path = @"C:\temp\"
        + FileUpload1.FileName;
    FileUpload1.PostedFile.SaveAs(path);
}
```

Here's the VB.NET version:

```
Protected Sub btnUpload_Click(ByVal sender As Object, _
        ByVal e As System.EventArgs) _
        Handles btnUpload.Click
    Dim path As String = "C:\temp\"
    path &= FileUpload1.FileName
    FileUpload1.PostedFile.SaveAs(path)
End Sub
```

Here are a few other quirks of the `FileUpload` control that are good to know:

✦ **You can check the size of the uploaded file using the** `PostedFile.` `ContentLength` **property.** This lets you put a size limit on uploads. Just don't call the `SaveAs` method if the file exceeds the maximum length.

✦ **The ASP.NET user account must have access rights to the location to which you save the file.**

✦ **The** `SaveAs` **method isn't what copies the file from the user's computer to the server.** Instead, the file is copied to the server when the user posts the page by clicking the Upload button. The `SaveAs` method merely directs the `FileUpload` control to save the file that has been copied to the server. If you don't call the `SaveAs` method, the uploaded file is discarded.

Chapter 5: Working with User Controls

In This Chapter

- ✔ Getting a handle on what user controls do
- ✔ Creating a simple user control
- ✔ Putting a user control in a page
- ✔ Adding properties to a user control
- ✔ Making use of user-control properties

*A*ll told, ASP.NET provides more than 50 different types of controls you can use on your Web pages. (You can learn the details of each control by looking them up in the Visual Studio help.) You'd think that would be enough, but some applications can benefit from controls that go beyond the basic capabilities provided by ASP.NET.

Fortunately, ASP.NET provides two ways you can create your own controls that build on and extend the standard controls: custom server controls and user controls. The most advanced type of custom control is called a *custom server control*. (Creating custom server controls is an advanced topic that's covered in Book 9.) *User controls* don't have all the bells and whistles of custom server controls, but they are much simpler to create and use.

All code listings used in this book are available for download at www.dummies. com/go/aspnetaiofd. Note that you'll find both C# and VB.NET versions of all the listings in this chapter available for download from the Web site.

Introducing User Controls

A *user control* is a special type of ASP.NET page that can be included in another ASP.NET page just as if it were a control — which (in fact) it is. Because a user control is just a type of ASP.NET page, creating one is as simple as creating a page. And putting a user control on your page is as simple as dragging it from the Solution Explorer onto the page.

Because a user control is simply a special type of ASP.NET page, it can include just about anything that a regular ASP.NET page can include. That includes other ASP.NET server controls. In fact, the most common way to put user controls to work is to create combinations of controls that are used together.

For example, how many Web applications have you seen that ask for your name, address, phone number, and e-mail address? Such a combination of labels, text boxes, and validation controls is ideal for a typical user control.

Figure 5-1 shows a Web page that uses just such a user control. As you can see, you can't tell from looking at this page that the three label controls and the five text-box controls are actually all a part of *one* user control.

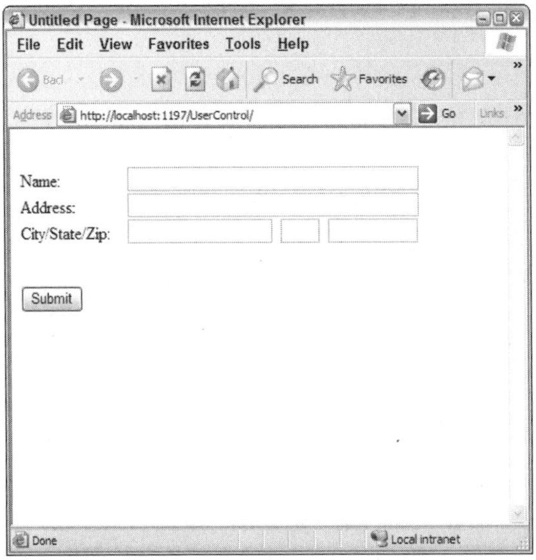

Figure 5-1:
A page with
a user
control.

An important benefit of using user controls is that you can *re*use them throughout your application. For example, suppose your application needs to get contact information for employees, clients, and vendors. Rather than code this function in three different places, you can create a single user control and reuse it three times. Is that easy, or what?

User controls have evolved in a handy, if ironic, way for ASP.NET 2.0. On the one hand, Visual Studio has been enhanced in a way that makes user controls much easier to work with. Previous versions of Visual Studio represented user controls as big gray boxes; you couldn't actually see what a page that included the actual controls looked like until you actually ran the application. Now you can show the contents of any user controls you've put on the page in the Web Designer — which makes 'em much easier to tweak.

And here's the irony: Although user controls are easier to work with these days, the new Master Pages feature has reduced the need for them. In previous versions of ASP.NET, user controls were a relatively convenient way to include common elements on each page of a Web site. For example, you could create a user control that not only represented a page banner, but also proceeded to add that user control to each page. Fortunately, now that the Master Pages feature makes it easy to create pages with common elements such as page banners, you don't have to whomp up specific user controls to serve that purpose.

Even so, there are plenty of *other* purposes for user controls. So it's worth a closer look at how they work and how to put them into effect.

Creating a User Control

To create a user control, call up the Add New Item dialog box by choosing Website⇨Add New Item command. Then choose Web User Control from the list of available templates, type a name for the user control in the Name text box, and click the Add button. This procedure adds a new user control (with the extension .aspx), and opens the user control in the Web Designer.

If you then switch to Source view, you'll see the following lines for C#:

```
<%@ Control Language="C#" AutoEventWireup="true"
    CodeFile="Contact.ascx.cs" Inherits="Contact" %>
```

The VB.NET version varies only slightly:

```
<%@ Control Language="VB" AutoEventWireup="false"
    CodeFile="Contact.ascx.vb" Inherits="Contact" %>
```

The Control directive takes the place of the Page directive found in a regular ASP.NET page.

Note that the user control is missing some of the other HTML elements that you'd normally see when you create a new Web page. For example, there are no <html>, <body>, <form>, or <div> tags. That's because a user control can't be displayed by itself; it can only be displayed by inserting it into a regular ASP.NET page. The <HTML>, <BODY>, <FORM>, and <DIV> tags are supplied by the ASP.NET page in which the user control is inserted.

To add content to an ASP.NET page, simply drag the controls you want from the toolbox onto the page in Design view. Or you can add HTML markup directly to any of those user controls by working in Source view. Listing 5-1 shows the complete C# markup for the Contact user control with three label controls, five text box controls, and five validation controls. (The only variation for the VB.NET version is that the `Control` directive specifies VB as the language, specifies `false` for `AutoEventWireup`, and names a .vb file as the code file.

Listing 5-1:   The .ascx file for the Contact user control (Contact.ascx)

```
<%@ Control Language="C#" AutoEventWireup="true"
    CodeFile="Contact.ascx.cs" Inherits="Contact" %>
<asp:Label ID="Label1" runat="server"
    Text="Name:" Width="100px" />
<asp:TextBox ID="txtName" runat="server"
    Width="272px" />
<asp:RequiredFieldValidator runat="server"
    ID="RequiredFieldValidator1"
    ControlToValidate="txtName"
    Display="Dynamic"
    ErrorMessage="*" />
<br />
<asp:Label ID="Label2" runat="server"
    Text="Address:" Width="100px" />
<asp:TextBox ID="txtAddress" runat="server"
    Width="272px" />
<asp:RequiredFieldValidator runat="server"
    ID="RequiredFieldValidator2"
    ControlToValidate="txtAddress"
    Display="Dynamic"
    ErrorMessage="*" />
<br />
<asp:Label ID="Label3" runat="server"
    Text="City/State/Zip:" Width="100px" />
<asp:TextBox ID="txtCity" runat="server"
    Width="134px" />
<asp:RequiredFieldValidator runat="server"
    ID="RequiredFieldValidator3"
    ControlToValidate="txtCity"
    Display="Dynamic"
    ErrorMessage="*" />
<asp:TextBox ID="txtState" runat="server"
    Width="30px" />
<asp:RequiredFieldValidator runat="server"
    ID="RequiredFieldValidator4"
    ControlToValidate="txtState"
    Display="Dynamic"
    ErrorMessage="*" />
<asp:TextBox ID="txtZipCode" runat="server"
    Width="79px" />
```

```
<asp:RequiredFieldValidator runat="server"
    ID="RequiredFieldValidator5"
    ControlToValidate="txtZipCode"
    Display="Dynamic"
    ErrorMessage="*" />
<br />
```

Adding a User Control to a Page

Once you've created a user control, you can add it to a page by simply dragging the user control from the Solution Explorer to the page while in Design view. When you do, Visual Studio *renders* (that is, gives you an on-screen look at) the controls you've put in the user control; they show up on the page, as shown in Figure 5-2.

**Book II
Chapter 5**

**Working with
User Controls**

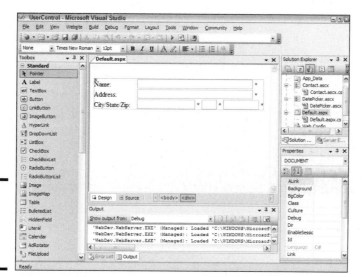

Figure 5-2:
A user
control
rendered
on a page.

Having the user control rendered on the page in the Web Designer is one of the handiest new features of Visual Studio 2005. In previous versions, user controls appeared as big gray boxes, and you had to actually run the application to see how the user controls looked on-screen.

If you switch to Source view, you'll see that two lines have been added to the markup for the page. The first is a `Register` directive that identifies the user control you've added to the page:

```
<%@ Register Src="Contact.ascx" TagName="Contact"
    TagPrefix="uc1" %>
```

The `Register` directive appears at the beginning of the `.aspx` file, right after the `Page` directive. It provides three bits of information:

✦ **The source file that defines the user control — in this case,** `Contact.ascx`.

✦ **The tag name that will be used to identify the user control — in this case,** `Contact`.

✦ **The prefix that will appear in front of the tag name instead of the standard asp prefix — in this case,** `uc1`.

Then, in the Body section of the Web page, you'll find the tag that actually inserts the user control. Here's what it looks like:

```
<uc1:Contact ID="Contact1" runat="server" />
```

Here you can see how the prefix and tag name are used in the tag that inserts the user control.

Adding Properties to a User Control

Okay, let's be practical here: A user control such as the `Contacts.ascx` control wouldn't be very useful if it didn't provide a way for you to get the contact information entered by the user. To do that, you need to add one or more *properties* to the user control. You do that by adding code to the code-behind file for the user control.

If you don't know how to code properties in C# or Visual Basic, fear not. You can learn how by reading Book 4 (C#) or Book 5 (Visual Basic).

Listing 5-2 shows the C# version of the code-behind file for the `Contact.ascx` control, and Listing 5-3 shows the Visual Basic version. The following list describes the highlighted lines of these code-behind files:

✦ **→1:** The `Name` property gets its value from the `Text` property of the `txtName` text box.

✦ **→2:** The `Address` property exposes the `Text` property of the `txtAddress` text box.

✦ **→3:** The `City` property exposes the `Text` property of the `txtCity` text box.

✦ →**4:** The State property exposes the Text property of the txtState text box.

✦ →**5:** The ZipCode property exposes the Text property of the txtZip code text box.

Listing 5-2: **The C# code-behind file for the Contact user control (Contact.ascx.cs)**

```
public partial class Contact : System.Web.UI.UserControl
{
    public string Name                                      →1
    {
        get
        {
            return txtName.Text;
        }
        set
        {
            txtName.Text = value;
        }
    }
    public string Address                                   →2
    {
        get
        {
            return txtAddress.Text;
        }
        set
        {
            txtAddress.Text = value;
        }
    }
    public string City                                      →3
    {
        get
        {
            return txtCity.Text;
        }
        set
        {
            txtCity.Text = value;
        }
    }
    public string State                                     →4
    {
        get
        {
            return txtState.Text;
```

(continued)

Listing 5-2 (continued)

```
        }
        set
        {
            txtState.Text = value;
        }
    }
    public string ZipCode                                        →5
    {
        get
        {
            return txtZipCode.Text;
        }
        set
        {
            txtZipCode.Text = value;
        }
    }
}
```

Listing 5-3:   The VB code-behind file for the Contact user control (Contact.ascx.vb)

```
Partial Class Contact
    Inherits System.Web.UI.UserControl
    Public Property Name() As String                             →1
        Get
            Return txtName.Text
        End Get
        Set(ByVal value As String)
            txtName.Text = value
        End Set
    End Property
    Public Property Address() As String                          →2
        Get
            Return txtAddress.Text
        End Get
        Set(ByVal value As String)
            txtAddress.Text = value
        End Set
    End Property
    Public Property City() As String                             →3
        Get
            Return txtCity.Text
        End Get
        Set(ByVal value As String)
            txtCity.Text = value
        End Set
    End Property
    Public Property State() As String                            →4
```

```
        Get
            Return txtState.Text
        End Get
        Set(ByVal value As String)
            txtState.Text = value
        End Set
    End Property
    Public Property ZipCode() As String          →5
        Get
            Return txtZipCode.Text
        End Get
        Set(ByVal value As String)
            txtZipCode.Text = value
        End Set
    End Property
End Class
```

Putting User-Control Properties to Work

After you've added properties to a user control, you can access those properties from any page that includes the user control. For example, here's the C# markup for a page that includes the Contact.ascx control along with a button and a label:

```
<uc1:Contact ID="Contact1" runat="server" />
<br /><br />
<asp:Button ID="btnSubmit" runat="server"
    OnClick="btnSubmit_Click"
    Text="Submit" />
<br /><br />
<asp:Label ID="Label1" runat="server" />
```

(The only difference for the VB.NET version is that it wouldn't include an OnClick attribute.)

Notice that the OnClick event for the button is handled by the btnSubmit_Click method in the code-behind file. This method uses the properties defined for the Contact user control to display the name and address entered by the user in the label, like this:

```
protected void btnSubmit_Click(object sender, EventArgs e)
{
    Label1.Text = Contact1.Name + "<br>"
        + Contact1.Address + "<br>"
        + Contact1.City + " "
        + Contact1.State + ", "
        + Contact1.ZipCode;
}
```

As you can see, the `Name`, `Address`, `City`, `State`, and `Zipcode` properties of the `Contact1` user control can be used in the same way you'd use the properties of any other type of control.

Here's the VB.NET version:

```
Protected Sub btnSubmit_Click( _
        ByVal sender As Object, _
        ByVal e As System.EventArgs) _
        Handles btnSubmit.Click
    Label1.Text = Contact1.Name & "<br>" _
        & Contact1.Address & "<br>" _
        & Contact1.City & " " _
        & Contact1.State & ", " _
        & Contact1.ZipCode
End Sub
```

Notice that it uses a `Handles` clause, so the `OnClick` attribute is necessary in the markup.

Book III

HTML

VISUAL WEB DEVELOPMENT TEAM

"Give him air! Give him air! He'll be okay. He's just been exposed to some raw HTML code. It must have accidentally flashed across his screen from the server."

Contents at a Glance

Chapter 1: HTML Basics

In This Chapter

✔ Generating the right type of HTML

✔ Microsoft support for XHTML

✔ Keeping your HTML clean and tidy

✔ Editing and formatting in Visual Web Developer

*M*odern Web browsers are far too forgiving. You can point them to any old HyperText Markup Language (HTML) markup and they'll do a creditable job of rendering what the programmer intended. If all browsers — starting with Mosaic and Lynx — had been sufficiently picky, there'd be almost no sloppy HTML out there. Imagine how precise Webmasters and graphical editors would have to be if browsers stopped cold at the first sign of illegal HTML. The browser would blast the viewer with the message `This HTML Violates Standards and Cannot be Viewed`.

This chapter looks at some basic HTML issues, especially the newer XHTML standard you should consider for your code. I'll show you features in Visual Web Developer that make editing code easier, analyze the structure of your HTML document, and beautify jumbled markup. I won't try to teach you HTML tags here because you probably know them already. At a minimum, a Web developer's goal should be to keep that pesky HTML close enough to standard usage that a strict browser won't choke on it. For my part, I try to keep my HTML clean enough that if some guy snoops at my source code, he won't die laughing. I don't want that on my conscience!

XHTML Rulez!

The popular HTML 4.01 specification is old by Internet standards. Anything Internet-related that was officially released at the end of 1999 (and existed long before) is probably today's has-been. After all, what browser did you use back in 1999? What search engine was in your Favorites in that browser? You get the picture; times change, and HTML is no exception.

The emerging standard is *eXtensible HyperText Markup Language (XHTML)*. XHTML tightens up the syntax rules so that its HTML meets XML standards.

XML is a cross-platform data format for publishing and exchanging structured documents. (For more on applying XML rules to Web pages, refer to sections "Making your HTML well-formed" and "More XHTML requirements," later in this chapter). When you create a Web site from scratch or do an overhaul, you might want to make the move to a higher standard as well.

Even if you don't see the point of moving to XHTML for today's browsers, consider it a way to future-proof your Web pages. Down the road, *user-agents* (Internet lingo for anything that reads or consumes XHTML) might require XML. You don't want to miss out if the Total Informational Computer Knowledge Leaving Earth (TICKLE) project accepts only valid XML documents. Once TICKLE is fully funded, it will beam all of Planet Earth's knowledge to distant solar systems. Okay, we're kidding about TICKLE (though what the heck, we use it in examples in this chapter) — but you never know what else might visit your site or want to parse its data.

XHTML and the W3C

The *World Wide Web Consortium (W3C)* is the organization that publishes all sorts of Web-related standards. Sadly, it can't enforce any of them. Instead of calling its January 26, 2000 specification on XHTML 1.0 a decree or ukase, the W3C ever so politely invited us to follow it as a *recommendation*. You can read the document at this address:

```
http://www.w3.org/TR/xhtml1
```

The dream of a common markup standard for browsers, document readers, TVs, PDAs, and mobile phones didn't grab our attention for several years. If the W3C had been really tough with us — like threatening to pull the plug on the Internet — compliance on the part of browser developers and Webmasters would have started much earlier.

Even though developers ignored XHTML 1.0 for years, the W3C wasn't deterred: XHTML 2.0 is currently in the works.

The strict upbringing of XHTML

As of this writing, there are four recommended flavors of XHTML.

+ **XHTML 1.0 Transitional:** This standard supports the tags and attributes in HTML 4.01, which makes it easier to use when updating existing Web pages. If your pages include `<font>` tags and attributes such as `bgcolor`, this one's for you. This is also the flavor of XHTML used by Visual Web Developer 2005 Express Edition (VWDE).

+ **XHTML 1.0 Strict:** This one requires you to use Cascading Style Sheets (CSS) to add color and style to pages. That's a very desirable goal for new sites because separating content from presentation lets you update the look of a site (for example, the entire color scheme) by swapping in a new CSS file. That said, getting that capability may require a lot of rework to get the `<font>` tags out of all legacy pages.

✦ **XHTML 1.0 Frameset:** The `<frameset>` tag isn't supported in the Transitional and Strict versions of XHTML 1.0. The Frameset standard is only for pages that act as frames or containers for other pages.

✦ **XHTML 1.1:** This one takes XHTML 1.0 Strict and adds support for modules and extensions such as the Scalable Vector Language (SVG) and the Mathematical Markup Language (MathML).

Making your HTML well-formed

XHTML is an XML application, which means it must abide by the strict rules of XML. A prime rule of XML is that the document must be *well-formed*. Here's what that means for HTML:

✦ **Close all tags:** Instead of just `<p>` or `<li>`, include the closing tag such as `</p>` and `</li>`.

✦ **Close empty tags:** Tags like `<img>` and `<br>` should be self-closing as in `<img />` and `<br />`. Think of them as screen doors — they're self-closing.

✦ **Nest tags properly:** Don't overlap start and end tags. Instead of this

```
<p>We are here to <b>help</p></b>
```

use

```
<p>We are here to <b>help</b></p>
```

✦ **Quote all attributes:** When you use an attribute like `id`, `name`, or `style`, its value must be inside quotation marks. For example, instead of

```
id=myvalue name=myvalue
```

use

```
id="myvalue" name="myvalue"
```

The HTML document below is an example of a well-formed document. You could pass it off as an XML document as well as HTML.

```
<html>
<head>
    <style></style>
    <script></script>
</head>
<body>
    <p id="formed">
        I'm well formed &amp; I know it.</p>
</body>
</html>
```

More XHTML requirements

As a "reformulation" of HTML 4.01 standards, XHTML retains the essentials of its predecessors. An HTML document includes an opening `<html>` tag and finishes with the closing `</html>` tag. Next is the `<head>` section that holds content that doesn't usually appear in the browser window but tells people about the page. Most visible content goes inside the `<body>` and `</body>` tags. Visual content includes plain text, image tags, forms, buttons for submitting data, and hyperlinks.

In XML, tag names are case-sensitive and the case of the opening and closing tags much match. Although legal in older HTML, the following is illegal markup in XML:

```
<P CLASS="sidebar">TICKLE Funding Begins</p>
```

To thwart errors related to the ups and downs of case, XHTML requires lowercase for HTML elements and attribute names:

```
<p class="sidebar">TICKLE Funding Begins</p>
```

Here's another issue where XHTML forces changes. Some HTML 4 tags require the `name` attribute as part of their construction. For example, you've doubtless seen hyperlink tags that look like this:

```
It is <a href="page.aspx#def">defined</a> here.<br />
```

The corresponding anchor (also known as a *bookmark*) in `page.aspx` looks like this:

```
<a name="def">Definition.</a><br />
```

The crosshatch (#) character in the hyperlink's URL (known as a fragment identifier) presents a problem. XML supports fragment identifiers as well, but the target needs to use `id` instead of `name`. The workaround that gives you backward compatibility while complying with XML rules is to add `id` and keep `name` for the XHTML, like this:

```
<a name="def" id="def">Definition.</a><br />
```

 You really can't win with the `name` and `id` compromise. XHTML 1.0 declares the `name` attribute to be technically legal but outdated (*deprecated* in geekspeak). However, the W3C warns that the `name` attribute in the a, `applet`, `form`, `frame`, `iframe`, `img`, and `map` elements will be booted from subsequent versions of XHTML. While trying to be compatible and compliant, you create problems in meeting a strict standard in the future.

Taking characters as an entity

XML (and remember XHTML is an XML application) reserves some characters such as < and > for its own purposes. In certain circumstances, you need to replace the actual character with a built-in *character entity*. (A character entity is a safe replacement sequence for reserved characters such as < for the reserved <.) This is to make sure the XML document doesn't mistake content or values for part of a tag. Here's an example of an ampersand in a Web page, converted to its legal form:

```
<h1>Rock &amp; Roll</h1>
```

For the most part, HTML editors fix these as you type. Here's what to watch for if you get a syntax error:

✦ < **replaces the less than symbol (<) in content**

✦ > **replaces the greater than symbol (>) in content**

✦ & **replaces the ampersand (&) in content**

✦ ' **replaces the apostrophe (') if the attributed value is quoted**

✦ " **replaces a quotation mark (" ") if the attribute value is quoted**

VWDE's Support for XHTML

**Book III
Chapter 1**

HTML Basics

ASP.NET 2.0 fully supports XHTML 1.0 Transitional. When server controls such as the `GridView`, `TreeView`, and `Menu` generate HTML tags and attributes, the markup conforms at least to the Transitional standard — and, in some cases, meets the XHTML 1.1 standard as well.

Visual Web Developer's page editor also generates code that complies with the XHTML 1.0 Transitional specification. As you see in the following sections, the page editor goes a long way toward keeping you compliant, whether it's a new page or an old one.

A solemn DOCTYPE declaration

When you add a new ASP.NET page to a Visual Web Developer Express project, you see VWDE's declaration of support for XHTML in the document-type declaration (`DOCTYPE`). The following code shows that the version is XHTML 1.0 Transitional (note also that the `<html>` tag identifies a supported namespace):

```
<%@ Page Language="VB" %>
<!DOCTYPE html PUBLIC "-//W3C//DTD XHTML 1.0
    Transitional//EN" "http://www.w3.org/TR/xhtml1/DTD/xhtml1-
    transitional.dtd">
```

```
<script runat="server">
</script>
<html xmlns="http://www.w3.org/1999/xhtml" >
<head runat="server">
    <title>Untitled Page</title>
</head>
<body>
    <form id="form1" runat="server">
    <div>
    </div>
    </form>
</body>
</html>
```

A *user agent* (geek-speak for a browser, screen reader, Web crawler, or other HTML parsing tool) that supports the same Document Type Definition (DTD) grammar should parse the content without stumbling over unknown syntax. If there's a dispute over the tags, case of characters, or overall structure, the referenced DTD is public for the entire world to see at the stated address:

```
http://www.w3.org/TR/xhtml1/DTD/xhtml1-transitional.dtd
```

The preceding referenced document is highly recommended reading for people who enjoy watching paint dry and grass grow.

If your document complies with its stated DTD, the document is said to be *valid*. That's why a geek can deny the authenticity of a Web page even while arguing to the last breath that the *document* is valid.

Validity spy

Visual Web Developer's editor is watching your every move as you develop pages. It constantly scans the markup and underlines problems with a red line. Exactly what is it checking? Well, that depends on what you selected as the target schema for validation. As shown in Figure 1-1, the choices are on the HTML Source Editing toolbar.

Figure 1-1:
HTML
Source
Editing
toolbar.

The editor determines which discrepancies to flag according to your choice of schema. Let's have some fun exploring this feature . . .

1. **Create a new ASP.NET page called** `xhtmlpg.aspx`.

2. **In Source view, type the following HTML markup (and try not to laugh):**

```
<blink>Netscape 3.0 supports this.</blink>
<marquee>Activate Internet Explorer 3.0</marquee>
```

3. **On the HTML Source Editing toolbar, from the drop-down list, select Netscape Navigator 4.0 (as you see in Figure 1-2).**

Figure 1-2:
Selecting
schema
validation.

ASP.NET controls and XHTML

Okay, a little clarity here: When we say that ASP.NET .2.0 supports the XHTML 1.0 specification, we mean that the *rendered* HTML is compliant, not necessarily the markup in an .aspx file. Thus the design-time code doesn't always pass XHTML muster. For example, here's what the XHTML 1.0 specification says about the attributes for the `<form>` element. Note especially the last column of the `action` attribute that's marked #REQUIRED.

```
<!ATTLIST form
  %attrs;
  action        %URI;
   #REQUIRED
  method        (get|post)
   "get"
  enctype       %ContentType;
   "application/x-www-form-
   urlencoded"
  onsubmit      %Script;
   #IMPLIED
  onreset       %Script;
   #IMPLIED
  accept        %ContentTypes;
   #IMPLIED
```

```
  accept-charset %Charsets;
   #IMPLIED
 >
```

But the `<form>` tag generated by VWDE doesn't match this specification. For example, it doesn't include the `action` attribute in the `<form>` tag as required. And it includes a `runat="server"` attribute that isn't in the spec.

Remember that the XHTML specification doesn't apply to the `<form>` element in the .aspx file, but to the code that ASP.NET renders for the page and sends to the browser. Here's what ASP.NET generates (and the browser sees) in the `<form>` tag:

```
<form name="form1"
   method="post"
   action="xhtmlpg.aspx"
   id="form1">
```

You can see that the `action` and `method` attributes have been added during server-side processing, and the `runat="server"` attribute has been removed.

**Book III
Chapter 1**

HTML Basics

4. In Source view, notice that there's no squiggly line under the `<blink>` tag.

This is because `<blink>` is a legal tag in Netscape 4.0.

5. Hover the mouse pointer over the opening `<marquee>` tag, which does have a squiggly line under it.

As shown in Figure 1-3, the validation tooltip advises that the tag is not supported in Netscape Navigator 4.0.

Figure 1-3:
Validating
against
Netscape
4.0.

6. On the HTML Source Editing toolbar, from the drop-down list, select Internet Explorer 6.0 (as you see in Figure 1-4).

Figure 1-4:
Validating
against IE 6.

7. Hover the cursor over the `<blink>` tag again. To IE 6.0, that's not a valid tag.

Figure 1-5 shows the result.

Figure 1-5:
Blink is
invalid but
marquee
is fine.

8. **Save and browse to** `xhtmlpg.aspx` **in Internet Explorer.**

As expected, the `<blink>` text doesn't blink but the `<marquee>` content scrolls across the page.

You can also set the validation target by going to Tools⇨Options⇨Text Editor⇨HTML⇨Validation, as shown in Figure 1-6.

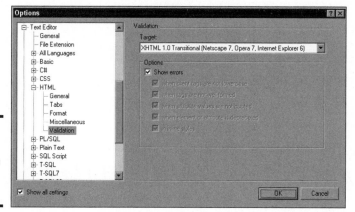

Figure 1-6:
Setting the validation in the Options dialog box.

Schema validation ignores the schema in the `DOCTYPE` declaration at the top of the ASP.NET page. Even when the `DOCTYPE` reads `XHTML 1.0 Transitional`, VWDE validates according to the selected schema (such as Internet Explorer 3.02 / Netscape Navigator 3.0). Be careful that the two don't get out of sync or you'll be assuming that `<blink>` is a valid tag (yikes) while declaring XHTML 1.0 compliance.

Letting VWDE fix old code

You don't need to memorize the XHTML specifications to update existing HTML as long as you pay attention to what the Visual Web Developer editor tells you — and follow suit. The Error List (View⇨Error List) nudges you towards best practices by pointing out the tags and other parts of the markup that aren't up to spec.

When you insert the following HTML code in the Visual Web Developer editor and set the validation schema to XHTML 1.1, the Error List comes alive. Here's what you get:

```
<!DOCTYPE html PUBLIC "-//W3C//DTD XHTML 1.1//EN"
"http://www.w3.org/TR/xhtml11/DTD/xhtml11.dtd">
<html>
<HEAD>
    <title>Go XHTML!</title>
```

```
</HEAD>
<body>
   My editor keeps me compliant!<br>
   <img src=http://www.gc.ca/images/flag.gif>
<hr>
</body>
</html>
```

As you see in the following list, the observant (some may say hypercritical) error checker has a lot to say about the code:

```
Error 1 Validation (XHTML 1.1): Element 'html' is missing
required attribute 'xmlns'.

Error 2 Validation (XHTML 1.1): This name contains upper-
case characters, which is not allowed.

Error 3 Validation (XHTML 1.1): Text is not allowed
between the opening and closing tags for element body'.

Error 4 Validation (XHTML 1.1): Text is not allowed
between the opening and closing tags for element body'.

Error 5 Validation (XHTML 1.1): Empty elements such as
'br' must end with />.

Error 6 Validation (XHTML 1.1): Attribute values must be
enclosed in quotation marks.

Error 7 Validation (XHTML 1.1): Element 'img' is missing
required attribute 'alt'.

Error 8 Validation (XHTML 1.1): Empty elements such as
'img' must end with />.

Error 9 Validation (XHTML 1.1): Empty elements such as
'hr' must end with />.
```

Ouch! We have more errors than code here. Fixing all this may seem like too much wasted time; after all, the page displays just fine. The good news is that you don't need to know anything in particular to write compliant XHTML — or, for that matter, to fix it. Just paste your old snippets into the VWDE editor and let it prompt you with the corrections. Hang in there; help is at hand in the following sections.

Fixing a missing attribute

Let's deal with the missing attribute in the html element. Try this in the HTML editor:

1. **Place your cursor just before the** `<html>` **tag's closing bracket (>) and insert a space.**

As shown in Figure 1-7, IntelliSense pops up a list of valid items.

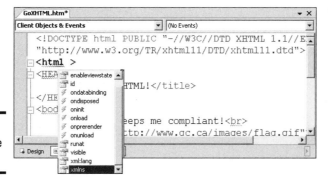

Figure 1-7:
IntelliSense
for HTML.

2. **Select** `xmlns` **(which is the missing attribute it was complaining about), and then press Tab.**

The `xmlns` namespace appears.

3. **Type the equals (=) sign.**

IntelliSense pops up again with the correct namespace value, as you see in Figure 1-8.

Figure 1-8:
Options for
attributes.

4. **Press Tab again.**

Not only does the value appear, the editor wraps it in quotation marks (see Figure 1-9) to make it all nice and legal.

Figure 1-9:
Tab when
you see
what you
want.

Crossing the great div (ide)

Another problem is in the body tag where the editor claims, "Text is not allowed between the opening and closing tags for element body." This rule sounds stupid at first blush — after all, if you don't put content between the body tags, you don't have much of a page. What it really means is that in XML, you must place all content inside a container tag. You'll notice that in its starter pages, Microsoft automatically provides a `<div>` right after `<body>` and closes it just before `</body>`.

Slashing squiggly lines

The editor's complaints about ending empty elements (such as `<br>` and `<img>`) without a closing slash are the easiest to fix. Just do what it says: Provide the forward slash and the squiggly line and error message go away. Often, when you type a closing bracket on its own, the editor tosses in the slash automatically as a freebie.

The error about the missing `alt` attribute is also a community service reminder. The description value of the `alt` tag ensures that you aren't excluding people with low or no vision or other disabilities from getting some value out of the graphical content.

Magical chorded keystrokes

You can fix some errors with magical keystrokes that geeky designers like to call *chords* because they are combined to perform one action. Hold down the Ctrl key and while it is down, press the K key and then (while still holding down the Ctrl key), press the D key. Bam! Here's what happened:

✦ **The illegal uppercase** `<HEAD></HEAD>` **turned lowercase.**

✦ **The missing quotation marks appeared around the value of the** `src` **attribute.**

✦ **The tags nested neatly inside their containers.**

Web tools have come a long way

In the late 1990s, Active Server Pages (ASP Classic) was the hot server-side technology. Microsoft introduced Visual InterDev (VID) as the development environment for dynamic, data-driven Web sites on Internet Information Server (now Internet Information Services).

The innovative Visual InterDev IDE introduced design-time controls to Web programmers, a Scripting Object Model, object-oriented development, and remote scripting. Remote scripting (using Java technology) let a page fetch new data without having to refresh. In 1998 it was ahead of its time and the precursor to AJAX (Asynchronous JavaScript And XML). Remote scripting was the brainchild of Nikhil Kothari, now a brilliant architect on the Web Platform and Tools team at Microsoft.

The one thing Visual InterDev *didn't* do well was abide by HTML standards. While I was admiring how Visual Web Developer flags non-compliant XHTML, I recalled the illegal markup that the VID editor generated. The following snippet is actual Visual InterDev code from a March 2000 sample. You can still download it from `http://msdn.microsoft.com/vstudio/previous/vinterdev/downloads/samples/`.

```
<FORM name=thisForm
    METHOD=post>
<html>
<head>
<title>Filtered Report</title>
</head>
<body>
<p>
</p>
. . .
</body>
</FORM>
</html>
```

As you can see, the `<FORM>` tag precedes the `<html>` tag and, at the end of the page, the two tags overlap instead of nesting.

Book III
Chapter 1

HTML Basics

The Ctrl+K, Ctrl+D sequence is a two-stroke shortcut that calls Visual Web Developer's built-in `Edit.FormatDocument` command. You can accomplish the same thing using the menus by going to Edit⇨Format Document.

For a complete list of default shortcut keys, chords, and assorted magical keystrokes, browse to this page:

`http://msdn2.microsoft.com/en-us/library/cftd38f0(VS.80).aspx`

You can go your own way

You can't corral hard-core mavericks into accepting imposed standards, and they buck at being shown the error of their ways. To remove the burr from under the saddle, you can set Visual Web Developer to turn a blind eye to faulty HTML.

Okay, it's not recommended for most of us to switch off syntax checking, but for the few who really want to, here's how:

1. From the Tools menu, click Options.

The Options dialog box appears, as shown in Figure 1-10.

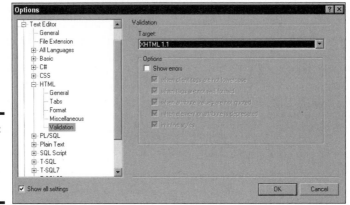

Figure 1-10: Don't nag me about every little mistake.

2. In the bottom-left corner of the dialog box, check Show all settings.

(Microsoft reserves many customizing options for people who are observant enough to find this check box.)

3. In the Options area hierarchy, drill down from Text Editor to HTML to the Validation node.

4. In the Validation area to the right, uncheck Show errors (shown in Figure 1-10) and then click OK.

Those pesky squiggly lines and error lists disappear.

Error checking isn't an all-or-nothing affair. As you can see by the choices in Figure 1-10, you can indulge your independent streak by allowing the IDE to nag you about missing closing tags and unquoted attributes but to keep its own counsel when it finds legal-but-outdated *(deprecated)* tags.

Extremely sloppy HTML with mismatched tags or dangling quotes can choke the Visual Web Developer editor. It's rare, but if parts of your code are indecipherable, the editor will refuse to go into Design mode. At that point, clean up the most grievous errors in Source view and try again.

Editing Code in Source View

Whether it's an accounting package, a word processor, or a programming environment, users' software demands are similar: They want the tool to make them more productive, not get in the way. Visual Web Developer offers hundreds of features that make editing HTML and ASP.NET code easier. This section looks at a few of them.

Preserving source code

People are pretty sensitive about their work — and especially about the way it looks. Microsoft heard that loud and clear when it came to the HTML code editor. "Don't touch my $#@% code!" became the ugly rallying cry for a bug-fix request. You see, in the bad old days, you could arrange your HTML very nicely in Source view — but the moment you switched to Design view to make a change, some very nasty gremlins went to work on your source code. While your code was out of view, the beasties realigned and reformatted the markup with someone else's choice of line breaks, white space, tabs, and tag case. It drove people crazy. The griping went on for years.

The complaints have finally paid off. A Microsoft insider tells us that preventing the editor from messing with source-code formatting "took several man-years to-do and a lot of engineering." The upshot is that in Visual Web Developer you can align your HTML any way you like and flip between Design and Source view without fear.

Book III
Chapter 1

HTML Basics

Source-code preservation, bah

Amaze the geeks by showing them that the much-vaunted editor *does* reformat HTML code despite lofty assurances. Here's how to make it happen:

Type the following markup for an unordered list into the HTML page in Code view.

```
<ul>
   <li>1234</li>
   <li>6789</li>
</ul>
```

Switch to Design view and then switch back to Code view. No change to the code, right?

Switch back to Design view and just after the number 4, type a space and the number **5**.

Go back to Source view. Look! The list item markup appears all on one line, like this:

```
<ul>
   <li>1234 5</li><li>6789</li>
</ul>
```

The seraphim of geekdom (geeks of the highest order) have a techy explanation for this anomaly: Browsers often ignore excess white space content (space characters, carriage returns, and tabs) in HTML. When white space doesn't matter, the page looks the same if you have everything on one line or in dozens of broken lines. In some instances, however, white space *does* affect the rendering. Apparently *not* reformatting the HTML source in the unordered list (that is, failing to tighten up the white space) would alter the way Internet Explorer renders the page. Microsoft decided to make an exception to the source-preservation rule in this case; therefore it reformats your code to save you from yourself.

Cleaning up source code

Then again, sometimes your markup ends up looking totally unkempt and disreputable as if it slept in a ditch all night. You wouldn't mind having someone straighten it up and run a comb through its hair. If you'd like Microsoft to make your HTML look pretty, go to the Edit menu and choose Format Document (or Format Selection if you just want a partial makeover).

The keyboard shortcut sequences to format HTML code are

> Ctrl+K, Ctrl+D to format the whole document
>
> Ctrl+K, Ctrl+F to format the selected area

By default, Visual Web Developer reformats any HTML pasted in from another source. You can change that by going to Tools➪Options➪Text Editor➪HTML➪ Miscellaneous➪Format HTML On Paste.

Using the Tag Navigator

Even professionally formatted HTML can be hard to navigate. For example, the end tag can fall outside of the visible surface and be hard to locate. Figure 1-11 shows the use of the Tag Navigator located next to the Source button along the bottom-right of the page editor. It shows the current tag and its ancestors. When you click a tag name, the editor highlights the corresponding code. As you hover the mouse pointer over the right end of a tag name (such as `<div>` in Figure 1-11) an arrow appears, letting you select the entire tag or just the inner content (as shown).

Figure 1-11:
The Tag
Navigator.

Collapsing and outlining

It's easier to concentrate on portions of your HTML code if you can dismiss the parts you don't need to see. The editor lets you reduce a vast area of code to a single line outline. Select the code you want to hide and right-click. Then, from the context menu, click Collapse Tag. The area shrinks to three dots, giving you room to maneuver. You can get it back by right-clicking the dots and clicking Stop Outlining Tag.

Tags that act as containers (such as `<div>` and `<p>`) are even easier to hide. Click the minus sign (-) in the margin to collapse the region and the plus sign (+) to expand it.

No Comment!

To take a whole section of HTML code out of commission (for example, so you can focus on what's happening elsewhere at runtime), select the area to *comment out* and press the keystroke sequence Ctrl+K, Ctrl+C. Doing so starts the process of identifying specified lines of code as comments so they won't be rendered. You can *uncomment* the code later to get it to appear in the browser again.

The way the editor comments out the code depends on the type of page:

**Book III
Chapter 1**

HTML Basics

✦ **If you are working in a page with the** `.aspx` **extension, the editor inserts** `<%--` **before the selection and** `--%>` **at the end.** The percent sign (%) indicates that these are server-side comments. ASP.NET bypasses the markup between the comments so it won't appear in the HTML output.

✦ **A plain HTML page with the** `.htm` **or** `.html` **extension gets pure HTML comments.** That is, the editor uses `<!--` before the section and `-->` after it. Ctrl+K, Ctrl+U uncomments the selected lines. HTML comments show up in the source code of the output but whatever's embedded in the comments isn't interpreted by the browser or rendered to the screen.

✦ **The same keystrokes for commenting and uncommenting work for Visual Basic and C# source code.** The editor uses the appropriate comment characters for the environment.

Keyboard commands are a very personal issue. The keystrokes we discuss in this text are Microsoft's default settings. You can customize the sequences to suit your fingers by going to Tools⇨Options⇨Environment⇨Keyboard.

Editing Pages in Design View

Hand-coding in Source view is fine for some tasks, but it's hard to beat the WYSIWYG (What You See Is What You Get) editor in Design view for rapid creation of Web pages. In the time you'd take to scroll to your work area in Source view, you can drag a button control from the toolbox, drop it on the design surface, hit F4 to set some properties, and go back for more controls. The Visual Web Developer editor writes massive amounts of clean, standards-compliant code whether you're working with plain HTML or complex ASP.NET server controls.

By default, the Web-page designer uses *flow layout*. In this mode, text, buttons, and other objects appear in the browser in the order that they appear in the source code. For example, if you drop a text box between two buttons at design time, the browser renders a button, the text box, and the second button in the same order. One element's position is always relative to another's spot when they're rendered. Web developers often use tables to keep elements above, below, or next to each other, even when the user resizes the browser.

Many sophisticated Web designs place elements very precisely on a page, using absolute positioning. Some call this mode *CSS positioning* or *layering*. In this mode, each control has horizontal and vertical coordinates as part of its style attributes. These coordinate values dictate an absolute position on the page.

If you attempt to write absolute positioning code in Source view, prepare for a monarch-sized unpleasant sensation in the buttocks. Calculating the control's coordinates becomes a frustrating exercise in trial and error — mostly the latter. Stick to Design view for CSS positioning where the IDE calculates the values as you drag the control around the design surface.

Establishing a position in Design view

When you start building a whole Web site that uses absolute positioning, you can set absolute positioning as the default mode for new pages. Here's how:

1. **Open an HTML or ASP.NET page in the editor.**

2. **From the Layout menu, click Position.**

3. **From the submenu click Auto-position Options.**

   The Options dialog box opens at the CSS Positioning node of the HTML Designer.

4. **Under Positioning options, check the check box and select Absolutely positioned from the drop-down list, as shown in Figure 1-12.**

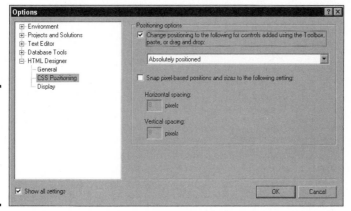

Figure 1-12:
Switch
on CSS
positioning
to the exact
location of
elements.

5. **Click OK.**

Freed from the constraints of flow layout, HTML controls slide easily across the design surface. Well, maybe not at first. You see, the default location for a control is the upper-left corner of the page. When you drag and drop a control from the toolbox, it snaps into the default position. Select the control and watch for the cursor to adopt the moveable icon (with arrows pointing in four directions) to indicate that you can put the control anywhere on the screen.

Some controls, like the horizontal rule (<hr />), nearly disappear into the upper-left corner when dropped onto a page. If you don't see the control in Design view, open Source view and set the control's top position to 50px (that's 50 pixels from the top of the page). You can grip an element more easily when it's away from the border.

Moving controls around the page at design time is much like arranging icons on your Windows desktop. The Visual Web Developer editor tracks the current position and writes parameters such as left and top, as shown in this input-button code:

```
<input id="Button1" style="z-index: 102; left: 218px;
position: absolute; top: 92px" type="button" value="OK" />
```

Figure 1-13 shows an HTML page in Design view with absolute positioning switched on. The controls include a horizontal rule, a block-level generic container with text, an input button, a text box, and a button. Notice the block containing text and the "moveable" cursor in its upper-left corner. You create a text block by wrapping the text in a `<div>` tag. (Web developers who work in FrontPage or Dreamweaver probably call these *layers*.)

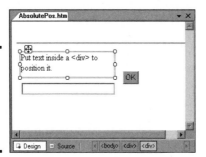

Figure 1-13:
Setting
exact
locations
with CSS
positioning.

Even without the positioning data, `<div>` tags are very handy. As you'll see in Chapter 4 of this mini-book, you can create interesting rollover and show/hide effects by adding a tiny bit of client-side code to `<div>` and its block mate, `<span>`.

When you compare the page in Design view (Figure 1-13) to the source code that follows, you see that the code for the horizontal rule is at the bottom of the markup but the rule appears at the top of the page in the designer. This arrangement highlights the difference between grid and flow — the order of the HTML makes no difference.

```
<!DOCTYPE html PUBLIC "-//W3C//DTD XHTML 1.0 Transitional//EN"
    "http://www.w3.org/TR/xhtml1/DTD/xhtml1-transitional.dtd">
<html xmlns="http://www.w3.org/1999/xhtml" >
<head>
    <title>Absolute Positioning</title>
</head>
<body>
<div>
    <input id="Text1"
        style="z-index: 106; left: 13px; width: 176px;
            position : absolute;top: 94px" type="text" />
    <input id="Button1" style="z-index: 102; left: 209px;
                    position: absolute; top: 65px"
        type="button" value="OK" />
    <div style="z-index: 105; left: 12px; width: 183px;
            position: absolute; top: 41px;
            height: 46px">
        Put text inside a &lt;div&gt; to position it.
```

```
        </div>
        <hr style="left: 1px; position: absolute; top: 23px" />
    </div>
    </body>
    </html>
```

Without the positioning information, the page would look like Figure 1-14.

Figure 1-14:
The render-
ing without
positioning
data.

Positioning a single control

Not all controls need absolute positioning. You can use flow layout for the basic page while adding CSS positioning for a special effect on one of your controls. Here's how:

1. **In Design view, select the control (or controls) to which you want to apply CSS positioning.**

2. **From the Layout menu, click Position and then click Absolute.**

3. **Drag the control to the place where you want it to appear.**

For more on using styles for visual effects, see Chapter 4 of this mini-book.

Viewing an HTML document's structure

The HTML specifications set out the basic structure for a document. For example, the `<style>` tag nests inside the `<head>` tag that always comes after `<html>`. Visual Web Developer provides the Document Outline window to view your document's logical structure. Here's how:

1. **Open an HTML or ASP.NET document in the Visual Web Developer editor.**

2. **From the View menu, click Document Outline. The Document Outline window opens, as shown in Figure 1-15.**

Figure 1-15:
The Document Outline window displays the logical structure of a page.

Document Outline

GoXHTML.htm
    <!DOCTYPE>
    <HTML>
        <HEAD>
            <TITLE>
        <BODY>
            <DIV>
                <P>
                http://www.gc.ca/images/flag.gif
                <HR>

3. **Expand the parent nodes to see the tags they contain.**

The Document Outline window offers a handy way to navigate very large documents and locate sections of code. Click a node to select the corresponding object in Design view or to mark the opening tag in Source view.

Manipulating the DOM

When loaded in the browser's memory, an HTML document appears as a *Document Object Model (DOM).* Although the DOM closely resembles the content of your page, it's actually the browser's interpretation of the page. For example, if you leave out a closing tag, the browser may add it while creating the DOM. Conversely, the horizontal rule tag (<br />) may be the fully XHTML-compliant version inside your code, but to the browser's DOM, it looks like an old-fashioned <BR>.

As client-side script executes within a Web page, it modifies the in-memory version of the DOM that controls what appears on the screen. For example, if a JavaScript command turns a heading red, the DOM knows about it immediately and the screen reacts. Obviously, the HTML file fetched from the Web server doesn't change.

DOM viewers like IEDocMon (www.cheztabor.com/IEDocMon/) act like a Computed Axial Tomography (CAT) scanner to take a snapshot of the browser's "mind" as it ponders the markup. When HTML or script doesn't produce what you expect to see on the page, a DOM viewer can help you analyze the browser's interpretation of your code.

Formatting Text

There are millions of ways to make text look appealing and readable on a Web page. You can change the size, font, color, background color, and spacing. But please, not all in one line! You've probably seen Web sites that overuse formatting and color and, like Figure 1-16, end up looking like a ransom note pasted together during a paint-shop explosion.

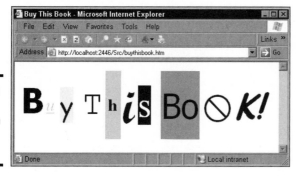

Visual Web Developer offers a reasonable set of formatting tools that should suit the average developer. That said, graphic artists (the ones wearing ponytails and working on Macs) and full-time page designers are often happier with Dreamweaver or even FrontPage for intricate formatting.

The Formatting toolbar

To format text with the least hassle, make sure the Formatting toolbar is showing. If you don't see a set of buttons like those in Figure 1-17, right-click in a blank area near the menus and make sure the Formatting item is checked. From left to right, the toolbar's controls and buttons set the tag (such as `<h1>` or `<p>`), font name, font size, bold, italics, underline, foreground color, background color, text alignment, bullets, numbering, and hyperlinking.

The Format menu

Some people prefer menu commands to toolbars, and sometimes the menu route is the only way to get to what you want. For example, superscript and subscript are items under Format that don't appear on the toolbar. Conversely, you'll have to look to the toolbar to format ordinary text as a bulleted or numbered list in Design view.

Properties pages

Properties pages provide yet another way to format text and especially for changing the appearance of HTML elements like buttons and boxes.

In the default keyboard scheme, you can open the properties page for a control by selecting the control and pressing F4.

To get a properties page to appear for lines of text, wrap the text in a container tag such as `<p>` or `<span>`. You usually find a `Style` property for formatting text inside tags. Most style tasks (such as assigning a font) lead to the Style Builder tool. Refer to Chapter 4 of this mini-book for more on that tool.

Chapter 2: Creating Tables

In This Chapter

✔ **The basic building blocks for tables**

✔ **Some table tags and attributes you might want to try**

✔ **Designing tables in Visual Web Developer Express**

✔ **Some alternatives to using tables for page layout**

✔ **Using tables for page layout anyway**

You can use tables as a great way to present columns of data, all neatly aligned. Accountants love tables because all those little cubbyholes for information appeal to a number cruncher's sense of order.

Web designers love tables, too, but perhaps for the wrong reasons. For years, designers have used tables to create the page layout because columns, rows, and cells work great for holding text and graphics in one spot.

Tsk, tsk, and shame on them. The World Wide Web Consortium's (W3C) advice about tables has been honored mainly in the breach: "Tables should not be used purely as a means to layout document content as this may present problems when rendering to non-visual media," says the W3C. "Authors should use style sheets to control layout rather than tables." (You can read about how to use style sheets for layout in Book 3, Chapter 4.)

Despite the W3C's scolding, people continue to use tables to align content. So you can find a discussion of the technique near the end of this chapter. However, most of this chapter concentrates on the `<table>` tag's forte — the presentation of organized, tabular data in rows and columns. A well-formatted grid has a pleasing structure that makes finding what you're after on a Web page easy.

All code listings used in this book are available for download at www.dummies. com/go/aspnetaiofd.

Some Basic Table Talk

To make a basic, simple, boring HTML table, you need only three unique tags, `<table>`, `<tr>`, and `<td>`. The table represented by the following code has four rows (each created by `<tr>`) and two columns (created by `<td>`):

```
<table>
    <tr>
        <td>Alberta</td>
        <td>T</td>
    </tr>
    <tr>
        <td>British Columbia</td>
        <td>V</td>
    </tr>
    <tr>
        <td>Québec</td>
        <td>H, J</td>
    </tr>
    <tr>
        <td>Yukon</td>
        <td>Y</td>
    </tr>
</table>
```

Figure 2-1 shows how this table looks in the Visual Web Developer Express's Design view.

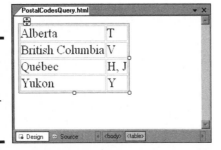

Figure 2-1:
Making a really basic HTML table in the designer.

Adding headers, a caption, and a summary

Table columns often include a header (by way of the `<th>` tag) to label the column's contents. The headers usually appear in the first row of the table, nested in the `<tr>` and `</tr>` tags as shown in bold in the following snippet:

```
<tr>
    <th>Province</th>
    <th>Prefix</th>
```

```
   </tr>
   <tr>
      <td>Alberta</td>
      <td>T</td>
   </tr>
```

Browsers automatically give headers a special look. For example, Figure 2-2 shows the rendered version of the preceding header code. Internet Explorer automatically centers the header text and makes it bold.

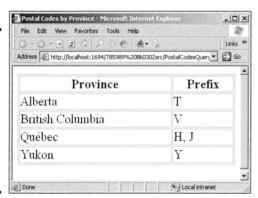

Figure 2-2: Browsers give header content special treatment such as rendering the text as bold.

Today's Internet doesn't often use the `<caption>` tag, which you have to place immediately after the `<table>` tag, even though this tag provides space for a blurb about a table's purpose. Why is this optional tag so rare? Browsers don't do much with it style-wise, which may help explain its absence in a lot of Web pages. `<caption>` needs a bigger public relations budget, like the one that `<div>` must have gotten. You see `<div>` everywhere! Anyway, if you use `<caption>`, you must place it right after the opening `<table>` tag.

Speaking of neglected HTML, the `summary` attribute for the `<table>` tag gets no attention at all. The W3C wants HTML authors to include `summary` content to assist Web surfers who use screen readers. Screen readers are computer programs that read text out loud for blind or low vision Internauts. In support of under-used and under-funded markup, we proudly include `<caption>` *and* `summary` in the following abbreviated example:

```
<table summary="A reference providing postal
  codes for Canadian provinces in alphabetical
  order.">
    <caption>Postal Codes by Province</caption>
    <tr>
        <th>Province</th>
        <th>Prefix</th>
```

```
        </tr>
        <tr>
            <td>Alberta</td>
            <td>T</td>
        </tr>
        <!--...-->
        <tr>
            <td>Yukon</td>
            <td>Y</td>
        </tr>
    </table>
```

Figure 2-3 shows how this markup looks in the browser.

Figure 2-3: Including a caption and summary in your page. The summary doesn't render on-screen.

Full disclosure

When you look at them in the browser, raw HTML tables seem drab and lifeless. By way of full disclosure, we add some style information to increase the visibility of the tables, cells, and text in this chapter's figures but haven't included the style markup in the chapter's listings. For instance, the following style information provides the grid lines and a larger font in Figure 2-3:

```
<style type="text/css">
    table,caption {border:
```

```
    darkgray 1px solid;font-
    size:large}
    td,th {border: darkgray 1px
    solid;}
</style>
```

The nice thing about cascading styles is that they don't intrude on the table's markup, so we don't need to show the code for the styles along with the table markup in this chapter's samples. See Book 3, Chapter 4 for a full discussion of making HTML stylish.

Grouping and spanning columns and rows

Tables often contain groups of related data. For example, Figure 2-4 shows hit songs grouped by bands and solo artists. The markup uses the `<thead>` and `<tbody>` tags and the `class` attribute to define areas of the grid. Instead of using `<th>` to indicate parts of the header, the top row is wrapped in `<thead>`, as you can see in the following code:

```
<thead>
<tr>
    <td>Artist</td>
    <td>Title</td>
    <td>Position</td>
</tr>
</thead>
```

Figure 2-4:
Using
<tbody>
to mark
sections
of a grid.

You often see `<tbody>` in database-driven grids that use categories. For example, by applying a style class to each `<tbody>` tag, you can create a distinctive look for a section without knowing how many items you need to include, as this code shows:

```
<tbody class="bands">
    <tr>
        <td colspan="3">Bands</td>
    </tr>
    <tr>
        <td>The Beach Boys</td>
        <td>Good Vibrations</td>
        <td>7</td>
```

```
        </tr>
        <tr>
            <td>The Temptations </td>
            <td>My Girl </td>
            <td>5 </td>
        </tr>
    </tbody>
```

The `<td>` tag's `colspan` attribute lets you merge the current cell with adjacent cells in the same row.

Just as rows can span columns, columns can span rows. As you can see in the code below (and Figure 2-5), the cell with The Beatles merges with the cell below it, indicating that both songs to the right were Beatles hits:

```
<table>
    <tr>
        <th>Artist</th>
        <th>Song</th>
        <th>No.</th>
    </tr>
    <tr>
        <td rowspan="2">The Beatles</td>
        <td>Hey Jude</td>
        <td>1</td>
    </tr>
    <tr>
        <td>I Want To Hold Your Hand</td>
        <td>8</td>
    </tr>
    <tr>
        <td>The Rolling Stones</td>
        <td>(I Can't Get No) Satisfaction</td>
        <td>3</td>
    </tr>
</table>
```

Figure 2-5: Row Span merges cells to create one cell for The Beatles.

Creating Tables in the Designers

You may find knowing how to create tables in Source view really useful — you never know when you may have to tweak a tag by hand. However, when you have to create tables quickly, the tools in Visual Web Developer Express type faster than a tax accountant at the filing deadline.

The graphical environment gives you three ways to add tables to ASP.NET pages. We look at these methods, from simplest to most advanced, in the following sections.

The Toolbox table

This table tool sits in the HTML tab of the Toolbox. When you drag and drop a table onto your page, you get a tiny, barebones table with three columns and three rows. As you can see in the upper-left corner of Figure 2-6, the measly starter table barely shows up in Design view. However, if you squint and hold the mouse button down on the table's selector icon (the four-way arrow in the upper-left area of Figure 2-6), you can bring the table's Properties page into view. The Properties page is also shown in Figure 2-6.

Book III
Chapter 2

Creating Tables

Figure 2-6:
The measly default table and its Properties page.

If you create quite a few tables by using a custom design, you may find selecting the HTML markup and dragging the selection into the Toolbox as a snippet faster. The markup behaves just like the table tool from the Toolbox, except it does more for you, such as retrieving your custom code.

The table designer

In addition to reaching into the Toolbox for a table, you can go to the Layout menu and click Insert Table. That brings up the Insert Table dialog box, which you can see in Figure 2-7. You can use the upper portion of the dialog box mainly for creating table-based page layouts, which we look at in the section "Creating a Table-Based Framework," later in this chapter. For now, we're interested in the lower Custom section.

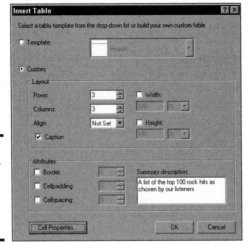

Figure 2-7: Design your table with the Insert Table dialog box.

In the Custom section, you can set the number of rows and columns, and you can indicate whether you want a caption. You even get a place to type in a summary. (It sure is nice to see <caption> and summary getting some attention from Microsoft after all these years.)

This designer does have a couple of annoying aspects — for one, it desperately wants to add its own style information to your table. For example, if you accept the default settings, it defines the rows with three cells, like this:

```
<tr>
    <td style="width: 100px"></td>
    <td style="width: 100px"></td>
    <td style="width: 100px"></td>
</tr>
```

Of course, a width value makes getting your cursor inside the cells to type some text easier, but if you're using a style sheet for the formatting, you need to go back into the code (or into the Properties page) to remove the style attributes. You can avoid this extra step by clicking the Cell Properties button in the lower-left corner of the Insert Table dialog box, as you can see in Figure 2-7. Clicking this button brings up another dialog box, which Figure 2-8 shows, where you can uncheck the Width check box. Unchecking this check box overrides the default behavior so that the designer doesn't insert a `style` attribute in the cells.

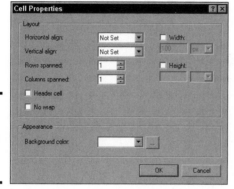

Figure 2-8:
Clear the
Width value
for cell
properties.

Another annoying feature of Layout➪Insert Table is that you only get one shot at it. If you insert a table with five rows and then realize that you need six rows, you can't just reopen the designer to add the extra row.

When you want to merge cells (that is, create a `rowspan` or `colspan`), follow these steps:

1. **Select the cells that you want to merge by holding the mouse button down in the starting cell while moving to the last cell to merge.**

2. **Right-click in the selected cells to bring up the context menu.**

3. **Select the Merge item from the menu that appears.**

If you explore the toolbars, you may discover one named Table Designer. Don't get excited. You use this toolbar to design database tables — it doesn't have anything to do with HTML.

The ASP.NET table tool

If you think the HTML table tool inserts minimal content, wait until you try the ASP.NET table tool. When you grab a table icon from the Standard tab of the Toolbox and drop it on your page, you get this skimpy markup — no rows at all:

```
<asp:table id="Table1" runat="server">
</asp:table>
```

You can barely make out the `Table` control on the design surface in Figure 2-9. (You wouldn't see it at all if not for the hash marks.) As they say, size isn't *that* important. What this table lacks in start-up size, it makes up for in its Properties page functions.

Figure 2-9:
The start-up content and properties page for an ASP.NET server-side table.

Follow these steps to build a server-side table in the graphical designer:

1. **Select the ASP.NET Table control by clicking on the control.**

2. **Open the control's Properties page. (The usual shortcut key is F4.)**

3. **In the Rows property, click the ellipsis button (. . .).**

   The TableRow Collection Editor opens.

4. **Click Add.**

   A TableRow appears in the left-hand pane, as you can see in Figure 2-10.

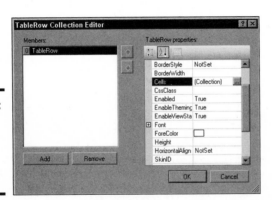

Figure 2-10:
Adding a row to an ASP.NET Table control.

5. **In the Cells property, click the ellipsis button (. . .).**

   The TableCell Collection Editor appears.

6. **Click Add.**

   A TableCell appears in the left-hand pane.

7. **Type the text of your first cell (for example, 1) next to the Text property.**

8. **Click Add again and type the text of the second cell (for example, Hey Jude).**

9. **Click Add again and type the text of the third cell (for example, The Beatles).**

10. **Continue adding TableRow objects and their TableCells until you've had enough.**

11. **When you finish, click OK to exit the TableCell Collection Editor.**

12. **Click OK again to exit the TableRow Collection Editor.**

In Design view, your ASP.NET Table control should look similar to Figure 2-11. (Remember, we add style information to the figures in this chapter to make them easier to see.)

Figure 2-11:
You can create an ASP.NET table in Design view.

The row and column designers generate ASP.NET tags and insert the text that you enter, as you can see in the following markup:

```
<asp:table id="Table1" runat="server">
  <asp:tablerow runat="server">
    <asp:tablecell runat="server">No.</asp:tablecell>
    <asp:tablecell runat="server">Artist</asp:tablecell>
    <asp:tablecell runat="server">Song</asp:tablecell>
  </asp:tablerow>
  <asp:tablerow runat="server">
    <asp:tablecell runat="server">1</asp:tablecell>
    <asp:tablecell runat="server">Hey Jude</asp:tablecell>
    <asp:tablecell runat="server">The Beatles</asp:tablecell>
```

```
    </asp:tablerow>
    <asp:tablerow runat="server">
      <asp:tablecell runat="server">3</asp:tablecell>
      <asp:tablecell runat="server">The Rolling
       Stones</asp:tablecell>
      <asp:tablecell runat="server">(I Can't Get No)
       Satisfaction</asp:tablecell>
    </asp:tablerow>
</asp:table>
```

An ASP.NET server-side `Table` control has more design-time features than the lowly basic tables. For example, you can reopen the server-side table's properties page at any time to add or remove cells or rows.

Creating a large table by using the collection editors doesn't make much sense because that approach is too time-consuming and boring. You're better off generating the table programmatically (which you can read about in the following section) or pointing a specialized grid control (such as the `GridView` control) to a separate data source. For more on the `GridView` control, see Book 6, Chapter 3.

Creating Tables Programmatically

The advantage of creating tables on the fly is that you don't need to know in advance how much data you have. You can choose from three main techniques for building grids using ASP.NET code. Most obviously, you can add a `GridView` or `DataGrid` control to your project and point it to a data source. The original ASP.NET 1.x `DataGrid` control works fine in ASP.NET 2.0, but its functions have been rolled into the enhanced `GridView` control. You can find coverage of the `GridView` control in Book 6, Chapter 3.

You can also build tables programmatically by using the ASP.NET `Repeater` control or the `Table`, `TableRow`, and `TableCell` objects. You can read more about these approaches in the following sections.

Building a table by using the Repeater control

You may find the ASP.NET `Repeater` control very useful for displaying lists of data. Because it's a templated control, you can mix in all sorts of HTML markup for the header, repeated content, and footer. Templated controls act as containers for other ASP.NET controls such as the `Label` control and `TextBox`.

You may find XML a useful file-based data source if the data is read-only and doesn't change very often. You can edit the data offline and upload the file to your Web site in seconds. You don't need to mess with the ASP.NET page to make a quick change. Listing 2-1 is an abbreviated version of the code listing for `topten.xml` (remember, you can get the full version from `www.dummies.com/go/aspnetaiofd`):

Listing 2-1:   Creating a Top Ten List

```xml
<?xml version="1.0" encoding="utf-8" ?>
<chart>
  <hit>
    <num>1</num>
    <song>Hey Jude</song>
    <artist>The Beatles</artist>
  </hit>
  <hit>
    <num>2</num>
    <song>American Pie</song>
    <artist>Don McLean</artist>
  </hit>
  <hit>
    <num>3</num>
    <song>(I Can't Get No) Satisfaction</song>
    <artist>The Rolling Stones</artist>
  </hit>
<!-- Content snipped here -->
  <hit>
    <num>9</num>
    <song>Runaway</song>
    <artist>Del Shannon</artist>
  </hit>
  <hit>
    <num>10</num>
    <song>Unchained Melody</song>
    <artist>The Righteous Brothers</artist>
  </hit>
</chart>
```

You can build this table entirely in the markup (*declaratively,* in geek-speak) by following these steps:

1. **Add the preceding XML content to your project's** App_Data **folder in a file called** topten.xml**.**

   The preceding XML code in Listing 2-1 is an abbreviated version. To get the complete version of the code, visit www.dummies.com/go/aspnetaiofd.

2. **From the Data tab of the Toolbox, drag an** XmlDataSource **control to the ASP.NET page. Configure the control as the following markup shows:**

```
<asp:xmldatasource id="XmlDataSource1"
  runat="server"
  datafile="~/App_Data/topten.xml"
  xpath="chart/hit">
</asp:xmldatasource>
```

Two key settings appear in the preceding `XmlDataSource` control. The `datafile` property points to the location of the XML file. The `xpath` property drills down into the XML file to the location of the data that you want to display. We'll cross the path (pun intended) of `xpath` again in Step 6.

3. **From the Data tab of the Toolbox, add a** `Repeater` **control to the page.**

4. **Configure the** `Repeater` **as the following code shows to use the** `XmlDataSource` **control that you add in Step 2 as its data source:**

```
<asp:repeater id="Repeater1" runat="server"
    datasourceid="XmlDataSource1">
```

5. **Inside the** `Repeater` **control, create a** `<headertemplate>` **section by using this code:**

```
<headertemplate>
    <table summary="A list of top songs as
    selected by our listeners">
    <caption>
        Top Hits and Artists
    </caption>
     <tr>
        <th>Number</th>
        <th>Song</th>
        <th>Artist</th>
    </tr>
</headertemplate>
```

This code creates the static content for the table, including the opening `<table>` tag, a summary, a caption, and the header row and cells.

6. **After the header template, add this** `<itemtemplate>` **section:**

```
<itemtemplate>
    <tr>
        <td><%#XPath("num")%></td>
        <td><%#XPath("song")%></td>
        <td><%#XPath("artist")%></td>
    </tr>
</itemtemplate>
```

This code adds the repeating content of the repeater. It includes the markup for the repeating rows and cells. The `<%#XPath("num")%>` statement tells ASP.NET to insert the content that it finds inside the current `<num>` node of the XML file. Recall that in Step 2 we used `xpath="chart/hit"` to navigate to the node level that contains the data we want.

7. **Add a** `<footertemplate>` **section to the** `Repeater` **control.**

In this case, you need only the closing `</table>` tag to finish off the table, as you can see in the following code:

```
<footertemplate>
    </table>
</footertemplate>
```

Remember that at the end of this sequence, you still need to have a closing tag for the `Repeater` control, such as this:

```
</asp:repeater>
```

When you browse the page, you get a fat-free table (as you can see in Figure 2-12) that leaps into the browser — even on the slowest dial-up connection.

Figure 2-12: You can create an HTML table by using the Repeater control.

Building an ASP.NET table from scratch

You can build a table, its rows, and its cells completely in code. In this example, you can create an ASP.NET `Table` object, add `TableRow` objects to it, and then add `TableCell` objects to the `TableRow` objects by following these steps:

1. **If you haven't already done so, add the XML content found in the previous section, "Building a table by using the Repeater control," to a file called** `topten.xml`.

2. **Add the file** `topten.xml` **to your project's** `App_Data` **folder.**

3. **In the page** `Load` **event, declare the variables to use in the routine, as this code shows:**

```
Dim tbl As Table
Dim tblrow As TableRow
Dim tblcell As TableCell
Dim intRows As Integer
Dim intCells As Integer
Dim strColNames() As String = _
{"No.", "Song", "Artist"}
Dim ds As New Data.DataSet
```

In this code, you add the content for the table's headings to a string array called `strColNames`. The variable `ds` creates a `DataSet` object to hold the XML data.

4. **Fetch the data from the XML file by using the** `DataSet` **object's** `ReadXml()` **method:**

```
ds.ReadXml(Server.MapPath("App_Data/topten.xml"))
```

The `MapPath` method of the `Server` object returns the physical path to the file when you supply a relative path.

5. **Create a** `Table` **object in the** `tbl` **variable and set its** `ID`, `EnableViewState`, **and** `Caption` **properties as this code shows:**

```
tbl = New Table
tbl.ID = "Table1"
tbl.EnableViewState = False
tbl.Caption = "Top Hits and Artists"
tbl.Attributes.Add("summary", _
  "A list of top songs as selected by our listeners")
```

The `Add` method of the `Attributes` property lets you include the `summary` content as a string value.

6. **Create a** `TableRow` **object to serve as the header row of the table:**

```
tblrow = New TableRow
```

7. **Add code that loops through the array of header names (three header names in this example).**

For each name, create a `TableCell` object. Set its `Text` property to the name and add the `TableCell` object to the `Cells` collection of the `TableRow`:

```
For Each s As String In strColNames
    tblcell = New TableCell
    tblcell.Text = s
    tblrow.Cells.Add(tblcell)
Next
```

8. Add the row that you create in Step 7 to the `Table` object's `Rows` collection by using its `Add()` method:

```
tbl.Rows.Add(tblrow)
```

9. Start looping through the rows of data that appear in the first table of the DataSet object.

For each row of data, create a new TableRow object and add it to the table's Rows collection by using this code:

```
For intRows = 0 To ds.Tables(0).Rows.Count - 1
    tblrow = New TableRow
    tbl.Rows.Add(tblrow)
```

10. Inside the preceding loop, create an inner loop to generate three `TableCell` objects. Within the inner loop, assign the value from the data as the cell's `Text` property and add the cell to the `Cells` collection of the `TableRow` by using this code:

```
For intCells = 0 To 2
    tblcell = New TableCell
    tblcell.Text = ds.Tables(0). _
        Rows(intRows).Item(intCells)
    tblrow.Cells.Add(tblcell)
Next
```

11. Finish off the outer loop and include the completed `Table` object in the page by adding it to the Controls collection of a `PlaceHolder` object. (If you don't have a `PlaceHolder`, on the .aspx page, drop one on the page from the Toolbox.):

12. Include the completed `Table` object in the page by adding it to the Controls connection of a `PlaceHolder` object. (If you don't have a `PlaceHolder`, drop one on the page from the Toolbox.)

```
Next
PlaceHolder1.Controls.Add(tbl)
```

When you browse to the page, you can see the identical HTML table that you can create by using the `Repeater` control (which you can read about in the preceding section, "Building a table by using the Repeater control").

Creating a Table-Based Framework

W3C doesn't recommend using the `<table>` tag for page layout, in part because tags are supposed to add structure to text. The other argument is more practical. Framing an entire page in a table makes it harder for screen readers and other specialized browsers for the disabled to parse the content.

The organization practices what it preaches — try to find a `<table>` tag in the HTML code of its home page at `www.w3.org`. Instead of using tables, the page generates its columns by using `<div>` tags, style sheet classes, and the `float` property. For more on using styles for layout, see Book 3, Chapter 4.

Web developers still do find that tables offer a quick, convenient, and browser-compatible way to set up a page. The fact that Microsoft puts the Insert Table item in the Layout menu of VWDE may give you a good indication that the table technique isn't going away soon.

When you use tables for page design (as opposed to positioning content with coordinates), your pages adopt a *flow layout*. The content flows from start to finish, top to bottom. If you want a copyright notice to appear at the bottom of the page when rendered in the browser, you need to put its markup near the end of the source code.

To use a designer to create the table-based framework for a page, follow these steps:

1. **Add a new HTML page to your project.**

2. **In Design view, from the Layout menu, click Insert Table.**

The Insert Table dialog box appears, as you can see in Figure 2-13. 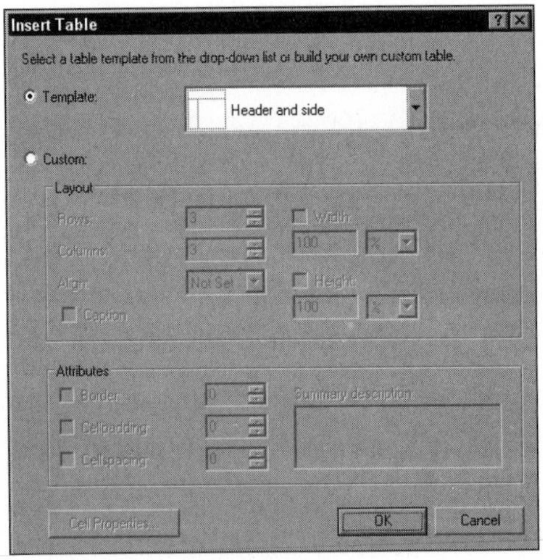

Figure 2-13: Use the Insert Table dialog box to create a framework for a page.

3. **Select the Template radio button.**

A drop-down list appears with a choice of layout templates. Figure 2-14 shows the available choices and has the Header and side template selected.

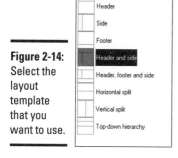

Book III
Chapter 2

Creating Tables

Figure 2-14: Select the layout template that you want to use.

4. **Select a template (for example, the Header and side template), and then click OK.**

The designer inserts the following table markup into the page:

```
<table border="0" cellpadding="0" cellspacing="0"
  style="width: 100%; height: 100%">
    <tr>
        <td colspan="2" style="height: 200px"></td>
    </tr>
    <tr>
        <td style="width: 200px"></td>
        <td></td>
    </tr>
</table>
```

The template creates two rows. The top row spans the entire table with one column that serves as the banner section for the page. The bottom row is divided into two columns. The left-hand column is 200 pixels wide to hold navigation links. The right-hand column takes up the rest of the width, providing space for page content.

5. **In Design view, open the Properties page.**

6. **Select the** Document **object and set its** BgColor **property to Black.**

7. **Move the row up so the banner area is 25 pixels high, as Figure 2-15 shows.**

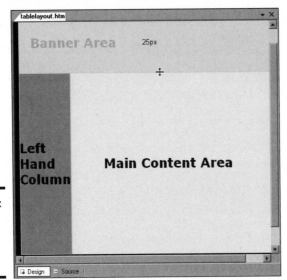

Figure 2-15:
Setting the height of the banner section.

8. **Adjust the left column until it's 100 pixels wide.**

It helps to add text and background colors to identify the layout's regions until the page takes shape with real content. The following code shows the final markup created by the preceding procedure with added placeholder text and shades of gray:

```
<table border="0" cellpadding="0"
cellspacing="0" style="width: 100%; height: 100%">
    <tr>
        <td valign="top" colspan="2"
        style="height: 10px; background-color: lightgrey;">
          Banner Area</td>
    </tr>
    <tr>
        <td style="width: 100px; background-color: dimgray;"
        valign="top">Left Hand Column </td>
        <td style="background-color: gainsboro"
        valign="top">
                Main Content Area </td>
    </tr>
</table>
```

Chapter 3: Working with Forms

In This Chapter

✔ Forming HTML forms

✔ Creating text boxes

✔ Punching radio buttons

✔ Buttoning down lists

✔ Processing form submissions with ASP.NET

✔ Keeping your tabs in order

A *form* is an HTML element that contains input controls through which a user can enter data that he or she wants to submit to the Web server. Using forms is the essence of ASP.NET Web programming, as all ASP.NET Web pages ultimately are rendered as HTML forms that are sent to the browser.

In this chapter, you can discover the ins and outs of forms. Even if you never code an HTML form on your own, understanding what HTML forms can and can't do may give you a better understanding of how ASP.NET server controls work.

Understanding Forms

In HTML, the `<form>` and `</form>` tags mark a specialized area of the document in which users can select items and type in data. The form collects user input and submits it somewhere, usually to a Web server for further processing.

The HTML form can hold several types of input controls, including text fields, drop-down lists, buttons, check boxes, and radio buttons. We look at each of these controls in detail in this chapter. For starters, here's the HTML markup for a typical form that lets the user make some choices:

```
<form
    action="http://www.kencox.ca/usubmitted.aspx"
    method="post">
Please tell us why you get
up in the middle of the night:<br /><br />
    <input id="Radio1" name="Radio1"
      type="radio" value="water" />
        To get a glass of water<br />
```

```
          <input id="Radio2" name="Radio2"
            type="radio" value="bathroom" />
             To go to the bathroom<br />
          <input id="Radio3" name="Radio3"
            type="radio" value="home" /> To go home<br />
          <input id="Radio4" name="Radio4"
            type="radio" value="other" /> Other
          <input name="Text1" id="Text1" type="text" /><br />
          <br />  
          <input id="submit" value="Send"
            type="submit" /> 
          <input id="reset" type="reset" />
</form>
```

Figure 3-1 shows the preceding code as rendered in Visual Web Developer's Design view. In this typical use for an HTML form, visitors make a selection, type some text, and click Send to send the data on its way.

Figure 3-1: You can use an HTML form for a survey.

HTML forms are very easy going because they allow almost any kind of HTML markup within their boundaries. In some Web pages, the `<form>` tag contains the page's entire visual markup, including text, tables, styles, and images.

Creating a Form

The tags `<form>` and `</form>` mark an HTML form. Forms get short shrift in Visual Web Developer and are completely taken for granted; you can't drag a form from the Toolbox and drop it on the design surface. When you add a new HTML page to your project, VWD doesn't ask, "Do you want a form with that?" — it just assumes that you don't and leaves it out.

In fact, you can put a `<form>` element into a regular HTML file only by typing it yourself, pasting it in, or dragging your own snippet from the Toolbox. Yes, ASP.NET pages do include the `<form>` element because server-side pages can't interact without a server-side form.

A call to action — sent by post

This code shows you how a minimal `<form>` element appears in a Web page:

```
<form action="http://www.kencox.ca/usubmitted.aspx" method="post">
```

The required `action` attribute specifies the address of the page or the script that processes the contents of the form. The `method` value can be `"get"` (the default) or `"post"`. The `method` determines the technical details on how the form's data travels to the destination. Here's a rundown on the submission methods:

✦ **get:** This submission method sends the data as part of the URL. You may have seen strange URLs with a jumble of text after a question mark — an alphabet soup of field names, values, equal signs, ampersands, percent signs, and more. (In geek-speak, the part after the question mark is a *query string*.) Here's a sample URL:

```
http://www.kencox.ca/usubmitted.aspx?Radio1=home&uptimes=1
```

You may think the "get" method is kind of ugly. It sends field names and values separated by ampersands. In the preceding example, the name parts are `Radio1` and `uptimes`. The value parts are `home` and `1`. (Geeks call the `Radio1/home` combination a *name/value pair*.)

✦ **post:** This submission method is much tidier and more discreet because it's embedded in a transaction rather than dangling as a query string. Like "posting" a letter in a mailbox, the data travels in a neat envelope within the body of the HTML. Here's an HTML form using `post` that achieves the same result as the preceding `get` method:

```
<html>
<body>
    <form action="http://www.kencox.ca/usubmitted.aspx"
            method="post">
        <input name="Radio1" checked="checked"
    type="radio" value="home">
```

```
                        <input name="uptimes" type="text" value="1" />
                        <input type="submit" />
                </form>
        </body>
        </html>
```

Staying on target

When you submit a form, you can control the browser's subsequent behavior by including the `target` property. The value of the `target` attribute determines how and where the browser opens the destination page. Here are the common values for the `target` attribute:

✦ `_blank`: The browser loads the destination page in a brand new, factory-fresh window or tab.

✦ `_self`: The browser reuses the current, slightly shop-worn window or tab to load the destination page. Not surprisingly, the destination page sweeps the window clean before moving in.

✦ `_parent`: This value works for browser windows that are no longer happy with living inside a frameset under their parent's roof. When the destination page loads, it takes over the parent's space.

✦ `_top`: Here, the destination page frees itself of all frames and appears in all its glory in an original, unsullied window.

✦ `_search`: An oddball target that may not work in all browsers, this value opens a small Search pane when you use it in Internet Explorer.

Your special events form

Forms have two unique attributes, `onsubmit` and `onreset`, that work great with JavaScript. When a user clicks a button to submit the form's data, the `onsubmit` attribute can run a script to verify that the form is complete and the data is valid. Another attribute, `onreset`, runs when the user clicks a Reset button. This attribute wipes out the data that the user entered on the form.

The following code presents a simple example of a form in which the text box must not be blank:

```
<html>
<head>
<script language="javascript"
   type="text/javascript">
function CheckFilled()
{
if (document.forms[0].txtbox.value=="")
 {
 alert('Ya gotta enter somethin\'');
 return false;
 }
```

```
}
function WipeOut()
{
return confirm('Wipe out what ya wrote?')
}
</script>
</head>
<body>
 <form
  onsubmit="return CheckFilled();"
  onreset="return WipeOut()"
  method="get"
  id="myform"
  action="http://www.kencox.ca/usubmitted.aspx">
 <input type="text" name="txtbox" id="txtbox" />
 <input type="submit" />
 <input type="reset" />
 </form></body></html>
```

The `onsubmit` attribute in the preceding code fires the `CheckFilled()` routine that does the checking and prevents a blank form from being submitted. The form also uses the `onreset` attribute to confirm that the user wants to abandon what he or she typed. Figure 3-2 shows what happens when a user tries to submit the form without typing anything in the text box.

**Book III
Chapter 3**

Working with Forms

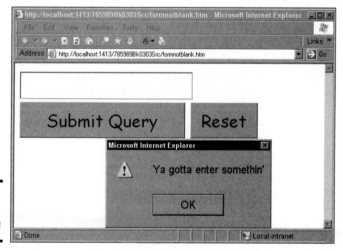

Figure 3-2:
Submit to
my demand!

Working with Text Boxes

Two types of controls in HTML let users enter text: the `<input>` and `<textarea>` elements. Let's look at their various forms and how you use them.

Creating text fields with <input>

You can most easily add a text field to your form by going to the Toolbox under the HTML tab and dragging the icon for Input (Text) to your page. (The Input icon shows a box with two letters and a cursor in it.) Make sure that you add the text box after the opening `<form>` tag and before the closing `</form>` tag.

You can drop an item from the Toolbox directly into Source view. Instead of seeing a graphical rendering, you see the item's markup.

Always add the `name` attribute, as in `name="Text1"`, to `<input>` tags. The Visual Web Developer environment inserts the newer `id` attribute automatically, but not the `name` attribute. Some form processors may expect the `name` attribute and refuse to cooperate. If a target page or script doesn't behave as you expect, check your form fields for `name`. It doesn't hurt to have both, and it may help avoid frustration. The syntax checker may complain that `name` is outdated, but use `name` anyway.

Here's the markup for a regular text box that uses some of the more common attributes:

```
<input id="Text1" name="Text1" value="The default."
type="text" size="20" maxlength="22" tabindex="1"
onblur="alert('Did the textbox blur?');">
```

Here are explanations for the attributes that appear in the preceding markup:

✦ `type="text"`: This attribute tells the browser that you want a regular text box. Technically, you don't need to provide this attribute to get a text box because a text box is the default value. If you leave it out, well, you get a text box.

✦ `size="20"`: The width of the control in characters. This sample makes the control wide enough for 20 characters. Beyond 20, you may not be able to see the text, or the text box may scroll.

✦ `maxlength="22"`: The maximum number of characters that the user can type into this text box. In this example, the text box stops accepting characters after it sees 22 of them.

✦ `tabindex="1"`: A number between 0 and 32767 that indicates the position in the tabbing order. You can read about tab order in the section "Setting the Tab Order," later in this chapter. If a form needs more than 32767 tab stops, it probably rates as user-hostile.

✦ `onblur="alert('Did the textbox blur?');"`: This attribute runs a JavaScript routine when the cursor or mouse moves out of the text box. (In geek-speak, the control *loses the focus.*) The other common event handlers are `onfocus` and `onchange`.

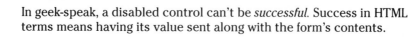

+ `value="The default.":` Provides the starting value for the text box.

+ `disabled="disabled":` This attribute prevents the text box from accepting text. Users can't put the cursor into a disabled text box or tab to it. The value in a disabled text box isn't sent when the form is submitted.

   In geek-speak, a disabled control can't be *successful.* Success in HTML terms means having its value sent along with the form's contents.

+ `readonly="readonly":` In this state, users can't change the value in the text box, but they can select the value and copy it to the clipboard. The value in a read-only text box is submitted as part of the form. Although users can't type into it, you can use JavaScript to programmatically add or change the value in a read-only text box.

Creating a password text box

The password text box is a one-line text box that you create by including `type="password"` in the `<input>` tag. Here's the basic markup:

```
<input name="Password1" id="Password1" type="password"
maxlength="18" value="supersecret" size="20" />
```

The main difference between the password text box and the standard text box is that password masks the text by replacing it with dots or asterisks. The password text box in the preceding example isn't all that secure because the password value often travels to its destination in clear, unencrypted text. A bad guy with a geeky tool called a sniffer can harvest passwords if he or she gets access to the network in the right place.

Super-sizing a text field

The ordinary `<input>` text box works fine for numbers and short bits of text, but its one-line block doesn't handle a long message well. That's a job for the multi-line `<textarea>`. Here's what this text box looks like in HTML markup:

```
<textarea name="txtarea" id="txtarea"
 rows="4" cols="35"  tabindex="2"
 title="Wisecrack about U-Know-Who">
Our software is 100% secure out-of-the-box...
If you load it onto the box to run it, you're on your own.
</textarea>
```

Figure 3-3 illustrates the use of a multi-line `<textarea>` for a joke.

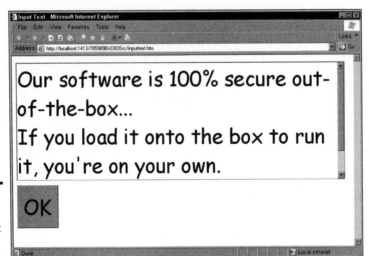

Figure 3-3:
Long jokes
need a <text
area>.

Unlike the <input> tag, <textarea> needs a separate closing tag. It uses the name, id, and tabindex attributes in the same way as <input>. No value attribute holds the default text content. Instead, the text goes between the opening and closing tags.

HTML usually ignores line breaks and multiple space characters in markup, but not in <textarea>. White space counts and makes a difference to the appearance. For example, if you put several line breaks in the default text, the user has to scroll to see the end of the message.

Most of the attributes, including name, id, disabled, readonly, and tabindex, are the same as for the <input> text box. Here are some of the more common attributes that <textarea> supports:

✦ rows="4": You can set the number of lines of text that appear on the page. If users type in more lines, they have to scroll to see the end of the text.

✦ cols="35": The number of columns determines the width of the control on the page. In this example, 35 is the number of character widths. This setting works like the size attribute in the regular text box.

✦ title="Wisecrack about U-Know-Who": In mainstream browsers, this attribute provides a tool tip.

All of the preceding attributes are in the code that generates Figure 3-3.

Working with Buttons

Some people call buttons "push-buttons," which is redundant, superfluous, and just plain needlessly wordy. If you found a pull-button somewhere, it might make sense to call a regular button a push-button. But, as everyone knows, an HTML button pulls itself back up.

At any rate, HTML buttons come in several varieties that we look at in the following sections.

Creating a submit button

The *submit button* is an input control with the power to submit a form. Here's how it looks in the markup:

```
<input type="submit" title="Sends the data" name="Submit1"
id="Submit1" value="OK" />
```

You don't have to use the `value` attribute on a submit button. If you leave it out, the browser puts a label on the button for you. Figure 3-4 shows two identical submit buttons, except that the upper one has the `value` of "OK" and the lower one has no `value` attribute at all. Internet Explorer inserts "Submit Query" as the text for the lower one. Oddly, if you leave out the `value` attribute for a regular button (shown in "Creating an ordinary button") you get only a sliver of a button because the browser doesn't invent text for regular buttons.

**Book III
Chapter 3**

Working with Forms

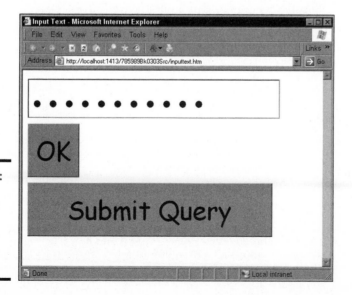

Figure 3-4:
When there's no value, IE inserts Submit Query.

Creating a reset button

The reset button switches all of the controls on the form back to their initial values — usually blank. You may find the reset button quite annoying if you spend 10 minutes filling out a long form and then accidentally click that button. Everything disappears in a millisecond click. (Actually, the correct technical term for the brief interval is an *onosecond*. An onosecond is the time between taking an action and realizing it was wrong and can't be undone. The term originates from the common expression "Oh No!" Just kidding, folks but we've all experienced it.)

The code below shows the basic markup for a reset button:

```
<input name="Reset1" id="Reset1" type="reset"
value="Wipe out!" />
```

If you don't provide the value attribute, Internet Explorer inserts the word "Reset."

Creating an ordinary button

You can put a plain, ordinary button on an HTML form by setting the type attribute's value to "button", as you can see in the following markup:

```
<input name="Button1" id="Button1" type="button"
value="Click me first!" />
```

But this kind of button is HTML's version of a drone. You can click an ordinary button all day without doing anything to the form. The button type only becomes useful when you add some client-side JavaScript to it as in the following:

```
<input name="button1" type="button"
onclick="alert('Nice click!');" value="Click Me!" />
```

Creating an image button

This button has class. It's a submit button that can look like whatever you want. Consider the form in Figure 3-5. You think you see a text box and a password box, right? Actually, what looks like a password box is actually an *image button*. It just uses the image of a password box but it's really a button in disguise.

Okay, this is a ridiculous example because nobody would use an image of a password box as a button. The point is that if you don't like the look of the standard HTML buttons, you can use anything you can draw as a button. You're only limited by your imagination and creative ability.

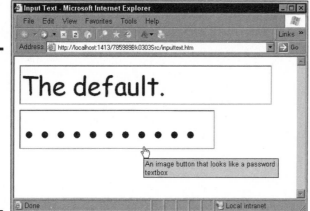

**Book III
Chapter 3**

Working with Forms

Figure 3-5:
Nobody
would
seriously
use a
picture of a
password
box as
an image
button!

When you click the image button, it sends the form's data to the server. Here's the markup that creates the image button:

```
<input id="btnImage" name="btnImage" src="imagebtn.png"
 alt="An image button that looks like a password textbox"
 type="image" />
```

As you can see, `type="image"` includes the `src` attribute that points to the name and address of the image that you want to use. This control has another interesting feature; the values it sends depend on where you click the image button. For example, the preceding markup can send the following data to the server:

```
btnImage.x=155
btnImage.y=41
```

The values for `btnImage.x` and `btnImage.y` are the coordinates where the click took place: 155 pixels from the left of the image and 41 pixels from the top of the image.

The ability to capture coordinates can be useful. For example, you might have a round image button showing the Zodiac. You can determine a user's astrological sign by calculating the coordinates of their click.

Creating submit, reset, and ordinary buttons another way

The buttons that you can read about in the earlier sections in this chapter are part of the `<input>` set. You can also create buttons by using the `<button>`

tag. The value of the `type` attribute determines the button's function: button, submit, or reset. According to the W3C specification, the default type is submit, but you may want to include the `type` attribute value at all times. Some versions of Internet Explorer use `type="button"` as the default behavior rather than `type="submit"`.

The syntax of the `<button>` tag is slightly different from the `<input>` button's syntax. The text for `<button>` goes between the opening and closing tags. Although `<button>` requires a closing tag, `<input>` forbids it. Here's the markup for a submit button:

```
<button id="btnReal" name="btnReal" type="submit">
Click Me!</button>
```

Visual Web Developer doesn't include `<button>` in its HTML Toolbox.

Working with Check Boxes and Radio Buttons

Check boxes and radio buttons are switches that users can toggle on and off. These controls are switched on when they include the `checked` attribute.

Creating a check box

The check box is part of the `<input>` family. You create it by setting the `type` attribute's value to `"checkbox"` as in `type="checkbox"`.

When its containing form is submitted, the check box sends its name and a value only when it's checked. Therefore, the page that processes the results has to assume that if it doesn't hear anything from a given check box, that check box is unchecked. The markup for a check box control looks like this:

```
<input name="Checkbox1" id="Checkbox1"
value="I have value only when checked!" type="checkbox" />
```

Creating a radio button

Radio buttons travel in groups of at least two and provide a mutually exclusive choice. If a user switches on one member of the group, all the others must turn off. The markup to create radio buttons looks like the following:

```
<input id="Radio1" name="Radio1" type="radio"
    value="Red" /> Red<br />
<input id="Radio1" checked="checked" name="Radio1"
    type="radio" value="Green" /> Green<br />
<input id="Radio1" name="Radio1" type="radio"
    value="Blue" /> Blue
```

The perverse check box

Pranksters can have some fun with a check box and a tiny bit of JavaScript. The following markup creates a perverse check box that switches on when you hover the mouse over it and off when the mouse goes away:

```
<input
    onmouseover="this.checked=t
    rue;"
onmouseout="this.checked=false
    ;" id="Checkbox2"
```

```
name="Checkbox2" type="check-
    box" value="Ha!" />
```

With this pesky check box, you can't make a choice stick! The preceding code uses the `onmouseover` and `onmouseout` events to change the checked state programmatically. Use at your own risk!

It may strike you as odd that all of the radio buttons have the same `id` and `name` values, `Radio1`. Sharing a name makes them act as a group. If your radio buttons act as rugged individualists and refuse to switch off, make sure that they have the same name as their group members.

Speaking of checking, notice that the second button (with the value `"Green"`) includes the `checked` property. That means the "Green" radio button is on by default.

Book III Chapter 3

Working with Forms

Using Drop-Down Lists and List Boxes

The `<select>` element creates a drop-down list or a list box, depending on the attribute settings. You add items to drop-down lists and list boxes by using embedded `<option>` tags.

Creating a drop-down list

A drop-down list, such as the one that you can see in Figure 3-6, creates a menu from which you can select one or more items.

The following code shows the default configuration that lets you select only one item at a time:

```
<select name="Select1" id="Select1">
  <option value="0">Red</option>
  <option value="1">Green</option>
  <option value="2" selected="selected">Blue</option>
  <option value="3">White</option>
  <option value="4">Black</option>
</select>
```

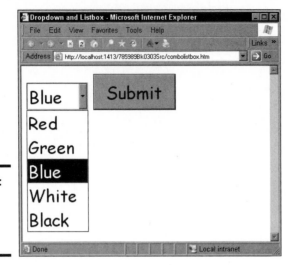

Figure 3-6:
Selecting
Blue in
a drop-
down list.

The preceding markup includes the `value` attribute. When the user submits the form, the corresponding value (0, 1, 2, 3, or 4) is sent to the server.

You don't have to use the `value` attribute. If you don't include it, as you can see in the following code, the form sends the text between the `<option>` and `</option>` tags, such as `Blue`:

```
<select name="Select1" id="Select1">
  <option>Red</option>
  <option>Green</option>
  <option selected="selected">Blue</option>
  <option>White</option>
  <option>Black</option>
</select>
```

You can set the default (that is, pre-selected) option by including the `selected` attribute in the `<option>` tag.

Creating a list box

A list box is a variation on the drop-down list that includes either the `multiple` attribute or the `size` attribute — or both. Figure 3-7 shows the browser rendering the following markup:

```
<select name="Select2" id="Select2"
  multiple="multiple" size="5">
    <option>Red</option>
    <option>Green</option>
```

```
    <option selected="selected">Blue</option>
    <option>White</option>
    <option>Black</option>
</select>
```

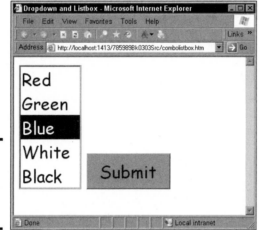

Figure 3-7:
You can set up a list box showing all five items.

**Book III
Chapter 3**

Working with Forms

Here's a short list of attributes that make a drop-down list a list box:

✦ `multiple`: When you include this attribute, users can select more than one item. In Windows, users select additional items by holding down the Ctrl key. When Internet Explorer sees `multiple`, it displays the control as a list box rather than as a drop-down list.

✦ `size="5"`: This attribute determines how many items you want to show in the control. If you have more items than indicated by the value (5 in this example), the user has to scroll to bring those additional items into view.

Creating a hierarchical drop-down list and list box

The `<select>` element lets you create hierarchical categories of options by using the `<optgroup>` tag. Users can select the options, but not the category names.

In the following code (which you can see rendered in Figure 3-8), the `<optgroup>` elements create three groups (Red, Green, and Blue):

```
<select name="shades" id="shades">
    <optgroup label="Red" >
        <option label="Pink" value="Pink">
        Pink</option>
```

```
                    <option label="Crimson" value="Crimson">
                    Crimson</option>
            </optgroup>
            <optgroup label="Green">
                <option label="Chartreuse" value="Chartreuse">
                Chartreuse</option>
                <option label="LightGreen" value="LightGreen">
                LightGreen</option>
                <option label="LawnGreen" value="LawnGreen">
                LawnGreen</option>
            </optgroup>
            <optgroup label="Blue">
                <option label="DarkSlateBlue" value="DarkSlateBlue">
                DarkSlateBlue</option>
                <option label="LightSteelBlue"
        value="LightSteelBlue">
                LightSteelBlue</option>
            </optgroup>
</select>
```

The `label` attribute in the preceding code holds the text for each group, for example `label="Green"`.

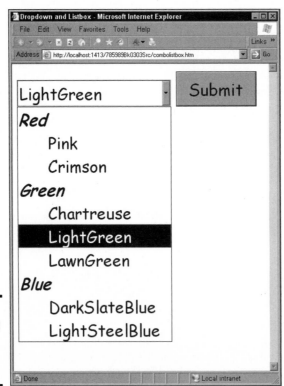

Figure 3-8:
You can add categories of menu items.

Checking Form Submissions with ASP.NET

Although this chapter talks about regular HTML controls and not ASP.NET controls, you may find some ASP.NET helpful in dealing with forms. As we discuss at the very beginning of this chapter, you need to have the contents of a form processed somewhere, usually by a program on a Web server, such as ASP.NET.

When you're developing and debugging forms, you may find it helpful to see just what names and values the server receives. The following code (put it in a page named `usubmitted.aspx`) displays the names of the controls and their corresponding values:

```
<%@ Page Language="VB" %>
<script runat="server">
    Protected Sub Page_Load _
      (ByVal sender As Object, _
      ByVal e As System.EventArgs)
        Dim loop1 As Integer
        Dim coll As NameValueCollection
        Dim sb As New System.Text.StringBuilder
        ' Load the Form Request variables into
        ' a NameValueCollection variable.
        coll = Request.Form
        For loop1 = 0 To coll.AllKeys.GetUpperBound(0)
            sb.Append(coll.GetKey(loop1) & "=" & _
                coll.GetValues(loop1).GetValue(0).ToString _
                & "<br />")
        Next loop1
        ' Load the Form Querystring variables into
        ' a NameValueCollection variable.
        coll = Request.QueryString
        For loop1 = 0 To coll.AllKeys.GetUpperBound(0)
            sb.Append(coll.GetKey(loop1) & "=" & _
                coll.GetValues(loop1).GetValue(0).ToString _
                & "<br />")
        Next loop1
        lblSubmitted.Text = sb.ToString
    End Sub
</script>
<html xmlns="http://www.w3.org/1999/xhtml" >
<head runat="server">
    <title>What you submitted</title>
</head>
<body>
    <form id="form1" runat="server">
    <div>
        <asp:label id="lblSubmitted"
        runat="server"></asp:label>
    </div>
    </form>
</body>
</html>
```

To see the preceding code in action, create an HTML page named `useform.htm` and put the processing page name as the `action` value in the form tag, such as:

```
<form id="myform" action="usubmitted.aspx" method="post"
name="myform">
```

Setting the Tab Order

Data entry professionals care passionately about tab order because the correct configuration makes forms usable. *Tab order* is the sequence in which controls are selected (in geek-speak, *receive the focus*) when the user presses the Tab key.

The value of a control's `tabindex` attribute (ranging from 0 to 32767) determines its place in the tab order. The browser starts at the lowest number and moves to the next higher. If two controls have the same `tabindex` value, the browser starts with the one whose markup comes first in the character stream.

The following code creates an HTML form with three controls and a poorly designed tab sequence that would drive a data entry clerk to toss the keyboard out the window:

```
<form id="myform"
 action="http://www.kencox.ca/usubmitted.aspx"
 method="post" name="myform">
    <input tabindex="1" id="Text1" name="Text1"
      type="text" /><br />
    <select tabindex="3" name="Select1"
      id="Select1" size="3">
        <option>Cool</option>
        <option>Hot</option>
        <option>Yeh, baby!</option>
    </select>
    <br />
    <input tabindex="2" name="Submit1" id="Submit1"
        onfocus="alert('You tabbed to me!');"
        type="submit" value="Go for it!" />
</form>
```

When the sequence reaches the Submit button, it fires a JavaScript function to open an `alert()` box, as you can see in Figure 3-9.

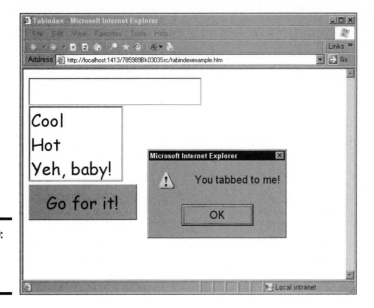

Figure 3-9:
Out-of-order tab ordering.

Notice that Internet Explorer tabs to the address bar first and then moves through the tab sequence on the page.

If you don't want a control to participate in the tab sequence, assign it the `tabindex` value -1 or disable the control.

Chapter 4: Using Styles and Style Sheets

*B*ack in the World Wide Web's Stone Age, the academics who roamed the Internet mainly concentrated on the exchange of information and data. They didn't mind if their brilliant research papers came across to colleagues in monotone, monochrome, and monotype text. Content was king and presentation very secondary. Of course, the early Web didn't offer that much in terms of style.

In the modern Web era, how a site looks can really make or break it. For a corporation, its site's colors, fonts, and images are important elements of company branding — the face that it presents to Joe and Jane Public. Even for individuals, Web site styles can reflect the owner's personality, hobbies, or tastes — much like fashion-sense with clothing.

This chapter can't turn you into a graphical designer. However, you can get a solid grasp of what Web page styles are all about. That way, if someone passes you an academic research paper and a professionally produced style sheet, you know what to do with them.

Understanding Styles

If you know how to work with a word processor, such as Microsoft Word, you already know a little bit about styles. They add fonts, formatting, color, borders, depth, and positioning to your HTML objects. Styles make Web pages visually attractive and, well, stylish. A Web site without style information is as exciting as a movie about the Microsoft End User License Agreement (EULA). Of course, you could always liven up the movie with a high-speed chase under the elevated railway in Brooklyn with Bill Gates screaming, "You may not reverse engineer, decompile, or disassemble the Product!" No such luck with a style-less Web site.

Cascading Style Sheets

The biggest style buzz right now is Cascading Style Sheets (CSS), especially versions 2.0 and higher. You can use *style sheets* to store formatting information in one place and have one set of styles trickle down (or *cascade*) to all pages on the site and all elements on the pages. For example, you can design a text box style in one place, and the browser applies that style to every text box that it renders.

CSS lets you separate presentation from content. A headline inside an `<h2>` tag and a paragraph of text within `<p>` or `<div>` tags sit naked in the markup because the information about the way that text looks comes from somewhere else. Overall, pages are cleaner, leaner, and more consistent when you don't mush the words and the styles together in the markup.

If you apply style sheets properly, you can give an entire Web site a makeover by swapping in new designs contained in one CSS file.

Will that be inline, embedded, or external?

Styles can live in three main places in a Web site. Each location has its advantages and disadvantages:

✦ **Inline:** These styles stick closely to the object that they're styling. Actually, some designers say they're too close and lose many of the benefits of style sheets. Here's an example of an inline style:

```
<input style="
color:black;
font-family:'Cooper Black',Fantasy;
background-color:lightgrey;
font-size: xx-large;"
id="Text1"
type="text"
value="Keep me inline" />
```

You can see that the style information, such as the color and font size, sits right inside the `<input>` tag. You may find that setup convenient at the outset, but if you have a page with many text boxes, you end up repeating the style information. Worse, on a big Web site with a lot of pages, you have to visit every page and every text box if you change your mind and decide to go with white rather than blue as the background color.

✦ **Embedded:** In this location, the styles sit inside `<style>` tags in the `<head>` area of the Web page. You can translate the preceding inline to the embedded format like this code:

```
<style type="text/css">
input {
        color:black;
        font-family:'Cooper Black',Fantasy;
```

```
background-color:lightgrey;
font-size: xx-large;
}
</style>
```

The embedded format works fine for individual pages because all of the text boxes on the page adopt the appearance characteristics. However, for a large site, it still means opening each page to change the overall look of the elements. If you have a large number of styles, you can probably think of a better use of your time. Each page has to have its own copy of the styles and can't share them with other pages.

✦ **External:** This technique puts all of the style information (but no HTML) in a separate file or files. Each Web page includes a link to that style sheet. Professional page designers prefer using this method for applying style sheets. You can make one change and have every page that references the style reflect that change. Also, browsers often cache (keep a copy on the user's computer) frequently used files like style sheets, which makes for faster browsing because the browser doesn't have to download the same content repeatedly.

External style sheets usually have the file extension `.css`. `Stylesheet1.css` may contain this content:

```
input
{
color:black;
font-family:'Cooper Black',Fantasy;
background-color:lightgrey;
font-size: xx-large;
}
```

Inside the HTML page, within the `<head>` tag, you include the link to the style sheet file as the following code shows:

```
<link
    href="stylesheet1.css"
    media="all"
    rel="stylesheet"
    type="text/css" />
```

The `href` attribute's value can be a fully qualified path such as `http://www.kencox.ca/styles/style.css`, or the name of the local file. If you reference more than one style sheet, the browser merges the styles before applying them.

In case of a dispute, the closest wins

When you use inline, embedded, and external styles, you may end up with conflicting instructions. What happens if the inline style declares the default font as Arial, the embedded font calls for Times New Roman, but the external style sheet uses Comic Sans MS? The rule is that the style declaration closest to the tag being styled wins out, so you get your font in Arial.

An inline style overrides the embedded style, which overrides the linked external style.

Style selectors and other syntax

CSS has its own terminology and syntax rules that keep everyone on the same Web page, so to speak. Don't worry, CSS isn't as complicated as Latin.

Each style rule starts with a selector. *Selectors* are somewhat like variables in programming. You load them up with the characteristics that you want to apply, such as the font, color, underlining, and so on. Geeks call them selectors because these variables reach into your HTML markup and select only those HTML elements (for example, <h2>) that belong to them. After they select the elements, the selectors paint those elements with their assigned styles.

The basic syntax for a style rule uses the selector's name followed by curly braces to mark the declaration block. Inside the block, each declaration has a property separated from its value by a colon. A semi-colon separates the declarations from each other. Here's the syntax:

```
selectorname {property: value; property: value;}
```

For example:

```
span {color: blue;font-size:x-large;}
```

CSS doesn't care about white space or case. Most designers find it easier to use line breaks and spaces for readability.

You can choose from three main types of selectors:

✦ **Type selector:** You recognize these because they use the same names as the regular HTML elements. In the following example, h1 is the selector that applies to all <h1> tags.

```
h1 {
    font-size: x-large;
    color: red;
    font-family: 'Courier New';
    }
```

The preceding h1 selector turns the following markup into large, red text using the Courier New font:

```
<h1>Select me! I'm your type!</h1>
```

✦ **Class selector:** This selector is very, er, selective about what it styles. It looks through the HTML and selects only those elements that have the same class name. As you can see in the example that follows, the class selector begins with a dot:

```
.blk {
        font-size:xx-large;
        color: white;
        background-color: black;
    }
```

When you use the preceding selector in the following code, it makes any element that has the attribute/value pair `class="blk"` white text on a black background.:

```
<input id="Button1" class="blk" type="button"
 value="Select Now!" />
```

✦ **Element ID selector:** You don't often find this selector used because it isn't as flexible as the others. It selects elements based on the ID value, such as `id="navitem"`. The selector name begins with a pound (#) sign, as you can see in the following code:

```
#Text1 {
        font-size:xx-large;
        color: white;
        background-color: red;
        }
```

The preceding code, when you use it in the following markup, applies white text with a red background to any element that has `Text1` as its id value:

```
<input id="Text1" type="text"
value="Natural selection" />
```

You can go crazy with selectors by mixing and matching them. For example, the following code starts by defining the basic look for a list item as a gray, supersized font. The next definition uses a *descendant selector* to select only list items that are in italics:

```
li {
    font-size:xx-large;
    color:gray;
    }
li i {
      color: red;
      background-color: silver;
    }
```

In the preceding, `li` is the selector and the `i` that follows is the descendant selector.

If you use the following markup, the first list item in the following code (Ocean) appears in red italics with a silver background, and the other two items appear gray. As you see in Figure 4-1, all of the items inherit the extra, extra large font as the styles merge.

```
<ol>
    <li><i>Ocean</i></li>
    <li>Lake</li>
    <li>Pond</li>
</ol>
```

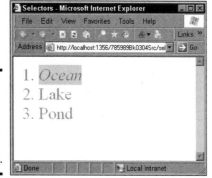

Figure 4-1: Using multiple selectors to add style to descendants.

Most CSS designers prefer the class selector with its `class="nameofclass"` format. It has the advantage that if your pages use ASP.NET controls, you can assign the class selector with this kind of code:

```
<asp:button cssclass="blk" id="Button1"
runat="server" text="Button" />
```

Working with Styles in Visual Studio 2005 and Visual Web Developer

Microsoft's developer tools help you design styles in a visual environment that spares you from looking up the syntax for colors, font sizes, and backgrounds. The following sections show you how the tools work for building inline styles and external style sheets.

Setting the CSS validation schema

Before getting too involved in CSS, you need to know what CSS level you intend to support. Then you can be sure that your definitions comply with the style sheet specification. Follow these steps to set the CSS validation schema:

1. **Create or open a style sheet (.css) file.**

2. **From the View menu, click Toolbars and add a check mark by the Style Sheet item if it isn't already checked.**

3. **On the Style Sheet toolbar, from the drop-down list, select a schema (for example, CSS 2.0) as Figure 4-2 shows.**

Figure 4-2:
Choosing
the CSS
validation
schema.

If you're using style sheets to position HTML objects, set the schema validation to CSS 2.0 or higher. You can read the CSS specifications (especially recommended for insomniacs) at www.w3.org/Style/CSS.

Visual Studio and Visual Web Developer constantly monitor the quality of your style sheets and syntax. Problems such as illegal syntax appear in the Error List window. You may find schema validation quite enlightening. For example, Figure 4-3 shows a style sheet that has validation initially set to Internet Explorer. When we change the validation to CSS 2.0, The Error List window reports that the color Gainsboro is "not a valid value for the 'background-color' property." The moral of the story is to set the schema validation level *before* you develop a style sheet. That way, the editor doesn't even offer you choices that don't comply with the schema.

**Book III
Chapter 4**

**Using Styles and
Style Sheets**

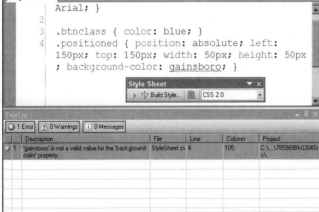

Figure 4-3:
The Error
List window
tells you
that Gains-
boro isn't
valid in
CSS 2.0.

You can switch schema validation off by going to Tools⇨Options⇨ Text Editor⇨CSS⇨CSS Specific⇨Detect errors.

Creating inline styles in Design view

You can most easily get started with creating style sheets by designing pages in a What-You-See-Is-What-You-Get (WYSIWYG) editor. Design view gives you a mostly faithful representation of what shows up in the browser, but you don't get a guarantee with this view. To create the page that you see in Figure 4-4, using the graphical environment, follow these steps:

Figure 4-4:
Add some inline style with white and silver.

1. **Add a Web page called** `inlinestyles.aspx` **to your project.**

The programming language and use of a separate code file don't make a difference in this procedure.

2. **In Design view, type "Show some style!" (without the quotes).**

3. **Select the line of text and, from the Format menu, click Style.**

The Style Builder dialog box opens.

4. **From the list of categories on the left of the Style Builder dialog box, click Background, as Figure 4-5 shows.**

5. **In the Background color area, from the drop-down list, select Silver.**

6. **From the list of categories on the left of the Style Builder, select the Font category.**

7. **In the Font name section, click the ellipsis button (. . .) to open the Font Picker dialog box.**

8. **In the Installed fonts list, select Arial and click the adjacent Add (>>) button.**

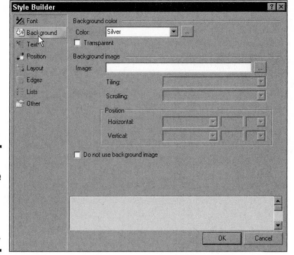

Figure 4-5:
You can give
your page a
silver lining
in the
background.

9. **Select Sans-Serif from the Generic fonts list, as you can see in Figure 4-6.**

**Book III
Chapter 4**

**Using Styles and
Style Sheets**

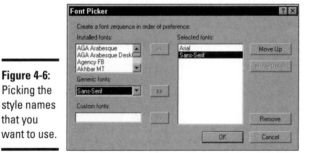

Figure 4-6:
Picking the
style names
that you
want to use.

10. **Click the Font Picker dialog box's Add (>>) button.**

11. **Click OK.**

The Style Builder comes back into view.

By including a generic font in the style, you have a better chance that
the browser renders the text closer to the way you want it to look. If the
user doesn't have the named font installed on his or her machine, the
browser matches its general type.

12. **In the Font attributes section, click the ellipsis button (. . .).**

The Color Picker dialog box appears.

13. **On the Named Colors tab, in the Basic area, click the square for White, as Figure 4-7 shows.**

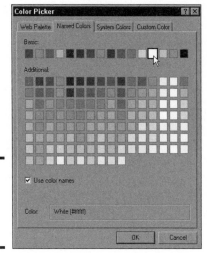

14. **Click OK.**

The Font Picker closes.

15. **In the Size area, click the Absolute radio button and select XX-Large as the size.**

The completed font section looks like Figure 4-8.

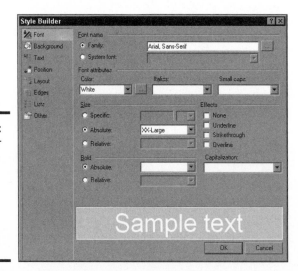

If you specify the exact font size (*hard code* it in geek-speak), such as 12 points, you may annoy some Web site visitors. Many people like to resize the text to suit their eyesight or the distance from the monitor. If the browser can't resize the text or zoom in, some users may find it hard to read. In that case, the visitor grumbles and moves on. You can leave room for customization by choosing one of these font sizes: XX-Small, X-Small, Small, Medium, Large, X-Large, or XX-Large.

16. **Click OK.**

Figure 4-9 shows the styled text of `inlinestyles.aspx` in Design view. You can experiment with many settings in the Style Builder dialog box. You can add effects such as underline, bold, centering, and much more. To change an existing style, select all of the text in Design view and, from the Format menu, click Style.

Figure 4-9:
Check out your styled text in Design view.

For faster styling, try setting common style options on the Formatting toolbar, which you can see in Figure 4-10. Some of the same functions also appear as items in the Format menu.

Figure 4-10:
Use the HTML Formatting toolbar for easy access to style options.

Creating inline styles in Source view

Hardcore geeks insist that for the leanest, tightest, most bloat-free HTML pages, you have to edit those pages with nothing more advanced than Notepad. That claim may be true, but most of us have better things to do than spend our days handcrafting opening and closing tags and removing line breaks to save a few bytes. That said, you may find a code editor essential for tweaking markup. You can type a few characters in HTML Source view more quickly than you can figure out which dialog box generates the attribute that you need.

Visual Web Developer's Source view offers many advantages over a simple text editor, such as Notepad. For example, you get plenty of syntax support and error checking. If you're a person who recognizes the tag, attribute, or value that you want when you see it in a list, the IntelliSense feature can help get you out of the office on time.

To use the built-in syntax support for styles, follow these steps:

1. **Add an HTML file to your project.**

2. **With the page in Source view, drag an** `Input (Button)` **control from the HTML tab of the Toolbox and drop the control between the** `<div>` **and** `</div>` **tags.**

3. **Place the mouse cursor just after the letter** `t` **in** `<input>` **and press the space bar.**

4. **In the IntelliSense window, click style (see Figure 4-11) and press the Tab key.**

The style attribute appears in the tag.

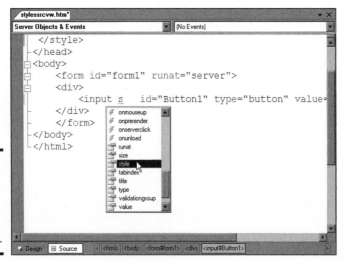

Figure 4-11: Inserting the style attribute by using IntelliSense.

5. Type the equals sign (=) and, in the IntelliSense window, click background-color (see Figure 4-12).

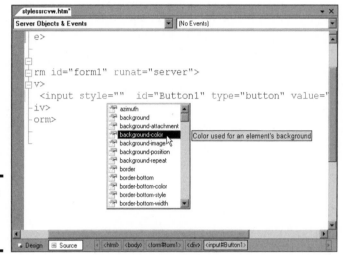

Figure 4-12:
Inserting the style property.

6. Press the Tab key.

The property appears inside the quotation marks.

7. Type a colon (:) and, in the IntelliSense window, click red (see Figure 4-13).

Figure 4-13:
Choosing the property value for background-color.

**Book III
Chapter 4**

Using Styles and
Style Sheets

8. **Press the Tab key.**

The value appears inside the quotation marks.

You can go on with the preceding steps by typing a semi-colon (`;`) and pressing the space bar. IntelliSense continues to prompt with property names and then values, such as `color` as the name and `red` as the value.

In places where there are so many possibilities that IntelliSense can't prompt you with acceptable names or values, IntelliSense shows the formatting syntax, as you can see in Figure 4-14.

Figure 4-14: IntelliSense can offer you syntax support for styles.

The following code shows a series of property/value pairs to fashion a button that sports white text on a red background with a five-pixel gray border:

```
<input style="
    background-color:Red;
    color:White;
    border:solid 5px gray;
    font-size:xx-large"
    id="Button1" type="button" value="button" />
```

Building external style sheets

Visual Web Developer includes graphical tools that help you build external cascading style sheets. For your first task, you need to create a style sheet and modify the default content by following these steps:

1. **Add a cascading style sheet called** `stylesheet.css` **to your Web project (File⇨@New File⇨Style Sheet).**

The style sheet file opens with a `body` selector and empty braces, as you can see in following code:

```
body {
}
```

2. **Place the cursor between the opening and closing braces (`{ }`) and right-click to bring up the context menu.**

3. **From the context menu, click Build Style.**

   The Style Builder dialog box opens.

4. **In the Font name section, click the Family button and then the ellipsis (. . .) button to open the Font Picker dialog box.**

5. **From the Installed fonts list, select Arial, click the Add (>>) button, and then click OK.**

   The Font Picker dialog closes.

6. **In the Size area, click the Absolute radio button and from the drop-down list, select X-Large (shown in Figure 4-15) and then click OK.**

   The Style Builder closes, and you return to the style sheet where the definition for the body selector has been inserted, as in the following code:

```
body { font-size: x-large; font-family: Arial; }
```

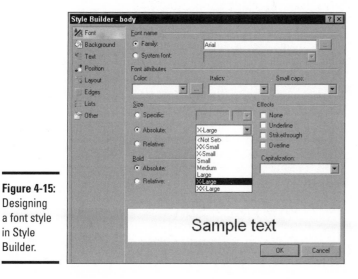

Figure 4-15:
Designing
a font style
in Style
Builder.

Creating a class with style

The barebones starter style sheet that you can find out how to create in the preceding section has only one type selector and no class selectors. You probably want to use class selectors most often. To add a class selector to the `.css` file, define the style, and use the style in a page, follow these steps:

1. **In a cascading style sheet (for example,** `stylesheet.css`**), place the cursor after the existing content.**

2. **Right-click, and from the context menu, click Add Style Rule.**

The Add Style Rule dialog box appears.

3. **Click the Class name radio button and type** `btnclass` **in the text box. You don't need to add the "dot" before** `btnclass` **because the designer adds it for you.**

4. **Click the adjacent Add button (>).**

The rule is included in the style rule hierarchy.

5. **Click OK.**

The dialog box closes, and the new class selector appears in the code:

```
.btnclass { }
```

6. **Place the cursor between the** `.btnclass` **style's braces (**`{ }`**) and right-click.**

7. **Select Build Style from the context menu that appears.**

8. **In the Font Attributes area, select Blue from the drop-down list and then click OK.**

The `.btnclass` definition now includes a definition for the text color, as you can see in the following code:

```
.btnclass { color: blue; }
```

9. **In Source view of an HTML file, drag the style sheet from Solution Explorer and drop it inside the** `<head>` **tag.**

This step produces the following link:

```
<link href="StyleSheet.css" rel="stylesheet"
    type="text/css" />
```

10. **From the HTML tab of the Toolbox, drag an** `Input` `(Button)` **control to the page.**

11. **Set the control's** `class` **attribute to** `btnclass`, **as the following markup shows:**

```
<input id="Button1" class="btnclass" type="button"
    value="button" />
```

The designer and the browser render the button's text in blue.

Using Span and Div for Styles and Positions

You can often see absolute positioning in those Web advertisements where the ad gets in your face by floating over the regular content. These ads get around pop-up blockers because they aren't separate windows. Rather, they're layers of dynamic HTML that use two very useful tags, `<span>` and `<div>`, plus a touch of inline JavaScript.

The demonstration page that you can create in the following sections rolls in topics from previous sections of this chapter, including `Type`, `Class`, and `ID Element` selectors. It adds in some position attributes and the important `visibility` property.

By way of preview, Figure 4-16 shows the page that you can build in the following sections in Design view. As the text on the page indicates, when the user passes the mouse over the highlighted text, the advertisement disappears.

Figure 4-16: You can create a peek-a-boo advertisement with CSS.

Highlighting text with <span>

For the most part, you want to add styles or style classes to the regular HTML tags, such as <p>, <h1>, <li>, and so on. However, you may find that sometimes regular tags don't provide what you want or need.

In the page that you can create in this section, you want to give two words within the sentence special treatment. Putting the style inside a paragraph tag doesn't work because the paragraph tag generates a line break in mid-sentence.

You can use the <span> tag as a generic way of creating an inline division. It marks the start and end of content that should have a special appearance or behavior. To create an area of colored text, follow these steps:

1. **In your HTML or ASP.NET page, add the following markup within the** <body> **tag:**

```
<p>Move the mouse over
<span id="mtext"
class="mtext">
 this text
</span>
to make the ad disappear.
</p>
```

The inline <span> tags set off the words "this text."

2. **Add a** <style> **section inside the** <head> **area of the page.**

3. **Insert the following style class and declaration to support the inline spanning of text:**

```
.mtext {font-weight:bold;background:black;color:white;}
```

4. **Browse to the page.**

The words within the <span> tags appear white with a black background, as you can see in Figure 4-17.

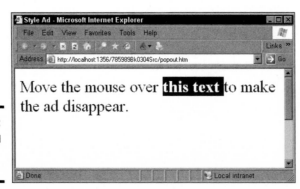

Figure 4-17: Highlighting words with <span>.

Creating a layer with <div>

You can use the <div> tag, like <span>, as an all-purpose container. Unlike
<span>, which is an inline tag, <div> marks large blocks of text such as
paragraphs. Working at that level makes <div> useful for creating layers of
independent content (such as advertisements) in neat boxes. Follow these
steps to create an advertisement as a layer inside a <div>:

1. **In your HTML or ASP.NET page, add the following markup within the**
   <body> **tag:**

```
<div id="slider" class="showing">
  Hello, I'm here to sell you something.
</div>
```

2. **In the** <style> **section of the page, add the following style classes to**
   support the block division:

```
#slider {position: absolute; left: 120px; top:120px;
         height: 118px; background-color: Yellow;
         font-family: Comic Sans MS; width: 146px;
         border-style: double;
         text-align: center}
.showing {visibility:visible}
.gone {visibility:hidden }
```

The preceding code uses an Element ID selector (#slider) to define the
advertisement, including its absolute position on the page. The layer sits
120 pixels down from the top of the pane and 120 pixels in from the left
side of the pane. The other properties and values in the code create the
layer's border and background color.

The .showing and .gone class selectors use the visibility property
to show and hide the layer by using the visible and hidden values,
respectively.

The Design view editor desperately wants to add inline style position
data to layers. If you select the layer in Design view, the editor may
insert a style attribute that you don't want. If your <div> stops obeying
the embedded style information, check to see whether the editor has
been up to mischief directly on the tag.

3. **Browse to the page and confirm that it now has a block of text with a**
   yellow background, as Figure 4-18 shows.

Book III
Chapter 4

Using Styles and
Style Sheets

Figure 4-18:
Using <div>
to create a
layer.

Showing and hiding the *<div>*

As it stands, the content of the <div> tag is visible because its style class
(.showing) sets it that way. In this procedure, you insert a tiny bit of
JavaScript to make the contents of the <div> tag disappear and reappear.
Follow these steps:

1. **Change the opening** <span> **tag so that it looks like the following
code:**

```
<span class="mtext"
        onmouseover="slider.className='gone'"
        onmouseout="slider.className='showing'">
```

The preceding code adds onmouseover and onmouseout attributes to the
tag with inline JavaScript as the values. When the mouse passes over
the text within the <span>, the JavaScript executes. It simply reassigns
the class value for the layer named slider. Instead of adopting the
showing style (which makes the layer visible), it assigns the gone style
where the layer is defined as hidden.

The onmouseout attribute does the reverse; it tells the element with the
class name of slider to go back to using the showing class.

2. **Browse to the page and pass the mouse over and out of the bold text
to confirm that the advertisement plays peek-a-boo.**

Creating and Applying Styles in Code

If you use ASP.NET pages, you have the added option of creating styles in code — or changing an existing style on the fly. You can also let users choose their own style sheet. The following sections show you how to put these ASP.NET options to work.

Applying inline styles in code

You can build a style from scratch in code and apply that style to any ASP.NET control that supports styles. Although you probably want to link to external style sheets when you can, you may run into times when you need to create a specific look for an ASP.NET control. To create an inline style using code, follow these steps:

1. **In the page** Load **handler or other subroutine, add the following code:**

```
Dim stylLabel As New Style
stylLabel.BackColor = Drawing.Color.Black
stylLabel.ForeColor = Drawing.Color.White
stylLabel.BorderColor = Drawing.Color.DarkSlateGray
stylLabel.BorderWidth = Unit.Pixel(4)
stylLabel.BorderStyle = BorderStyle.Double
stylLabel.Font.Bold = True
stylLabel.Font.Size = FontUnit.XXLarge
Label1.ApplyStyle(stylLabel)
```

Book III
Chapter 4

Using Styles and
Style Sheets

The preceding code declares the variable stylLabel as a Style type and creates an instance of the Style object. The subsequent lines set various properties, including the colors, border width, and font size. The last line uses the Label control's ApplyStyle method to apply the style to the object.

2. **Use the** Label **control's** Attributes **property and its** Add **method to include positioning information in the style, as the following code shows:**

```
Label1.Attributes.Add("style", _
  "position: absolute; left: 120px; top:120px;")
```

3. **Assign a string of text to the** Label **control's** Text **property, as the following code shows:**

```
Label1.Text = "I've been given a style!"
```

4. **Browse to the** .aspx **page.**

Figure 4-19 shows the styled text that you create in these steps in server-side code.

Figure 4-19:
You can
create
styles
program-
matically.

If you look at the browser's source code (View⇨Source), you can see the following markup (formatted for easy viewing on this printed page):

```
<span id="Span1"
style=
"display: inline-block;
color: White;
background-color: Black;
border-color: DarkSlateGray;
border-width: 4px;
border-style: Double;
font-size: XX-Large;
font-weight: bold;
position: absolute;
left: 120px;
top: 120px;">
I've been given a style!
</span>
```

Inserting embedded styles with code

You can use ASP.NET code to insert a `<style>` tag into a page. You just need to create a literal string containing the markup and definitions. Then, inject the string into the `<head>` section of the page. To add a `<style>` tag to your page, follow these steps:

1. **In an** `.aspx` **page, in the Load or other event handler, create a** `Literal` **control by using the following code:**

```
Dim genStyle As New Literal
genStyle.ID = "lit1"
```

2. **Assign the complete content of the style sheet (tags included) to the** `Literal` **control's** `Text` **property, as the following snippet of code shows:**

```
genStyle.Text = "<style>body {color:red}</style>"
```

If you have a long string in the preceding code, use the `Append()` method of the `StringBuilder` class to build the string. `StringBuilder` uses less memory and runs faster. For more, see http://msdn2.microsoft.com/en-us/library/system.text.stringbuilder.aspx.

3. **Use the** `Add()` **method of the** `Header.Controls` **collection to insert the literal markup, as this code shows:**

```
Page.Header.Controls.Add(genStyle)
```

At runtime, the code creates a normal-looking `<style>` tag inside the `<head>` tag, as you can see in the following snippet of rendered code:

```
<head>
  <title>Style Section</title>
  <style>body {color:red}</style>
</head>
```

In ASP.NET 2.0, you can turn almost any HTML tag into a server-side tag by adding `runat="server"` to it, including the `<head>` and `<style>` tags.

Letting users choose their style sheet

If you enjoy designing style sheets, you can let Web site visitors sample your creations and choose the one that they prefer while browsing your site. To let users choose a style sheet, follow these steps:

1. **Add two style sheets with style information to your project.**

   For the example that we include with these steps, you can use the samples that follow:

```
[blue.css]
body { font-size: xx-large; color: pink;
    font-family:Comic Sans MS;background: blue;}

[pink.css]
body { font-size: xx-large; font-family:Arial;
  color:blue; background-color: pink; }
```

2. **In your** `.aspx` **page, add an ASP.NET** `Label` **and two** `RadioButton` **controls, as you can see in the following markup:**

```
<asp:label cssclass="defaulttext" id="Label1"
runat="server" text="Choose your style sheet!">
```

```
</asp:label><br /><br />
<asp:radiobutton id="radPink"
runat="server" autopostback="True"
groupname="stylegrp" checked="true"
oncheckedchanged="radCSS_Changed"
text="Pink Style" /><br />
<asp:radiobutton id="RadioButton1"
runat="server" autopostback="True"
groupname="stylegrp"
oncheckedchanged="radCSS_Changed"
text="Blue Style" />
```

The preceding code sets the autopostback property of the radio buttons to true so they execute the radCSS_Changed subroutine when someone changes the buttons by clicking one.

3. **Add a link to one of the style sheets, including the** runat="server" **and** id="style1" **portions, as the following code shows:**

```
<link id="style1" href="pink.css" runat="server"
  rel="stylesheet" type="text/css" />
```

4. **Add the following** radCSS_Changed() **subroutine that swaps the referenced style sheet according to the selected radio button:**

```
Protected Sub radCSS_Changed _
(ByVal sender As Object, _
ByVal e As System.EventArgs)
    If radPink.Checked Then
        style1.Href = "pink.css"
    Else
        style1.Href = "blue.css"
    End If
End Sub
```

5. **Browse to the page and click the radio buttons.**

As you can see in Figure 4-20, the page changes according to the style sheet in use.

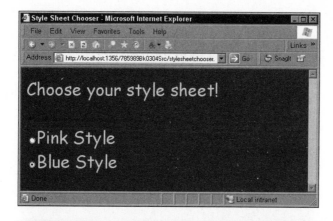

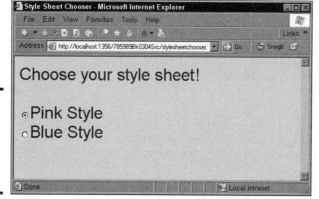

Figure 4-20:
Let users
decide
if they're
blue or in
the pink.

If you want to store a user's changes between settings, check out Book 8, Chapter 2.

Chapter 5: Using Client-Side Script

In This Chapter

✔ Peering into Microsoft.com's use of browser script

✔ Inserting client-side script using server code

✔ Warnings and confirmations

✔ Validating with client-side script

✔ Refreshing part of a page using callbacks

*C*lient-side scripting refers to a program that runs inside the browser page rather than on the Web server. One of the oldest uses of client-side script is rollover effects on HTML buttons. When the mouse passes over an image, the browser raises an event flag. A handler executes a tiny piece of code that points to a different image than the one originally displayed. The second image usually has a slightly different appearance.

By running code inside the browser, you can harness the local computer's horsepower and bypass the page refreshes that slow down server-side applications. Reloading everything that appears on a page just to validate whether the user enters a value in a text box doesn't make much sense. If you use enough client-side script, a browser page can give you the responsiveness of a typical Windows forms program while keeping the advantage of easy code updates on the server.

ASP.NET 2.0 uses client-side scripting extensively. That may sound odd for a server-side programming technology, but it makes sense. Server-side code can deliver custom markup to each user's browser. Included in that individual markup, you can find content that generates custom client-side script. As you can see in this chapter, architects are working magic to create stunning effects with client-side JavaScript.

All code listings used in this book are available for download at www.dummies. com/go/aspnetaiofd.

Sampling Client-Side Script on Microsoft.com

You don't have to go far to find examples of client-side script — almost every Web page has some. You can check out the script by selecting View⇨ Source from the browser. For example, the home page at www.microsoft. com has quite a few snippets of JavaScript. You may have to do some reverse engineering and detective work to find out what the JavaScript does, but you can really get a handle on client-side capabilities by snooping around. The following sections walk you through some code (that you can find on just one page of Microsoft's site) to look at a few uses for client-side scripting.

Compensating for browser differences

The first evidence of client-side script on the page www.microsoft.com turns out to be a reference to more script. In the following code, you can see the <script> tag that refers to an address where the actual script file (hp.js) resides:

```
<script type="text/javascript"
src="http://i2.microsoft.com/h/all/s/hp.js">
</script>
```

 Including JavaScript in a separate file helps speed the loading of a page on subsequent visits because browsers often store files in a cache (that is, a copy of the file) on the user's machine. If the user has downloaded hp.js, the browser fetches the local version, saving time and bandwidth.

You can explore the external JavaScript file by typing the URL in the browser. This entry generally starts a download, and you may get some security warnings. hp.js is a library of short functions. One of the functions, which you can see in the following code, helps the page deal with the differences in the way browsers handle script:

```
function wrT(){document.write("<!"+"--");}
```

When executed in a page, the preceding code inserts the opening of an HTML comment (<!--) to shield portions of script from a browser's idiosyncrasies, as shown in Figure 5-1.

Figure 5-1:
The tiny
perfect
browser
window

Embedding multimedia content

In the script in Microsoft's home page, you discover that Microsoft uses Macromedia ShockWave in its pages. One of the scripts, a portion of which follows, adjusts for the version of the Flash player on the user's machine:

Beware of Microsoft JavaScript

Microsoft uses many very appealing JavaScript features. For example, say that you discover the following JavaScript built onto a button:

```
<input
onclick="window.showModalDialo
   g('http://www.dummies.com',
null,'dialogHeight:100px;dialo
   gWidth:100px;edge:sunken;
unadorned:yes;status:no;scroll
   :no');"
type="button" value="Click
   Me!" />
```

This code pops up a tiny browser window (shown in Figure 5-1) that sits on top of every other window on the computer. (In geek-speak, the term for this window is *modal*.) Don't you need exactly this kind of little window? Wait until you read the fine print in the Microsoft reference material for the showModalDialog() function:

```
"There is no public standard
   that applies to this
   method."
```

You see, Microsoft's proprietary version of JavaScript includes the window.showModalDialog() method, but you can't be sure that any other browser supports the method. The fact is, the code only works in Internet Explorer. You may not have a problem with this restriction if you're in an environment (like some companies) where you can guarantee that everyone has a recent version of Internet Explorer.

You can safely use Microsoft's extensions only if you detect the browser type and emit the proprietary codes for only Internet Explorer. Substitute standards-based syntax for all other browsers.

**Book III
Chapter 5**

Using Client-Side Script

```
for(var gVer=2;gVer<=10;gVer++)
  {try
   {var gFlash=eval("new ActiveXObject
   ('ShockwaveFlash.ShockwaveFlash."+gVer+"');");
    if(gFlash)
      {
       gFV=gVer+".0";
```

You can use scripts to control embedded objects. For example, buttons with JavaScript can start, pause, and stop movies running in Windows Media Player.

Tracking page views and statistics

Commercial Web sites do a tremendous amount of tracking. The owners want to know how many page hits they get, where the visitor comes from, what kind of browser he or she has, and the amount of money in his or her wallet. Scripts can provide *almost* all of the preceding statistics.

Microsoft's home page is no exception to the tracking rule. You can find a script (in the following code) that sends information about your browsing to a company called WebTrends (www.webtrends.com) that specializes in "Web analytics" (which means they analyze Web site statistics for you):

```
var gDomain="statse.webtrendslive.com";
<SCRIPT SRC="http://i2.microsoft.com/h/all/s/webtrends.js"
TYPE="text/javascript"></SCRIPT>
```

Client-side scripts do much of the tracking. These scripts create and read browser cookies that record where you go on the Web site and how much time you spend there.

Making the page interactive

Some JavaScript may look almost invisible to you because you don't see any <script> tags. Instead, Web developers add the JavaScript as values to some of the attributes in an HTML object.

The following code shows part of the markup that makes the Site Map link on Microsoft's home page:

```
<td class="gt0" nowrap onmouseover="this.className='gt1'"
onmouseout="this.className='gt0'">
```

When the mouse hovers over the link (firing onmouseover), the style class name changes to gt1, which generates a lighter cell color and a border. When the mouse moves back out (firing onmouseout), the cell returns to its original class, gt0.

You can often recognize inline script by the fact that it uses JavaScript keywords, such as this. (We mean this the keyword, not "this" the word-word.)

Creating random content and surveys

Some of the script in Microsoft's home page creates content that appears at random intervals — a plea to take part in a survey. If you decline, the script passes a cookie to your browser so that the survey request doesn't bug you again — or, at least, it doesn't bug you too soon.

The script builds the content of a Web page, including links that you can see in the following code:

```
SRC.invitations[1] = new
      SiteRecruit_InvitationConfiguration();
SRC.invitations[1].weight = 57;
SRC.invitations[1].projectId = '2944mt';
SRC.invitations[1].invitationType = 0;
```

```
SRC.invitations[1].acceptUrl =
 'http://web.survey-poll.com/bin/survey.asp';
SRC.invitations[1].viewUrl =
 'http://web.survey-poll.com/bin/survey.asp';
```

If you accept the survey invitation, the script passes information to the specialized page, hosted by SurveySite (www.surveysite.com). This company does online market research, and it arranges focus groups, collects and analyzes data, and produces reports.

Embedding Script in an ASP.NET Page

Because client-script is so important to ASP.NET, you may not be surprised to see a .NET Framework class dedicated to it. The ClientScriptManager class, implemented through the ClientScript property of the Page object, lets you generate client-side script from server-side code.

Even when the script in a page doesn't need to be generated dynamically, some developers prefer to keep script as part of the ASP.NET code rather than hard-coded inside the client-side <head> and </head> tags. For one thing, the technique keeps page logic in one location instead of splitting it by including some in with the HTML code. Keeping script with the server-side code also ensures that an HTML page designer doesn't accidentally change the script while creating an attractive layout.

The following sections show you the main features of the ClientScript Manager class. Figure 5-2 shows a page in which you build a client-side script to continuously display the time by using dynamic HTML (DHTML).

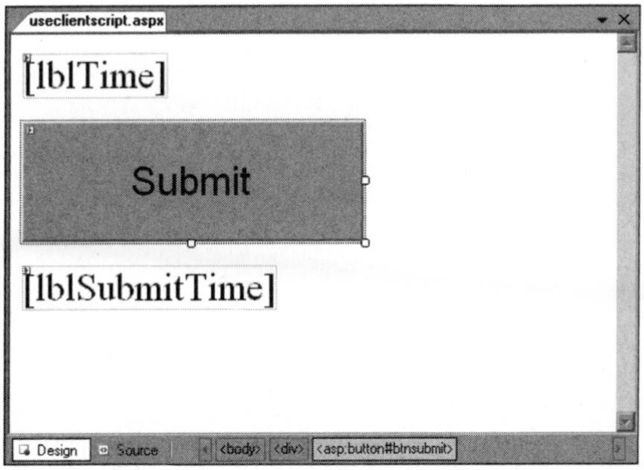

Book III
Chapter 5

Using Client-Side
Script

Figure 5-2:
Design view of a page that uses client-side script.

Embedding a block of script

The ASP.NET `RegisterClientScriptBlock()` method inserts a block of custom JavaScript into a page. Usually, the content of the script is a function that you call from elsewhere in the page. To insert script into a page, follow these steps:

1. **Add an ASP.NET page named** `useclientscript.aspx` **to your project using VB and no code-behind.**

2. **Add two ASP.NET Label controls called** `lblTime` **and** `lblSubmitTime` **to the page.**

3. **Add an ASP.NET** `Button` **control named** `btnSubmit` **to the page.**

4. **In an empty area of Design view, double-click to create a handler for the** `Load` **event.**

5. **Insert the following server-side code as part of the** `Load` **event handler:**

```
Protected Sub Page_Load _
  (ByVal sender As Object, _
   ByVal e As System.EventArgs)
   Dim cs As ClientScriptManager
   cs = Page.ClientScript
   cs.RegisterClientScriptBlock _
     (Me.GetType, "clockfunction", BuildClock(), True)
End Sub
```

The preceding code runs when the page loads. The first line of the routine declares `cs` as a variable to hold an instance of the `ClientScript Manager` class. The following line gets a reference to the `ClientScript` property of the `Page` class.

Using the reference, the code calls the `RegisterClientScriptBlock()` method, which inserts whatever JavaScript you want to include. `RegisterClientScriptBlock()` takes four parameters:

- **The type of client script to register:** In this case, the type is the page itself.

- **A keyword:** This sample uses the keyword `clockfunction` so that you can track the function programmatically.

- **The contents of the JavaScript routine:** For this parameter, you can use any object that produces a string of JavaScript. The parameter can be the literal script in quotes, a string variable, or, in this case, a call to a function that produces a string.

- **A** `Boolean` **value to indicate whether ASP.NET includes or excludes** `<script>` **and** `</script>` **tags as it inserts the JavaScript:** When true, `RegisterClientScriptBlock()` wraps the script in `<Script>`

</Script> tags for you. In the example in this section, you want the tags added because they aren't included in the string that you supply.

6. Add the following subroutine to generate the JavaScript code:

```
Public Function BuildClock() As String
    Dim sb As New StringBuilder
    Dim nl As String = Environment.NewLine
    sb.Append("function clock() " & nl)
    sb.Append("{" & nl)
    sb.Append("if (!document.layers && ")
    sb.Append("!document.all) return;" & nl)
    sb.Append("var dt=new Date();" & nl)
    sb.Append("var hr=dt.getHours();" & nl)
    sb.Append("var min=dt.getMinutes();" & nl)
    sb.Append("var sec=dt.getSeconds();" & nl)
    sb.Append("if (hr<10){ hr=""0"" + hr;}" & nl)
    sb.Append("if (min<10){ min=""0"" + min;}" & nl)
    sb.Append("if (sec<10){sec=""0"" + sec;}" & nl)
    sb.Append("shw="" "" + hr + "":"" + ")
    sb.Append("min + "":"" + sec +  "" "" ;" & nl)
    sb.Append("document.forms[0].")
    sb.Append("submittime.value=shw;" & nl)
    sb.Append("if (document.layers) {" & nl)
    sb.Append("document.layers(""lblTime"").")
    sb.Append("document.write(shw);" & nl)
    sb.Append("document.layers(""lblTime"").")
    sb.Append("document.close();" & nl)
    sb.Append("}" & nl)
    sb.Append("else " & nl)
    sb.Append("if (document.all) " & nl)
    sb.Append("lblTime.innerHTML = shw;" & nl)
    sb.Append("setTimeout(""clock()"", 1000);" & nl)
    sb.Append("}" & nl)
    Return sb.ToString
End Function
```

Although you can add all the JavaScript to a string variable, the StringBuilder object and its Append() method give you faster performance using less memory.

You don't have to add Environment.NewLine at the end of a JavaScript line, but the line breaks that Environment.NewLine inserts make the code easier for humans to read. The browser doesn't require line breaks.

7. Browse to the page.

You don't have much to see yet, other than the Submit button. However, you can explore plenty of code that's hidden behind the scenes.

8. **In the browser, view the source code (View⇨Source).**

Inside the browser's source code, you can see the JavaScript `clock()` function. The abbreviated version that follows shows that ASP.NET has added the `<script>` tags and some HTML comment tags (`<!--` and `// -->`) to the HTML stream, in addition to the JavaScript that you provide in Step 6:

```
<script type="text/javascript">
<!--
function clock()
{
if (!document.layers && !document.all) return;
var dt=new Date();
//... code removed here for brevity
lblTime.innerHTML = shw;
setTimeout("clock()", 1000);
}
// -->
</script>
```

The comment tags prevent browsers that might misinterpret the script from doing so.

Inserting a hidden field into a page

In the preceding section, you can find out how to get the JavaScript clock code in place, but you still have to start it running.

Web developers often store bits of data in the page, hidden from the user. If the content is dynamic, such as a variable, a hidden form field works very well as a storage location. In this example, you want to capture a time stamp to use later. The `RegisterHiddenField()` method is made for this sort of procedure. To create and use a hidden form field, follow these steps:

1. **In Source view of** `useclientscript.aspx`, **locate the** `Load` **event handler and add the following statement:**

```
cs.RegisterHiddenField("submittime", "")
```

This code assumes that you completed the steps in the preceding section to add a script block.

`RegisterHiddenField()` takes two parameters. The first is the name of the hidden field, and the second is the value of the field. In this case, you don't need a default value, so you insert an empty string (`""`).

2. **Browse to the page and open the browser's source code (View⇨ Source).**

In the source code, ASP.NET adds the following HTML markup to create the hidden field:

```
<input type="hidden" name="submittime"
id="submittime" value="" />
```

You can also see where the JavaScript `clock()` function makes use of this field:

```
document.forms[0].submittime.value=shw;
```

This inserts the hidden field but doesn't do anything significant with it. The field reappears in the following section as a storage location.

Embedding code so that it executes on startup

You need to keep timing and placement in mind when writing client-side script. The browser reads the incoming HTML stream from start to finish and may begin rendering the markup before the last characters arrive. Modern browsers show you text and images long before the final `</html>` tag arrives.

If client-side script at the beginning of the page calls a function at the end of the page, you need to be sure that all of the code has arrived and is available to the browser. If not, users see a script error and effects such as rollovers stop working.

In addition, you may sometimes want to take some action such as initialize objects as soon as the page is fully loaded. Timing is important.

The `RegisterStartupScript()` method does exactly what its name says: It inserts a script and then runs that script on page startup. This method uses four parameters:

✦ **The script type (usually** `Me.GetType` **works)**

✦ **The script's name**

✦ **A string that contains the script itself**

✦ **A** `Boolean` **that indicates whether you want to add script tags (usually** `True`, **which means add the script tags)**

For this demonstration, you want to start the clock as soon as everything's loaded into the browser — but not before. To add content that executes in the correct sequence, follow these steps:

1. **In Source view of** `useclientscript.aspx`, **locate the** `Load` **event handler and add the following statement:**

```
cs.RegisterStartupScript _
  (Me.GetType, "clock", "clock();", True)
```

This code assumes that you complete the steps in the preceding section to add a script block.

This code tells ASP.NET to insert a call to the JavaScript `clock()` function and wrap it in `<script>` tags because you haven't included the `<script>` tags yourself.

2. **Browse to the page.**

The clock appears on the page, as you can see in Figure 5-3.

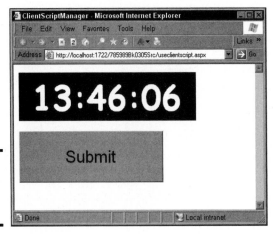

Figure 5-3:
Running the clock on startup.

3. **View the HTML source code (View⇨Source) and locate the following markup:**

```
<script type="text/javascript">
<!--
clock();// -->
</script>
</form>
</body>
</html>
```

Notice the placement of the preceding JavaScript? The `Register StartupScript()` inserts the startup code as close as possible to the end of the HTML markup. This placement ensures that the client-side function that the JavaScript calls precedes it. You know that the technique works because the clock starts.

Embedding code to catch a page submit

You often may need to perform client-side validation before submitting the page to the server. To validate at the right moment, you need to know when the page is about to be submitted. That way, you can intervene and run your validation or other code such as an error handler.

The `RegisterOnSubmitStatement()` lets you designate the routine that you want to run when the user clicks the Submit button. To designate the code to run, follow these steps:

1. **In Source view of** `useclientscript.aspx`, **locate the** `Load` **event handler and add the following statement:**

```
cs.RegisterOnSubmitStatement _
  (Me.GetType, "submitstmte", _
   "alert('The Test is Beginning!')")
```

This code assumes that you complete the steps starting way back in the section "Embedding a block of script."

The preceding code supplies three parameters:

- The type of client script to register

- An identifier so that you can interact with the script programmatically

- The script that you want to run when the page is about to be submitted

   In this case, the script is a call to the built-in JavaScript `alert()`, but you can use the name of a homegrown function already in the page.

2. **Browse to the page and click the Submit button.**

The `alert()` box pops up, as you can see in Figure 5-4.

**Book III
Chapter 5**

Using Client-Side Script

Figure 5-4:
You see an alert before the page is submitted.

3. **Dismiss the** `alert()` **box by clicking the button.**

4. **View the HTML source code (View⇨Source).**

`RegisterOnSubmitStatement()` generates client-side code in two places. The first is an added attribute in the `<form>` tag. Notice the `onsubmit()` attribute (in bold) in the rendered markup:

```
<form name="form1" method="post"
action="useclientscript.aspx"
 onsubmit="javascript:return WebForm_OnSubmit();"
id="form1">
```

When the form is being submitted, the page executes code in a second location — a routine called `WebForm_OnSubmit()` that you can find just after your own `clock()` script. Wrapped inside ASP.NET's code, you can see the `alert()` function that you passed as a parameter to `RegisterOnSubmit Statement()`:

```
function WebForm_OnSubmit() {
alert('The Test is Beginning!');
return true;
}
```

Capturing the hidden field

In the previous sections, you can embed a hidden field to store the time on the client. During a postback, you can capture the value for display in a server-side control. A *postback* is the action of submitting data to the server for processing. To submit hidden data to the server, follow these steps:

1. **In Design view, double-click the** `Button` **control (**`btnSubmit`**) to create a default handler.**

2. **In Source view, configure the handler to look like the following code:**

```
Protected Sub btnSubmit_Click _
  (ByVal sender As Object, _
   ByVal e As System.EventArgs)
     lblSubmitTime.Text = "Submitted at " & _
     Request.Form("submittime")
End Sub
```

The preceding code gets the value of the hidden field `submittime` and displays the value of that field as the `Text` property of the second `Label` control (`lblSubmitTime`).

3. **Browse to the page.**

4. **Click Submit.**

5. **Dismiss the alert that appears.**

The top label shows the time of the page refresh. The stored time appears in the bottom label, as you can see in Figure 5-5.

Figure 5-5:
Capturing
the hidden
field value.

Referencing external scripts

Instead of embedding blocks of client-side script with the server-side
`RegisterClientScriptBlock()` method, you may want to reference an
external script. The `RegisterClientScriptInclude()` method lets you
add the reference (such as the URL and name of the script library) in code.
Using references programmatically lets you swap in a different script library,
depending on conditions that you choose.

In this example, the following code uses one JavaScript library if the page
appears for the first time, and a different set of functions if the page is
posted back by a button click or other event:

```
if IsPostBack Then
    cs.RegisterClientScriptInclude("inclscrpt", _
    "http://i.microsoft.com/h/en-us/r/" & _
    "SiteRecruit_PageConfiguration_HomePage_Page.js")
Else
    cs.RegisterClientScriptInclude _
    ("inclscrpt", "http://i2.microsoft.com/h/all/s/hp.js")
End If
```

Storing an array of values in a page

If you're using client script, you may want to access data from within the page. The data may come from a server-side process, such as a database. ASP.NET's `RegisterArrayDeclaration()` inserts a comma-delimited string of values into client-side script as an array.

The following code, when you use it in the `Page_Load` procedure, creates and uses a client-side array. The embedded comments (look for the apostrophes) explain the purpose of each section of this code:

```
'Create a comma-delimited string to provide the data
'for the array
Dim s As String
s = "1, 2, 3, 4, 5, 6, 7, 8, 9, 10"
'Get a reference to the ClientScript property for the page
Dim cs As ClientScriptManager
cs = Page.ClientScript
'Register the array
cs.RegisterArrayDeclaration _
    ("myarray", s)
'Register a startup script that uses the array
cs.RegisterStartupScript(Me.GetType, _
    "arry", "for (x=0; x<10; x++)document.write" & _
    "(myarray[x] + '<br>')", True)
```

Notice that the startup script uses the `document.write` method, which is the JavaScript equivalent to ASP.NET's `Response.Write`.

When you browse to the page, the values appear as you see them in Figure 5-6.

ASP.NET generates the `<script>` tags, an array variable that uses the name that you supply in first parameter, and an array object initialized with the values. The following code shows the ASP.NET-generated routine that puts the array values on the page:

```
<script type="text/javascript">
<!--
var myarray =  new Array(1, 2, 3, 4, 5, 6, 7, 8, 9, 10);
// -->
</script>
<script type="text/javascript">
<!--
for (x=0; x<10; x++)document.write(myarray[x] + '<br>')// -->
</script>
```

If you try to use array items before the complete HTML is loaded, you may generate a JavaScript syntax error, such as this line:

```
"Error: 'myarray' is undefined
```

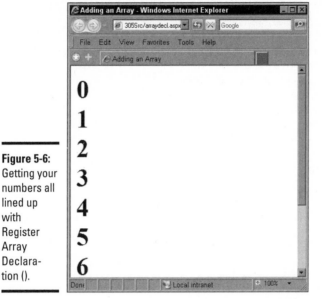

Figure 5-6:
Getting your
numbers all
lined up
with
Register
Array
Declara-
tion ().

REMEMBER

You can't count on arrays being in place until you have the page fully loaded
in the browser. So you may want to go the safe route and use `Register`
`StartupScript()` to insert startup code.

Using Client-Side Scripts in ASP.NET

In ASP.NET, client-side script and server-side programs exist in separate
domains. You can, however, build bridges between them so they can play
nicely together. The following sections show a few of the common techniques to do just that.

Identifying page elements by using script

One of the advantages of using server-side code to insert client-side script is
that the server-side code knows a lot about what's on the page and the name
of everything that it has built.

If you want to manipulate objects by using client-side script, you need to
know the object's name. Of course, you can loop through everything on a
page to find what you want, but that's messy. The identification becomes
more complicated when your page includes user controls because object
names change by the time they go to the client.

For example, a `TextBox` control known as `Textbox1` at the time you drop it into the user control shows up with a different identity when that user control appears on the Web page. ASP.NET supplies its own names as it generates the code.

To be sure that you're getting the right name for an object when you need to refer to it on the client-side, follow these steps:

1. **Create a user control named** `txtboxusr.ascx` **and include the following code:**

   ```
   <%@ Control Language="VB" ClassName="txtboxusr" %>
   <asp:textbox id="TextBox1" runat="server">
   </asp:textbox>
   ```

2. **Add an ASP.NET Web form called** `identif.aspx` **to your project.**

3. **Add a** `Button` **control to the form and configure that control with the following code:**

   ```
   <asp:button id="Button1"
   runat="server"
   onclientclick="FillBox();return false;"
   text="Fill Box" />
   ```

   We discuss the use of the `onclientclick` property in the sidebar "onclick, onclientclick, onserverclick," later in this chapter.

4. **From Solution Explorer, drag** `txtboxusr.ascx` **and drop it on the design surface of the Web form.**

5. **Add the following code in the page** `Load` **event:**

   ```
   Protected Sub Page_Load _
   (ByVal sender As Object, _
   ByVal e As System.EventArgs)
       Dim usrcntrl As UserControl
       Dim txtbx As TextBox
       usrcntrl = Page.FindControl("Txtboxusr1")
       txtbx = usrcntrl.FindControl("TextBox1")
       Dim cs As ClientScriptManager
       cs = Page.ClientScript
       cs.RegisterClientScriptBlock _
       (Me.GetType, "fillusr", _
        "function FillBox(){document.forms[0]." & _
        txtbx.ClientID & ".value='" & _
        txtbx.ClientID & "';}", True)
   End Sub
   ```

   The preceding code determines the exact name of the `TextBox` control and makes that name available to client-side script.

The routine declares instances of the UserControl and TextBox objects. Next, it gets a reference to the user control by using the Page object's FindControl() method. Using that reference (stored in usrcntrl), it searches inside the user control (using usrcntrl.FindControl()) to return a reference to the TextBox control.

The third parameter of the RegisterClientScriptBlock() method builds a JavaScript function by adding the strings together. The function that you assemble in this code includes the ClientID property of the TextBox object twice, once as a programming reference, and the second time as a value for display.

6. **Browse to** identif.aspx **and click the button.**

As you can see in Figure 5-7, the real name of the text box is Txtboxusr1_TextBox1, as the server-side ClientID property tells you.

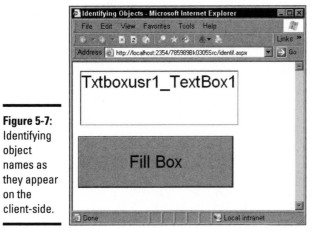

Figure 5-7: Identifying object names as they appear on the client-side.

7. **View the source code (View⇨Source) and locate the JavaScript** FillBox() **function.**

The JavaScript written to the page includes the real name of the TextBox control. As it turns out, the final name is predictable. When you combine the name of the user control, an underscore, and the TextBox name, you get Txtboxusr1_TextBox1, as you can see in the following code:

```
<script type="text/javascript">
<!--
function FillBox()
{document.forms[0].Txtboxusr1_TextBox1.value=
'Txtboxusr1_TextBox1';}// -->
</script>
```

Using alert( ) to stop users cold

You can really make the JavaScript `alert()` function get the user's attention. He or she can't move on until he or she dismisses the alert.

This in-your-face characteristic also makes `alert()` highly annoying when you overuse or abuse it. That said, you may find times when you simply have to prevent users from continuing. Check out this example:

1. **In Source view, add the following markup to create two** `DropDownList` **controls and a** `Button` **control:**

```
<p><asp:dropdownlist  id="DropDownList1"
runat="server" autopostback="True">
</asp:dropdownlist>
<asp:dropdownlist id="DropDownList2"
runat="server" autopostback="True">
</asp:dropdownlist></p>
<p><asp:button id="Button1" runat="server"
text="OK" onclick="Button1_Click" /> </p>
```

2. **In the page** `Load` **event, add the following code to fill the** `DropDownList` **controls with all of the colors known to .NET:**

```
Private Sub Page_Load _
 (ByVal sender As System.Object, _
 ByVal e As System.EventArgs) _
 Handles MyBase.Load
  If Not IsPostBack Then
   Dim enumColor As New Drawing.KnownColor
   Dim Colors As Array = _
   [Enum].GetValues(enumColor.GetType())
   DropDownList1.DataSource = Colors
   DropDownList1.DataBind()
   DropDownList2.DataSource = Colors
   DropDownList2.DataBind()
  End If
End Sub
```

3. **Add the following code to handle the** `Button` **control's server-side** `onclick` **event:**

```
Protected Sub Button1_Click _
(ByVal sender As Object, _
ByVal e As System.EventArgs)
   If Left(DropDownList1.SelectedValue, 1) = _
      Left(DropDownList2.SelectedValue, 1) Then
      Dim cs As ClientScriptManager
      cs = Page.ClientScript
      cs.RegisterStartupScript _
```

```
        (Me.GetType, "alrt", "alert('Never choose " & _
        "colours that start with the same letter!');", _
        True)
    End If
End Sub
```

4. **Browse to the page, select Firebrick in one** `DropDownList` **control, select ForestGreen in the other, and then click OK.**

   The page refreshes and the `alert()` appears, as you can see in Figure 5-8.

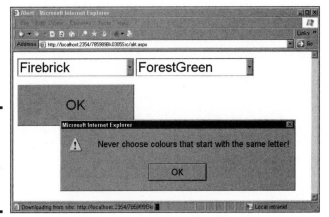

Figure 5-8:
Issuing a
fashion
alert() from
the server-
side.

confirm ( ) a drastic action

Friendly user interfaces are forgiving. A user interface can let users bail out of an action before it's too late. The JavaScript `confirm()` function is a handy way to alert a user to a drastic action. You can use `confirm()` with server-side controls by adding code to the ASP.NET `onclientclick` property.

The following code prompts the user to make a conscious decision about a very drastic action, as Figure 5-9 shows:

```
<asp:button id="btnDelete"
 runat="server"
 onclientclick="return confirm('Delete' +
 ' your life\'s work\n' +
 'even though there\'s no \n' +
 'back-up version and \n' +
 'no hope of recovery?');"
 text="Delete" />
```

Figure 5-9:
The program asks if you really want to delete your life's work.

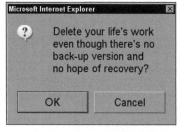

The `confirm()` function returns the value `true` if the user clicks OK and `false` if he or she clicks Cancel. By using the construction `return confirm()`, you effectively tell the button not to carry out the action if the value returned from `confirm()` is `false`.

In JavaScript strings, use the backslash as an escape code before the apostrophe to keep the apostrophe from causing trouble by being misinterpreted:

```
your life\'s
```

You can break long lines in the `confirm()` box by adding the escape code for a new line. Just use a backslash and the letter "n" for a new line. Here's how it looks in the code:

```
work\n
```

Creating a rollover effect

Web pages commonly offer interesting *rollover effects,* where a control's appearance changes as you pass the mouse over it. You can add these effects to ASP.NET server controls by injecting inline JavaScript as an attribute. To create a rollover, follow these steps:

1. **Add an ASP.NET** `Image` **control named** `Image1` **to your page.**

2. **In the page** `Load` **event, add the following code:**

```
Protected Sub Page_Load _
(ByVal sender As Object, _
ByVal e As System.EventArgs)
    Image1.Attributes.Add _
    ("onmouseover", _
    "src='http://www.gc.ca/images/francaisbt.gif'")
    Image1.Attributes.Add _
    ("onmouseout", _
    "src='http://www.gc.ca/images/englishbt.gif'")
End Sub
```

This code uses the `Add()` method of the `Image` control's `Attributes` collection to insert `onmouseover` and `onmouseout` event handlers. The `src` attribute points to the images on the Internet.

3. **Browse to the page and hover the mouse over the image and then out again.**

The graphic toggles between the English and Français versions.

When rendered in the browser, the inline JavaScript appears as follows:

```
<img id="Image1"
onmouseover="src='http://www.gc.ca/images/francaisbt.gif'"
onmouseout="src='http://www.gc.ca/images/englishbt.gif'"
src="http://www.gc.ca/images/englishbt.gif" />
```

You can use this technique for many events, depending on what the object supports. Some frequently used events include `onload`, `onsubmit`, `onselect`, `onchange`, `onfocus`, and `onblur`.

Client-Side Script and Validation Controls

ASP.NET's server-side validation controls always validate on the server. For example, if you set the `RangeValidator`'s `MaximumValue` property to 100 and `MinimumValue` property to 1, those values need to pass inspection when the page is submitted to the server. However, the validation controls also do client-side validation, using JavaScript, to improve performance.

If the browser supports JavaScript, the page renders some sophisticated client-side script that stops the values in the page from being sent back to the server until all the validation passes. For example, if you drop a `RangeValidator` control on a page, browse to it, and view the rendered output, you find blocks of script like this:

```
<script type="text/javascript">
<!--
var RangeValidator1 = document.all ?
  document.all["RangeValidator1"] :
  document.getElementById("RangeValidator1");
RangeValidator1.controltovalidate = "TextBox1";
RangeValidator1.focusOnError = "t";
RangeValidator1.errormessage =
  "Must be from 1 to 100!";
RangeValidator1.display = "Dynamic";
RangeValidator1.evaluationfunction =
  "RangeValidatorEvaluateIsValid";
RangeValidator1.maximumvalue = "100";
RangeValidator1.minimumvalue = "1";
// -->
</script>
```

The preceding script uses client-side properties and values that parallel those on the server-side validation. For example, notice the minimum and maximum values and error message text.

Client-side validation goes to work even before you click Submit to send the form to the server. In Figure 5-10, we typed 1001 in the text box and then hit the Tab key to move on. The client-side validation detects that change and displays the warning message dynamically.

Figure 5-10:
Dynamic
warning
script tells
you when
you
overstep
your
bounds.

The warning message in Figure 5-10 was in the page all along, but we can't see it until we enter bad data. The following markup hides the error message by setting the style to `display:none` as you see here:.

```
<span id="RangeValidator1" style="color:Red;display:none;">
Must be from 1 to 100!</span>
```

ASP.NET's client-side logic makes the error text visible by changing the style value programmatically.

How Auto-Postback Uses Client-Side Script

Although you call them ASP.NET *server* controls, a lot happens on the client side using JavaScript. `AutoPostback` uses client-side script a lot. The Auto Postback technique allows a client-side event — such as selecting a different item in a drop-down list — to trigger a postback to the server.

ASP.NET can process changes to the page only during a postback. This section looks at what ASP.NET does to make postbacks happen.

Our sample page for this section consists of one control, a server-side `CheckBox` control with the `AutoPostBack` property set to `true`. When you browse to the page, you see only the `CheckBox` control. You don't get a peek at the magic until you view the source code (View⇨Source) that ASP.NET has generated.

ASP.NET has added JavaScript to the `CheckBox` control on the client. As you can see in the following code, ASP.NET added the `onclick` attribute with the instruction to immediately evaluate (using `setTimeout()` with zero delay) a function called `__doPostBack()`:

```
<input id="CheckBox1" type="checkbox" name="CheckBox1"
onclick="javascript:setTimeout
('__doPostBack(\'CheckBox1\',\'\')', 0)" />
<label for="CheckBox1">AutoPostBack</label>
```

**Book III
Chapter 5**

**Using Client-Side
Script**

The `__doPostBack()` function (yes, the function name starts with two underscores) takes two arguments. The first is the name of the `CheckBox` control in single quotes (`'CheckBox1'`) and an empty string as two apostrophes. The backslashes (`\`) act as escape codes to tell JavaScript to treat these apostrophe characters as actual apostrophes.

You can find the `__doPostBack` function elsewhere in the rendered markup. As you can see in the code that follows, `eventTarget` is the name of the control that is triggering the postback, and `eventArgument` is additional data to go with it:

```
function __doPostBack(eventTarget, eventArgument) {
    if (!theForm.onsubmit ||
        (theForm.onsubmit() != false)) {
        theForm.__EVENTTARGET.value = eventTarget;
        theForm.__EVENTARGUMENT.value = eventArgument;
        theForm.submit();
    }
}
```

Our example has no additional data.

When the preceding code runs, it stores the value it receives in two hidden fields that ASP.NET generates within the page. Consistent with the convention of using two underscores at the beginning of the name, the input controls are called __EVENTTARGET and __EVENTARGUMENT. On the face of it, you'd say their value is empty. In reality, as the page runs, the script provides the name of the control and perhaps additional data. Here's how the hidden fields appear within the markup:

```
<input id="__EVENTTARGET" name="__EVENTTARGET"
    type="hidden" value="" />
<input id="__EVENTARGUMENT" name="__EVENTARGUMENT"
    type="hidden" value="" />
```

The last line of __doPostBack() calls the JavaScript submit() function. It programmatically simulates the click of a Submit button. Thanks to scripting, the event (onclick on the CheckBox control) becomes a full-fledged postback that includes the name and optional arguments of the control that caused the postback to happen.

You can determine the control that caused the postback by adding the following code into the Load event handler for the page:

```
Protected Sub Page_Load _
    (ByVal sender As Object, _
    ByVal e As System.EventArgs)
        If IsPostBack Then
            Response.Write("Postback by: " & _
                Request.Form("__EVENTTARGET") & "<br />")
        End If
End Sub
```

This code reads the value of the hidden __EVENTTARGET control and displays the name of the control that caused the postback, similar to Figure 5-11.

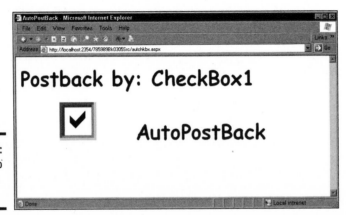

Figure 5-11:
Seeing who caused the postback.

Using Client-Side Callbacks

Imagine that you're in a restaurant and discover an egg spot on a fork. You ask the server to replace the fork with a clean one. Instead of just bringing one clean fork, the server clears the whole table. While you sit and wait, she replaces everything in sight—the tablecloth, candleholder, dishes, and cutlery. That's a lot of effort and wasted time when all you wanted was a clean fork! Given the possible delay, you'd think twice about asking for a coffee refill.

Surprisingly, most Web pages work in this inefficient manner. If you update a single value on the page from No to Yes, the browser wipes out everything in view. The Web server resends all of the page content including the background, images, and text.

Fortunately, an alternative technology lets you update a page without creating huge amounts of overhead. ASP.NET 2.0 supports *callbacks*. Using a callback, a specific part of the Web page, such as a radio button, communicates directly with the Web server by combining a sophisticated mix of client-side JavaScript and server-side requests. The control sends and receives updated data independently from the other controls on the page. Only the specific control changes, so there's no page refresh and a minimal delay. Client-side callbacks translate into snappy page performance that's well worth the programming effort.

Client-side callbacks are the basis for a new ASP.NET technology that goes by the code name *Atlas.* The goal of Atlas is to make Web applications act more like Windows forms programs, where displaying fresh data on the screen takes no time at all. At the time of publication, Atlas was still pre-release software, but complete enough to offer a Go Live license for use on production sites. Get the latest at `http://atlas.asp.net`.

The material that follows is quite advanced. Although you can make the sample work by following the steps, you may need a solid grasp of ASP.NET programming to get the most out of the rest of the chapter.

In the following sections, you find out how to build a page that uses a callback to create and display a hash value. A *hash value* is a small, unique representation of a piece of data. It ensures data integrity because the same input always returns the identical hash value. When you use the hash value properly for passwords, figuring out the value that went into creating the hash value is almost impossible.

This callback demonstration is broken into edible morsels in the following sections. If you're impatient and want to gobble down the source code in one swallow, jump to the section "Callback source code," later in this chapter.

Creating the Web page interface

In this section, you create the Web page that accepts the input value and displays the hash value that the server sends back. As you can see in Figure 5-12, you have a few labels, a text box, and a button.

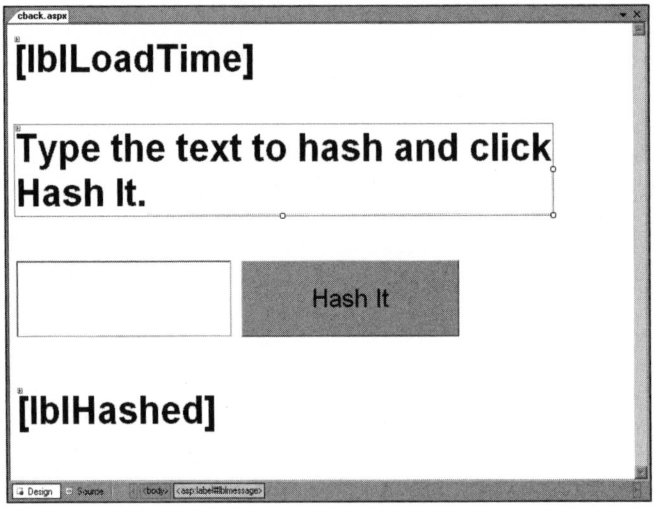

Figure 5-12:
A basic user interface for callbacks.

To create the Web page, follow these steps:

1. **Add an ASP.NET Web form called** cback.aspx **to your project by using VB and no separate code file.**

2. **Build the interface that Figure 5-12 shows by using the following markup:**

```
<asp:label id="lblLoadTime" runat="server">
</asp:label><br /><br />
<asp:label id="lblMessage" runat="server"
text="Type the text to hash and click Hash It.">
</asp:label><br /><br />
<input id="txtHash" name="txtHash" type="text"/> 
<button id="btnHash"
 onclick="HashText(document.forms[0].
  txtHash.value,'txthash')">
 Hash It
 </button>
<br /><br />
<asp:label id="lblHashed" runat="server">
</asp:label>
```

The exact name and case of the id attribute value is important here because you're implementing case-sensitive JavaScript functions.

To show that you have nothing up your sleeves during this callback magic act, you display the time in `lblLoadTime` each time the page loads. If the whole page refreshes, it updates the time. That flags any attempt to cheat by slipping a server postback into the deck.

The button (`btnHash`) starts the whole process by calling the JavaScript routine `HashText()` that you can add in the following section.

Preparing the JavaScript

A page that uses ASP.NET 2.0 callbacks has to include at least three client-side JavaScript functions to process the outgoing and incoming data. Your page uses four functions because it also implements error handling.

Here are the names of the functions and their roles:

✦ `HashText()`: Kicks off the process by calling `WebForm_DoCallback()` and passing arguments to it. You create the `HashText()` routine on the fly by using server-side code. You see the routine in the source code of the rendered page.

✦ `WebForm_DoCallback()`: ASP.NET generates this function for you based on parameters that your code provides. This function appears only in the rendered page.

✦ `ClientCallback()`: Receives and displays the result. In this section's example, `ClientCallback()` dynamically updates the text in a label with the string it receives. You put this function into the HTML as static script.

✦ `ClientErrorCallback()`: Displays an error message if something goes wrong. As with the `ClientCallback()` function, embed this static JavaScript in the page.

To put the script into the file, follow these steps:

1. **Open** `cback.aspx` **in Source view.**

2. **Add the following script markup just before the closing** `</head>` **tag:**

```
<script language="javascript"
    type="text/javascript">
function ClientCallback( result, context )
{
 document.all.lblHashed.innerHTML=result;
}
function ClientErrorCallback( err, context )
{
 document.all.lblHashed.innerHTML("Problem!: " & err);
}
</script>
```

**Book III
Chapter 5**

**Using Client-Side
Script**

That's all you need by way of static client-side code. You require additional client-side JavaScript to implement callbacks, but you can insert that script using server-side code.

Building the server-side algorithm

The callback sample that you can create in the preceding section takes a string value from the client and submits that value to a server-side function. You can find very elaborate server-side functions in a sophisticated application, generating huge amounts of data from a database and returning it as HTML or XML. However, to keep the demonstration simple, your function in this section (called `Make_Hash()`) creates a quick hash value and returns that string to the caller. To build the server-side hash, follow these steps:

1. **Open in** `cback.aspx` **in Source view.**

2. **Add the following function:**

```
Public Shared Function Make_Hash _
(ByVal strInval As String) As String
   Dim strHashed As String
   strHashed = FormsAuthentication. _
   HashPasswordForStoringInConfigFile(strInval, "SHA1")
   Return strHashed
End Function
```

The preceding code reads the text that it finds in `strInval` and creates a hash value by using a standard called the Secure Hash Algorithm-1 (SHA1).

Implementing ICallbackEventHandler

Talking about an interface like `ICallbackEventHandler` can get a bit technical — but don't worry, we keep it moving. The implementation of a .NET interface reminds me of this old joke:

At the end of the party, two guests ask the host if they can stay overnight rather than drive home. The host says he'd be pleased to have them stay in a spare room, "But you have to make your own bed."

"No problem," reply the grateful guests.

"Great," says the host. "Take these hammers and some nails. You can find the boards in the garage. Good night!"

What's the joke's connection with a .NET interface? At the core, an interface describes methods and properties that a object makes available — but it only does half the job, providing only the outline and not the full code. You can only use the interface if you declare and implement the members that the interface sets out for you. In other words, "Here are the names of some properties and methods you can use. Just write your own code for them, and you're done. Good night!"

To write your interface code, follow these steps:

1. In cback.aspx**, declare the interface using the** implements **directive.**

Because all of the implementation code is in the .aspx page rather than in a code-behind file, you can declare the implementation with a directive in the page. Put the following code after the @page directive:

```
<%@ implements
    interface="System.Web.UI.ICallbackEventHandler" %>
```

If you prefer the code-behind model put this code below the Partial Class line:

```
Implements System.Web.UI.ICallbackEventHandler
```

2. Declare a public variable to hold the returned value as you see below.

```
Public retVal As String
```

3. Implement the RaiseCallbackEvent() **subroutine.**

After you implement an interface, you have to implement the functions that go into it. The following subroutine does the trick:

```
Public Sub RaiseCallbackEvent _
  (ByVal eventArgs As String) _
   Implements ICallbackEventHandler.RaiseCallbackEvent
   Dim strInput As String = eventArgs
   retVal = Make_Hash(strInput)
End Sub
```

RaiseCallbackEvent() is a handler subroutine that takes a string as the parameter. In this implementation, the parameter is the string that you want to hash. You pass the string to the Make_Hash() function that you wrote previously in building the server-side algorithm. You get back the hashed value and store it in the variable retVal.

4. Implement the GetCallbackResult() **function, as the following code shows:**

```
Function GetCallbackResult() As String _
   Implements ICallbackEventHandler.GetCallbackResult
   Return retVal
End Function
```

This code doesn't do much more than pass along the value stored in the public variable `retVal`.

You don't need to do anything else to keep the implementation of the `ICallbackEventHandler` from complaining.

Generating the callback code

If you followed the steps starting back at "Using Client-Side Callbacks," you're in the home stretch in the callback project. Now you need to put ASP.NET to work by connecting the pieces. To complete the callback code, follow these steps:

1. **In the** `Load` **event of** `cback.aspx`, **add the following code to display the time that the page loaded:**

```
lblLoadTime.Text = "Page loaded at: " & _
Now.ToLongTimeString
```

2. **Generate a client-side function in server-side code to send the callback.**

This line uses the `GetCallbackEventReference()` method, as you can see in the following code:

```
Dim strCB As String = Page.ClientScript. _
  GetCallbackEventReference(Me, "arg", _
  "ClientCallback", _
  "ctx", "ClientErrorCallback", False)
```

The preceding code has a lot going on. This list breaks down the code, parameter by parameter:

- `Me`: The first parameter is a reference to the page (`Me` in Visual Basic, `this` in C#).

- `"arg"`: This string is the name of the variable that passes the value from the client-side part of the code to the server-side part.

- `"ClientCallback"`: The name of the client-side event handler that accepts the result of the server-side event. You can find out how to add this function in the section "Preparing the JavaScript," earlier in this chapter.

- `"ctx"`: The name of the client-side script that the client evaluates prior to starting the callback.

- `"ClientErrorCallback"`: The name of the client-side event handler that accepts an error message if the server can't be found, the data is too slow arriving, or there's some other calamity in the process.

- `False`: Indicates whether to do the callback synchronously or asynchronously. These steps do the callback asynchronously.

When you execute it, the preceding code returns a string containing a JavaScript function. Here's what you get back, stored in the variable `strCB`:

```
"WebForm_DoCallback('__Page',arg,ClientCallback,
ctx,ClientErrorCallback,false)"
```

3. **Build a client-side function that calls the** `WebForm_DoCallback()` **function.**

You can do this step by concatenating your own function and inserting in it the string that you create in Step 2:

```
Dim strJS As String = _
  "function HashText(arg, ctx)" & _
  Environment.NewLine & "{" & strCB & ";}"
```

If you set a breakpoint and look at `strJS` at runtime, it builds this JavaScript string:

```
function HashText(arg, ctx)
{
WebForm_DoCallback('__Page',arg,ClientCallback
,ctx,ClientErrorCallback,false);
}
```

4. **Use the** `RegisterClientScriptBlock()` **method to inject the string of JavaScript code into the page, including the** `<script>` **tags, as you can see in the following code:**

```
        Page.ClientScript.RegisterClientScriptBlock _
        (Me.GetType(), "HashText", strJS, True)
End Sub
```

Making the callback call

Building all of this client callback code takes a fair bit of effort, but after you install the plumbing into a page, adding more fixtures doesn't take as long. To give your new page a run, follow these steps:

1. **Browse to** `cback.aspx` **and note the time that it displays.**

2. **Type** `aarrgghh!` **in the text box.**

3. **Click the** `Hash It` **button.**

The page returns a hash value, as you can see in Figure 5-13.

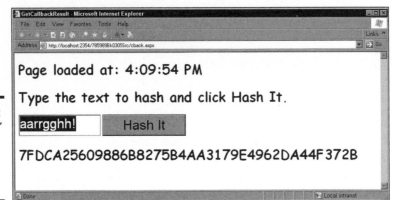

Figure 5-13: "aarrgghh!" looks very different in its hashed value.

If you type the exact text that appears in Step 2 (without the quotes — and letter case, spaces, and punctuation count!), you see the exact same hash code. That's how hash codes work. Anyone can verify that you type "aarrgghh!" simply by comparing its hash code.

4. **Check whether the time on the page changes after you click the button.**

   It doesn't, right? The time doesn't update because this interaction with the server is a callback, not a postback. The only part of the page that changes is the text of lblHashed.

The ASP.NET component industry is making a lot of developments around callbacks. The major vendors are using the technique in many innovative and attractive ASP.NET add-ons.

Callback source code

Listing 5-1 shows the complete VB source code for the callback demonstration that the preceding sections cover, without commentary or commercial interruption.

Listing 5-1:   Complete source code for callback implementation (VB)

```
<%@ page language="vb" %>
<%@ implements
    interface="System.Web.UI.ICallbackEventHandler" %>
<script runat="server">
    Public retVal As String
    Public Sub RaiseCallbackEvent _
      (ByVal eventArgs As String) _
```

```
        Implements ICallbackEventHandler.RaiseCallbackEvent
            Dim strInput As String = eventArgs
            retVal = Make_Hash(strInput)
        End Sub
        Function GetCallbackResult() As String _
          Implements ICallbackEventHandler.GetCallbackResult
            Return retVal
        End Function
        Public Sub Page_Load _
        (ByVal sender As Object, ByVal e As EventArgs)
            lblLoadTime.Text = "Page loaded at: " & _
            Now.ToLongTimeString
            Dim strCB As String = Page.ClientScript. _
             GetCallbackEventReference(Me, "arg", _
                "ClientCallback", _
              "ctx", "ClientErrorCallback", False)
            Dim strJS As String = _
             "function HashText(arg, ctx)" & _
             Environment.NewLine & "{" & strCB & ";}"
            Page.ClientScript.RegisterClientScriptBlock _
            (Me.GetType(), "HashText", strJS, True)
        End Sub
        Public Shared Function Make_Hash _
        (ByVal strInval As String) As String
            Dim strHashed As String
            strHashed = FormsAuthentication. _
            HashPasswordForStoringInConfigFile _
            (strInval, "SHA1")
            Return strHashed
        End Function
</script>
<html xmlns="http://www.w3.org/1999/xhtml">
<head id="Head1" runat="server">
    <title>GetCallbackResult</title>
<script language="javascript"
    type="text/javascript">
function ClientCallback( result, context )
{
    document.all.lblHashed.innerHTML=result;
}
function ClientErrorCallback( err, context )
{
    document.all.lblHashed.innerHTML("Problem!: " & err);
}
</script>
</head>
<body>
<form id="Form1" runat="server">
<asp:label id="lblLoadTime" runat="server">
</asp:label><br /><br />
```

Book III
Chapter 5

Using Client-Side
Script

(continued)

Listing 5-1 (continued)

```
<asp:label id="lblMessage" runat="server"
text="Type the text to hash and click Hash It.">
</asp:label><br /><br />
<input id="txtHash" name="txtHash" type="text"/> 
<button id="btnHash"
 onclick="HashText(document.forms[0].
  txtHash.value,'txthash')">
 Hash It
 </button>
<br /><br />
<asp:label id="lblHashed" runat="server">
</asp:label>
</form>
</body>
</html>
```

Book IV

C#

"We're here to clean the code."

Contents at a Glance

Chapter 1: C# Programming Basics

In This Chapter

✔ Examining keywords

✔ Inspecting statements

✔ Perusing blocks

✔ Reviewing comments

✔ Surveying classes

✔ Investigating variables

✔ Considering data types

✔ Observing operators

✔ Experiencing expressions

In this chapter, you find the basics of writing C# code. If you've been browsing around in the book, you've already seen plenty of C# code examples, so I won't start with a basic "Hello World!" program (the way most introductory C# programming books do). Instead, I'll dive right into the building blocks of C# programs, such as keywords, statements, blocks, and so on.

So jump in and hang on!

Dealing with Keywords

A *keyword* is a word that has special meaning defined by the C# programming language. In all, C# has 77 keywords. They're listed in alphabetical order in Table 1-1.

Like everything else in C#, keywords are case-sensitive. Thus, if you type `If` instead of `if` or `For` instead of `for`, the compiler complains about your error. Because *Visual Basic keywords begin with capital letters,* you may be prone to make this mistake frequently if you've programmed in Visual Basic.

Table 1-1		The C# Keywords	
abstract	event	new	struct
as	explicit	null	switch
base	extern	object	this
bool	false	operator	throw
break	finally	out	true
byte	fixed	override	try
case	float	params	typeof
catch	for	private	uint
char	foreach	protected	ulong
checked	goto	public	unchecked
class	if	readonly	unsafe
const	implicit	ref	ushort
continue	in	return	using
decimal	int	sbyte	virtual
default	interface	sealed	volatile
delegate	internal	short	void
do	is	sizeof	while
double	lock	stackalloc	
else	long	static	
enum	namespace	string	

Working with Statements

Like most programming languages, C# uses *statements* to build programs. A statement is a command that causes C# to do something, such as calculate an amount or perform a test. Unlike most programming languages, statements are not the fundamental unit of code in C#. Instead, that honor goes to the class. However, every class must have a body, and the body of a class is made up of one or more statements. In other words, you can't have a meaningful C# program without at least one statement. The following sections describe the ins and outs of working with C# statements.

Types of statements

C# has many different types of statements. Some statements simply create variables that you can use to store data. These types of statements are often called *declaration statements,* and tend to look like this:

```
int i;
string s = "This is a string";
decimal amount = 33.4m;
```

Another common type of statement is an *expression statement*, which performs calculations. Here are some examples of expression statements:

```
i = a + b;
salesTax = invoiceTotal * taxRate;
Response.Write("Hello, World!");
```

There are many other kinds of statements besides these two. For example,
`if-then` statements execute other statements only if a particular condition
has been met. And statements such as `for`, `while`, or `do` execute a group of
statements one or more times.

White space

In C#, the term *white space* refers to one or more consecutive space characters, tab characters, or line breaks. All white space is considered the same.
In other words, a single space is treated the same as a tab or line break or
any combination of spaces, tabs, or line breaks.

If you've programmed in Visual Basic, white space is different from what
you're used to. In Visual Basic, line breaks mark the end of statements unless
special continuation characters are used. In C#, you don't have to do anything
special to continue a statement onto a second line. Thus, the statement

```
x = (y + 5) / z;
```

is identical to this statement:

```
x =
(y + 5) / z;
```

In fact, you could write the above statement like this if you wanted:

```
x
=
(
y
+
5
)
/
z
;
```

I wouldn't advise it, but the statement would compile and execute properly.

Using white space liberally in your programs is a good idea. In particular, you should get into the habit of using line breaks to place each statement on a separate line and use tabs to line up elements that belong together. The compiler ignores the extra white space, so it doesn't affect your program's performance in any way. However, it does make the program's source code easier to read — and future troubleshooters happier.

Working with Blocks

A *block* is a group of one or more statements that's enclosed in braces. A block begins with an opening brace ({) and ends with a closing brace (}). Between the opening and closing brace, you can code one or more statements. For example, here's a block that consists of three statements:

```
{
    int i, j;
    i = 100;
    j = 200;
}
```

A block is itself a type of statement. As a result, any time the C# language requires a statement, you can substitute a block to execute more than one statement. For example, in Chapter 2 of this mini-book, you discover that the basic syntax of an `if` statement is this:

```
if ( expression ) statement
```

Here, the *statement* can be a single statement or a block.

You can code the braces that mark a block in two popular ways. One is to place both braces on separate lines, and then indent the statements that make up the block — as in this example:

```
if ( i > 0)
{
    string s = "The value of i is " + i;
    Response.Write(s);
}
```

The other style is to place the opening brace for the block on the same line as the statement the block is associated with, like this:

```
if ( i > 0) {
    string s = "The value of i is " + i;
    Response.Write(s);
}
```

Which style you use is a matter of personal preference. I prefer the first style (mostly because I once had a programming job where I got paid by the line).

Creating Identifiers

An *identifier* is a word that you make up to refer to a C# programming element by name. Although you can assign identifiers to many different types of C# elements, they're most commonly used for the following elements:

✦ **Classes**

✦ **Methods**

✦ **Variables**

✦ **Parameters**

You must follow a few simple rules when you create identifiers:

✦ **Identifiers are case-sensitive.** As a result, `SalesTax` and `salesTax` are distinct identifiers.

✦ **Identifiers can be made up of upper- or lowercase letters, numerals, underscore characters (_), and dollar signs ($).**

✦ **All identifiers must begin with a letter or an underscore.** Thus, `a15` is a valid identifier, but `13Unlucky` isn't because it begins with a numeral.

✦ **An identifier can't be the same as any of the C# keywords listed in Table 1-1.** Thus you can't create a variable named `for` or a class named `public`.

Crafting Comments

A *comment* is a bit of text that provides explanations of your code — for the human beings who may want them. The compiler ignores comments completely; you can place any text you want in a comment. Using plenty of comments in your programs to explain what they do and how they work is a good idea — and merciful to troubleshooters.

C# has two basic types of comments: *single-line* and *delimited.* I describe these styles of comments in the following sections.

Single-line comments

A *single-line comment* begins with the sequence `//` and ends at the end of the line. You can place this type of comment at the end of any line. Everything you type after the `//` is ignored by the compiler. Here's an example:

```
total = total * discountPercent; // calculate the discounted total
```

If you want, you can also place single-line comments on separate lines, like this:

```
// calculate the discounted total
total = total * discountPercent;
```

You can also place single-line comments in the middle of statements that span two or more lines, as in this example:

```
total = (total * discountPercent)   // apply the discount first
     + salesTax;                    // then add the sales tax
```

Delimited comments

A *delimited comment* can span multiple lines — so it begins with the sequence /* and ends with the sequence */ (as in this example):

```
/* Simple Calculator application.
   This program demonstrates a simple one-pageprogram
   Web application. */
```

A delimited comment can begin and end anywhere on a line. If you want, you can even sandwich a comment between other C# programming elements, like this:

```
x = (y + /* a strange place for a comment */ 5) / z;
```

Normally delimited comments appear on separate lines. One common use for these traditional comments is to place a block of comment lines at the beginning of a class to indicate information about the class — such as what the class does, who wrote it, and so on.

Introducing Object-Oriented Programming

After presenting some basic elements of the C# programming language, most C# books plunge into variables and data types — and though those are important topics, classes are really the heart of object-oriented programming. After all, C# is an inherently object-oriented programming language — so here's where I look at how classes play an important role in creating objects. (I get to variables and data types in the next chapter.)

Understanding classes and objects

Okay, quick briefing on some vital terms: A *class* is code that defines the behavior of a distinct C# programming element called an *object* — which has two essential characteristics:

✦ **State:** This is, in effect, what the object knows; it consists of any data that the object might be keeping track of.

✦ **Behaviors:** These are what the object does; they're represented in the class by one or more methods that can be called upon to perform actions.

The difference between a class and an object is similar to the difference between a blueprint and a house. A blueprint is a plan for a house; a house is an implementation of a blueprint. One set of blueprints can be used to build many houses. Likewise, a class is a plan for an object, and an object is — in C# terms — an *instance* of a class. You can use a single class to create more than one object.

When an object is created, C# sets aside an area of computer memory that's sufficient to hold all the data stored by the object. As a result, each instance of a class has its own data, independent of the data used by other instances of the same class.

Classes and objects are vital to ASP.NET applications for two basic reasons:

✦ **Every page — as well as every control on the page — is an object that's defined by a class.** When you write the code that handles events for an ASP.NET page, you're actually writing the code for the class that defines the page.

✦ **Most ASP.NET applications use one or more of the classes that are a part of the .NET Framework class library.** You have to know how to work with classes and objects to write even the simplest ASP.NET applications.

Coding a class

ASP.NET programming depends on understanding the basic form of a class, since every ASP.NET page is defined by a class. The ins and outs of coding your own custom classes show up later in this mini-book (in Chapters 5 and 6); for now, first things first: a quick look at what goes into coding a class.

Every ASP.NET page is represented by two C# source files that define a single class. The ASP.NET runtime generates the first of these files from the `.aspx` file. You never actually see this file, so you don't have to worry about it other than to realize that the markup in your .aspx file is automatically translated by ASP.NET into C# code.

The second file defines the part of the class that contains the methods called to respond to events — say, when a page loads or a user clicks a button. This file follows this general format:

```
using System;
using System.Data;
```

```
using System.Configuration;
using System.Web;
using System.Web.Security;
using System.Web.UI;
using System.Web.UI.WebControls;
using System.Web.UI.WebControls.WebParts;
using System.Web.UI.HtmlControls;
public partial class _Default : System.Web.UI.Page
{
    // methods that handle events go here
}
```

The thing to notice about this code is how the class itself is structured. The first nine statements are using statements that let your code access nine of the most commonly used groups of .NET Framework classes. Then, the next line — called the *class declaration* — marks the start of the class. The following list describes each of the elements on this line:

✦ public **indicates that the class is a public class, which means it can be accessed throughout the application.**

✦ partial **indicates that this is a partial class, which means that this code defines a part of the class.** The rest of the class is defined by the C# code generated from the .aspx file.

✦ class **indicates that a class is being defined.**

✦ _Default **provides the name of the class.** In most cases, the class name is the same as the name of the page. But Visual Studio adds an underscore to the class name for the Default.aspx page.

✦ System.Web.UI.Page **indicates that this class is based on a .NET Framework class called** System.Web.UI.Page **— that is, the** _Default **class *inherits* the** System.Web.UI.Page **class.** (For more about inheritance and why it's important, have a look at Chapter 6 of this mini-book.)

After the class declaration is the actual code that makes up the class. In C#, the class is defined by code that appears within a block marked by a set of curly braces {}. Everything between those braces is considered part of the class. The most common elements you'll see in this block are *method definitions,* which tell the program which methods to run when an event occurs. (For more about defining methods, refer to Chapter 4 of this mini-book.)

Creating an object from a class

In C#, you can create an object from a class in several ways. But the most straightforward happens in three stages:

1. **You create a variable that provides a name you can use to refer to the object.**

2. **You use the** `new` **keyword to create an instance of the class.**

3. **You assign the resulting object to the variable.** The general form of a statement that does that job looks like this:

```
ClassName variableName = new ClassName();
```

For example, to create an object instance of a class named `Class1` and assign it to a variable named `myClass1Object`, you would write a statement like this:

```
Class1 myClass1Object = new Class1();
```

Okay, but why list the class name twice? The first time, you're providing a *type* for the variable — saying that the variable you're creating here can be used to hold objects created from the `Class1` class. The second time, you're creating an object from the class. The `new` keyword tells C# to create an object; the class name identifies which class to use when creating the object.

The equals sign (=) is an *assignment operator*. It says to take the object created by the `new` keyword and assign it to the variable. Thus the statement given here actually does *three* things:

✦ **It creates a variable named** `myClass1Object` **that can be used to hold objects created from the** `Class1` **class.** At this point, no object has been created — just a variable that can be used to store objects.

✦ **It creates a new object in memory from the** `Class1` **class.**

✦ **It assigns this newly created object to the** `myClass1Object` **variable.** That way, you can use the `myClassObject` variable to refer to the object that was created.

Using .NET Framework Classes

You've probably noticed that the code-behind file for an ASP.NET Web page begins with a bunch of statements that look like this:

```
using System;
using System.Data;
using System.Configuration;
using System.Web;
using System.Web.Security;
using System.Web.UI;
using System.Web.UI.WebControls;
using System.Web.UI.WebControls.WebParts;
using System.Web.UI.HtmlControls;
```

These `using` statements are required to grant you access to the various collections of classes within the .NET Framework. For example, the first `using` statement lets you use general-purpose system classes; the second lets you use data-handling classes; the third lets you use configuration classes; and so on.

Strictly speaking, using statements are never required per se — but they can save you a lot of hassle. If you don't use using statements to access the classes your program uses, you must *fully qualify* the names of the classes when you use them — that is, list the complete class path in front of the class name. So, if your code didn't include the using System.Web statement, any reference to the Response class would have to be coded like this:

```
System.Web.Response.Write("This is some text.");
```

Declaring Variables

In C#, you must explicitly declare all variables before using them. This rule is in contrast to some languages — most notably Basic and Visual Basic — which let you use variables that haven't been automatically declared. So what's the big deal? Allowing you to use variables that you haven't explicitly declared might seem like a good idea at first glance. But it's a common source of bugs that result from misspelled variable names. C# requires that you explicitly declare variables so that if you misspell a variable name, the compiler can detect your mistake and display a compiler error.

The basic form of a variable declaration looks like this:

```
type name;
```

Here are some typical examples:

```
int x;
string lastName;
double radius;
```

In these examples, variables named x, lastName, and radius, are declared. The x variable holds integer values, the lastName variable holds string values, and the radius variable holds double values. For more information about what these types mean, see the section "Working with Built-in Data Types," later in this chapter. Until then, just keep in mind that int variables can hold whole numbers (such as 5, 1,340, and -34), double variables can hold numbers with fractional parts (such as 0.5, 99.97, or 3.1415), and string variables can hold text values (such as "Hello, World!" or "Jason P. Finch").

Notice that a variable declaration has to end with a semicolon. That's because the variable declaration is itself a type of statement.

Declaring two or more variables in one statement

You can declare two or more variables of the same type in a single state-ment, by separating the variable names with commas. Here's an example:

```
int x, y, z;
```

It declares three variables of type int, using the names x, y, and z.

As a rule, I suggest you avoid declaring multiple variables in a single state-ment. Your code is easier to read and maintain if you give each variable a separate declaration.

Declaring instance variables

An *instance variable* is a variable that any method in a class can access. When declaring a class variable, you must place the declaration within the body of the class, but not within any of the class methods.

The following program shows the proper way to declare and use an instance variable named CompanyName:

```
public partial class _Default : System.Web.UI.Page
{
    string CompanyName;
    protected void Page_Load(object sender, EventArgs e)
    {
        txtCompanyName.Text = CompanyName;
    }
}
```

You don't *have* to place class-variable declarations at the beginning of a class. Some programmers prefer to place them at the end of the class, as in this example:

```
public partial class _Default : System.Web.UI.Page
{
    protected void Page_Load(object sender, EventArgs e)
    {
        txtCompanyName.Text = CompanyName;
    }
    string CompanyName;
}
```

Here the class variable is declared *after* the class methods.

I think classes are easier to read if the variables are declared first, so that's where you seem them in this book.

Declaring local variables

A *local variable* is a variable declared within the body of a method. When that's done, you can use the variable only within that method. Other methods in the class aren't even aware that the variable exists.

Here's an example of a class with a local variable:

```
public partial class _Default : System.Web.UI.Page
{
    protected void Page_Load(object sender, EventArgs e)
    {
        string CompanyName;
        txtCompanyName.Text = CompanyName;
    }
}
```

Unlike instance variables, local variables are fussy about the placement of the declaration. In particular, you must place the declaration prior to the first statement that actually uses the variable. Thus the following code won't compile:

```
public partial class _Default : System.Web.UI.Page
{
    protected void Page_Load(object sender, EventArgs e)
    {
        txtCompanyName.Text = CompanyName;
        string CompanyName;
    }
}
```

When it gets to the first line of the `Page_Load` method, the compiler generates an error message complaining that it can't find the symbol `"CompanyName"`. That's because it hasn't yet been declared.

Although most local variables are declared near the beginning of a method's body, you can also declare local variables within smaller blocks of code marked by braces. This makes more sense when considered in terms of statements that use blocks, such as `if` and `for` statements (for more about those, refer to "Working with Blocks," earlier in this chapter). But here's an example:

```
if (taxRate > 0)
{
    decimal taxAmount;
    taxAmount = subTotal * taxRate;
    total = subTotal + total;
}
```

Here the variable `taxAmount` exists only within the set of braces that belongs to the `if` statement.

Initializing Variables

In C#, local variables are not given initial default values. The compiler checks to make sure that you have assigned a value before you use a local variable. For example, the following code won't compile:

```
int i;
Response.Write(i);
```

If you try to compile this code, you get an error message indicating that the variable i hasn't been assigned a value. To avoid such an error message, you must *initialize* local variables before you can use them. Initializing a variable sets an initial value for the variable. You can do that by using an assignment statement or an initializer, as I describe in the following sections.

Unlike local variables, instance variables are given default values. Numeric types are automatically initialized to zero; String variables are initialized to empty strings. As a result, you don't have to initialize a class variable or an instance variable (although you can if you want them to have an initial value other than the default).

Initializing variables with assignment statements

One way to initialize a variable is to code an *assignment statement* following the variable declaration. Assignment statements have this general form:

```
variable = expression;
```

Here, the *expression* can be any C# expression that yields a value of the same type as the variable. The following code correctly initializes the i variable before using it:

```
int i;
i = 0;
Response.Write(i);
```

In this example, the variable is initialized to a value of zero before the variable is written to the page. In this example, the 0 in the second line is called a *literal*. Literals provide hard-coded values in your program.

Initializing variables with initializers

C# also allows you to initialize a variable in the same statement that declares the variable. To do that, you use an *initializer,* a useful little piece of code that has the following general form:

```
type name = expression;
```

In effect, the initializer lets you combine a declaration and an assignment statement into one concise statement. Here are some examples:

```
int x = 0;
string lastName = "Lowe";
decimal price = 15.99m;
```

In each case, the variable is both declared and initialized in a single statement.

Working with Built-in Data Types

The term *data type* refers to the type of data that can be stored in a variable. C# is sometimes called a *strongly typed* language — not because you hit the keyboard hard, but because you must specify the variable's type when you declare the variable. Then the compiler ensures that you don't try to assign data of the wrong type to the variable. For example, the following code generates a compiler error:

```
int x;
x = 3.1415;
```

Because x is declared as a variable of type int (which holds whole numbers), you can't assign the value 3.1415 to it.

In C#, there are two basic kinds of data types: *value types* and *reference types*. A key difference between a value type and a reference type is what's in the memory location associated with the type. With a value type variable, it contains the actual value of the variable (which is why primitive types are sometimes called *value types*). By contrast, the memory location associated with a reference type variable contains an address (called a *pointer*) that indicates where the actual object is in memory.

It isn't quite true that reference types are defined by the .NET Framework and not by the C# language specification. A few reference types, such as Object and String, are defined by classes in the API (Application Programming Interface), but those classes are specified in the C# Language Specification. And a special type of variable called an *array* — which can hold multiple occurrences of variables, whether they're value or reference types — is itself considered a reference type.

C# defines a total of 13 value types — they're called *built-in value types* because they are built into the language. For your reference, Table 1-2 lists them. Of the 13 value types, 11 are for numbers, 1 is for characters, and 1 is for true/false values. Of the 11 number types, 8 are types of integers, 2 are types of floating-point numbers, and 1 is the decimal type. I describe each of the value types in the following sections.

Table 1-2	C#'s Built-in Value Types
Type	*Explanation*
int	A 32-bit (4-byte) signed integer value
uint	A 32-bit (4-byte) unsigned integer value
short	A 16-bit (2-byte) signed integer value
ushort	A 16-bit (2-byte) unsigned integer value
long	A 64-bit (8-byte) signed integer value
ulong	A 64-bit (8-byte) unsigned integer value
byte	An 8-bit (1-byte) unsigned integer value
sbyte	An 8-bit (1-byte) signed integer value
float	A 32-bit (4-byte) floating-point value
double	A 64-bit (8-byte) floating-point value
decimal	A 128-bit (16-byte) decimal value
char	A 16-bit character using the Unicode encoding scheme
boolean	A true or false value

A *bit* is a single binary digit which can have a value or either 0 or 1. A *byte* is a collection of eight bits.

Integer (int) types

An *integer* is a whole number — that is, a number with no fractional or decimal portion. C# has eight different integer types, which you can use to store numbers of varying sizes. The integer types come in pairs — one signed, the other unsigned. For example, the int type is a signed type, meaning it can represent negative as well as positive numbers. It can hold values roughly between negative 2.15 billion and positive 2.15 billion. However, its counterpart uint is unsigned, so it doesn't distinguish between negative and positive. It can hold values between 0 and just under 4.4 billion.

If you're writing the application that counts how many hamburgers McDonald's has sold, an int variable might not be big enough. In that case, you can use a long integer instead. Long is a 64-bit integer that can hold numbers ranging from about negative 9,000 trillion to positive 9,000 trillion. (That's a big number, even by Federal Deficit standards.)

In some cases, you may not need integers as large as the standard int type provides. For those cases, C# provides smaller integer types. The short type represents a two-byte integer, which can hold numbers from –32,768 to +32,767. And the byte type defines an 8-bit integer that can range from –128 to +127.

C# allows you to *promote* an integer type to a larger integer type. For example, C# allows the following:

```
int xInt;
long yLong;
xInt = 32;
yLong = xInt;
```

Here you can assign the value of the `xInt` variable to the `yLong` variable because `yLong` is larger than `xInt`. However, C# does not allow the converse, which would look like this (and fail to compile):

```
int xInt;
long yLong;
yLong = 32;
xInt = yLong;
```

The value of the `yLong` variable cannot be assigned to the `xInt` because `xInt` is smaller than `yLong`. Because such an assignment might result in a loss of data, C# doesn't allow it.

Floating-point types

Floating-point numbers are numbers that have fractional parts. Floating-point types can represent numbers with decimals, such as 19.95 or 3.1415.

C# has two primitive types for floating-point numbers: `float`, which uses four bytes, and `double`, which uses eight bytes. In almost all cases, you should use the `double` type whenever you need numbers with fractional values.

The *precision* of a floating-point value indicates how many significant digits the value can have. The precision of a `float` type is only about 6 or 7 decimal digits, which isn't sufficient for most types of calculations. In contrast, `double` variables have a precision of about 15 decimal digits, which is enough for most purposes.

Floating-point numbers actually use *exponential notation* (also called *scientific notation*) to store their values. In effect, a floating-point number actually records *two* numbers: a *base value* (also called the *mantissa*) and an *exponent* (that little superscript number). You calculate the actual value of the floating-point number by multiplying the mantissa by two raised to the power that the exponent indicates. For `float` types, the exponent can be from –127 to +128. For `double` types, the exponent can be from –1023 to +1024. Thus, both `float` and `double` variables are capable of representing very large and very small numbers.

When you use a floating-point literal, you should always include a decimal point, like this:

```
double period = 99.0;
```

If you omit the decimal point, the C# compiler treats the literal as an integer. Then, when it sees that you're trying to assign the literal to a `double` variable, it generates a compiler error message.

You can add an F or D suffix to a floating-point literal to indicate whether the literal itself is of type `float` or `double`. For example:

```
float value1 = 199.33F;
double value2 = 200495.995D;
```

If you omit the suffix, D is assumed. As a result, you can usually omit the D suffix for `double` literals. But you must always use an F suffix when assigning a value to a float variable.

The decimal type

Because of their limited precision, floating-point types are not really appropriate for representing currency amounts in business applications. Instead, these types of applications should use the `decimal` data type, which is designed to accurately store decimal data. The `decimal` type uses 128 bits for each number and can accurately store decimal numbers with as many as 28 digits.

One oddity of the decimal type is that if you want to use a decimal number as a literal value, you must follow the value with the letter m, as in this example:

```
decimal taxRate = 0.075m;
decimal price = 19.99m;
```

If you omit the m suffix, the C# compiler will assume the literal is a double, not a decimal.

The char type

The `char` type represents a single character from the Unicode character set. It is important to keep in mind that a character is not the same as a string. You find out about strings later in this chapter, in the section "Working with Strings." For now, just realize that a `char` variable can store just *one* character, not a sequence of characters (as a string can).

To assign a value to a `char` variable, you use a *character literal,* which is always enclosed in apostrophes rather than quotes. Here's an example:

```
char code = 'X';
```

Here the character X is assigned to the variable named `code`.

The following statement won't compile:

```
char code = "X";   // error -- should use apostrophes, not quotes
```

That's because quotation marks are used to mark strings, not character constants.

Unicode is a two-byte character code that can represent the characters used in most languages throughout the world. Currently, about 35,000 codes in the Unicode character set are defined. That leaves another 29,000 codes unused. The first 256 characters in the Unicode character set are the same as the characters of the *ASCII character set,* the most commonly used character set for computers that work with Western languages.

For more information about the Unicode character set, see the official Unicode Web site at `www.unicode.org`.

The boolean type

A `boolean` type can have one of two values: `true` or `false`. Booleans are used to perform logical operations, most commonly to determine whether some condition is true. For example:

```
boolean enrolled = true;
boolean credited = false;
```

Here a variable named `enrolled` of type `boolean` is declared and initialized to a value of `true`, and another `boolean` named `credited` is declared and initialized to `false`.

Working with Strings

A *string* is a sequence of text characters (whether numerals, operators, or letters). In C#, strings are an interesting breed. C# doesn't define strings as a primitive type. Instead, strings are a *reference type*. That means that strings are defined by a class named `string`, and a string variable doesn't contain the actual value of the string, but instead contains a pointer to the memory location where the string's value is stored. The following sections present the bare essentials of working with strings so you can incorporate simple strings in your programs.

Declaring and initializing strings

Strings are declared and initialized much like primitive types. The following statements define and initialize a string variable:

```
string s;
s = "Hello, World!";
```

Here, a variable named s of type `string` is declared and initialized with the *string literal* `"Hello, World!"` Notice that string literals are enclosed in quotation marks, not apostrophes. Apostrophes are used for character literals (mentioned earlier), which are different from string literals.

Like any variable declaration, a string declaration can include an initializer. Thus you can declare and initialize a string variable in one statement, like this:

```
string s = "Hello, World!";
```

Class variables and instance variables are automatically initialized to empty strings — but local variables aren't. To initialize a local string variable to an empty string, use a statement like this:

```
string s = "";
```

Combining strings

Combine two strings by using the plus sign (+) as a *concatenation operator*. (In C#-speak, combining strings is called *concatenation*.) For example, the following statement combines the value of two string variables to create a third string:

```
string hello = "Hello, ";
string world = "World!";
string greeting = hello + world;
```

The final value of the greeting variable is `"Hello, World!"`

When C# concatenates strings, it doesn't insert any blank spaces between strings. As a result, if you want to combine two strings *and* want a space to appear between them, make sure that the first string ends with a space or the second string *begins* with a space. (In the previous example, the first string ends with a space.)

Alternatively, you can concatenate a string literal along with the string variables. For example:

```
string hello = "Hello";
string world = "World!";
string greeting = hello + ", " + world;
```

Here the comma and the space that appear between the words `Hello` and `World` are inserted as a string literal.

Note that when you use a primitive type in a concatenation, C# automatically converts the value to a string. Thus the following is allowed:

```
string s = "There are " + i + " items in your basket.";
```

Converting strings to primitives

Converting a primitive value to a string value is pretty easy. Going the other way — converting a string value to a primitive — is a little more complex because it doesn't always work. If a string contains the value 10 (for example), you can easily convert it to an integer. But if the string contains the string `thirty-two`, you can't.

Fortunately, the .NET Framework contains a class that corresponds to each data type, and this class provides a Parse method that converts a string value to the correct type. Table 1-3 lists these classes. For example, to convert a string value to an integer, you use statements like this:

```
string s = "10";
int x = Int32.Parse(s);
```

Note that if the string does not contain a valid representation of the desired type, an error will occur. You can avoid this error by using the `TryParse` method instead of the `Parse` method. This method accepts two parameters. The first contains the string to be parsed, and the second is a value parameter that receives the resulting value if the string is valid. The `TryParse` method itself returns a `boolean` that indicates whether or not the string could be parsed.

Here's an example:

```
string s = "10";
int x, y;
if (Int32.TryParse(s, x))
    y = x;   // The string contains a valid integer
else
    y = 0;   // The string does not contain a valid integer
```

Table 1-3		Methods that Convert Strings to Numeric Primitive Types	
Type	*Class*	*Parse Method*	*TryParse Method*
Int	Int32	Parse(String)	TryParse(String, Int32)
Short	Int16	Parse(String)	TryParse(String, Int16)

Type	Class	Parse Method	TryParse Method
Long	Int64	`Parse(String)`	`TryParse(String, Int64)`
Byte	Byte	`Parse(String)`	`TryParse(String, Byte)`
Float	Single	`Parse(String)`	`TryParse(String, Single)`
Double	Double	`Parse(String)`	`TryParse(String, Double)`
Decimal	Decimal	`Parse(String)`	`TryParse(String, Decimal)`

Working with Arithmetic Operators

An *arithmetic operator* is a special symbol or keyword used to designate a mathematical operation performed on one or more values (called *operands*). Arithmetic operators perform basic arithmetic operations, such as addition, subtraction, multiplication, and division. In all, there are 7 arithmetic operators. Table 1-4 summarizes them.

Table 1-4	C#'s Arithmetic Operators
Operator	**Description**
+	Addition
–	Subtraction
*	Multiplication
/	Division
%	Remainder
++	Increment (adding 1 to a variable)
--	Decrement (subtracting 1 from a variable)

The following section of code can help clarify how these operators work for `int` types:

```
int a = 21, b = 6;
int c = a + b;      // c is 27
int d = a - b;      // d is 15
int e = a * b;      // e is 126
int f = a / b;      // f is 3   (21 / 6 is 3 remainder 3)
int g = a % b;      // g is 3   (20 / 6 is 3 remainder 3)
a++;                // a is now 22
b--;                // b is now 5
```

Notice that for division, the result is truncated. Thus, `21 / 6` returns `3`, not `3.5`. For more information about integer division, see the section "Dividing Integers," later in this chapter.

**Book IV
Chapter 1**

**C# Programming
Basics**

Here's how the operators work for `double` values:

```
double x = 5.5, y = 2.0;
double m = x + y;          // m is 7.5
double n = x - y;          // n is 3.5
double o = x * y;          // o is 11.0
double p = x / y;          // p is 2.75
double q = x % y;          // q is 1.5
x++;                       // x is now 6.5
y--;                       // y is now 1.0
```

Note that you'd get the same results if you used `decimal` types instead of `double` types.

When you divide two `int` values, the result is an integer value, even if you assign it to a `double` variable. Here's an example:

```
int a = 21, b = 6;
double answer = a / b;    // answer = 3.0
```

If that's not what you want, you can cast one of the operands to a `double` before performing the division, like this:

```
int a = 21, b = 6;
double answer = (double)a / b;    // answer = 3.5
```

The moral of the story is that if you want to divide `int` values and get an accurate `double` or `decimal` result, you must cast at least one of the `int` values to a `double` or `decimal`.

Here are a few additional things to think about tonight as you lay awake pondering the wonder of the C# arithmetic operators:

✦ **In algebra, you can write a number right next to a variable to imply multiplication.** For example, *4x* means "four times x." Not so in C#. The following statements do not compile:

```
int x;
y = 4x;    // error, won't compile
```

✦ **The remainder operator (%) is also called a *modulus* operator.** It returns the remainder when the first operand is divided by the second operand. The remainder operator is often used to determine whether one number is evenly divisible by another, in which case the result is 0. For more information, see the section "Dividing Integers," later in this chapter.

✦ All operators, including the arithmetic variety, are treated as separators in C#. As a result, any use of white space in an expression is optional. Thus, the following two statements are equivalent:

```
a = ( (x + 4) * 7 ) / (y * x);
a=((x+4)*7)/(y*x);
```

Just remember that a little bit of white space never hurt anyone, and sometimes it helps make your C# code a little more readable.

Dividing Integers

When you divide one integer into another, the result is always another integer. Any remainder is simply discarded, and the answer is *not* rounded up. For example, 5 / 4 gives the result 1, and 3 / 4 gives the result 0. If you want to know that 5 / 4 is actually 1.25 or that 3 / 4 is actually 0.75, you need to use floating-point values, doubles, or decimals instead of integers.

Categorizing operators by the number of operands

A common way to categorize operators is by the number of operands the operator works on. Categorizing the operators in this way, there are three types:

✔ **Unary operators:** Operators that work on just one operand. Examples of unary operators are negation (−x, which returns the negative of x) and increment (x++, which adds 1 to x).

A unary operator can be a prefix operator or a postfix operator. A *prefix operator* is written before the operand, like this:

```
operator operand
```

A *postfix operator* is written after the operand:

```
operand operator
```

✔ **Binary operators:** Operators that work on two operands. Examples of binary operators are addition (x + y), multiplication (invoiceTotal * taxRate), and comparison operators (x < leftEdge). In C#, all binary operators are *infix operators*, which means they appear between the operands, like this:

```
operand1 operator operand2
```

✔ **Ternary operators:** Operators that work on three operands. C# has only one ternary operator, called the *conditional operator* (? :). As with the binary operators, the conditional operator is also infix, appearing between operands:

```
operand1 ? operand2 : operand3
```

If you need to know what the remainder is when you divide two integers, use the remainder operator (%). For example, suppose you have a certain number of marbles to give away and a certain number of children to give them to. Here's a code snippet to show how you might calculate how many marbles to give to each child, and how many marbles you'll have left over:

```
int numberOfMarbles = 38;
int numberOfChildren = 4;
int marblesPerChild;
int marblesLeftOver;
marblesPerChild = numberOfMarbles / numberOfChildren;
marblesLeftOver = numberOfMarbles % numberOfChildren;
```

After this code runs, `marblesPerChild` will be 9 and `marblesLeftOver` will be 2.

It's probably obvious if you think about it, but you should realize that if you use integer division to divide a by b, then the result times b plus the remainder equals a. Here's what that looks like in code:

```
int a = 29;          // any value will do
int b = 3;           // any value will do
int c = a / b;
int d = a % b;
int e = (c * b) + d; // e will always equal a
```

Combining Operators

You can combine operators to form complicated expressions. When you do, the operations are carried out in a specific order, determined by the *precedence* of each operator in the expression. Here's the order of precedence for applying the arithmetic operators, from first to last:

1. **Increment (++) and decrement (--) operators are evaluated.**

2. **Sign operators (+ or -) are applied.**

3. **Multiplication (*), division (/), and remainder (%) operators are evaluated.**

4. **Addition (+) and subtraction (-) operators are applied.**

For example, in the expression a + b * c, multiplication has a higher precedence than addition. Thus, b is multiplied by c first. Then, the result of that multiplication is added to a.

If an expression includes two or more operators at the same order of precedence, the operators are evaluated from left to right. Thus, in the expression a * b / c, a is first multiplied by b, and then the result is divided by c.

If you want, you can use parentheses to change the order in which operations are performed. *Operations within parentheses are always performed before operations that aren't in parentheses.* Thus, in the expression `(a + b) * c`, a is added to b first. Then the result is multiplied by c.

If an expression has two or more sets of parentheses, the operations in the innermost set are performed first. For example, in the expression `(a * (b + c)) / d`, b is first added to c. Then the result is multiplied by a. And finally, that result is divided by d.

Apart from the increment and decrement operators, these precedence rules and the use of parentheses are the same as they are for basic algebra. So if you were paying attention in eighth grade, precedence should make sense.

With `decimal`, `double`, or `float` values, changing the left-to-right order for operators with the same precedence doesn't affect the result. However, with integer types, it can make a huge difference if division is involved. For example, consider these statements:

```
int a = 5, b = 6, c = 7;
int d1 = a * b / c;      // d1 is 4
int d2 = a * (b / c);    // d2 is 0
```

This difference occurs because integer division always returns an integer result — which is a truncated version of the actual result. Thus, in the first expression, a is first multiplied by b, giving a result of 30. Then, this result is divided by c. Truncating the answer gives a result of 4. But in the second expression, b is first divided by c — which gives a truncated result of 0. Then this result is multiplied by a, giving a final answer of 0.

Using the Unary Plus and Minus Operators

The plus and minus unary operators let you change the sign of an operand. *Note:* The actual operator used for these operations is the same as the binary addition and subtraction operators. The compiler figures out whether you mean to use the binary or the unary version of these operators by examining the expression.

The unary minus operator doesn't necessarily force an operand to have a negative value. Instead, it changes whatever sign the operand has to start with. Thus, if the operand starts with a positive value, the unary minus operator changes the sign to negative; if the operand starts with a negative value, the unary minus operator makes it positive. The following examples illustrate this point:

```
int a = 5;      // a is 5
int b = -a;     // b is -5
int c = -b;     // c is +5
```

You can also use these operators with more complex expressions, like this:

```
int a = 3, b = 4, c = 5;
int d = a * -(b + c);    // d is -27
```

Here, b is added to c, giving a result of 9. Then the unary minus operator is applied, giving a result of -9. Finally, -9 is multiplied by a and you get a result of -27.

Using Increment and Decrement Operators

One of the most common operations in computer programming is adding or subtracting 1 from a variable. Adding 1 to a variable is called *incrementing* the variable. Subtracting 1 is called *decrementing*. One way to increment a variable is like this:

```
a = a + 1;
```

Here the expression a + 1 is calculated and the result is assigned to the variable a.

C# provides an easier way to do this type of calculation: the increment (++) and decrement (--) operators. These are unary operators that apply to a single variable. Thus, to increment a variable a, you can code just this:

```
a++;
```

Note that an expression that uses an increment or decrement operator is a statement by itself. That's because the increment or decrement operator is also a type of assignment operator; it changes the value of the variable it applies to. That makes placement of the operator crucial — and tricky.

The increment and decrement operators are unusual because they're unary operators that you can place either before *(prefix)* or after *(postfix)* the variable they apply to. Whether you place the operator before or after the variable can have a major effect on how an expression is evaluated.

✦ **If you place an increment or decrement operator before its variable, the operator is applied *before* the rest of the expression is evaluated.** As a result, the incremented value of the variable is used in the expression.

✦ **If you place the operator after its variable, the operator is applied *after* the expression is evaluated.** The original value of the variable is used in the expression.

Confused yet? A simple example can clear it up. First, consider these statements with an expression that uses a postfix increment:

```
int a = 5;
int b = 3;
int c = a * b++;    // c is set to 15
```

When the expression in the third statement is evaluated, the original value of b — 3 — is used in the multiplication. Thus c is set to 15. Then b is incremented to 4.

Now consider this version, with a prefix increment:

```
int a = 5;
int b = 3;
int c = a * ++b;    // c is set to 20
```

This time b is incremented before the multiplication is performed, so c is set to 20. Either way, b ends up set to 4.

Because the increment and decrement operators can be confusing when used with other operators in an expression, I suggest you use them on their own lines. Whenever you're tempted to incorporate an increment or decrement operator into a larger expression, well, don't. Instead, pull the increment or decrement out of the expression and make it a separate statement, putting it either before or after the expression. In other words, code this:

```
b++;
c = a * b;
```

instead of this:

```
c = a * ++b;
```

In the first version, it's crystal clear that b is incremented before the multiplication is done. The second version presumes that whoever reads your code a year from now understands the subtle nuances of prefix-versus-postfix operators.

Using the Assignment Operator

The standard assignment operator — the equal sign (=) — is used to assign the result of an expression to a variable. In its simplest form, you code it like this:

```
variable = expression;
```

Here's a typical example:

```
int a = (b * c) / 4;
```

You've already seen plenty of examples of assignment statements like this one, so I won't belabor that point any further. However, I do want to point out — just for the record — that you *cannot* code an arithmetic expression on the left side of an equal sign. Thus the following statements do not compile:

```
int a;
a + 3 = (b * c);
```

In the rest of this section, I point out some unusual ways in which you can use the assignment operator. *I don't actually recommend that you use any of these techniques,* as they are rarely necessary and almost always confusing. However, knowing about them can shed light on how C# expressions work, help you spot shortcuts that other programmers may have taken, and can sometimes help you find sneaky problems in your code.

The key to understanding the rest of this section is realizing that in C#, assignments are expressions, not statements. In other words, a = 5 is an assignment expression, not an assignment statement — yet. It becomes an assignment statement only when you add a semicolon to the end.

The result of an assignment expression is the value that's assigned to the variable. For example, the result of the expression a = 5 is 5. Likewise, the result of the expression a = (b + c) * d is the result of the expression (b + c) * d.

The implication is that you can use assignment expressions in the middle of other expressions. For example, the following is legal:

```
int a;
int b;
a = (b = 3) * 2;    // a is 6, b is 3
```

As in any expression, the part of the expression inside the parentheses is evaluated first — thus b is assigned the value 3. Then the multiplication is performed, and the result (6) is assigned to the variable a.

Now consider a more complicated case:

```
int a;
int b = 2;
a = (b = 3) * b;    // a is 9, b is 3
```

Here the expression in the parentheses is evaluated first — which means b is set to 3 before the multiplication is performed.

The parentheses are important in the previous example; without them, the assignment operator is the last operator to be evaluated in the C# order of precedence. Watch what happens without the parentheses:

```
int a;
int b = 2;
a = b = 3 * b;   // a is 6, b is 6
```

This time the multiplication 3 * b is performed first, giving a result of 6. Then this result is assigned to b. Finally, the result of that assignment expression (6) is assigned to a.

Incidentally, the following expression is also legal:

```
a = b = c = 3;
```

This expression assigns the value 3 to all three variables.

Using Compound Assignment Operators

A *compound assignment operator* is an operator that performs a calculation and an assignment at the same time. In C#, all binary arithmetic operators (that is, the ones that work on two operands) have compound assignment operators that are equivalent. Table 1-5 lists them.

Table 1-5	Compound Arithmetic Operators
Operator	**Description**
+=	Addition and assignment
-=	Subtraction and assignment
*=	Multiplication and assignment
/=	Division and assignment
%=	Remainder and assignment

For example, this statement

```
a += 10;
```

is equivalent to

```
a = a + 10;
```

And this statement

```
z *=2;
```

is equivalent to

```
z = z * 2;
```

To avoid confusion, compound assignment expressions are best used by themselves, not in combination with other expressions. For example, consider these statements:

```
int a = 2;
int b = 3;
a *= b + 1;
```

Is a set to 7 or 8? In other words, is the third statement equivalent to

```
a = a * b + 1;      // This would give 7 as the result
```

or

```
a = a * (b + 1);    // This would give 8 as the result
```

At first glance, you might expect the answer to be 7 because multiplication has a higher precedence than addition. But assignment has the lowest precedence of all — and here the multiplication is performed *as part of the assignment*. As a result, the addition is performed before the multiplication — and the answer is 8. (Gotcha!)

In this chapter, you've learned the basics of creating C# statements, using variables, and creating expressions. In the next chapter, you'll learn how to use *conditional statements*, which let you test for certain conditions such as whether a user entered a value or how one variable's value compares with another variable's value.

Chapter 2: Doing Things Conditionally in C#

In This Chapter

✔ Telling true from false with boolean expressions

✔ Keeping your options open with if expressions

✔ Operating logically with (you guessed it) logical operators

✔ Knowing when to pull the (logical) switch

So far in this book, all the programs have run straight through from start to finish, without making any decisions along the way. In this chapter, you discover two C# statements that let you create some variety in your programs. The `if` statement lets you execute a statement or a block of statements only if some conditional test turns out to be true. And the `switch` statement lets you execute one of several blocks of statements, depending on the value of variable.

These statements rely heavily on the use of *boolean expressions* — expressions that yield a simple `true` or `false` result. Because you can't do even the simplest `if` statement without a boolean expression, this chapter begins by showing you how to code simple boolean expressions that test the value of a variable. Later, after looking at the details of how the `if` statement works, I revisit boolean expressions and show how to combine them to make complicated logical decisions. Then I get to the `switch` statement.

You're going to have to put on your thinking cap for much of this chapter — most of it plays with logical puzzles. Find yourself a comfortable chair in a quiet part of the house, turn off the TV, and pour yourself a cup of coffee.

All code listings used in this book are available for download at `www.dummies.com/go/aspnetaiofd`.

Using Simple boolean Expressions

Most of the statements presented in this chapter use boolean expressions to determine whether to execute or skip a statement (or a block of statements). A *boolean expression* is a C# expression that, when evaluated, returns a boolean value — either `true` or `false`.

As explained later in this chapter, boolean expressions can be very complicated (though for very logical reasons). Most of the time, however, you use simple expressions that compare the value of one variable with the value of some other value — a variable, a literal, or a simple arithmetic expression. This comparison uses one of the *relational operators* listed in Table 2-1. All these operators are *binary operators,* which means they work on two operands.

Table 2-1		Relational Operators
Operator	*Name*	*Description*
==	Equal	Returns `true` if the expression on the left evaluates to the same value as the expression on the `right`.
!=	Not Equal	Returns `true` if the expression on the left does not evaluate to the same value as the expression on the `right`.
<	Less Than	Returns `true` if the expression on the left evaluates to a value that is less than the value of the expression on the right.
<=	Less Than or Equal	Returns `true` if the expression on the left evaluates to a value that is less than or equal to the expression on the right.
>	Greater Than	Returns `true` if the expression on the left evaluates to a value that is greater than the value of the expression on the right.
>=	Greater Than or Equal	Returns `true` if the expression on the left evaluates to a value that is greater than or equal to the expression on the right.

A basic boolean expression has this form:

```
expression relational-operator expression
```

C# evaluates a boolean expression by first evaluating the expression on the left, then evaluating the expression on the right, and finally applying the relational operator to determine whether the entire expression evaluates to `true` or `false`.

Here are some simple examples of relational expressions. For each example, assume that the following statements were used to declare and initialize the variables:

```
int i = 5;
int j = 10;
```

Okay. Here are the sample expressions, along with their results (which are based on the values supplied):

Expression	Value	Explanation
i == 5	true	The value of i is 5.
i == 10	false	The value of i is not 10.
i == j	false	i is 5 and j is 10, so they are not equal.
i == j - 5	true	i is 5 and j - 5 is 5.
i > 1	true	i is 5, which is greater than 1.
j == i * 2	true	j is 10 and i is 5, so i * 2 is also 10.

Note that the relational operator that tests for equality is easy to spot: It's two equal signs in a row (==). A single equal sign is the *assignment operator.* When you're first learning C#, it's easy to goof and type the assignment operator when you mean the equals operator, getting a statement that looks like this:

```
if (i = 5)
```

C# won't let you get away with this; you'd have to correct that mistake and recompile the program. At first, doing so seems like a nuisance. The more you work with C#, the more you realize that it really *is* a nuisance, but one you can get used to.

If you're familiar with Java, you might be pleased to know that you can use the good ol' == operator to compare string values. For example, the following is acceptable in C#:

```
string s1 = "John"
string s2 = "John"
if (s1 == s2)
    Response.Write("s1 is equal to s2");
```

Using if Statements

The if statement is one of the most important statements in any programming language, and C# is no exception. The following sections describe the ins and outs of using the various forms of the powerful C# if statement.

Simple if statements

In its most basic form, an if statement lets you execute a single statement (or block of statements) only if a boolean expression evaluates to true. In its most basic form, the if statement looks like this:

```
if (boolean-expression)
    statement
```

Note that the boolean expression comes with a few requirements:

✦ **The statement must be enclosed in parentheses.**

✦ **If only a single statement is used, it must end with a semicolon.**

✦ **The statement can also be a statement block enclosed by braces.** In that case, each statement within the block needs a semicolon, but the block itself doesn't.

Here's an example of a typical `if` statement:

```
decimal commissionRate = 0.0m;
if (salesTotal > 10000.0m)
    commissionRate = 0.05m;
```

In this example, a variable named `commissionRate` is initialized to `0.0`, and then set to `0.05` if `salesTotal` is greater than $10,000 (but don't use a dollar sign or a comma when you specify that value in your code).

Indenting the statement under the `if` statement is customary to make the structure of your code more obvious. It isn't necessary, but always a good idea.

Some programmers find it helpful to visualize the operation of an `if` statement in a flowchart, as shown in Figure 2-1. In this flowchart, the diamond symbol represents the condition test. If the sales total is greater than 10,000, the statement in the rectangle is executed. If not, that statement is bypassed.

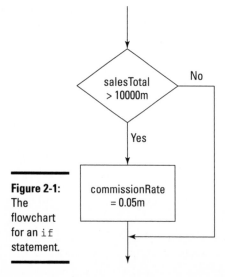

Figure 2-1:
The
flowchart
for an `if`
statement.

Here's an example that uses a block rather than a single statement:

```
decimal commissionRate = 0.0m;
if (salesTotal > 10000.0m)
{
    commissionRate = 0.05m;
    commission = salesTotal * commissionRate;
}
```

In this example, the two statements within the braces are executed if `salesTotal` is greater than \$10,000. Otherwise, neither statement is executed.

Here are a few additional points about simple `if` statements:

✦ **Some programmers prefer to code the opening brace for the statement block on the same line as the `if` statement itself, like this:**

```
if (salesTotal > 10000.0m) {
    commissionRate = 0.05m;
    commission = salesTotal * commissionRate;
}
```

This method is simply a matter of style, so either technique is acceptable.

✦ **Indentation by itself doesn't create a block.** For example, consider this code:

```
if (salesTotal > 10000.0m)
    commissionRate = 0.05m;
    commission = salesTotal * commissionRate;
```

Here, I didn't use the braces to mark a block, but indented the last statement as if it were part of the `if` statement. Don't be fooled; the last statement is executed whether or not the expression in the `if` statement evaluates to `true`.

✦ **Some programmers like to code a statement block even for `if` statements that conditionally execute just one statement.** For example

```
if (salesTotal > 10000.0m)
{
    commissionRate = 0.05m;
}
```

That's not a bad idea because it makes the structure of your code a little more obvious by adding extra white space around the statement. And if you later decide you need to add a few statements to the block, the braces are already there.

✦ **If only one statement needs to be conditionally executed, some programmers put it on the same line as the `if` statement, like this:**

```
if (salesTotal > 10000.0) commissionRate = 0.05;
```

This method works, but I'd avoid it. Your code is easier to follow if you use line breaks and indentation to highlight their structure.

if-else statements

An `if-else` statement adds an additional element to a basic `if` statement: a statement or block that's executed if the boolean expression is not `true`. Its basic format is

```
if (boolean-expression)
    statement
else
    statement
```

Here's an example:

```
decimal commissionRate;
if (salesTotal > 10000.0m)
    commissionRate = 0.05m;
else
    commissionRate = 0.02m;
```

In this example, the commission rate is set to `5%` if the sales total is greater than $10,000. If the sales total is not greater than 10,000, the commission rate is set to `2%`.

Figure 2-2 shows a flowchart for this `if-else` statement.

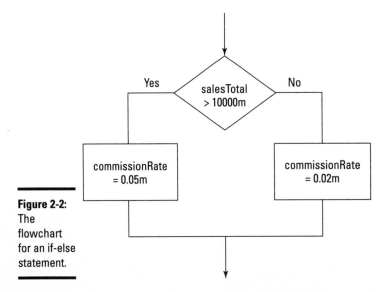

Figure 2-2:
The flowchart for an if-else statement.

In some cases, you can avoid the need for the else part of an `if-else` statement by cleverly rearranging your code. For example, this code has the same effect as the previous `if-else` statement:

```
decimal commissionRate = 0.05m;
if (salesTotal <= 10000.0m)
    commissionRate = 0.02m;
```

You can use blocks for either or both of the statements in an `if-else`. For example, here's an `if-else` statement in which both statements are blocks:

```
decimal commissionRate;
if (salesTotal <= 10000.0m)
{
    commissionRate = 0.02m;
    rate1Count++;
}
else
{
    commissionRate = 0.05m;
    rate2Count++;
}
```

In this example, the `if` and `else` blocks require two statements each: one to set the `commissionRate` variable, the other to increment counter-variables named `rate1Count` and `rate2Count` that count the number of sales made at each commission rate.

Nested if statements

The statement that goes in the if or else part of an `if-else` statement can be any kind of C# statement, including another `if` or `if-else` statement. This is called *nesting*, and an `if` or `if-else` statement that includes another `if` or `if-else` statement is called a *nested if statement*.

The general form of a nested `if` statement is this:

```
if (expression-1)
    if (expression-2)
        statement-1
    else
        statement-2
else
    if (expression-3)
        statement-3
    else
        statement-4
```

**Book IV
Chapter 2**

**Doing Things
Conditionally in C#**

In this example, *expression-1* is first evaluated. If it evaluates to true, *expression 2* is evaluated. If that expression is true, *statement-1* is executed; otherwise, *statement-2* is executed. But if *expression-1* is false, then *expression-3* is evaluated. If *expression-3* is true, *statement-3* is executed; otherwise, *statement-4* is executed.

An if statement that's contained within another if statement is called an *inner if statement*, and an if statement that contains another if statement is called an *outer if statement*. Thus, in the previous example, the if statement that tests *expression-1* is an outer if statement, and the if statements that test *expression-2* and *expression-3* are inner if statements.

Nesting can be as complex as you want, but try to keep it as simple as possible. And be sure to use indentation to indicate the structure of the nested statements.

As an example, suppose your company has two classes of sales representatives (class 1 and class 2), and they get a different sales commission for sales below $10,000 and sales equal to or above $10,000 according to this table:

Sales	Class 1	Class 2
$0–$9,999	2%	2.5%
$10,000 and over	4%	5%

You could implement this commission structure with a nested if statement:

```
if (salesClass == 1)
    if (salesTotal < 10000.0m)
        commissionRate = 0.02m;
    else
        commissionRate = 0.04m;
else
    if (salesTotal < 10000.0m)
        commissionRate = 0.025m;
    else
        commissionRate = 0.05m;
```

This example assumes that if the salesClass variable isn't 1, it must be 2. If that's not the case, you have to use an additional if statement for class-2 sales reps:

```
if (salesClass == 1)
    if (salesTotal < 10000.0m)
        commissionRate = 0.02m;
```

```
    else
        commissionRate = 0.04m;
else if (salesClass == 2)
    if (salesTotal < 10000.0)
        commissionRate = 0.025m;
    else
        commissionRate = 0.05m;
```

Notice that I place this extra `if` statement on the same line as the `else` keyword. That's a common practice for a special form of nested `if` statements called `else-if` statements. You find more about this type of nesting in the next section.

You could also just use a pair of separate `if` statements:

```
if (salesClass == 1)
    if (salesTotal < 10000.0m)
        commissionRate = 0.02m;
    else
        commissionRate = 0.04m;
if (salesClass == 2)
    if (salesTotal < 10000.0m)
        commissionRate = 0.025m;
    else
        commissionRate = 0.05m;
```

The result is the same. However, this technique works only if the `if` statement itself doesn't change the variable being tested. If the first `if` statement changed the value of the `salesClass` variable, this statement doesn't work.

else-if statements

This type of statement isn't really a type, but it *is* really useful for something that doesn't officially exist. It's simply a common pattern for nested `if` statements: a series of `if-else` statements includes another `if-else` statement in each `else` part:

```
if (expression-1)
    statement-1
else if (expression-2)
    statement-2
else if (expression-3)
    statement-3
```

These are sometimes called *else-if* statements, although that's an unofficial term. Officially, all that's going on is that the statement in the `else` part happens to be another `if` statement, so this statement is just a type of a nested `if` statement — an especially useful form of nesting.

For example, suppose you want to assign four different commission rates based on sales total, according to this table:

Sales	Commission
$10,000 and over	5%
$5,000 to $9,999	3.5%
$1,000 to $4,999	2%
Under $1,000	0%

You can do that pretty easily if you implement a series of else-if statements:

```
if (salesTotal >= 10000.0m)
    commissionRate = 0.05m;
else if (salesTotal >= 5000.0m)
    commissionRate = 0.035m;
else if (salesTotal >= 1000.0m)
    commissionRate = 0.02m;
else
    commissionRate = 0.0m;
```

Figure 2-3 shows a flowchart for this sequence of else-if statements.

You have to carefully think through how you set up these else-if statements. For example, at first glance, this sequence looks like it might also work:

```
if (salesTotal > 0.0m)
    commissionRate = 0.0m;
else if (salesTotal >= 1000.0m)
    commissionRate = 0.02m;
else if (salesTotal >= 5000.0m)
    commissionRate = 0.035m;
else if (salesTotal >= 10000.0m)
    commissionRate = 0.05m;
```

But no, this scenario won't work. These if statements always set the commission rate to 0% because the boolean expression in the first if statement always tests true (assuming the salesTotal isn't zero or negative — and if it is, none of the other if statements matter). As a result, none of the other if statements are ever evaluated.

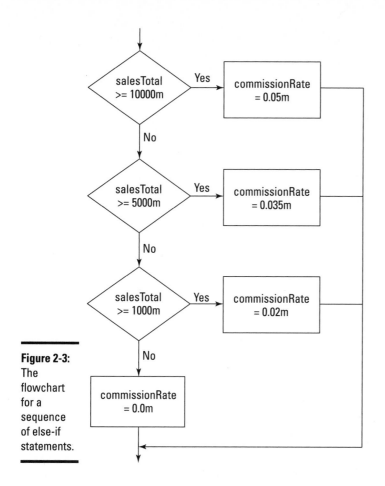

Figure 2-3:
The
flowchart
for a
sequence
of else-if
statements.

Mr. Spock's Favorite Operators (the Logical Ones, of Course)

A *logical operator* (sometimes called a *boolean operator*) is an operator that returns a boolean result that's based on the boolean result of one or two other expressions. Expressions that use logical operators are sometimes called *compound expressions* because (in effect) the logical operators let you combine two or more condition tests into a single expression. Table 2-2 lists the logical operators.

Table 2-2			Logical Operators
Operator	*Name*	*Type*	*Description*
!	Not	Unary	Returns `true` if the operand to the right evaluates to `false`. Returns `false` If the operand to the right is `true`.
&	And	Binary	Returns `true` if both of the operands evaluate to `true`. Both operands are evaluated before the And operator is applied.
|	Or	Binary	Returns `true` if at least one of the operands evaluates to `true`. Both operands are evaluated before the Or operator is applied.
^	Xor	Binary	Returns `true` if one and only one of the operands evaluates to `true`. If both operands evaluate to `true` or if both operands evaluate to `false`, returns `false`.
&&	Conditional And	Binary	Same as &, but if the operand on the left returns `false`, returns `false` without evaluating the operand on the right.
||	Conditional Or	Binary	Same as |, but if the operand on the left returns `true`, returns `true` without evaluating the operand on the `right`.

The following sections describe these operators in excruciating detail.

Using the ! operator

The simplest of the logical operators is *not* (!) — honest, it's called "not." Technically, it's a *unary prefix operator,* which means you use it with one operand, and you code it immediately in front of that operand. (Also, this operator is technically called the *complement operator,* not the "not operator." But in real life, everyone calls it *not.* Honest. Never mind.)

The "not" operator reverses the value of a boolean expression. Thus, if the expression is `true`, not changes it to `false`. If the expression is `false`, not changes it to `true`.

For example:

```
!(i == 4)
```

This expression evaluates to `true` if i is any value other than 4. If i is 4, then it evaluates to `false`. It works by first evaluating the expression (i == 4). Then it reverses the result of that evaluation.

Don't confuse the "not" logical operator (!) with the "not-equals" relational operator (!=). Although they are sometimes used in similar ways, the "not" operator is more general. For example, I could have written the previous example like this:

```
i != 4
```

The result is the same. However, the "not" operator can be applied to any expression that returns a `true` or `false` result; it isn't limited to equality tests.

Note: You must almost always enclose the expression that the ! operator is applied to in parentheses. For example, consider this expression:

```
! i == 4
```

If `i` is an integer variable, the compiler won't allow this expression — and that's because it looks like you're trying to apply the ! operator to the variable, instead of to the result of the comparison. A quick set of parentheses solves that problem:

```
!(i == 4)
```

Using the & and && operators

(I don't recommend reading that heading aloud.) The *and* (&) and *conditional and* (&&) operators combine two boolean expressions and return `true` only if both expressions are `true`. This is called an *and operation* because both the first expression *and* the second expression must be `true` for this particular operator to return a `true`.

For example, suppose the sales commission rate should be 2.5% if the sales class is 1 and the sales total is $10,000 or more. You could perform this test with two separate `if` statements (as I did earlier in this chapter), or you could combine the tests into one `if` statement:

```
if ( (salesClass == 1) & (salesTotal >= 10000.0) )
    commissionRate = 0.025m;
```

Here the expressions (salesClass == 1) and (salesTotal >= 10000.0) are evaluated separately. Then the & operator compares the results. If they're both `true`, then the & operator returns `true`. If one or both are `false`, then the & operator returns `false`.

Notice that I used parentheses liberally to clarify where one expression ends and another begins. Using parentheses isn't always necessary, but when you use logical operators, I suggest you always use parentheses to clearly identify the expressions being compared. Saves on aspirin.

The && (conditional "and") operator is similar to the & operator, but leverages our knowledge of logic. It all has to do with a limitation of the & operator: Because both expressions compared by the & operator must be true for the entire expression to be true, there's no reason to evaluate the second expression if the first one returns false. The & isn't aware of this, so it blindly evaluates both expressions before determining the results. The && operator is smart enough to stop when it knows what the outcome is.

As a result, it's prudent (almost always) to use && instead of &. Here's the previous example, this time coded smartly with &&:

```
if ( (salesClass == 1) && (salesTotal >= 10000.0) )
    commissionRate = 0.025m;
```

Why do I say you should *almost* always use &&? Because sometimes the expressions themselves have side effects that are important. For example, expressions can call methods, as you'll learn in Chapter 4 of this mini-book. If the second expression (the one after the && operator) calls a method that updates a database, the method will be called only if the first expression evaluates to true. That's because the second expression won't be evaluated at all if the first expression is false. If you want the database to be updated regardless of the result of the first expression, you should use & instead of && to ensure that both expressions always get evaluated.

Relying on the side effects of expressions can be risky — and you can almost always find a better way to write your code so the side effects are avoided. In other words, placing an important call to a database update method inside a compound expression buried in an if statement probably isn't a good idea.

Using the | and || operators

The *or* (|) and *conditional or* (||) operators are called so because they return true if the first expression is true *or* if the second expression is true. They also return true if both expressions are true. (You'll find the | symbol on your keyboard just above the Enter key. Note that you need to hold down the shift key to type these symbols.)

Suppose that sales representatives get no commission if the total sales are less than $1,000 or if the sales class is 3. You can do this calculation with two separate if statements, like this:

```
if (salesTotal < 1000.0m)
    commissionRate = 0.0m;
if (salesClass == 3)
    commissionRate = 0.0m;
```

But with an "or" operator, you can do the same thing with a compound condition, which looks like this:

```
if ( (salesTotal < 1000.0) | (salesClass == 3) )
    commissionRate = 0.0m;
```

To evaluate the expression for this `if` statement, C# first evaluates the expressions on either side of the `|` operator. Then, if at least one of them is `true`, the whole expression is `true`. Otherwise the expression is `false`.

In most cases, you should use the conditional "or" operator (`||`) instead of the regular "or" operator (`|`), like this:

```
if ( (salesTotal < 1000.0) || (salesClass == 3) )
    commissionRate = 0.0m;
```

Like the conditional "and" operator (`&&`), the conditional "or" operator stops evaluating as soon as it knows what the outcome is. For example, suppose the sales total is $500. At that point, there's no need to evaluate the second expression. Because the first expression evaluates to `true` and only one of the expressions *needs* to be `true`, C# can skip the second expression altogether.

Of course, if the sales total is $5,000, the second expression must still be evaluated.

As with the and operators, you should use the regular or operator only if your program depends on some side effect of the second expression, such as work done by a method call as described in Chapter 4 of this mini-book.

Pulling the Ol' Switch-er-oo

Besides the `if` statement, C# offers another statement that's excellent for decision-making; the `switch` statement. The `switch` statement excels at one particular type of decision-making: choosing one of several actions based on a value stored in an integer or string variable. As it turns out, the need to do just that comes up a lot. So you want to keep the `switch` statement handy when such a need arises.

Creating else-if monstrosities

Many applications call for a simple logical selection of things to be done depending on some value that controls everything. Such tasks are often handled with big chains of `else-if` statements all strung together.

If you feel a moment of creeping unease here, you're not alone; these things can quickly get out of hand. Else-if chains can end up looking like DNA double-helix structures, or those strings of symbols that dribble down from the tops of the computer screens in *The Matrix*.

For example, Listing 2-1 shows a bit of an application that might be used to decode error codes in a Florida or Ohio voting machine.

Listing 2-1:   The else-if Version of the Voter-Error-Code Decoder Program (C#)

```
public string GetError(int err)
{
    string msg;
    if (err==1)
        msg = "Voter marked more than one candidate. "
                + "Ballot rejected.";
    else if (err==2)
        msg = "Box checked and write-in candidate "
                + "entered. Ballot rejected.";
    else if (err==3)
        msg = "Entire ballot was blank. "
                + "Ballot filled in at random. ";
    else if (err==4)
        msg = "Nothing unusual about the ballot. "
                + "Voter selected for tax audit.";
    else if (err==5)
        msg = "Voter filled in every box. "
                + "Ballot counted twice.";
    else if (err==6)
        msg = "Voter drooled in voting machine. "
                + "Beginning spin cycle.";
    else if (err==7)
        msg = "Voter lied to pollster after voting. "
                + "Voter's ballot changed "
                + "to match polling data.";
    else
        msg = "Voter filled out ballot correctly. "
                + "Ballot discarded anyway.";
    return msg;
}
```

Wow! And this program has to decipher only 7 different error codes. What if the machine had 500 different codes?

Using the switch statement

Fortunately, C# has a special statement that's designed just for the kind of task represented by the Voter-Error-Code Decoder program: the switch statement. Specifically, the switch statement is sometimes useful when you have to select one of several alternatives according to the value of an integer or character-type variable.

The basic form of the `switch` statement looks like this:

```
switch (expression)
{
    case constant:
        statements;
        break;
  [ case constant-2:
        statements;
        break;  ] ...
  [ default:
        statements;
        break;  ] ...
}
```

The expression must evaluate to an integer or string.

You can code as many case groups as you want or need. Each begins with the word `case` followed by a constant (usually a simple numeric literal) and a colon. Then you code one or more statements that you want to execute when (or if) the value of the `switch` expression equals the constant. The last line of each case group is a `break` statement, which causes the entire `switch` statement to end.

The `default` group, which is optional, works like a catch-all case group. Its statements are executed only if *none* of the previous case constants match the `switch` expression.

Note that the case groups are not true blocks (those would be marked with braces). Instead, each case group begins with the `case` keyword and ends with the `case` keyword that starts the next case group. However, all the case groups together are defined as a block — and that's marked with a set of braces.

The last statement in each case group usually is a `break` statement. A `break` statement causes control to skip to the end of the `switch` statement. If you omit the `break` statement, control falls through to the next case group — an instant headache. Accidentally leaving out `break` statements is the most common cause of trouble with the `switch` statement.

A better version of the Voter-Error-Code Decoder program

Listing 2-2 shows a version of the Voter-Error-Code Decoder program that uses a `switch` statement instead of a big `else-if` structure.

Listing 2-2:   The switch Version of the Voter-Error-Code Decoder Program (C#)

```csharp
public string GetError(int err)
{
    string msg;
    switch (err)
    {
        case 1:
            msg = "Voter marked more than one "
                + "candidate. Ballot rejected.";
            break;
        case 2:
            msg = "Box checked and write-in candidate "
                + "entered. Ballot rejected.";
            break;
        case 3:
            msg = "Entire ballot was blank. "
                + "Ballot filled in at random.";
            break;
        case 4:
            msg = "Nothing unusual about the ballot.\n"
                + "Voter selected for tax audit.";
            break;
        case 5:
            msg = "Voter filled in every box.\n"
                + "Ballot counted twice.";
            break;
        case 6:
            msg = "Voter drooled in voting machine.\n"
                + "Beginning spin cycle.";
            break;
        case 7:
            msg = "Voter lied to pollster after "
                + "voting. Voter's ballot changed "
                + "to match polling data.";
            break;
        default:
            msg = "Voter filled out ballot correctly.\n"
                + "Ballot discarded anyway.";
            break;
    }
    return msg;
}
```

I think you'll agree that this version of the program is a bit easier to follow. The switch statement makes it clear that the messages are all selected according to the value of the err variable.

Chapter 3: Going Around in Circles (Or, Looping in C#)

In This Chapter

- The thrill of while loops
- The brilliance of break statements
- The rapture of infinite loops
- The ecstasy of the continue statement
- The splendor of do loops
- The wonder of for loops
- The joy of nested loops

So far, all the programs in this book have started, run quickly through their `main` method, and then ended. If Dorothy from *The Wizard of Oz* were using these programs, she'd probably say, "My, programs come and go quickly around here!"

In this chapter, you find out how to write programs that *don't* come and go so quickly. They hang around by using *loops,* logical constructions that let them execute the same statements more than once.

Or, put another way, loops are like the instructions on your shampoo: Lather. Rinse. *Repeat.*

Like `if` statements, loops rely on conditional expressions to tell them when to stop looping. Without conditional expressions, loops would go on forever, and your users would grow old watching them run. So, if you haven't yet read Chapter 2 of this mini-book, I suggest you do so before continuing much farther.

Your Basic while Loop

The most basic of all looping statements in C# is `while`. The `while` statement creates a type of loop (called, you guessed it, a *while loop*) that executes continuously as long as some conditional expression evaluates to true. Since `while` loops are useful in all sorts of programming situations, you will end up using them a lot. (I take a spin through other kinds of loops later in this chapter.)

The while statement

The basic format of the `while` statement is like this:

```
while (expression)
    statement
```

The `while` statement begins by evaluating the expression. If the expression is `true`, then *statement* (whatever it may be) is executed. Then the expression is evaluated again and the whole process repeats. If the expression is `false`, then *statement* is not executed, and the `while` loop ends.

Note that the statement part of the `while` loop can either be a single statement or a block of statements contained in a pair of braces. Loops that have just one statement aren't very useful, so nearly all the `while` loops you code use a block of statements. (Well, okay, sometimes loops with a single statement are useful. It isn't unheard of — just not all that common.)

A counting loop

Here's a simple program that uses a `while` loop to list the even numbers from 2 through 20 on a Web page by using `Response.Write`. My `EvenCounter` loop looks like this:

```
int number = 2;
while (number <= 20)
{
    Response.Write(number + "...");
    number += 2;
}
```

If you incorporate this code into a Web page (for example, in the `Load` event), the following output will be included on the page:

```
2...4...6...8...10...12...14...16...18...20...
```

The conditional expression in this program's `while` statement is `number <= 20`. That means the loop repeats as long as the value of `number` is less than or equal to `20`. The body of the loop consists of two statements. The first prints the value of `number` followed by a space to separate this number from the next one. Then the second statement adds 2 to `number`.

Figure 3-1 shows a flowchart for this program — a handy way to visualize the basic decision-making process of a loop.

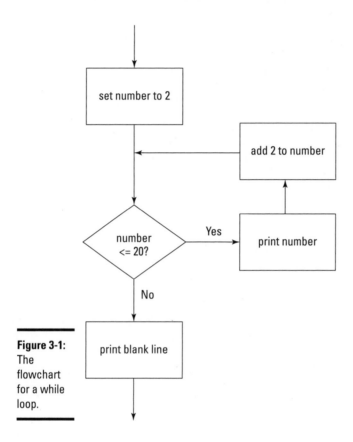

Figure 3-1:
The flowchart for a while loop.

Breaking Out of a Loop

Many programs need a loop that has some kind of escape clause to tell the program to get back to its business. In C#, you can set up that escape clause by using the `break` statement. When a `break` statement is executed in a `while` loop, the loop ends immediately. Any remaining statements in the loop are ignored, and the next statement executed is the statement that follows the loop.

For example, suppose you're afraid of the number 12. (I'm not a doctor and I don't play one on TV, but I think the scientific name for this condition would be *dodecaphobia*.) You could modify the `EvenCounter` program shown in the previous section so that when it gets to the number 12, it panics and aborts the loop. My `Dodecaphobia` loop looks like this:

```
int number = 2;
while (number <= 20)
{
    if (number == 12)
        break;
    Response.Write(number + " ...");
    number += 2;
}
```

When you run this program, the following line is displayed in the browser:

```
2...4...6...8...10...
```

Whew! That was close. Almost got to 12 there.

Looping Forever

One common form of a loop — the *infinite loop* goes on forever — or would if it had its druthers. You can create infinite loops in many ways in C# (not all of them intentional), but the easiest is to just specify `true` for the `while` expression, like this:

```
int number = 2;
while (true)
{
    Response.Write(number + " ...");
    number += 2;
}
```

Of course, if you were to run this code, the application would run forever without actually *doing* anything. If that seems, well, counterproductive, you can stop an infinite loop four ways:

+ **Close the browser window.**

+ **Switch to the Visual Studio window and choose Debug⇨Break All.**

+ **Turn off your computer.**

+ **Hit your computer with an ax or other heavy object.**

The first two are probably the ones you want to go with here. Call it a hunch.

TIP

Obviously, infinite loops are something you want to avoid in your programs. So whenever you use a `while` expression that's always `true`, be sure to throw in a `break` statement to give your loop some way to terminate. For example, if you put an infinite loop with a `break` statement in the Dodecaphobia loop, it would look like this:

```
int number = 2;
while (true)
{
    if (number == 12)
        break;
    Response.Write(number + "...");
    number += 2;
}
```

Here the loop looks like it might go on forever, but the `break` statement panics out of the loop when it hits 12.

Using the continue Statement

The `break` statement is rather harsh: It completely bails out of the loop. Sometimes that's what you need, but just as often, you don't really need to quit the loop; you just need to skip a particular iteration of the loop (an *iteration* is a single execution of a loop). For example, the Dodecaphobia program presented earlier in this chapter stops the loop when it gets to 12. What if you just want to skip the number 12 and go straight from 10 to 14?

To do that, you can use the `break` statement's kinder, gentler relative: the `continue` statement. The `continue` statement sends control right back to the top of the loop, where the expression is immediately evaluated again. If the expression is still `true`, the loop's statement or block is executed again.

Here's a version of the Dodecaphobia loop that uses a `continue` statement to skip the number 12 rather than stop counting altogether when it reaches 12:

```
int number = 0;
while (number < 20)
{
    number += 2;
    if (number == 12)
        continue;
    Response.Write(number + "...");
}
```

Run this code and you get the following output on the page:

```
2...4...6...8...10...14...16...18...20...
```

Notice that I had to make several changes to this loop to get it to work with a `continue` statement instead of a `break` statement. If I had just replaced the word `break` with `continue`, the program wouldn't have worked. That's because the statement that added 2 to `number` came after the `break` statement in the original version. As a result, if you just replace the `break` statement with a `continue` statement, you end up with an infinite loop once you reach 12 (eek!) because the statement that added 2 to `number` never gets executed.

To make this code work with a `continue` statement, I rearranged the statements in the loop body so that the statement that adds 2 to `number` comes *before* the `continue` statement. That way, the only statement skipped by the `continue` statement would be the one that prints `number` to the console. Sounded promising, but . . .

Unfortunately, this change affected other statements in the program as well. Because 2 is added to `number` before `number` is printed, I had to change the initial value of `number` from 2 to 0, and I had to change the `while` expression from `number <= 20` to `number < 20`.

Understanding do-while Loops

A *do-while loop* (sometimes just called a *do loop*) is similar to a `while` loop, but with a critical difference: In a `do-while` loop, the condition that stops the loop isn't tested until after the statements in the loop have executed. The basic form of a `do-while` loop looks like this:

```
do
    statement
while (expression);
```

Note that the `while` keyword and the expression aren't coded until *after* the body of the loop. As with a `while` loop, the body for a `do-while` loop can be a single statement — or a block of statements — enclosed in braces.

Also, notice that the expression is followed by a semicolon. The `do-while` statement is the only looping statement that ends with a semicolon.

Here's a version of the `EvenCounter` loop that uses a `do-while` loop instead of a `while` loop:

```
int number = 2;
do
{
    Response.Write(number + "...");
    number += 2;
} while (number <= 20);
```

Here's the most important thing to remember about do-while loops: Every statement in the body of a do-while loop is *always executed at least once.* In contrast, the statement or statements in the body of a while loop aren't executed at all if the while expression returns false the first time it is evaluated.

Look at the flowchart in Figure 3-2 to see what I mean. You can see that execution starts at the top of the loop and flows through to the decision test after the loop's body has been executed once. Then, if the decision test is true, control flies back up to the top of the loop. Otherwise, it spills out the bottom of the flowchart.

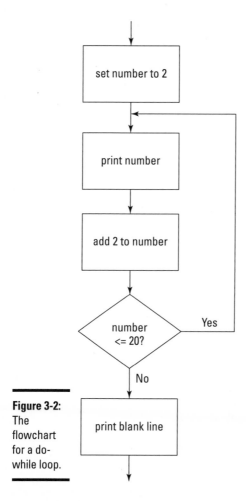

Figure 3-2:
The flowchart for a do-while loop.

Here are a few other quirks you'll run into when you use do-while loops:

✦ **You can use** break **and** continue **statements in a** do-while **loop just as you can in a** while **loop.**

✦ **Some programmers like to place the brace that begins the loop body on the same line as the** do **statement, and the** while **statement that ends the** do-while **loop on the same line as the brace that marks the end of the loop body.** Whatever makes you happy is fine with me. Just remember that the compiler is agnostic when it comes to matters of indentation and spacing.

The Famous for Loop

In addition to while and do-while loops, C# offers one more kind of loop: the *for loop*. You may have noticed that many of the loops presented so far in this chapter have involved counting. It turns out that counting loops are quite common in computer programs, so long ago, in a computer room far, far away, the people who design computer programming languages (they're called "computer-programming-language designers") concocted a special kind of looping mechanism designed just for counting.

The basic principle behind a for loop is that the loop itself maintains a *counter-variable* — that is, a variable whose job is counting. Its value is increased each time the body of the loop is executed. For example, if you want a loop that counts from 1 to 10, you'd use a counter-variable that starts with a value of 1 and is increased by 1 each time through the loop. Then you'd use a test to end the loop when the counter-variable reaches 10. The for loop lets you set this up all in one convenient statement.

People who majored in computer science call the counter-variable an *iterator* because they think we don't know what it means. (We know perfectly well that the iterator is where you put your beer to keep it cold.)

The formal format of the for loop

I would now like to inform you of the formal format for the for loop, so you know how to form it from now on. The for loop follows this basic format:

```
for (initialization-expression; test-expression; count-expression)
    statement;
```

See those three expressions in the parentheses that follow the keyword for? They control how the for loop works. Here's a rundown on what the three expressions are and what they do:

✦ **The *initialization expression* is executed before the loop begins.**
Usually, you use this expression to initialize the counter-variable. If you
haven't declared the counter-variable before the `for` statement, you can
declare it here.

✦ **The *test expression* is evaluated each time the loop is executed to
determine whether the loop should keep looping.** Usually this expression tests the counter-variable to make sure it's still less than or equal to
the value you want to count to. The loop keeps executing as long as this
expression evaluates to `true`. When the test expression evaluates to
`false`, the loop ends.

✦ **The *count expression* is evaluated each time the loop executes.** Its job
is usually to increment the counter-variable.

Figure 3-3 shows a flowchart for visualizing how a `for` loop works.

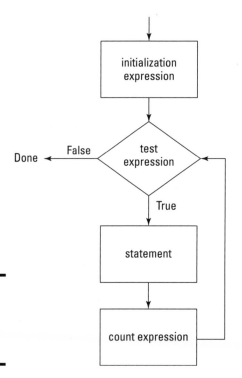

Figure 3-3:
The
flowchart
for a for
loop.

Here's a simple `for` loop that writes the numbers 1 to 10 to the page:

```
for (int i = 1; i <= 10; i++)
    Response.Write(i + "<br>");
```

Here's how the output from this code will be rendered on the page:

```
1
2
3
4
5
6
7
8
9
10
```

If you take this `for` loop apart, it has the following pieces:

+ **The initialization expression is** `int i = 1`. This expression declares a variable named `i` of type `int` and assigns it an initial value of `1`.

+ **The test expression is** `i <= 10`. As a result, the loop continues to execute as long as `i` is less than or equal to `10`.

+ **The count expression is** `i++`. As a result, each time the loop executes, the variable `i` is incremented.

+ **The body of the loop is the single statement** `Response.Write(i + "<br>")`. As a result, each time the loop executes, the value of the `i` variable is written to the page, followed by a `<br>` tag (the `<br>` tag creates a line break).

Scoping out the counter-variable

If you declare the counter-variable in the initialization statement, then the scope of the counter-variable is limited to the `for` statement itself. That means you can use the same variable in the other expressions that appear within the parentheses — and in the body of the loop — but you can't use it outside the loop. For example, code that looks like this causes a build error:

```
for (int i = 1; i <=10; i++)
    Response.Write(i + "<br>");
Response.Write ("The final value is " + i);
```

That's because the last statement refers to the variable `i`, which has gone *out of scope* because it was declared within the `for` loop and has no business wandering off elsewhere.

Note, however, that you don't have to declare the counter-variable in the `for` statement itself. Thus the following code works just fine:

```
int i;
for (i = 1; i <=10; i++)
```

```
        Response.Write(i + "<br>");
Response.Write ("The final value is " + i);
```

Here's why: The i variable is declared before the `for` statement — so the initialization expression doesn't name the variable's data type, and the variable doesn't go out of scope. When you run this program, here's what you get on the page:

```
1
2
3
4
5
6
7
8
9
10
The final value of i is 11
```

Counting even numbers

Earlier in this chapter, you saw a program that counts even numbers up to 20. You can do that with a `for` loop as well. All you have to do is adjust the count expression. For example, here's a version of a `for` loop that counts even numbers only:

```
for (int number = 2; number <= 20; number += 2)
    Response.Write(number + "...");
```

Run this code and sure enough, the page renders the following:

```
2...4...6...8...10...12...14...16...18...20...
```

Counting backward

There's no rule that says `for` loops can count only forward. To count backward, you simply adjust the three `for` loop expressions appropriately. As usual, the initialization expression specifies the starting value for the counter-variable. The test expression uses a greater-than test instead of a less-than test. And the count expression subtracts from the counter-variable instead of adding to it.

Here's an example:

```
for (int count = 10; count >= 1; count--)
{
    Response.Write(count + "<br>");
}
```

Run this program and you see this result on the page:

```
10
9
8
7
6
5
4
3
2
1
```

for loops without bodies

Some programmers get a kick out of writing code that's as terse as possible. (I think *Seinfeld* did an episode about that . . . Jerry had a girlfriend who was one of these *terse coders,* but he had to dump her because he couldn't understand her code.)

Anyway, terse coders sometimes like to play with `for` statements in an effort to do away with the body of a `for` loop altogether. To do that, they take advantage of a really handy fact: You can code any expression you want as part of the count expression in a `for` statement — including method calls as described in the next chapter. For example, here's a loop that writes the numbers 1 to 10 to the page, using a `for` statement that has no body:

```
for (int i = 1; i <=10; Response.Write(i++));
```

Here, the count expression is a call to `Response.Write`. The parameter to the `Write` method cleverly uses the increment operator so the variable is both printed *and* incremented in the same expression. (Somebody's just asking for trouble.)

Stay away from terse coders! Seinfeld was right to dump her.

Ganging up your expressions

An obscure aspect of `for` loops is that their initialization and count expressions don't have to be individual expressions; either one can actually be a *list* of expressions separated by commas. This quirk can be useful if you need to keep track of two counter-variables at the same time. For example, here's a loop that counts from 1 to 10 *and* from 10 to 1 at the same time, using two counter-variables. I call it my `CountBothWays` loop, and it looks like this:

```
int a, b;
for (a = 1, b = 10; a <= 10; a++, b--)
    Response.Write(a + " " + b
        + "<br>");
```

The output from this loop will render like this in the browser:

```
1  10
2  9
3  8
4  7
5  6
6  5
7  4
8  3
9  2
10 1
```

Keep the following rules in mind when you use more than one expression for the initialization and counter expressions:

+ **In the initialization expression, you can't declare variables if you use more than one expression.** (That's why I declared the a and b variable *before* the for statement in the CountBothWays example.)

+ **The expressions in an expression list can be assignment statements, increment or decrement statements (such as a++), method calls, or object-creation statements that use the new keyword to create an object from a class.** Other types of statements (such as if statements or loops) are not allowed.

+ **You can't list more than one expression in the test expression.** However, you can use compound conditions created with boolean operators, so you don't need to use an expression list.

Omitting expressions

Yet another oddity about for loops is that all three of the expressions (initialization, test, and count) are optional. If you omit one or more of the expressions, you just code the semicolon as a placeholder so the compiler knows.

Omitting the test expression or the count expression is not common, but omitting the initialization expression *is* common. For example, the variable you're incrementing in the for loop may already be declared and initialized before you get to the loop. In that case, you can omit the initialization expression, as in this example:

```
int a = 10;
for ( ; a >= 0; a--)
    Response.Write(a + "<br>");
```

This `for` loop simply counts down from whatever number the user enters, and keeps at it till it gets to zero.

If you omit the test expression, you'd better throw a `break` statement into the loop somewhere. Otherwise you find yourself in an infinite loop.

You can even omit all three of the expressions if you want to, as in this example:

```
for(;;)
    Response.Write("Infinite loop!");
```

This program also results in an infinite loop. There's little reason to do it this way because `while(true)` has the same effect and is more obvious.

Breaking and continuing your for loops

You can use a break in a `for` loop just as you can in a `while` or `do-while` loop. For example, here I revisit the `Dodecaphobia` loop from earlier in the chapter, this time with a `for` loop:

```
for (int number = 2; number <=20; number += 2)
{
    if (number == 12)
        break;
    Response.Write(number + "...");
}
```

As before, this version counts by 2s until it gets to 20. But when it hits 12, it panics and aborts the loop, so it never actually gets to 14, 16, 18, or 20. Thus the page looks like this:

```
2...4...6...8...10...
```

And here's a version that uses a `continue` statement to skip 12 instead of aborting the loop:

```
for (int number = 2; number <=20; number += 2)
{
    if (number == 12)
        continue;
    Response.Write(number + "...");
}
```

This code renders the following on the page:

```
2...4...6...8...10...14...16...18...20...
```

Nesting Your Loops

Loops can contain loops. The technical term for this is Loop-de-Loop. (Just kidding.) Actually the technical term is *nested loop* — a loop completely contained inside another loop. The loop that's inside is called the *inner loop*, and the loop that's outside is called the *outer loop*.

To demonstrate the basics of nesting, here's a simple little code snippet that uses a pair of nested `for` loops:

```
for(int x = 1; x < 10; x++)
{
    for (int y = 1; y < 10; y++)
    {
        Response.Write(x + "-" + y + "  ");
    }
    Response.Write("<br>");
}
for(int x = 1; x < 10; x++)
{
    for (int y = 1; y < 10; y++)
    {
        Response.Write(x + "-" + y + "  ");
    }
    Response.Write("<br>");
}
```

This program consists of two `for` loops. The outer loop uses x as its counter-variable; the inner loop uses y. For each execution of the outer loop, the inner loop executes 10 times and prints a line that shows the value of x and y for each pass through the inner loop. When the inner loop finishes its work, a call to `Response.Write` with no parameters starts a new line. Then the outer loop cycles so the next line can be printed.

When you run this program, the page displays this text:

```
1-1   1-2   1-3   1-4   1-5   1-6   1-7   1-8   1-9
2-1   2-2   2-3   2-4   2-5   2-6   2-7   2-8   2-9
3-1   3-2   3-3   3-4   3-5   3-6   3-7   3-8   3-9
4-1   4-2   4-3   4-4   4-5   4-6   4-7   4-8   4-9
5-1   5-2   5-3   5-4   5-5   5-6   5-7   5-8   5-9
6-1   6-2   6-3   6-4   6-5   6-6   6-7   6-8   6-9
7-1   7-2   7-3   7-4   7-5   7-6   7-7   7-8   7-9
8-1   8-2   8-3   8-4   8-5   8-6   8-7   8-8   8-9
9-1   9-2   9-3   9-4   9-5   9-6   9-7   9-8   9-9
```

Chapter 4: Using Methods and Exceptions

In This Chapter

✓ Introducing methods

✓ Pondering some good reasons to use methods in your programs

✓ Creating methods that return values

✓ Creating methods that accept parameters

✓ Dealing with exceptions

In C#, a *method* is a block of statements that has a name and can be executed by *calling* (also called *invoking*) it from some other place in your program. If you've coded some of the examples in this mini-book, then you're already experienced with using methods; when you use `Response.Write` to write data to the page (for example), you're calling a method.

In addition, the code that responds to events such as button clicks is written in methods. Besides such event-handling methods, you can put other methods in the code-behind file to handle other tasks. This chapter shows how.

Another important aspect of C# programming is working with *exceptions* — those pesky times when the program (like the universe) balks at following the rules you've so carefully created. This chapter covers that important detail as well.

The Basics of Making Methods

All methods must begin with a *method declaration,* a statement that identifies the method for the program. Here's the basic form for a method declaration, at least for the types of methods I talk about in this chapter:

```
protected return-type method-name (parameter-list)
{
        statements...
}
```

Here's a rundown of the parts that make up a method declaration, defined piece by piece:

✦ `protected`: This keyword indicates that the method's existence should be kept hidden from most of the classes in your ASP.NET application, but that the method should be available to certain classes. If hiding a method seems a little weird, not to worry; Chapter 6 of this mini-book delves into what `protected` means and why it works.

All methods that handle events must be declared as `protected`. For other methods you add to a code-behind file, you can specify `protected` if you want, or you can specify `private` (which means you can't call the method from outside the current class).

✦ *return-type*: This part of the declaration indicates whether the method returns a value when it's called — and, if so, what type the value is. If the method doesn't return a value, specify `void`. (For more about methods that return values, flip ahead in this chapter to the "Methods that Return Values" section.)

✦ *method-name*: Now comes the name of your method. The rules for making up method names are the same as the rules for creating variable names: You can use any combination of letters and numbers, but the name has to start with a letter. It can include a dollar sign ($) and/or an underscore character (_), but no other special characters are allowed.

Always try to give your method a name that's relatively short but descriptive. Okay, `calculateTheTotalAmountOfTheInvoice` is a little long, but just `calc` is pretty ambiguous. Something along the lines of `calculateInvoiceTotal` seems more reasonable to me.

✦ *parameter list*: You can pass one or more values to a method by listing the values in parentheses following the method name. The parameter list in the method declaration lets C# know what types of parameters a method should expect to receive and provides names so the statements in the method's body can access the parameters as local variables. (You can get a closer look at parameters in the "Using Methods that Take Parameters" section later in this chapter.)

If the method you're using doesn't accept parameters, you still have to code the parentheses that surround the parameter list — you just leave 'em empty.

✦ **Method body:** The method body consists of one or more C# statements enclosed in a set of braces. Unlike C# statements such as `if`, `while`, and `for`, the method body requires those braces even if it consists of only one statement.

A Simple Example

Okay, the previous section was a little abstract. Now, for a concrete example, I offer the code-behind file (with the `using` statements omitted) for a simple page that uses the `Response.Write` method to write the stock `"Hello,`

`World!"` greeting to a Web page when the page is posted. But instead of writing the message in the `Page_Load` method, you have to use a second method to write the message — like this:

```
public partial class _Default : System.Web.UI.Page
{
    protected void Page_Load(object sender, EventArgs e)
    {
        WriteMessage();
    }
    private void WriteMessage()
    {
        Response.Write("Hello, World!");
    }
}
```

This program is admittedly trivial, but it illustrates the basics of creating and using methods in C#. Here the statement in the `Page_Load` method calls the `WriteMessage` method, which in turn writes the greeting message to the page.

The order in which methods appear in your C# source file doesn't matter. The only rule is that *all methods must be declared within the body of the class —* that is, between the first left brace and the last right brace. For example, here's a version of the previous code-behind file in which I reversed the order of the methods:

```
public partial class _Default : System.Web.UI.Page
{
    private void WriteMessage()
    {
        Response.Write("Hello, World!");
    }
    protected void Page_Load(object sender, EventArgs e)
    {
        WriteMessage();
    }
}
```

This version works exactly like the previous version.

Methods that Return Values

Methods that just do work without returning any data are useful only in limited situations. The real utility of methods comes when they can perform some mundane task such as a calculation, and then return the value of that calculation to the calling method so the calling method can do something with the value. The following sections explain how to get all that done.

Declaring the method's return type

To create a method that returns a value, you simply indicate the type of value you want the method to return; this declaration of a *return type* goes in the method declaration in place of the `void` keyword. For example, here's a method declaration that creates a method that returns an `int` (integer) value:

```
private int GetRandomNumber()
```

Here, the `GetRandomNumber` method calculates a random number, and then returns the number to the caller.

The return type of a method can be a C# primitive return type (as described in Chapter 1 of this mini-book) or a reference type that includes a class defined by the .NET Framework (or a class you create yourself).

Using the return statement to return the value

When you specify a return type other than `void` in a method declaration, the body of the method must include a `return` statement that specifies the value you want returned. The `return` statement has this form:

```
return expression;
```

The expression must evaluate to a value whose type matches the type listed in the method declaration. If the method returns (say) an `int`, the expression in the `return` statement must evaluate to an `int`.

For example, here's a program that uses a method to provide the text of a greeting message that's displayed on the page:

```
protected partial class _Default
{
    protected void Page_Load(object sender, EventArgs e)
    {
        string greeting = GetGreeting();
        Response.Write(greeting);
    }
    private string GetGreeting()
    {
        return "Hello, World!";
    }
}
```

In this program, the `Page_Load` method calls a method named `GetGreeting` to set the value of a string written to the page.

Using Methods that Take Parameters

A *parameter* is a value that you can pass to a method. The method can then use the parameter as if it were a local variable initialized with the value of the variable passed to it by the calling method.

For example, here's a method that returns a greeting message that incorporates a string passed as a parameter:

```
private string GetGreeting(string name)
{
    return "Hello, " + name;
}
```

Suppose you call this method with the following statement:

```
string msg = GetGreeting("Bob!");
```

Then the variable `msg` will be set to the string `"Hello, Bob!"`

Declaring parameters

A method that accepts parameters must list the parameters in the method declaration. The place to put those parameters is in the *parameter list* — the space between the parentheses that follow the method name. For each parameter used by the method, you list the parameter type followed by the parameter name. If you need multiple parameters, you separate them with commas.

For example, here's a method that determines which of two integer values is larger:

```
private int GetLarger(int i, int j)
{
    if (i > j)
        return i;
    else
        return j;
}
```

Here the method uses two parameters, both of type `int`, named `i` and `j`. Then, within the body of the method, these parameters can be used as if they were local variables.

The names you use for parameters can be the same as the names you use for the variables you pass to the method when you call it, but they don't have to be. For example, you could call the `GetLarger` method like this:

```
int i = 1;
int j = 10;
int number = GetLarger(i, j);
```

Or you could call it like this:

```
int foo = 1;
int bar = 10;
int number = GetLarger(foo, bar);
```

Or you can dispense with the variables altogether and just pass literal values to the method:

```
int number = GetLarger(1, 10);
```

You can also specify expressions as the parameter values, like this:

```
int i = 1;
int j = 10;
int number = GetLarger(i * 5, j * 2);
```

Understanding pass-by-value

When C# passes a value-type variable to a method via a parameter, the method itself receives a copy of the variable's value — but not the variable itself. This copy is called a *pass-by-value*, and it has an important consequence: If a method changes the value it receives as a parameter, that change is *not* reflected in the original variable that was passed to the method. The following code can help clear up what this looks like:

```
protected void Page_Load(object sender, EventArgs e)
{
    decimal subtotal = 14.99m;
    decimal tax = GetTax(subtotal);
    Response.Write(tax + "<br>");
    Response.Write(subtotal);
}
private decimal GetTax(decimal subtotal)
{
    decimal tax = subtotal * 0.05m;
    subtotal = 0.0m;
    return tax;
}
```

Here's how it works: When you run this code, the following will be written to the page:

```
0.7495
14.99
```

Notice that the value of the subtotal variable has not been changed in the `Page_Load` method.

Note that pass-by-value is used only for value-type variables. If you pass a reference type, a pointer to the value is passed, not the actual value itself. This is called *pass by reference.*

Understanding Exceptions

An *exception* is what happens when an error occurs in a C# program and C# can't automatically fix the error. Then a special type of object called — you guessed it, an *exception* — is created to contain all the necessary information about the error that occurred.

Each type of exception that can occur is represented by a different exception class. For example, here are some typical exceptions:

✦ `ArgumentException`: You passed an incorrect argument to a method.

✦ `ArithmeticException`: You tried an illegal type of arithmetic operation, such as dividing an integer by zero.

✦ `IOException`: A method that performs I/O encountered an unrecoverable I/O error.

✦ `ClassNotFoundException`: A necessary class couldn't be found.

Here are a few things you need to know about exceptions:

✦ **When an error occurs and an exception object is created, C# is said to have *thrown an exception.*** C# has a pretty good throwing arm, so the exception is always thrown right back to the statement that caused it to be created.

✦ **The statement that caused the exception can *catch* the exception if it wants it.** But it doesn't have to catch the exception if it doesn't want it. Instead, it can duck and let someone else catch the exception — namely, the statement that called the method that's currently executing.

✦ **If everyone ducks and the exception is never caught by the program, the program ends abruptly and displays a nasty-looking exception message instead of the page the user was expecting.**

You should *never* let an ASP.NET Web application throw an unhandled exception.

Catching Exceptions

Whenever you use a statement that might throw an exception, you should write special code to anticipate and *catch* the exception. You catch an exception by using a `try` statement, which has this general form:

```
try
{
    statements that can throw exceptions
}
catch (exception-type identifier)
{
    statements executed when exception is thrown
}
```

Here, you place the statements that might throw an exception within a *try block*. Then you catch the exception with a *catch block*.

Here are a few things to note about `try` statements:

+ **The .NET Framework defines several different types of exceptions.** You can use a specific exception type in a `catch` block to catch just that type of exception, or you can just specify `Exception` as the exception type to catch exceptions of any type.

+ **You can code more than one** `catch` **block.** That way, if the statements in the `try` block throw more than one type of exception you can catch each type of exception in a separate `catch` block.

+ **For scoping purposes, the** `try` **block is its own self-contained block, separate from the** `catch` **block.** As a result, any variables you declare in the `try` block are not visible to the `catch` block. If you want them to be, declare them immediately before the `try` statement.

+ **You can also code a special block called a *finally block* after all the** `catch` **blocks.** The finally block is always executed, whether or not an exception occurs. For more information about coding `finally` blocks, see the section "Using a finally Block," later in this chapter.

+ **The various exception classes in the C# API (Application Programming Interface) are defined in different packages.** If you use an exception class that isn't defined in the standard `C#.lang` package that's always available, you need to provide an `using` statement for the package that defines the exception class.

To illustrate how to provide for an exception, here's a snippet of code that divides two numbers and uses `try` and `catch` statements to catch an exception if the second number turns out to be zero:

```
int a = 5;
int b = 0;                   // you know this won't work
```

```
try
{
    int c = a / b;     // but you try it anyway
}
catch (Exception ex)
{
    Response.Write("Oops, you can't divide by zero.<br>");
}
```

Here the division occurs within a `try` block, and a `catch` block handles `ArithmeticException`. Note that `ArithmethicException` is defined by `C#.lang`, so an `import` statement for it isn't necessary.

When you run this program, the following line is written to the page:

```
Oops, you can't divide by zero.
```

There's nothing else to see here. The next section shows a more complicated example, though.

Catching Different Exception Types

If you have some code that might throw several different types of exceptions — and you want to provide specific processing for some, but general processing for all the others — code the `try` statement like this:

```
try
{
    // statements that might throw several types of exceptions
}
catch (ArgumentException ex)
{
    // statements that process ArgumentException
}
catch (IOException ex)
{
    // statements that process IOException
}
catch (Exception ex)
{
    // statements that process all other exception types
}
```

In this example, imagine that the code in the `try` block might throw an `InputMismatchException`, an `IOException`, and perhaps some other type of unanticipated exception. Here, the three `catch` blocks provide for each of these possibilities.

When you code more than one `catch` block on a `try` statement, always list the more specific exceptions first. If you include a `catch` block to catch `Exception`, list it last.

Using the Exception Message

In most cases, the `catch` block of a `try` statement won't do anything at all with the exception object passed to it. However, exception objects do have a `Message` property you can use to get additional information about the exception. The following example shows how you might print the message for an exception in a `catch` block:

```
try
{
    int c = a / b;
}
catch (Exception e)
{
    Response.Write(e.Message + "<br>");
}
```

This code displays the text `Attempted to divide by zero` on the page if `b` has a value of zero.

Using a finally Block

A `finally` block is a block that appears after all the `catch` blocks for a statement. It's executed whether or not any exceptions are thrown by the `try` block — or (for that matter) caught by any `catch` blocks. The `finally` block is like a mop; its purpose is to let you clean up any mess that might be left behind by the exception, such as open files or database connections.

The basic framework for a `try` statement with a `finally` block is this:

```
try
{
    statements that can throw exceptions
}
catch (exception-type identifier)
{
    statements executed when exception is thrown
}
finally
{
    statements that are executed whether or not exceptions
    occur
}
```

Usually the place to look for code that closes database connections and does other clean-up chores is the `finally` block.

Chapter 5: Getting into Object-Oriented Programming

In This Chapter

✔ Looking at what object-oriented programming is

✔ Understanding objects and classes

✔ Creating your own classes

✔ Working with fields and properties

✔ Overloading your methods

✔ Concocting constructors

✔ Using static members

*T*his chapter is a basic introduction to the object-oriented programming features of C#. We're talking basic here, not comprehensive; object-oriented programming is easily enough for a book of its own. But you've come to the right place for a look at creating and using your own classes.

What Is Object-Oriented Programming?

The term *object-oriented programming* means many different things — but at its heart, this type of computer programming organizes code into logical objects, on the premise that all programs are essentially computer-based simulations of real-world objects — or of abstract concepts that can be made to work like objects. Here are some examples:

✦ **Flight-simulator programs attempt to mimic the behavior of real airplanes.** Some do an amazingly good job; military and commercial pilots train on them. In the 1960s, the Apollo astronauts used a computer-controlled simulator to practice moon landings — these days, even inexpensive flight simulator programs that run on PCs (and cost about $50) do a pretty credible job.

✦ **Many computer games are simulations of actual games humans play, such as baseball, NASCAR racing, and chess.** But even abstract games such as Pacman or World of Warcraft attempt to model the behavior of creatures and objects that *could* exist somewhere, but don't; they are imaginary objects with consistent behaviors. Those programs simulate conceptual games that can't actually be played anywhere in the real world, but can be simulated by a computer.

✦ **Business programs can be thought of as simulations of business processes — such as order-taking, customer service, shipping, and billing.** For example, an invoice isn't just a piece of paper; it's a document that represents a transaction that has occurred between a company and one of its customers. In essence, no paper is required; a computer-based invoice is really just a simulation of that transaction.

The notion of a programming language having a premise of this sort isn't new. Traditional programming languages such as C and its predecessors, including even COBOL, are based on the premise that computer programs are ways to get a computer to implement specific, consistent *procedures* — the electronic equivalent of "Step 1: Insert Tab A into Slot B." The LISP programming language is based on the idea that all programs can be looked at as different ways of manipulating lists. And the ever-popular database-manipulation language, SQL, views programs as ways to manipulate mathematical sets.

Using computer programs to simulate real-world objects, processes, or abstract concepts has lead to a fairly odd relationship between the real world and the simulated world:

✦ **Sometimes the simulation is better than the real thing.** Word processing programs started out as simulations of typewriters, but a modern word processing program is far superior to any typewriter.

✦ **This sort of simulation isn't new; computer programs have been doing it for decades.** In fact, the first object-oriented programming language (Simula) was developed in the 1960s. By 1967, this language had many of the features we now consider fundamental to object-oriented programming, including classes, objects, inheritance, and virtual methods.

✦ **Suddenly you can see simulations everywhere.** For instance, manual business record-keeping systems are simulations too. A file cabinet full of printed invoices doesn't hold the actual objects that the orders are for (where would you get one big enough to hold a hundred cars?); it holds written *representations* of those orders. A computer is a better simulation device than a file cabinet, but both are simulations.

✦ **Is anything real?** Hmm. I think I am, but I might just be a simulation of myself. (I wonder if I can get me to work better . . .).

Understanding Objects

All this talk of simulations is getting a little existential for me, so let's turn to the nature of the objects that make up object-oriented programming. Whether you find them in the real world or in the world of programming, objects have certain basic characteristics; the following sections describe some of the most important; identity, type, behavior, and state.

Objects have identity

Every object in an object-oriented program has an *identity*. In other words, every occurrence of a particular type of object — called an *instance* — can be distinguished from every other occurrence of the same type of object, as well as from objects of other types.

In the real world, object identity is a pretty intuitive and obvious concept. Pick up two apples, and you know that although both of them are apples (that's the object *type*, described in the next section), they aren't the *same* apple. Each has a distinct identity. They're both roughly the same color, but not exactly. They're both more or less round, but have minor variations in shape. Either one (or both) could have a worm inside.

Open a file cabinet that's full of invoices and you'll find page after page of papers that look almost identical to one another — but each one has an invoice number printed somewhere near the top. This number isn't what actually gives each of these invoices a unique identity, but it does give us an easy way to identify each individual invoice, just as our names give us an easy way to identify each other.

In object-oriented programming, each object has its own location in the computer's memory. Thus two objects, even though they may be of the same type, have two distinct memory locations. The address of the starting location for an object provides us with a way of distinguishing one object from another, since no two objects can occupy the same location in memory. Object identity in C# has two other especially important aspects:

✦ **C# pretty much keeps each object's identity to itself.** In other words, there's no easy way to get the memory address of an object. C# figures that's none of your business, and rightfully so. If C# made that information readily available to you, you'd be tempted to tinker with it — humans are hardwired that way — which can cause all sorts of problems (as any C or C++ programmer will tell you).

✦ **When used with objects, the equality operator (==) actually tests the object identity of two variables or expressions.** If those refer to the same object instance, then the two variables or expressions are considered equal.

Objects have type

Back when I was an English major in college, I remember studying *Naming of Parts*, a fine poem written by Henry Reed in 1942:

> *Today we have naming of parts. Yesterday,*
> *we had daily cleaning. And tomorrow morning,*
> *we shall have what to do after firing. But today,*
> *today we have naming of parts. Japonica*
> *glistens like coral in all of the neighboring gardens,*
> *and today we have naming of parts.*

Sure, it's a fine antiwar poem and all that, but it's also a little instructive about object-oriented programming. After the first stanza, the poem goes on to name the parts of a rifle, though it inexplicably keeps interjecting strange details about flowers and bees too:

> *This is the lower sling swivel. And this*
> *is the upper sling swivel, whose use you will see,*
> *when you are given your slings. And this is the piling swivel,*
> *which in your case you have not got. The branches*
> *hold in the gardens their silent, eloquent gestures,*
> *which in our case we have not got.*

I never got that part the part about the Japonica gardens. (I said I was an English major; I didn't say I was good at it.) But back to the other parts . . .

Imagine a whole room of new soldiers taking apart their rifles, while the drill sergeant tells them "This is the lower-sling swivel. And this is the upper-sling swivel . . ." Each soldier's rifle has one of these parts — in object-oriented terms, an object of a particular type. The lower-sling swivels in each soldier's rifle are different objects, but all are of the type `LowerSlingSwivel`.

As if you were the drill sergeant in this poem, object-oriented programming lets you assign names to the different kinds of objects in a program. In C#, types are defined by classes — sections of code that define the objects that make up a program. (You'll learn how to create classes later in this chapter, in the section "Declaring a Class.") So when you create an object from a type, you're saying that the object will be of the type specified by the class. Here's an example:

```
Invoice i = new Invoice();
```

The statement creates a object of type `Invoice`. Then the identity of this object (that is, its address in memory) is assigned to the variable `i`, which the compiler knows can hold references to objects of type `Invoice`.

Objects have state

Let's switch gears to another literary genius:

> *One fish, two fish,*
> *Red fish, Blue fish*

In object-oriented terms, Dr. Seuss here is enumerating information about a pair of objects of type Fish. The Fish type apparently has two attributes — we'll call them Number and Color. These two objects have differing values for these attributes:

Attribute	Object 1	Object 2
Number	One	Two
Color	Red	Blue

The type of an object determines what attributes the object has. Thus, all objects of a particular type have the same attributes — but they don't necessarily have the same *values* for those attributes. In this example, all Fish have attributes named Number and Color, but the two Fish objects have different values for these attributes.

The combination of the values for all of the attributes of an object is called the object's *state*. Unlike its identity, an object's state can, and usually does, change over its lifetime. For example, some fish change colors — and other changing states are everywhere: The total sales for a customer will change each time the customer buys another product. The grade-point average for a student changes each time a new class grade is recorded. And the address and phone number of an employee changes if the employee moves.

Here are a few more interesting details about object state:

✦ **In C#, the state of an object is represented by class variables, which are called *fields*.** A *public field* is a field that's declared with the public keyword so the variable can be visible to the outside world.

✦ **Some of the attributes of an object are publicly known, but others can be private.** The private attributes may be vital to the internal operation of the object, but no one outside of the object knows they exist. They're like your private thoughts: They affect what you say and do, but nobody knows them but you. (I discuss fields in more detail in the section "Using Fields," later in this chapter. My thoughts about that are private.)

Objects have behavior

Another characteristic of objects is their *behavior* — which means they can do things. As with state, the specific behavior of an object depends on its type; unlike a state, a behavior doesn't vary for each instance of a type. For example, suppose all the students in a classroom have calculators of the same type. Ask them all to pull out those calculators and add two numbers — any two numbers of their choosing. All the calculators will display different numbers — but they all do addition. In other words, they all have a different state (the answers they get), but the same behavior (addition).

In C#, what provides the behavior of an object is its methods. Thus the `HttpResponse` class — which defines the object you can access via the `Response` property of the `Page` class — has a behavior that enables it to write data directly to the page being rendered. This is the behavior you access when you call the `Response.Write` method.

Here are a couple of other notable points about object behavior to keep in mind:

✦ **Objects have to be available.** The *interface* of a class is the set of methods and fields that the class makes public so they can be accessed by other objects.

✦ **An object works best as a "black box."** Exactly how an object does what it does can — and should — be hidden within the object. Someone who uses the object needs to know what the object does, but doesn't need to know how it works. If you later find a better way for the object to do its job, you should be able to swap in the new improved version without anyone knowing the difference.

The Life Cycle of an Object

As you work with objects in C#, it's important to understand how objects are born, live their lives, and die. This topic is called the *life cycle* of an object, and it goes something like this:

✦ **Before an object can be created from a class, the class must be *compiled* and *loaded*.** The C# compiler is responsible for creating executable code based on the class; then the .NET runtime reads the compiled class into memory, which loads it.

✦ **An object is created from a class when you use the `new` keyword.** To initialize the class, the .NET runtime allocates memory for the object and sets up a reference to the object to keep track of the object. Then, the class *constructor* is called. The constructor is like a method but is called only once — when the object is created. The constructor is responsible for doing any processing required to initialize the object (such as initializing variables, opening files or databases, and so on).

✦ **The object lives its life, providing access to its** `public` **methods and fields to whomever wants and needs them.**

✦ **When it's time for the object to die, the object is removed from memory and .NET drops all internal reference to it.** Note that you don't have to do anything about this yourself. A special part of the .NET runtime called the *garbage collector* takes care of deciding when objects should die and handling the details of destroying those objects.

Working with Related Classes

The real power of object-oriented programming lies in the distinctions it can make when you create classes to describe objects that are closely related to each other. For example, baseballs are similar to softballs. Both are specific types of balls. They both have a diameter and a weight. And both can be thrown, caught, or hit. However, they have different characteristics which cause them to behave differently when thrown, caught, or hit.

If you were creating a program that simulated the way baseballs and softballs work, you'd need a way to represent these two types of balls. One option would be to create separate classes to represent each type of ball. These classes would be similar, so you could just copy most of the code from one class to the other.

Another option would be to use a single class to represent both types of balls. Then, you could pass a parameter to the constructor to indicate whether an instance of the class should behave like a baseball or like a softball. (Parameters are discussed in Chapter 4 of this mini-book.)

However, C# has two object-oriented programming features that are designed specifically to handle classes that are related like this: *inheritance* and *interfaces*. These features are briefly described in the following sections.

Inheritance

As in biology, *inheritance* is a way of passing along characteristics. In object-oriented programming, it's a technique that uses one class as the basis for another. The existing class is called the *base class*, *superclass*, or *parent class*, and the new class that's derived from it is called the *derived class*, *subclass*, or *child class*.

The moment you create a subclass, it automatically acquires all the methods and fields defined by its superclass. You can use these methods and fields just as they are, or you can override them to alter their behavior. You can also add methods and fields that define data and behavior unique to the subclass.

**Book IV
Chapter 5**

**Getting into
Object-Oriented
Programming**

You could use inheritance to solve our baseball/softball problem by creating a class named `Ball` that provides the basic features of all types of balls, and then use it as the base class for separate classes named `BaseBall` and `SoftBall`. To provide appropriate behaviors for their types of balls, these classes could override the methods in `Ball` that need to behave differently for each type of ball.

One way to think of inheritance is as a way to implement *is-a-type-of* relationships. For example, a softball is a type of ball, as is a baseball, so inheritance is an appropriate way to implement these related classes.

ASP.NET uses inheritance in an important way: Each page you create for an application is a child class of a .NET Framework class called `System.Web.UI.Page`. As a result, all the pages you create inherit properties and methods from this base `Page` class. One of these properties is named `Response`; this property refers to an object of type `HttpResponse`, which in turn provides a method named `Write`. Thus, when you code `Response.Write` in a code-behind file, you're actually using the `Response` property that your page inherited from the `System.Web.UI.Page` class.

Interfaces

An *interface* is a set of methods and fields that a class must provide for implementation. What creates the interface is a set of `public` method and field declarations; the set is given a specific name. Note that the interface itself doesn't provide any code that implements those methods; it just provides the declarations. Then a whole other class implements the interface by providing an implementation for each method that the interface defines.

You could use an interface to solve the baseball/softball problem by creating an interface named `Ball` that specifies all the methods and fields that a ball should have. Then you could create the `SoftBall` and `BaseBall` classes so that they both implement the `Ball` interface.

Interfaces work in a way closely related to inheritance, but there are two key differences:

✦ **The interface itself doesn't provide code that implements any of its methods.** An interface is, essentially, just a set of method and field signatures. In contrast, a base class can provide the implementation for some or all of its methods.

✦ **A class can have only one base class — but a class can implement as many interfaces as necessary.**

Interfaces are also commonly used through the .NET Framework, but creating your own interface is a somewhat advanced C# programming topic. That's beyond what we need for this little overview of what they are.

Declaring a Class

Okay, class, it's time to learn how to create your own (ahem) classes. To start, all classes must defined by a *class declaration* that provides the name for the class and the body of the class. Here's the most basic form of a class declaration:

```
[public] [partial] class ClassName {class-body}
```

The `public` keyword indicates that this class is available for use by other classes. Although it is optional, you usually include it on your class declarations. After all, the main reason you write class declarations is so other classes can create objects from the class.

The `partial` keyword is optional and is used only when the class definition is spread over two or more files. ASP.NET Web pages use the `partial` keyword to keep the code that's generated by ASP.NET from the `.aspx` file separate from the code-behind file. In other words, ASP.NET generates a C# source file from the `.aspx` file that defines part of the same class defined by the code-behind file. (Fortunately, you don't need to worry about this generated source file. Just know it exists.)

Picking class names

The class name that usually looks like this: `ClassName`) is an identifier that provides a name for your class. You can use any identifier you want to name a class, but the following three guidelines can simplify your life:

✦ **Begin the class name with a capital letter.** If the class name consists of more than one word, capitalize each word — for example, `Ball`, `RetailCustomer`, and `GuessingGame`.

✦ **Whenever possible, use nouns for your class names.** Classes create objects, and nouns are the words that identify objects; most class names should be nouns.

✦ **Avoid using the name of a .NET Framework class.** Life will be much simpler if you avoid using the names of common .NET Framework classes (like String or TextBox) for your own classes. You'll run into conflicts if you create classes with these names.

What goes in the class body

The *class body* of a class is everything that goes within the braces at the end of the class declaration. The `public partial class ClassName` part of a class declaration takes just one line, but the body of the class declaration may take hundreds of lines. (Or thousands if you get carried away.)

The class body can contain the following elements:

✦ **Fields:** Variable declarations define the `public` or `private` fields of a class.

✦ **Properties:** Properties are a more sophisticated form of fields and are the preferred way to grant access to data associated with an object.

✦ **Methods:** Method declarations define the methods of a class. Most of the code in a code-behind file consists of methods that handle events raised by the page — such as the `Load` event that's raised when the page is loaded or the `Click` event that's raised when the user clicks a button.

✦ **Constructors:** A *constructor* is a block of code that's similar to a method but is run to initialize an object when an instance is created. A constructor must have the same name as the class itself and, although it resembles a method, it doesn't have a return type.

✦ **Other classes and interfaces:** A class can include another class, which is then called an *inner class* or a *nested class*. (This advanced programming technique is beyond the scope of this book.)

Unlike some programming languages, the order in which items appear in the class body doesn't matter. Still, being consistent about the order in which you place things in your classes is a good idea. That way you know where to find them. I usually code all the fields together at the start of the class, followed by constructors and then by methods.

Some programmers like to place the fields at the end of the class, rather than at the beginning. Whatever brings you happiness is fine with me.

The field, properties, constructors, and methods contained within a class are called the *members* of the class.

Using Fields

A *field* is a variable that's defined in the body of a class, outside any of the class's methods. Fields, which are also called *class variables,* are available to all the methods of a class. In addition, if the field specifies the `public` keyword, then the field is visible outside the class. If you don't want the field to be visible outside the class, use the `private` keyword instead.

Fields are defined the same as any other C# variable, but can have a modifier that specifies whether the field is `public` or `private`. Here are some examples of `public` field declarations:

```
public int trajectory = 0;
public string name;
public Player player;
```

To create a `private` field, specify `private` instead of `public`, like this:

```
private int x_position = 0;
private int y_position = 0;
private string error_message = "";
```

Creating Properties

Although `public` fields provide a rudimentary way to grant access to the data of a class, a better way is to create *properties*. Simply put, a property is a special type of method that can be accessed as if it were a field. For example, suppose you have an `Employee` class with a property called `Name`. Then, when you set the `Name` property of an `Employee` object, a method defined by the `Employee` class is called to set the employee's name.

The methods associated with a property are called *accessors*, and there are two types of accessors: *get accessors* and *set accessors*. A `get` accessor is a method that's called when the value of a property is retrieve; while a `set` assessor is a method that's called to set a property value.

Here's the basic syntax for creating a property:

```
public type property-name
{
    get
    {
        // Statements executed when property is retrieved.
        // Should end with return statement that returns
        // the property value
    }
    set
    {
        // statements executed when the property value is
        // set. The value to be set is passed as a
        // parameter named value.
    }
}
```

Here's a simple example:

```
public class Employee
{
    private string _name;
    public string Name
    {
        get
        {
            return _name;
        }
```

```
        set
        {
            _name = value;
        }
    }
}
```

Here, the employee's name is represented by a `private` field called _name. (It's common, but not required, to use underscores for fields that are used to store property values.) The `get` accessor for this property simply returns the value of the _name property, while the `set` accessor uses the special parameter named `value` to set the _name field.

Note that `set` accessors are optional. If you omit them, the property is read-only. (The value of a read-only property can be read but not set.) For example, here's a read-only version of the `Name` property:

```
public string Name
{
    get
    {
        return _name;
    }
}
```

You can also omit the `set` accessor to create a write-only property — that is, a property that can be set but not retrieved. But that's uncommon.

The code in the `get` and `set` accessors can do more than simply get or set the value of a private field. For example, suppose an `Invoice` class has a property named `Total` that's calculated by adding the invoice subtotal, sales tax, and shipping charges. Here's how you might define this property:

```
public decimal Total
{
    get
    {
        return _subtotal + _tax + _shipping;
    }
}
```

Here, the total is recalculated each time the `Total` property is retrieved.

You can also do data validation in the `set` accessor. For example, suppose a `Quantity` property must be between 0 and 1000. You could write a `set` accessor that restricts the value, like this:

```
private int quantity;
public int Quantity
{
```

```
get
{
    return _quantity;
}
set
{
    if (value < 0)
        _quantity = 0;
    else if (value > 1000)
        _quantity = 1000;
    else
        _quantity = value;
}
}
```

Using Methods

You define methods for a class using the same techniques that I describe in Chapter 4 of this mini-book. To declare a method that's available to users of your class, add the `public` keyword to the method declaration:

```
public boolean IsActive()
{
    return this.isActive;
}
```

To create a private method that can be used within the class but isn't visible outside the class, use the `private` keyword, like this:

```
private void CalculateLunarTrajectory()
{
    // code to calculate the lunar trajectory
}
```

A class can contain two or more methods with the same name, provided those methods accept different parameters. When it does so, the class is *overloaded* — and this technique is one of the keys to building flexibility into your classes. By overloading a class, you can anticipate different ways someone might want to invoke an object's methods, and then provide overloaded methods for each alternative.

The term *overloading* is accurate, but a little unfortunate. Normally, when you say something is overloaded, there's a problem — as in that picture I once saw of a Volkswagen Jetta loaded down with 3,000 pounds of lumber. (You can find the picture courtesy of Snopes.com, the Urban Legend Reference Page Web site, at `www.snopes.com/photos/lumber.asp`.) That's a classic example of overloading. You don't have to worry about C# collapsing under the weight of overloaded methods.

Understanding visibility

In the preceding sections, I mention that fields, properties, and methods can use the `public` or `private` keywords to indicate whether the field or method can be accessed from outside the class. This is called the *visibility* of the field or method.

The combination of all members that have `public` access is sometimes called the *public interface* of your class. These members are the only means that other objects have to communicate with objects created from your class. As a result, carefully consider which public fields, properties, and methods your class declares. By doing so, you expose them.

In this context, to *expose* is to create `public` fields and methods that make a property visible — which simply means that the method is available to other classes. For example,

if a class has a `public` property named `IsActive`, you could say that the class exposes the `IsActive` property.

You can use private fields, properties, and methods within a class but not from other classes. They're used to provide implementation details that may be crucial to the operation of your class, but that shouldn't be exposed to the outside world. Private fields and methods are sometimes called *internal members* because they're available only from within the class.

Another type of visibility you'll encounter often is `protected` — which is used along with inheritance to create members that can be accessed by a child class but not by other classes. For more about how this works, see the next chapter.

The basic rule for creating overloaded methods is that every such method must have a unique *signature* — which is the combination of its name and the number and types of parameters it accepts.

Two things that are *not* a part of a method's signature are

+ **The method's return type:** You can't code two methods with the same name and parameters but with different return types.

+ **The names of the parameters:** All that matters to the method signature are the types of the parameters and the order in which they appear. Thus, the following two methods have the same signature:

```
double SomeMethodOfMine(double x, boolean y)
double SomeMethodOfMine(double param1, boolean param2)
```

Creating Constructors

A *constructor* is a block of code that's called when an instance of an object is created. A constructor is similar to a method, but with a few telling differences:

✦ **A constructor doesn't have a return type.**

✦ **The name of the constructor must be the same as the name of the class.**

✦ **A constructor is called when a new instance of an object is created.** In fact, it's the `new` keyword that calls the constructor.

Here's the basic format for coding a constructor:

```
public ClassName (parameter-list)
{
    statements...
}
```

The `public` keyword indicates that other classes can access the constructor, and `ClassName` must be the same as the name of the class that contains the constructor. And you code the parameter list the same as you code it for a method.

Basic constructors

Probably the most common reason for coding a constructor is to provide initial values for class fields when you create the object. For example, suppose you have a class named `Actor` that has fields named `firstName` and `lastName`. You can create a constructor for the `Actor` class like this:

```
private string firstName, lastName;
public Actor(string first, String last)
{
    firstName = first;
    lastName = last;
}
```

Then you create an instance of the `Actor` class by calling this constructor:

```
Actor a = new Actor("Arnold", "Schwarzenegger");
```

A new `Actor` object for Arnold Schwarzenegger is created.

Like methods, constructors can be overloaded. In other words, you can provide more than one constructor for a class, provided that each constructor has a unique signature. For example, here's another constructor for the `Actor` class:

```
public Actor(string first, string last, boolean good)
{
    firstName = first;
    lastName = last;
    goodActor = good;
}
```

This constructor lets you create an `Actor` object with additional information besides the actor's name, like this:

```
Actor a = new Actor("Arnold", "Schwarzenegger",
    IsArnoldGoodActor);
```

I'll let you decide how you want to set the `IsArnoldGoodActor` variable before you create the `Actor` object.

Default constructors

I grew up on *Dragnet*. I can still hear Joe Friday reading some thug his rights: "You have the right to have an attorney present during questioning. If you desire an attorney and cannot afford one, an attorney will be appointed to you free of charge."

C# constructors are like that. Every class has a right to a constructor. If you don't provide a constructor, C# appoints one for you, free of charge; it's called the *default constructor*. It doesn't accept any parameters and it doesn't do anything, but it does allow you to create an object from the class.

Thus the following two classes are identical:

```
public Class1
{
    public Class1() { }
}

public Class1 { }
```

In the first example, the class explicitly declares a constructor that doesn't accept any parameters and has no statements in its body. In the second example, C# creates a default constructor that works just like the constructor shown in the first example.

The default constructor is *not* created if you declare any constructors for the class. As a result, if you declare a constructor that accepts parameters and still want to have an empty constructor (with no parameters and no body), you must explicitly declare an empty constructor for the class.

Using this

One of the most confusing keywords in C# is `this`. Simply put (if that's possible), the `this` keyword refers to the current instance of the current class.

The `this` keyword is usually used to qualify references to instance variables of the current object. For example, here's how you might use it in a constructor:

```
public Actor(string Last, string First)
{
    this._LastName = Last;
    this._FirstName = First;
}
```

Here `this` isn't really necessary because the compiler can tell that `_LastName` and `_FirstName` refer to class variables. However, it does help to clarify that these variables refer to class fields.

You can also use `this` in a method body. Here's an example:

```
public string getFullName()
{
    return this._FirstName + " " + this._LastName;
}
```

Because this particular example has no ambiguity, `this` isn't really required. However, many programmers like to use `this` even when it isn't necessary; what better way to make clear that you're referring to an instance variable?

Working with Static Members

According to my handy Webster's dictionary, the word *static* has several meanings. Most of them relate to the idea of being stationary or unchanging. For example, a *static display* is a display that doesn't move. *Static electricity* is an electrical charge that doesn't flow. A *static design* is a design that doesn't change. And the kind of static that mucks up radio reception never goes away when you want it to.

As used in C#, however, the term *static* doesn't mean unchanging. For example, you can create a static field, and then assign values to it as a program executes. Thus the value of the `static` field can change. In C#, *static* means something more like "a member that holds still so you can reference it regardless of instance." It describes a special type of member that isn't associated with a particular instance of a class. Static members are associated with the class itself. That means you don't have to create an instance of the class to access a static member; you need only specify the class name — no need for a variable that references an object.

Static members have many common uses. Here are but a few:

✦ **To provide constants or other values that aren't related to class instances.** For example, a `Billing` class might have a constant named `SALES_TAX_RATE` that provides the state sales tax rate.

✦ **To keep a count of how many instances of a class have been created.** For example, a `BadGuy` class used in a game might have a `static` field that counts how many bad guys currently exist. This count doesn't belong to any one instance of the `BadGuy` class.

✦ **In a business application, to keep track of a reference or serial number that's assigned to each new object instance.** For example, an `Invoice` class might maintain a `static` field that holds the invoice number that is assigned to the next `Invoice` object created from the class.

Working with static fields or properties

A *static field* is a field that's declared with the `static` keyword, like this:

```
public static int BadGuyCount;
```

You can provide an initial value for a `static` field, like this:

```
public static string District = "Northwest";
```

Static fields are created and initialized automatically when the class is first loaded. That happens when a `static` member of the class is referred to, or when an instance of the class is created, whichever comes first.

Properties can be declared as `static` in much the same way as fields. Here's an example:

```
private static string _District;
public static string District
{
    get
    {
        return _District;
    }
}
```

Using static methods

A *static method* is a method declared with the `static` keyword. Like static fields, `static` methods are associated with the class itself, and not with any particular object created from the class. As a result, you don't have to create an object from a class before you can use a `static` method that's defined by the class.

One basic rule of `static` methods is a limitation on what they can access; you can't access a non-static method or field from a `static` method. That's because the `static` method doesn't have an instance of the class to use, so it can't reference instance methods or fields. For example, the following code won't compile:

```
public class TestClass
{
    private int x = 5;        // an instance field
    public static void main(String[] args)
    {
        int y = x;            // error: won't compile
    }
}
```

Here the `TestClass` method is static, so it can't access the instance variable `x`.

Note: However, you *can* access static methods and fields from an instance method. For example, the following code works fine:

```
public class Invoice
{
    private static double taxRate = 0.75;
    private double salesTotal;
    public double getTax()
    {
        return salesTotal * taxRate;
    }
}
```

Here the instance method named `salesTotal` has no trouble accessing the static field `taxRate`.

This chapter has introduced you to the basics of writing your own classes and creating objects from them. In the next chapter, you'll learn how to work with inheritance, one of the most important features of classes in C#.

Chapter 6: Working with Inheritance

In This Chapter

✔ **Explaining inheritance**

✔ **Creating derived classes**

✔ **Using protected access**

✔ **Demystifying polymorphism**

You probably already know that a C# class can be based on another class. When that happens, the class becomes like a child to the parent class: It inherits all the characteristics of the parent class, good and bad. All the fields, properties, and methods of the parent class are passed on to the child class. The child class can use these members as is, or it can override them to provide its own versions. In addition, the child class can add fields, properties, or methods of its own.

Inheritance is considered by some to be an advanced topic of object-oriented programming, but it's a topic that can't be ignored when you work in ASP.NET because every ASP.NET page you create inherits a .NET Framework class called `System.Web.UI.Page`. To write even a trivial program, you need to understand the implications of this fact.

Understanding Inheritance

The word *inheritance* conjures up several different non-computer meanings:

✦ **Children inherit certain characteristics from the parents.** For example, two of my three children have red hair. Hopefully, they won't be half bald by the time they're 30.

✦ **Children can also inherit behavior from their parents.** As they say, the apple doesn't fall far from the tree.

✦ **When someone dies, their heirs get their stuff.** Some of it is good stuff, but some of it may not be. My kids are going to have a great time rummaging through my garage deciding who gets stuck with my junk.

✦ **You can inherit rights as well as possessions.** For example, you may be a citizen of a country by virtue of being born to parents who are citizens of that country.

In C#, *inheritance* refers to a feature of object-oriented programming that lets you create classes that are derived from other classes. A class that's based on another class is said to *inherit* the other class. The class that is inherited is the *base class* or the *parent class*. The class that does the inheriting is the *derived class* or the *child class*.

You need to know a few important things about inheritance:

✦ **A derived class automatically takes on all the behavior and attributes of its base class.** Thus, if you need to create several different classes to describe types that aren't identical but have many features in common, you can create a base class that defines all the common features. Then, you can create several derived classes that inherit the common features.

✦ **A derived class can add features to the base class it inherits by defining its own methods and fields, which is one way a derived class distinguishes itself from its base class.**

✦ **Inheritance is best used to implement an *is-a-type-of* relationships.** For example: Solitaire is a type of game; a truck is a type of vehicle; an invoice is a type of transaction. In each case, a particular kind of object is a specific type of a more general category of objects.

The following sections provide some examples that help illustrate these points.

A real-world explanation

Inheritance is often explained in terms of real-world objects such as cars and motorcycles, birds and reptiles, or other familiar objects. For example, consider various types of vehicles. Cars and motorcycles are two distinct types of vehicles. If you're writing software that represents vehicles, you could start by creating a class called `Vehicle` that describes the features that are common to all types of vehicles, such as wheels, a driver, the ability to carry passengers, and the ability to perform actions such as driving, stopping, and turning.

A motorcycle is a type of vehicle that further refines the `Vehicle` class. The `Motorcycle` class inherits the `Vehicle` class, so it can have wheels, a driver, possibly passengers, and the ability to drive, stop, turn, or crash. In addition, it can have features that differentiate it from other types of vehicles. For example, it has two wheels and uses handlebars for steering control.

A car is also a type of vehicle. The `Car` class inherits the `Vehicle` class, so it too can have wheels, a driver, possibly some passengers, and the ability to drive, stop, turn, or crash. Plus, it can have some features of its own, such as four wheels and a steering wheel, seat belts and air bags, and an optional automatic transmission.

A fun explanation

Because you're unlikely to ever write a program that simulates cars, motorcycles, or other vehicles, take a look at a more common example: games. Suppose you want to develop a series of board games such as *Life*, *Sorry*, or *Monopoly*. Most board games have certain features in common:

✦ **A playing board that has locations the players can occupy.**

✦ **Players that are represented by objects.**

✦ **Rules for how the game is played: namely, each player taking a turn, one after the other.** After the game starts, it keeps going until someone wins. (If you don't believe me, ask the kids who tried to stop a game of Jumanji before someone won.)

Each specific type of game has these basic characteristics but adds features of its own. For example, Life adds features such as money, insurance policies, spouses and children, and a fancy spinner in the middle of the board. Sorry has cards you draw to determine each move as well as safety zones within which other players can't attack you. And Monopoly has Chance and Community Chest cards, properties, houses, hotels, and money.

If you were designing classes for these games, you might create a generic `BoardGame` class that defines the basic features common to all board games and then use it as the base class for classes that represent specific board games, such as `LifeGame`, `SorryGame`, and `MonopolyGame`.

A business-world explanation

If vehicles or games don't make inheritance clear, here's an example from the world of business. Suppose you're designing a payroll system and you're working on the classes that represent the employees. You realize that the payroll basically includes two types of employees: salaried employees and hourly employees. So, you decide to create two classes, sensibly named `SalariedEmployee` and `HourlyEmployee`.

You quickly discover that most of the work done by these two classes is identical. Both types of employees have names, addresses, Social Security numbers, and totals for how much they've been paid for the year, how much tax has been withheld, and so on.

However, they have important differences. The most obvious is that salaried employees have an annual salary and hourly employees have an hourly pay rate. However, other differences exist as well. For example, hourly employees may have a schedule that changes week to week, and salaried employees may have a benefit plan that isn't offered to hourly employees.

So, you decide to create three classes instead of just two. A class named `Employee` handles all the features that are common to both types of employees. This class is the base class for the `SalariedEmployee` and `Hourly Employee` derived classes. These derived classes provide the additional features that distinguish salaried employees from hourly employees.

Inheritance hierarchies

One of the most important aspects of inheritance is that a class derived from a base class can in turn be used as the base class for another derived class. Thus, you can use inheritance to form a *hierarchy* of classes.

For example, you can read in the preceding section how an `Employee` class can be used as a base class to create two types of child classes: a `SalariedEmployee` class for salaried employees and an `HourlyEmployee` class for hourly employees. If salaried employees fall into two categories — management and sales — you can use the `SalariedEmployee` class as the base class for two more classes, named `Manager` and `SalesPerson`. Thus, a `Manager` is a type of `SalariedEmployee`. Because a `SalariedEmployee` is a type of `Employee`, a `Manager` is also a type of `Employee`.

All classes ultimately derive from the .NET Framework class `Object`. Any class that doesn't specifically state what class it is derived from is assumed to derive from the `Object` class. This class provides some of the basic features that are common to all classes, such as the `ToString` method.

Creating Derived Classes

The basic procedure for creating a derived class is simple. You just code a colon after the class name on the declaration for the derived class and then list the name of the base class. Here's the syntax:

```
public class ClassName : BaseClass
{
    // class body goes here
}
```

You can see this syntax in use in your code-behind files:

```
public partial class _Default : System.Web.UI.Page
```

Here, the `_Default` class inherits the class named `System.Web.UI.Page`.

The derived class automatically has all the methods and fields of the class that it extends. Thus, the `_Default` class can use properties such as `Response` and `IsPostBack` because those properties are defined by the `System.Web.UI.Page` class.

You need to know some important details in order to use inheritance properly:

✦ **The visibility (**`public` **or** `private`**) of any members inherited from the base class is the same in the derived class.** This means that you can't access methods or fields that are declared in the base class as `private` from the derived class.

  • **A special type of visibility,** `protected`**, hides fields and methods from other classes but makes them available to derived classes.** For more information, see "Protecting Your Members" later in this chapter.

✦ **You can** *override* **a method by declaring a new member with the same signature in the derived class.** For more information, see the next section, "Overriding Methods."

✦ **You can also add additional methods or fields,** `public`, `private` **or** `protected`**, to a derived class.** For example, most code-behind files add methods to handle various types of ASP.NET events.

Overriding Methods

If a derived class declares a method that has the same signature as a public method of the base class, the derived class version of the method overrides the base class version of the method. This technique lets you modify the behavior of a base class to suit the needs of the derived class.

For example, suppose you have a base class named Game that has a method named Play. The base class, which doesn't represent any particular game, implements this method:

```
public class Game
{
    public virtual void Play()
    {
    }
}
```

The `virtual` keyword is required on the Play method to indicate that it can be overridden by any class that inherits the Game class.

Next, you declare a class named Chess that extends the Game class but provides an implementation for the Play method:

```
public class Chess : Game
{
    public override void Play()
    {
        //code to play chess game goes here
    }
}
```

Here, the `override` keyword is required to indicate that the Play method is overriding a virtual method from the Game class. Then, when you call the `Play` method of a `Chess` object, the game announces that it gives up. (I was going to provide a complete implementation of an actual chess game program for this example, but it would have made this chapter about 600 pages long, so I opted for the simpler version here.)

Note that to override a method, three conditions have to be met:

+ **The class must extend the class that defines the method you want to override.**

+ **The method must be declared in the base class with** `public` **or** `protected` **access and with the** `virtual` **keyword.** You can't override a `private` method. (For more about `protected` access, see the next section.)

+ **The method in the derived class must have the same signature as the method in the base class.** In other words, the name of the method and the parameter types must be the same.

Protecting Your Members

You can read earlier in this chapter about `public` and `private` keywords, which are used to indicate whether class members are visible outside of the class. When you inherit a class, all the `public` members of the base class are available to the derived class, but the `private` members aren't. Although `private` members do become a part of the derived class, you can't access them directly in the derived class.

C# provides a third visibility option that's useful when you create derived classes: `protected`. A member with `protected` visibility is available to derived classes but not to other classes. Consider this example:

```
public class Ball
{
    private double _Weight;
    protected double Weight
    {
        get
        {
            return this._Weight;
        }
        set
        {
            this._Weight = value;
        }
    }
}
```

```
public class BaseBall : Ball
{
    public BaseBall()
    {
        Weight = 5.125;
    }
}
```

Here, the `Weight` property is declared with `protected` access, which means it is visible in the derived class `BaseBall`. However, this property isn't visible to classes that don't extend `Ball`.

Using this and base in Your Derived Classes

In Chapter 5 of this mini-book, you learned about the `this` keyword: It provides a way to refer to the current object instance. `this` is used to refer to the current instance of the current class. For example:

```
private double _Velocity;
protected double Velocity
{
    get
    {
        return this._Velocity;
    }
    set
    {
        this._Velocity = value;
    }
}
```

Here, the `this` keyword indicates that the `_Velocity` variable referred to in the `get` and `set` accessors is an instance variable. For a refresher on the `get` and `set` accessors, see Chapter 5 of this mini-book.

If you need to refer to a field or method that belongs to a base class, you use the `base` keyword. It works similarly to `this` but refers to the instance of the base class rather than the instance of the current class.

For example, consider these two classes:

```
public class Ball
{
    protected virtual string Description;
    public string Hit()
    {
```

```
            return "You hit it a mile!";
        }
    }
    public class BaseBall : Ball
    {
        public override string Hit()
        {
            return base.Hit() + " And it's still going!";
        }
    }
```

Here, the `Hit` method in the `BaseBall` class calls the `Hit` method of its base class object. Suppose you place the following code in the `Page_Load` method of a code-behind file:

```
BaseBall b = new BaseBall();
Response.Write(b.Hit());
```

The following will display on the page:

```
You hit it a mile! And it's still going!
```

You can also use the `base` keyword in the constructor of a derived class to explicitly call a constructor of the base class. For more information, see the next section.

Inheritance and Constructors

When you create an instance of a derived class, C# automatically calls the default constructor of the base class before it executes the derived class constructor. If you want to call a base class constructor that uses parameters, you must use the `base` keyword. Do that by creating a constructor in the derived class and following the constructor definition with a colon and a call to the base constructor.

For example, here's a version of the `Ball` and `BaseBall` classes in which the `BaseBall` constructor calls a `Ball` constructor that uses a parameter:

```
public class Ball
{
    public double Weight;
    public Ball(double Weight)
    {
        this.Weight = Weight;
    }
}
public class BaseBall : Ball
{
    public BaseBall() : base(5.125)
```

```
            {}
    }
```

Here, the `BaseBall` constructor calls the `Ball` constructor to supply a default weight of 5.125 for the ball.

Casting Up and Down

An object of a derived type can be treated as if it were an object of its base type. For example, if the `BaseBall` class extends the `Ball` class, a `BaseBall` object can be treated as if it were a `Ball` object. This is *upcasting,* and C# does it automatically, so you don't have to code a casting operator. Thus, the following code is legal:

```
Ball b = new BaseBall();
```

Here, an object of type `BaseBall` is created. Then, a reference to this object is assigned to the variable b, whose type is `Ball`, not `BaseBall`.

Now suppose you have a method named `Hit` that's declared like this:

```
public void Hit(Ball b)
```

In other words, this method accepts a `Ball` type as a parameter. When you call this method, you can pass it either a `Ball` object or a `BaseBall` object because `BaseBall` is a derived class of `Ball`. Thus, the following code works:

```
BaseBall b1 = new BaseBall();
Hit(b1);
Ball b2 = b1;
Hit(b2);
```

Downcasting — the opposite of upcasting — doesn't happen automatically, however. Thus, you can't use a `Ball` object where a `BaseBall` object is called for. For example, suppose your program has a method declared like this:

```
public void Toss(BaseBall b)
```

In this case, the following code does not compile:

```
Ball b = new BaseBall();
Toss(b);     // error: won't compile
```

However, you can explicitly cast the b variable to a `BaseBall` object, like this:

```
Ball b = new BaseBall();
Toss((BaseBall) b);
```

Note that the second statement throws an exception if the object referenced by the b variable isn't a BaseBall object. Thus, the following code doesn't work:

```
Ball b = new SoftBall();
Toss((BaseBall) b);          // error: b isn't a Baseball
```

What if you want to call a method that's defined by a derived class from an object that's referenced by a variable of the base class? For example, suppose the SoftBall class has a method named RiseBall that isn't defined by the Ball class. How can you call it from a Ball variable? One way is to create a variable of the derived class and then use an assignment statement to cast the object:

```
Ball b = new SoftBall();
SoftBall s = (SoftBall)b;    // cast the Ball to a SoftBall
s.RiseBall();
```

Here's a better way: C# lets you cast the Ball object to a SoftBall class and call the RiseBall method in the same statement. All you need is an extra set of parentheses:

```
Ball b = new SoftBall();
((SoftBall) b).RiseBall();
```

Here, the expression ((SoftBall) b) returns the object referenced by the b variable, cast as a SoftBall. You can then call any method of the SoftBall class. (An exception will be thrown if b is not a SoftBall object.)

Determining an Object's Type: The is Operator

You can see in the preceding section that a variable of one type can possibly hold a reference to an object of another type. For example, if Salaried Employee is a derived class of the Employee class, the following statement is perfectly legal:

```
Employee emp = new SalariedEmployee();
```

Here, the type of the emp variable is Employee, but the object it refers to is a SalariedEmployee.

Suppose you have a method named ReadEmployee whose return type is Employee, but that actually returns either a SalariedEmployee or an HourlyEmployee object:

```
Employee emp = ReadEmployee();
```

In many cases, you don't need to worry about which type of employee this method returns, but sometimes you do. For example, suppose the Salaried

Employee class extends the Employee class by adding a method named Get FormattedSalary, which returns the employee's salary formatted as currency. Similarly, the HourlyEmployee class extends the Employee class with a Get FormattedRate method that returns the employee's hourly pay rate formatted as currency. You need to know which type of employee a particular object is in order to determine whether you should call the GetFormattedSalary method or the GetFormattedRate method to obtain the employee's pay rate.

To tell what type of object has been assigned to the emp variable, you can use the is operator, which is designed specifically for this purpose. Here's how you can use the is operator to determine the type of an object:

```
Employee emp = ReadEmployee();
string msg;
if (emp is SalariedEmployee)
{
    msg = "The employee's salary is ";
    msg += ((SalariedEmployee) emp).GetFormattedSalary();
}
else
{
    msg = "The employee's hourly rate is ";
    msg += ((HourlyEmployee) emp).GetFormattedRate();
}
Response.Write(msg);
```

Here, the is operator is used in an if statement to determine the type of the object returned by the GetEmployee method. Then, the emp variable can be cast without fear of throwing an exception.

Poly What?

Polymorphism refers to the ability of C# to use base class variables to refer to derived class objects, keep track of which derived class an object belongs to, and use overridden methods of the derived class even though the derived class isn't known when the program is compiled. This sounds like a mouthful, but it's not that hard to understand when you see an example.

Suppose you're developing an application that can play the venerable game tic-tac-toe. You start out by creating a class named Player that represents one of the players. This class has a public method named Move that returns an int value to indicate which square of the board the player wants to mark:

```
class Player
{
    public int Move()
    {
        int square = 0;
        // code to find the first open square goes here
```

```
        return square;
    }
}
```

This basic version of the Player class uses a simple strategy to determine what its next move should be: It chooses the first open square on the board. This strategy stokes your ego by letting you think you can beat the computer every time. (To keep the illustration simple, I omitted the code that actually chooses the move.)

Next, you need to create a derived class of the Player class that uses a more intelligent method to choose its next move:

```
class BetterPlayer : Player
{
    public int Move()
    {
        int square;
        // code to find the best move goes here
        return square;
    }
}
```

As you can see, this version of the Player class overrides the Move method and uses a better algorithm to pick its move. (Again, to keep the illustration simple, I don't show the code that actually implements the better algorithm.)

Now suppose you code a method like this:

```
public static void PlayARound(Player p1, Player p2)
{
    p1.Move();
    p2.Move();
}
```

Notice that the PlayARound method doesn't know which of the two players is the basic player and which is the better player. It simply calls the Move method for each Player object.

C# knows to call the Move method of the BetterPlayer derived class because it uses a technique called *late binding*. Late binding simply means that when the compiler can't tell for sure what type of object a variable references, it doesn't hardwire the method calls when the program is compiled. Instead, the compiler waits until the program is executing to determine exactly which method to call.

Book V

Visual Basic

Contents at a Glance

Chapter 1: Mastering the Basics of Visual Basic

In This Chapter

- ✔ Containing your code in classes, structures, and modules
- ✔ Establishing home base with source files
- ✔ Dealing with events via sub-procedures
- ✔ Making efficient statements
- ✔ Handling changeable values with variables
- ✔ Specifying data types
- ✔ Writing usable strings
- ✔ Using the right operators for the job
- ✔ Specifying tasks with assignment statements

*T*his chapter outlines some basic elements of Visual Basic programming. Here you get a grip on the basic structure of Visual Basic programs and the most efficient ways to code elements such as classes, modules, Sub and Function routines, variables, and statements.

Hang on and have fun!

Looking at Classes, Structures, and Modules

Visual Basic is, frankly, a strange beast. It has evolved over many decades from a once-simple programming language known as BASIC. BASIC was invented back in 1963 at Dartmouth College as a way to teach computer programming to students who were not Computer Science majors. Of course, BASIC has changed dramatically over the years, and Visual Basic today bears almost no resemblance to the original 1963 version of BASIC. Even so, there are many elements of today's Visual Basic that have their roots in early versions of BASIC.

In Visual Basic .NET (which I refer to as VB.NET from now on), there are three basic "containers" for your code:

✦ **Classes:** These are the most commonly used coding elements in ASP.NET applications. Every page in an ASP.NET application is defined as a class. Thus an ASP.NET application has at least one class for each of its pages.

✦ **Structures:** These are similar to classes but are different in several key ways (about which more in a minute).

✦ **Modules:** These are also similar to classes and structures, but with key differences in the way they organize and keep the data.

Since classes are the most common coding elements in ASP.NET applications, I focus on them in this chapter. For more about structures and modules, consult the Visual Studio help.

Working with Source Files

As with any other programming language, VB.NET programs are written in *source files* that contain the statements and other elements that make up a program. VB.NET source files always end with the extension .vb.

In most cases, each VB.NET source file contains a single class, structure, or module. Of course, you can code more than one class, structure, or module in a source file, but it's best to limit each source file to just one so you can easily locate the file that contains each class.

Besides classes, structures, and modules, a source file can contain two file-level elements:

✦ Option **statements:** These specify options that affect how your code is compiled. Most VB.NET programs should include two option statements:

   • Option Explicit means that all variables used by the program must be explicitly declared.

   • Option Strict means the compiler won't automatically convert data from incompatible types.

I highly recommend that you include both these statements at the start of every VB.NET source file. (Option Explicit is on by default, but I like to code it anyway so there's no confusion about whether this option is on or off.)

If you're using the single-file model in which the page markup and executable code are in the same file, you can specify these options using the Page directive, like this:

```
<%@ Page explicit="true" strict="true" Language="VB" %>
```

✦ Imports **statements:** These provide a convenient way to refer to other classes. By default, VB.NET code-behind files have access to most of the .NET Framework libraries they need. However, you may occasionally need to add an Imports statement to gain access to infrequently used .NET classes.

Here's what a typical VB.NET code-behind file looks like after the two Option statements and an Imports statement have been added:

```
Option Explicit On
Option Strict On
Imports System.Collections.Generic
Partial Class _Default
    Inherits System.Web.UI.Page
    'Additional code will go here
End Class
```

Creating Sub Procedures

The most common way to write VB.NET code in an ASP.NET application is to create a Sub procedure that responds to an event such as the current page loading or the user clicking a button. You can create a Sub procedure automatically in Visual Studio by double-clicking a control in the Web designer. For example, if you double-click a button control, a Sub procedure that handles the Click event for the button will be created, like this:

```
Protected Sub Button1_Click(ByVal sender As Object, _
    ByVal e As System.EventArgs) Handles Button1.Click
End Sub
```

When that's done, you can flesh out this Sub procedure by adding VB.NET programming statements between the Protected Sub and End Sub lines.

Here are a few noteworthy things to point out about this example:

✦ **The name of the** Sub **procedure (in this case,** Button1_Click**) tells you both the name of the control it is associated with (**Button1**) and the event it handles (**Click**). This is simply a convention — ASP.NET** doesn't actually use the `Sub` procedure name to associate the procedure with a particular event — but it does make troubleshooting easier.

✦ **The `Handles` part of the `Sub` procedure heading is what associates a procedure with a particular event.** In this case, `Button1.Click` indicates that this procedure is an event handler for the `Click` event of the `Button1` button.

✦ **This procedure accepts two *parameters*, named `sender` and `e`.** In some cases, you may need to use these parameters; in most cases, you can ignore them.

Chapter 3 of this mini-book delves deeper into `Sub` procedures, including the use of parameters and a related type of procedure called a `Function` procedure.

If you're using the single-file model in which the markup and executable code are together in the same file, the Visual Studio IDE doesn't use a `Handles` clause when you create an event handler. Instead, the control you double-click will have an attribute that specifies the method to be invoked if the event is triggered. For example, if you double-click a button control, an `onclick` attribute will be generated to provide the name of the method that handles the button's click event.

Working with Statements

Like most programming languages, VB.NET uses *statements* to get things done. VB.NET has many different types of statements. Here are two of the most important general types:

✦ *Declaration statements* **create variables that you can use to store data.** Such statements tend to look like this:

```
Dim i As Integer
Private s As String
Public Amount As Decimal = 33.4D
```

✦ *Executable statements* **actually perform some action (that is, they're executed) when the program comes to them.** Among such statements, an *assignment statement* is a particular type that assigns a value to a variable — as in this example:

```
i = 0
s = "This is a string"
```

You'll see many other examples of VB.NET statements in the rest of this chapter and throughout this mini-book.

Some general rules govern how you write VB.NET statements, but the most important one is that every VB.NET statement must be coded on a single line. If you must extend a statement to a second line, you must end the first line with a space followed by an underscore and a return character. Here's how that looks:

```
string message = "The total invoice amount is " _
    & "shown at the bottom of the page."
```

In this example, an assignment statement is continued onto a second line.

Okay, technically you *can* code more than one statement on a single line — but I don't recommend it because it makes your code less readable. If you absolutely have to do that, you just separate the statements with a colon, like this:

```
i = 0 : s = "This is a string"
```

Creating Identifiers

An *identifier* is a name you use to refer to a VB.NET programming element. Identifiers are used to refer to elements such as variables, Sub procedures, and classes.

Here are some important points to keep in mind regarding identifiers:

+ **In VB.NET, identifiers are *not* case-sensitive.** As a result, SalesTax and salesTax refer to the same variable. This is unlike C#, in which identifiers *are* case-sensitive.

+ **Identifiers can be made up of upper- or lowercase letters, numerals, and underscore characters (_).**

+ **All identifiers must begin with a letter or an underscore.** Thus a15 is a valid identifier, but 13Unlucky isn't because it begins with a numeral.

+ **An identifier can't be the same as a VB.NET keyword.** Don't worry: The compiler will let you know — and will tell you "no dice" — if you try to create a variable named If or a Sub procedure named Public.

+ **If you absolutely must use an identifier name that is the same as a VB.NET reserved word, you can get away with it if you enclose that name in brackets ([ ]).** For example, the following is legal, but not recommended:

```
Dim [Public] As String
[Public] = "This variable has the same name as a keyword"
Response.Write([Public])
```

Adding Comments to Your Code

A *comment* is a bit of text that provides explanations of your code for the human beings who may read it (and puzzle over it) later on. Comments are completely ignored by the compiler, so you can place any text you wish in a comment. Tucking plenty of comments into your programs is a good idea to explain what your program does and how it works.

To mark a comment in VB.NET, simply code an apostrophe. When the compiler encounters an apostrophe, it ignores any text from the apostrophe to the end of the line. For example:

```
Dim i As Integer     'This line declares the i variable
```

If you want an entire line to be a comment, just start the line with an apostrophe:

```
' Calculate the discounted total
```

Declaring Variables

In VB.NET, you don't necessarily have to declare variables before you use them. For example, the following is legal in VB.NET:

```
Message = "This is a string"
```

If the `Message` variable hasn't been previously declared, VB.NET will declare it automatically. If that sounds tempting, consider . . .

Allowing VB.NET to declare variables automatically may be convenient, but it's a recipe for trouble. One of the most common problems caused by this practice is misspelled variable names. For example, consider this sequence:

```
TaxRate = 0.05D
SalesTax = Subtotal * TaxRate
InvoiceTotal = Subtotal + SalseTax
```

Here the customer will never be charged sales tax because the `SalesTax` variable is misspelled in the third line. With VB.NET's normal behavior, a new variable named `SalseTax` will be defined automatically — and initialized to zero — and you'll never know until you notice that no sales tax is applied.

This sort of debacle is why I recommend you always specify `Option Explicit On` in your VB.NET programs. That way, you must always explicitly declare variables before you can use them.

The basic form of a variable declaration is this:

```
Dim name As type
```

Here are some examples:

```
Dim x As Integer
Dim LastName As String
Dim Radius As Double
```

In these examples, variables named x, LastName, and Radius are declared. The x variable holds integer values, the lastName variable holds string values, and the radius variable holds double values. (For more about what these types mean, see the section "Working with Data Types," below.)

Here are a few additional details worth knowing about Dim statements:

✦ **You can declare two or more variables of the same type in a single statement if you separate the variable names with commas, as in this example:**

```
Dim x, y, z As Integer
```

✦ **If you declare a variable outside any procedure in the class, the variable is made available to** *all* **procedures — in which case, it's called an** *instance variable.*

✦ **If you declare a variable within a procedure, it's made available only to that procedure — in which case, it's called a** *local variable.*

✦ **You can assign an initial value to a variable like this:**

```
Dim i As Integer = 5
```

Here the value 5 is assigned to the variable i.

✦ **Instead of the word** Dim, **you can use an** *access modifier* **that indicates whether the variable is visible outside the class.** The access modifiers are Private, Public, and Protected. (There's more about these access modifiers in Chapter 5 of this mini-book.)

Working with Data Types

The term *data type* refers to the type of data that can be stored in a variable. VB.NET is very loose about keeping data confined to any one data type — in fact, it goes to great lengths to convert data automatically from one type to another whenever necessary. Note, however, that if you include Option Strict On in your programs (which you should), VB.NET suddenly gets a lot more picky about the correct use of data types. So here's a word to the wise: To deal with VB.NET when it gets persnickety, pay careful attention to the information in this section.

Table 1-1 lists the data types you're most likely to use in VB.NET. (There are other data types available, but they aren't commonly used so I don't include them in the table. You can find out about the other types by searching Visual Studio help for "data types.")

Table 1-1	Commonly Used VB.NET Types
Type	*Explanation*
Integer	A 32-bit (4-byte) signed integer value.
Short	A 16-bit (2-byte) signed integer value.
Long	A 64-bit (8-byte) signed integer value.
Byte	An 8-bit (1-byte) unsigned integer value.
Single	A 32-bit (4-byte) floating-point value.
Double	A 64-bit (8-byte) floating-point value.
Decimal	A 128-bit (16-byte) decimal value.
Char	A 16-bit character using the Unicode encoding scheme.
Boolean	A True or False value.

Integer types

An *integer* is a whole number — that is, a number with no fractional or decimal portion. VB.NET has several different integer types, which you can use to store numbers of varying sizes.

If you're writing the application that counts how many hamburgers McDonald's has sold, an Integer variable might not be big enough. The largest number an Integer can hold is a little over two billion, and McDonald's passed that many years ago. Fortunately, Visual Basic provides a Long integer type that can hold large numbers. Long is a 64-bit integer that can hold numbers ranging from about –9 quadrillon (that's a nine with fifteen zeros after it) to +9 quadrillon. That's a big number, even by Federal Deficit standards.

In some cases, you may not need integers as large as those the standard Integer type provides. For those situations, VB.NET provides smaller integer types. The Short type represents a two-byte integer, which can hold numbers from –32,768 to +32,767. And the Byte type defines an 8-bit integer that can range from –128 to +127.

VB.NET allows you to *promote* an integer type to a larger integer type. For example, VB.NET allows the following:

```
Dim xInt As Integer
Dim yLong As Long
xInt = 32
yLong = xInt
```

Here you can assign the value of the `xInt` variable to the `yLong` variable because `yLong` is a larger size than `xInt`. However, VB.NET does not allow the converse:

```
Dim xInt As Integer
Dim yLong as Long
yLong = 32
xInt = yLong
```

The value of the `yLong` variable cannot be assigned to the `xInt` because `xInt` is smaller than `yLong`. Because this assignment might result in a loss of data, VB.NET doesn't allow it if you have specified `Option Strict On`.

Floating-point types

Floating-point numbers are numbers that have fractional parts expressed in decimal form; the decimal point can move (or *float*) as needed. Floating-point data types can represent numbers such as 19.95 or 3.1415.

✦ **VB.NET has two built-in types for floating-point numbers:** `Single`, **which uses four bytes, and** `Double`, **which uses eight bytes.** In almost all cases, you should use the `Double` type whenever you need numbers with fractional values.

✦ **The** *precision* **of a floating-point value indicates how many significant digits the value can have.** The precision of a `Single` type is only about 6 or 7 decimal digits, which isn't sufficient for most types of calculations. That's why you should almost always use `Double` instead.

The decimal type

Because of their limited precision, floating-point types are not really appropriate for representing currency amounts in business applications. Instead, these types of applications should use the `Decimal` type, which is designed to store decimal data accurately. The decimal data type uses 128 bits for each number, and can accurately store decimal numbers with as many as 28 digits.

One oddity of the decimal type is that if you want to use a decimal number as a literal value (that is, a number hard-coded into your program), you must follow that value with the letter D. Here's an example:

```
Dim TaxRate As Decimal = 0.075D
Dim Price As Decimal = 19.99D
```

The D is required because `Option Explicit` prevents Visual Basic from automatically converting a double to a decimal, and numbers without the trailing D are assumed to be doubles.

The char type

The `char` type represents a single character. Note that a character is not the same as a string; a string is a collection of one or more individual characters. A `char` represents just a single character. The lowdown about strings appears below, in the section "Working with Strings." For now, just realize that a `char` variable can store only one character, not a sequence of characters (as a string can).

To assign a value to a `Char` variable, you follow the character literal with the letter `c` to indicate that the literal is a character rather than a string. Here's an example:

```
Dim Code As Char = "X"c
```

Here the character `X` is assigned to the variable named `Code`.

The Boolean type

A `Boolean` type can have one of two values: `True` or `False`. Booleans are used to perform logical operations, most commonly to determine whether some condition is true. For example:

```
Dim Enrolled As Boolean = True
Dim Credited As Boolean = False
```

Here a variable named `Enrolled` of type `Boolean` is declared and initialized to a value of `True`, and another `Boolean` named `Credited` is declared and initialized to `False`.

Working with Strings

A *string* is a sequence of text characters. The following sections present the bare essentials of working with strings so you can incorporate simple strings in your programs.

Declaring and initializing strings

Strings are declared and initialized like other data types. The following statements define and initialize a string variable:

```
Dim s As String
s = "Hello, World!"
```

Here, a variable named `s` of type `String` is declared and initialized with the following *string literal* (that is, an unchanging string that corresponds exactly to what appears on-screen): `"Hello, World!"`

As with any variable declaration, you can declare and initialize a string variable in one statement, like this:

```
Dim s As String = "Hello, World!"
```

Combining strings

If you want to combine two strings, you can use an ampersand (&) or a plus sign (+) as a *concatenation operator* (so called because in VB.NET-speak, combining strings is called *concatenation*). For example, the following statement combines the value of two string variables to create a third string:

```
Dim Hello As String = "Hello, "
Dim World As String = "World!"
Dim Greeting As String = Hello & World
```

Here the final value of the `Greeting` variable is `"Hello, World!"`

When VB.NET concatenates strings, it doesn't insert any blank spaces between the strings. As a result, if you want to combine two strings and have a space appear between them, you need to make sure that either the first string ends with a space or the second string begins with a space. In the previous example, the first string ends with a space.

Converting strings

Converting a numeric data value to a string value is pretty easy. You can always use the `ToString` method, as in this example:

```
Dim i As Integer = 53
Dim s As String = i.ToString()
```

In addition, VB.NET automatically converts numeric values to strings when you use them in a concatenation. For example, the `Integer` variable i converts automatically to a string in this statement:

```
Dim s As String = "The value of i is " & i
```

However, going the other way — converting a string value to a numeric type — is a little more involved. And unfortunately, it doesn't always work. For example, if a string contains the value 10 you can easily convert it to an integer. But if the string contains thirty-two, you can't.

The good news is that the .NET Framework contains a class that corresponds to each data type — and every one of these classes provides a `Parse` method for converting string values to the correct type. For example, to convert a string value to an integer, you use statements like this:

```
Dim s As String = "10"
Dim x As Integer = Integer.Parse(s)
```

Working with Arithmetic Operators

An *operator* is a special symbol or keyword that's used to designate a mathematical operation (or some other type of logical operation, for example, `And` or `Or`) that can be performed on one or more values. Those values are called *operands*. In all, VB.NET has about 35 different operators. This chapter focuses on the operators that do arithmetic. These *arithmetic operators* perform basic arithmetic operations such as addition, subtraction, multiplication, and division. In all, there are 7 of them; Table 1-2 summarizes them.

Table 1-2	VB.NET's Arithmetic Operators
Operator	**Description**
+	Addition
–	Subtraction
*	Multiplication
/	Division
\	Integer Division (returns an integer result)
Mod	Remainder
^	Exponentiation

The following section of code illustrates how these operators work for `Integer` types:

```
Dim a As Integer = 21
Dim b As Integer = 6
Dim c As Integer = a + b      ' c is 27
Dim d As Integer = a – b      ' d is 15
Dim e As Integer = a * b      ' e is 126
Dim f As Integer = a / b      ' Not allowed!
Dim g As Integer = a Mod b    ' g is 3
```

Notice that you can't assign the result of normal division to an `Integer` variable because not all results of division are integers; thus the / operator returns a floating-point result.

Chapter 1

Mastering the
Basics of
Visual Basic

Here's how the operators work for `Double` values:

```
Dim x As Double = 5.5
Dim y As Double = 2.0
Dim m As Double = x + y         ' m is 7.5
Dim n As Double = x - y         ' n is 3.5
Dim o As Double = x * y         ' o is 11.0
Dim p As Double = x / y         ' p is 2.75
Dim q As Double = x Mod y       ' q is 1.5
```

Note that the same results would be obtained if you used `Decimal` types instead of `Double` types.

The Exponentiation operator can be used to raise one number to the power of another, as in this example:

```
Dim a As Integer = 5
Dim answer As Double = a ^ 2    'answer is 25
```

Note that the result of the Exponentiation operator is always a `Double` value.

Here are a few additional things to think about tonight as you lie awake pondering the wonder of VB.NET's arithmetic operators:

✦ **In algebra, you can write a number right next to a variable to imply multiplication.** For example, *4x* means "four times x." Not so in VB.NET. Statements such as the following do not compile:

```
Dim x As Integer
Dim y As Integer
y = 4x               ' error, won't compile
```

✦ **The `Mod` operator is often used to determine whether one number is evenly divisible by another, in which case the result is** 0.

✦ **C# has** *increment* (++) **and** *decrement* (--) **operators.** If you're looking for the equivalent operators in VB.NET, get used to disappointment. VB.NET doesn't have increment or decrement operators.

Combining Operators

You can combine operators to form complicated expressions. When you do, the order in which the operations are carried out is determined by the *precedence* of each operator in the expression. The order of precedence for the arithmetic operators follows a six-step sequence:

1. Exponentiation (^) is done first.

2. Sign operators (+ or -) are applied next.

3. Multiplication (*) and floating-point division (/) happen next.

4. Integer division (\) is the next operation performed.

5. The Mod operator is applied next.

6. Finally, addition (+) and subtraction (-) operators are applied.

For example, in the expression a + b * c, multiplication has a higher precedence than addition. Thus b is multiplied by c first; then the result of that multiplication is added to a.

Here are three more aspects of precedence to keep in mind:

✦ **If an expression includes two or more operators that have the same order of precedence, the operators are evaluated left to right.** Thus, in the expression a * b / c, a is first multiplied by b, and then the result is divided by c.

✦ **If you want to change the order in which operations occur, you can use parentheses to do so.** Operations within parentheses are always performed before operations that aren't in parentheses. Thus, in the expression (a + b) * c, a is added to b first. Then the result is multiplied by c.

✦ **If an expression has two or more sets of parentheses, the operations in the innermost set are performed first.** For example, in the expression (a * (b + c)) / d, b is first added to c. Then, the result is multiplied by a. And finally, that result is divided by d.

Using Assignment Statements

You use the standard assignment operator (=) to assign the result of an expression to a variable. In its simplest form, you code it like this:

```
variable = expression;
```

Here's a typical example:

```
a = (b * c) / 4
```

You've already seen plenty of examples of assignment statements like this one, so I won't belabor this point further. However, I do want to point out — just for the record — that you *cannot* code an arithmetic expression on the left side of an equal sign; thus the following statement doesn't compile:

```
a + 3 = (b * c)
```

If you've worked with older versions of BASIC, you may have seen assignment statements prefixed with the word Let, as in this example:

```
Let a = (b * c) / 4
```

Like Dim, the Let statement goes all the way back to the original 1963 version of BASIC. But that's where VB.NET parts company from its ancestor: Unlike the Dim statement, VB.NET doesn't allow you to use the word Let in an assignment statement. Oddly enough, Microsoft seems to assume that some VB.NET programmers are in the habit of typing Let at the beginning of an assignment statement — so there's an added built-in quirk: If you use the word Let in an assignment statement, the Visual Studio code editor automatically removes it for you.

Using Assignment Operators

An *assignment operator* is an operator that performs a calculation and an assignment at the same time. Most of VB.NET's arithmetic operators have corresponding assignment operators; Table 1-3 lists them.

Table 1-3	Assignment Operators
Operator	*Description*
+=	Addition assignment
-=	Subtraction assignment
*=	Multiplication assignment
/=	Division assignment
\=	Integer division assignment

As an example, this statement

```
a += 10
```

is equivalent to

```
a = a + 10
```

and this statement

```
z *=2
```

is equivalent to

```
z = z * 2
```

To avoid confusion, compound assignment expressions are best used by themselves — not in combination with other expressions. For example, consider these statements:

```
Dim a As Integer = 2
Dim b As Integer = 3
a *= b + 1
```

Is a set to 7 or 8?

In other words, is the third statement equivalent to

```
a = a * b + 1     ' This would give 7 as the result
```

or

```
a = a * (b + 1)   ' This would give 8 as the result
```

At first glance, you might expect the answer to be 7 because multiplication has a higher precedence than addition. But assignment has the lowest precedence of all, and the multiplication here is performed as part of the assignment. As a result, the addition is performed before the multiplication. Thus the answer is 8. (Gotcha!)

Chapter 2: Controlling Your Programs

In This Chapter

✓ Setting conditions with the If statement

✓ Zeroing in on the Select Case statement

✓ Reaching a particular value with the For statement

✓ Setting a time limit with the While statement

✓ Specifying tasks with the Do statement

*O*nly the most trivial of programs execute their tasks one at a time, in the exact sequence in which the statements are listed in the program. Life, even in the world of programming, just isn't that simple. Most programs require more control over the sequence in which statements are executed. For example, you may need to skip over some statements based on the results of a condition test. Or, you may need to create a loop of statements that repeats itself a given number of times or until a certain condition is met.

This chapter describes the VB.NET statements that let you control the flow of execution for your ASP.NET programs.

Using If Statements

The Robert Frost poem that begins, "Two roads diverged in a yellow wood . . ." is an apt description of how the If statement works. The program is rolling along, executing one statement after another, until it comes to an If statement. The If statement represents a fork in the road; a choice must be made about which path to take.

Many programs have to make such either/or decisions as they execute. For example, a program that writes data entered by the user into a database has to make a determination first: Did the user actually enter some data? If so, the program writes the data to the database. If not, the program displays an error message saying something along the lines of, "Yo! You didn't enter anything!" To process this decision, the program uses an If statement.

VB's `If` statement is remarkably flexible, with several formats to choose from. All these forms involve three basic parts:

✦ **A *condition test,* in which a conditional expression is evaluated to yield a value of** `True` **or** `False`**.** (There's more about conditional expressions later in this chapter.)

✦ **A *Then part*, which supplies one or more statements that execute only if the result of the condition test is** `True`**.**

✦ **An *Else part*, which supplies one or more statements that execute only if the result of the condition test is** `False`**.**

For example, consider these lines:

```
If txtLastName.Text <> "" Then
    ' Add the last name to the database
Else
    ' Display an error message
End If
```

Here the `If` statement begins with a condition test that checks to see whether the user entered anything in the `txtLastName` text box. If so, that data is written to the database; if not, an error message is displayed.

The `If` statement takes various useful forms, with varying degrees of complexity. The following sections dig deeper into the basics of using them.

The basic If statement

The most basic form of the `If` statement looks like this:

```
If expression Then
    statements executed if true
End If
```

Each component of the `If` statement must fall on a separate line, as shown in the preceding structure. In other words, you shouldn't place the statements on the same line as the `Then` or `Else` keywords.

Here's an example of a typical `If` statement:

```
Dim CommissionRate As Decimal
If SalesTotal > 10000D Then
    CommissionRate = 0.05D
End If
```

In this example, a variable named `CommissionRate` is set to `0.05` if `Sales Total` is greater than $10,000.

Here's an example that executes more than one statement if the condition test is `True`:

```
Dim CommissionRate As Decimal
If SalesTotal > 10000D Then
    CommissionRate = 0.05D
    Commission = SalesTotal * CommissionRate
End If
```

The single-line If

VB.NET also allows you to use a single-line form of the `If` statement, which looks like this:

If *condition* **Then** *statement* [**Else** *statement*]

To use this form of the `If` statement, the condition, `Then` clause, and `Else` clause (if any) must all be coded on the same line. Here's an example:

```
If x > 0 Then Response.Write("X is " & x)
```

The preceding example displays the message `X is` *n,* where *n* is the value of x. But the message appears only if x is greater than zero.

You can include more than one statement in the `Then` part by separating the statements with colons. But if more than one statement is required, or if an `Else` part is required, I suggest you use the basic multiline `If` form instead of the single-line form.

The Else clause

The optional `Else` clause adds an element that qualifies a basic `If` statement by saying (in effect), "otherwise do this." The `Else` clause executes one or more statements if the conditional expression is not `True`. When an `If` statement includes an `Else` clause, the basic structure of the `If` statement looks like this:

```
If expression Then
    Statements executed if true
Else
    statements executed if false
End If
```

When an `Else` clause is used, the `If` statement is sometimes called an *If-Then-Else* statement. Here's an example:

```
Dim CommissionRate As Decimal
If SalesTotal <= 10000.0D Then
    CommissionRate = 0.02D
```

```
Else
    CommissionRate = 0.05D
End If
```

In this example, the commission rate is set to 2 percent if the sales total is less than or equal to $10,000. If the sales total is greater than 10,000, the commission rate is set to 5%.

In some cases, you can avoid the need for the `Else` clause by cleverly rearranging your code. For example, this code has the same effect as the previous `If-Then-Else` statement:

```
Dim CommissionRate As Decimal = 0.05D
If SalesTotal <= 10000.0D Then
    CommissionRate = 0.02D
End If
```

Nesting If statements

You can *nest* `If` statements — that is, include an `If` statement within the `Then` or `Else` part of another. Here's a typical example:

```
If expression Then
    If expression Then
        statements
    Else
        statements
    End If
Else
    If expression Then
        statements
    Else
        statements
    End IF
End If
```

Nesting can be as complex as you want — just remember that you need an `End If` for every `If`. And be certain to use indentation so that each set of matching `If`, `Else`, and `End If` lines are properly aligned.

The ElseIf structure

VB.NET supports a special type of `If` structure, using the `ElseIf` keyword. The `ElseIf` form is a shorthand notation that allows you to simplify `If` structures that follow this form:

```
If expression Then
    statements
```

```
Else
    If expression Then
        statements
    Else
        If expression Then
            statements
        End If
    End IF
End If
```

Using the ElseIf keyword, you can express the same structure like this:

```
If expression Then
    statements
ElseIf expression Then
    statements
ElseIf expression Then
    statements
End If
```

If that's a little too abstract, consider a program that writes one of three messages to the page, depending on the day of the week. For Sunday, the program writes Time for football! For Saturday, it writes Time to mow the lawn!! And for any other day, it writes Time to go to work!!! (An automatic nag — now, that's progress.)

Here's how to code this program using ordinary If statements:

```
Dim DayOfWeek As Integer
DayOfWeek=Weekday(Now())
If DayOfWeek = 1 Then
    Response.Write("Time for football!")
Else
    If DayOfWeek = 7 Then
        Response.Write("Time to mow the lawn!!")
    Else
        Response.Write("Time to go to work!!!")
    End IF
End If
```

Here's how you would code this using ElseIf:

```
Dim DayOfWeek As Integer
DayOfWeek=Weekday(Now())
If DayOfWeek = 1 Then
    Response.Write("Time for football!")
ElseIf DayOfWeek = 7 Then
    Response.Write ("Time to mow the lawn!!")
Else
    Response.Write ("Time to go to work!!!")
End If
```

In this example, only one `End If` line is required because it has only one `If` statement. In other words, the `ElseIf` keyword does not require its own matching `End If`.

You can chain as many `ElseIf` statements together as you need. For example, suppose you want to assign four different commission rates based on a sales total, according to this table:

Sales	Commission
Over $10,000	5%
$5,000 to $9,999	3.5%
$1,000 to $4,999	2%
Under $1,000	0%

You can easily implement a series of `ElseIf` statements, like this:

```
If SalesTotal >= 10000.0D Then
    CommissionRate = 0.05D
ElseIf SalesTotal >= 5000.0D Then
    CommissionRate = 0.035D
ElseIf SalesTotal >= 1000.0D Then
    CommissionRate = 0.02D
Else
    CommissionRate = 0.0D
End If
```

You have to carefully think through how you set up these `ElseIf` statements. For example, at first glance, this sequence looks like it *might* also work:

```
If SalesTotal > 0.0D Then
    CommissionRate = 0.00D
ElseIf SalesTotal >= 1000.0D Then
    CommissionRate = 0.03D
ElseIf SalesTotal >= 5000.0D Then
    CommissionRate = 0.035D
ElseIf SalesTotal >= 10000D Then
    CommissionRate = 0.05D
End If
```

In a word (okay, two words), no way. The snag is that these `If` statements always set the commission rate to `0%` because the expression in the first `If` statement always tests `True` (assuming the `SalesTotal` isn't zero or negative — and if it is, none of the other `If` statements matter). As a result, none of the other `If` statements ever get evaluated.

In many cases, a `Select Case` statement implements `If` structures that require `ElseIf` clauses more easily. (There's more about the `Select Case` statement later in this chapter.)

Using Conditional Expressions

The If statements presented so far have used simple *conditional expressions* — that is, expressions that return a value of True or False. (Such expressions are also called *Boolean expressions*.) This section shows you the basics of crafting these types of expressions, which are essential ways to tell the computer exactly how to proceed.

Simple conditional expressions use one of the *relational operators* (listed in Table 2-1) to compare two values — which can be simple variables, literal values, or expressions that perform calculations.

Table 2-1	Relational Operators
Operator	*Description*
=	Returns True if the expression on the left evaluates to the same value as the expression on the right.
!=	Returns True if the expression on the left does not evaluate to the same value as the expression on the right.
<	Returns True if the expression on the left evaluates to a value that is less than the value of the expression on the right.
<=	Returns True if the expression on the left evaluates to a value that is less than or equal to the expression on the right.
>	Returns True if the expression on the left evaluates to a value that is greater than the value of the expression on the right.
>=	Returns True if the expression on the left evaluates to a value that is greater than or equal to the expression on the right.

A basic conditional expression has this form:

```
expression relational-operator expression
```

VB.NET evaluates a Boolean expression by evaluating the expression on the left first, and then evaluating the expression on the right, after which it applies the relational operator to determine whether the entire expression evaluates to True or False.

Here are some simple examples of relational expressions. For each example, assume that the following statements were used to declare and initialize the variables:

```
Dim i As Integer = 5
Dim j As Integer = 10
Dim k As Integer = 15
```

Now, here are the sample expressions along with their results based on the values supplied:

Expression	Value	Explanation
`i = 5`	`True`	The value of `i` is 5.
`i = 10`	`False`	The value of `i` is not 10.
`i = j`	`False`	`i` is 5 and `j` is 10, so they are not equal.
`i = j - 5`	`True`	`i` is 5 and `j - 5` is 5.
`i > 1`	`True`	`i` is 5, which is greater than 1.
`j = i * 2`	`True`	`j` is 10 and `i` is 5, so `i * 2` is also 10.

Getting Logical

A *logical operator* (sometimes called a *Boolean operator*) is an operator that returns a `True` or `False` result that's based on a combination of two `True`/`False` expressions. Table 2-2 lists the logical operators.

Table 2-2	Logical Operators
Operator	*Description*
`Not`	Returns `True` if the operand to the right evaluates to `False`. Returns `False` If the operand to the right is `True`.
`And`	Returns `True` if both of the operands evaluate to `True`. Both operands are evaluated before the `And` operator is applied.
`Or`	Returns `True` if at least one of the operands evaluates to `True`. Both operands are evaluated before the `Or` operator is applied.
`Xor`	Returns `True` if one — and only one — of the operands evaluates to `True`. If both operands evaluate to `True` or if both operands evaluate to `False`, this operator returns `False`.
`AndAlso`	Same as `And`, but if the operand on the left returns `False`, this operator returns `False` without evaluating the operand on the right.
`OrElse`	Same as `Or`, but if the operand on the left returns `True`, this operator returns `True` without evaluating the operand on the `right`.

The following sections describe these operators (with the exception of `Xor`, which isn't used often) in excruciating detail.

Using the Not operator

The simplest of the logical operators is the `Not` operator — which reverses the value of a `True/False` expression. Thus, if the expression is `True`, this operator changes it to `False`. If the expression is `False`, the `Not` operator changes it to `True`.

Here's a typical example:

```
If Not (i = 4) Then
```

This expression evaluates to `True` if `i` is any value other than `4`. If `i` is `4`, it evaluates to `False`. It works by first evaluating the expression `(i = 4)`. Then it reverses the result of that evaluation.

Although it isn't always required, I suggest you always use parentheses with the `Not` operator to clearly indicate the expression that the `Not` operator is applied to. Can't hurt. Computers do exactly as they're told.

Working with the And operator

You can use the `And` operator to combine two `True/False` conditions. The result is `True` only if both of the conditions are `True`. If either condition is `False`, the result of the `And` condition is also `False`.

For example, suppose the sales commission rate should be 2.5 percent if the sales class is `1` and the sales total is `$10,000` or more. You could use two separate `If` statements to do this check, or you could use the `And` operator to combine them, like this:

```
If SalesClass = 1 And SalesTotal >= 10000.0D Then
    CommissionRate = 0.025D
End If
```

Here the conditions `SalesClass = 1` and `SalesTotal >= 10000.0` are separately tested. Then the `And` operator compares the results. If they're both `True`, the entire expression is `True`. If one or both are `False`, the entire expression returns `False`.

Utilizing the AndAlso operator

The `AndAlso` operator is similar to the `And` operator, but it takes an important shortcut. Because both expressions that the `And` operator compares must be `True` for the entire expression to be `True`, there's no reason to evaluate the second expression if the first one returns `False`. The regular `And` operator isn't aware of this, so it blindly calculates the result of the second condition even though the entire expression can't possibly be True. The And Also operator is smart enough to stop when it knows what the outcome is.

You can almost always use AndAlso instead of And. Consider this example:

```
If SalesClass = 1 AndAlso SalesTotal >= 10000.0D Then
    CommissionRate = 0.025D
End If
```

Here the second condition (SalesTotal >= 1000.0D) isn't tested if the first condition proves to be False. The only time you shouldn't use AndAlso is if the second expression calls a method that returns a Boolean result but also has a side effect, such as a method that updates a database. If you use AndAlso in this case, the method won't be called if the first expression returns True.

Using the Or and OrElse operators

The Or operators combine two conditions and return True if either condition is true, or if both conditions are True. Suppose (for example) that sales representatives get no commission if the total sales are less than $1,000 or if the sales class is 3. Here's how you could use the Or operator to solve this problem:

```
If SalesTotal < 1000.0D Or SalesClass = 3 Then
    CommissionRate = 0.0D
End If
```

The OrElse operator is similar to the AndAlso operator, in that it takes a shortcut — it skips evaluating the second condition if it knows the final result is based on the first condition. The second condition is evaluated only if the first condition is False. Here's an example:

```
If SalesTotal < 1000.0D OrElse SalesClass = 3 Then
    CommissionRate = 0.0D
End If
```

Using the Select Case Statement

Life would be easy if it consisted entirely of either/or choices. But in the real world, you're often faced with many alternatives to choose from. And so it is in VB.NET.

For example, suppose you need to translate letter grades into grade points. You're given a string that contains the letter grade, and want to determine an Integer value for each grade.

You could do this task via a series of `ElseIf` statements, like this:

```
Dim GradePoints As Integer
If LetterGrade = "A" Then
    GradePoints = 4
ElseIf LetterGrade = "B" Then
    GradePoints = 3
ElseIf LetterGrade = "C" Then
    GradePoints = 2
ElseIf LetterGrade = "D" Then
    GradePoints = 1
ElseIf LetterGrade = "F" Then
    GradePoints = 0
End If
```

Okay, that'll get the job done, but VB.NET has a better way: The `Select Case` statement.

The `Select Case` statement lets you test an expression for various values — and execute different statements depending on the result. Its general form is as follows:

```
Select Case expression
    Case values
        statements
  [ Case values
        statements ]
  [ Case Else
        statements ]
End Select
```

The `Select Case` statement starts by evaluating the expression. Then it compares the result with the case conditions listed in the `Case` clauses, one at a time. When it finds a match, it executes the statements listed for the `Case` clause that matches, and skips the rest of the `Select Case` statement. If none of the case conditions match, the statements in the `Case Else` clause execute. The key point here is that only one of the `Case` clauses is selected for execution.

Here's a `Select Case` statement that determines the grade points for a given letter grade:

```
Dim GradePoints As Integer
Select Case LetterGrade
    Case "A"
        GradePoints = 4
    Case "B"
        GradePoints = 3
```

```
    Case "C"
        GradePoints = 2
    Case "D"
        GradePoints = 1
    Case "F"
        GradePoints = 0
End Select
```

In the preceding example, each of the Case clause specifies a single value. However, there are other ways you can code the Case clause. To wit:

✦ **A list of expressions, such as** Case 4, 8, 12, 16. The Case clause is selected if the expression equals any of the listed values.

✦ **A range of values, separated with the keyword** To, **such as** Case 4 To 8. The Case clause is selected if the expression falls between the two values, inclusively.

✦ **The word** Is **followed by a relational comparison, such as** Is > 4. The relation is tested against the expression, and the Case clause is selected if the result of the comparison is True.

You can use Case Else to handle any values that aren't specifically mentioned in Case clauses.

The Select Case statement is one of the few aspects of VB.NET that is undeniably superior to the equivalent feature in C#. If you don't believe me, turn to Book 4, Chapter 2, and compare VB.NET's Select Case statement with C#'s switch statement. VB.NET has C# beat hands down in this department.

Working with For/Next Loops

For/Next loops allow you to set up a basic looping structure in which a series of statements execute over and over again, increasing the value of a counter-variable by one each time, until the counter-variable reaches a certain value.

As a simple — if not very practical — example, the following snippet inserts the numbers 1 through 100 on the page, one number on each line:

```
Dim x As Integer
For x = 1 To 100
    Response.Write(x.ToString() & "<br>")
Next x
```

This For/Next loop calls Response.Write 100 times. The first time through, the variable x is set to the value 1. The second time, x is 2; the third time, 3; and so on, all the way up to 100.

The general form of a `For/Next` loop is

```
For counter-variable = start To end [Step increment]
    statements...
Next [counter-variable]
```

As you can see, you can specify any starting and ending value you want for the counter-variable. In addition, you can specify an increment value using the `Step` clause. You can use `Step` to create `For/Next` loops that count by twos, threes, or any other value you want. If you omit `Step`, the default is 1.

If you want to get clever (or launch a rocket), you can use a `For/Next` loop to count backward by using a negative step value. In that case, the *start* value should be greater than the *end* value. Here's an example:

```
Dim x As Integer
For x = 100 To 1 Step -1
    Response.Write(x & "<br>")
Next x
```

The term *iteration* is often used to refer to each time a `For/Next` loop executes. For example, a `For/Next` loop that starts with the line `For x = 1 To 10` iterates ten times.

Using While loops

`While` loops provide a more general form of looping: The loop continues as long as a specified condition remains `True`. The general form is

```
While condition
    statements
End While
```

The `While` loop starts by evaluating the condition. If it is `True`, the statements in the loop execute. When the End While statement is encountered, the condition is evaluated again. If it is still `True`, the statements in the loop execute again. This cycle continues until the condition evaluates as `False`.

For example:

```
Dim x As Integer = 10
While x > 0
    Response.Write(x & "<br>")
    x = x - 1
End While
```

This loop continues to execute as long as x is greater than zero. The moment x becomes zero, VB.NET considers the condition expression to be `False` and the loop terminates. So this `While` loop displays five lines, showing the values 5, 4, 3, 2, 1, and then it terminates.

To continue a loop as long as an expression evaluates to `False`, use `Not` as part of the condition test. For example:

```
Dim x As Integer = 0
While Not x = 5
    Response.Write(x & "<br>")
    x = x + 1
End While
```

Here the loop repeats as long as `x` is not equal to `5`.

Utilizing Do loops

A `Do` loop is like a `While` loop, but it has more flexibility in determining exactly when the condition that signals the end of the loop is tested. The `Do` loop can actually take one of four different forms:

```
Do While condition
    statements
Loop

Do
    statements
Loop While condition

Do Until condition
    statements
Loop

Do
    statements
Loop Until condition
```

Two of these variations use the word `While` to state the condition; the other two use the word `Until`. Two of them place the condition at the beginning of the loop; the other two place the condition at the end.

If the word `While` is used, the loop is repeated as long as the condition tests `True`. But if you specify `Until` instead, the loop repeats itself for as long as the condition tests `False`. In other words, the loop repeats until the condition becomes `True`.

The position of the condition determines whether the condition is tested before or after the loop executes once. If you place the condition at the beginning of the loop, the condition is evaluated before any statements in the loop are executed. As a result, it's possible that the statements in the loop will never be executed.

In contrast, placing the condition at the end of the loop causes the test to be executed *after* the statements in the loop are executed. As a result, the statements in the loop will always be executed at least once.

Exiting a loop

Many loops require an escape clause. VB.NET's escape clause is the Exit For, Exit While, or Exit Do statement (depending on the type of loop you want to get out of). When the program encounters one of these statements, the loop ends immediately. Any remaining statements in the loop are ignored, and the next statement executed is the one that follows the loop.

For example, suppose you have an aversion to the number 12. Here's a For-Next loop that looks like it's going to count to 20, but it exits when it gets to the number 12:

```
Dim Number As Integer
For Number = 1 to 20
    If Number = 12 Then
        Exit For
    End If
    Response.Write(Number & " ...")
Next
```

When you run this program, the following line is displayed on the browser:

```
1...2...3...4...5...6...7...8...9...10...11...
```

Whew! That was close. Almost got to 12 there.

Nesting your loops

It's not uncommon for a loop to contain other loops, which can lead to vertigo if you're not careful. The proper term for a loop completely contained inside another loop is *nested loop*. The contained loop — the one that's inside — is called the *inner loop;* the loop doing the containing is called the *outer loop.*

Here's a basic example of a nested loop:

```
Dim x, y As Integer
For x = 1 To 9
    For y = 1 To 9
        Response.Write(x & "-" & y & "  ")
    Next y
    Response.Write("<br>")
Next x
```

The outer loop in this code snippet uses x as its counter-variable; the inner loop uses y. For each execution of the outer loop, the inner loop executes 9 times and prints a line that shows the value of x and y for each pass through the inner loop. When the inner loop finishes, a call to `Response.Write` (`"<br>"`) starts a new line. Then the outer loop cycles so the next line is printed.

When you run this program, the page will display this text:

```
1-1   1-2   1-3   1-4   1-5   1-6   1-7   1-8   1-9
2-1   2-2   2-3   2-4   2-5   2-6   2-7   2-8   2-9
3-1   3-2   3-3   3-4   3-5   3-6   3-7   3-8   3-9
4-1   4-2   4-3   4-4   4-5   4-6   4-7   4-8   4-9
5-1   5-2   5-3   5-4   5-5   5-6   5-7   5-8   5-9
6-1   6-2   6-3   6-4   6-5   6-6   6-7   6-8   6-9
7-1   7-2   7-3   7-4   7-5   7-6   7-7   7-8   7-9
8-1   8-2   8-3   8-4   8-5   8-6   8-7   8-8   8-9
9-1   9-2   9-3   9-4   9-5   9-6   9-7   9-8   9-9
```

Chapter 3: Working With Procedures, Exceptions, and Arrays

In This Chapter

✔ Working with Sub procedures

✔ Using Function procedures to best effect

✔ Examining the nuances of parameters

✔ Dealing with exceptions

✔ Getting arrays to work right

This chapter introduces you to three individually important but unrelated aspects of Visual Basic.Net (VB.NET) programming: procedures and functions, exceptions, and arrays.

A *procedure* is a group of sequential statements that have a name in common — and can be executed by calling the group (by name, of course) from some other place in the program. VB.NET lets you use two distinct types of procedures: Sub procedures and Function procedures. The difference between the two is that a Function procedure returns a calculated value, while a Sub procedure doesn't return a value.

Sub procedures are used extensively in ASP.NET to handle events such as the Load event for a page or the Click event for a button. In addition, you can create your own Sub or Function procedures. This often helps you simplify your code by enabling you to break a long Sub procedure into several shorter Sub or Function procedures.

Note that Sub procedures are often called *subroutines*, and both Sub and Function procedures are often called *methods*. The only difference between a Sub procedure and a Function procedure is that a Function procedure returns a value, while a Sub procedure does not.

Another highly useful (okay, indispensable) aspect of VB.NET programming is handling exceptions. This chapter lays out the details of exception handling as well.

Finally, you'll learn about arrays, which are like variables on steroids. An array can hold not only a single value, but a whole set of values.

Using Sub Procedures

A Sub procedure begins with a Sub statement and ends with an End Sub statement. The statements that make up the procedure go between the Sub and End Sub statements. The Sub command supplies the name of the procedure and any parameters that can be passed to the subroutine. Here's an example:

```
Sub SayHello
    Response.Write("Hello, World!")
End Sub
Sub SayWhatever(Message As String)
    Response.Write(Message)
End Sub
```

In this example, the SayHello procedure writes the text "Hello, World!" to the page. The SayWhatever message writes the text you pass via a parameter to the page.

Notice that if the procedure uses parameters, you must provide both the name and the type of the parameter (in parentheses) following the procedure name. For example, in the second procedure above, one parameter is used. The name of the parameter is Message, and its type is String.

You can invoke a Sub procedure simply by listing the procedure's name, almost as if the procedure had become its own VB.NET statement. Here's a simple example:

```
SayHello
```

If the Sub procedure uses parameters, you list the values you want to pass to the parameters following the procedure name, like this:

```
SayWhatever("Greetings, Planet!")
```

Besides literal values, you can also pass variables or complex expressions. For example, both of the following calls are allowed:

```
Dim Msg As String
Dim Part1 As String
Dim Part2 As String
Part1 = "Hello"
Part2 = "World!"
Msg = Part1 & ", " & Part2
SayWhatever(Msg)
SayWhatever(Part1 & ", " & Part2)
```

Here the Sub procedure SayWhatever is called twice. In both cases, the same value is passed to the Message parameter: The first time, the value is passed via a variable named `Msg`; the second time, the value is passed as an expression.

If you want to be just a bit of a neatness freak, you can type the keyword `Call` before the subroutine name when calling the subroutine — as in this example:

```
Call SayWhatever("Hello World!")
```

Okay, the `Call` keyword is optional, but some VB.NET programmers like to use it to help distinguish user-written subroutines from built-in VB.NET commands.

`Sub` procedures (as well as `Function` procedures, described in the next section) can begin with an *access modifier* that specifies whether the procedure is available to other classes in the application. The three most common access modifiers are

✦ **Public:** The procedure is visible throughout the application.

✦ **Private:** The procedure is visible only within the current class, which means it can't be used from other classes.

✦ **Protected:** The procedure is hidden from other classes in the project, with the exception of any classes derived from the current class. (If you find that statement confusing, not to worry: Turn to Chapter 5 of this mini-book for a briefing on derived classes and why they're worth bothering with.)

Working with Functions

A `Function` procedure is similar to a `Sub` procedure, with one crucial difference: A `Function` procedure returns a value. Here's an example:

```
Function CalculateDiscount(Amount As Decimal, _
        Percent As Decimal) As Decimal
    Dim Discount As Decimal
    Discount = Amount * Percent
    Return Discount
End Function
```

Here the `CalculateDiscount` function uses two parameters — an amount and a percentage — to calculate a discount amount. The amount and percentage are multiplied to determine the `Discount` amount. Then a `Return` statement is used to exit the function and return the value.

If you prefer, you can return a value by assigning a value to the function name as if it were a variable. Then you don't have to use the `Return` statement;

instead, the assigned value is returned when the end of the function is reached. Here's a handy example:

```
Function CalculateDiscount(Amount As Decimal, _
        Percent As Decimal) As Decimal
    CalculateDiscount = Amount * Percent
End Function
```

Both of these versions of the `CalculateDiscount` function return the same value.

Getting Finicky about Parameters

As you've seen in the previous sections, both the `Sub` and `Function` procedures can accept parameters. If a `Sub` or `Function` procedure does accept parameters, its `Sub` or `Function` statement must list the name and type of each parameter it expects — as in this example:

```
Sub SayWhatever(Message As String)
```

Here the `Sub` procedure `SayWhatever` accepts one parameter named `Message`. The type of this parameter is `String`.

When you call a procedure that takes parameters, you must supply an *argument* for each parameter that the procedure expects. Here's a handy example:

```
SayWhatever("Hello, World!")
```

In this case, the argument is a string literal (a *literal* is a value that's hard-coded into the program — in this case, the string value `"Hello, World!"`.

Although the terms *parameter* and *argument* are often used interchangeably, technically they're not the same thing. I know, picky, picky, but consider: A *parameter* represents data that is expected by a `Sub` or `Function` procedure; an *argument* represents data that is passed to a parameter.

The most important thing to know about parameters is the distinction between *pass-by-value* and *pass-by-reference*.

✦ **When data is passed-by-value, a copy of the variable's data is sent to the `Sub` or `Function` procedure.** This prevents the `Sub` or `Function` procedure from changing the contents of a variable passed as an argument.

✦ **When data is passed-by-reference, what's passed is merely a reference to the original argument variable.** Then, if the `Sub` or `Function` procedure changes the parameter, the argument is changed as well.

In VB.NET, the `ByVal` and `ByRef` keywords are used to indicate whether data is passed-by-value or passed-by-reference. Here's an example that should help clear things up:

```
Sub MySub(ByVal string1 As String, _
        ByRef string2 As String)
    string1 = "Gotcha!"
    string2 = "Gotcha!"
    Response.Write(string1 & string2 & "<br>")
End Sub
Sub TestIt
    Dim s1, s2 As String
    s1 = "Hello, "
    s2 = "World!"
    Response.Write(s1 & s2 & "<br>")
    MySub(s1, s2)
    Response.Write(s1 & s2 & "<br>")
End Sub
```

Here the `MySub` procedure takes two parameters: `string1` is passed-by-value, and `string2` is passed-by-reference. The `MySub` procedure changes the value of both parameters — and then writes them to the page via `Response.Write`. Then the `TestIt` procedure creates two strings, assigns the values `"Hello, "` and `"World!"` to the strings, writes the strings to the page, calls `MySub`, and writes the strings again. (Busy, busy, busy.)

If you add this code to a page and call the `TestIt` procedure, the following three lines appear on the page:

```
Hello, World!
Gotcha! Gotcha!
Hello, Gotcha!
```

The first line shows the original value of the two string variables. The second line shows that both parameters have changed within the `MySub` procedure. And the third line shows that when the `MySub` procedure ends and control returns to the `TestIt` procedure, the `MySub` procedure managed to change the `s2` argument but not the `s1` argument. That's because `s1` was passed-by-value, but `s2` was passed-by-reference.

If you omit `ByVal` and `ByRef` when you specify a parameter, VB.NET assumes `ByVal`.

To clarify the default, the Visual Studio code editor automatically inserts `ByVal` to force pass-by-values for all parameters. For example, suppose you type the following line in the code editor:

```
Sub SaySomething(Message As String)
```

It won't stay that way; Visual Studio automatically changes the line to

```
Sub SaySomething(ByVal Message As String)
```

Understanding Exceptions

Face it, sometimes bad things happen to good programs. Sometimes a file you need to open is missing, or sometimes the data that you thought was the unit price of a product turns out to be random gibberish that isn't even a number.

When that happens in VB.NET, the program will crash with an unsightly error message — unless you write your code to anticipate such errors. This anticipation is called *exception handling*, and you accomplish this bit of magic by using a statement called `Try/Catch`.

Before we get into the details of using the `Try/Catch` statement, here are some things you need to know about exceptions:

✦ **When an error occurs and an exception object is created, VB.NET has *thrown an exception.*** Of course, VB.NET has good aim, so the exception is always thrown right back to the statement that caused it to be created.

✦ **If you want to, you can use a `Try/Catch` statement so the statement that caused the exception can *catch* the exception.** But the offending statement doesn't have to catch the exception if it doesn't want it. Instead, it can duck and let someone else catch the exception. That someone else is the statement that called the procedure that's currently executing.

✦ **If everyone ducks and the exception is never caught by the program, the program ends abruptly — and displays a nasty-looking exception message instead of the page the user was expecting.** And the moral is . . .

Never let an ASP.NET Web application throw an unhandled exception.

Catching exceptions

You can catch an exception by using placing a `Try/Catch` statement around the statement (or statements) that might throw an exception. The `Try/Catch` statement follows this overall form:

```
Try
    statements that can throw exceptions
Catch [Exception As ExceptionType]
    statements executed when exception is thrown
End Try
```

The statements that follow the `Try` statement are called the *Try block*, and the statements that follow the `Catch` statement are called the *Catch block*. If any of the statements in the `Try` block cause an exception to be thrown, the rest of the statements in the `Try` block aren't executed. Instead, the statements in the `Catch` block are executed.

Here's a little piece of code that divides two numbers and uses a `Try/Catch` statement to catch an exception if the second number turns out to be zero:

```
Dim a, b, c As Integer
a = 5
b = 0    'You know darn well this won't work!
Try
    c = a / b
Catch
    Response.Write("Oops, you can't divide by zero.<br>")
End Try
```

Here the division occurs within a `Try` block and a `Catch` block catches the exception and displays an error message if an exception is thrown.

When you run this program, the following line is written to the page:

```
Oops, you can't divide by zero.
```

Here are a few additional things you should know about what `Try/Catch` statements can and can't do:

✦ **There are many different types of exceptions.** You can code a `Catch` statement by itself to catch any and all exceptions — or you can list a specific exception type to catch just one type of exception, as in this example:

```
Dim a, b, c As Decimal
a = 5
b = 0 'You know this won't work!
Try
    c = a / b
Catch DivEx As DivideByZeroException
    Response.Write("Oops, you can't divide by
    zero.<br>")
End Try
```

Here only a `DivideByZeroException` type of exception will be caught.

✦ **You can code more than one `Catch` block.** That way, if the statements in the `Try` block might throw more than one type of exception, you can catch each type of exception in a separate `Catch` block.

✦ **In most cases, the** `Catch` **block doesn't do anything with the exception object passed to it.** However, exception objects do have a `Message` property that you can use to get additional information about the exception. Consider this example:

```
Try
    c = a / b
Catch DivEx As DivideByZeroException
    Response.Write(div-ex.Message)
End Try
```

This code displays the text `Attempt to divide by zero` on the page if b has a value of zero.

Using a Finally block

After you've included all the `Catch` blocks in a `Try` statement, you can code a `Finally` block to finish things up. This block is executed whether or not any exceptions are thrown by the `Try` block or caught by any `Catch` blocks. You can use the `Finally` block to clean up any mess that might be left behind by the exception, such as open files or database connections.

Here's the basic structure of a `Try` statement with a `Finally` block:

```
Try
    statements that can throw exceptions
Catch [Exception As ExceptionType]
    statements executed when exception is thrown
Finally
    statements executed whether or not exceptions occur
End Try
```

Most of the time, a `Finally` block isn't needed because you can just place any clean-up code after the `End Try`, and the effect is the same. No surprise that you probably won't use the `Finally` block very often.

Using Arrays

An *array* is a set of variables referred to by a single variable name combined with an index number. Each item of an array is called an *element*. All the elements in an array must be of the same type. Thus the array itself has a type that specifies what kind of elements it can contain. For example, an array of `Integer` values can contain only integers, and an array of type `String` can contain only strings.

The *index number* is written after the variable name and enclosed in parentheses. So, if the variable name is x, you could access a specific element of the array with an expression like x(5).

You might think x(5) would refer to the fifth element in the array. But index numbers start with zero for the first element, so x(5) actually refers to the *sixth* element. This little detail is one of the chief causes of problems when working with arrays.

The real power of arrays comes from the simple fact that you can use a variable or even a complete expression as an array index. So, for example, instead of coding x(5) to refer to a specific array element, you can code x(i) to refer to the element indicated by the index variable i. This little trick lets you use arrays along with loops (such as For Next loops) to process all of the elements in the array.

Creating an array

Before you can create an array, you have to define it by using a Dim statement. In the Dim statement, you list the largest index value that can be used to access the array, like this:

```
Dim Names(3) As String
```

As confusing as it might be, this Dim statement creates an array that can hold *four* strings, not three. That's because the largest index can be 3, but the index of the first element is zero. Thus the array contains 4 elements.

Initializing an array

Like any other variable, an array must be initialized by setting the values of its individual elements before the array can be used. One way to initialize the values in an array is to simply assign them one by one, like this:

```
Dim Days(6) As String
Days(0) = "Sunday"
Days(1) = "Monday"
Days(2) = "Tuesday"
Days(3) = "Wednesday"
Days(4) = "Thursday"
Days(5) = "Friday"
Days(6) = "Saturday"
```

Of course, that *is* a tad labor-intensive. VB.NET has a shorthand way to create an array and initialize it with constant values:

```
Dim Days() As String = {"Sunday", "Monday", "Tuesday", _
    "Wednesday", "Thursday", _
    "Friday", "Saturday"}
```

Here each element to be assigned to the array is listed within braces ({}).

Using For loops with arrays

One of the most common ways to process an array is with a For loop. In fact, For loops were invented specifically to deal with arrays. For example, here's a For loop that uses the Visual Basic Rnd function to create an array of 100 random Integer values:

```
Dim numbers(99) As Single
Dim i As Integer
For i = 0 To 99
    numbers(i) = Rnd()
Next i
```

You can also use a For loop to display the contents of an array, as in this example:

```
For i = 0 To 99
    Response.Write(i & "<br>")
Next
```

As an alternative, you can use a For Each loop, like this:

```
For Each num In numbers
    Response.Write(num & "<br>")
Next
```

Using two-dimensional arrays

The arrays described so far in this chapter have been *one dimensional*, which means they use a single index to access their values. Arrays can have more than one dimension — for example, you could use a two-dimensional array to represent data in the form of a table: One dimension refers to the rows of the table and the other refers to the columns. Then the array works a lot like a spreadsheet.

For example, suppose you're working on a program that tracks five years' worth of sales (2002 through 2006) for a company, with the data broken down for each of their four sales territories (North, South, East, and West). You could create 20 separate variables, with names such as sales2002 North, sales2002South, sales2002East, and so on. But that gets a little tedious.

Alternatively, you could create an array with 20 elements, like this:

```
Dim Sales(19) As Decimal
```

But then, how would you organize the data in this array so you know the year *and* sales region for each element?

Going beyond two dimensions

Those of you who feel at home with the multiple dimensions of mathematics, rejoice: VB.NET doesn't limit you to two-dimensional arrays. You can nest arrays within other arrays, to as many as 32 levels. To declare an array with more than two dimensions, you just specify as many extra dimensions as you need. For example:

```
Dim Cubicle(2, 2, 2) As Integer
```

Here a three-dimensional array is created, with each dimension having three elements. You can think of this array as a cube. Each element requires three indexes to access.

You can access an element in a multidimensional array by specifying as many indexes as the array needs. For example:

```
Cubicle(0, 1, 2) = 100
```

This statement sets element 1 in column 2 of row 3 to 100.

You can also use multiple nested For statements to process an array that has three or more dimensions. For example, here's one way to initialize a three-dimensional array with the numbers 1 to 27:

```
Dim Cubicle(2, 2, 2) As Integer
Dim Value As Integer
Value = 1
Dim i, j, k As Integer
For i = 0 to 2
    For j = 0 to 2
        For k = 0 to 2
            Cubicle(i, j, k) = Value
            Value += 1
        Next k
    Next j
Next i
```

There's a *lot* more you can do with arrays, but the information in the preceding few sections should be enough to get you going. In addition, you should realize that for many applications, you're better off using one of the .NET collection classes rather than arrays to hold collections of data. For more about collection classes, dig into Book 7, Chapter 3.

With a two-dimensional array, you can create an array with an element for each year. Each of those elements, in turn, is another array with an element for each region. Here's an example:

```
Dim Sales(4, 3) As Decimal
```

Here, Sales is a two-dimensional array of type Decimal. The first dimension has 5 elements (0 through 4) that correspond to the years (2002 through 2006); the second dimension has four elements (0 through 3) for the four sales territories (North, South, East, and West).

To access the elements of a two-dimensional array, you use two indexes. For example, this statement sets the 2002 sales for the North region:

```
Sales(0, 0) = 23853.0D
```

As you might imagine, accessing the data in a two-dimensional array by hard-coding each index value can get tedious. So For loops are usually used instead. For example, the following bit of code uses nested For loops to initialize each of the elements of the Sales array to 10,000:

```
Dim i, j As Integer
For i = 0 to 4
    For j = 0 to 3
        Sales(i, j) = 10000D
    Next j
Next i
```

Chapter 4: Exploring Object-Oriented Programming

In This Chapter

✔ **Understanding object-oriented programming**

✔ **Creating your own objects and classes**

✔ **Working with shared members**

*V*isual Basic.NET (VB.NET) traces its roots way back to the early 1960s, long before anyone had ever conceived of object-oriented programming. However, unlike most programming languages from that era (such as FORTRAN and COBOL), Visual Basic evolved into a thoroughly object-oriented programming language.

In this chapter, I introduce some of the basic concepts of object-oriented programming and show you how these basic concepts work in VB.NET.

Introducing Object-Oriented Programming

One of the oldest concepts of programming is the idea of *modularity*. The basic idea of modularity is that you can often solve a large problem by breaking the problem down into several smaller problems. You can easily write code to implement each of the smaller pieces and then combine the pieces to solve the entire problem. But how do you keep track of the pieces?

In early programming languages, the pieces were simple procedures. Procedures are useful, but it's difficult to coordinate programs that consist of hundreds, thousands, or even *tens* of thousands of procedures. Object-oriented programming attempts to ease this burden by applying additional structure to the individual pieces that make up an application.

In object-oriented programming, the pieces that make up an application are called *objects*, and they have certain basic characteristics. The following sections describe some of the more important object characteristics: identity, type, behavior, and state.

Objects have identity

Every object has an *identity* that serves to uniquely identify the object. Identity is important because it lets you distinguish one occurrence of a particular type of object from another occurrence of the same type.

Objects in the real world have a self-apparent notion of identity. For example, people have names that serve to identify them — though there aren't really enough names (you'd need billions) to give every person on the planet a *unique* name. But modern science can tell people apart by their DNA, which provides more than enough uniqueness.

One way to tell two objects apart in an object-oriented program is to use the objects' memory location. This is possible because objects exist within computer memory — and to do that, each object must have its own memory location. After all, everything's got to be somewhere.

Note, however, that memory location isn't a very reliable way to identify objects; an object can change memory locations without changing its identity. That's why VB.NET uses a more sophisticated way to keep track of objects — but let's skip the details of that topic for now. Just keep in mind that every object has a unique identity.

Objects have type

The *type* of an object is an overall category used to group objects together into classes. To use an analogy from biology, cats and dogs are types of objects. If you walk into the waiting room of a busy veterinarian's office, you'll probably find several cats and several dogs. The cats will be cowering in their owner's arms, and the dogs will be straining against their leashes trying to get at the cats. The waiting room contains two *types* or *classes* of objects: cats and dogs.

However, not all the dogs are alike. There may be a couple of Labrador Retrievers, a Great Dane, and a Siberian Husky. All three are types of dogs, but they are *different* types of dogs. As detailed in Chapter 5 of this mini-book, this is the basic idea behind the concept of inheritance in object-oriented programming: An object can inherit a type, but not a state.

Objects have state

The *state* of an object is the data that's held by the object. Pushing our veterinary-office analogy just a little bit, imagine that there are two Golden Retrievers in the waiting room. One of them is a nine-month-old puppy with light hair. The other is a six-year-old adult with reddish hair. The nine-month-old hasn't eaten since this morning, so he is hungry. But the six-year-old ate just before coming to the vet, so he isn't hungry. If these dogs were objects, I have just identified three aspects of these objects' state: age, hair color, and hunger level.

All dogs have an age, a hair color, and a hunger level. But these state values aren't what uniquely identifies a dog. There might be two three-year-old Labs with chocolate-brown hair who haven't eaten in a week, but that doesn't make them the same dog. (Of course, we all know that *all* three-year-old chocolate Labs *act* like they haven't eaten in a week, even if they just wolfed down an entire package of cookies left unattended on the table. But that's another story.)

Unlike its identity, an object's state can — and usually does — change over its lifetime. For example, dogs get older with time, and their hair might turn gray. The sales total for a customer changes each time the customer buys another product. The grade-point average for a student changes each time a new class grade is recorded. And the address and phone number of an employee changes if the employee moves.

Note that the exact combination of items that make up an object's state is determined by the object's type. For example, Golden Retrievers have traits such as color, height, and weight. But an object such as an invoice doesn't have color, height, or weight to speak of; it can exist as pure information. Instead, it has characteristics such as a subtotal, a sales tax amount, and an invoice total. And an object such as a doctor appointment might have a time, date, and patient name. In other words, an object's type determines what items make up the object's state.

In VB.NET, an object's state is represented by its fields and properties. For example, you might use statements like these to set the hair color for a Golden Retriever named `Penny`:

```
Dim Penny As GoldenRetriever
Penny = New GoldenRetriever()
Penny.Color = Blond
```

Objects have behavior

The final basic characteristic of objects is *behavior*, which refers to the things an object can do. Like state, the specific behavior of an object depends on its type. But unlike state, the behavior isn't different for each instance of a type. For example, dogs have a favorite behavior called *eating*. All dogs eat pretty much the same. Put food or anything vaguely resembling food in front of a dog, and the dog will eat.

In VB.NET, object behavior is the behavior of an object provided by its methods — that is, by its `Sub` and `Function` procedures. For example, to make the (logical) dog called `Penny` eat, you might call the `Eat` method:

```
Penny.Eat()
```

This calls the `Eat` method, which is implemented as a `Sub` or `Function` procedure. (For more about `Sub` and `Function` procedures, see Chapter 3 of this mini-book.)

Creating Objects from Classes

Before we get into the details of how to create your own classes, you need to know how to create objects from classes. Okay, maybe that sounds a little backward — the difference between an object and a class is one of the most confusing aspects of object-oriented programming — but bear with me: A *class* is the code that defines the data and behavior associated with an object. An *object* is an instance of a class that's created when the program runs; it exists in memory for as long as it's needed.

To create an object from a class, you use the `New` keyword. For example, suppose you have a class named `SomeClass`, and you want to create an instance of this class and refer to it using a variable named `MyObject`. First, you must define the `MyObject` variable. You use the `As` clause to specify that the type of the variable is `SomeClass`, like this:

```
Dim MyObject As SomeClass
```

This doesn't create an object. Instead, it just creates a variable that you can use later to refer to an object.

To create an object from a class, you use the `New` keyword, like this:

```
MyObject = New SomeClass()
```

This creates an instance of the `SomeClass` class, and assigns the resulting object to the `MyObject` variable.

You can combine variable declaration and object creation into a single statement, like this:

```
Dim MyObject As SomeClass = New SomeClass()
```

Or, you can shorten it even more by coding it like this:

```
Dim MyObject As New SomeClass()
```

Declaring Classes

Classes are one of the basic building blocks of ASP.NET applications. In fact, most of the coding you do when you develop an ASP.NET application will be in the form of classes, each of which represents a page of the application.

Declaring Classes **459**

Book V
Chapter 4

Exploring
Object-Oriented
Programming

A VB.NET class begins with a *class declaration* that provides the name for
the class and a class body that contains the code that implements the class.
Here's the most basic form of a class declaration:

```
Public [Partial] Class ClassName
Class body
End Class
```

You use the `Public` keyword to indicate that the class can be referred to from
other classes throughout your application. You can also create `Private`
classes, but they aren't very useful for ASP.NET applications.

The optional `Partial` keyword indicates that the definition of the class
is spread over two or more files. You probably won't use this keyword
for classes you create yourself, but ASP.NET relies on `Partial` classes to
create page classes — including the code-behind file.

The body of the class — that is, that sequence of statements that appears
between the `Class` and `End Class` statements — can contain the following
elements:

+ **Fields, which are variables that can be accessed throughout the class.**
  Fields can be private (used only within the class), or public (usable
  outside the class).

+ **Properties, which are an advanced type of field.**

+ **Methods, which are simply** `Sub` **and** `Function` **procedures associated
  with the class.**

+ **Constructors, which are special Sub procedures that are executed
  whenever a new object is created from the class.**

The field, properties, methods, and constructors of a class are called its
members.

The next few sections take a closer look at using these class members.

Using fields

A variable that's defined in the body of a class, outside any of the class's
methods is called a *field* or a *class variable*. Fields are available throughout
the class. Although you can create a field by coding a `Dim` statement, the
usual approach is to omit the keyword `Dim` and (instead) specify `Public` or
`Private` to indicate whether the field is visible outside its class.

For example, here's a class that uses a private field to represent a sales tax:

```
Public Class SomeClass
    Private TaxRate As Decimal = 0.075D
    Public Function CalculateTax(Amount As Decimal) _
            As Decimal
        Return Amount * TaxRate
    End Function
End Class
```

Here the `CalculateTax` method uses a private field named `TaxRate`, which contains the sales tax rate.

If you want the tax rate to be available outside the class, you can define it as `Public` instead, like this:

```
    Public TaxRate As Decimal
```

Then, when you create an object from the class by using the New keyword, you can access the `TaxRate` field — like this:

```
Dim MyObject As SomeClass = New SomeClass()
MyObject.TaxRate = 0.075D
```

Creating properties

A *property* is a procedure — actually, a pair of procedures — that looks like a field. When you set the value of a property, one of the two procedures — called the *set procedure* — is executed to set the property's value. And when you retrieve the value of the property, the other procedure — called the *get procedure* — is executed to calculate the property's value. This turns out to be extremely useful, as you'll see in a few moments.

To create a property, you follow this basic syntax:

```
Public name As type
    Get
        'Statements executed to get the property value
    End Get
    Set (ByVal Value As type)
        'Statements executed to set the property value
    End Set
End Property
```

As you can see, a property contains one or two procedures. The `Get` procedure is executed when the property value is retrieved; it must use a `Return` statement to return the value of the property. The `Set` procedure is executed when the property value is set; a parameter is passed to it that indicates the value to be set.

Declaring Classes **461**

**Book V
Chapter 4**

Exploring
Object-Oriented
Programming

Here's a simple example:

```
Private _LastName As String
Public Property LastName As String
    Get
        Return _LastName
    End Get
    Set
        _LastName = Value
    End Set
End Property
```

Here a person's last name is represented by a private field called _LastName. It's common to use a private field to hold the value of a property, and to give the field the same name as the property, starting the field name with an underscore so you can tell them apart.

The Set method is optional. You can create a read-only property by omitting it. For example:

```
Private _TaxRate As Decimal
Public ReadOnly Property TaxRate As Decimal
    Get
        Return _TaxRate
    End Get
End Property
```

Here the TaxRate property value can be read but not set.

The real power of properties is that you can use them to perform calculations in the Get or Set procedures. For example, here's a read-only property named InvoiceTotal that calculates the total for an invoice from several fields:

```
Public ReadOnly Property InvoiceTotal As Decimal
    Get
        Return _Subtotal + _SalesTax + _Shipping
    End Get
End Property
```

Then, the InvoiceTotal property is recalculated each time it is accessed.

Another handy trick is to validate data in the Set procedure. For example, suppose a Quantity property must be between 0 and 1000. You could write a Set procedure that enforces those limits; it would look like this:

```
Private _Quantity As Integer
Public Property Quantity As Integer
    Get
        Return _Quantity
```

```
      End Get
      Set (ByVal Value As Integer)
         If Value < 0 Then
            _Quantity = 0
         ElseIf Value > 1000
            _Quantity = 1000
         Else
            _Quantity = Value
         End If
      End Set
   End Property
```

Using methods

Methods are simply `Sub` or `Function` procedures defined within a class. (For more about `Sub` and `Function` procedures, see Chapter 3 of this minibook.) You can use the `Private` or `Public` keywords to indicate (respectively) that a method is available only within the class, or that it's visible outside the class. Here's an example of a `Function` procedure defined as a `Public` function:

```
Public Function CalculateSalesTax(Amount As Decimal) _
      As Decimal
   Return Amount * _TaxRate
End Function
```

Here's an example of a private function:

```
Private Sub CalculateLunarTrajectory()
   'Code to calculate the lunar trajectory goes here
End Sub
```

You can create two or more methods with the same name, provided those methods accept different parameters. For example, suppose you're planning to bounce a laser beam off the moon — hey, some people do that — and that sometimes you need to provide an argument when you calculate lunar trajectories, and sometimes you don't. To handle both situations, you could provide two versions of the `CalculateLunarTrajectory` method:

```
Public Sub CalculateLunarTrajectory()
   'Code to calculate the lunar trajectory goes here
End Sub

Public Sub CalculateLunarTrajectory(Mass As Double)
   'Code to calculate the lunar trajectory goes here
End Sub
```

This technique is called *overloading* — and it's one of the keys to building flexibility into your classes. Overloading enables you to anticipate the different ways someone might want to invoke an object's methods, and then provide overloaded methods for each alternative.

An important rule you must follow when you overload methods is that each method in a class must have a unique signature. A method's *signature* is the combination of its name with the number and types of parameters it accepts — but the signature does *not* include the method's return type or the specific names of its parameters.

Creating constructors

A *constructor* is a Sub procedure that's executed via the New keyword when a new object instance is created. A constructor is simply a Public Sub procedure named New. For example, here's a class with a constructor that initializes the value of a field:

```
Public Class SomeClass
    Public TaxRate As Decimal
    Public Sub New()
        TaxRate = 0.075D
    End Sub
End Class
```

In the previous example, the constructor is called a *default* constructor because it doesn't accept arguments. It's called when you create an object without specifying parameters, like this:

```
Dim MyObject As SomeClass = New SomeClass()
```

You can also create constructors that accept parameters, as in this example:

```
Public Class SomeClass
    Public TaxRate As Decimal
    Public Sub New(Rate As Decimal)
        TaxRate = Rate
    End Sub
End Class
```

Here the constructor sets the TaxRate field to the value passed via the Rate parameter. Here's how you can pass an argument to this constructor:

```
Dim MyObject As SomeObject = New SomeClass(0.075D)
```

Using the Me keyword

The `Me` keyword has a specific use within a class: It refers to the current instance of the class. Typically it qualifies references to fields or methods, as in this constructor:

```
Public Sub New(LastName As String,
          FirstName As String)
    Me._LastName = LastName
    Me._LirstName = FirstName
End Sub
```

In this case, `Me` isn't really necessary — the compiler can tell that `_LastName` and `_FirstName` refer to class fields — but it does help clarify that these variables refer to class fields.

When you use `Me` in a code-behind file, it refers to the page itself. ASP.NET Web pages are defined by the class `System.Web.UI.Page`, and this class has many methods and properties you can use. For example, the `Page` class has a property called `IsPostBack`, which you can test to see whether a page is being posted back to itself, like this:

```
If Me.IsPostBack Then
```

You can almost always omit the `Me` keyword because it is assumed. Thus the following works just as well:

```
If IsPostBack Then
```

Using Shared Members

Shared members are members that aren't associated with a particular instance of a class. Instead, they are associated with the class itself; you don't have to create an instance of the class to access a shared member. Instead, you use the class name (rather than an object reference) to access the shared member.

One common use for shared members is to provide constants or other values that aren't related to a particular instance of a class. For example, a `Billing` class might have a constant named `SalesTaxRate` that provides the state sales-tax rate. This rate is the same for all `Billing` objects.

To create a shared member, you use the `Shared` keyword on the declaration for a field, property, or procedure. Here's a typical example:

```
Public Shared BadGuyCount As Integer
```

And here's an example of a shared property:

```
Private Shared _District As String
Public Shared Property ReadOnly District As String
    Get
        Return _District
    End Get
End Property
```

Notice that a shared procedure (including the Get or Set procedure for a shared property) can't refer to any class variable that isn't also shared. That's why the _District field in the previous example is declared as Shared.

Here's an example of a shared method that violates this rule:

```
Public Class TestClass
    Private x As Integer = 5 'Note that this is not shared
    Public Shared Sub TestSub()
        Dim y As Integer
        y = x                  'Error!
    End Sub
End Class
```

Here the TestSub method is shared, so it can't access the non-shared class field x. You can, however, create and use non-shared variables within a shared procedure — which is why the previous example creates and uses the variable y without any problems.

In the next chapter, I expand on these object-oriented programming basics by presenting an important — but relatively advanced — feature of object-oriented programming called *inheritance*.

Chapter 5: Demystifying Inheritance in VB.NET

In This Chapter

✔ Demystifying inheritance

✔ Creating derived classes

✔ Using protected access

✔ Understanding polymorphism

*I*nheritance is typically thought of as an advanced feature of object-oriented programming, as if it were something you shouldn't confront until your third year of grad school. Nonsense! Inheritance is actually a pretty simple idea, and one that you must deal with even in the simplest of ASP.NET applications.

In this chapter, you come to grips with the basics of inheritance. You get the lowdown on how ASP.NET takes advantage of inheritance for every Web page you create — and on how you can use inheritance in your own classes. After you finish this chapter, you may want to glance over Book 4, Chapter 6, to get a taste of some of the other things you can do with inheritance.

Understanding Inheritance

The very first line of a typical VB.NET code-behind file looks something like this:

```
Partial Class _Default Inherits System.Web.UI.Page
```

Okay, it's fairly obvious what the `Partial` keyword means — that only part of the class is defined by this source file. The rest of the class is defined elsewhere. (In the case of an ASP.NET code-behind file, the rest of the class is defined by a source file that's generated automatically by ASP.NET from the `.aspx` file for the page.)

But what about the `Inherits` keyword? It says that this class is *based on* — or *derives from* — another class. In this case, that other class is `System.Web.UI.Page`.

The `System.Web.UI.Page` class provides all the basic functionality that is available to every ASP.NET page. For example, here are just some of the more obvious benefits that the `System.Web.UI.Page` class gives us:

✦ **The `IsPostBack` property lets you tell whether the page is being loaded in response to a postback of the same page, or whether it's being loaded for the first time.**

✦ **The `Response` property lets you access the `HttpResponse` object associated with the page.** Among other things, the `HttpResponse` object provides a `Write` method you can use to write text directly to the response page. Thus, when you code `Response.Write` in an ASP.NET page, you're actually using the `Response` property of the inherited `System.Web.UI.Page` object.

✦ **The `Load` event is handled automatically when the constructor of the `System.Web.UI.Page` sets up the `Page_Load` method as the event handler for the `Load` method.**

Inheritance is the magic that makes these features work for your Web pages. If it weren't for inheritance, you'd have to write your own code to provide these features — *and* all the other features that `System.Web.UI.Page` would otherwise provide automatically. But because the `Class` statement specifies `Inherits System.Web.UI.Page`, your page class automatically inherits all these features.

Here are a few other important details you should know about inheritance:

✦ **A class that inherits another class is called a *derived class* or a *subclass*.**

✦ **The class that is inherited is called the *base class* or a *superclass*.**

✦ **A derived class automatically takes on all the behavior and attributes of its base class.** Thus, if you need to create several different classes to describe types that aren't identical but have many features in common, you can create a base class that defines *all* the common features. Then you can create several derived classes that inherit the common features.

✦ **A derived class can add features to the base class it inherits by defining its own methods and fields.** This is one way a derived class distinguishes itself from its base class.

✦ **When you create a class, you can specify just about any class in the .NET Framework to serve as the base class.** Or, if your program has unusual needs, you can create your own base class and derive a class from it.

Understanding Inheritance Hierarchies

Inheritance can be used in hierarchies, where one class is based on a second class, which in turn is based on a third class. For example, class A might be the base class for class B, while class B is the base class for class C. In that case, class C inherits features not only from class B, but also from class A.

Note that all classes except one must use inheritance. The only class that doesn't use inheritance is System.Object. If you don't specify the Inherits clause when you create a class, the class inherits System.Object by default.

Because of these requirements, all classes ultimately derive from the System. Object class. Here's how that works: In our A-B-C example, class C inherits class B and class B inherits class A, but what class does class A inherit? The granddaddy of 'em all: System.Object. Thus all three classes — A, B, and C — inherit the features of System.Object.

The System.Object class defines just a few rudimentary features that are common to all classes. Of these features, one of the best known is the ToString method. Because all classes inherit the System.Object class, the ToString method is available to all classes.

Creating a Derived Class

To create a derived class, you simply add an Inherits statement at the beginning of a class, right after the Class statement. Here's the basic syntax:

```
Class ClassName
    Inherits BaseClass
    ' The class body goes here
End Class
```

Note that the Inherits statement is not a part of the Class statement. Thus you can't code it on the same line as the Class statement. Instead, it must be on a separate line, and it must be the first statement (other than a blank line or comment) in the class.

The body of a derived class contains properties, fields, and methods that *extend* the capabilities of the base class. For example, if you add a method named Button1_Click to handle the Click event for a button, you have extended the System.Web.UI.Page class by providing an event handler for a control on the page.

Here are a few important details you need to know to use inheritance correctly:

✦ **The *visibility* (`Public` or `Private`) specified for members in the base class determines whether those members are available in the derived class.** That means you can't access `Private` methods, fields, or properties that are declared in the base class. However, you can access `Public` members.

✦ **You can *override* a method by declaring a new member with the same signature in the derived class.** (There's more about this technique coming up in the next section, "Overriding Methods.")

✦ **A special type of visibility, called `Protected`, hides members from other classes but makes them available to derived classes.** (For more about how this works, see "Using Protected Members" later in this chapter.)

Overriding Methods

An *override* is a `Sub` or `Function` procedure that makes a derived class behave differently from a base class. You get this to happen by specifying the `Overrides` keyword; otherwise, the override procedure has the same parameters and return type as a `Public` or `Protected` method of the base class. When you've specified an override and called the method, the override version that lives in the derived class will be used instead of the original method that was inherited from the base class. This technique lets you modify the behavior of a base class to suit the needs of the derived class.

For example, suppose you create a class named `Employee` and don't specify an `Inherits` clause. Remember that if you don't specify `Inherits`, the class inherits `System.Object` by default. Thus, in this case, the `Employee` class has a `ToString` method that it inherits from `System.Object`.

The `ToString` method defined by the `System.Object` class returns the name of the class, which isn't very helpful in most situations. Fortunately, you can override the default `ToString` class inherited from `System.Object` by providing your own `ToString` method.

Here's how the `Employee` class that overrides the `ToString` method might look:

```
Public Class Employee
    Private LastName, FirstName As String
    Public Sub New(ByVal First As String, ByVal Last As String)
        FirstName = First
        LastName = Last
```

```
      End Sub
      Public Overrides Function ToString() As String
          Return FirstName + " " + LastName
      End Function
  End Class
```

Now, when you call the `ToString` method of an `Employee` object, the employee's name is returned.

To override a method, you have to make sure four conditions are met:

+ **The class must extend the class that defines the method you want to override.**

+ **The method must be declared in the base class with** `Public` **or** `Protected` **access.** You can't override a `Private` method. (For more about `Protected` access, see the next section.)

+ **The method in the derived class must have the same signature as the method in the base class.** In other words, the derived class must have the same method name and the same parameter types as the base class.

+ **The method in the base class must specify the** `Overridable` **keyword to indicate that it can be overridden.**

Using Protected Members

You can use the `Public` and `Private` keywords to indicate whether class members are visible outside the class. All `Public` members of the base class are available to any derived classes, but the `Private` members aren't (they stay inside the class).

The `Protected` keyword provides a third option that's useful when you create derived classes. A `Protected` member is available to derived classes, but not to other classes — as in this example:

```
Public Class Ball
    Protected Weight As Double
End Class
Public Class BaseBall
    Inherits Ball
    Public Sub New()
        Weight = 5.125
    End Sub
End Class
```

Here the `Weight` field is given `Protected` access so it's visible to the `BaseBall` class. Note, however, that the `Weight` field won't be visible to classes that don't inherit the `Ball` class.

Using the MyBase Keyword

The MyBase keyword provides a convenient way to reference the members of a base class. One of the most common uses for MyBase is when you have overridden a method, but then need to call the original method defined by the base class.

For example, suppose you have a class called SuperBall that inherits a class named Ball. A SuperBall object is similar to a Ball object, but goes twice as fast. As a result, the Ball class has a method named ThrowBall that returns the speed, and the SuperBall class overrides this method to double the speed.

Here's how you might code the SuperBall class:

```
Public Class SuperBall
    Inherits Ball
    Public Overrides Function ThrowBall() As Double _
        Return MyBase.ThrowBall() * 2
    End Function
End Class
```

Here the overridden ThrowBall method calls the ThrowBall method of the base class, and then returns the result multiplied by two.

Note that for this to work, the ThrowBall method must be declared with the Overridable keyword in the base class. Here's how the base class would look:

```
Public Class Ball
    Public Overridable Function ThrowBall() As Double
        Return 5.5
    End Function
End Class
```

Using Casting with Inheritance

Casting is another somewhat advanced topic of object-oriented programming. Casting can come into play whenever you work with classes that use inheritance, including not only classes you create yourself but also classes provided by the .NET Framework.

Simply put, an object of a derived type can be treated as if it were an object of its base type. For example, suppose you create a class named BaseBall that extends the Ball class. Then, a BaseBall object can be treated as if it were a Ball object. This type of casting is called *upcasting* because the BaseBall object gets treated as a more general type of object, and that happens automatically so you don't have to do anything special to make it work. Here's an example:

```
Dim b As Ball
b = New BaseBall()
```

Here a variable of type `Ball` is created. Then an object of type `BaseBall` is created and assigned to the b variable. Although the b variable is a `Ball` rather than a `BaseBall` type, this code works because `BaseBall` is derived from `Ball`.

It doesn't work the other way around, though — at least, not automatically. For example, the following code won't work:

```
Dim b As BaseBall
b = New Ball()
```

Here's why: You can't create an object of type `Ball` and then assign it to a variable defined with type `BaseBall`. That's because you don't know what type of ball is represented by a `Ball` object.

A common use for upcasting is to provide general-purpose method parameters. For example, you might define a method that can hit any type of ball, like this:

```
Public Sub Hit(b As Ball)
```

Here the `Hit` method accepts a `Ball` type as a parameter. When you call this method, you can pass it either a `Ball` object or a `BaseBall` object because `BaseBall` is a derived class of `Ball`. So the following code works:

```
Dim b1 As BaseBall
b1 = new BaseBall()
Hit(b1)
Ball b2 = b1
Hit(b2)
```

As I already mentioned, VB.NET does upcasting automatically. But *downcasting* is a different story: An object gets treated as a more specific type of object. For example, suppose you have a method that tosses baseballs:

```
Public Sub Toss(b As BaseBall)
```

If you want to call this method with a `Ball` object, you have to use the `CType` function to *cast* the `Ball` object to a `BaseBall` object, like this:

```
Dim b2 As Ball
b2 = New BaseBall()
Toss(CType(b2, BaseBall));
```

Here the CType function casts the b2 variable to an object of type BaseBall. Note that this results in an exception if the object referenced by the CType function can't be cast to the specified type. Thus the following code doesn't work:

```
Dim b3 As Ball
b3 = New SoftBall()
Toss(CType(b3, BaseBall))        ' error: b3 isn't a Baseball
```

Determining an Object's Type

As the previous section points out, a variable of one type may actually hold an object of a different type. For example, a Ball object may refer to an object of type BaseBall.

In some cases, you may need to find out the exact type of an object. For example, suppose you have a method named GetEmployee whose return type is Employee, but that actually returns either a SalariedEmployee or an HourlyEmployee object:

```
Dim emp As Employee = GetEmployee()
```

In this case, you don't know whether the GetEmployee method has returned a SalariedEmployee or an HourlyEmployee object. Fortunately, VB.NET provides a special operator called TypeOf that lets you find out. Here's an example of how you might use this operator:

```
Dim emp As Employee
emp = GetEmployee()
Dim msg As String
If TypeOf emp Is SalariedEmployee Then
    msg = "The employee is a salaried employee."
Else
    msg = "The employee is an hourly employee"
End If
Response.Write(msg)
```

Here the TypeOf operator is used in an If statement to determine the type of the object returned by the GetEmployee method.

Confronting Polymorphism

If you were to take a college class on object-oriented programming, the term *polymorphism* would be on the final exam. Polymorphism sounds like it might be some abstract concept that's difficult to understand, but really the concept is pretty simple: it's VB.NET's capability that lets you use the base class to declare variables that can hold objects created from derived classes. VB.NET keeps track of which type of object is actually referred to by the variable, and calls the appropriate override methods when necessary.

Let's consider a simple example. Suppose a payroll system has a class named Employee, with a method named CalculatePay. The method accepts the number of hours worked as a parameter, and returns the amount of pay. The Employee class calculates the pay by multiplying the number of hours worked by the pay rate (which is stored by the Employee class as a property).

Here's the code for the Employee class (not including the HourlyRate property):

```
Public Class Employee
    Public Function CalculatePay(Hours As Integer)
            As Decimal
        Return Hours * HourlyRate
    End Function
End Class
```

Now suppose you have another class named SalariedEmployee. This class overrides the CalculatePay method and calculates the employee's pay differently: Instead of multiplying the hours worked by the hourly rate, the SalariedEmployee's CalculatePay method pays a base salary and only pays the hourly rate for hours worked over 40 — in other words, overtime pay.

Here's the code for the SalariedEmployee class:

```
Public Class SalariedEmployee
    Public Function CalculatePay(Hours As Integer)
            As Decimal
        Dim OvertimeHours As Integer = 0
        If Hours > 40 Then
            OvertimeHours = Hours - 40
        End If
        Return BaseSalary + OvertimeHours * HourlyRate
    End Function
End Class
```

Now, suppose you have a method somewhere named GetEmployee that returns an Employee object. After you call it, you call the Employee object's CalculatePay method to determine the employee's pay:

```
Dim Hours As Integer = 43
Dim emp As Employee = GetEmployee()
Dim pay As Decimal = emp.CalculatePay(Hours)
```

Because of polymorphism, the `Employee` class `CalculatePay` method will be executed if the `GetEmployee` object returns an object created from the `Employee` class. But if the object is created from the `SalariedEmployee` class, the `SalariedEmployee` version of the `CalculatePay` method will be called instead.

Book VI

Database Programming

The 5th Wave   By Rich Tennant

IT WAS THE LAST TIME EMILY SERVED ALPHABET SOUP TO HER WORD PUZZLE PLAYING HUSBAND.

Contents at a Glance

Chapter 1: Accessing Data with ADO.NET

In this chapter

✔ Relating to the basics of relational databases

✔ Using databases using SQL

✔ Manipulating your databases with SQL

✔ Issuing database commands with a .NET application

✔ Displaying data on a Web page

✔ Adding security to your SQL statements

*I*f you're creating software to run on the Web, chances are good that you're also going to have to store data in a database. Thereby hangs a tale: Long before Microsoft's .NET technology, Microsoft gave us the ADO (which originally stood for ActiveX Data Objects, although today the controls have little to do with ActiveX). The original ADO objects were controls you could use in programs built with Visual Basic 6.0 (or even C++); they provided easy access to your data.

Today, Microsoft has given us ADO.NET, the .NET version of data-access controls. Now, with the second version of .NET, we have ADO.NET 2.0.

ADO.NET 2.0 is a set of classes that you can use in your .NET programs. These classes allow you to access data stored in various places such as in SqlServer. But these classes do more than just access data. They are high-performance classes that Microsoft built with the Web in mind. If you have a high-volume Web server, you want to make sure that your data access is fast and efficient, and that the server won't be brought to its knees trying to access too much data for too many users. Microsoft built the ADO.NET classes to *conserve resources*. When a Web session accesses the data using ADO.NET, the classes make a quick connection to the database, do what they need to do, and get out as soon as possible, leaving room for other sessions and programs to get to the data.

In this chapter, you'll explore the fundamentals of database development and how to use the ADO.NET controls and classes to access your data. To get the ball rolling, the first section covers the concept of relational databases in general.

Understanding the Basics of Relational Databases

By far the most common way to store data these days is by using relational databases. A *database* is a place where you store data. A *relational database* is a type of database that allows you to make connections between the data. For example, you might store a bunch of information about your customers in a database, and you might also store all your sales information in the database. For each sale, you might want to know which customer the sale was with. Or — for each customer — you might want to know all the sales that customer had in the past year. Thus you would have a relationship between the customer information and the sales information. Further, one customer might have multiple sales, whereas one sale would likely go with only one customer. All this amounts to a relational database.

Strictly speaking, the word *relational* in *relational database* does not refer to the fact that the tables that make up the database can have relationships. Instead, it is derived from the mathematical concept of a *relation*, which is something you learn in grad school in pursuit of your Ph.D. in Set Theory. Relational databases do let you create relationships among the various tables that make up the database — but that's not why they are called relational databases. So now you know.

Gathering data into tables

Relational databases are typically organized in a gridlike fashion called a *table*. A table is really a very natural way of storing data. You see it all the time. A teacher might have a grade book organized as a table with names of students down the left column, and information for the different tests for a particular student arranged across the top of the page. Table 6-1 shows this idea.

Table 6-1	Student Scores			
Student	*Test 1*	*Test 2*	*Test 3*	*Final Exam*
Abe Lincoln	100	80	85	95
Ben Franklin	105	100	98	102
Jamie Foxx	100	98	90	82
Hilary Swank	95	90	80	85
Sean Penn	80	83	97	87
Charlize Theron	90	100	82	89

Even data that might not quite appear in this same gridlike fashion can often be represented in a table. For example, if you go to the grocery store and buy a bunch of groceries, your receipt might look like a list, but it could be stored in a table, as in Table 6-2.

What about records and fields?

The terms *records* and *fields* are really just synonyms for *rows* and *columns*, respectively. You might hear people using these terms when talking about data stored in tables: The table contains several records (corresponding to the rows of data), and each record contains several fields (corresponding to the columns). These are actually older terms with their history in older-style databases. They're perfectly acceptable terms, and until a few years ago, I always used them. Over time, however, most people in the relational-database field have agreed that the terms *rows* and *columns* more clearly describe their role in a table structure. Thus I've switched to using the terms *rows* and *columns* as well, and use them here in this book.

Table 6-2	Grocery Receipt	
Item	*Price*	*Taxable (Y/N)*
Milk	1.50	N
Bread	1.25	N
Pencils	0.99	Y
Donuts	1.99	N
Car	21,000	Y
Boat	500,000	Y

Organizing with rows and columns

Data is organized into tables, and tables by nature have both rows and columns. As is typical of a table of data on paper, the columns of a table in a database often have names. For example, if you look back to Table 6-1 you can see that the columns are named Student, Test 1, Test 2, Test 3, and Final Exam.

The concept of rows and columns transcends the whole database concept. As you work with data, you'll always be organizing your tables into rows and columns. When you create a table, you specify the name of the table and you describe the columns. Then as you add data, you're adding rows to the table.

Distinguishing data with primary keys and foreign keys

When you mentally keep track of data in your head, you usually use some method of distinguishing the data. For example, if you're a schoolteacher, you have to know the students in your class. When the students take a written test, they write their names on the test — and if two students happen to have the same name, you'll want to do something to ensure that the scores they get end up with the right students in your grade book. For example, you might want the students to also write their middle names in such a case. This concept of the student's name is the idea behind a *primary key*. Each student gets a unique name; from there, you can relate the right test to the right student.

In most colleges and high schools (even some elementary schools), each student gets a unique ID number. That way, in the likely event of students having the same name (even the same middle name), you can be sure to uniquely identify the particular student in your grade book. Instead of getting confused over *which* of the two unrelated students named Aloisius Benedict Forbes in your class got the A — the tall blonde one or the short red-haired one — you can simply track the students by their student ID. Since student IDs are unique, there's no question which student got the A — and which one didn't.

When you identify rows in a database, you use the same method. Although you might have data that doesn't require you to uniquely identify each row, more often than not, you'll need to do that chore. That's where the concept of a primary key comes in.

Understanding the primary key

A *primary key* is a column whose value is always unique from row to row. Each primary key value can occur only once in the table.

The primary key doesn't have to be a number; it might be unique text such as a scientific name for an animal, like *Homo sapiens*. Or it might be a text string such as a *vehicle ID number (VIN)* for a car — a long string of letters and numbers that uniquely identifies a particular car. Regardless, it is a piece of data that applies only to the particular row: Each car gets a unique VIN, and no two cars share the same VIN. That way, when you refer to a VIN, you are talking about one particular car and no other car.

In some cases, the rows in a table are uniquely identified by a combination of two column values. For example, suppose you have a table that stores line item information for invoices. Each line item has an `InvoiceNumber` column, but since each invoice can have more than one line item, the invoice number isn't by itself able to uniquely identify a particular row in the table. In this case, you might add a second column called `RowNumber` that gives a number to each row. Then the combination of `InvoiceNumber` and `RowNumber` can be used to uniquely identify each row. This type of key is called a *composite key*.

Sometimes, however, you might not be able to come up with a unique number for your data. For example, a particular combination of first and last name isn't always unique, so you can't always use it reliably to identify customers. In such cases, you'll likely want to let the database system assign a unique number to each row. This number can serve as the primary key. All decent database systems today (including SQL Server, Oracle, Access, and others) can generate unique numbers to serve as primary keys. In SQL Server, this type of key is called an *identity column* because it generates a unique identifier for each row in the table.

Creating a primary key, whether you are creating it yourself or having the database system assign it, is discussed in the section "Specifying a primary key," later in this chapter.

Utilizing the foreign key

One advantage to using primary keys are foreign keys, which allow you to relate data between tables. A *foreign key* is a column in a table that refers to a primary key in another table. For example, if you have a list of customers in one table (and each customer has a unique number serving as a primary key), and you have purchases in another table, you can simply use the customer's number with each of their purchases.

The `Purchases` table would have a list of purchases in it. But with each purchase you would also have a customer so you know who made the purchase. You could store the customer's name, address, and other information in the `Purchases` table. But then you'd have to duplicate that information each time the customer made a purchase. A much better solution is to simply store the customer's unique number in the `Purchases` table. Then, the customer data is stored in just one place — in the `Customer` table. So if the customer moves and gets a new address and phone number, you would only need to update the information in the customer table.

The unique number identifying the customer serves as the primary key in the `Customer` table. That unique number is also used in the `Purchases` table. But that unique number does not refer to a specific purchase. In fact, if a customer makes multiple purchases, you would have several rows in the `Purchases` table with the `Customer` table's primary key. Still, that key refers to a specific row in the `Customer` table. When used in the `Purchases` table, that unique customer number is a foreign key. In the `Purchases` table, the customer number is a primary key in the `Customer` table — thus it's a foreign key in the `Purchases` table.

For information on adding a foreign key, see the section "Implementing a foreign key," later in this chapter.

Normalizing your data

Suppose you weren't very experienced at designing databases, and you were putting together a program that tracks customer purchases for the local dry cleaner. In your haste, you create a `Purchases` table that includes the name, address, and phone number of the customer who made the purchase.

Now suppose a customer makes a purchase. That cool software you wrote updates the `Purchases` table, inserting a row describing the purchase along with the name, address, and phone number of the customer.

The next day, the same customer comes in and makes another purchase. Once again, you enter the information on the purchase, as well as the same information you entered the day before about the customer — the name, the address, and the phone number. Uh-oh.

As you can see, you'll have a great deal of duplicate data. If that one customer makes 1,000 purchases, you'll have the customer's name repeated 1,000 times in the database, the customer's address repeated 1,000 times, and the customer's phone number repeated 1,000 times. There's a word for that kind of database: *wasteful*.

A much better approach is to use primary and foreign keys. You would have a separate customer table that lists the customer's name, address, and phone number. Each customer would appear only once in the table, and would have a unique number: the primary key.

The `Purchases` table, instead of having all the customer information for each purchase, would just have the unique customer number alongside the purchase information. In other words, you've separated data that would otherwise be repeated out into its own table, allowing the data to only be stored a single time. This process of separating data out to avoid repeating data is called *normalization*, and the act is called *normalizing the data*.

Indexing your data for fast retrieval

If you're going to be searching through your data a lot, you want to make sure you set up the table to allow for easy searching. For example, suppose you have a table containing customer information. Each row in the customer table has a unique number (the primary key; see "Distinguishing data with primary keys and foreign keys," earlier in this chapter), but when a customer calls on the phone you want to be able to look up information in the customer table, even if the customer doesn't know his or her unique number. You might want to be able to look up the customer information by last name. In that case, you might ask for a last name — you type it in, and then the computer shows a list of all customers with that last name. Then you scan through the list and find the right customer.

If you have two million customers, they call on the phone all the time, and you have to look them up by last name, you'll want to make sure you don't bog down the database with these searches. All this rummaging could get extremely time-consuming if the database had to search row-by-row through every row in the table looking for a last name.

Instead, you'll want to set up an index. An *index* is an organizational tool that the database system manages, allowing it to find data quickly. In the case of the last name of a customer, you could set up an index on that field. The database would manage the index, and would keep it sorted. If you need all rows that have the last name `Forbes`, for example, the database system can quickly locate the entry in the index for `Forbes` — and that entry would point to all the rows in the table that have `Forbes` for a last name. (To find out how to set up an index, see the section "Creating an index with CREATE INDEX," later in this chapter.)

What's nice about indexes is that you don't have to really do anything with them other than create them. The database system does all the rest. In fact, if you're dealing with a small amount of data, you might not even notice any difference if you forget to create an index. But with large volumes of data (or small volumes but lots of data accesses), you'll definitely notice that system performance slows down until you add an index. Thus, when you create an index, the database system takes care of the details of managing it — and you don't have to worry about it again. But your life will be easier because your searches will be faster.

Working with Databases Using SQL

When you're working with databases, you'll almost always use a standard language called *Structured Query Language*, or *SQL* for short. (People are pretty much equally divided in half on how they pronounce *SQL*. Half say "sequel" and half say "Es-Queue-El." For me, it's my left half that says *sequel*.)

SQL is a declarative language in that you state what you want to do to the database: You might want to get data from the database (that is, "select" data from the database), or you might want to insert data into the database, update the existing data, or delete data. As for what happens afterwards, that's up to your program. The database server might go and select the data for you, but it's up to your program to decide what to do with the data that comes from the database.

The cool thing about SQL is you don't have to specify how to do all this. You just issue the command and the database server knows how to make it happen. However, this presents a bit of a problem because while you might write your ASP.NET code in VB.NET or C#, your database speaks a different language — SQL. How do you communicate with the database? You put your SQL statements in strings, which are then interpreted by the database system.

In this section, I talk about the four major SQL statements: `SELECT`, `INSERT`, `UPDATE`, and `DELETE` — as well as two more important statements for creating and deleting tables: `CREATE TABLE` and `DROP TABLE`. I'll talk about the two table statements first.

Most SQL database servers let you use any case for your SQL statements. You can type SELECT, select, Select, or even sElEcT. However, traditionally, most people use all-uppercase letters, as in SELECT. If other people are going to be reading your code, I suggest you follow the same standard of all-uppercase letters.

Creating a table with CREATE TABLE

Creating a table is easy with SQL. (The whole idea behind SQL was to make data management easy, after all.) You simply issue the statement CREATE TABLE followed by your table name and a description of the columns in the table.

Suppose you want to create a table called Scores containing the columns StudentID, Test1, Test2, Test3, and FinalExam. In addition to the names of the columns, you have to specify a type. (Specifying a name and type is just what you'd do if you created a variable in any programming language.)

The types you can use for the columns of a table vary from database system to database system. In these examples, I'm using SQL Server, so the types I use apply to SQL Server. (Fortunately, most of the types you use are the same between systems.)

In the case of the Scores table, all the columns we want are integers. In SQL, the integer is specified with int. Here's an example in SQL of the CREATE TABLE statement:

```
CREATE TABLE Scores (
    StudentID int,
    Test1 int,
    Test2 int,
    Test3 int,
    FinalExam int
)
```

You can see the format of this statement. First is the CREATE TABLE portion, followed by the name of the table you're creating. What follows inside the set of parentheses are a set of columns separated by commas, with each column consisting of a name followed by a type.

Specifying a primary key

When you're creating tables, you'll probably want one of your columns to be the primary key for your table. To do so, you simply tack on the words PRIMARY KEY after the column's type, before the comma, like so:

```
CREATE TABLE Scores (
    StudentID int PRIMARY KEY,
    Test1 int,
```

```
    Test2 int,
    Test3 int,
    FinalExam int
)
```

What if you want the database server to automatically assign a number for the primary key? Then you tack on a couple more words before PRIMARY KEY. Here goes:

```
CREATE TABLE Scores (
    StudentID int IDENTITY(1,1) PRIMARY KEY,
    Test1 int,
    Test2 int,
    Test3 int,
    FinalExam int
)
```

The IDENTITY(1,1) means the column is an *identity column*, — meaning it gets a unique number assigned by the database system. The first of the two numbers in parentheses is the first number that the column will get, in this case 1. The second number is how much to increment that number as you add rows to the table; again, in this case the value is also 1. Thus, in this example, as you add rows, the first one gets a 1 for the StudentID, the second row gets 2, the third row gets a 3, and so on.

Implementing a foreign key

Depending on which database system you are using (such as SQLServer or Oracle), the process for creating a foreign key differs. Since this mini-book focuses primarily on SQLServer, I'll show you the SQLServer syntax.

Remember, a foreign key relates a field in a table to a key in another table. Of these two tables, the former is where you define your foreign key. Suppose you have two tables, a Teachers table and a Courses table. Here's the SQL for creating both tables:

```
CREATE TABLE Teachers (
    TeacherID int IDENTITY(1,1) PRIMARY KEY,
    FirstName varchar(20),
    LastName varchar(20)
)
CREATE TABLE Courses (
    CourseID int IDENTITY(1,1) PRIMARY KEY,
    Title varchar(30),
    Description varchar(100),
    TeacherID int,
    foreign key(TeacherID) references Teachers(TeacherID)
)
```

The types of data

The column types available to you vary from database system to database system. SQL Server has a set of basic types that include a set specified in a standard for the SQL language. The usual types are `int` for integer, `datetime` for a date and a time, `bit` for a single bit that can represent true and false, and `money` to store currency.

Additionally, SQL Server supports two types for strings, `char` and `varchar`. To use them, you follow the word `char` or `varchar` with a number in parentheses, like so:

```
char(100)
varchar(100)
```

Both of these hold strings that are 100 characters long. The difference, however, is that `char(100)` always uses 100 characters, even if the string you store in the column doesn't take up 100 characters. (Can you say, "Waste of space?") The `varchar(100)`, on the other hand, only uses as much space as is needed. If your string is only 5 characters, that's all the space the string uses up. As you can see, `varchar` is much better for saving space. So when do you use `char`? Only if you know that every string will be exactly the same size. Otherwise opt for `varchar`.

Notice that the Teachers table simply consists of an ID for each teacher, and a first and last name. The Courses table provides an ID for each course, along with a title and description. However, the Courses table also includes a `TeacherID` for each course, specifying who teaches that course. When you add rows to the Courses table, you want to make sure that the value you specify in the `TeacherID` column is an actual value existing in the `TeacherID` of the Teachers table. In other words, you want to make sure you only add actual teachers to the course.

The line following the `TeacherID` line in the Courses table maintains the integrity, ensuring that only actual teacher ID's go inside the `TeacherID` column. This line is the foreign key declaration. Notice that this line is not part of the preceding line; the preceding line ends with a comma. To create the foreign key, you put the words "foreign key" (they can be in either uppercase or lowercase) followed by the name of the field in parentheses of the field within the Courses table, in this case `TeacherID`. Next you put the word "references" (again, uppercase or lowercase is fine), followed by the field in the other table. To specify the field in the other table you specify the other table's name followed by its field in parentheses.

The foreign key line then ensures that only values available from the Teachers table will be allowed in the `TeacherID` column of the Courses table. What happens if you put in some other value that's not allowed? You'll get an error back from the database server stating that the foreign key is violated.

But the whole idea of foreign keys opens up some serious cans of worms. For example, what happens if you try to delete a table whose keys are used as foreign keys elsewhere? You can't. The database won't allow it. You have to first delete the tables using the foreign keys. Once those tables are gone, then you can delete your table whose keys are used as foreign keys.

What about deleting rows from a table whose keys are used as foreign keys? Again, you can't if the row you're trying to delete is referenced elsewhere. Thus, as before, you have to make sure you delete the rows elsewhere before deleting the rows you're really trying to delete.

In short, working with foreign keys can make life a bit more cumbersome, but foreign keys force you to keep all your data organized, thus ensuring that you have data integrity.

Creating an index with CREATE INDEX

If you want to add an index to your table, you just issue a single statement after you issued your CREATE TABLE statements. You need to specify what table you're adding an index for, and what column or columns you want to use in the index. Here's an example:

```
CREATE INDEX test1index ON Scores(test1)
```

The format is the statement CREATE INDEX followed by a unique name for the index. The name for the index can be whatever you want, provided each index within your table is named differently. Next comes the word ON, followed by the name of the table you're creating the index for, and (placed in parentheses) the names of the columns you want to include in the index. (For multiple columns, separate the names of the columns with commas.)

That's it — after you create the index, you don't have to do anything else. The database server uses the index to make your searches easier, and you don't have to do anything else to it.

Deleting a table with DROP TABLE

If you need to get rid of a table, use the DROP TABLE statement. It's effective, if a bit drastic.

This statement doesn't just empty out the table; it removes the table altogether. That means before you can put data for the table back in, you need to create the table again by using CREATE TABLE.

Here's an example of the DROP TABLE statement:

```
DROP TABLE Scores
```

This statement deletes the table called Scores.

Be careful with the DROP TABLE statement! You don't get an "Are you sure?" question before the table actually gets dropped. When you issue the DROP TABLE statement, the table is gone, done deal. Be careful!

Getting data with SELECT

The SELECT statement is by far the most common SQL statement. Remember: Databases are organized into tables, and tables are organized into columns and rows. When you want to get data out of a table, you issue the SELECT statement, specifying which table you want, and which columns; and you get back a set of rows.

For example, suppose you have a table called Scores that contains student test scores throughout the semester. The table has the following columns: StudentID, Test1, Test2, Test3, and FinalExam. Now, suppose you want to find out the scores from the first test. Here's the SELECT statement that gets that data:

```
SELECT Test1 FROM Scores
```

This SELECT statement returns just the Test1 column for every row in the Scores table. If the table contains the data shown in Table 6-1 from earlier in this chapter, then here's the data you'll get back from this SELECT statement:

```
100
105
98
95
83
90
```

If you want to get back more than one column of data, separate the column names with a comma, like so:

```
SELECT Test1, Test2 FROM Scores
```

If you want to get back all the columns, you can either type all the column names (again, separated by commas), or just use an asterisk like this:

```
SELECT * FROM Scores
```

Selecting only specific rows with the WHERE clause

When you use the SELECT statement, by default you'll get back the columns you specify for every single row in the table. Often that's way more information than you want; you probably only want some of the rows, not all of them. Suppose you have a table filled with the million-or-so users who have signed up with your Web site and are paying you $200 per month, and you need to look up one user. You don't want to have to grind through a million or so records looking for the data — after all, the database is supposed to do that for you! The SELECT statement makes such a search easy by letting you specify exactly which rows you want back.

The way you specify the rows is by using what's called a WHERE clause. Here's an example:

```
SELECT Test1 from Scores WHERE StudentID = 1
```

This statement returns the row that has a 1 for the StudentID column. (If, for some reason, you put two rows in your table with a StudentID of 1, then you get back the values in both rows.)

You can put all sorts of conditions in the WHERE clause. For numbers you can use less-than (<), greater-than (>), equals (=), and so on. You can combine your conditions with Boolean operators such as AND and OR, like so:

```
SELECT StudentID from Scores WHERE Test1 >= 90 AND Test2 > =90
```

This SELECT statement will return all StudentID's where both Test1 is greater than or equal to 90 and Test2 is greater than or equal to 90; that is, you'll find out which students got As on the first two tests (assuming an A is 90 or better).

Adding data with INSERT

To add data to a database, you use the INSERT statement. This statement is easy to use — except it's kind of wordy, and you can only enter one row of data at a time. Here's an example:

```
INSERT Scores
(StudentID, Test1, Test2, Test3, FinalExam)
VALUES (1, 100, 100, 90, 95)
```

You start with the word INSERT, followed by the table name. Then you list the column names you wish to set for this row you're inserting. You put the whole set of column names inside parentheses, and separate the names with commas.

Then you type the word VALUES, followed by the corresponding values for the columns. The values are also separated by commas and the whole set is surrounded by parentheses.

Note that the previous example applies only to tables where you *don't* have an identity column. If you do have identity column in your table, you can't specify it in the INSERT statement because only the database server is allowed to fill in the value for such a column. Thus the preceding INSERT would have to be modified like so:

```
INSERT Scores
(Test1, Test2, Test3, FinalExam)
VALUES (100, 100, 90, 95)
```

Notice I'm only specifying the remaining four columns, and not the identity column; the database server will fill that column in with the next available value for the column.

In the preceding two INSERT samples, I wrote the statement over three lines. You don't have to do that; if you can fit the whole thing on one line, it's okay to do so. Or you can break it up as much as you want and add extra spaces — provided you don't break up individual words or numbers. Thus the following is acceptable as well:

```
INSERT Scores
    (StudentID, Test1, Test2,
    Test3, FinalExam)
VALUES
    (1, 100, 100,
    90, 95)
```

Modifying data with UPDATE

If you need to modify existing data, use the UPDATE statement. Here's an example:

```
UPDATE Scores
SET Test1=10, Test2=20
WHERE
StudentID = 1
```

The format of this statement is easy, but different from the INSERT statement. You type UPDATE followed by the name of the table you're modifying. Then you type SET followed by the new values for the columns. For each of these values, you specify the column name, followed by the new value; you separate each column from the others with a comma.

Next comes the WHERE clause, which is how you describe the rows you want to change. In this example, I'm changing the row that has a 1 for StudentID.

Be careful with your UPDATE statements! It's very easy to accidentally modify more rows than you intend to. The UPDATE statement will modify all rows that satisfy the condition in your UPDATE statement. Thus, your best bet is to stick to the primary key in the UPDATE statement. The primary key is always unique per row; thus, if you use the primary key, you can be assured you'll only update the row you want. If (for example) you use the following for your UPDATE statement

```
UPDATE Scores
SET Test1=10, Test2=20
WHERE
Test3 = 100
```

then you modify all rows that have 100 in the Test3 column. Be careful!

Removing data with DELETE

Removing data from a table is easy, but also dangerous; it's almost too easy to remove too much data. So before I show you how to remove data, I just want to remind you to *always be careful when removing data*. When it's gone, it's gone!

There are two parts to the DELETE statement: The main clause and the WHERE clause. Here's an example:

```
DELETE Scores WHERE StudentID = 1
```

The format of the statement is the DELETE statement followed by the name of the table you're deleting records from; then comes the word WHERE, followed by a condition describing the rows you want to delete.

The condition for the WHERE clause is where you have to be extremely careful. Your best bet is to stick to the primary key in the WHERE clause. Otherwise, you'll want to make sure you construct your statement carefully so you're only deleting the rows you want to get rid of. For example, take a look at this statement:

```
DELETE Scores WHERE Test1 = 100
```

This statement deletes all rows having 100 for the Test1 field.

I'll say it again: Pay close attention to the WHERE clause in your DELETE statement. The WHERE clause is the only way to specify which rows to delete. If you get the WHERE clause wrong, you could easily delete the wrong rows.

Piecing Together SQL Statements

What I'm about to discuss here is possibly one of the biggest "gotchas" when working with SQL, regardless of the programming language you're using, and regardless of which database server you're working with.

Look closely at the following VB.NET code, where I'm attempting to insert data into the names table using the INSERT statement:

```
Dim mysql As String = _
    "INSERT" & _
    "names" & _
    "(first_name, last_name)" & _
    "VALUES" & _
    "('Jennifer', 'Wood')"
```

I'm storing my INSERT statement in a single string, but for readability, I'm attempting to break it up onto multiple lines of code. In VB.NET, you can break up lines by putting underscores (_) at the end of each line as I do here. And you can piece together strings with the ampersand (&) character.

But it doesn't work here. Why not? Because after these strings get pieced back together, here's the string I end up with:

```
INSERTnames(first_name, last_name)VALUES('Jennifer', 'Wood')
```

Notice the problem? There are no spaces in between the pieces — I have a mess. Really, though, there's only one place where there's a problem: in between the first two strings I pieced together. I ended up with INSERTnames, when I wanted INSERT names, with a space between them. If I try to execute this SQL code, the database server gives me back a beautiful error message that I can print up and hang on the wall.

(Interestingly, the other lines are fine; the database server doesn't care about the missing spaces because it can figure everything out — thanks to the parentheses. That's just dumb luck on my part — when I made this example, I was shocked to see it actually executed after I fixed the first line!)

Here's a better version of the same code:

```
Dim mysql As String = _
    "INSERT " & _
    "names " & _
    "(first_name, last_name) " & _
    "VALUES " & _
    "('Jennifer', 'Wood')"
```

In this code, I added spaces to the end of each string, just inside the double quotes. That fixes the problem!

As an alternative, if I'm going to piece together SQL statements that aren't always the same, I find the `String` class's `Format` method to be extremely helpful. (For a full discussion of the `Format` method, check out Book 7, Chapter 1.)

Here's an example where I might want to issue the same `INSERT` statement in different situations. Here I piece together my string using some other strings:

```
Protected Function BuildInsert _
  (ByVal firstname As String, ByVal lastname As String) _
As String
    Return String.Format( _
        "INSERT names (first_name, last_name) " & _
        "VALUES ('{0}', '{1}')", _
        firstname, lastname)
End Function
```

The `Format` method takes the first string and replaces the `{0}` with the contents of the next string (in this case, `firstname`) and then replaces the `{1}` with the contents of the second string (in this case, `lastname`). The end result is a nice `INSERT` string that contains the correct values.

Connecting to Data with ADO.NET

You have all this amazing data stored away on a database, but how do you put it to use in your ASP.NET application? The data doesn't do much good just sitting out there ruminating on the nature of the universe unless you can display such ruminations on the Web for your users to interact with by viewing 'em — or even modifying and adding to them.

To get to the data, you use what's called a connection. (Life is good when the computer terms actually make sense!) A *connection* is a mechanism by which you get to your data. Conceptually, think of a connection in the same way that a Web browser opens up a connection to a Web site, or your e-mail program opens up a connection to an e-mail server. ASP.NET manifests a connection through a class called `SQLConnection`, found in the `System.Data.SqlClient` namespace.

The `SQLConnection` class is strictly for connecting to SQLServer databases. To connect to Oracle databases, you use the `OracleConnection` class, found in the namespace `System.Data.OracleClient`. (Interestingly, ADO.NET doesn't have an abstract class from which these connection classes are derived.)

One step better for the Oracle controls

If you're using Oracle in your ASP.NET application, you're free to use the Oracle controls that are built into the .NET Framework, found in the `System.Data.OracleClient` namespace. However, these controls were built by Microsoft — and they don't take full advantage of the power of Oracle client software. If you want to get the full power of *the Oracle* (sounds impressive!) you can download a rather powerful set of controls made by Oracle. These controls and documentation are available at

```
www.oracle.com/technology/
    tech/dotnet/index.html
```

Please be aware, however, that if you already have Oracle client software installed on your computer, and then you install the Oracle controls, some of youregistry settings might get changed. If you find other software breaking, you might need to reinstall your previous Oracle client software.

Since a connection is how your program connects to a database, you can probably predict what might be required to open up a connection. Let's see:

✦ **You need to tell the connection what computer (or server) to connect to.**

✦ **You need to specify what database on that server to connect to.**

✦ **You're accessing a database, so you need a username and password.**

That's it! Here's a sample call that creates and then opens a connection to a database:

```
Dim connect As New SqlConnection( _
    "Server=mycomp;UID=jeff;password=yeah;database=Dummies")
connect.Open()
```

To create a new connection, you specify all that stuff I just described, and you can see it in the preceding code. You can also see, however, that it's bizarre; I'm not passing it as individual parameters. Instead, I'm using something that has confused the world left and right and upside down. It's the one and only . . .the mysterious . . . *connection string*.

Just what the heck is that? A *connection string* is a bunch of parameters stuffed together inside a single string, written in pieces of the form `name=value`, separated by semicolons. Yes, all in a single string. And no, I'm not defending it as the world's greatest idea. In fact, personally I think it's kind of stupid. But like it or not, I'm stuck with it (and so are you).

Look carefully at how the connection string is constructed. Notice that it's several of those `name=value` pairs I just mentioned. Here's what each does:

✦ `Server=mycomp`: This is where you specify which computer to connect to. Note that this can either be a computer name (such as `mycomp`), the local name (such as `localhost`), an IP address (such assss `127.0.0.1`), or a full IP name (such as `server.wiley.com`).

✦ `UID=jeff`: This is the username by which you log in to the database. Remember, that's supposed to be the username for the database itself; for some computers, you might also have a separate username for logging in to the computer. Make sure you keep straight which is which, and use the database username when you log in to the database.

✦ `password=yeah`: This is the password that goes with the username.

✦ `database=Dummies`: This is the name of the database running on the computer.

The computer itself has a name (which you specify for the `Server` value), and the computer has a database holding your data, which you specify for the `database` value.

Connection sharing and pooling

If you're creating a Web site that's going to have at least a fair amount of traffic, then you might be concerned about the number of open connections to your database server. The usual way of dealing with such situations is to use *connection pooling* — maintaining a set of connections to a database. Then, whenever you need a new connection, you draw from one of the available open connections in the pool. If a connection is not available, your application waits until one becomes available. This has the advantage that you don't have to constantly open and close connections; in the end, you increase performance by not having to keep opening and closing connections.

Now for the cool part: When you use the `SQLConnection` class, connection pooling takes place automatically for you. You just create `SQLConnection` instances as you need them, and call `Open`, just as you normally would as described in the rest of this section.

The key to making connection pooling work, however, is that you follow two easy rules:

✔ **Make sure you specify the exact same connection string for each connection you want to participate in the pool.**

✔ **Call** `Close()` **each time you're done using the connection.**

By calling `Close()`, you will release the connection back into the pool. The .NET Framework will then decide whether to actually close the connection.

Remember: Each unique connection string gets its own pool.

You can have multiple databases on a single computer. That's why you need to specify *both* the name of the computer and database.

Issuing Database Commands

When you have an open connection, you can issue SQL statements from your ASP.NET program to access and manipulate data by using the SQLCommand class — or you can use this same class to call a stored procedure. For that matter, you can even execute multiple SQL statements, all in a single SQL Command instance.

Calling statements that return no data

Statements that return no data are the easiest kind of statements to call — because you don't need to do anything after you issue the statement. In a nutshell, all you do is create an instance of SQLCommand with your statement, and you call the SQLCommand's ExecuteNonQuery method. (The name here makes sense, too. Statements that return data are called *queries;* statements that do not return data are *non-queries.*)

For example, if you're inserting data, then you'll want to call ExecuteNon Query. Here's some sample code that opens up a database connection and sends a command to insert data into the names table.

```
Dim connect As New SqlConnection( _
    "Server=mycomp;UID=jeff;password=yeah;database=Dummies")
connect.Open()
Dim cmd As New SqlCommand( _
    "INSERT NAMES (first_name, last_name) " & _
    "VALUES ('Jennifer', 'Wood')", _
    connect)
cmd.ExecuteNonQuery()
connect.Close()
```

This code first opens a connection to the database. Next, it creates a new SQLCommand instance that contains an INSERT statement, calls Execute NonQuery to run the command, and (finally) closes the connection.

Generally speaking, for security reasons, you don't want to just issue INSERT statements from within your ASP.NET program. This is a topic I discuss in more detail later in this chapter (in the section "Adding Security to Your SQL Statements — Read This!") The idea here is that you're wise to use stored procedures and pass the data you're inserting as parameters to a stored procedure.

In such a case, you can code your stored procedure as just an `INSERT` statement, and then you would still use `ExecuteNonQuery`. However, with stored procedures, you have more flexibility because you can code the stored procedure to return something — such as a number representing whether the insert succeeded, or the value of an identity column for the inserted data. Or, as in the case of another non-query statement such as `UPDATE`, you might return a number representing the number of rows that were updated. In any of these cases, you're getting data back — which means, technically, that it's not "*not* a query" — that is, it's a query. In these cases, I recommend using `ExecuteScalar` (which I discuss in the section "Calling statements that return one data item," later in this chapter).

Calling a stored procedure

If you do a great deal of database work, most likely you'll also have a lot of stored procedures, which are SQL code stored right on the database server. Calling stored procedures is easy from within a .NET program, except for one little part that's annoying: gathering the parameters for the stored procedure.

First off, if you look at the online help for the `SqlCommand` class, you'll see there's a member called `CommandType`. You use this member to specify that you're using a stored procedure. (By default, this member is set to `Text` — which simply means the SQL you're issuing is, in fact, SQL, and not a stored procedure.) To use a stored procedure, you need to set the `CommandType` to `StoredProcedure`. Then the name you specify for the SQL is interpreted by the framework as the name for a stored procedure, rather than SQL statements. Here's some code that does the work:

```
Dim connect As New SqlConnection( _
"Server=mycomp;UID=jeff;password=yeah;database=Dummies")
connect.Open()
Dim cmd As New SqlCommand("GetInfo", connect)
cmd.CommandType = CommandType.StoredProcedure
cmd.ExecuteNonQuery()
connect.Close()
```

The first three lines create a connection and open it; the next line creates the command. The first parameter to the `SqlCommand` constructor is the name of the stored procedure you're calling, in this case `GetInfo`. The second parameter is the `SqlConnection` instance.

Next, I set the command type — in this case, `StoredProcedure`, which is an enumeration of type `CommandType`.

To use the preceding code, you'll need to include two `Imports` statements at the beginning of your code file, the first for the `SqlConnection` and `SqlCommand` classes, and the second for the `CommandType` enumeration:

```
Imports System.Data.SqlClient
Imports System.Data
```

Calling statements that return one data item

When you have an SQL statement that returns only one data item — and I don't mean one row, I mean only one *value* — then your best bet is to call the `ExecuteScalar` method of the `SQLCommand` class.

There are many ways that you can get back one data item from a database. The most obvious is if you select a single column and get back only a single row, such as this:

```
select nameid from names where first_name = 'Jeff'
```

But other times you might only get back one data item — as when you're counting rows in a table, like this:

```
SELECT count(*) FROM names
```

Having said that, how do you actually use `ExecuteScalar`? Here's some sample code:

```
Dim connect As New SqlConnection( _
 "Server=mycomp;UID=jeff;password=yeah;database=Dummies")
connect.Open()
Dim cmd As New SqlCommand( _
    "select nameid from names where first_name = 'Jeff'", _
    connect)
Dim id As Int32
id = cmd.ExecuteScalar()
connect.Close()
Response.Write(id)
```

The first three lines of this code open up a connection to the database. Next, this code creates an instance of the `SQLCommand` class containing the query that returns a single value; this value is the `nameid` from the row in the `names` table where the first name is `Jeff`.

Then I called `ExecuteScalar`, which is the meat of the code. This function does the dirty work of sending the command to the database server, and getting back the single value. I store that single value in the `id` variable; then I close the connection and write out the value to my ASP.NET Web page, using the `Response.Write` method.

Notice one interesting tidbit, however: I took the result of `ExecuteScalar` and stored it in an `Int32` variable, and the compiler didn't complain. That's because `ExecuteScalar` returns an instance of `Object`, the top level class from which everything else is derived. The .NET system will then attempt to cast the object to an `Int32`. In this case, that worked fine because I did, in fact, get back an integer, meaning casting worked.

But what if I got back a string and tried to save it in an `Int32`? Then I would have gotten a *runtime* error — that is, the error would happen when I run the program, but not when I compile it. That's not a good thing because run-time errors are too easy to miss during development, and often find their way into the laps of the unsuspecting and short-tempered users. The moral here, then, is to mind your Ps and Qs, set up your data correctly, and know the data types you'll be getting back from the database. If you know that your table contains a string for a certain column, don't just save it into an `Int32` variable. Know your data; make sure it plays well with others.

Book VI
Chapter 1

Accessing Data with ADO.NET

What if you use `ExecuteScalar` and call a `SELECT` statement that ends up giving you more than one data item when you thought you'd only get one? In that case, you'll just get back the very first data item in the result set. If you have multiple columns, you'll end up with the first column in the result set; if you have more than one row, you'll get back the first column of the first row. In general, though, you'll want to avoid this situation — if you retrieve large amounts of data but only use one item from the result set, that's extra overhead you don't need. You can avoid this situation by carefully constructing your `SELECT` statement so you only get exactly what you want and nothing more.

Displaying Data on a Web Page

Getting data from a database is all well and good, and a nice exercise, but what good is it if you can't show it to anybody? In this section I get you started with displaying the data on a Web page.

For much more discussion on displaying data on a Web page, check out Chapter 2 of this mini-book.

The quickest and easiest way to display your data on a Web page as soon as you get the data is through the `Response.Write` method. In this case, you can either embed the VB.NET or C# code right inside the `.aspx` file, or put it in the separate code file and call the `Response.Write` function right from your `.aspx` file.

Although you can do your `Response.Write` calls from within the `Form_Load` method for your page, the ordering of events makes that approach undesirable. Here's why: The `Form_Load` method takes place before the rendering of the page, so any writing you do there happens at the very top of your Web page. Here's a VB.NET example:

```
<%@ Page Language="VB" AutoEventWireup="false"
 CodeFile="Connection1.aspx.vb" Inherits="Connection1" %>
<%@ Import Namespace="System.Data.SqlClient" %>
<html>
<body>
    Here comes the data!<br />
<%
    Dim connect As New SqlConnection( _
    "Server=mycomp;UID=jeff;password=yeah;database=Dummies")
    connect.Open()
    Dim cmd As New SqlCommand( _
      "select nameid from names where first_name = 'Jeff'", _
      connect)
    Dim id As Int32
    id = cmd.ExecuteScalar()
    connect.Close()
    Response.Write(id)
%>
    <br />How about that?<br />
</body>
</html>
```

This is just a simple `.aspx` file with a bunch of HTML in it. But right smack in the middle is some ASP.NET code that does the data access. The code, in fact, is identical to the code in the previous section; it opens a connection, creates `SQLCommand` for a `SELECT` statement, issues the statement by calling `ExecuteScalar`, and (finally) closes the connection. Further, this code calls `Response.Write` to write out what it gets back from the database.

Now, thanks to the magic of ASP.NET (or at least the careful work of the people at Microsoft), the output of the code that you see here will appear right where it is in the Web page — in this case, after the words `Here comes the data!` and before the words `How about that?` — like so:

```
Here comes the data!
5
How about that?
```

Notice, in the preceding code, that in order to use the data classes, I had to tell the Web page about the namespace containing the classes. To do so, I used included the following line:

```
<%@ Import Namespace="System.Data.SqlClient" %>
```

If you don't like bogging down your `.aspx` file with a lot of code, you can put the code in a protected function in the class that accompanies the `.aspx` file. Then all you have to do is call the function from the `.aspx` file. Here's an example. First, here's the code, which is in a separate `.vb` file:

```
Imports System.Data.SqlClient
Partial Class Connection1
    Inherits System.Web.UI.Page
    Protected Sub WriteMyData()
        Dim connect As New SqlConnection( _
        "Server=mycomp;UID=jeff;password=yeah;database=Dummies")
        connect.Open()
        Dim cmd As New SqlCommand( _
        "select nameid from names where first_name = 'Jeff'",
        connect)
        Dim id As Int32
        id = cmd.ExecuteScalar()
        connect.Close()
        Response.Write(id)
    End Sub
End Class
```

**Book VI
Chapter 1**

**Accessing Data
with ADO.NET**

The subroutine `WriteMyData` does the same work as before, and calls `Response.Write` to write out the results. Now here's the `.aspx` file, which calls the following subroutine:

```
<%@ Page Language="VB" AutoEventWireup="false"
    CodeFile="Connection1.aspx.vb" Inherits="Connection1" %>
<%@ Import Namespace="System.Data.SqlClient" %>
<html>
<body>
    Here comes the data!<br />
<%
    WriteMyData()
%>
    <br />How about that?<br />
</body>
</html>
```

There — that's a bit simpler (which works better for my brain, personally!).

Retrieving Data from a Table

Retrieving a result set from a `SELECT` statement is probably one of the easiest tasks in .NET database programming. That's because you get to use a really nifty class called `SQLDataAdapter` — which takes care of a ton of work for you.

Have a gander at this code:

```
Dim adapt As New SqlDataAdapter( _
   "select * from names", _
   "Server=mycomp;UID=jeff;password=yeah;database=Dummies")
Dim table As New DataTable
adapt.Fill(table)
```

The first three lines make up a single statement that creates a new SqlData Adapter. You pass to the constructor the SELECT statement that retrieves the result set, and you pass the connection string. Pretty easy.

Next you call Fill. The Fill method is part of the SqlDataAdapter, and you pass to it an instance of DataTable.

Now be careful here. The Fill method does not create an instance of DataTable. Instead — and first — you have to create an instance by calling New DataTable, and then pass that existing instance to Fill. Otherwise you'll get a runtime error.

After you call Fill, what do you do with it? You can actually read the data by stepping through the rows in the table. Here's code that continues from the preceding code:

```
Dim row As DataRow
For Each row In table.Rows
    Response.Write(row("nameid"))
    Response.Write(" ")
    Response.Write(row("first_name"))
    Response.Write(" ")
    Response.Write(row("last_name"))
    Response.Write("<br>")
Next
```

Adding Security to Your SQL Statements — Read This!

Think about this situation: You have a form on your Web page for users to enter a first and last name for entry into a table. Then you use the name in an INSERT statement, like so:

```
INSERT names (first_name, last_name) VALUES ('bob', 'smith')
```

The first name comes from a field on the form, and the last name comes from a separate form. Now, suppose that somebody who's particularly crafty visits your Web page and types this in for the first name:

```
bob
```

and this for the last name:

```
smith') delete from names
```

That's a little strange, but look what your SQL statement is going to end up as:

```
INSERT names (first_name, last_name) VALUES ('bob', 'smith') delete from names
```

Yikes! What you get is one line that executes two separate SQL statements. Here they are, each shown separately:

```
INSERT names (first_name, last_name) VALUES ('bob', 'smith')
delete from names
```

The first line inserts the data, but the next line deletes everything from the table! (And yes, if you combine two statements into one line like this, they run individually — doing exactly what the hacker wanted: *Deleting all the data from your table.* This type of hacker attack is called *SQL Injection* because it injects covert SQL instructions into the form's input data.)

Now suppose you have a guest-book page where the user can enter his or her name and a short comment — and all the names and comments show on a single page. Everything is fine until one day, all of a sudden, from one message on, the text suddenly changes to a huge font and the rest of the page is like that? Nope, it isn't the Curse of the Nearsighted Mummy; it's what happens if the user types in a message that looks like this:

```
<h1>Hi everybody
```

Do you see the problem? The user put an opening `<h1>` tag in there — but no closing `</h1>` tag — so all the text from that point on gets rendered as extremely large. Given how easy such a goof is, you probably won't want people to put HTML tags in their messages.

So how do you prevent these two kinds of problems, known as SQL and HTML *abuses?* Here's the short form:

✦ **To prevent SQL abuses, the best way is to use stored procedures to insert all your data.** Then you're not even piecing together SQL. If the user enters SQL, it'll just go into the database and end up treated as if it were any other text.

✦ **To prevent HTML abuses, the easiest way is to call the function**
`Server.HtmlEncode`. This function converts the special characters
(such as < and >) into their HTML equivalents (such as `&lt;` and `&gt;`
respectively). Then, when written out to the browser, such characters
appear as their actual characters, rather than as HTML tags. (For a full
discussion on `HtmlEncode`, check out Book 7, Chapter 1.)

Finally, ASP.NET has a mechanism that automatically handles such situations. Unfortunately, this mechanism somewhat limits how much you can
use the two techniques I just described. The mechanism is as follows: If
ASP.NET detects something suspicious such as JavaScript or SQL in a form,
it'll trigger an exception and display a not-so-lovely error page to your users.

If you want to use all the techniques you can to prevent abuses, then
you can turn off the built-in protection. However, make sure you're careful
to cover all your bases! To turn off the built-in protection, modify your
`web.config` file by adding the following line to your `<system.web>` section:

```
<pages validateRequest="false" />
```

Chapter 2: Displaying and Editing Data for the Web

In this chapter

✓ Binding: Displaying data with server-side controls

✓ Creating and using data sources

✓ Repeating through a result set

✓ Creating a data-entry page

*W*hen you're writing the code that displays data on a Web page, it's worth your time to think carefully through the order in which everything takes place: when the form loads, when the data is read, when the server controls write their text — and when, in the midst of all this, you want to write your data. Further, there's the practical matter of formatting the data: Do you write out each data item manually — specifying Cascading Style Sheet information and using HTML tags as well — or do you rely on a server control that writes CSS styles for you? Well, that depends. In this chapter I present different ways to get your data out of the database and onto the Web page.

All code listings used in this book are available for download at www.dummies.com/go/aspnetaiofd.

Writing Data to a Page with a Label

A `Label` server control lets you write dynamic text to a page. But you can also use it to write out data from a database. But why is this any better than just using `Response.Write`? It's neither better nor worse, just an alternate way of writing your data with its own pros and cons, which I tell you about here.

Here's a sample `Page_Load` event that stores a data item in a `Label`'s `Text` property. First, here's the `.aspx` file:

```
<%@ Page Language="VB" AutoEventWireup="false"
CodeFile="LabelDemo.aspx.vb" Inherits="LabelDemo" %>
<html>
<body>
    Welcome! We have had
    <asp:Label ID="WriteData" runat="server" />
    page hits.
</body>
</html>
```

Notice how I have a `Label` control, and I've put the closing slash right inside the tag itself; I've also provided no text. Now here's the Visual Basic (VB) example of the file:

```
Imports System.Data.SqlClient
Partial Class LabelDemo
    Inherits System.Web.UI.Page
    Protected Sub Page_Load(ByVal sender As Object, _
    ByVal e As System.EventArgs) Handles Me.Load
        Dim connect As New SqlConnection( _
        " Server=mycomp;UID=jeff;password=yeah;database=Dummies ")
        connect.Open()
        Dim command As New SqlCommand( _
            "SELECT hitcount FROM hits WHERE pagename = 'login.aspx'", _
            connect)
        Dim count As Int32
        count = command.ExecuteScalar()
        WriteData.Text = count
        connect.Close()
    End Sub
End Class
```

This code retrieves a single data item from the `hits` table, and then sets the label's `Text` property to the retrieved value.

Notice that I'm relying on some automatic data-casting here. That's because the `Text` property is a `String` instance, and the data retrieved is an `Int32` data type — but I'm not putting an exception handler in there, for two reasons: Okay, the first one (as this is just an example) is no big deal. But the second reason is a real programming issue: I've taken care to make sure that I'm retrieving data that actually exists — and in this case, I know that data is an integer, which will safely cast to a string.

In the preceding code, the database read takes place in the `Page_Load` event, and the result is sent to the `Label` server control to be written when the `Label` control renders.

This approach of doing the SQL query from within the `Page_Load` event and storing the result in a server control's property works great if you have a single SQL query and want to populate several controls. But if you only have to do one query and write one data item, you can either use the method I just described, or you can simply call `Response.Write` to write out the data, which is discussed in Chapter 1 of this mini-book.

Binding to Data

If you do a great deal of database access in your Web pages, then you will want to make use of a feature known as *data binding*. It's a technique that involves selecting the place(s) where the data comes from (each of which is a *data source*), and then specifying which fields will be rendered by which controls. The rest takes place "automagically," which means your life (that part of it, anyway) becomes pretty easy.

Creating a data source

The different incarnations of Visual Studio.NET provide a wizard for creating data sources that you can then use for supplying data to the controls on your Web page. The wizard makes displaying data incredibly easy — but first you have to make sure your database, tables, and users are all set up. Otherwise the wizard will fail and you'll have to start over.

To create a data source using the wizard, follow these steps:

1. **Drag the SQLDataSource from the toolbox onto a Web form and click the triangle in the upper-right corner.**

Doing so expands the Smart Tag, as shown in Figure 6-1.

Figure 6-1:
Expand the
Smart Tag
by clicking
the little
triangle.

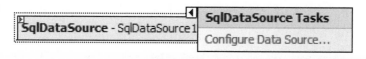

2. **In the Smart Tag, click Configure Data Source... to open the Configure Data Source Wizard, shown in Figure 6-2.**

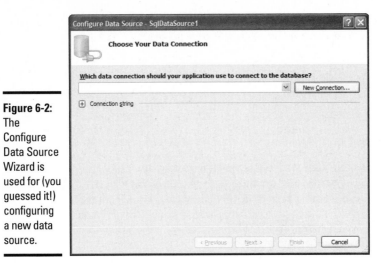

Figure 6-2:
The
Configure
Data Source
Wizard is
used for (you
guessed it!)
configuring
a new data
source.

3. In the Configure Data Source Wizard, click the New Connection... button.

This opens the Add Connection dialog box, shown in Figure 6-3.

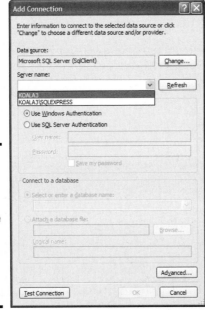

Figure 6-3:
The Add
Connection
dialog box
contains the
items for
specifying
a connec-
tion to a
database.

4. **In the Add Connection dialog box, click the Server Name drop-down list box, and choose the server where your data lives.**

If you don't see any names in the Server Name drop-down box, head over to the Start menu of your computer and start up your SQLServer. (Choose Start⇨Microsoft SQL Server 2005⇨Configuration Tools⇨SQL Server Configuration Manager; then select SQL Server 2005, right-click the server instance you want to start, and choose Start.) Then, come back to the Add Connection dialog box and click the Refresh button.

5. **Next click the radio button for the type of authentication you're using for your database.** I'm using SQL Server Authentication; thus I entered my SQL username and password, as shown in Figure 6-4.

**Book VI
Chapter 2**

**Displaying and
Editing Data
for the Web**

Figure 6-4:
Enter the username and password to your database.

6. **Next, click the Select Or Enter a Database Name radio button.**

7. **Click the drop-down list box just below the radio button.**

You will see a list of available databases, as shown in Figure 6-5. Choose the one holding your data.

8. **To make sure you can log in to the database, click the Test Connection button in the lower-left corner of the Add Connection dialog box.**

Figure 6-5:
Choose your
database.
Choose it
wisely.
Choose it
well.

You should see a friendly message appear, as shown in Figure 6-6.

Figure 6-6:
Looks like it
worked!

9. **Close the friendly message by clicking OK; back in the Add
Connection box, click OK.**

Doing so completes the new connection, and you're returned to the
Configure Data Source dialog box.

At this point, you haven't really configured anything, nor have you created a connection. Instead, you've created a connection string. Yup, it's
true. That's all you've really accomplished at this point — but don't feel
too bad about it. Piecing together connection strings can be a royal pain;
the Add Connection process ensures that you get it right. So fear not —
no time was wasted.

10. **You can now see the connection string that you created; to see it, in
the Configure Data Source dialog box, click the little plus sign to the
left of Connection String.**

You can see my connection string in Figure 6-7.

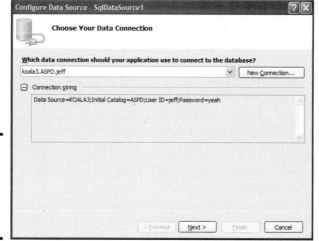

Figure 6-7:
The dialog box created the connection string.

11. **Click Next.**

A screen appears, asking whether you want to save the connection string you created (as shown in Figure 6-8). If you click the Yes, Save This Connection As check box, you can then either accept the default name for the new connection or specify a new name.

Figure 6-8:
You can optionally save the connection string to your web.config file.

TIP

What is the default name? Inside your `web.config` file for this Web application you can specify connection strings, and each one gets a name. That's what the default name is. I accepted the default name. Here's the entry that the wizard wrote to my `web.config` file:

```
<connectionStrings>
    <add name="ASPDConnectionString" connectionString=
        "Data Source=mycomp;Initial Catalog=Dummies;
        User ID=jeff;Password=yeah"
    providerName="System.Data.SqlClient" />
</connectionStrings>
```

Now the fun part begins (which also happens to be the easiest part because you already did all the hard work!). The next pages in the Configure Data Source Wizard allow you to specify the tables or stored procedures in your database that contain the data you want to display on the Web page. Remember, once again, you're setting up a *data source* (a source of data for your Web page). While the connection string was cool and all, the `SQLDataSource` that you're configuring is what supplies the data to the controls on your Web page.

12. **Click Next in the Configure Data Source Wizard.**

The page that opens allows you to choose a stored procedure or table, as shown in Figure 6-9.

Figure 6-9: After creating the connection string, you can set up the data retrieval.

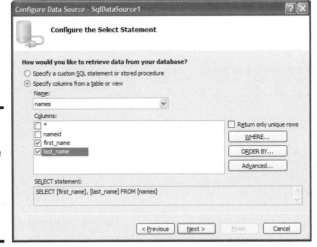

As shown in Figure 6-9, I chose to get my data from a table. I clicked the Specify Columns From a Table or View radio button, which activated the drop-down list below the radio button. This drop-down list contains a list of all the tables and views in the database. I chose the names table, and the columns from the table appear in a checked list box. You can select which columns you will feed to your controls; as you can see in the figure, I chose the first_name and last_name columns.

What does it mean that I'm choosing the first_name and last_name columns? It means I want the controls I'm setting on my form to access those specific columns when they make use of this data source I'm configuring. The controls will get their data from the first_name and last_name columns of the names table. And the data source will get its data using the connection string that I created.

If you look at the .aspx file and the code that the wizard inserts into the file, you can see a little more deeply into what's happening. Here are the lines that were inserted into my form:

```
<asp:SqlDataSource ID="SqlDataSource1" runat="server"
ConnectionString="<%$ ConnectionStrings:ASPDConnectionString %>"
SelectCommand="SELECT [first_name], [last_name] FROM [names]">
</asp:SqlDataSource>
```

**Book VI
Chapter 2**

Displaying and Editing Data for the Web

The first line identifies the SqlDataSource. The second line specifies the connection string. Notice the special <%$ and %> syntax, which allows access to special expressions — including connection strings.

The third line shows the SELECT statement that the data source will use to access the data. (Notice that the column and table names are inside brackets [ ]. They guarantee the statement will run, even if the column names are the same as reserved SQL words.) The fourth line is the closing tag for the control.

If you think it was a lot of work just to get those four measly lines, fear not: If you're so inclined, you can skip the wizard, go right to the .aspx source file, and type in the code yourself, manually. Really, that's not so hard, either — because the editor gives you plenty of tips as you go along. After you type <asp:SqlDataSource and press the spacebar, a list will appear showing you the different parameters — such as ID, runat, ConnectionString, and SelectCommand.

13. **Finally, click Next to test out the query.**

What I see for mine is shown in Figure 6-10 — a table that shows the rows from the table and only the columns I selected. (Looks to me like it worked.)

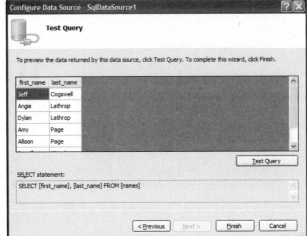

Figure 6-10: When you test the query, you'll see the results here.

Using a data source

Once you have a data source created and configured, you can put it to use on your form. But first think about one small issue: Your data source is linked to a table, a view, or a stored procedure that returns data. And the data that's returned, though it possesses columns, probably has multiple rows as well. To show all this data, typically you have to use a control that can show multiple items — for example, a ListBox.

Here's some sample .aspx code that displays the data in a ListBox control (I'm assuming you already have a SQLDataSource control on your form, that it's all configured, and that you've already dropped a ListBox control on your form):

```
<%@ Page Language="VB" AutoEventWireup="false"
CodeFile="DatasourceDemo.aspx.vb" Inherits="DatasourceDemo" %>
<!DOCTYPE html PUBLIC "-//W3C//DTD XHTML 1.0 Transitional//EN"
"http://www.w3.org/TR/xhtml1/DTD/xhtml1-transitional.dtd">
<html xmlns="http://www.w3.org/1999/xhtml" >
<head runat="server">
    <title>Untitled Page</title>
</head>
<body>
    <form id="form1" runat="server">
    <div>
        <asp:SqlDataSource ID="SqlDataSource1" runat="server"
        ConnectionString="<%$ ConnectionStrings:ASPDConnectionString %>"
        SelectCommand="SELECT [first_name], [last_name] FROM [names]">
```

```
        </asp:SqlDataSource>
        <asp:ListBox ID="ListBox1" runat="server"
        DataTextField="first_name"></asp:ListBox>
    </div>
    </form>
</body>
</html>
```

Inside the `<div>` and `</div>` tags you can see the `SqlDataSource` and `ListBox` controls. Notice the `DataTextField` property of the `ListBox` control; it specifies the field from the data source that will show up when the page renders.

Note also, however, that so far I haven't specified which data source to use. That task has to happen in the code. Here's the VB example of the file:

```
Partial Class DatasourceDemo
    Inherits System.Web.UI.Page
    Protected Sub Page_Load(ByVal sender As Object, _
    ByVal e As System.EventArgs) Handles Me.Load
        ListBox1.DataSource = SqlDataSource1
        ListBox1.DataBind()
    End Sub
End Class
```

Here the code takes place in the `Page_Load` event. The first thing this code does is specifies the data source to use by setting the `ListBox` control's `DataSource` property. Next the code calls the `DataBind` method, which does the actual work of obtaining the data from the database.

Here, the `SqlDataSource` control is configured to select all the rows in the `names` table, and the `ListBox` control is configured to display the `first_name` column from the result set. Figure 6-11 shows what you'll see when you open this page in the browser.

**Book VI
Chapter 2**

**Displaying and
Editing Data
for the Web**

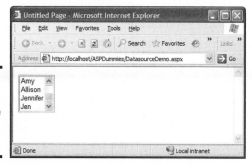

Figure 6-11:
This list box
contains the
results from
a query.

Repeating Through a Result Set

If you want to display several rows of data and do a lot of custom formatting in your displaying of the data, then the `Repeater` control is for you. (Do I sound like a salesman yet?) The `Repeater` control is nothing fancy; you simply supply the HTML and ASP.NET controls for each row, and the `Repeater` control displays your HTML and controls for each row in the data set. Pretty simple.

An example will help make this clear. I have a table called `names`, and each row contains an identifier, a first name, and a last name. Take a look at this `.aspx` file:

```
<%@ Page Language="VB" AutoEventWireup="false"
CodeFile="RepeaterDemo.aspx.vb" Inherits="RepeaterDemo" %>
<html>
<body>
    <asp:SqlDataSource ID="SqlDataSource1" runat="server"
    ConnectionString="<%$ ConnectionStrings:ASPDConnectionString %>"
    SelectCommand="SELECT [first_name], [last_name] FROM [names]">
    </asp:SqlDataSource>
    <asp:Repeater ID="MyRepeater" runat="server"
        DataSourceID="SqlDataSource1" >
    <ItemTemplate>
        <%# Eval(""first_name")%>
        <br />
    </ItemTemplate>
    </asp:Repeater>
</body>
</html>
```

This `.aspx` file includes a `SQLDataSource` that retrieves data from the `names` table. Next comes the `Repeater` control that I've been raving about. Look carefully at the format. It has an opening `asp:Repeater` tag and the associated closing tag. The opening tag specifies an `ID` for the `Repeater` control, and the requisite `runat="server"` property. Then, the `DataSourceID` attribute provides the name of the data source (in this case, `SqlDataSource1`) that the `Repeater` control is bound to — that is, the data source that the `Repeater` control retrieves its data from.

Inside the `asp:Repeater` tag is an opening and closing `ItemTemplate` tag, in which you put the HTML and server controls that will render for each item in the data set. Inside the `ItemTemplate` tag is the following line:

```
<%# Eval("first_name")%>
```

This line uses the `Eval` method to retrieve the value of a field in the data source. It simply provides the name of the column whose value should be displayed.

The <%# and #> symbols and the Eval method that appears between them is called a *binding expression*. Binding expressions that use the Eval method are not particularly efficient. In fact (for technical reasons that I'd explain if I had another 10 pages to spare), the Eval method is actually quite inefficient. There's a more efficient technique that's explained in Chapter 5 of this minibook, in case you're interested in writing code that not only works, but works well. But Eval is fine while you're just getting started.

Figure 6-12 shows what my browser looks like with the data retrieved from the names table.

Figure 6-12:
The Repeater control lets you iterate though data.

The Repeater control is a bit of an oddity in that it's not particularly useful in the Design view. It really doesn't have any visual aspect to it. For that reason, I usually just type its code into the source editor for the .aspx files.

Setting server control properties in a Repeater control

If you put a server control inside a Repeater control, setting its properties to values from the data is easy. You just use a binding expression to set the property. Take a look at the following code to see how this works:

```
<%@ Page Language="VB" %>
<html>
<body>
    <form id="form1" runat="server">
    <asp:SqlDataSource ID="SqlDataSource1" runat="server"
    ConnectionString="<%$ ConnectionStrings:ASPDConnectionString %>"
    SelectCommand="SELECT [first_name], [last_name] FROM [names]">
    </asp:SqlDataSource>
    <asp:Repeater ID="MyRepeater" runat="server"
        DataSourceID="SqlDataSource1" >
    <ItemTemplate>
```

```
        <asp:CheckBox runat="server" Text=
            <%# Eval(first_name")%>
        /><br />
        </ItemTemplate>
        </asp:Repeater>
        </form>
</body>
</html>
```

This code creates a data source and a `Repeater` control, and binds the `Repeater` control to the data source. Take a careful look, however, inside the `Repeater` control, as well as at the `CheckBox` control, and (specifically) at the `Text` property. The `Text` property is set to a value that comes from the data set:

```
<%# Eval"first_name")%>
```

What will this look like on-screen, then? Each iteration of the `Repeater` control creates a check box, and then sets the check box's text to the `first_name` column from the `names` table. Figure 6-13 shows what this page looks like in the browser.

Figure 6-13:
Inside the Repeater, you can include server controls and set their properties to the data values.

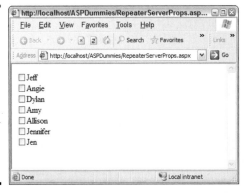

Adding some style to the Repeater control

With the basics of the `Repeater` control under your belt, you can easily make each row in the `Repeater` control show as many columns as you want in your data set, and you can format the lines as you want. Take a look at this example:

```
<%@ Page Language="VB" %>
<html>
<body>
    <asp:SqlDataSource ID="SqlDataSource1" runat="server"
```

```
ConnectionString="<%$ ConnectionStrings:ASPDConnectionString %>"
SelectCommand="SELECT [first_name], [last_name] FROM [names]">
</asp:SqlDataSource>
<div style="width:300px;border:solid 2px #404040">
<asp:Repeater ID="MyRepeater" runat="server"
    DataSourceID="SqlDataSource1" >
<ItemTemplate>
    <div style="font-family:Verdana;font-size:12px;border-bottom:solid 2px
#A0A0FF">
    <%# Eval"first_name")%>
    <%# Eval("last_name")%>
    </div>
</ItemTemplate>
</asp:Repeater>
</div></body>
</html>
```

**Book VI
Chapter 2**

Displaying and
Editing Data
for the Web

You can see that prior to the opening `asp:Repeater` tag I have an opening `div` tag, and I provide some style information. Specifically, I provide a width and a border around the `div`.

For each iteration of the `Repeater` control, I provide another `div` tag and some style information; specifically, I set the font size and give a border at the bottom of the `div` of a color `#A0A0FF` (a light blue). Then I have two data casts to display the first name and the last name from the table.

Figure 6-14 shows what all this code looks like when rendered in a browser.

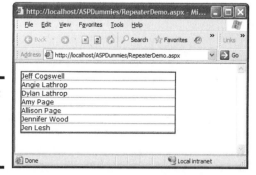

Figure 6-14:
Now the
Repeater
control has
some style.

Altering the look of the Repeater control's rows

When you're displaying lots of data, sometimes reading the data can be difficult on the eyes. You might want to provide an alternating style, such as an alternating background or alternating font color from row to row. Doing so helps make the data more readable (or just nicer to look at on-screen).

The `Repeater` control provides two different templates, one for the first line and all odd-numbered lines, and one for all the other lines. The one for the first and all odd-numbered lines is the standard template that you normally use — `ItemTemplate`. For the other lines, you use a template called `AlternatingItemTemplate`. Here's an example:

```
<%@ Page Language="VB" %>
<html>
<body>
    <asp:SqlDataSource ID="SqlDataSource1" runat="server"
    ConnectionString="<%$ ConnectionStrings:ASPDConnectionString %>"
    SelectCommand="SELECT [first_name], [last_name] FROM [names]">
    </asp:SqlDataSource>
    <div style="width:300px;border:solid 2px #404040">
    <asp:Repeater ID="MyRepeater" runat="server"
        DataSourceID="SqlDataSource1" >
    <ItemTemplate>
        <div style="font-family:Verdana;font-size:12px;background-color:#A0A0FF">
        <%# Eval"first_name")%>
        <%# Eval("last_name")%>
        </div>
    </ItemTemplate>
    <AlternatingItemTemplate>
        <div style="font-family:Verdana;font-size:12px;background-color:#FFFFFF">
        <%# Eval("first_name")%>
        <%# Eval("last_name")%>
        </div>
    </AlternatingItemTemplate>
    </asp:Repeater>
    </div>
</body>
</html>
```

Here I use two templates inside the `asp:Repeater` tag. The first is `ItemTemplate`, and the second is `AlternatingTemplate`. The only difference between them is the style property of the `div` tag — the first one has a bluish background color, and the second has a white background color. The on-screen result is alternating dark and light lines, as shown in Figure 6-15.

Figure 6-15:
Using the Alternating Template tag, you can choose what appears in alternating rows.

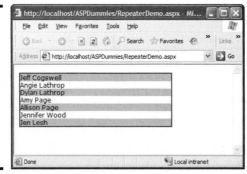

Creating a Data-Entry Page

Chances are you want an interactive site where your users can actually enter data into your database, rather than just look at the data. Here I show you how you can make a data entry form that lets users add data.

Creating a data-entry form requires you to think about the postback process. Remember that when you present your users with a data-entry page, you are presenting them with controls through which they enter their data. When they've entered the data, they click a button to post the data. What happens then? The data gets sent back to your Web server for processing — which takes place inside a postback of your page, in the form of a button control's `Click` event. (For more information on postback, see Book 1, Chapter 4.)

Before I show you an example, you'll need to set up a sample table. Here's the VB code that creates the table I'm using for this sample:

```
CREATE TABLE member (
    custid int IDENTITY(1,1),
    first_name varchar(20),
    last_name varchar(20),
    malefemale bit,
    yearborn int
)
```

This table includes an ID column, a first name, a last name, whether the person is male or female, and an integer representing the year the person was born. The male or female column is a `bit`, meaning it can be 1 or 0, so I'll randomly choose 0 to mean *male* and 1 to mean *female*.

Listing 2-1 provides the entire VB code for the sample, all in one compact `.aspx` file.

**Book VI
Chapter 2**

Displaying and
Editing Data
for the Web

Listing 2-1:   Data-Entry Page Demo (VB)

```
<%@ Page Language="VB" %>
<script runat="server">
    Protected Sub Page_Load(ByVal sender As Object, _
    ByVal e As System.EventArgs) Handles Me.Load
        Dim year As Int32
        For year = 1900 To 2005
            YearDropDown.Items.Add(year.ToString)
        Next
    End Sub
    Protected Sub Save_Click(ByVal sender As Object, _
    ByVal e As System.EventArgs) Handles Save.Click
        SqlDataSource1.Insert()
```

(continued)

Listing 2-1 *(continued)*

```
    End Sub
</script>
<html>
<body>
    <form id="form1" runat="server">
    <div style="border: solid 1px black;width:350px;
    font-family:Tahoma;font-size:12px;padding:5px;">
    Welcome! Please enter your information to add to the database.<br />
    First name:
        <asp:TextBox ID="FirstTextBox" runat="server"></asp:TextBox><br />
    Last name:
        <asp:TextBox ID="LastTextBox" runat="server"></asp:TextBox><br />
    <asp:RadioButtonList ID="MFRadioButton" runat="server"
        Font-Names="Tahoma" Font-Size="12px">
        <asp:ListItem Text="Male" Value="0"></asp:ListItem>
        <asp:ListItem Text="Female" Value="1"></asp:ListItem>
    </asp:RadioButtonList><br />
    Year born:
        <asp:DropDownList ID="YearDropDown" runat="server">
        </asp:DropDownList><br />
    <asp:Button ID="Save" runat="server" Text="Save" />
    </div>
        <asp:SqlDataSource ID="SqlDataSource1" runat="server"
            ConnectionString=
            "<%$ ConnectionStrings:ASPDConnectionString %>"
            InsertCommand=
            "INSERT INTO
            [member] ([first_name], [last_name], [malefemale], [yearborn])
            VALUES
            (@first_name, @last_name, @malefemale, @yearborn)">
            <InsertParameters>
                <asp:FormParameter Name="first_name" Type="String"
                    FormField="FirstTextBox" />
                <asp:FormParameter Name="last_name" Type="String"
                    FormField="LastTextbox" />
                <asp:FormParameter Name="malefemale" Type="Int32"
                    FormField="MFRadioButton" />
                <asp:FormParameter Name="yearborn" Type="Int32"
                    FormField="YearDropDown" />
            </InsertParameters>
        </asp:SqlDataSource>
    </form>
</body>
</html>
```

Before I describe this code, take a look at it in the browser. Figure 6-16 shows what it looks like.

You can see I tried to make it look nice as opposed to just using the default font in the Web browser. I even put a pretty box around it! (Seriously, though, appearance does matter with Web sites.) This form gives you a field for first name, last name, male/female, and year of birth.

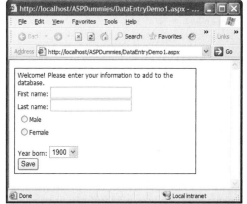

Figure 6-16:
A data-entry form is easy to construct with the server controls.

In the code, you can see the parts that I used to create these fields. I provided two `TextBox` controls, one `RadioButtonList` control, and one `DropDownList` control.

To fill the `DropDownList` control, I provided some code in the `Page_Load` event that loops through the numbers `1900` through `2005`, adding each year as a string to the `DropDownList` control's items.

The important part here is the whole business inside the `SqlDataSource` tag. That's where the meat of the work gets done. Sure, it'd be nice if you didn't have to do any coding and could just use the Configure Data Source Wizard instead — but in fact the wizard only helps you so far. I started with some basic tags that the wizard created for me, but then I modified it by hand to get it just the way I wanted. (In general, however, I don't even bother with the wizards; it's faster and easier just to type in the tags and properties.)

Following is a breakdown of the parts of the `SqlDataSource` tag in Listing 2-1:

✦ **Here's the opening tag for the** `SqlDataSource`:

```
<asp:SqlDataSource ID="SqlDataSource1" runat="server"
```

This tag specifies the `ID` and the usual `runat` property; nothing too mysterious there.

✦ **Next is the** `ConnetionString` **property:**

```
ConnectionString=
"<%$ ConnectionStrings:ASPDConnectionString %>"
```

This is the connection string created for another section of this chapter, and it lives in the `web.config` file. To see how it came together, see the section "Creating a data source," earlier in this chapter.

✦ **Then we have the** `InsertCommand` **property:**

```
InsertCommand=
"INSERT INTO
 [member] ([first_name], [last_name], [malefemale], [yearborn])
VALUES
 (@first_name, @last_name, @malefemale, @yearborn)">
```

This property specifies the SQL `INSERT` statement that will be used to insert the data into the database. Since I started out with code generated by the wizard, this `INSERT` statement has the brackets around the names, as in `[member]`. That's fine, although not really necessary in this case since none of the names are reserved SQL words. No biggie.

The important thing here is the `VALUES` clause of the `INSERT` statement. Notice that they aren't actual values; instead, they're words preceded by @ symbols. These are placeholders (or *parameters*) that will be replaced by the values the user enters into the form.

✦ **As for what controls in the form go with what parameters; the following tags specify such information:**

```
<InsertParameters>
    <asp:FormParameter Name="first_name" Type="String"
    FormField="FirstTextBox" />
    <asp:FormParameter Name="last_name" Type="String"
    FormField="LastTextbox" />
    <asp:FormParameter Name="malefemale" Type="Int32"
    FormField="MFRadioButton" />
    <asp:FormParameter Name="yearborn" Type="Int32"
    FormField="YearDropDown" />
</InsertParameters>
```

These tags detail exactly which control data goes into which parameters. The first `FormParameter` tag says that the data from the `FirstTextBox` control will go into the `first_name` parameter. The next `FormParameter` tag puts the data from `LastTextBox` into the `last_name` parameter. Data for the `malefemale` parameter comes from the `MFRadioButton` control, and `yearborn` comes from the `YearDropDown` control.

Notice one little caveat: If you start with the wizard, all these `FormParameter` tags will actually be just `Parameter` tags; I had to manually change them. And second, the `Parameter` tag for `malefemale` specified a data type of `Boolean`. That didn't work either; technically, the only way to do `Boolean` types in SQL Server are with `bit` fields, which are single-bit integers that can have either the integer value 0 or the integer value 1. So I changed the type from `Boolean` to `Int32`.

If you want the visitors to your site to choose between two items (such as Large and Small or perhaps Inches and Centimeters), then you'll likely either use two radio buttons, one for each item, or a single check box. For example, if you're selling a product that comes in two sizes, Large and Small, you might have two radio buttons, one labeled `Large` and one labeled `Small`. Or you might automatically ship a Small unless the users explicitly check a check box labeled `Large`.

Note that if you choose to use radio buttons, most usability experts agree that your form must start with one of the radio buttons selected (the default). The purists feel that radio buttons have rules: One must always be selected (you can't have both blank) — and you can't select both. Thus, when your page opens, you should have either the Small or Large radio button checked by default.

That's all fine and dandy except for one special situation: Imagine that your users must choose an item describing themselves — such as `male` or `female`, or perhaps a race. You can't win on this one. You don't want *default* to either male or female (or a particular race) if you want to avoid offending people; thus you might display your Web page with initially *neither* radio button checked (in the case of male/female) or with no radio buttons checked for race. But on the other hand, if you're concerned about adhering strictly to usability rules, then setting up the radio buttons that way would be in violation.

Personally, I'm fine with letting the form appear on-screen with neither the male or female radio buttons checked — and then throwing in some Javascript that shows a message if the user tries to submit the form without choosing male or female. But here's another option: You can always use a drop-down box with the first selection being "Choose one." Then you would also have some Javascript that prevents the form from posting unless the user has chosen one option. (Or you could allow a "prefer not to answer" option, depending on your particular application.)

Chapter 3: Displaying and Editing with the GridView Control

In This Chapter

↙ Viewing simple data with GridView

↙ Changing the appearance of the display

↙ Adding edit and delete capabilities for data

↙ Sorting and paging

↙ Defining fields

*I*f you've done database programming with ASP.NET in the past, you might have worked with the `DataGrid` control. The `DataGrid` control was a useful control for displaying and editing data in a grid fashion on a Web page. But that was just Microsoft's first take. Now, Microsoft has given us a much more powerful control, the `GridView` control. In this chapter I introduce the two of you: Meet `GridView`. `GridView`, meet Reader.

Setting Up the AdventureWorks Database

In many of the examples throughout this chapter, I refer to the `AdventureWorks` database. That's a database that ships with the various 2005 editions of SQL Server.

If you don't have a copy of the `AdventureWorks` database, you can download it from Microsoft for free at:

```
www.microsoft.com/downloads/details.aspx?familyid=E719ECF7-9F46-4312-
    AF89-6AD8702E4E6E
```

Or, instead of typing that in, simply go to `www.microsoft.com/downloads` and type `SQL Server 2005 Samples` into the search box, and click Go. In the results, choose *SQL Server 2005 Samples and Sample Databases*. When you've found this page, click the link labeled `AdventureWorksDB.msi`, then follow the instructions to download and install the sample database.

After you've downloaded and installed the database, you need to create a connection from Visual Studio 2005. To do that, follow these steps:

1. **Open the Server Explorer window.**

2. **Right-click Data Connections and choose Add Connection.**

3. **In the Add Connection dialog box, enter your SQL server name in the Server name box.**

   In most cases, `localhost\SQLExpress` will do the trick.

4. **Select the Attach a Database File option.**

5. **Click the Browse button, then locate the** `AdventureWorks` **database file and click Open.**

6. **Click OK to create the connection.**

Creating a GridView Control

The `GridView` control makes data display incredibly easy. In this example, I'm using the `Address` table from the `AdventureWorks` database. (Note, however, that the owner of this table by default is a user called `Person` — I'm not making that up — and so you need to refer to the table as `Person.Address`.)

To get started, make sure you have the `AdventureWorksConnectionString` set up as described in the previous section.

Next, follow these steps.

1. **Create a new Web Form and call the form whatever you like. (I called mine** `GridViewSample1.aspx`**.)**

2. **Switch to Design view, then open the Data section of the toolbox and drag a** `SqlDataSource` **control over to the page.**

3. **Click Configure Data Source in the Smart Tag menu.**

   This summons the familiar Configure Data Source Wizard dialog box.

4. **Choose the connection string for the** `AdventureWorks` **database in the drop-down list, then click Next.**

   The Wizard now asks for the table and columns you want to select.

5. **Choose the Specify a Custom SQL Statement option, then click Next.**

6. **Enter the following** `SELECT` **statement, then click Next.**

   ```
   SELECT * FROM Person.Address WHERE AddressID < 50
   ```

7. **Click Finish.**

Now the data source has been configured.

8. **Drop a** `GridView` **control on your form; expand its Smart Tag by click-ing the little arrow in the upper-right corner, as shown in Figure 3-1.**

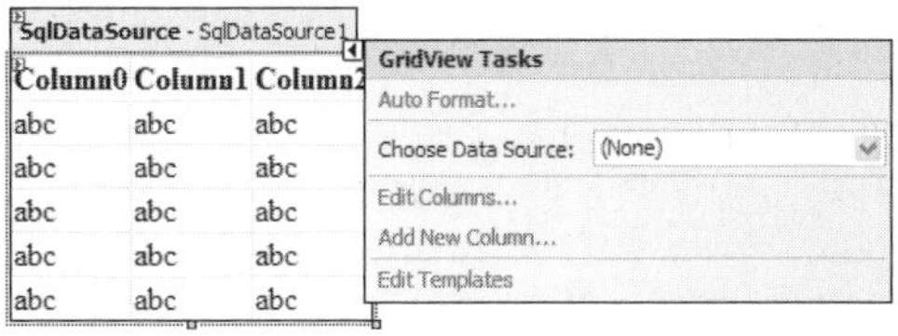

Figure 3-1:
Open the
smart tag to
configure
the
GridView
control.

9. **Click the Choose Data Source drop-down list, and select**
`SqlDataSource1`.

That's it! Open this page in the Web browser and you'll see a grid of data; it will look like Figure 3-2.

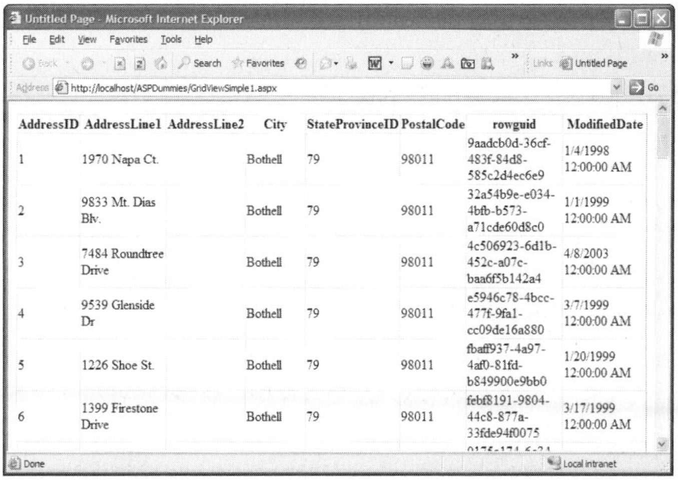

Figure 3-2:
Here's a
simple
GridView
example in
the browser.
It isn't all
that fancy
yet.

Of course, the screen you see in Figure 3-2 isn't very pretty. Formatting the display is something we address in the next section.

Want to know the fastest way to create a data source and `GridView` control? Work your way over to the Server Explorer, double-click the database that contains the data you want to show, and then double-click Tables. Finally, drag the table you want to display in the data grid onto a blank form. This procedure creates both a data source and a `GridView` control that's bound to the data source. Pretty neat.

Formatting the Display

In this section, I'm making use of the `GridView` control created in the preceding section. Displaying data on a Web page is important, but typically you'll want it to look nice. Users are easily put off by an ugly display with poorly formatted text, ugly fonts, and no color (or too much color!).

Assuming you've followed the steps in the preceding section and created the `GridView` control, switch to Design view. To set the format of the header row in the `GridView`:

1. **Left-click the GridView in Design view. In the properties window, expand the `HeaderStyle` property by double-clicking the `HeaderStyle` property or single-clicking the + sign next to the property name.**

2. **Set HorizontalAlign to Left.**

3. **Under `HeaderStyle`, expand Font by double-clicking the Font property.**

4. **Set Bold to True.**

5. **For Name, choose Tahoma.**

6. **For Size, type** `12px`.

Now, here's how you format alternating lines in the grid, first the first row and every other (essentially all the odd-numbered rows):

1. **Click the GridView in Design view. In the properties window, expand the `RowStyle` property by double-clicking the `RowStyle` property.**

2. **Under `RowStyle`, expand the `Font` property by double-clicking the word Font that's under `RowStyle`.**

3. **For Name, chose Tahoma.**

4. **For Size, type** `11px`.

And here's how you set the second row and every other (the even-numbered rows):

1. **Click the GridView in Design view. In the Properties window, expand the `AlternatingRowStyle` property by double-clicking the `AlternatingRowStyle` property.**

2. **Set BackColor to LightGray. This will cause all even-numbered lines to have a light-gray background.**

3. **Under `RowStyle`, expand the `Font` property by double-clicking the word Font that's under `RowStyle`.**

4. **For Name, chose Tahoma.**

5. **For Size, type `11px`.**

That's good enough. Now try opening the form in the browser. Figure 3-3 shows what you get.

**Book VI
Chapter 3**

**Displaying and
Editing with the
GridView Control**

Figure 3-3:
This example of the GridView in the browser is a lot easier on the eyes.

AddressID	AddressLine1	AddressLine2	City	StateProvinceID	PostalCode	rowguid	ModifiedDate
1	1970 Napa Ct.		Bothell	79	98011	9aadcb0d-36cf-483f-84d8-585c2d4ec6e9	1/4/1998 12:00:00 AM
2	9833 Mt. Dias Blv.		Bothell	79	98011	32a54b9e-e034-4bfb-b573-a71cde60d8c0	1/1/1999 12:00:00 AM
3	7484 Roundtree Drive		Bothell	79	98011	4c506923-6d1b-452c-a07c-baa6f5b142a4	4/8/2003 12:00:00 AM
4	9539 Glenside Dr		Bothell	79	98011	e5946c78-4bcc-477f-9fa1-cc09de16a880	3/7/1999 12:00:00 AM
5	1226 Shoe St.		Bothell	79	98011	fbaff937-4a97-4af0-81fd-b849900e9bb0	1/20/1999 12:00:00 AM
6	1399 Firestone Drive		Bothell	79	98011	febf8191-9804-44c8-877a-33fde94f0075	3/17/1999 12:00:00 AM
7	5672 Hale Dr.		Bothell	79	98011	0175a174-6c34-4d41-b3c1-4419cd6a0446	1/12/2000 12:00:00 AM
8	6387 Scenic Avenue		Bothell	79	98011	3715e813-4dca-49e0-8f1c-31857d21f269	1/18/1999 12:00:00 AM
9	8713 Yosemite Ct.		Bothell	79	98011	268af621-76d7-4c78-9441-144fd139821a	7/1/2002 12:00:00 AM
10	250 Race Court		Bothell	79	98011	0b6b739d-8eb6-4378-8d55-fe196af34c04	1/3/1999 12:00:00 AM
11	1318 Lasalle Street		Bothell	79	98011	981b3303-aca2-49c7-9a96-fb670785b269	4/1/2003 12:00:00 AM
12	5415 San Gabriel Dr.		Bothell	79	98011	1c2c9cfe-ab9f-4f96-8e1f-d9666b6f7f22	2/6/2003 12:00:00 AM
13	9265 La Paz		Bothell	79	98011	e0ba2f52-c907-4553-a0db-67fc67d28ae4	1/15/2004 12:00:00 AM

The `GridView` control gives you a great deal of control with the formatting and style. Go ahead and browse through the Properties window to see what different styling options exist. Don't be afraid to modify different settings to see how the `GridView` changes appearance. Play with it until it looks just the way you want it!

Editing and Deleting Data with a GridView

One of the cool things about the GridView control is it lets you add editing capabilities to your Web page. With the GridView control, if you turn on such functionality, your users can edit existing rows and delete rows of data. To try out my example in this section, you will want to create a table and put some initial data in it. Here's the table I created:

```
CREATE TABLE member (
    memberid int IDENTITY(1,1)
        PRIMARY KEY,
    first_name varchar(20),
    last_name varchar(20),
    malefemale bit,
    yearborn int
)
```

In this CREATE TABLE statement, you can see that I included a primary key. The primary key is required in order to make editing work. The reason is that when you're using a GridView control to edit data, the GridView control needs to know how to update a row you're editing. The only way it can make sure it updates the correct row with your changes is to keep track of the primary key. (Remember, primary keys are unique; thus a single primary key refers specifically to a single row, not more than one row.) Thus, you need a primary key in your table. For more on primary keys, see Chapter 1 of this mini-book.

Here's some sample data you can start out with for your table:

```
INSERT member
    (first_name, last_name, malefemale, yearborn)
    VALUES
    ('George', 'Washington', 0, 1732)
INSERT member
    (first_name, last_name, malefemale, yearborn)
    VALUES
    ('Elizabeth', 'Windsor', 1, 1926)
INSERT member
    (first_name, last_name, malefemale, yearborn)
    VALUES
    ('Thomas', 'Jefferson', 0, 1743)
INSERT member
    (first_name, last_name, malefemale, yearborn)
    VALUES
    ('Abe', 'Lincoln', 0, 1809)
```

```
INSERT member
    (first_name, last_name, malefemale, yearborn)
    VALUES
    ('Betsy', 'Ross', 1, 1752)
GO
```

You'll also need a connection string in your `web.config` file to get to the database that uses the table. (To find out more about connection strings see Chapter 1 of this mini-book.) For this particular connection I'm using this connection string; you'll need to use one appropriate for your database:

```
<add name="ASPDConnectionString" connectionString=
"Data Source=KOALA3;Initial Catalog=ASPD;
User ID=jeff;Password=yeah"
providerName="System.Data.SqlClient" />
```

Following are the steps to create a project that demonstrates a `GridView` control in Edit mode. First, these steps create the necessary `SqlDataSource` control:

1. **Create a new Web Form, and name it whatever you like.**

   I named mine `GridviewEditDemo1.aspx`.

2. **Drop a `SqlDataSource` control on your form.**

   Expand the Smart Tag by clicking the triangle in the upper-right corner of the control on the form. Choose Configure Data Source.... The Configure Data Source Wizard will open.

3. **In the Configure Data Source dialog box, choose your connection string (or create one if one doesn't exist).**

   Then click Next to open the Configure the Select Statement page of the wizard.

4. **Select the Specify Columns from a Table or View radio button.**

5. **In the Name drop-down list, choose member.**

6. **In the Columns drop-down list, click * to choose all columns.**

7. **Click the Advanced button.**

   The Advanced SQL Generation Options dialog box opens.

8. **Check the Generate INSERT, UPDATE, and DELETE Statements check box (shown in Figure 3-4); and then click OK to close this dialog box.**

9. **Back in the Configure Data Source Wizard, click Next to move to the Test Query page of the wizard.**

10. **In the Test Query page, you can test the page if you would like by clicking the Test Query button.**

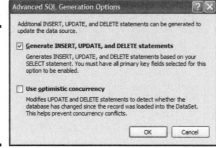

Figure 3-4:
Check the
top check
box to
generate all
the SQL
statements.

11. **Click Finish to close the wizard.**

The `SqlDataSource` control is now ready. Next, the following steps create
and configure the `GridView` control.

1. **Drag a `GridView` control onto the form.**

2. **Left-click on the `GridView` in the designer if it's not already selected,
and then click the little triangle in the upper-right corner to show the
Smart Tag.**

3. **In the Smart Tag window, click the Choose Data Source drop-down
list, and choose `SqlDataSource1`.**

The `GridView` control redraws the screen to show the columns in the
member table, as shown in Figure 3-5.

	memberid	first_name	last_name	male	female	yearborn
	0	abc	abc	☐		0
	1	abc	abc	☑		1
	2	abc	abc	☐		2
	3	abc	abc	☑		3
	4	abc	abc	☐		4

DataSource - SqlDataSource1

GridView Tasks

Auto Format...

Choose Data Source: SqlDataSource1

Configure Data Source...

Refresh Schema

Edit Columns...

Add New Column...

☐ Enable Paging

☐ Enable Sorting

☐ Enable Editing

☐ Enable Deleting

☐ Enable Selection

Edit Templates

Figure 3-5:
The
GridView
control has
redrawn to
reflect the
changes.

4. **Still in the Smart Tag window, click Edit Columns, which opens the
Fields dialog box, as shown in Figure 3-6.**

You're going to remove the `memberid` column from the GridView because although the `GridView` control keeps track of it so it can update the rows, you don't want users to be able to modify the `memberid`.

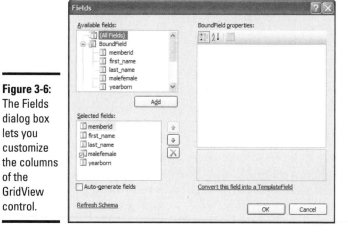

Figure 3-6:
The Fields dialog box lets you customize the columns of the GridView control.

5. **In the Selected Fields list towards the lower-left of the dialog box, click** `memberid`.

   Then click the box with a red X in it to delete the column.

   Yes, I know, the dialog box calls them *fields*, but I call them *columns*. Most database experts these days prefer *columns*, and so I quit saying *fields* and started saying *columns* so people would think I'm an expert. It's all about image, you know.

6. **Click OK to close the Fields dialog box.**

7. **Back in the Smart Tag dialog box, click Add New Column.**

   You're going to add a button column (this time it really isn't a field!) that allows users to edit the row. The Add Field dialog box opens, wasting a whole lot of on-screen real estate (it's shown in Figure 3-7).

8. **In the Choose a Field Type drop-down list, choose Command Field.**

   Some new fields (not columns) will open in the Add Field dialog box, as shown in Figure 3-8. For Header Text, type `Edit`. For Button Type, you can choose whichever you want; I'm choosing Button type. For Command Buttons, check Delete, Edit/Update, and Show Cancel Button.

Figure 3-7:
The Add Field dialog box lets you create a new column.

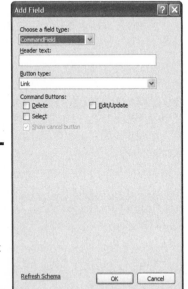

Figure 3-8:
When you choose Command Field, you get options for different types of commands.

TIP

That's it! You're done.

At this point I recommend choosing File⇨Save All. Then, open the page in your browser; it should look like Figure 3-9.

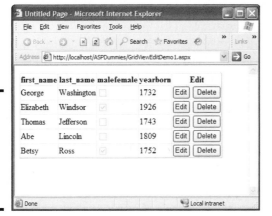

Figure 3-9:
Your grid
now has
Edit and
Delete
buttons
on it.

Go ahead and click the Edit button for Elizabeth Windsor (for the Americans reading this, that's the name of the British Queen). The row for the Queen will change to Edit mode, as shown in Figure 3-10. Try making some changes. Change the birth year to something like 1975, and uncheck the `malefemale` check box. (Don't worry, we'll change the Queen back to a woman later.)

Figure 3-10:
When you
click Edit,
the grid goes
into edit
mode for a
single row.

Then click Update. The grid switches back to regular mode, and you can see the changes are there. If you close the page and reopen it again later, the changes will still be there, meaning the database really did change.

Now open the page again and change the Queen back to `female` (by check-ing the `malefemale` check box) and her birth year back to 1926.

Sorting and Paging the Data in Your Grid

One of the great features of the `GridView` control is that you can display pages of data. For example, if you have hundreds of rows of data to display, you might not want to display all of them in a single HTML page. Instead, you might want to show just 10 rows per HTML page, and provide a list of page numbers at the bottom; this is called "paging," where your users can nagivate through several pages of data in the grid. You might also want to allow your users to click on a column header to sort the grid by that column. Take a look at Figure 3-11.

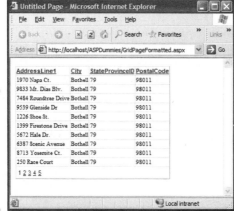

Figure 3-11:
You can easily turn on the sorting and paging mechanism.

Notice in Figure 3-11 that the grid shows 10 rows of data, along with five clickable page numbers below the grid. When you click a number, the page refreshes with the set of data corresponding to the page.

Notice also that each column name is underlined; each is a link. If you click a column header, the rows sort in ascending order by that column. But one cool thing is that rows don't just sort for that page; the entire data sorts, and then you see the appropriate page.

Now for the great part: This sample was incredibly easy to create! Woohoo! Here's the entire code:

```
<%@ Page Language="VB" %>
<!DOCTYPE html PUBLIC "-//W3C//DTD XHTML 1.0 Transitional//EN"
    "http://www.w3.org/TR/xhtml1/DTD/xhtml1-transitional.dtd">
```

```html
<html xmlns="http://www.w3.org/1999/xhtml" >
<head runat="server">
    <title>Untitled Page</title>
    <link href="GridFormats.css" rel="stylesheet" type="text/css" />
</head>
<body>
    <form id="form1" runat="server">
    <div>
    <div>
        <asp:SqlDataSource ID="SqlDataSource1" runat="server"
            ConnectionString=
            "<%$ ConnectionStrings:AdventureWorksConnectionString %>"
            SelectCommand=
            "SELECT AddressLine1,City, StateProvinceID, PostalCode FROM
    Person.Address WHERE AddressID < 50">
        </asp:SqlDataSource>
        <asp:GridView ID="GridView1" runat="server"
            AllowPaging="True" AllowSorting="True"
            DataSourceID="SqlDataSource1">
            <RowStyle CssClass="gridline" />
            <PagerStyle CssClass="gridpaging" />
            <HeaderStyle CssClass="gridheader" />
        </asp:GridView>
    </div>
    </div>
    </form>
</body>
</html>
```

To create this code, I started with the default `.aspx` file created by Visual Studio. I then dragged a `SqlDataSource` control onto the form, and used its Smart Tag to open the Configure Data Source Wizard. Within the wizard, I selected the connection string (as described in the section "Setting up the AdventureWorks Database," at the beginning of this chapter). Next, I used the wizard to enter my `SELECT` statement manually.

After closing the wizard, I dropped a `GridView` control on the form. I opened its Smart Tag, selected `SqlDataSource1`, and then checked the Enable Paging and Enable Sorting check boxes, as shown in Figure 3-12.

Figure 3-12:
Check the
Enable
Paging
and Enable
Sorting
check boxes
to turn on
these two
features.

But to make sure the grid looks pretty good, I made use of a style sheet (for more on style sheets see Book 3, Chapter 4). Although I could have put the style definitions right in the `.aspx` file itself, I wanted to put them in a separate `.css` file in case I want to use them again elsewhere. Notice the link line in the `.aspx` file linking the `.css` file. Here, then, is the `.css` file, which I called GridFormats.css, and put in the same directory as the `.aspx` file:

```
.gridheader
{
    font-family:Arial;
    font-size:11px;
    text-align:left;
}
.gridline
{
    font-family:Ariel;
    font-size:11px;
    text-align:left;
}
.gridpaging
{
    font-family:Arial;
    font-size:11px;
}
```

This file defines three styles (`.gridheader`, `.gridline`, and `.gridpaging`), and gives a font size and font family to each style. For the `.gridheader` style, the file also provides a text alignment, as does the `.gridline` style. (You might notice the `.gridheader` and `.gridline` styles are identical. I made them separate in case I want to later modify the style of the lines or the page numbers without modifying the other.)

Customizing the Columns in a Grid

Yes, you read that right — once again, the columns are called *fields*. (Microsoft isn't making this easy on a lowly writer and the hardworking editors.) Either way, the `GridView` control provides a way to customize exactly what data will appear in its columns.

To get started with the examples in this section, follow these steps:

1. **Create a new** `.aspx` **file, and name it what you wish.**

I called mine `GridViewFields.aspx`.

2. Add a `SqlDataSource` **control.**

You can type it manually, copy it from another example in this chapter, or use the wizard to create it. Here's the code; I've shown the `SqlDataSource` code in bold:

```
<%@ Page Language="VB" %>
<!DOCTYPE html PUBLIC "-//W3C//DTD XHTML 1.0 Transitional//EN"
    "http://www.w3.org/TR/xhtml1/DTD/xhtml1-transitional.dtd">
<script runat="server">
</script>
<html xmlns="http://www.w3.org/1999/xhtml" >
<head runat="server">
    <title>Untitled Page</title>
</head>
<body>
    <form id="form1" runat="server">
    <div>
        <asp:SqlDataSource ID="SqlDataSource1" runat="server"
            ConnectionString=
            "<%$ ConnectionStrings:AdventureWorksConnectionString %>"
            SelectCommand=
            "SELECT * FROM Person.Address WHERE AddressID < 50">
        </asp:SqlDataSource>
    </div>
    </form>
</body>
</html>
```

3. Next, drop a `GridView` **control on your form.**

You can do this from either Design view or Source view; if you do it in Source view, drop it after the closing tag of the `SqlDataSource`. But then you'll want to switch to Design view for the next part.

4. Open the `GridView` **control's Smart Tag.**

The Smart Tag opens.

5. Click the SqlDataSource1 for the data source, and then click Refresh Schema in the Smart Tag.

6. Click Edit Columns in the Smart Tag.

This brings up the Fields dialog box, as shown in Figure 3-13. The Fields dialog box lets you choose exactly what the columns of the grid will look like and what data will appear in them.

TIP

If you don't see a list of column names under `BoundField` in the Available Fields area, here's how to handle it:

1. Click Cancel to get out of the Fields dialog box.

2. Back in the Smart Tag, click Refresh Schema again.

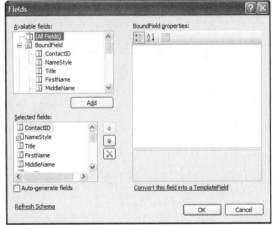

Figure 3-13:
The Fields
dialog box
now has
your fields
already in it,
ready for you
to work on.

3. **Still in the Smart Tag, Click Edit Columns.**

4. **This takes you back into the Fields dialog box.**

5. **Check for a list of column names under** `BoundField`.

You'll notice there are several types of fields available. (The box labeled "Available fields" is actually misnamed; it should be called "Available field types" because it refers to *types* of fields, not existing fields.) Here's a list of the types and what they do:

- `BoundField`: The data in a column of this type appears simply as text.

- `CheckBoxField`: Every row of a column of this type contains a check box.

- `HyperLinkField`: Each row in a column of this type contains a clickable link.

- `ImageField`: Each row in a column of this type contains an image.

- `ButtonField`: Each row in a column of this type contains a button.

- `CommandField`: This is a special type of column that can contain buttons or links that allow you to edit or delete a column. (Check out the "Editing and Deleting Data with a GridView" section earlier in this chapter to see an example.)

- `TemplateField`: A template field is kind of cool; you can put all kinds of your own controls inside a column of this type.

When you chose the data source for the `GridView` control, the designer automatically created a set of columns for your control. The type of column depends on the type of data: If the data is a `bit` type, then the column will be a `CheckBoxField`. Otherwise, the column will be a `BoundField`.

Each field gets a tag inside the `GridView` control's tag. Here's how the `GridView` control's code looked after I chose its data source and clicked Refresh Schema:

```
<asp:GridView ID="GridView1" runat="server" AutoGenerateColumns="False"
DataKeyNames="ContactID"
    DataSourceID="SqlDataSource1">
    <Columns>
        <asp:BoundField DataField="ContactID" HeaderText="ContactID"
            InsertVisible="False"
            ReadOnly="True" SortExpression="ContactID" />
        <asp:CheckBoxField DataField="NameStyle" HeaderText="NameStyle"
            SortExpression="NameStyle" />
        <asp:BoundField DataField="Title" HeaderText="Title"
            SortExpression="Title" />
        <asp:BoundField DataField="FirstName" HeaderText="FirstName"
            SortExpression="FirstName" />
        <asp:BoundField DataField="MiddleName" HeaderText="MiddleName"
            SortExpression="MiddleName" />
        <asp:BoundField DataField="LastName" HeaderText="LastName"
            SortExpression="LastName" />
        <asp:BoundField DataField="Suffix" HeaderText="Suffix"
            SortExpression="Suffix" />
        <asp:BoundField DataField="EmailAddress"
            HeaderText="EmailAddress" SortExpression="EmailAddress" />
        <asp:BoundField DataField="EmailPromotion"
            HeaderText="EmailPromotion"
            SortExpression="EmailPromotion" />
        <asp:BoundField DataField="Phone" HeaderText="Phone"
            SortExpression="Phone" />
        <asp:BoundField DataField="PasswordHash"
            HeaderText="PasswordHash" SortExpression="PasswordHash" />
        <asp:BoundField DataField="PasswordSalt"
            HeaderText="PasswordSalt"
            SortExpression="PasswordSalt" />
        <asp:BoundField DataField="AdditionalContactInfo"
            HeaderText="AdditionalContactInfo"
            SortExpression="AdditionalContactInfo" />
        <asp:BoundField DataField="rowguid" HeaderText="rowguid"
            SortExpression="rowguid" />
        <asp:BoundField DataField="ModifiedDate"
            HeaderText="ModifiedDate" SortExpression="ModifiedDate" />
    </Columns>
</asp:GridView>
```

**Book VI
Chapter 3**

Displaying and
Editing with the
GridView Control

You can see there's a whole bunch of tags. Most of them are `BoundField` tags, except for the second one, which is a `CheckBoxField` tag. Each tag corresponds to a column in the data, and you can see the name of the column by the `DataField` property. Notice also that the very first `BoundField` tag, for `ContactID`, has a property of `ReadOnly` set to `True`. The reason for making this column read-only is the column is the primary key in the table, and you don't want to be modifying that column if you turn on the edit capabilities of the `GridView` control.

If you like, you can open the `.aspx` page in the browser, although it's not particularly interesting. So I'm going to go ahead and have some fun with these columns. In the sections that follow I'll demonstrate some ways you can format your data with the Fields dialog box.

Specifying headers

Probably the easiest thing you can do with the Fields dialog box is specify the headers for your columns. When you click a field in the Selected Fields box, you can go over to the BoundField Properties box on the right. Inside that box is a property called `HeaderText`, as shown in Figure 3-14.

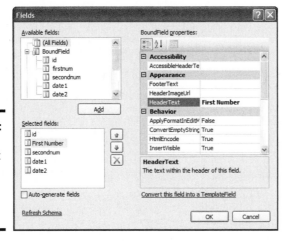

Figure 3-14: Set the HeaderText property to specify a column's header.

To change the header, simply type your text for that property. The text appears as a header in the rendered HTML.

Displaying formatted text with the BoundField type

The `BoundField` type simply takes the text that's in the data column and displays it on the Web page in the grid's column. Okay, you can get fancy if you want by sending the text through the `String.Format` function. Note, however, that you don't actually call the `Format` function yourself; the `GridView` control does that for you. All you do is specify the format string in the `DataFormatString` column, putting in a `{0}` in your format string where you want the text from the data to appear. The `{0}` represents the location in the string where you want the data to appear; then, when the grid control creates the HTML page, the grid will replace the {0} with the string that's in the database.

For example, suppose your text field contains the string "200 Main St" and you make the format string read "Address: {0} Cincinnati, OH". Then your text ultimately renders in the browser as

```
Address: 200 Main St Cincinnati, OH
```

In other words, the string {0} was replaced with the data, which was "200 Main St" resulting in the aforementioned string. That's not all that terribly useful; but where this concept shines is in formatting other types of data such as numbers and dates. If, for example, your data column contains a date and you want this to appear as $1.23, you can use this format string:

```
{0:c}
```

This pattern is just like the {0} I just mentioned, except now the pattern contains some formatting information, the :c part. The :c means "currency." Thus, your number will appear formatted as currency, with a dollar sign and a decimal point and two digits to the right of the decimal.

> **TIP**
>
> If you're new to the .NET way of specifying format strings, open up the online help, go to its index, and open Composite Formatting.

Displaying images from a URL with the ImageField type

Let me first make clear that the ImageField type does not pull images out of a database — unfortunately. Rather, this column generates IMG tags in the resulting HTML, with the SRC attribute's URL coming from your database. (Remember, an IMG tag is simply the HTML tag for displaying an image. The SRC attribute tells the IMG tag where to find the image.) For example, it might generate an IMG tag such as this:

```
<img src="www.wiley.com/mypic.jpg" style="border-width:0px;" />
```

Here, the mypic.jpg name came from your database.

Suppose you have a table with a column that holds VARCHAR data (that is, a string type), such as the imagefile column in this table definition and sample data:

```
CREATE TABLE thumbnails (
    photoid int IDENTITY(1,1)
```

```
        PRIMARY KEY,
    description varchar(50),
    imagefile varchar(255)
)
GO
INSERT thumbnails (description, imagefile)
VALUES ('mountain', 'mountainthumb.jpg')
INSERT thumbnails (description, imagefile)
VALUES ('car', 'carthumb.jpg')
INSERT thumbnails (description, imagefile)
VALUES ('tree', 'treethumb.jpg')
INSERT thumbnails (description, imagefile)
VALUES ('house', 'housethumb.jpg')
INSERT thumbnails (description, imagefile)
VALUES ('boat', 'boatthumb.jpg')
GO
```

The `ImageField` can take this data and turn it into IMG tags, such as this:

```
<img src="www.dummies.com/mountainthumb.jpg" style="border-width:0px;" />
<img src="www.dummies.com/carthumb.jpg" style="border-width:0px;" />
<img src="www.dummies.com/treethumb.jpg" style="border-width:0px;" />
<img src="www.dummies.com/housethumb.jpg" style="border-width:0px;" />
<img src="www.dummies.com/boatthumb.jpg" style="border-width:0px;" />
```

Then, as these tags are rendered, the browser will show the images defined by the `src` property URLs. But where does the `GridView` get the rest of the URL? You define that in the field editor. Start with the following code:

```
<%@ Page Language="VB" %>
<!DOCTYPE html PUBLIC "-//W3C//DTD XHTML 1.0 Transitional//EN"
    "http://www.w3.org/TR/xhtml1/DTD/xhtml1-transitional.dtd">
<script runat="server">
</script>
<html xmlns="http://www.w3.org/1999/xhtml" >
<head runat="server">
    <title>Untitled Page</title>
</head>
<body>
    <form id="form1" runat="server">
    <div>
        <asp:SqlDataSource ID="SqlDataSource1" runat="server"
            ConnectionString=
            "<%$ ConnectionStrings:ASPDConnectionString %>"
            SelectCommand = "SELECT * FROM thumbnails">
        </asp:SqlDataSource>
        <asp:GridView ID="GridView1" runat="server" AutoGenerateColumns="False"
            DataKeyNames="photoid"
            DataSourceID="SqlDataSource1">
        </asp:GridView>
    </div>
    </form>
</body>
</html>
```

I created a new form and put a `SqlDataSource` control on it, as well as a `GridView` control. I selected `SqlDataSource1` for the `GridView` control's data source. Back in Design view, I opened the Smart Tag for the `GridView` control, refreshed the schema, and then clicked Edit Columns to get to the Fields dialog box. In the Available Fields box of the Fields dialog box, I scrolled down to description (found under BoundField), clicked description, and then clicked Add. This added a simple text column that contains text from the description column of the data.

Next, I clicked `ImageField`, and then Add. This adds an image field, as shown in Figure 3-15.

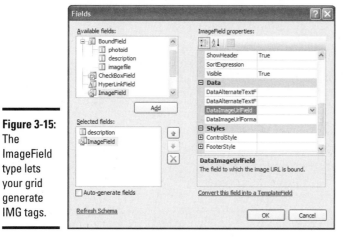

Figure 3-15: The ImageField type lets your grid generate IMG tags.

You can also see in Figure 3-15 two properties in the ImageField Properties list called `DataImageUrlfield` and `DataImageUrlFormatString` (the latter is chopped off a bit because it doesn't quite fit, but it's there). These two fields let you define what text appears in the SRC property of the generated IMG tag. The IMG tag will automatically have this in it:

```
<img src="" style="border-width:0px;" />
```

Your job here is to specify what exactly goes inside the double quotes after the `src=` part. Of the two properties I just mentioned, `DataImageUrlField` is the name of the column containing the data. In this example, that's `imagefile`. This property has a drop-down list box in the Fields editor; if you select it, you'll see the data columns and you can choose `imagefile`.

The second property, `DataImageUrlFormatString`, specifies the format. This is where you put the rest of the URL. Internally, the `GridView` control passes this to the `String.Format` method, meaning you use the standard string formatting rules here. Use `{0}` in the string to specify the `DataImageUrlField` text. For example, you might use this for your `DataImageUrlFormatString`:

```
http://localhost/{0}
```

This will generate SRC properties that look like this for the sample data:

```
http://localhost/mountainthumb.jpg
http://localhost/carthumb.jpg
http://localhost/treethumb.jpg
http://localhost/housethumb.jpg
http://localhost/boatthumb.jpg
```

Notice you don't need to specify the rest of the IMG tag; the `GridView` will generate that for you. That means these five images will appear on the Web page. Pretty easy!

Chapter 4: Displaying and Editing Detail Data

In This Chapter

✔ Viewing data with a DetailsView control

✔ Managing a DetailsView and a GridView together

✔ Editing data with a DetailsView control

✔ Viewing data in a custom layout with a FormView control

✔ Managing a FormView and a GridView together

✔ Editing data in a custom layout with a FormView control

A common way to display data on a computer screen is to show only a single record arranged in a table format, with a left column showing names of the fields, and a right column showing the data in the fields. The standard result looks something like this:

Name	Abraham Lincoln
Position	President
Salary	$5,000

This is quite different from showing records from a result set, where you show many records, each on a single row. Instead, in the case at hand, only a single record is visible, and the single record does not occupy a single row on the screen.

In this chapter, I show you different ways to display a single record of data on the screen. Please note that throughout this chapter I typically use the term *row* (as I have throughout the book) to mean *a single record in a result set*. At times such terminology can become confusing — in which case, I use the term *record* just to keep my words unambiguous. Similarly, I sometimes use the term *field* instead of *column* to avoid ambiguity.

All code listings used in this book are available for download at www. dummies.com/go/aspnetaiofd.

Introducing the DetailsView and FormView Controls

ASP.NET 2.0 provides two controls for displaying individual records. The `DetailsView` control displays records in a tabular fashion, like the Abraham Lincoln example earlier in this chapter. The `DetailsView` control requires very little work — it displays your data for you automatically.

The second control is the `FormView` control. The `FormView` control does not display data automatically; instead, you provide the individual controls that will display the data. The `FormView` control, in turn, acts as a container, providing your controls with the data obtained from a data source.

In the sections that follow, I discuss these two controls. I created a table called `customers` to hold the sample data used in the examples. Listing 4-1 provides the SQL code for the table:

Listing 4-1: SQL code for the customers table

```
CREATE TABLE customers (
    id int IDENTITY(1,1) PRIMARY KEY,
    first_name varchar(20),
    last_name varchar(20),
    phone varchar(12),
    credit int,
    address varchar(50),
    city varchar(20),
    state char(2)
)
GO
INSERT customers (first_name, last_name, phone, credit, address, city, state)
values ('George','Washington','202-555-1212','10000',
    '1600 Pennsylvania Avenue NW','Washington','DC')
INSERT customers (first_name, last_name, phone, credit, address, city, state)
values ('Frank','Smith','513-555-5432','5000','100 Main St','Cincinnati','OH')
INSERT customers (first_name, last_name, phone, credit, address, city, state)
values ('Julie','Williams','313-555-1234','6000',
    '100 1st Street','Los Angeles','CA')
GO
```

This `CREATE TABLE` statement creates a table called `customers`, which holds an identity column along with a first name, last name, phone number, credit limit, and address (composed of a street address, city, and state). Next comes a set of three `INSERT` statements to fill the table with some sample data.

Displaying a Record with a DetailsView Control

If you want to display a single record of data in a table form with the field names in the left column and the field data in the right column, then the `DetailsView` control is for you.

If you want to just display data without editing, the DetailsView control requires very little work. In fact, you don't even have to provide any functions; you can set everything up strictly declaratively, which is incredibly cool because it leaves little room for errors!

To create a simple example, I started out with a fresh page, and dropped a SqlDataSource and a DetailsView control onto it. I then opened the Configure Data Source dialog box from the SqlDataSource control's Smart Tag. (I used a connection string that I created in Listing 4-1, earlier in this chapter, although you're free to create a new one or use an existing one.) I specified the table, customers, and all the fields (the star (*) symbol). I clicked Next and Finish, and that was it. I had the data source set up.

Setting up the DetailsView was just as easy. I dropped it in on the form, and opened the control's Smart Tag; I then selected its data source, as shown in Figure 4-1.

**Book VI
Chapter 4**

**Displaying and
Editing Detail Data**

Figure 4-1:
Use the
Smart Tag to
choose the
data source
for a Details
View
control.

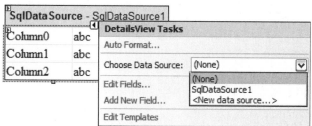

As soon as I selected the data source, the DetailsView control updated its display, showing the columns in the data source, as shown in Figure 4-2.

Figure 4-2:
The Details
View control
automa-
tically
updated its
appearance
after
receiving its
data source.

SqlDataSource - SqlDataSource1	
id	0
first_name	abc
last_name	abc
phone	abc
credit	0
address	abc
city	abc
state	abc

Next I saved my form (any name works), ran it in the browser, and *Shazam!* It worked! Check out Figure 4-3 to see the form in my browser. It's not the prettiest (it could use some formatting), but it's pretty good considering I didn't have to do any programming to get there.

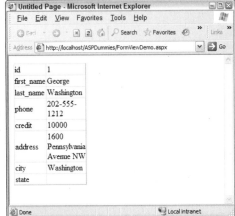

Figure 4-3:
The Details
View control
was easy
to set up
and use.

Even though I didn't do any programming in this case, Visual Studio created a certain amount of code for me. This, of course, is all declarative, as I didn't have to provide any functions. Listing 4-2 shows the code that Visual Studio has created.

Listing 4-2: A page that uses a DetailsView control (VB)

```
<%@ Page Language="VB" %>
<!DOCTYPE html PUBLIC "-//W3C//DTD XHTML 1.0 Transitional//EN"
"http://www.w3.org/TR/xhtml11/DTD/xhtml11-transitional.dtd">
<script runat="server">
</script>
<html xmlns="http://www.w3.org/1999/xhtml" >
<head runat="server">
    <title>Untitled Page</title>
</head>
<body>
    <form id="form1" runat="server">
    <div>
        <asp:SqlDataSource ID="SqlDataSource1" runat="server"
        ConnectionString="<%$ ConnectionStrings:ASPDConnectionString %>"
        SelectCommand="SELECT * FROM [customers]"></asp:SqlDataSource>
        <asp:DetailsView ID="DetailsView1" runat="server"
        AutoGenerateRows="False" DataKeyNames="id"
            DataSourceID="SqlDataSource1" Height="50px" Width="125px">
            <Fields>
                <asp:BoundField DataField="id" HeaderText="id"
                    InsertVisible="False" ReadOnly="True"
                    SortExpression="id" />
                <asp:BoundField DataField="first_name" HeaderText="first_name"
                    SortExpression="first_name" />
                <asp:BoundField DataField="last_name" HeaderText="last_name"
                    SortExpression="last_name" />
```

```
                <asp:BoundField DataField="phone" HeaderText="phone"
                    SortExpression="phone" />
                <asp:BoundField DataField="credit" HeaderText="credit"
                    SortExpression="credit" />
                <asp:BoundField DataField="address" HeaderText="address"
                    SortExpression="address" />
                <asp:BoundField DataField="city" HeaderText="city"
                    SortExpression="city" />
                <asp:BoundField DataField="state" HeaderText="state"
                    SortExpression="state" />
            </Fields>
        </asp:DetailsView>
    </div>
    </form>
</body>
</html>
```

Remember, as with any ASP.NET application, you're free to type this code in manually, or you can let the designer create it for you. Either way, however, you should make sure you understand what the code does so you can modify and enhance it.

The heart of this code is inside the `<div>` tag, and the code consists of two parts, the `SqlDataSource` control and the `DetailsView` control. The `SqlDataSource` control here just includes a connection string reference and a select statement to obtain the data.

The `DetailsView` control includes the required `ID` and `runat` tags. Additionally, it contains the following properties:

✦ `AutoGenerateRows`: This is set to false because inside the `DetailsView` tag are tags specifying the individual fields from which to access the data. (Remember, the designer did all this for us.)

✦ `DataSourceID`: This is the ID of the data source I added in the designer.

✦ `Height` **and** `Width`: This is just the size of the control in the Web page.

Additionally, the `DetailsView` control contains a field called `DataKeyNames`. This is a string that represents the name of the primary key field in the data source. The designer added this field automatically, although it's not used in this example. (It's used when you edit data; it lets the `UPDATE`, `INSERT`, and `DELETE` SQL statements know which row of data to modify.)

After the properties come the `Field` tags. These tags specify exactly what fields you want to appear in the form.

Now if you've read other portions of this book, you might be able to predict what I'm about to say. The terminology used in .NET isn't particularly consistent. These `Field` tags are not fields in the data set; they are fields on the form. Each field tag does, however, get its data from a particular column in the data set.

Each `Field` has the same format; here's an example:

```
<asp:BoundField DataField="first_name" HeaderText="first_name"
SortExpression="first_name" />
```

This field is a `BoundField`, meaning the field on the screen is bound to a particular column in the data set. In this particular case, the field is bound to the `first_name` column of the data set, as denoted by the `DataField` property; the value from this column will appear on the right side of the `DetailsView` on the page.

The `HeaderText` property is the text that appears in the left side of the `DetailsView` on the page. The `SortExpression` specifies the expression used for sorting the data (note, however, that I'm not actually using this feature in the current example).

Moving through data by paging

By itself, the `DetailsView` control isn't particularly useful if you only display a single record and don't give your users the ability to view different records. Thus, the `DetailsView` control includes a handy feature called *paging*. When `Paging` is on, you get a list of record numbers at the bottom of the form; these numbers are clickable, allowing your users to look at different records of data.

The `DetailsView` provides you with different ways to turn on paging. The first is in the designer through the `FormView` control's Smart Tag. (For more on the `FormView` control see the section "Displaying Record Details with a FormView Control," later in this chapter.) Simply check the `Enable Paging` check box. The second is to turn paging on declaratively in the code by setting the `AllowPaging` property to `True`, as in the following code:

```
<asp:DetailsView ID="DetailsView1" runat="server" Height="50px"
Width="125px" AllowPaging="True">
```

Using GridView and DetailsView controls together

A common use of the `DetailsView` control is to use it in conjunction with a `GridView` control. The idea is that the `GridView` will display only a couple columns from a data set; the user then clicks on a row in the `GridView`, and then a `DetailsView` opens showing all the columns for the selected row. That way you don't have to cram a gazillion columns into your grid; all you need are enough for the user to know which row he or she is looking at.

To make all this happen, you need two data sources. The first data source is for the grid, and the second is for the `DetailsView` control. The one for the grid selects only the columns needed for display in the grid — and this data source is bound to the grid, so the grid updates itself automatically when the form opens.

The second data source takes the unique key for the selected row in the grid, and then selects only that row from the data set. However, this data source selects all the columns for the particular row. Then the DetailsView control is manually bound to this second data source; as a result, the DetailsView control displays all the details for the selected column.

To create the page that contains all these controls, then, you need two data sources, a grid, and a DetailsView. Listing 4-3 shows these four controls.

Listing 4-3:   A page that uses a DetailsView and GridView control together (VB)

```
<%@ Page Language="VB" %>
<!DOCTYPE html PUBLIC "-//W3C//DTD XHTML 1.0 Transitional//EN"
"http://www.w3.org/TR/xhtml1/DTD/xhtml1-transitional.dtd">
<script runat="server">
    Protected Sub GridView1_SelectedIndexChanged( _
    ByVal sender As Object, ByVal e As System.EventArgs)
        DetailsSqlDataSource.SelectParameters("id").DefaultValue _
            = GridView1.SelectedValue
        DetailsView1.DataBind()
    End Sub
</script>
<html xmlns="http://www.w3.org/1999/xhtml" >
<head runat="server">
    <title>Untitled Page</title>
</head>
<body>
    <form id="form1" runat="server">
    <div>
        <asp:SqlDataSource ID="GridSqlDataSource" runat="server"
        ConnectionString="<%$ ConnectionStrings:ASPDConnectionString %>"
        SelectCommand="SELECT * FROM [customers]">
        </asp:SqlDataSource>
        <asp:SqlDataSource ID="DetailsSqlDataSource" runat="server"
        ConnectionString="<%$ ConnectionStrings:ASPDConnectionString %>"
        SelectCommand="SELECT * FROM [customers] WHERE [id] = @id">
            <SelectParameters>
                <asp:Parameter Name="id" Type="Int32" />
            </SelectParameters>
        </asp:SqlDataSource>
        <asp:GridView ID="GridView1" runat="server"
        AutoGenerateColumns="False" DataKeyNames="id"
        DataSourceID="GridSqlDataSource"
        OnSelectedIndexChanged="GridView1_SelectedIndexChanged">
            <Columns>
                <asp:CommandField ShowSelectButton="True"
                    ButtonType="Button" SelectText="Details" />
                <asp:BoundField DataField="first_name"
                    HeaderText="first_name" SortExpression="first_name" />
```

(continued)

Listing 4-3 *(continued)*

```
                <asp:BoundField DataField="last_name"
                    HeaderText="last_name" SortExpression="last_name" />
            </Columns>
            <SelectedRowStyle BackColor="Silver" />
        </asp:GridView>
        <asp:DetailsView ID="DetailsView1" runat="server"
        Height="50px" Width="500px" DataSourceID="DetailsSqlDataSource">
        </asp:DetailsView>
    </div>
    </form>
</body>
</html>
```

Look carefully at the SELECT statements in the two data sources. The first selects only the unique ID, the first name, and the last name — which is enough information for the grid:

```
SELECT [id], [first_name], [last_name] FROM [customers]
```

The second SELECT statement selects all the columns, but only a particular row:

```
SELECT * FROM [customers] WHERE [id] = @id
```

The SqlDataSource lets you use parameters in your SQL statements. The parameters are basically like variables in your SQL statements. The WHERE portion of the SELECT statement contains a parameter, @id. Parameters start with an *at* symbol (@). When you call the SQL statement, you must specify a value to replace the parameter with. For example, if you replace the @id parameter with the number 3, then the SELECT statement becomes

```
SELECT * FROM [customers] WHERE [id] = 3
```

This SELECT statement retrieves only a particular row whose ID is 3. When you use a parameter in a SqlDataSource — in addition to specifying the parameter in the SQL — you also have to describe the parameter using some <SelectParameters> tags, like so:

```
<SelectParameters>
    <asp:Parameter Name="id" Type="Int32" />
</SelectParameters>
```

This tag specifies the name of the parameter (given by the Name property) and the type of data (given by the Type property).

When you're ready to retrieve data, first you fill in a value for the parameter, and then bind it to the data. To fill in the value, you access the parameter through the data source, like so:

```
DetailsSqlDataSource.SelectParameters("id").DefaultValue _
= GridView1.SelectedValue
```

This code takes the selected value from the grid and fills that selected value into the parameter. What is the selected value? When you set up the grid, you can specify which column in the row represents the unique key. Since the data uses the id column as the unique key, that's the column I used. To specify this column in the grid, you use the DataKeyNames property:

```
DataKeyNames="id"
```

Further, to make the grid and DetailsView work together, you have to include a way to select a row in the grid. The way to do that is to include a command button, like so:

```
<asp:CommandField ShowSelectButton="True"
ButtonType="Button" SelectText="Details" />
```

Putting everything together, the whole process works. However, before running the code, I want to make one more quick change. When you drop a DetailsView control onto a form, the control defaults to 125 pixels wide — and that's not enough. So I changed the width to 500, as you can see in the code for the Width property of the DetailsView control.

When you run the form, you see Figure 4-4.

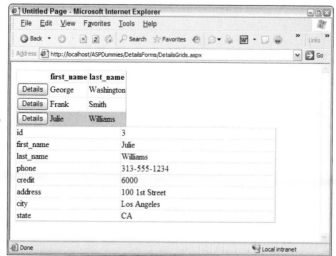

Figure 4-4:
The Details
View control
plays well
together
with the
GridView
control.

Editing Data with a DetailsView

The DetailsView is one of my favorite controls because it exemplifies the nature of laziness inherent in every bone of my body. (Hey, just being honest!) I don't like to write long lines of code when I don't have to. And what's cool about the DetailsView — in addition to displaying data — is that you can easily set up the control for modifying (that is, editing, inserting, and deleting) data.

To modify data with a DetailsView control, you have to do two things:

✦ **Configure your data source for editing, inserting, and deleting (or any combination thereof).**

✦ **Turn on the corresponding features in the DetailsView control.**

Both tasks are easy to do; you can do everything from the designer.

To turn on these data-modification features in the data source, you simply click the Advanced button in the Configure Data Source dialog box, and then click to put a check mark next to Generate INSERT, UPDATE, and DELETE statements (as shown in Figure 4-5).

You then exit the Configure Data Source dialog box and move to the DetailsView control's Smart Tag, as shown in Figure 4-6. In this figure, you can see that I checked the Enable Inserting, Enable Editing, and Enable Deleting options, as well as the Enable Paging options.

That's it! You don't have to do anything else; from there you can just open the form in the browser and go to town. Figure 4-7 shows what you get when you open the form. Notice, in addition to the record of data, you also get Edit, New, and Delete links for — you guessed it — (editing data, creating new data, and deleting data.)

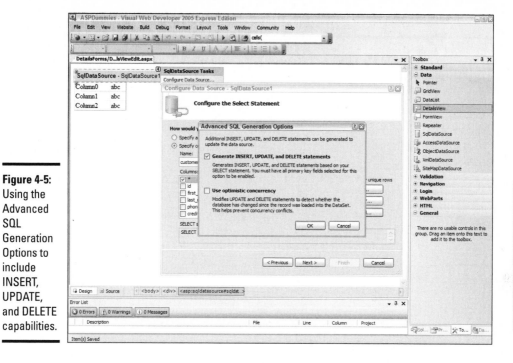

**Book VI
Chapter 4**

Displaying and
Editing Detail Data

Figure 4-5:
Using the
Advanced
SQL
Generation
Options to
include
INSERT,
UPDATE,
and DELETE
capabilities.

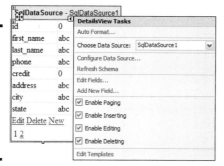

Figure 4-6:
Turning on
the INSERT,
UPDATE,
and DELETE
capabilities
in Details
View.

When you click the Edit link, the form switches to Edit mode, where you can
type in data (as shown in Figure 4-8). To get out of Edit mode, you either
click Update (to save the changes) or click Cancel (to get out without saving
your changes).

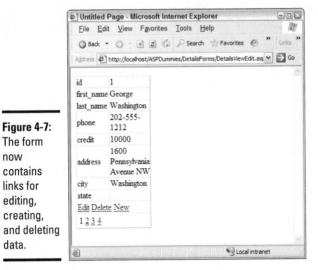

Figure 4-7:
The form
now
contains
links for
editing,
creating,
and deleting
data.

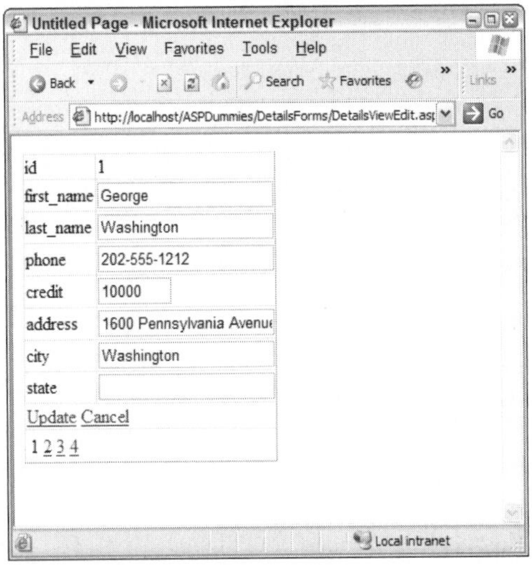

Figure 4-8:
In Edit
mode, you
can modify
the existing
data.

When you click New, you get a form similar to that shown in Figure 4-7 — except the place for the data is empty, ready for you to enter new data. When you click Delete, the data gets deleted.

Listing 4-4 shows the complete code generated by the designer.

Listing 4-4: A page that that uses an editable DetailsView control (VB)

```
<%@ Page Language="VB" %>
<!DOCTYPE html PUBLIC "-//W3C//DTD XHTML 1.0 Transitional//EN"
"http://www.w3.org/TR/xhtml1/DTD/xhtml1-transitional.dtd">
<script runat="server">
</script>
<html xmlns="http://www.w3.org/1999/xhtml" >
<head runat="server">
    <title>Untitled Page</title>
</head>
<body>
    <form id="form1" runat="server">
    <div>
        <asp:SqlDataSource ID="SqlDataSource1" runat="server"
        ConnectionString="<%$ ConnectionStrings:ASPDConnectionString %>"
        DeleteCommand="DELETE FROM [customers] WHERE [id] = @id"
        InsertCommand="INSERT INTO [customers] ([first_name], [last_name],
[phone], [credit], [address], [city], [state]) VALUES (@first_name,
@last_name, @phone, @credit, @address, @city, @state)" SelectCommand="SELECT
* FROM [customers]" UpdateCommand="UPDATE [customers] SET [first_name] =
@first_name, [last_name] = @last_name, [phone] = @phone, [credit] = @credit,
[address] = @address, [city] = @city, [state] = @state WHERE [id] = @id">
            <DeleteParameters>
                <asp:Parameter Name="id" Type="Int32" />
            </DeleteParameters>
            <UpdateParameters>
                <asp:Parameter Name="first_name" Type="String" />
                <asp:Parameter Name="last_name" Type="String" />
                <asp:Parameter Name="phone" Type="String" />
                <asp:Parameter Name="credit" Type="Int32" />
                <asp:Parameter Name="address" Type="String" />
                <asp:Parameter Name="city" Type="String" />
                <asp:Parameter Name="state" Type="String" />
                <asp:Parameter Name="id" Type="Int32" />
            </UpdateParameters>
            <InsertParameters>
                <asp:Parameter Name="first_name" Type="String" />
                <asp:Parameter Name="last_name" Type="String" />
                <asp:Parameter Name="phone" Type="String" />
                <asp:Parameter Name="credit" Type="Int32" />
                <asp:Parameter Name="address" Type="String" />
                <asp:Parameter Name="city" Type="String" />
                <asp:Parameter Name="state" Type="String" />
            </InsertParameters>
        </asp:SqlDataSource>
        <asp:DetailsView ID="DetailsView1" runat="server" Height="50px"
        Width="125px" AllowPaging="True" AutoGenerateRows="False"
        DataKeyNames="id" DataSourceID="SqlDataSource1">
            <Fields>
                <asp:BoundField DataField="id" HeaderText="id"
                    InsertVisible="False" ReadOnly="True"
                    SortExpression="id" />
                <asp:BoundField DataField="first_name" HeaderText="first_name"
                    SortExpression="first_name" />
                <asp:BoundField DataField="last_name" HeaderText="last_name"
                    SortExpression="last_name" />
                <asp:BoundField DataField="phone" HeaderText="phone"
```

(continued)

Listing 4-4 *(continued)*

```
                SortExpression="phone" />
            <asp:BoundField DataField="credit" HeaderText="credit"
                SortExpression="credit" />
            <asp:BoundField DataField="address" HeaderText="address"
                SortExpression="address" />
            <asp:BoundField DataField="city" HeaderText="city"
                SortExpression="city" />
            <asp:BoundField DataField="state" HeaderText="state"
                SortExpression="state" />
            <asp:CommandField ShowDeleteButton="True" ShowEditButton="True"
                ShowInsertButton="True" />
        </Fields>
    </asp:DetailsView>
</div>
</form>
</body>
</html>
```

Searching and displaying details

When you use parameters in a SELECT statement, you can easily put together a search form. Here's what the example will do: First, the user will be presented with a text box in which to enter a string. After entering some text, the user clicks a button; a grid appears, listing the names that match. From there, the user can click a Details button in the grid to see a DetailsView appear, showing the details from the selected row. Figure 4-9 shows the results of a sample session.

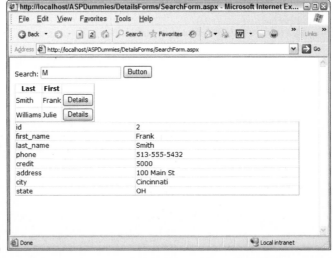

Figure 4-9:
Using parameters, you can create a search form.

Listing 4-5 shows the code for a search form.

Listing 4-5: A page that creates a search form (VB)

```
<%@ Page Language="VB" %>
<script runat="server">
    Protected Sub Button1_Click(ByVal sender As Object, _
    ByVal e As System.EventArgs)
        GridSqlDataSource.SelectParameters("name").DefaultValue = _
            "%" + TextBox1.Text + "%"
    End Sub
    Protected Sub GridView1_SelectedIndexChanged( _
    ByVal sender As Object, ByVal e As System.EventArgs)
        DetailsSqlDataSource.SelectParameters("id").DefaultValue _
            = GridView1.SelectedValue
        DetailsView1.DataBind()
    End Sub
</script>
<html>
<body style="font-family:Verdana,Arial,Sans-Serif;font-size:12px;">
    <form id="form1" runat="server">
        <div>
            Search: <asp:TextBox ID="TextBox1" runat="server"></asp:TextBox>
            <asp:Button ID="Button1" runat="server" _
            Text="Button" OnClick="Button1_Click" />
        </div>
        <div style="padding-top:8px;">
            <asp:SqlDataSource ID="GridSqlDataSource" runat="server"
            ConnectionString="<%$ ConnectionStrings:ASPDConnectionString %>"
            SelectCommand="SELECT id, first_name, last_name FROM [customers] WHERE
    [last_name] like @name">
                <SelectParameters>
                    <asp:Parameter Name="name" Type="String" />
                </SelectParameters>
            </asp:SqlDataSource>
            <asp:GridView ID="GridView1" runat="server"
            DataSourceID="GridSqlDataSource" AutoGenerateColumns="False"
            DataKeyNames="id"
            OnSelectedIndexChanged="GridView1_SelectedIndexChanged">
                <Columns>
                    <asp:BoundField DataField="last_name"
                        HeaderText="Last" SortExpression="last_name" />
                    <asp:BoundField DataField="first_name"
                        HeaderText="First" SortExpression="first_name" />
                    <asp:CommandField ShowSelectButton="True"
                        ButtonType="Button" SelectText="Details" />
                </Columns>
                <RowStyle Font-Size="12px" />
                <HeaderStyle Font-Size="12px" />
            </asp:GridView>
        </div>
        <div>
            <asp:SqlDataSource ID="DetailsSqlDataSource" runat="server"
            ConnectionString="<%$ ConnectionStrings:ASPDConnectionString %>"
            SelectCommand="SELECT * FROM [customers] WHERE [id] = @id">
                <SelectParameters>
                    <asp:Parameter Name="id" Type="Int32" />
```

(continued)

Listing 4-5 *(continued)*

```
            </SelectParameters>
        </asp:SqlDataSource>
        <asp:DetailsView ID="DetailsView1" runat="server"
            Height="50px" Width="550px" DataSourceID="DetailsSqlDataSource">
            <RowStyle Font-Size="12px" />
        </asp:DetailsView>
    </div>
    </form>
</body>
</html>
```

This code contains a data source for the grid; the data source contains a parameter that does the searching for the last name. When the user clicks the button, the `Button1_Click` method runs; this method sets the parameter for the search, which causes the grid to update.

The grid has three fields — two that are bound (those for first name and last name), and one that is a command button. The command button selects the row in the grid. When the user clicks the button, the selected row changes, causing the `SelectedIndexChanged` event to occur. The code includes a handler for this event.

In addition to the first `SqlDataSource` control and `GridView` control, the code contains another `SqlDataSource` and a `DetailsView` control. This second `SqlDataSource` retrieves a single, entire row of data containing all the details for the selected name. The second `DetailsView` control then displays the data retrieved by the second `SqlDataSource` control.

Now look back at the `SelectedIndexChange` event handler; this code is what brings out the details of the data. The code in this handler sets the parameter for the second `SqlDataSource` control's `SELECT` statement, and then calls `DataBind` to retrieve the data.

Displaying Record Details with a FormView Control

If you're not happy with the generic grid format of the `DetailsView` control, you can customize your presentation by using a `FormView` control. The `FormView` control operates much like the `DetailsView` control, except the `FormView` doesn't automatically display anything at all. Instead, you provide the controls that go in the `FormView` control.

In the following sections, I demonstrate first how to use a `FormView` in conjunction with a `GridView`. Then I wrap up the chapter with a demonstration of a custom edit form that includes some custom drop-downs and other means of entering data.

Using GridView and FormView controls together

In this section, I'm assuming you're familiar with how to use two data sources along with parameters. If you're not, check out the section "Using GridView and DetailsView controls together," earlier in this chapter.

Listing 4-6 uses two data sources, each with its own tasks:

✦ One retrieves all the rows in a data set and places the results in a grid.

✦ One retrieves only a particular row from the data set, and places the results in a `FormView` control.

This code is nearly identical to that in Listing 4-3 — except instead of using a `DetailsView`, I'm using a `FormView` control.

Listing 4-6:   A page that uses a FormView and GridView control together (VB)

```vb
<%@ Page Language="VB" %>
<script runat="server">
    Protected Sub GridView1_SelectedIndexChanged( _
    ByVal sender As Object, ByVal e As System.EventArgs)
        DetailsSqlDataSource.SelectParameters("id").DefaultValue _
            = GridView1.SelectedValue
        FormView1.DataBind()
    End Sub
</script>
<html>
<body>
    <form id="form1" runat="server">
    <div>
        <asp:SqlDataSource ID="GridSqlDataSource" runat="server"
        ConnectionString="<%$ ConnectionStrings:ASPDConnectionString %>"
        SelectCommand="SELECT * FROM [customers]">
        </asp:SqlDataSource>
        <asp:SqlDataSource ID="DetailsSqlDataSource" runat="server"
        ConnectionString="<%$ ConnectionStrings:ASPDConnectionString %>"
        SelectCommand="SELECT * FROM [customers] WHERE [id] = @id">
            <SelectParameters>
                <asp:Parameter Name="id" Type="Int32" />
            </SelectParameters>
        </asp:SqlDataSource>
        <asp:GridView ID="GridView1" runat="server"
        AutoGenerateColumns="False" DataKeyNames="id"
        DataSourceID="GridSqlDataSource"
        OnSelectedIndexChanged="GridView1_SelectedIndexChanged">
            <Columns>
                <asp:CommandField ShowSelectButton="True"
                    ButtonType="Button" SelectText="Details" />
                <asp:BoundField DataField="first_name"
                    HeaderText="first_name" SortExpression="first_name" />
                <asp:BoundField DataField="last_name"
                    HeaderText="last_name" SortExpression="last_name" />
            </Columns>
```

(continued)

Listing 4-6 *(continued)*

```
        <SelectedRowStyle BackColor="Silver" />
      </asp:GridView>
      <asp:FormView ID="FormView1" runat="server"
      DataSourceID="DetailsSqlDataSource">
        <ItemTemplate>
          <%#Eval("first_name")%> <%#Eval("last_name")%><br />
          Credit Limit: $<%#Eval("credit")%><br />
          <%#Eval("address")%><br />
          <%#Eval("city")%> <%#Eval("state")%><br />
        </ItemTemplate>
      </asp:FormView>
    </div>
    </form>
</body>
</html>
```

In the preceding code, you can see how I had to describe exactly what I want to appear inside the FormView, using Eval statements like so:

```
<%#Eval("first_name")%>
```

This bit of code retrieves the first_name column from the data set and displays the results on the page. All these Eval statements go inside an ItemTemplate tag in the FormView control.

As you can see, the FormView is actually quite easy to use; it requires a bit more finagling than the DetailsView, but not a lot. Figure 4-10 shows you what the form looks like when it opens and you select an item in the grid.

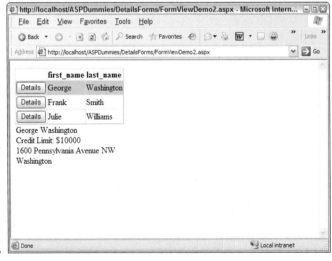

Figure 4-10:
Using parameters, you can create a search form.

Editing data with a FormView

Listing 4-7 shows a complete Web page that lets you edit data in a `FormView`. This chapter covers everything in this program except for two techniques: the way the data is bound in the `FormView` and the way I use several templates within the `FormView`, an `ItemTemplate`, and an `EditTemplate`.

Listing 4-7:   A page with a FormView control that can be edited

```
<%@ Page Language="VB" %>
<script runat="server">
</script>
<html>
<body>
    <form id="form1" runat="server">
    <div style="font-family:Arial;border:solid 1px black;width:500px;">
        <asp:SqlDataSource ID="SqlDataSource1" runat="server"
        ConnectionString="<%$ ConnectionStrings:ASPDConnectionString %>"
        SelectCommand="SELECT * FROM [customers]"
        DeleteCommand="DELETE FROM [customers] WHERE [id] = @id"
        InsertCommand="INSERT INTO [customers] ([first_name], [last_name],
    [phone], [credit], [address], [city], [state]) VALUES (@first_name,
    @last_name, @phone, @credit, @address, @city, @state)" UpdateCommand="UPDATE
    [customers] SET [first_name] = @first_name, [last_name] = @last_name,
    [phone] = @phone, [credit] = @credit, [address] = @address, [city] = @city,
    [state] = @state WHERE [id] = @id">
            <DeleteParameters>
                <asp:Parameter Name="id" Type="Int32" />
            </DeleteParameters>
            <UpdateParameters>
                <asp:Parameter Name="first_name" Type="String" />
                <asp:Parameter Name="last_name" Type="String" />
                <asp:Parameter Name="phone" Type="String" />
                <asp:Parameter Name="credit" Type="Int32" />
                <asp:Parameter Name="address" Type="String" />
                <asp:Parameter Name="city" Type="String" />
                <asp:Parameter Name="state" Type="String" />
                <asp:Parameter Name="id" Type="Int32" />
            </UpdateParameters>
            <InsertParameters>
                <asp:Parameter Name="first_name" Type="String" />
                <asp:Parameter Name="last_name" Type="String" />
                <asp:Parameter Name="phone" Type="String" />
                <asp:Parameter Name="credit" Type="Int32" />
                <asp:Parameter Name="address" Type="String" />
                <asp:Parameter Name="city" Type="String" />
                <asp:Parameter Name="state" Type="String" />
            </InsertParameters>
        </asp:SqlDataSource>
        <asp:FormView ID="FormView1" runat="server"
        DataSourceID="SqlDataSource1" DataKeyNames="id" AllowPaging="true">
        <EditItemTemplate>
        <table cellpadding="0" cellspacing="0">
            <tr>
                <td style="height:10px;"></td>
                <td style="font-size:10px;height:10px;">First</td>
```

(continued)

**Book VI
Chapter 4**

**Displaying and
Editing Detail Data**

Listing 4-7 *(continued)*

```
        <td style="font-size:10px;height:10px;padding-left:3px;">
            Last</td>
    </tr>
    <tr>
        <td>Name</td>
        <td>
            <asp:TextBox ID="TextBox1" runat="server"
            Text='<%# Bind("first_name") %>' />
        </td>
        <td style="padding-left:3px;">
            <asp:TextBox ID="TextBox2" runat="server"
            Text='<%# Bind("last_name") %>' />
        </td>
    </tr>
    <tr>
        <td style="padding-top:3px;">Phone:</td>
        <td style="padding-top:3px;">
            <asp:TextBox ID="TextBox3" runat="server"
            Text='<%# Bind("phone") %>' />
        </td>
        <td style="padding-top:3px;"></td>
    </tr>
    <tr>
        <td style="padding-top:3px;">Credit Limit: $</td>
        <td style="padding-top:3px;">
            <asp:TextBox ID="TextBox4" runat="server"
            Text='<%# Bind("credit") %>' />
        </td>
        <td style="padding-top:3px;">.00</td>
    </tr>
    <tr>
        <td style="height:10px;"></td>
        <td colspan="2" style="font-size:10px;height:10px;">
            Street</td>
    </tr>
    <tr>
        <td>Address:</td>
        <td colspan="2">
            <asp:TextBox ID="TextBox5" runat="server"
            Text='<%# Bind("address") %>' />
        </td>
    </tr>
    <tr>
        <td style="height:10px;"></td>
        <td style="font-size:10px;height:10px;">City</td>
        <td style="font-size:10px;height:10px;padding-left:3px;">
            State</td>
    </tr>
    <tr>
        <td></td>
        <td>
            <asp:TextBox ID="TextBox7" runat="server"
                Text='<%# Bind("city") %>' />
        </td>
        <td style="padding-left:3px;">
            <asp:DropDownList ID="DropDownList1" runat="server"
            SelectedValue='<%# Bind("state") %>'>
```

```
    <asp:ListItem>AK</asp:ListItem><asp:ListItem>AL</asp:ListItem>
    <asp:ListItem>AR</asp:ListItem><asp:ListItem>AS</asp:ListItem>
    <asp:ListItem>AZ</asp:ListItem><asp:ListItem>CA</asp:ListItem>
    <asp:ListItem>CO</asp:ListItem><asp:ListItem>CT</asp:ListItem>
    <asp:ListItem>DC</asp:ListItem><asp:ListItem>DE</asp:ListItem>
    <asp:ListItem>FL</asp:ListItem><asp:ListItem>GA</asp:ListItem>
    <asp:ListItem>HI</asp:ListItem><asp:ListItem>IA</asp:ListItem>
    <asp:ListItem>ID</asp:ListItem><asp:ListItem>IL</asp:ListItem>
    <asp:ListItem>IN</asp:ListItem><asp:ListItem>KS</asp:ListItem>
    <asp:ListItem>KY</asp:ListItem><asp:ListItem>LA</asp:ListItem>
    <asp:ListItem>MD</asp:ListItem><asp:ListItem>ME</asp:ListItem>
    <asp:ListItem>MI</asp:ListItem><asp:ListItem>MN</asp:ListItem>
    <asp:ListItem>MO</asp:ListItem><asp:ListItem>MS</asp:ListItem>
    <asp:ListItem>MT</asp:ListItem><asp:ListItem>NC</asp:ListItem>
    <asp:ListItem>ND</asp:ListItem><asp:ListItem>NE</asp:ListItem>
    <asp:ListItem>NH</asp:ListItem><asp:ListItem>NJ</asp:ListItem>
    <asp:ListItem>NM</asp:ListItem><asp:ListItem>NV</asp:ListItem>
    <asp:ListItem>NY</asp:ListItem><asp:ListItem>OH</asp:ListItem>
    <asp:ListItem>OK</asp:ListItem><asp:ListItem>OR</asp:ListItem>
    <asp:ListItem>PA</asp:ListItem><asp:ListItem>RI</asp:ListItem>
    <asp:ListItem>SC</asp:ListItem><asp:ListItem>SD</asp:ListItem>
    <asp:ListItem>TN</asp:ListItem><asp:ListItem>TX</asp:ListItem>
    <asp:ListItem>UT</asp:ListItem><asp:ListItem>VA</asp:ListItem>
    <asp:ListItem>VT</asp:ListItem><asp:ListItem>WA</asp:ListItem>
    <asp:ListItem>WI</asp:ListItem><asp:ListItem>WV</asp:ListItem>
    <asp:ListItem>WY</asp:ListItem>
        </asp:DropDownList>
    </td>
  </tr>
</table>
<asp:LinkButton ID="UpdateButton" Text="Update"
CommandName="Update" RunAt="server" />
<asp:LinkButton ID="CancelButton" Text="Cancel"
CommandName="Cancel" runat="server" />
</EditItemTemplate>
<InsertItemTemplate>
<table cellpadding="0" cellspacing="0">
    <tr>
        <td style="height:10px;"></td>
        <td style="font-size:10px;height:10px;">First</td>
        <td style="font-size:10px;height:10px;padding-left:3px;">
            Last</td>
    </tr>
    <tr>
        <td>Name</td>
        <td>
            <asp:TextBox ID="TextBox1" runat="server"
            Text='<%# Bind("first_name") %>' />
        </td>
        <td style="padding-left:3px;">
            <asp:TextBox ID="TextBox2" runat="server"
            Text='<%# Bind("last_name") %>' />
        </td>
    </tr>
    <tr>
        <td style="padding-top:3px;">Phone:</td>
        <td style="padding-top:3px;">
            <asp:TextBox ID="TextBox3" runat="server"
            Text='<%# Bind("phone") %>' />
```

(continued)

Listing 4-7 *(continued)*

```
        </td>
        <td style="padding-top:3px;"></td>
    </tr>
    <tr>
        <td style="padding-top:3px;">Credit Limit: $</td>
        <td style="padding-top:3px;">
            <asp:TextBox ID="TextBox4" runat="server"
            Text='<%# Bind("credit") %>' />
        </td>
        <td style="padding-top:3px;">.00</td>
    </tr>
    <tr>
        <td style="height:10px;"></td>
        <td colspan="2" style="font-size:10px;height:10px;">
            Street</td>
    </tr>
    <tr>
        <td>Address:</td>
        <td colspan="2">
            <asp:TextBox ID="TextBox5" runat="server"
            Text='<%# Bind("address") %>' />
        </td>
    </tr>
    <tr>
        <td style="height:10px;"></td>
        <td style="font-size:10px;height:10px;">City</td>
        <td style="font-size:10px;height:10px;padding-left:3px;">
            State</td>
    </tr>
    <tr>
        <td></td>
        <td>
            <asp:TextBox ID="TextBox7" runat="server"
                Text='<%# Bind("city") %>' />
        </td>
        <td style="padding-left:3px;">
            <asp:DropDownList ID="DropDownList1" runat="server"
            SelectedValue='<%# Bind("state") %>'>
        <asp:ListItem>AK</asp:ListItem><asp:ListItem>AL</asp:ListItem>
        <asp:ListItem>AR</asp:ListItem><asp:ListItem>AS</asp:ListItem>
        <asp:ListItem>AZ</asp:ListItem><asp:ListItem>CA</asp:ListItem>
        <asp:ListItem>CO</asp:ListItem><asp:ListItem>CT</asp:ListItem>
        <asp:ListItem>DC</asp:ListItem><asp:ListItem>DE</asp:ListItem>
        <asp:ListItem>FL</asp:ListItem><asp:ListItem>GA</asp:ListItem>
        <asp:ListItem>HI</asp:ListItem><asp:ListItem>IA</asp:ListItem>
        <asp:ListItem>ID</asp:ListItem><asp:ListItem>IL</asp:ListItem>
        <asp:ListItem>IN</asp:ListItem><asp:ListItem>KS</asp:ListItem>
        <asp:ListItem>KY</asp:ListItem><asp:ListItem>LA</asp:ListItem>
        <asp:ListItem>MD</asp:ListItem><asp:ListItem>ME</asp:ListItem>
        <asp:ListItem>MI</asp:ListItem><asp:ListItem>MN</asp:ListItem>
        <asp:ListItem>MO</asp:ListItem><asp:ListItem>MS</asp:ListItem>
        <asp:ListItem>MT</asp:ListItem><asp:ListItem>NC</asp:ListItem>
        <asp:ListItem>ND</asp:ListItem><asp:ListItem>NE</asp:ListItem>
        <asp:ListItem>NH</asp:ListItem><asp:ListItem>NJ</asp:ListItem>
        <asp:ListItem>NM</asp:ListItem><asp:ListItem>NV</asp:ListItem>
        <asp:ListItem>NY</asp:ListItem><asp:ListItem>OH</asp:ListItem>
        <asp:ListItem>OK</asp:ListItem><asp:ListItem>OR</asp:ListItem>
        <asp:ListItem>PA</asp:ListItem><asp:ListItem>RI</asp:ListItem>
```

```
                <asp:ListItem>SC</asp:ListItem><asp:ListItem>SD</asp:ListItem>
                <asp:ListItem>TN</asp:ListItem><asp:ListItem>TX</asp:ListItem>
                <asp:ListItem>UT</asp:ListItem><asp:ListItem>VA</asp:ListItem>
                <asp:ListItem>VT</asp:ListItem><asp:ListItem>WA</asp:ListItem>
                <asp:ListItem>WI</asp:ListItem><asp:ListItem>WV</asp:ListItem>
                <asp:ListItem>WY</asp:ListItem>
                    </asp:DropDownList>
                </td>
            </tr>
        </table>
        <asp:LinkButton ID="InsertButton" Text="Insert"
        CommandName="Insert" RunAt="server" />
        <asp:LinkButton ID="CancelButton" Text="Cancel"
        CommandName="Cancel" runat="server" />
        </InsertItemTemplate>
        <ItemTemplate>
            <%#Eval("first_name")%> <%#Eval("last_name")%><br />
            Credit Limit: $<%#Eval("credit")%><br />
            <%#Eval("address")%><br />
            <%#Eval("city")%> <%#Eval("state")%><br />
            <asp:LinkButton ID="EditButton" Text="Edit"
            CommandName="Edit" RunAt="server" />
            <asp:LinkButton ID="NewButton" Text="Add New"
            CommandName="New" RunAt="server" />
        </ItemTemplate>
        </asp:FormView>
    </div>
    </form>
</body>
</html>
```

Figure 4-11 shows the code in action. In this figure, the form is in Edit mode, meaning I'm editing existing data.

A FormView control maintains multiple modes depending on what action the control is taking. For example, when you are simply viewing data, the form is in ReadOnly mode. If you're editing existing data, the form is in Edit mode; if you're inserting new data, the form is in Insert mode.

You can find out the current mode of a FormView control by checking its CurrentMode property. Valid values are Edit, Insert, and ReadOnly.

Remember, you have complete control over the appearance of a FormView control. It doesn't automatically put any controls on-screen; instead, you have to specify what the controls are and where they appear. Since you probably want different controls when in ReadOnly mode versus when in Edit mode, the FormView control provides you with three different templates in which you describe the controls: ItemTemplate for viewing data, EditItemTemplate for editing existing data, and InsertItemTemplate for inserting new data.

Take a look at Listing 4-7 and you can see how I made use of all three of these templates. Inside each template I provided several controls for manipulating the data.

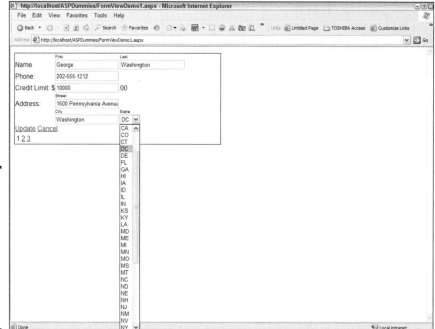

Figure 4-11:
The FormView control includes templates for viewing, inserting, and editing data.

Now look inside the `ItemTemplate` template: Here I'm just displaying data using the `Eval` function, in which I retrieve the data for a particular column in the data. The `Eval` function does nothing more than retrieve the data.

But in the case of the other two templates, I want to actually modify data that's in the data set — so I don't use `Eval` with these templates. Instead, I put my controls on the page (mostly `TextBox` controls) and instead of using `Eval` to simply retrieve data, I bind the control to the `SqlDataSource` using the `Bind` function. The `Bind` function causes the control to work as a two-way street, meaning data is retrieved for the current record (via the `SqlDataSource` control's `SELECT` statement) and sent back to the database (via the `SqlDataSource` control's `INSERT` or `UPDATE` statement).

One particularly handy feature of the `Bind` function is that it also works with drop-down lists. Notice that I'm providing a drop-down in two of the templates for the state. I bind to the drop-down when the form opens, and then the control will update itself with whatever is in the current record. When I select a new state, the drop-down control sends the correct data to the database for the state. It works pretty well!

Chapter 5: Advanced Data Retrieval

In This Chapter

✔ Steering clear of the Eval method

✔ Attaching to different kinds of data

✔ Advanced Repeater usage

In this chapter, I explore several advanced topics of data retrieval in your ASP.NET programs. Although I tag this section "advanced," everything is relative. If you've mastered the rest of the data-access topics in this mini-book, I strongly encourage you to master these topics as well; they offer some deeper insight into getting the most power out of your data-ready Web sites.

In this chapter, I look at how to bind to different types of data — including your own `ArrayList` containers — as well as how to skip the somewhat cumbersome `SqlDataSource` control. I also talk about how to get more out of your `Repeater` controls (a control I personally find incredibly powerful through its simplicity). I begin the chapter with a discussion of the elusive concept of binding — and a convoluted, but worthwhile, alternative to the `Eval` method that was presented in Chapter 2 of this mini-book.

All the code listings that are used in this book are available for download at www.dummies.com/go/aspnetaiofd.

Ditching the Eval Method

When you bind to data using the `<%# %>` tags in a typical `.aspx` file, you're making use of a special ASP.NET syntax. Inside these constructs, what you can do is pretty limited. This is a source of a lot of confusion among ASP.NET programmers. Further, with ASP.NET 2.0, Microsoft added a way of binding to data within the `<%# %>` tags. The previous ASP.NET 1.0 way still exists, however. But what exactly is the `<%# %>` tag? In this section I look at the tag in more detail. When you understand what exactly it is and how it works, you're less likely to make mistakes with your data.

In Chapter 2 of this mini-book, I introduce the `Eval` method and mentioned that although it is convenient, it is anything but efficient. In fact, it's excruciatingly inefficient. So inefficient, in fact, that you should never use it in a real program. Let me repeat, in case you didn't get it the first time: Don't use `Eval`!

Here's why: The `Eval` method is a *static* (also called *shared*) method of a class called `DataBinder`. It takes an object for a first parameter and a name as a string for the second parameter. The `Eval` method then uses the built-in functionality of the .NET Framework to dig through the object passed in, locate a data member having the given name, and retrieve the member's value.

Such access is costly and time-consuming. Suppose the variable `inst` in the upcoming lines of code is an instance of a class called `MyClass`, and that class has a member called `Size`. Normally you would access the `Size` member through code, like so:

```
value = inst.Size
```

Such an expression gets figured out by the compiler — and the resulting compiled code is neat, short, and fast. However, the .NET system has the capability to ask an object at runtime for the names of all its members — and the system also lets you retrieve the members based on their names, like so:

```
membername = "Size"
value = inst.FindMemberByName(membername)
```

Note that the method isn't actually called `FindMemberByName`; it's actually a bit more involved than just one line of code, but this is the basic idea. (If you really want to know all the gory details, go to the online help, look up `Reflection` namespace, and read as much as you can to your heart's content.)

Now to make things messier, imagine that the value of `membername` is filled in by a user at runtime through a form. In other words, when you compile the code, the compiler doesn't yet know which member to access. The member might be `Size`, or it might be something else. Only after the program runs does the program know which member to access. Big-time yuck.

As you can imagine, such access is slooooooooow. Accessing members like this takes time. And this approach is *exactly* what the `Eval` method uses. Have I said enough? Don't use it!

So what should you use instead? I'm glad you asked. And after you see what the preferred method is, you'll understand why I didn't have the heart to spring this on you so early in your growing years as a database programmer. It would have scarred you for life.

Where does the <%# %> get processed?

One really annoying thing about the `<%# #>` tag (in addition to looking like a censored swear word to the uninitiated) is that the processing takes place elsewhere from the rest of the code in your `.aspx` file. For example, suppose you have this snippet within your code:

```
<%
    Dim myvar As Int32 = 5
    Response.Write(myvar)
%>
<asp:Repeater ID="Repeater1"
    runat="server">
<ItemTemplate>
    <asp:LinkButton
    runat="server"
    CommandName="Details"
        Text = <%# myvar %> />
```

(This isn't a complete `Repeater`; but it's enough to make my point.) Notice that I'm declaring a variable `myvar`, and then attempting to use it in the `<%# %>` tag. This code might look fine, but, in fact, it isn't because the `<%# %>` tags are not processed in the same place

and time as the rest of the code. When ASP.NET goes through an `.aspx` file and an associated code file, ASP.NET generates a big, long code file that gets compiled. The code you insert into your `.aspx` file between `<%` and `%>` gets copied into one function, and the code you put in your `<%# %>` tags gets put into a *separate* function. Not the best situation; a separate function means separate scooping, as well as execution at a different time.

The way to get around this problem, then, is to develop your `.aspx` file in such a way that you don't need to rely on variables inside the `<%# %>` tags that you declare elsewhere. Instead, if you need to use variables and such, you can create a protected member function in the associated code file — and call the function from within your `<%# %>` tags, passing any data retrieved from the bind that you might need. It looks like this:

```
<%#CreateDetailString(CType
    (Container.DataItem,
    DataRowView))%>
```

Here's what you should code instead of a simple expression such as `<%# Eval("first_name") %>`:

```
<%#CType(Container.DataItem, System.Data.DataRowView).Item("first_name")%>
```

The data-bound control that contains the binding expression is currently processing a row that's available via `Container.DataItem`. However, the type of the `DataItem` object depends on the data you're using. As a result, the `DataItem` property is defined as an `Object` type.

So, to use the `DataItem` property in any meaningful way, you must cast it to the correct type. In the case of data bound to a database, the type of object returned by the `DataItem` property is `System.Data.DataRowView`. Thus the `CType` expression casts it to `System.Data.DataRowView`.

Once the object has been cast to `System.Data.DataRowView,` you can use the `Item` property to retrieve the column you're interested in.

Granted, this code is convoluted compared to `<%# Eval("first_name") %>`. But the improved efficiency for any but the most trivial applications is enough to merit going to the extra trouble.

What if, instead of repeating through data from a database, you're climbing through an `ArrayList` containing instances of your own structures — such as those we see in Listings 5-1 and 5-2 later in this chapter? In that case, the `DataItem` property is not an instance of `DataRowView`; instead, it's an instance of whatever class is in the `ArrayList`. In Listings 5-1 and 5-2, the class is `Employee`. But again, `Container.DataItem` is declared as `Object`, so you must cast:

```
<%#CType(Container.DataItem, Employee).Name%>
```

Thus you have in hand an instance of `Employee`, and can access its individual members.

Binding to Different Kinds of Data

The ASP.NET data controls are extremely powerful. Sure, that sounds like an advertisement, but it's true. I have coded in many different Web languages — including PHP, Perl, and many others — and I can tell you that of all the advanced languages, ASP.NET is by far the easiest for doing data access. You can put together entire systems without any coding. But you can also roll up your sleeves and get down to some serious programming as well to get the most out of your data. Case in point: Here I show you how to skip one control that I'm not particularly fond of, the `SqlDataSource` control.

Skipping the SQLDataSource

If you've been exploring the previous four chapters of this mini-book, you've seen that to get data in and out of a database, the examples use a `SqlDataSource` control. However, if you find that control a bit cumbersome, you can skip it altogether — and just write code to get to the data. My personal preference is to skip it, as I find the code quite easy to write.

The data classes in ASP.NET provide several ways to access the data. One way is to access all the rows and columns in a single table (or a set of tables). Another way is to simply code your own SQL with the help of the data classes.

First, here's an example that uses two important classes, the `SqlDataAdapter` and the `DataTable`. The `SqlDataAdapter` class is a "do-everything" class that includes various kinds of data classes — all combined into a single class. It includes data commands for handling SQL statements; it also contains a connection string for connecting to the database.

The `SqlDataAdapter` returns its data specifically in the form of either a single `DataTable` instance or a set of `DataTable` instances collected together into a class called `DataSet`. It returns its data by filling an instance of `DataTable`, or by creating `DataTable` instances of a `DataSet` and filling them.

The following code is a quick demonstration of `SqlDataAdapter`:

```
Dim da As New SqlDataAdapter( _
    "SELECT * FROM member", _
    "Data Source=KOALA3;Initial Catalog=ASPD;User ID=sa;Password=")
Dim dt As New DataTable
da.Fill(dt)
```

Book VI Chapter 5

Advanced Data Retrieval

The first three lines of this code create the new instance of `SqlDataAdapter`. Look at the parameters; the first is the SELECT statement for acquiring the data. Although you can see I'm getting all the rows from a specific table (and thus the `DataTable` I'm filling corresponds exactly to a table in the database), this need not always be the case. You can use any SQL statement that retrieves data; the result set will come back in a row-column form and be placed in a `DataTable`.

The forth line creates a new instance of `DataTable`. Notice that I'm creating a new instance! The `SqlDataAdapter` doesn't create one for me. The final line of this code does the work; the `Fill` method connects to the database using the connection you supplied to the `SqlDataAdapter`, and then retrieves the data using the SQL statement you also supplied to the `SqlDataAdapter`.

Always create the `DataTable` manually by calling `New`. If you forget `New`, the code will compile, but you'll be passing an empty object into the `SqlDataAdapter` upon the call to `Fill` — and you'll get a nice, big, beautiful exception error when the program runs.

Notice how easy the code is. I didn't have to go through a bunch of trouble creating a `SqlDataSource` control, nor did I have to step through a wizard. I just typed the code in quickly and got it working. Personally, I like that kind of coding — but use whatever method you prefer and find easiest: You can either type code manually (as I did here) or use the `SqlDataSource` control and its wizards.

The `SqlDataAdapter` is in the `SqlClient` namespace. Thus you need to import `System.Data.SqlClient`. But the `DataTable` is in a more general-purpose namespace, `Data`. To use it, you must import `System.Data.SqlClient`.

Binding SqlDataAdapter results to controls

After you have retrieved data from a `SqlDataAdapter`, you probably want to do something with the data. Its not of much use just sitting there on your hard drive.

Getting the data into the controls is easy; you simply bind it, which takes two lines of code. The first line tells the control where the data comes from; the second line tells the control to go get the data.

Following is a complete `.aspx` file that creates a `SqlDataAdapter`, retrieves data through the adapter into a `DataTable` object, and tells a `GridView` control to bind to the data:

```
<%@ Page Language="VB" %>
<%@ Import Namespace="System.Data" %>
<%@ Import Namespace="System.Data.SqlClient" %>
<script runat="server">
    Protected Sub Page_Load(ByVal sender As Object, ByVal e As System.EventArgs)
        Dim da As New SqlDataAdapter( _
            "SELECT * FROM member", _
            "Data Source=KOALA3;Initial Catalog=ASPD;User ID=sa;Password=")
        Dim dt As New DataTable
        da.Fill(dt)
        GridView1.DataSource = dt
        GridView1.DataBind()

    End Sub
</script>
<html>
<body>
    <form id="form1" runat="server">
    <div>
        <asp:GridView ID="GridView1" runat="server">
        </asp:GridView>
    </div>
    </form>
</body>
</html>
```

The first thing I want to say about this code, before explaining it in detail, is that I typed it all in without using the designer. I started with a default `.aspx` file, and then I removed a few things I didn't want (which Visual Studio inserts automatically), such as the DOCTYPE line and the `namespace` parameter to the HTML tag. (Okay, technically it's good policy to *include* those in a sound Web-page design for the real world — they define the exact breed of

HTML you're using — but I usually remove them from samples to keep the samples from getting bogged down with too many lines of code.)

Now, moving on to the code itself, you can see that I included the two necessary `Import` statements at the top, one for `System.Data` and one for `System.Data.SqlClient`.

Moving on, I'll describe the code in the order I created it (as opposed to the order it appears in the code.) I added the `GridView` control that's visible toward the bottom of the form. I put it inside the `<div>` tag, which is inside the `<form>` tag because the `GridView` control must be inside a `<form>` tag as per Microsoft's requirements. Notice that I didn't actually supply anything inside the `GridView` tag. I just specified the `GridView` tag itself, a name, and the required `runat="server"` property.

Next, higher up in the code, I added the `Page_Load` event handler. This takes place when the page first loads, as the name implies. In this method, I create a new `SqlDataAdapter` instance, passing a connection string and a `SELECT` statement. Next, I create a new `DataTable`, and then call the `Fill` method on the data adapter, passing the table. That gets the data for me.

Now comes the cool part. Look at the next two lines of code:

```
GridView1.DataSource = dt
GridView1.DataBind()
```

The first of these two lines tells the `GridView` where it will get its data and what the source of the data will be. This code sets the `DataSource` property to the data table.

The second of these two lines calls `DataBind`, which gets the `GridView` control's ball rolling.

That's it! Figure 5-1 shows what you get in the browser when you run this code.

Attaching arrays to data-bound controls

One of the big secrets about data controls like the `Repeater` is that you don't have to bind them to instances of other data controls such as `DataTable`. You can, in fact, attach a data control to almost any general-purpose .NET container. That allows for some really cool data-viewing-and-manipulation features.

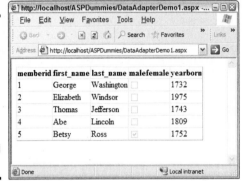

Figure 5-1:
The SqlData Adapter and DataTable can easily fill a Grid Control with the help of the DataBind method.

For this example, I decided to separate the code into its own file away from the .aspx file. The reason is practical: The code is more than just a few lines, and separating makes it easier to manage.

First, take a look at the code, shown in Listing 5-1.

Listing 5-1:   ContainerBind1.aspx.vb (VB)

```vb
Structure Employee
    Dim Name As String
    Dim Salary As Int32
    Dim Phone As String
    Sub New(ByVal AName As String, ByVal ASalary As Int32, _
    ByVal APhone As String)
        Name = AName
        Salary = ASalary
        Phone = APhone
    End Sub
End Structure
Partial Class ContainerBind1
    Inherits System.Web.UI.Page
    Protected Sub Page_Load(ByVal sender As Object, ByVal e As System.EventArgs)
    Handles Me.Load
        Dim mylist As New ArrayList
        mylist.Add(New Employee("Jeff", 100000, "513-555-1234"))
        mylist.Add(New Employee("Angie", 110000, "859-555-1555"))
        mylist.Add(New Employee("Dylan", 105000, "269-555-9876"))
        mylist.Add(New Employee("Jennifer", 115000, "404-555-1029"))
        Repeater1.DataSource = mylist
        Repeater1.DataBind()
    End Sub
End Class
```

The first half of Listing 5-1 defines a new structure called Employee. This structure is quite simple — it has just three members, called Name, Salary, and Phone. Additionally, it includes a constructor to simplify initializing the members with a single call to New.

Next, Listing 5-1 defines the main class for the form, `ContainerBind1`. The class includes a `Page_Load` method that creates a new instance of `ArrayList`. That's the almost-magical structure here that we'll be binding to the data control. (Okay, maybe not magical, but pretty cool at least.) The first thing I do after creating this `ArrayList` is fill it with four instances of `Employee`.

Then I just bind the `ArrayList` instance to the `Repeater` by setting the `Repeater`'s `DataSource` member, and then call `DataBind`.

Now take a look at the `.aspx` file, shown in Listing 5-2.

Listing 5-2:   ContainerBind1.aspx (VB)

Book VI
Chapter 5

Advanced Data
Retrieval

```
<%@ Page Language="VB" AutoEventWireup="false" CodeFile="ContainerBind1.aspx.vb"
    Inherits="ContainerBind1" %>
<!DOCTYPE html PUBLIC "-//W3C//DTD XHTML 1.0 Transitional//EN"
    "http://www.w3.org/TR/xhtml1/DTD/xhtml1-transitional.dtd">
<html xmlns="http://www.w3.org/1999/xhtml" >
<head runat="server">
    <title>Untitled Page</title>
</head>
<body>
    <form id="form1" runat="server">
    <div>
        <asp:Repeater ID="Repeater1" runat="server">
            <ItemTemplate>
                <%#CType(Container.DataItem, Employee).Name%>
                <%#CType(Container.DataItem, Employee).Salary%>
                <%#CType(Container.DataItem, Employee).Phone%>
                <br />
            </ItemTemplate>
        </asp:Repeater>
    </div>
    </form>
</body>
</html>
```

The only thing I added to this code — beyond what was created by Visual Studio — is the `Repeater` control. Also, please note that I typed this in manually, although you're welcome to drag one onto the form to get it started.

Inside the `Repeater` tag I added the `ItemTemplate` tag (which is required), and inside the `ItemTemplate` tag I added the three mysterious lines that extract the members out of the data as it comes in. Remember, the data that comes into the control is an `ArrayList`. With each iteration of the `Repeater`, the `Repeater` receives another instance of whatever is in the `ArrayList`.

In this case, each item inside the `ArrayList` is an instance of my class `Employee`. However, in the eyes of the `Repeater`, the instance is of a class called `DataItem`. And so I must cast the item to `Employee`; then I can access the individual members, like so:

```
<%#CType(Container.DataItem, Employee).Name%>
```

When you open this page in the browser, you get the following text:

```
Jeff 100000 513-555-1234
Angie 110000 859-555-1555
Dylan 105000 269-555-9876
Jennifer 115000 404-555-1029
```

Advanced Usage of Repeater Controls

Although the `Repeater` control at heart seems pretty simple (you just put code and controls inside it and they repeat), in truth you can do some pretty sophisticated data display with it.

For example, you can carefully type the necessary HTML tags (`TABLE`, `TR`, `TD`) to generate a table. Why would you do that instead of using a `GridView`? Because you might need more flexibility than the `GridView` gives you, but still want your data organized in a table. You can also inject some VB.NET or C# code into your `Repeater` control, allowing for more programmability. The following sections take you through a variety of different ways you can get a `Repeater` control to do your bidding.

Creating a table around a Repeater

Often, when using a `Repeater` control, I need the output to be aligned — I like it nice and neat. That's when I throw in some HTML table tags all around, and throughout, the control.

Take a look at the following code:

```
<%@ Page Language="VB" %>
<%@ Import Namespace="System.Data" %>
<%@ Import Namespace="System.Data.SqlClient" %>
<script runat="server">
    Protected Sub Page_Load(ByVal sender As Object, ByVal e As System.EventArgs)
        Dim da As New SqlDataAdapter( _
            "select * from member", _
            "Data Source=KOALA3;Initial Catalog=ASPD;User ID=sa;Password=")
        Dim dt As New DataTable
        da.Fill(dt)
        Repeater1.DataSource = dt
        Repeater1.DataBind()
    End Sub
</script>
```

```
<html>
<body>
    <form id="form1" runat="server">
    <div>
        <table>
        <tr>
            <th style="font-weight:bold;border-bottom:1px solid black">
                First Name</th>
            <th style="font-weight:bold;border-bottom:1px solid black">
                Last Name</th>
            <th style="font-weight:bold;border-bottom:1px solid black">
                Year Born</th>
        </tr>
        <asp:Repeater ID="Repeater1" runat="server">
            <ItemTemplate>
            <tr>
            <td style="border-bottom:1px solid #808080">
                <%#CType(Container.DataItem, DataRowView).Item("first_name")%>
            </td>
            <td style="border-bottom:1px solid #808080">
                <%#CType(Container.DataItem, DataRowView).Item("last_name")%>
            </td>
            <td style="border-bottom:1px solid #808080">
                <%#CType(Container.DataItem, DataRowView).Item("yearborn")%>
            </td>
            </tr>
            </ItemTemplate>
        </asp:Repeater>
        </table>
    </div>
    </form>
</body>
</html>
```

This code includes a `Page_Load` method that retrieves data from a table and binds the data to a `Repeater` control. The `Repeater` control, in turn, has a table around it. Notice how the code includes a `<table>` tag before the `Repeater`, and a closing `</table>` tag after the `Repeater`.

Make sure you remember to put the `Import` lines in the `.aspx` file. Otherwise the compiler won't be able to find such words as `DataRowView` — and you'll see errors throughout the file.

Now remember, each iteration of the `Repeater` is a single row. Thus, I have included a single `<tr>` and closing `</tr>` tag inside the `ItemTemplate` opening and closing tag; the repeating part is a single row.

Now, I want each column of the data to appear in its own column in the table that will appear in the browser — so I surrounded each data item with an opening `<td>` and closing `</td>` tag.

In the end, this code renders nicely as a table in the browser, as shown in Figure 5-2.

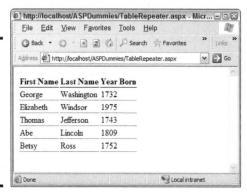

Figure 5-2:
Using the
HTML table
tags, you
can format
your
Repeater
neatly into
a table.

At this point, you might wonder why I didn't just use a `GridView` control. In
fact, what I did in this section I could also have done in a `GridView` control.
However, in the following section I take this sample code and add in some
server-side controls that appear in the table. I want everything formatted, but I
want controls in the table as well, making a `Repeater` an ideal control to use.

Handling Repeater events

If you put a control that provides events (such as a `Button` or a
`LinkButton`) inside a `Repeater`, you can still respond to those events as
well as know which row the event took place in. For example, if you put a
`LinkButton` in the `Repeater`, a `LinkButton` will appear in each row of the
output. If you include in your code a handler for the `LinkButton`, you'll
probably want to know *which* `LinkButton` was clicked (there are several,
one for each row).

Before plunging into the code, I'll explain how it works: The events from
the controls in a `Repeater` control come through the `Repeater` control's
`ItemCommand` event. Inside that event, you can check which item was
clicked. To know that, however, you have to set some properties in the
control. With that little tidbit in mind, take a look at Listing 5-3 — and
look closely at the declaration of the `LinkButton` control.

Listing 5-3: RepeaterEvents.aspx (VB)

```
<%@ Page Language="VB" AutoEventWireup="false" CodeFile="RepeaterEvents.aspx.vb"
    Inherits="RepeaterEvents" %>
<%@ Import Namespace="System.Data" %>
<html>
<body>
    <form id="form1" runat="server">
    <div>
        <table>
        <tr>
```

```
                <th style="font-weight:bold;border-bottom:1px solid black">
                    First Name</th>
                <th style="font-weight:bold;border-bottom:1px solid black">
                    Last Name</th>
                <th style="font-weight:bold;border-bottom:1px solid black">
                    Year Born</th>
            </tr>
            <asp:Repeater ID="Repeater1" runat="server">
                <ItemTemplate>
                <tr>
                <td style="border-bottom:1px solid #808080">
                    <asp:LinkButton runat="server" CommandName="Details"
                    CommandArgument=
                    <%#CreateDetailString(CType(Container.DataItem, DataRowView))%>
                    Text =
                    <%#CType(Container.DataItem, DataRowView).Item("first_name")%>
                    />
                </td>
                <td style="border-bottom:1px solid #808080">
                    <%#CType(Container.DataItem, DataRowView).Item("last_name")%>
                </td>
                <td style="border-bottom:1px solid #808080">
                    <%#CType(Container.DataItem, DataRowView).Item("yearborn")%>
                </td>
                </tr>
                </ItemTemplate>
            </asp:Repeater>
            </table>
    </div>
        <asp:Label ID="ResultsLabel" runat="server" Text="" />
    </form>
</body>
</html>
```

In addition to the `LinkButton`'s usual properties (`runat` and `Text`), I've also set two additional properties: `CommandName` and `CommandArgument`. The values of these two properties are passed into the `ItemCommand` event. Look closely at how I set these two properties in Listing 5-3. Here they are by themselves:

```
CommandName="Details"
```

and

```
CommandArgument=
<%#CreateDetailString(Container.DataItem)%>
```

The first one sets the `CommandName`. You can make up whatever command name you want here; the idea is that if you have more than one `LinkButton` within a single row, you can find out which `LinkButton` was clicked by checking the `CommandName`. For example, you might have an `Edit` button and a `Details` button. The `LinkButton` for `Edit` could have a `CommandName` of `"Edit"`, and the `LinkButton` for `Details` could have a `CommandName` of `"Details"`. Then you just check the `CommandName` to know which of the two was clicked.

Now the second property, CommandArgument, is for knowing which row was clicked. Again, you can put whatever you want in this property — but whatever it is, somehow it has to uniquely identify the row or have information applicable to that row.

For this example, I'm setting the CommandArgument to a string that's unique to the row; I set that string using a CreateDetailString, which is in Listing 5-4.

Listing 5-4:   RepeaterEvents.aspx.vb (VB)

```
Imports System.Data.SqlClient
Imports System.Data
Partial Class RepeaterEvents
    Inherits System.Web.UI.Page
    Protected Sub Page_Load(ByVal sender As Object, ByVal e As System.EventArgs)
    Handles Me.Load
        Dim da As New SqlDataAdapter( _
            "select * from member", _
            "Data Source=KOALA3;Initial Catalog=ASPD;User ID=sa;Password=")
        Dim dt As New DataTable
        da.Fill(dt)
        Repeater1.DataSource = dt
        Repeater1.DataBind()
    End Sub
    Function CreateDetailString(ByVal row As DataRowView) 'ByVal firstnams As
    String, ByVal lastname As String, ByVal yearborn As Int32) As String
        Dim firstname As String = row.Item("first_name")
        Dim lastname As String = row.Item("last_name")
        Dim yearborn As Int32 = row.Item("yearborn")
        Return String.Format("{0} {1} was born in {2}", _
            firstname, lastname, yearborn)
    End Function
    Protected Sub Repeater1_ItemCommand(ByVal source As Object, ByVal e As
    System.Web.UI.WebControls.RepeaterCommandEventArgs) Handles
    Repeater1.ItemCommand
        If e.CommandName = "Details" Then
            ResultsLabel.Text = e.CommandArgument
        End If
    End Sub
End Class
```

In Listing 5-4, you can see how I set the string for the CommandArgument in the CreateDetailString. I passed in a Container.DataItem property, which represents the current row in the Repeater's data set. In the method, I then grab out the first_name, last_name, and yearborn columns of the data row that came in, and piece together a friendly message to store in a string. Then I return that string.

Now look at the Repeater1_ItemCommand method. This one is pretty simple; it just checks if the CommandName is Details, and if so, sets the ResultsLabel text to the CommandArgument — the very same thing created by the CreateDetailString method. (As for the CommandName, technically I didn't have to check its value because there's only one LinkButton per row. Thus the `LinkButton` that comes into the `Repeater1_ItemCommand` method will always have a `CommandName` of `Details`. But I'm providing the code here so you can expand on it.)

So what does all this code do? Here's a summary: The `Repeater` command generates a table of data in an HTML document. Included in that table is a column containing a clickable link. When you click the link, the VB.NET code detects which item you clicked, and then displays a label showing a message about the row where you clicked.

Figure 5-3 shows the result of listings 5-3 and 5-4 when it initially opens in the browser. Notice the first names are underlined — meaning they're clickable. (Although this book is black and white, in my browser the clickable text is blue.)

Figure 5-3:
The initial grid from Listing 5-3.

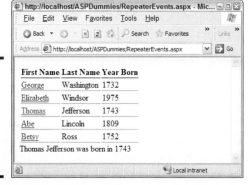

Figure 5-4 shows what the browser looks like after I click the word `Thomas`. Notice the message appears under the grid as planned.

Figure 5-4:
After I click on Thomas Jefferson, I get detail information on him.

Chapter 6: Reading XML and Generic Data

In This Chapter

✔ Creating an XML file for use in a data application

✔ Transforming an XML file for viewing in a browser

✔ Connecting to XML as a data source

✔ Using the `ObjectDataSource` control to connect to generic data

*I*n recent years, XML has become a common format for storing and transferring data. As a result, you may well encounter some requirements where your Web site has to process XML data.

ASP.NET has some advanced XML handling features that will make your XML work easier. The idea behind the XML features is that your application treats XML data simply as data — just like the data from a database. Thus you use a data source whose specific job is to handle XML data.

In addition to XML, another data source that ASP.NET provides is a general object data source, which can handle data from any kind of object. In this chapter, I cover these two kinds of data sources.

All the code listings that are used in this book are available for download at www.dummies.com/go/aspnetaiofd.

Putting Together Some XML

In order to use the samples in this chapter, you will need some XML. If you happen to have an old pile of XML lying around the living room, feel free to use it. Otherwise, you can use the sample data I provide here.

Listing 6-1 shows an XML file that contains a list of animals arranged hierarchically by type (mammals, birds, amphibians, reptiles, and fish). Each `animal` entry contains two pieces of information — a common name and a scientific name (okay, so the science is a little weird). You can type this data into any text editor, and then save it with the filename `animals.xml`. (For simplicity, put it in the same directory where you'll be putting the sample `.aspx` files for this chapter.)

Listing 6-1:   A sample XML file

```
<?xml version="1.0" encoding="ISO-8859-1"?>
<animals>
    <class>
        <name>mammals</name>
        <animal>
            <name>dog</name>
            <species>eatus scrappingus</species>
        </animal>
        <animal>
            <name>cat</name>
            <species>sleepus allthetimeus</species>
        </animal>
        <animal>
            <name>horse</name>
            <species>runus jumpus</species>
        </animal>
        <animal>
            <name>cow</name>
            <species>moous moous</species>
        </animal>
        <animal>
            <name>pig</name>
            <species>pigpenna messyus</species>
        </animal>
        <animal>
            <name>gorilla</name>
            <species>grumpyus hairiest</species>
        </animal>
        <animal>
            <name>monkey</name>
            <species>climbus allovertheplaceus</species>
        </animal>
        <animal>
            <name>tiger</name>
            <species>stalkingus bestus</species>
        </animal>
        <animal>
            <name>bear</name><species>roaringus loudingus</species>
        </animal>
    </class>
    <class>
        <name>birds</name>
        <animal>
            <name>hummingbird</name>
            <species>singus beautifulus</species>
        </animal>
        <animal>
            <name>chicken</name>
            <species>tastius pluckedist</species>
        </animal>
        <animal>
            <name>flamingo</name>
            <species>pinkus featherus</species>
        </animal>
        <animal>
            <name>parrots</name>
            <species>talkbacking atus</species>
        </animal>
```

```
        <animal>
            <name>penguins</name>
            <species>handsomus outfitus</species>
        </animal>
        <animal>
            <name>owl</name>
            <species>hootus hootus</species>
        </animal>
        <animal>
            <name>woodpecker</name>
            <species>eatingus woodus</species>
        </animal>
    </class>
    <class>
        <name>amphibians</name>
        <animal>
            <name>frog</name>
            <species>kissmeus froggus</species>
        </animal>
        <animal>
            <name>toad</name>
            <species>jumpus treeus</species>
        </animal>
        <animal>
            <name>salamander</name>
            <species>slidingus sneakeus</species>
        </animal>
    </class>
    <class>
        <name>reptiles</name>
        <animal>
            <name>turtle</name>
            <species>shellus hardest</species>
        </animal>
        <animal>
            <name>tortoise</name>
            <species>biggus turtlelus</species>
        </animal>
        <animal>
            <name>crocodile</name>
            <species>biggus teethus</species>
        </animal>
        <animal>
            <name>komodo dragon</name>
            <species>rahrahus spookius</species>
        </animal>
        <animal>
            <name>boa</name>
            <species>huggmeus squeezemeus</species>
        </animal>
    </class>
    <class>
        <name>fish</name>
        <animal>
            <name>catfish</name>
            <species>meowingus swimmerus</species>
        </animal>
        <animal>
            <name>sunfish</name>
            <species>brightskyus fishius</species>
```

(continued)

Listing 6-1 *(continued)*

```
        </animal>
        <animal>
            <name>goldfish</name>
            <species>goldenpondius swimmerus</species>
        </animal>
    </class>
</animals>
```

You can see the general format of this file. The first line is required to specify that the file is an XML file. The remaining lines are the data.

Of the data lines, the first is the opener for the outermost or *root* tag. XML requires that you only have one root tag in a document, and this one is it; the tag is `animals`.

Inside the `animals` tag are five tags called `class`. These tags contain two types of embedded tags, a `name` and a list of animals. The `name` contains the name of the `class`, such as `mammals`. Each animal is a tag called `animal`, and this tag contains two tags, a name (called `name`) and a scientific name (called `species`). In all, you have a hierarchy that looks like this:

```
Animals
        Class 1
                Name
                Animal 1
                        Name
                        Species
                Animal 2
                        Name
                        Species
        Class 2
```

In the following section, I use this XML file as-is to display the XML in a browser. Then (in the section "Displaying XML in a TreeView Control," later in this chapter), I modify the file slightly to make it a bit more robust and suitable for more general uses.

Transforming XML into a Formatted Table

ASP.NET supports *transformation files* for style sheets. Such files allow an XML processor to take a given XML file (in this case, `animals.xml`) and use the information provided in the transformation file to create a new XML file. Typically such transformations create an XML file that is really an XHTML file — which can be viewed in a browser — and often you'll include style-sheet information to provide formatting and colors. (For more on style sheets, see Book 3, Chapter 4.)

Listing 6-2 shows a sample transformation file named `animals.xsl` (note the filename extension is `.xsl`, which stands for XML Stylesheet Language):

Listing 6-2: Animals.xsl

```
<?xml version="1.0" encoding="ISO-8859-1"?>
<xsl:stylesheet version="1.0" xmlns:xsl="http://www.w3.org/1999/XSL/Transform">
<xsl:template match="/">
<div>
<style type="text/css">
    .head {
        background-color:#B0B0FF;
        font-family:Arial;
        font-weight:bold;
        font-size:14px;
    }
    .head2 {
        background-color:#B0B0FF;
        font-family:Arial;
        font-weight:bold;
        font-size:10px;
    }
    .datum {
        background-color:#FFB0B0;
        padding:2px;
        font-family:Arial;
        font-size:14px;
        border: 1px solid white;
    }
</style>
    <table cellspacing="0" cellpadding="0">
        <xsl:for-each select="animals/class">
            <tr>
                <td colspan="2" class="head">
                    <xsl:value-of select="name" />
                </td>
            </tr>
            <tr>
                <td class="head2">Name</td>
                <td class="head2">Species</td>
            </tr>
            <xsl:for-each select="animal">
                <tr>
                    <td class="datum">
                        <xsl:value-of select="name" />
                    </td>
                    <td class="datum">
                        <xsl:value-of select="species" />
                    </td>
                </tr>
            </xsl:for-each>
        </xsl:for-each>
    </table>
</div>
</xsl:template>
</xsl:stylesheet>
```

Like the `animals.xml` file, this XML file starts with a line that tells the world it's an XML file. Then comes information about which transformation is being used — and that information fills up the rest of the text missing.

Although this book isn't a treatise on XML Stylesheet Language (XSL), a quick rundown of the highlights of this file will come in handy. So here goes . . .

The file contains what looks like standard HTML, including a `<div>` tag, and some style information, including styles called `head1`, `head2`, and `datum`.

Inside the body tag is where you find the most important aspects of the transformation. XSL files are like programs that tell the XML system how to transform a file. XSL files even have constructs such as `for` loops, which you can see I'm using in this file, like so:

```
<xsl:for-each select="animals/class">
```

A `for` loop in an XSL file simply means iterating over the data of a certain path type in XML. (XML files have paths much like those you find in a directory structure on a hard drive. The paths are the names of the tags separated by forward slashes; the `animals.xml` file has paths such as `animals/ class/animal/name`.)

This particular `for` loop iterates through all elements in the `animals/class` path. The `animals.xml` file has five entries in the `animals/class` path, one entry for `mammals`, one for `birds`, and so on.

To access the parts of a path, you use a tag like this:

```
<xsl:value-of select="name" />
```

If you're iterating through classes, then this will be the name tag for the class, such as `"mammals"` or `"birds"`.

Each class has several animal entries, which I then iterate through. Thus I have an embedded `for-each` tag:

```
<xsl:for-each select="animal">
```

This tag iterates through each item called `animal` inside the current path. Thus, if the current path is the one for `mammals`, then this tag will iterate through each `animal` tag under `mammals`, starting with the tag for `dog`, then `cat`, and so on.

For each iteration, I provide some style information to give some color and formatting to the resulting XML. Listing 6-3 shows the XML that results after the transformation. Note that the result is also valid XHTML

Displaying XML using the XML control

Here I demonstrate how you can view your data as XML in a Web browser using a transformation. In the code, I simply grab an instance of `XmlDocument` and write out the XML right to the Web page.

ASP.NET includes an XML control that does a similar task; it reads XML data and writes the data out to a Web page. You're free to use either method; both require very little code and effort. If you want to use the XML control, all you do is drop it on your form, and set its properties to point to the XML file and the transformation file. Here's an example:

```
<asp:Xml ID="Xml1"
    runat="server"
DocumentSource="~/animals.xml"
TransformSource="~/animals.
    xsl">
</asp:Xml>
```

In this case, the `animals.xml` file and `animals.xsl` file are in the root directory of my application; thus they are preceded with the `~/` sequence of characters. The end result of this code is identical to that shown in Figure 6-1.

Listing 6-3: The transformed XML file

```
<div><style type="text/css">
    .head {
        background-color:#B0B0FF;
        font-family:Arial;
        font-weight:bold;
        font-size:14px;
    }
    .head2 {
        background-color:#B0B0FF;
        font-family:Arial;
        font-weight:bold;
        font-size:10px;
    }
    .datum {
        background-color:#FFB0B0;
        padding:2px;
        font-family:Arial;
        font-size:14px;
        border: 1px solid white;
    }
</style>
<table cellspacing="0" cellpadding="0">
    <tr><td colspan="2" class="head">mammals</td></tr>
    <tr><td class="head2">Name</td>
        <td class="head2">Species</td></tr>
    <tr><td class="datum">dog</td>
```

(continued)

Listing 6-3 *(continued)*

```
        <td class="datum">eatus scrappingus</td></tr>
<tr><td class="datum">cat</td>
        <td class="datum">sleepus allthetimeus</td></tr>
<tr><td class="datum">horse</td>
        <td class="datum">runus jumpus</td></tr>
<tr><td class="datum">cow</td>
        <td class="datum">moous moous</td></tr>
<tr><td class="datum">pig</td>
        <td class="datum">pigpenna messyus</td></tr>
<tr><td class="datum">gorilla</td>
        <td class="datum">grumpyus hairiest</td></tr>
<tr><td class="datum">monkey</td>
        <td class="datum">climbus allovertheplaceus</td></tr>
<tr><td class="datum">tiger</td>
        <td class="datum">stalkingus bestus</td></tr>
<tr><td class="datum">bear</td>
        <td class="datum">roaringus loudingus</td></tr>
<tr><td colspan="2" class="head">birds</td></tr>
<tr><td class="head2">Name</td>
        <td class="head2">Species</td></tr>
<tr><td class="datum">hummingbird</td>
        <td class="datum">singus beautifulus</td></tr>
<tr><td class="datum">chicken</td>
        <td class="datum">tastius pluckedist</td></tr>
<tr><td class="datum">flamingo</td>
        <td class="datum">pinkus featherus</td></tr>
<tr><td class="datum">parrots</td>
        <td class="datum">talkbacking atus</td></tr>
<tr><td class="datum">penguins</td>
        <td class="datum">handsomus outfitus</td></tr>
<tr><td class="datum">owl</td>
        <td class="datum">hootus hootus</td></tr>
<tr><td class="datum">woodpecker</td>
        <td class="datum">eatingus woodus</td></tr>
<tr><td colspan="2" class="head">amphibians</td></tr>
<tr><td class="head2">Name</td>
        <td class="head2">Species</td></tr>
<tr><td class="datum">frog</td>
        <td class="datum">kissmeus froggus</td></tr>
<tr><td class="datum">toad</td>
        <td class="datum">jumpus treeus</td></tr>
<tr><td class="datum">salamander</td>
        <td class="datum">slidingus sneakeus</td></tr>
<tr><td colspan="2" class="head">reptiles</td></tr>
<tr><td class="head2">Name</td>
        <td class="head2">Species</td></tr>
<tr><td class="datum">turtle</td>
        <td class="datum">shellus hardest</td></tr>
<tr><td class="datum">tortoise</td>
```

```
        <td class="datum">biggus turtlelus</td></tr>
    <tr><td class="datum">crocodile</td>
        <td class="datum">biggus teethus</td></tr>
    <tr><td class="datum">komodo dragon</td>
        <td class="datum">rahrahus spookius</td></tr>
    <tr><td class="datum">boa</td>
        <td class="datum">huggmeus squeezemeus</td></tr>
    <tr><td colspan="2" class="head">fish</td></tr>
    <tr><td class="head2">Name</td>
        <td class="head2">Species</td></tr>
    <tr><td class="datum">catfish</td>
        <td class="datum">meowingus swimmerus</td></tr>
    <tr><td class="datum">sunfish</td>
        <td class="datum">brightskyus fishius</td></tr>
    <tr><td class="datum">goldfish</td>
        <td class="datum">goldenpondius swimmerus</td></tr>
</table></div>
```

As a very quick demo of how you can use the XML tools in .NET to transform the preceding .xml and .xsl files into the preceding HTML code, try out the following. Make sure the animals.xml and animals.xsl files are in the same directory where you put your .aspx files, and create a new .aspx file. Following is the code; the part you add is shown in **bold**.

```
<%@ Page Language="VB" %>
<!DOCTYPE html PUBLIC "-//W3C//DTD XHTML 1.0 Transitional//EN"
"http://www.w3.org/TR/xhtml1/DTD/xhtml1-transitional.dtd">
<script runat="server">
</script>
<html xmlns="http://www.w3.org/1999/xhtml" >
<head runat="server">
    <title>Untitled Page</title>
</head>
<body>
    <form id="form1" runat="server">
    <div>
      <asp:xmldatasource
        id="XmlDataSource1"
        runat="server"
        datafile="animals.xml"
        TransformFile="animals.xsl" />
    <%
        Dim doc As System.Xml.XmlDocument
        doc = XmlDataSource1.GetXmlDocument
        Response.Write(doc.InnerXml)
    %>
    </div>
    </form>
</body>
</html>
```

The code you add first includes a new XmlDataSource control. The file that the data source reads is animals.xml, as specified in the datafile property. The transformation is animals.xsl, as specified in the TransformFile property.

The code after the data source obtains an `XmlDocument` instance from the data source, and then writes out the XML from the document. This XML is not the original XML in the `animals.xml` file, but rather the resulting transformed XML.

If you open the preceding `.aspx` file in a browser, you'll see something like Figure 6-1.

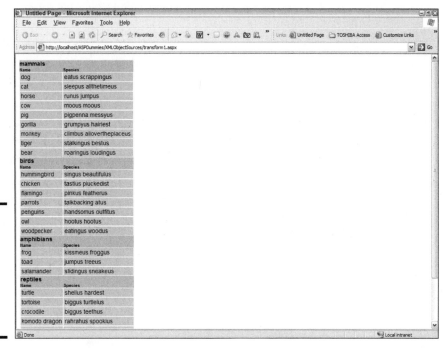

Figure 6-1:
You can transform an XML file into a nicely formatted table.

Displaying XML in a TreeView Control

XML provides several different ways to express the same set of data. Take, for example, the a file called `animals.xml` described earlier in this chapter, where the general format is

```
<animals>
    <class>
        <name>class name</name>
        <animal><name>name1</name><species>species1</species>
        <animal><name>name2</name><species>species2</species>
```

An alternate way to express this same data is to make use of parameters, like so:

```
<animals>
    <class name="mammals">
        <animal name="dog" species="eatus scrappingus\" />
        <animal name="cat" species="sleepus allthetimeus\" />
```

This type of XML lends itself nicely to displaying in a `TreeView` control. When you use an `XmlDataSource` as the data source for a `TreeView`, you must tell the `TreeView` how to map the different data items to nodes on the `TreeView`.

The `TreeView` allows for tags called `treenodebinding` tags that let you describe the mapping between the incoming XML and the nodes in the tree. You can have multiple `treenodebinding` tags; you provide different tags for the different types of data in your XML.

Take a look at the complete XML shown in Listing 6-4 — which you can save as `animals2.xml`. Pay special attention to the attributes I'm providing for the different types of tags.

Book VI Chapter 6

Reading XML and Generic Data

Listing 6-4:   The transformed XML file

```xml
<?xml version="1.0" encoding="ISO-8859-1"?>
<animals>
    <class name="mammals">
        <animal name="dog" species="eatus scrappingus" />
        <animal name="cat" species="sleepus allthetimeus" />
        <animal name="horse" species="runus jumpus" />
        <animal name="cow" species="moous moous" />
        <animal name="pig" species="pigpenna messyus" />
        <animal name="gorilla" species="grumpyus hairiest" />
        <animal name="monkey" species="climbus allovertheplaceus" />
        <animal name="tiger" species="stalkingus bestus" />
        <animal name="bear" species="roaringus loudingus" />
    </class>
    <class name="birds">
        <animal name="hummingbird" species="singus beautifulus" />
        <animal name="chicken" species="tastius pluckedist" />
        <animal name="flamingo" species="pinkus featherus" />
        <animal name="parrots" species="talkbacking atus" />
        <animal name="penguins" species="handsomus outfitus" />
        <animal name="owl" species="hootus hootus" />
        <animal name="woodpecker" species="eatingus woodus" />
    </class>
    <class name="amphibians">
        <animal name="frog" species="kissmeus froggus" />
        <animal name="toad" species="jumpus treeus" />
        <animal name="salamander" species="slidingus sneakeus" />
    </class>
    <class name="reptiles">
```

(continued)

Listing 6-4 *(continued)*

```
        <animal name="turtle" species="shellus hardest" />
        <animal name="tortoise" species="biggus turtlelus" />
        <animal name="crocodile" species="biggus teethus" />
        <animal name="komodo dragon" species="rahrahus spookius" />
        <animal name="boa" species="huggmeus squeezemeus" />
    </class>
    <class name="fish">
        <animal name="catfish" species="meowingus swimmerus" />
        <animal name="sunfish" species="brightskyus fishius" />
        <animal name="goldfish" species="goldenpondius swimmerus" />
    </class>
</animals>
```

In this XML, I'm using three different tags:

✦ `animals` has no parameters.

✦ `class` has one parameter, `name`.

✦ `animal` has two parameters, `name` and `species`.

In the code, then, I provide three different `treenodebinding` tags to describe how to handle each type of tag in the `TreeView`. Listing 6-5 shows the code for the `.aspx` file that displays the XML in a `TreeView`.

Listing 6-5:   Using a TreeView control to display an XML file

```
<%@ Page Language="VB" %>
<!DOCTYPE html PUBLIC "-//W3C//DTD XHTML 1.0 Transitional//EN"
"http://www.w3.org/TR/xhtml1/DTD/xhtml1-transitional.dtd">
<script runat="server">

</script>
<html xmlns="http://www.w3.org/1999/xhtml" >
<head runat="server">
    <title>Untitled Page</title>
</head>
<body>
    <form id="form1" runat="server">
    <div>
      <asp:xmldatasource
        id="XmlDataSource1"
        runat="server"
        datafile="animals2.xml" />
      <asp:treeview
        id="TreeView1" runat="server" datasourceid="XmlDataSource1">
        <databindings>
          <asp:treenodebinding DataMember="animals"
            Text="animals" />
          <asp:treenodebinding DataMember="class"
            TextField="name" />
          <asp:treenodebinding DataMember="animal"
            TextField="name" />
        </databindings>
```

```
      </asp:TreeView>
    </div>
    </form>
</body>
</html>
```

This code includes an `XmlDataSource` control that simply connects to the `animals2.xml` file. The code then has a `TreeView` control. The data source for the `TreeView` control is the `XmlDataSource` control. The tags that follow are the `treenodebinding` tags I was just discussing:

✦ **The first tag provides the** `TreeView` **information on how to handle tags of type animals.** The text to appear in the `TreeView` is the word `"animals"`, which I specify with the `TextField` property.

✦ **The second tag provides information for the tags of type** `class`. For these tags, the text to appear in the `TreeView` is whatever text is stored in the `name` attribute for the tag.

✦ **The third tag tells the** `TreeView` **how to handle tags of type** `animal`. In this case, just like the `class` tags, the text to appear in the `TreeView` node is whatever text is stored in the `name` attribute for the tag.

Figure 6-2 shows what you see when you open this file in the browser.

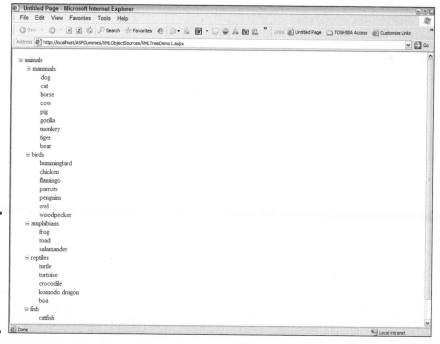

Figure 6-2:
A TreeView can display the hierarchy of the data in the XML.

Accessing Generic Data with an ObjectDataSource Control

The ObjectDataSource is a generic data-source component that lets you connect to any kind of data, so long as you provide a way to access the data. You provide methods for accessing the data, and then give the ObjectDataSource control the information for the methods; the control will then call the methods to retrieve the data. This allows you to connect to any type of data, so long as you have methods to access the data.

Listing 6-6 shows a page that demonstrates the ObjectDataSource control.

Listing 6-6: Using an ObjectDataSource control (VB)

```
<%@ Page Language="VB" AutoEventWireup="false"
CodeFile="ObjData1.aspx.vb" Inherits="XMLObjectSources_ObjData1" %>
<!DOCTYPE html PUBLIC "-//W3C//DTD XHTML 1.0 Transitional//EN"
"http://www.w3.org/TR/xhtml1/DTD/xhtml1-transitional.dtd">
<html xmlns="http://www.w3.org/1999/xhtml" >
<head runat="server">
    <title>Untitled Page</title>
</head>
<body>
    <form id="form1" runat="server">
    <div>
        <asp:ObjectDataSource ID="ObjectDataSource1" runat="server"
            SelectMethod = "SelectData">
            <SelectParameters>
                <asp:ControlParameter Name="TheClass" Type="String"
                ControlID="DropDownList1" />
            </SelectParameters>
        </asp:ObjectDataSource>
        <asp:DropDownList ID="DropDownList1" runat="server">
            <asp:ListItem Text="All" Value="*" />
            <asp:ListItem Text="Mammals" Value="mammal" />
            <asp:ListItem Text="Birds" Value="bird" />
            <asp:ListItem Text="Amphibians" Value="amphibian" />
        </asp:DropDownList>
        <asp:Button ID="Button1" runat="server" Text="Go" />
        <table cellspacing="2">
        <asp:Repeater ID="Repeater1" runat="server">
            <ItemTemplate>
                <tr>
                <td style="font-family:Arial;background-color:#A0A0FF">
                  <%#CType(Container.DataItem, Animals.AnimalItem).Name%>
                </td>
                <td style="font-family:Arial;background-color:#FFA0A0">
                  <%#CType(Container.DataItem, Animals.AnimalItem).Species%>
                </td>
                </tr>
```

```
            </ItemTemplate>
          </asp:Repeater>
          </table>
     </div>
     </form>
</body>
</html>
```

Look carefully at the controls I've included here:

◆ `ObjectDataSource`: This control attaches to the methods that retrieve the data. You can see that I'm using the control to retrieve data; I specify the method's name in the `SelectMethod` property. Additionally, I provide some tags to specify a parameter to be passed to the `SelectMethod`. The parameter is a single parameter called `TheClass`, and the information for the parameter comes from the `DropDownList` I'm providing.

◆ `DropDownList`: This control contains three values that are types of animals: `mammals`, `birds`, and `amphibians`. The item selected is used in the `SelectMethod` of the `ObjectDataSource`.

◆ `Button`: The handle for this button, which appears in Listing 6-7, will attach the `Repeater` control to the data source and call `Bind()` to start the ball rolling.

◆ `Repeater`: This control retrieves incoming data by casting each item to an object (which I also describe in Listing 6-7).

Listing 6-7 provides the code that supplies the objects and methods for retrieving the data.

Listing 6-7:   ObjData1.aspx.vb (VB)

```
Namespace Animals
    Public Structure AnimalItem
        Dim TheClass As String
        Dim Name As String
        Dim Species As String
        Public Sub New(ByVal AClass As String, ByVal AName As String, _
        ByVal ASpecies As String)
            TheClass = AClass
            Name = AName
            Species = ASpecies
        End Sub
    End Structure
    Public Class AnimalData
        Public Shared Function SelectData(ByVal TheClass As String) As
    ICollection
```

(continued)

Listing 6-7 *(continued)*

```
            Dim result As New ArrayList
            If TheClass = "" Or TheClass = "*" Or TheClass = "mammal" Then
                result.Add(New AnimalItem("mammal", _
                    "dog", "eatus scrappingus"))
                result.Add(New AnimalItem("mammal", _
                    "cat", "sleepus allthetimeus"))
                result.Add(New AnimalItem("mammal", _
                    "horse", "runus jumpus"))
                result.Add(New AnimalItem("mammal", _
                    "cow", "moous moous"))
                result.Add(New AnimalItem("mammal", _
                    "pig", "pigpenna messyus"))
            End If
            If TheClass = "" Or TheClass = "*" Or _
            TheClass = "bird" Then
                result.Add(New AnimalItem("bird", _
                    "hummingbird", "singus beautifulus"))
                result.Add(New AnimalItem("bird", _
                    "chicken", "tastius pluckedist"))
                result.Add(New AnimalItem("bird", _
                    "flamingo", "pinkus featherus"))
            End If
            If TheClass = "" Or TheClass = "*" Or _
            TheClass = "amphibian" Then
                result.Add(New AnimalItem("amphibian", _
                    "frog", "kissmeus froggus"))
                result.Add(New AnimalItem("amphibian", _
                    "toad", "jumpus treeus"))
            End If
            Return result
        End Function
    End Class
End Namespace
Partial Class XMLObjectSources_ObjData1
    Inherits System.Web.UI.Page
    Protected Sub Button1_Click(ByVal sender As Object, _
    ByVal e As System.EventArgs) Handles Button1.Click
        Dim mytype As Type = Type.GetType("Animals.AnimalData")
        ObjectDataSource1.TypeName = mytype.AssemblyQualifiedName
        Repeater1.DataSource = ObjectDataSource1
        Repeater1.DataBind()
    End Sub
End Class
```

In this code, I create a namespace to hold the function that retrieves the data, as well as a class that will hold instances of the data. The class is called `Animal`, and it contains an animal class name, a name for the animal, and a species for the animal. Additionally, the class contains a constructor for easy creation of objects of the class.

Tearing up your data into multiple tiers

If you're building a large Web site that will have a lot of traffic, most likely you won't want to use the `SqlDataSource` control. The reason is that you're probably working on a team, and other members of the team (or even a different group within your company) might have already written code for accessing the database. Further, the data might be divided among multiple servers to provide higher performance. In such cases, the `SqlDataSource` simply doesn't cut it because the normal way to use the `SqlDataSource` is to hard-code SQL statements right in your `.aspx` file.

In the case of the large organization, your data calls are broken out into other classes. Some people like the term *tier* because it separates the classes into their own layers. Also, some people refer to tiers that hold such classes as the "business logic tier." You can call it what you like, but the point is that the classes retrieving the data are somewhere other than your `.aspx` file, or its associated code file.

Next comes the class that contains the function for retrieving the data. This function doesn't do much, as the program we're dealing with here is just a demo. In this code, I'm just creating an `ArrayList` and filling it with instances of the `Animal` class. However, I'm inspecting the incoming parameter to see whether a request for a specific animal class came in. If that's the case, I only fill the `ArrayList` object with instances for the particular animal class. Finally, I return the `ArrayList` — but simply as an instance of `ICollection`. The object is still an `ArrayList` instance, but the object calling the function sees the object only as an `ICollection`.

Next comes the code for the button's click handler. This code tells the `ObjectDataSource` control where to find the class containing my data retrieval methods:

```
Dim mytype As Type = Type.GetType("Animals.AnimalData")
ObjectDataSource1.TypeName = mytype.AssemblyQualifiedName
```

In order to tell the `ObjectDataSource` object where to find the method, I must specify exactly where the class lives — not just the class name, but the assembly containing the class. The easiest way to obtain such information is to simply call `Type.GetType`, passing the fully qualified name of the class. This call will return an instance of `Type`, which you can then use to get the full `Assembly` name by calling `AssemblyQualifiedName`.

In the end, when you run the preceding code in the browser, what you get is a form with a nice drop-down list containing three kinds of animals — and a choice for `All`. When you make your selection and then click the button, you get a nicely formatted list, as shown in Figure 6-3.

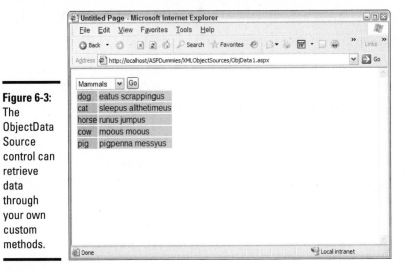

Figure 6-3:
The
ObjectData
Source
control can
retrieve
data
through
your own
custom
methods.

If you try out some samples to demonstrate the `ObjectDataSource`, you may well end up with an annoying error message that tells you the type specified in the `TypeName` property cannot be found. ASP.NET 2.0 does some strange things with assemblies; the default is to compile each `.aspx` file into a separate assembly. As a result, the runtime might have trouble locating a class if you don't specify the full name. The problem is you probably don't know what the assembly name is when you type in your code. So instead of putting the type name right in the `.aspx` file — like so —

```
<asp:ObjectDataSource ID="ObjectDataSource1" runat="server"
TypeName="animals.animal"
SelectMethod = "SelectData" />
```

a better, safer bet is to determine the assembly name at runtime, as I do in the button's `Click` event handler:

```
Dim mytype As Type = Type.GetType("Animals.AnimalData")
ObjectDataSource1.TypeName = mytype.AssemblyQualifiedName
```

Book VII

Using the .NET Framework

The 5th Wave   By Rich Tennant

"You know how cats love to play with strings? Well, Mittens would rather write them."

Contents at a Glance

Chapter 1: Handling Strings

In This Chapter

✔ Setting up Strings

✔ Working with special HTML characters

✔ Taking apart and putting together strings

✔ Converting to and from strings

✔ Connecting strings with StringBuilder

*T*he .NET framework includes hundreds of classes that range from general-purpose classes (which you'll use all the time) to specialized classes that you might use only on rare occasions. In this mini-book, I cover several of the general-purpose classes.

In this chapter, the focus is on the various classes that support string manipulation. This includes the `String` class itself, as well as a few others including `RegEx`, which is for testing whether a string matches a pattern.

In this chapter, I cover a class called `StringBuilder`. This class is for piecing together strings. However, the more traditional class `String` also includes methods for piecing together strings. In the section "Piecing Together Strings with a StringBuilder" at the end of this chapter, I discuss exactly why Microsoft gave us a separate class for piecing together strings. (Make sure you read that section; it tells you some extremely important stuff for developing high-performance Web sites.)

Formatting Strings

The .NET framework includes a powerful string-formatting mechanism that you can access through the `String` class's `Format` method. The formatting mechanism shows itself in many places, including the formatting of columns in the `GridView` control.

The idea behind the formatting mechanism is that you supply a special string called the *format string,* which describes in detail what your final string will look like. Included in the format string are various placeholders that will be replaced by the variables you specify, in a separate operation.

An example will help show you what I mean. Look at the following code:

```
Protected Sub Page_Load(ByVal sender As Object, _
ByVal e As System.EventArgs)
    Dim result As String
    Dim firstname As String = "Harold"
    Dim lastname As String = "Lloyd"
    result = String.Format( _
        "My first name is {0} and my last name is {1}.", _
        firstname, lastname)
    Response.Write(result)
End Sub
```

This code creates three strings, including one for a first name and one for a last name. Now look closely at the call to String.Format. This method takes a format string for its first parameter:

```
"My first name is {0} and my last name is {1}."
```

I then supplied two more strings to the String.Format method, the first name and the last name. The String.Format method takes the format string and replaces the {0} with the firstname and the {1} with the last name. To be more precise, String.Format replaces the {0} with the first parameter following the format string, and {1} with the second parameter following the format string.

The final resulting string that's placed in the result variable looks like this:

```
My first name is Harold and my last name is Lloyd.
```

You don't have to follow the format string with exactly two parameters; you can have as many as you want. The first one you supply always gets the number 0 in the format string as in {0}, the second one always gets {1}, the third one always gets {2}, and so on. (If you have a mismatch in counts, you'll get an error when you run your program.)

If you come from a C/C++ background, you might be familiar with the printf function in C — and wonder of wonders, it's a function that uses a formatting string. Unfortunately, the characters and specifiers you use in the printf function bear no similarity to those in the .NET String.Format method. (Oh well, such is life.)

Supplying parameters other than strings

The String.Format method can take more than just strings as its additional parameters. Have a look at this example:

```
Protected Sub Page_Load(ByVal sender As Object, _
ByVal e As System.EventArgs)
```

```
        Dim result As String
        Dim firstname As String = "Harold"
        Dim pi As Double = Math.PI
        result = String.Format( _
            "My first name is {0} and my value is {1}.", _
            firstname, pi)
        Response.Write(result)
End Sub
```

The `String.Format` method in this example takes the following format string:

```
"My first name is {0} and my value is {1}."
```

The two parameters supplied are then `firstname` and `pi`, where `firstname` is a string, and `pi` is a double-precision number (that is, a floating-point number that takes up 64 bits). Here's the resulting string:

```
My first name is Harold and my value is 3.14159265358979.
```

The `Format` method accepts any kind of variable as a parameter provided the type of variable includes a `ToString` method. A `ToString` method is used to convert a type to a string, and I discuss it in the "Converting to Strings with the ToString Method" section, later in this chapter. All the basic, built-in .NET types provide a `ToString` method. For your own classes, you have to provide your own `ToString` methods; doing so enables the instances of your class to work as parameters in the `Stirng.Format` method.

Formatting the numeric parameters

The `String.Format` method is useful for splicing together your variables inside a format string, but the method becomes even more useful when you use it to format your variables.

For example, in the preceding section I demonstrated inserting a double variable into a format string. The resulting output showed the value of pi (π) to 14 digits to the right of the decimal place. What if you want fewer or more digits? Then you can modify the format specifier. Here's a short example:

```
Protected Sub Page_Load(ByVal sender As Object, _
ByVal e As System.EventArgs)
    Dim result As String
    Dim pi As Double = Math.PI * 1000
    result = String.Format( _
        "The value is {0:c} or {0:F5} or {0:e4}.", pi)
    Response.Write(result)
End Sub
```

**Book VII
Chapter 1**

Handling Strings

This code uses the same variable (`{0}`) three times in the format string, providing a different format each time. Here's the output:

```
The value is $3,141.59 or 3141.59265 or 3.1416e+003.
```

✦ **The first version of the variable appears in the final string as a currency value.** Notice that I used the notation `{0:c}` to specify currency. The `c` character means *currency*, and you throw in a colon in between the `0` and `c`.

✦ **The second shows the value as a fixed-point number with five digits to the right of the decimal.** For that one, I used `{0:F5}` where the `F` means "fixed point" and the `5` specifies how many digits to the right of the decimal I want displayed.

✦ **The third version shows the value in scientific notation with four digits to the right of the decimal.** Notice that the format specifier is `{0:e4}`, where `e` refers to scientific notation (the `e` is for *exponent*, I guess) and `4` specifies how many digits to the right of the decimal.

Table 1-1 shows some of the format specifiers you can use with numbers.

Table 1-1		Number Specifiers	
Specifier	*Description*	*Example*	*Result*
C or c	Currency	String.Format ("{0:c}", 31415.9)	$31,415.90
D or d	Decimal	String.Format ("{0:d}", 31415)	31415
E or e	Scientific notation	String.Format ("{0:e3}", 31415.9)	3.142e+004
F or f	Fixed-point	String.Format ("{0:f3}", 31415.9)	3.142e+004
G or g	General number	String.Format ("{0:g}", 31415.9)	31415.9
N or n	Number	String.Format ("{0:n}", 31415.9)	31415.9
X or x	Hexadecimal	String.Format ("{0:X}", 31415)	7AB7

You can use either integers or floating-point numbers for any of the specifiers in Table 1-1, except for the D (decimal) and X (hexadecimal) specifiers, which allow only integers.

Formatting dates and times

Just as you can use String.Format to format numbers, you can also use it to format DateTime variables. The idea is the same; you use a specifier such as {0:d} to format the date. The letters (such as d), however, have different meanings from those of the numeric specifiers. First, take a look at the following code.

```
Protected Sub Page_Load(ByVal sender As Object, _
ByVal e As System.EventArgs)
    Dim dt As DateTime
    dt = Now
    Response.Write(String.Format("{0}", dt))
    Response.Write("<br>")
    Response.Write(String.Format("{0:d}", dt))
    Response.Write("<br>")
    Response.Write(String.Format("{0:D}", dt))
    Response.Write("<br>")
    Response.Write(String.Format("{0:f}", dt))
    Response.Write("<br>")
    Response.Write(String.Format("{0:g}", dt))
    Response.Write("<br>")
End Sub
```

Here's the output from this code:

```
1/15/2006 2:07:15 PM
1/15/2006
Sunday, January 15, 2006
Sunday, January 15, 2006 2:07 PM
1/15/2006 2:07 PM
```

The first format string doesn't have any specifiers, and you can see — in the first line of the output — what you get. The second format string uses the specifier d, which means "short date" and gives you a date in a numerical form with the month first (for example, 1/15/2006). The third example uses a capital D for the specifier, which means "long date" and gives you a date written out in words (as in Sunday, January 15, 2006). Both the little d and the big D give you the date without the time.

The f specifier gives a "full" date/time output (such as "Sunday, January 15, 2006 2:07 PM) and the g specifier gives a "general" output such as 1/15/2006 2:07 PM.

Now, keep in mind that those words "full," "general," and so on don't really have any specific technical meanings — but the kind folks at Microsoft tried to give these format specifiers at least *some* sort of intuitive meaning. In reality, the format specifiers are a bunch of letters, each providing a different type of output. Table 1-2 shows several of the format specifiers for dates and times.

Table 1-2	Date Specifiers	
Specifier	*Example*	*Output*
a	`String.Format("{0}", dt)`	1/15/2006 2:13:01 PM
d	`String.Format("{0:d}", dt)`	1/15/2006
t	`String.Format("{0:t}", dt)`	2:13 PM
T	`String.Format("{0:T}", dt)`	2:13:01 PM
f	`String.Format("{0:f}", dt)`	Sunday, January 15, 2006 2:13 PM
F	`String.Format("{0:F}", dt)`	Sunday, January 15, 2006 2:13:01 PM
g	`String.Format("{0:g}", dt)`	1/15/2006 2:13 PM
G	`String.Format("{0:G}", dt)`	1/15/2006 2:13:01 PM
M	`String.Format("{0:M}", dt)`	January 15
R	`String.Format("{0:R}", dt)`	Sun, 15 Jan 2006 14:13:01 GMT
s	`String.Format("{0:s}", dt)`	2006-01-15T14:13:01
t	`String.Format("{0:t}", dt)`	2:13 PM
T	`String.Format("{0:T}", dt)`	2:13:01 PM
u	`String.Format("{0:u}", dt)`	2006-01-15 14:13:01Z
U	`String.Format("{0:U}", dt)`	Sunday, January 15, 2006 7:13:01 PM
Y	`String.Format("{0:Y}", dt)`	January, 2006

Rather than trying to memorize the meaning of each date-format specifier, what I find easier is to scan through Table 1-2 and find the format you want, and then use that string.

Technically speaking, the output you see in Table 1-2 isn't fixed. That is, you can configure certain variables to specify how you want each date to look. The specifiers in Table 1-2 are simply shortcuts to longer, more detailed specifiers. In the following section, "Customizing data formats," I show you how to create your own data formatters, and, in turn, how to modify the behavior of those format specifiers shown in Table 1-2.

Customizing data formats

If you find that the standard date formats in the previous section aren't enough for you — or that you need a format that's not present in the table — you can use an extended set of format specifiers to describe exactly how you want your date and time to look.

Here's an example:

```
Protected Sub Page_Load(ByVal sender As Object, _
ByVal e As System.EventArgs)
    Dim dt As DateTime
    dt = Now
    Response.Write( _
        String.Format("{0:ddd, MMM d yyyy}", dt))
    Response.Write("<br>")
    Response.Write( _
        String.Format("{0:yyyy-dd-MM HH:mm:ss}", dt))
    Response.Write("<br>")
End Sub
```

Notice the two different format strings I'm using. They're more complex than single characters because they describe in detail how the date should be formatted. Here's the first format string in the code:

```
{0:ddd, MMM d yyyy}
```

And here's the output from the first format string:

```
Sun, Jan 15 2006
```

The ddd part of the format string says to print the day of the week as three characters, as in Sun for Sunday. The format string then includes a comma and a space that are written out exactly as they're coded. Next the string has a MMM, which means to print the month as three characters, as in Jan for January. Then a space follows. Next is a d which simply means to print the numbered day of the month; if the number is 1 through 9, it won't have a preceding 0. Again there is a space, and finally yyyy, which means to print the year as four digits.

Now here's the second format string:

```
{0:yyyy-dd-MM HH:mm:ss}
```

And here's the output from the second format string:

```
2006-15-01 18:20:39
```

The second format string starts with yyyy, which (again) means the year in four digits. Then comes a hyphen, which prints as is. Next is dd, which means to print the numbered day of the month, but always as two digits — thus the dates 1 through 9 print as 01 through 09. Again there is a hyphen, and then the month's number. As with the date, MM means to always print the month's number as two digits. Thus, January prints as 01, February as 02, and so on. A space follows, and then the hour (as two digits), a colon, the minutes (as two digits), a colon, and finally the seconds (as two digits).

Table 1-3 lists all the format specifiers you can use for these dates.

Table 1-3	Date-Time Format Specifiers
Specifier	*Description*
d	The numbered day of the month as 1, 2, 3, and so on up to 31. A single d means the numbers 1 through 9 show up as a single digit. A double dd means to show them as 01 through 09.
ddd	The day of the week as three letters, as in Mon, Tue, Wed, and so on. Use four of them, dddd, to show the full day of the week (Monday, Tuesday, and so on).
f	Fractions of a second. If the time is 1:25 and 30.5 seconds, the f is for the .5 part. To show more digits, specify more f's, as in ffff to show four digits (such as .5432). Note that trailing 0 characters *are* shown, as in .5000.
F	A capital F is the same as a little f except the trailing 0 characters are not shown, as in .5 (as opposed to .5000).
g	Shows "A.D." after the date.
h	The hour number as a single digit. The hours go from 1–12. Thus one o'clock in the afternoon or in the morning would show up as a single digit (1). To specify two digits (as in 01), use hh.
H	The hour number in a 24-hour clock. The hours go from 1–24. Thus one o'clock a.m. would show up as 1, whereas one o'clock p.m. would show up as 13. The numbers 1 through 9 are single digits. To have them show up as two digits (01 through 09), use HH.
m	The minute number. The numbers 1–9 show as a single digit. To show them as double digits (01 through 09), use mm.
M	The month number, from 1 through 12. The numbers 1–9 show as a single digit. To show these values as double digits (01 through 09), use MM.
MMM	The three-letter abbreviated name of the month (Jan, Feb, Mar, and so on).
MMMM	The full name of the month (January, February, March, and so on).
s	The seconds of the time. The numbers 0–9 show up as a single digit. To show the numbers 0–9 as a double digit (00 through 09), use ss.
t	A.M. or P.M. Shows A for A.M. and P for P.M. times. To show the full A.M. and P.M., use tt.
y	The year as one or two digits. Years 2000–2009 show up as a single digit (0, 1, 2, and so on). The years 2010, 2011, and so on show up as two digits, (10, 11, and so on).
yy	The year as two digits, as in 00 for 2000, 01 for 2001, and so on, or 89 for 1989, 90 for 1990, and so on.

Specifier	Description
yyyy	The full four digits of the year, as in `2001`.
z	The time zone offset. For example, Eastern Time Zone is –5 degrees from Greenwich Mean Time, thus the number `-5` shows up. If you always want to show this value as two digits (for example, –05), then use `zz`. To show the offset as a full number of hours and minutes (written, for example –05:00), use `zzz`. (Remember: Some time zones are a half hour off from others, so these would show `30` in the `minutes` portion.)

Pay close attention to the uppercase and lowercase of the formatting characters. If you reverse the case, .NET will display the string formatted differently from what you expect!

Handling Special HTML Characters in Strings

If you need to display on a Web page characters that are normally part of HTML tags, you might run into some problems. The Web browser might get confused and choke. It won't die or explode, but it will choke, and that can be bad.

For example, suppose you have the following `.aspx` file:

**Book VII
Chapter 1**

Handling Strings

```
<%@ Page Language="VB" %>
<script runat="server">
    Protected Sub Page_Load(ByVal sender As Object, _
    ByVal e As System.EventArgs)
        Label1.Text = "<The Moon!>"
    End Sub
</script>
<html>
<body>
    <form id="form1" runat="server">
        Greetings from
        <asp:Label ID="Label1" runat="server" Text="Label" />
    </form>
</body>
</html>
```

The label's text is set to the string `<The Moon!>`. Unfortunately, the `<` and `>` make up an HTML tag — and the browser interprets them as such. Since `<The Moon!>` is not a legitimate HTML tag, the browser just ignores it and displays nothing. Thus you get the following in your browser:

```
Greetings from
```

The way to remedy the situation is to replace the special HTML characters with special codes called *HTML entities*. Change the label assignment line to this:

```
Label1.Text = Server.HtmlEncode("<The Moon!>")
```

Now the text shows up properly in the browser, like so:

```
Greetings from <The Moon!>
```

If you look at the source in the browser, you'll see the codes that the < and > characters got replaced by:

```
&lt;The Moon!&gt;
```

Thus the `&lt;` denotes a less-than character and the `&gt;` denotes a greater-than character.

Splitting and Combining Strings

Splitting and combining strings is a common activity in programming. I can think of dozens of times in the past couple of years I've had to do such a thing. For example, suppose you want to give your user the capability to enter one full name into a single text box, instead of supplying two separate boxes, one for the first name and one for the last name. To get that done, you can simply take the string containing the first and last name and split it up into two separate strings — one for the first name and one for the last.

Or, going the other way, if you have a first name and a last name stored as separate columns in a data table, you can piece them together to form a single string.

Of course, piecing together two strings into one isn't all that complicated — but what if you have to piece together a dozen strings, all stored in an *array* (remember, an array is simply a variable that stores several items of the same type all in a row; for more information see Book 5, Chapter 3)? The .NET Framework provides functions for combining groups of strings as well as splitting up single strings.

Splitting strings

The `String` class includes a `Split` method that makes splitting strings easy. `Split` operates on a given string, and takes as a parameter an array of characters. This character array specifies the characters used to split the string. For example, if the array of characters consists of

```
, . ;
```

and the string you want to split is

```
Hello.there;everybody,how.are;you
```

then the resulting array will have six entries containing the words `Hello`, `there`, `everybody`, `how`, `are`, and `you`.

Here's an example in VB.NET that demonstrates how to use the `Split` method:

```
<%@ Page Language="VB" %>
<script runat="server">
    Protected Sub Page_Load(ByVal sender As Object, _
    ByVal e As System.EventArgs)
        Dim chars As Char() = ",.;".ToCharArray()
        Dim mystring As String = _
            "Hello.there;everybody,how.are;you"
        Dim strings As String()
        strings = mystring.Split(chars)
        Dim word As String
        For Each word In strings
            Response.Write(word)
            Response.Write("<br>")
        Next
    End Sub
</script>
<html>
<body>
    <form id="form1" runat="server">
    </form>
</body>
</html>
```

This code does exactly as I just described: It creates an array of characters and then splits a string based on those characters. Notice how I create the array of characters by starting with a string and then calling the `ToCharArray` method on that string. Then I call `Split` on the string I'm splitting, passing the array of characters. The `Split` method returns an array, which I then iterate through, printing out each word to the browser.

Here's the output:

```
Hello
there
```

```
everybody
how
are
you
```

Because arrays are declared a little differently in both C# and VB.NET, I'll give you a look at the code in C#. Here it is:

```
<%@ Page Language="C#" %>
<script runat="server">
    protected void Page_Load(object sender, EventArgs e)
    {
        char[] chars = ",.;".ToCharArray();
        string mystring =
            "Hello.there;everybody,how.are;you";
        string[] strings = mystring.Split(chars);
        foreach (string word in strings) {
            Response.Write(word);
            Response.Write("<br>");
        }
    }
</script>
<html>
<body>
    <form id="form1" runat="server">
    </form>
</body>
</html>
```

The Split method is a member of a specific instance of string. Thus you type the Split method as you would call any other method of an object: You type the string you're splitting, followed by the dot (.) character, and then add Split followed by its parameters. This technique is in contrast to the way you combine strings, as you see in the next section.

Combining strings

If you have a set of strings you've stored in an array, you can easily combine them into a single string. To do so, you start with an array of strings and then call the Join method of the String class. The Join method returns a single string containing the combined strings. The following code demonstrates the Join method:

```
<%@ Page Language="VB" %>
<script runat="server">
    Protected Sub Page_Load(ByVal sender As Object, _
    ByVal e As System.EventArgs)
        Dim words As String() = _
            {"Greetings", "From", "Planet", "Earth"}
```

```
        Dim bigstring As String

        bigstring = String.Join(" ", words)
        Response.Write(bigstring)
    End Sub
</script>
<html>
<body>
    <form id="form1" runat="server">
    </form>
</body>
</html>
```

This code creates an array of strings and saves it in the variable called words. Then the code creates a string called `bigstring` and calls the `String.Join` method, passing two parameters. The first parameter is a string of a single space; this puts single spaces in between words in the final string. The second parameter to `Join` is the array of strings you're combining. Here's the output:

```
Greetings From Planet Earth
```

The `Join` method is a *static* (also called *shared*) method. This means it's a member of the `String` class, but does not operate on a particular instance of `String`. Thus, to call it, you type the class `String`, followed by the dot (`.`), and then the word `Join`. This is in contrast to the `Split` method, which is a member of a particular instance of `String`.

Converting to Strings with the ToString Method

When you want to use a variable's value inside a call to `String.Format`, you have to make sure that the value can actually be converted to a string; that converted string is what appears inside the final result. How can a variable be converted to a string? Easy: The class it belongs to includes a `ToString` method.

All the basic classes in the .NET framework have a `ToString` method. For example, the `Int32` type has a `ToString` method. When you call `String.Format`, the formatting engine calls `ToString` on the variables passed in as parameters. That `ToString` method supplies a string version of the variable. Otherwise the `Format` will have no way to generate a string from the variable.

So why is this useful knowledge? Because you can supply a `ToString` method in your own classes, making them formattable! Imagine the possibilities! Strings everywhere!

Consider this code:

```
<%@ Page Language="VB" %>
<script runat="server">
    Class MyPoint
        Public X As Integer
        Public Y As Integer
        Public Overrides Function ToString() As String
            Return String.Format("({0},{1})", X, Y)
        End Function
    End Class
    Protected Sub Page_Load(ByVal sender As Object, _
    ByVal e As System.EventArgs)
        Dim point1 As New MyPoint
        point1.X = 10
        point1.Y = 20
        Dim point2 As New MyPoint
        point2.X = 15
        point2.Y = 16
        Dim descrip As String
        descrip = String.Format("Point 1 is {0}<br>", point1)
        Response.Write(descrip)
        descrip = String.Format("Point 2 is {0}<br>", point2)
        Response.Write(descrip)
    End Sub
</script>
<html>
<body>
    <form id="form1" runat="server">
    </form>
</body>
</html>
```

This code declares a class that simply contains two member variables, X and Y, both integers. The class also contains a ToString method that returns a string of the form (X,Y). (Notice that just to be clever, I used the Format method inside the ToString method. You're perfectly allowed to do that.)

Then to test out the class, I provided a Page_Load method that creates two instances of my class, point1 and point2. I set the X and Y values of each instance, and then pass each to a String.Format function to see if it works. And it did! (If it hadn't, I'd have had to delete this section of the book.) Here's the output:

```
Point 1 is (10,20)
Point 2 is (15,16)
```

Converting Strings to Numbers

If you have a string containing text in the form of a number (such as a string containing "3.1415926") and you want to convert the string to a number, you need to call the Parse method of the type you're converting to. Each of the .NET number types has a Parse method that takes a String as a parameter and returns a number. In fact, just for good measure, all the the number types actually have two Parse methods (Parse and TryParse), each with different purposes.

Here's an example with the Int32 type:

```
Dim digits As String = "54321"
Dim num As Int32 = Int32.Parse(digits)
```

This code creates a string with the text "54321". Then the code converts the string "54321" to the number 54321 by using the Int32.Parse method. (Notice that the Parse method is a shared — that is, static — member of the class Int32 itself.)

But what happens if the string you pass to Parse doesn't contain a number? The Parse method throws an exception. When you're writing apps for the Web, those unsightly exceptions can be a problem. You don't want to have a big horrible exception page appear in the browser when somebody's visiting your Web site. But writing an exception handler around every call to Parse would be annoying, too. Thus Microsoft has given us an alternative to the Parse method — the TryParse method.

The TryParse method doesn't throw an exception if it encounters a string that doesn't contain a number. Instead, it returns a Boolean value of True or False depending on if the conversion to a number succeeded.

Here's some sample code that demonstrates the TryParse method:

```
Dim digits As String = "54321"
Dim num As Int32
If Int32.TryParse(digits, num) Then
    Response.Write(num)
Else
    Response.Write("Please enter a number.")
End If
```

Look at how the TryParse method works. I used it in an If statement because it returns a True or False that represents whether I gave it a valid string. The first parameter to TryParse is the string I'm trying to parse. The second parameter is the name of the Int32 variable in which I'm going to save the resulting number if the parse succeeds.

Inside the `If` block, I process the number (in this case, I just print it out). In the `Else` block, I provide an error message that asks the user to try again.

Piecing Together Strings with a StringBuilder

As you do Web development, you'll want to keep in mind an extremely important situation regarding the `String` class: Instances of the `String` class are *immutable*. What that means is when you have an instance of class `String` and you store some text in the instance, that text *cannot change*. The only way to change the string is by getting rid of the original string and creating a new string in its place. If you want to change an individual character of the string, say from WALK to TALK, the only way this can be done is to throw away the entire WALK string and replace it with the string TALK.

In fact, if you look closely at the `String` class, you'll see there are no methods to modify the string. Instead, the methods that seem to modify the string actually return a new string, which you can store in place of the original string. Consider this code:

```
Dim mystr As String
mystr = "Jump"
mystr = mystr.Replace("J", "L")
```

I'm calling the `Replace` method to replace the letter J with the letter L. However, I'm not actually replacing anything at all. Instead, I'm creating a new string with the changes and storing it back in the original string. So for a moment there are two strings in memory: Jump and Lump.

Consider what happens if (instead) I decide to save the string to a different variable, like so:

```
Dim first As String
Dim second As String
first = "Jump"
second = first.Replace("J", "L")
```

If you try out this code, you'll see that the original string variable, `first`, remains intact. It didn't change. It can't: The `String` type is immutable. Knowing this, if you look through all the methods of the `String` class, you'll see that not one of them actually changes the string; instead, each one returns a *copy* of the string with the requested changes.

While immutability might seem like it's not a problem, when dealing with a high-performance Web site, immutability can be a major problem. Suppose you're using a loop to continually add large amounts of text to an already-large string. This loop might run, say, 100 times. With each iteration of the loop, the string grows.

Now, that's where the problem comes in. Each time the loop runs, the `String` class creates an entirely new string — and your code throws away the old string. If you have a Web site that gets thousands of hits every hour, you could see a major performance penalty in terms of speed and memory.

The solution to this performance problem is the `StringBuilder` class instead of the `String` class. An instance of `StringBuilder` is *mutable*, meaning you *can* change it. And the cool thing about `StringBuilder` is that you can instantly convert it to a `String` instance.

Here's a good example of when you might use `StringBuilder`: Suppose you're piecing together a long string of HTML, such as in the following:

```
Protected Function BuildHTML() As String
    Dim bigstring As New _
        StringBuilder("<h1>Numbers</h1>")
    Dim i As Int32
    For i = 0 To 100
        bigstring.Append(i.ToString)
        bigstring.Append("<br>")
    Next
    Return bigstring.ToString
End Function
```

The `StringBuilder` class works much like `String`, except you can change instances of `StringBuilder`. You can see, I'm calling the `Append` method, which actually modifies the string stored in the `StringBuilder` instance, adding on the text I supply. Thus I'm appending together a string piece-by-piece — but saving the memory overhead of `String`. Then, at the end of the function, I simply cast the result to a `String` by calling `ToString` — and return the result as a `String`.

The `StringBuilder` class also supports a handy `Format` function. Here I'm modifying the preceding `BuildHTML` function just a tad to make use of the handy `Format` function:

```
Protected Function BuildHTML() As String
    Dim bigstring As New _
        StringBuilder("<h1>Numbers</h1>")
    Dim i As Int32
    For i = 0 To 100
        bigstring.AppendFormat("{0}<br>", i.ToString)
    Next
    Return bigstring.ToString
End Function
```

The `AppendFormat` function works just like the `String.Format` function.

If you're piecing together a string and considering switching to `String Builder`, take another mental step and see whether you can skip both `String` and `StringBuilder` altogether and just use `Response.Write`. For example, when I call `BuildHTML`, if I just call `Response.Write` with the result, then really I can skip `StringBuilder` and call `Response.Write` directly, like so:

```
Protected Sub WriteHTML()
    Response.Write("<h1>Numbers</h1>")
    Dim i As Int32
    For i = 0 To 100
        Response.Write(i.ToString)
        Response.Write("<br>")
    Next
End Sub
```

While this might seem a bit obvious, many times I've written a function that carefully pieces together some HTML, thinking I'd have to save it for later — only to realize I could have skipped all that and just called `Response.Write`.

Chapter 2: Manipulating Dates and Times

In This Chapter

✔ Getting the current date and time anywhere on the planet

✔ Reading the components of a DateTime structure

✔ Streaming a DateTime structure

✔ Handling local times versus universal times

✔ Calculating with dates

✔ Parsing a string containing a date and time

*T*he .NET Framework includes a `DateTime` structure that stores and manipulates — you guessed it — dates and times. With .NET 2.0, the `DateTime` structure has improved a bit, adding further support for handling time zones. For example, suppose you have an application that grabs the current date and time, which is stored in a `DateTime` variable. The application then sends the `DateTime` off to another computer via the Internet, and that other computer is in another time zone. The receiving computer can take the data in the `DateTime` structure, recognize the time zone, and then adjust the value so it's correct for the new time zone.

In this chapter, I cover various aspects of the `DateTime` structure.

All code listings used in this book are available for download at www.dummies.com/go/aspnetaiofd.

Getting the Current Date and Time

The `DateTime` structure contains a handy *static* or shared property for obtaining the current date and time. The property is simply called `Now`. Because it's a property, you call it from the `DateTime` structure itself — and this property is available regardless of which .NET language you're using. Here's a quick sample in VB.NET:

```
Dim dt As DateTime = DateTime.Now
```

And here's the same code in C#:

```
DateTime dt = DateTime.Now;
```

In the case of VB.NET, however, you also have a remnant of older versions of Visual Basic that you're free to use. VB.NET has a function called Now that provides the same information as the Now property in the DateTime structure. The Now function is a standalone function; here's a sample call:

```
Dim dt As DateTime = Now
```

In VB.NET, you're free to use either DateTime.Now or the Now function; they both function exactly the same. Personally, I usually just call Now. The reason is pure, raw, unadulterated laziness mixed with a hint of impatience: It's faster to just type Now than it is to type DateTime.Now.

Reading the Components of a DateTime Structure

The DateTime structure includes several properties for accessing the individual components of a date and time. By *components* I mean, for example, the individual hour or the individual month of a date and time. Table 2-1 is a list of what's available.

Table 2-1	The Components of a DateTime Structure
Property	*Description*
DayOfWeek	The day of the week as an enumeration, specifically of the type DayOfWeek — which contains the values Sunday, Monday, Tuesday, Wednesday, Thursday, Friday, and Saturday.
DayOfYear	The day of the year, written as an integer. January 1st is Day 1, January 2nd is Day 2, February 1st is Day 32, and so on.
Hour	The exact hour as a portion of the time, written as an integer.
Kind	The kind of time stored. This is an enumeration of type DateTimeKind, and has values Local, Unspecified, and Utc. (Utc stands for Universal Time-Coordinated, which is basically a fancy name for Greenwich Mean Time.)
Millisecond	The exact millisecond as a poriton of the time, written as an integer.
Minutes	The exact minute as a portion of the time, written as an integer.
Month	The exact month as a portion of the time, written as an integer.
Second	The exact second as a portion of the time, written as an integer.
Ticks	The time as a number of *ticks* (nanoseconds since the date 1/1/0001).

Property	Description
TimeOfDay	The amount of time that has passed since midnight local time. The value is given as a `TimeSpan` structure.
Year	The exact year as a portion of the time, written as an integer.

Remember that for all properties in Table 2-1, *except for* `Ticks`, the names are given in the singular — for example, `Second` (not `Seconds`). This is in contrast to various English dialects, where these words are usually spoken in plural, as in "The number of seconds." `Ticks`, on the other hand, is given in plural.

Note also that the `Ticks` property represents the time as the number of nanoseconds since January 1, 0001. (I didn't know they even *had* computers back then.) A nanosecond, remember, is one *billionth* of a second. In one nanosecond, light travels about 11.8 inches — a tad less than a foot.

The following code demonstrates each of these calls. The code is a function that you can call from a `Page_Load` method.

```
Public Sub WriteDateComponents(ByVal dt As DateTime)
    Response.Write("Date Components:<br>")
    Response.Write(dt)
    Response.Output.Write("", dt)
    Response.Write("<br>")
    Response.Write(String.Format("{0:f}", dt))
    Response.Output.Write("Date: {0}<br>", dt.Date)
    Response.Output.Write("DayOfWeek: {0}<br>", dt.DayOfWeek)
    Response.Output.Write("DayOfYear: {0}<br>", dt.DayOfYear)
    Response.Output.Write("Hour: {0}<br>", dt.Hour)
    Response.Output.Write("Kind: {0}<br>", dt.Kind)
    Response.Output.Write("Milliseconds: {0}<br>", dt.Millisecond)
    Response.Output.Write("Minutes: {0}<br>", dt.Minute)
    Response.Output.Write("Month: {0}<br>", dt.Month)
    Response.Output.Write("Seconds: {0}<br>", dt.Second)
    Response.Output.Write("Ticks: {0}<br>", dt.Ticks)
    Response.Output.Write("TimeOfDay: {0}<br>", dt.TimeOfDay)
    Response.Output.Write("Year: {0}<br>", dt.Year)
End Sub
```

Here's a sample output from this code:

```
Date Components:
3/14/2006 12:50:12 PM
Tuesday, March 14, 2006 12:50 PMDate: 3/14/2006 12:00:00 AM
DayOfWeek: Tuesday
DayOfYear: 73
Hour: 12
Kind: Local
Milliseconds: 984
Minutes: 50
Month: 3
Seconds: 12
```

```
Ticks: 632779374129843750
TimeOfDay: 12:50:12.9843750
Year: 2006
```

Streaming a DateTime Structure

Occasionally you may find that you need to save a `DateTime` structure — whether to a file or into a database — or transmit the data over a network connection. You could store the individual components of the `DateTime` (the year, the month, the day, the hour, and so on) and then reconstruct a `DateTime` component when you read the data back later on. Fortunately, however, the `DateTime` structure provides a handy alternative that takes time-zone conversions into account automatically.

Suppose, for example, that you're in the Eastern Time Zone of the United States. You've written some software that saves information to a file, including the value of the current date and time. A friend of yours in the Pacific Time Zone has a copy of this software.

You run the software on your computer in the Eastern Time Zone. At exactly 12:00 noon, you create a file, save it to your hard drive, and then e-mail the file to your friend in the Pacific Time Zone.

When your friend opens the file, she wants to know what time you created the file. The software reads the date from the file. But should the software say 12:00? This might lead your friend to believe that you created the file at 12:00 her time, when in fact, you created the file at 9:00 her time (which is 12:00 *your* time).

The `DateTime` structure in .NET 2.0 is smart enough to detect the time zone, and, should you want it to, automatically adjusts the time for the time zone. Further, when you save a `DateTime` structure to a file, the information you save includes a time zone. Thus, using the `DateTime` structure, you can write the current time to a file as 12:00 Eastern Standard Time. Then, when your friend opens the file and the software reads the time, the `DateTime` structure can take an automatic look at the computer's configured time zone — along with the time zone information in the file — and adjust accordingly. You can then display the time as either 12:00 EST or 9:00 PST. That way there won't be any question about what time it was when the information was saved.

Demonstrating such a feat is (unfortunately) difficult to do in a book. One way might be to arrange for a bunch of readers in different parts of the planet to all agree to try out a really cool demo at a particular time. But alas, that's just not going to happen. As it happens, however, the Web server I use for one of my own hosting arrangements is in the Pacific Time Zone — while I'm in the Eastern Time Zone. That's a perfect way to demonstrate this amazing technology for you. So here goes . . .

Listing 2-1 shows how you can make that transformation happen. To stream the `DateTime` instance, I call the `ToBinary` method, which returns the `DateTime` instance as an `Int64` number. You can write this number to a file, or simply paste it into a box (as I allow for in this code).

Listing 2-1:   Time transformation demo (VB)

```
<%@ Page Language="VB" %>
<!DOCTYPE html PUBLIC "-//W3C//DTD XHTML 1.0 Transitional//EN"
"http://www.w3.org/TR/xhtml1/DTD/xhtml1-transitional.dtd">
<script runat="server">
    Protected Sub Button1_Click(ByVal sender As Object, _
    ByVal e As System.EventArgs)
        Dim value As Int64
        If Int64.TryParse(TextBox1.Text, value) Then
            Response.Write(String.Format("You entered {0}<br>", value))
            Response.Write("This number converts to time ")
            Dim dt As DateTime
            dt = DateTime.FromBinary(value)
            Response.Write(String.Format( _
                "{0:MM/dd/yy HH:mm:ss zz}<br><hr>", dt))
        End If
    End Sub
</script>
<html xmlns="http://www.w3.org/1999/xhtml" >
<head runat="server">
    <title>Untitled Page</title>
</head>
<body>
    <form id="form1" runat="server">
    <div>
        The current time as binary is:
        <%
            Response.Write(Now.ToBinary.ToString())
        %>
        <br />
        Enter a binary value here and click Transform!:
        <asp:TextBox ID="TextBox1" runat="server"></asp:TextBox>
        <asp:Button ID="Button1" runat="server" Text="Transform!"
        OnClick="Button1_Click" />
    </div>
    </form>
</body>
</html>
```

Book VII
Chapter 2

Manipulating Dates
and Times

In this code, I print out the current date and time, streamed as an `Int64` value. You can highlight that number with the mouse pointer, copy it to the clipboard, and paste it into the form — or into the same form running on a different server thousands of miles away. Figure 2-1 shows the form running on my own computer in the Eastern Time Zone. Figure 2-2 shows what happens when I run the form on a Web server that's in the Pacific Time Zone. I pasted the same number into both browser windows; notice how the form displayed the time but *adjusted to the local time zone*. Still, the time displayed on-screen represents the same time, regardless of time zone.

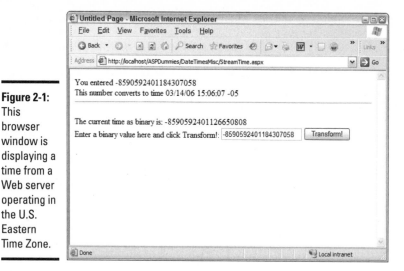

Figure 2-1:
This browser window is displaying a time from a Web server operating in the U.S. Eastern Time Zone.

Figure 2-2:
This browser window is displaying a page from a Web server operating in the U.S. Pacific Time Zone.

Handling Local Times Versus Universal Times

New with the DateTime structure in .NET version 2.0 is a special property called Kind and a function called SpecifyKind. When you store a date, you want to specify (somehow) whether the date is local to a specific time zone, or whether the time is instead universal time. The Kind property specifies exactly this information.

To find out whether a `DateTime` structure refers to a local time zone or to universal time, check the `Kind` property. To specify whether a `DateTime` is local or universal, you create a new `DateTime` structure, specifying the kind.

Note that you don't use a constructor to create a `DateTime` structure; instead, you call the static (shared) method `SpecifyKind`, which is part of the `DateTime` structure.

If you put all this talk about `Kind` and `SpecifyKind` together, you might come to the conclusion that you cannot modify an existing `DateTime` structure's `Kind` property. That is indeed the case. To get around this limitation, you create a new `DateTime` structure with the `Kind` property set the way you want.

Listing 2-2 demonstrates how you can read a `DateTime` structure's `Kind` property — and then how you can create a new `DateTime` structure with a different `Kind` property. This code makes use of the `WriteDateComponents` function (which I created in the section "Reading the Components of a DateTime Structure," earlier in this chapter).

Listing 2-2:   Converting between kinds of dates (VB)

```
<%@ Page Language="VB" %>
<!DOCTYPE html PUBLIC "-//W3C//DTD XHTML 1.0 Transitional//EN"
"http://www.w3.org/TR/xhtml1/DTD/xhtml1-transitional.dtd">
<script runat="server">
    Public Sub WriteDateComponents(ByVal dt As DateTime)
        Response.Write("Date Components:<br>")
        Response.Write(dt)
        Response.Output.Write("", dt)
        Response.Write("<br>")
        Response.Write(String.Format("{0:f}", dt))
        Response.Output.Write("Date: {0}<br>", dt.Date)
        Response.Output.Write("DayOfWeek: {0}<br>", dt.DayOfWeek)
        Response.Output.Write("DayOfYear: {0}<br>", dt.DayOfYear)
        Response.Output.Write("Hour: {0}<br>", dt.Hour)
        Response.Output.Write("Kind: {0}<br>", dt.Kind)
        Response.Output.Write("Milliseconds: {0}<br>", dt.Millisecond)
        Response.Output.Write("Minutes: {0}<br>", dt.Minute)
        Response.Output.Write("Month: {0}<br>", dt.Month)
        Response.Output.Write("Seconds: {0}<br>", dt.Second)
        Response.Output.Write("Ticks: {0}<br>", dt.Ticks)
        Response.Output.Write("TimeOfDay: {0}<br>", dt.TimeOfDay)
        Response.Output.Write("Year: {0}<br>", dt.Year)
    End Sub
    Public Sub ConvertDateKinds()
        Dim dt As DateTime = DateTime.Now
        Dim utctime As DateTime = DateTime.SpecifyKind( _
            dt.ToUniversalTime, DateTimeKind.Utc)
        Response.Output.Write("Local time: {0}<br>", dt)
        WriteDateComponents(dt)
        Response.Write("<hr>")
        Response.Output.Write("As a UTC time: {0}<br>", utctime)
        WriteDateComponents(utctime)
    End Sub
```

Book VII
Chapter 2

Manipulating Dates
and Times

(continued)

Listing 2-2 *(continued)*

```
    Protected Sub Page_Load(ByVal sender As Object, _
    ByVal e As System.EventArgs) Handles Me.Load
        ConvertDateKinds()
    End Sub
</script>
<html xmlns="http://www.w3.org/1999/xhtml" >
<head runat="server">
    <title>Untitled Page</title>
</head>
<body>
    <form id="form1" runat="server">
    <div>
    </div>
    </form>
</body>
</html>
```

The heart of this code is in its `ConvertDateTimes` function. This function creates a new `DateTime` structure, filling the structure with the current `DateTime`. Next, the code creates a second `DateTime` structure, taking the time that's currently in the first `DateTime` structure; in this case, however, `Kind` is set to `Universal Time`.

Next, the code writes out the components of each time, the local `Now` time, and the `Universal Time` version. Figure 2-3 shows what you see when you run this on your computer.

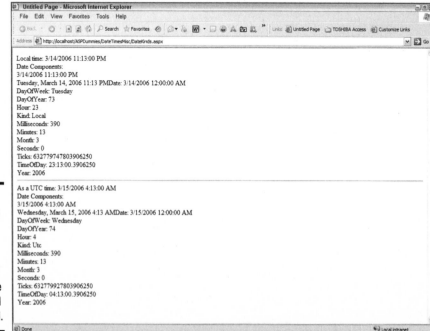

Figure 2-3:
A DateTime structure has a Kind property specifying whether the time is local or universal.

Modifying Kind (or any other property)

You can't modify the `Kind` property. In fact, if you look into the different properties of the `DateTime` structure, you'll notice that you actually can't modify any of the properties. Once you create a `DateTime` structure, what you set is what you get. A `DateTime` structure is, therefore, *immutable*. It holds a date and a time, and from there you can't change the date and time in it.

So what if you need to modify the date and time in a `DateTime` structure? After all, you will probably have good reason to do so sooner or later. To modify a date or a time, you simply create a new `DateTime` structure. If you have a variable holding your `DateTime` structure, then you place your new `DateTime` structure in that same variable, allowing the previous one to be deleted by the .NET system.

Below is a section called "Calculating with Dates." The same concept applies there as well. You can make calculations with dates, adding days, minutes, months — whatever — to a `DateTime` structure. After the calculation, you get back a new `DateTime` structure, which you can store in the same variable that previously had the previous `DateTime` structure. This situation may give you the impression that you're modifying the `DateTime` structure — but in fact, you aren't. You're creating a new one altogether, and throwing away the old one. (And just for completeness, I should mention that the `String` class has this same immutable quality. You don't actually modify a `String` instance; instead, functions that *seem* to modify a `String` are simply throwing the old instance away and returning a new `String` instance.)

Before ending the topic of the `Kind` property, you might remember from Table 2-1 that the `Kind` property also has a third possibility besides `Local` and `Utc`. This third value is simply called `Unspecified`. You're free to pass this third value to the `SpecifyKind` function. Why would you use it? If you're simply not concerned with the time zone. If you just want to store a time without regard for local versus universal time, then you can specify `Kind` as `Unspecified`. (Or would that be "unspecify the time as `Unspecified`?" On second thought, let's not go there.)

Calculating with Dates

When you're working with dates, you may well run into a case where you need to perform a calculation on a date. But hold on: What exactly *is* a calculation on a date? The following are examples of date calculations:

Two weeks from now

Three days after March 1, 2010

Six seconds before March 1, 2010

Seven minutes ago

Before showing you how to do calculations with dates, however, I need to clarify a tiny-but-important detail. Unlike regular arithmetic, in which you perform operations on two *items of the same type* (say, an integer plus an integer), date calculations get weird in a hurry: You're not doing operations on two items of the same type. In the phrase "three days after March 1, 2010," for example, you're dealing with *two different types of data:*

1. A date (in this case, March 1, 2010)

2. A time span (three days)

You're not actually dealing with two dates because adding two dates doesn't really make sense. What does it mean (to anybody but a time traveler making tourist stops) if you try to add March 1, 2010 to April 1, 2006? Sure, a mathematician with a lot of extra time to waste could come up with an algebraic system for adding dates — but under normal circumstances, adding dates to dates doesn't make sense. Instead, you add a time span to a date — and get another date (farther along in time) as a result.

It's just as easy to imagine how to take the difference between two dates — that is, to subtract two dates. For example, the difference between March 1, 2010 11:05 and March 2, 2010 11:05 is exactly 24 hours. Thus you might express it like this:

"March 2, 2010 11:05 *minus* March 1, 2010 11:05 *equals* 24 hours"

The .NET Framework includes two types for adding dates. The first is the type I've talked about throughout this chapter, the `DateTime` structure. The second is a structure used for storing time spans, called (fittingly enough) `TimeSpan`.

The `DateTime` structure, in turn, offers two important operations for adding and subtracting a `TimeSpan` from an existing `DateTime` structure:

+ **Add:** This operation takes a `TimeSpan` structure as a parameter. This function returns a new `DateTime` structure.

+ **Subtract:** This operation also takes a `TimeSpan` structure as a parameter (thus returning a new `DateTime` structure) or another `DateTime` as a parameter (thus returning a `TimeSpan` structure).

Adding a `TimeSpan` to a date and time yields a time in the future, counting forward from the existing date and time. Subtracting a `TimeSpan` from a date and time yields a time in the past, counting backward from the existing date and time.

`TimeSpan` structures can also be negative. A negative value simply reverses the direction of the `TimeSpan`; that is, adding a negative `TimeSpan` to an existing date and time yields a time prior to the existing date and time, while subtracting a negative `TimeSpan` yields a time after. (That's kind of confusing, though — here's hoping you keep your code nice and simple for us mere humans to read!)

The .NET library provides you with four different constructors for creating a `TimeSpan` structure, each with a different set of parameters. Here they are:

- ✦ `New TimeSpan(ticks as Int64)`

- ✦ `New TimeSpan(hours as Int32, minutes as Int32, seconds as Int32)`

- ✦ `New TimeSpan(days as Int32, hours as Int32, minutes as Int32, seconds as Int32)`

- ✦ `New TimeSpan(days as Int32, hours as Int32, minutes as Int32, seconds as Int32, milliseconds as Int32)`

You use the first type if you're dealing with ticks, which are nanoseconds. That's a pretty small amount of time, a billionth of a second. You use the second if you need to specify a time span in terms of hours, minutes, and seconds, such as 23 hours, 59 minutes, and 59 seconds from now. Use the third if you need a days term, such as 5 days, 20 hours, 59 minutes, and 40 seconds. And finally, use the fourth if you want to specify a time span as days, hours, minutes, seconds, and milliseconds.

The `DateTime` structure is immutable. Thus, when calling the `Add` or `Subtract` function, you are not modifying any existing `DateTime` structure; instead, you're getting back a *new and separate* `DateTime` structure.

In addition to using a `TimeSpan` with the `DateTime` structure's `Add` and `Subtract` functions, you can also make use of some specialized `DateTime` calculation functions. These functions are members of the `DateTime` structure and, like `Add` and `Subtract`, return a new instance of `DateTime`:

- ✦ `AddDays`: Pass a floating-point number such as 3.5, which adds 3 days and 12 hours to the value in `DateTime`, and returns the new `DateTime`.

- ✦ `AddHours`: Pass a floating-point number such as 6.5, which adds six hours and 30 minutes to the value in `DateTime`, returning a new `DateTime`.

- ✦ `AddMilliseconds`: Pass a floating-point number. This one gets confusing; if you use decimals you end up with a portion of milliseconds in ticks, where one millisecond is equivalent to 10,000 ticks. For example, if you pass 1.5 to the `AddMilliseconds` function, you'll get back a time 1 millisecond and 5,000 ticks later.

- ✦ `AddMonths`: This function takes a whole number only (that is, an integer). Apparently Microsoft didn't want to deal with the headache of figuring fractions of months since the months are different sizes! (I don't blame them!)

+ `AddSeconds`: Pass a floating-point number. For fractions of a second, remember that 1,000 milliseconds is one second. Thus, 1.5 seconds from now is 1 second and 500 milliseconds later.

+ `AddTicks`: Pass a whole number, an integer. Fractions of ticks don't really have much meaning to the computer, since a tick is the smallest portion of time the computer understands.

+ `AddYears`: Pass a whole number, an integer. Like the `AddMonths` method, Microsoft understandably didn't want to have to deal with fractions of years.

As you can see, these functions are easy to use, but not as flexible as using the `Add` and `Subtract` functions. If you're just adding a number of days, for example, the `AddDays` function is easier than trying to create a `TimeSpan` structure and using the `Add` function. If you're trying to add years, you're pretty much forced to use the `AddYears` function, as the length of a year varies depending on whether the year is a leap year or not. (Additionally, occasionally we have leap seconds!)

These specialized `Add` functions can take as a parameter either a positive value, meaning time in the future from the original date and time, or a negative value, meaning a time preceding the original date and time. (Thus, passing –10 to `AddDays` means "ten days before the date and time.")

Listing 2-3 demonstrates several examples of the `Add`, `Subtract`, and specialized `Add` functions.

Listing 2-3:   Adding and Subtracting dates and times (VB)

```
<%@ Page Language="VB" %>
<!DOCTYPE html PUBLIC "-//W3C//DTD XHTML 1.0 Transitional//EN"
"http://www.w3.org/TR/xhtml1/DTD/xhtml1-transitional.dtd">
<script runat="server">
    Sub DemoDateTimeCalc()
        Dim dt As DateTime
        ' Two minutes from now
        Response.Write("Two minutes from now is ")
        dt = Now.Add(New TimeSpan(0, 2, 0))
        Response.Write(dt)
        Response.Write("<br>")
        ' Two days, fourteen hours, three minutes ago
        Response.Write("Two days, fourteen hours, three minutes ago was ")
        dt = Now.Subtract(New TimeSpan(2, 14, 3, 0))
        Response.Write(dt)
        Response.Write("<br>")
        ' Three weeks, two days, two hours after July 4, 2010 at 11:05 am.
        ' Three weeks and two days is 23 days.
        dt = New DateTime(2010, 7, 4, 11, 5, 0)
        Response.Write("Three weeks, two days, two hours after ")
        Response.Write("July 4, 2010 at 11:05 am is ")
        dt = dt.Add(New TimeSpan(23, 2, 0, 0))
        Response.Write(dt)
        Response.Write("<br>")
```

```
            ' The time span between
            ' July 4, 2010 11:05 am and
            ' July 20, 2000 8:07 pm (8:07 pm is 20:07)
            dt = New DateTime(2010, 7, 4, 11, 5, 0)
            Dim dt2 As New DateTime(2000, 7, 20, 20, 7, 0)
            Response.Write("The time span between ")
            Response.Write(" July 4, 2010 11:05 am and ")
            Response.Write(" July 20, 2000 8:07 pm is ")
            Dim ts As TimeSpan
            ts = dt.Subtract(dt2)
            Response.Write(ts)
            Response.Write("<br>")
            ' Some specialized functions
            ' One year before July 4, 2010 at 11:05 am
            dt = New DateTime(2010, 7, 4, 11, 5, 0)
            Response.Write("One year before July 4, 2010 11:05 am is ")
            dt = dt.AddYears(-1)
            Response.Write(dt)
            Response.Write("<br>")
            ' Six minutes after July 4, 2010 at 11:05 am.
            dt = New DateTime(2010, 7, 4, 11, 5, 0)
            Response.Write("Six minutes after July 4, 2010 11:05 am is ")
            dt = dt.AddMinutes(6)
            Response.Write(dt)
            Response.Write("<br>")
        End Sub
</script>
<html xmlns="http://www.w3.org/1999/xhtml" >
<head runat="server">
    <title>Untitled Page</title>
</head>
<body>
    <form id="form1" runat="server">
    <div>
        <%
            DemoDateTimeCalc()
        %>
    </div>
    </form>
</body>
</html>
```

In this code, I provide a `DemoDateTimeCalc` function that does all the work. First, I declare a `DateTime` structure that I use throughout. Then I demonstrate the concept of *two minutes from now*. To do so, I start with the results of the `Now` function; then I need to create a `TimeSpan` structure, using the constructor that takes three parameters, hours, minutes, then seconds. To specify two minutes, I simply pass 2 for the middle paramter, and 0 for the others.

I then call `Add`, all in the same line of code. The result is a new `DateTime` structure, which I store back in the `dt` variable. Then I print out the results.

Next I demo *two days, fourteen hours, three minutes ago*. To do so, I start with the results of `Now`; then I use the form of the `TimeSpan` constructor that takes four parameters. The first parameter is the number of days, so I pass 2. Next comes hours; I pass 14. Then comes minutes; I pass 3. The final parameter is seconds, to which I pass 0. In this case, I call the `Subtract` function; I then print out the results.

Next comes the demo of *Three weeks, two days, two hours after July 4, 2010 at 11:05 am*. For this, I start with my `dt` variable, filling it with the given date in 2010. Then I create a `TimeSpan` structure, using the four-parameter constructor. The first parameter is days, so I pass 23 to represent three weeks and two days. I pass 2 for the hours, 0 for the minutes, and 0 for the seconds parameter. I pass the `TimeSpan` structure to `Add`, and print out the results.

The next example shows how to do the time span between two `DateTime` structures. For this example, I need to create two `DateTime` structures to hold the two dates. I then take the later of the two dates, calling its `Subtract` function, passing the earlier date. I get back a `TimeSpan` structure, which I then write out.

Before moving on, however, I need to say a few words about printing out a `TimeSpan` structure. Take a look at the output here:

```
3635.14:58:00
```

This number translates to 3,635 days, 14 hours, 58 minutes, and 0 seconds.

The following two examples demonstrate how to use the specialized `Add` functions. The first example simply calls `AddYears(-1)` to find one year ago from the given date. The second example calls `AddMinutes(6)` to calculate six minutes later from the given date.

Here's the output from the code:

```
Two minutes from now is 3/14/2006 10:07:35 PM
Two days, fourteen hours, three minutes ago was 3/12/2006 8:02:35 AM
Three weeks, two days, two hours after July 4, 2010 at 11:05 am
    is 7/27/2010 1:05:00 PM
The time span between July 4, 2010 11:05 am and July 20, 2000 8:07 pm
    is 3635.14:58:00
One year before July 4, 2010 11:05 am is 7/4/2009 11:05:00 AM
Six minutes after July 4, 2010 11:05 am is 7/4/2010 11:11:00 AM
```

Parsing a Date-Time String

When you have a Web page and you want to allow users to enter a date, a really nice touch is to allow flexibility on the format of the date. The `DateTime` structure includes some handy functions for parsing a string for a date and time. The functions are extremely flexible, allowing for a wide variety of formats. The functions are

✦ `Parse:` This function attempts to parse the string based on one of many different formats. If the string cannot be parsed, .NET throws an exception.

✦ `ParseExact:` This function attempts to parse the string only for a particular format that you specify. Again, if the string cannot be parsed, you'll get an exception.

✦ `TryParse:` This function works just like `Parse`, except it doesn't throw an exception. Instead, the function returns a `Boolean` value of `True` if the parse succeeds, and `False` otherwise.

✦ `TryParseExact:` Like `TryParse`, this function doesn't throw an exception; instead, it returns `true` if the parse succeeds. Also (as with `ParseExact`), you specify the particular format for the string being parsed.

Listing 2-4 demonstrates the `Parse` function:

Listing 2-4:   Parsing strings for dates and times (VB)

```
<%@ Page Language="VB" %>
<!DOCTYPE html PUBLIC "-//W3C//DTD XHTML 1.0 Transitional//EN"
"http://www.w3.org/TR/xhtml1/DTD/xhtml1-transitional.dtd">
<script runat="server">
    Sub DemoParse()
        Dim dt As DateTime
        dt = DateTime.Parse("July 4, 2010")
        Response.Write(dt)
        Response.Write("<br>")
        dt = DateTime.Parse("July 4, 2010 8:00 AM")
        Response.Write(dt)
        Response.Write("<br>")
        dt = DateTime.Parse("1 Jan 2000 23:00:00")
        Response.Write(dt)
        Response.Write("<br>")
    End Sub
</script>
<html xmlns="http://www.w3.org/1999/xhtml" >
<head runat="server">
    <title>Untitled Page</title>
</head>
<body>
    <form id="form1" runat="server">
    <div>
        <%
            DemoParse()
        %>
    </div>
    </form>
</body>
</html>
```

This code is somewhat contrived, as I'm hard-coding date and time strings that I *know* will pass the `Parse` without throwing an exception. Not (really) cheating, just an illustrating.

Here are the results you see in the browser when you run this code:

```
7/4/2010 12:00:00 AM
7/4/2010 8:00:00 AM
1/1/2000 11:00:00 PM
```

As you can see, the dates and times were correctly read. When I printed them, the format reverted to the default for the DateTime structure.

But what if you pass a string that cannot be parsed? The Parse function throws an exception, which you'll see when it shows up in your browser:

```
The string was not recognized as a valid DateTime.
There is a unknown word starting at index 0.
```

As I mentioned, the preceding example was rather contrived; a real example would let the users enter a date and time. Listing 2-5 gets real (okay, a bit more real); it's an example that uses TryParse to avoid throwing an exception.

Listing 2-5:   Parsing (almost) any string for a date and time (VB)

```vb
<%@ Page Language="VB" %>
<!DOCTYPE html PUBLIC "-//W3C//DTD XHTML 1.0 Transitional//EN"
"http://www.w3.org/TR/xhtml1/DTD/xhtml1-transitional.dtd">
<html xmlns="http://www.w3.org/1999/xhtml" >
<head runat="server">
    <title>Untitled Page</title>
</head>
<body>
    <form id="form1" runat="server">
    <div>
        <%
            Dim finished As Boolean = False
            If IsPostBack Then
                Dim dt As DateTime
                If DateTime.TryParse(TextBox1.Text, dt) Then
                    Response.Write(dt)
                    finished = True
                Else
                    Response.Write( _
                    "Sorry, I was unable to parse that date/time.<br>")
                End If
        %>
        <%
            End If
            If Not finished Then
        %>
            Please enter your favorite date and time:
        <asp:TextBox ID="TextBox1" runat="server" />
        <asp:Button ID="Button1" runat="server" Text="Button" />
        <%
            End if
        %>
    </div>
```

```
    </form>
</body>
</html>
```

This example lets the user enter in a date and time, which is then passed to `TryParse`. If the `TryParse` call succeeds, the page prints out the resulting date and time. If the call fails, then the page prints out a message that says so, and allows the user to try again. Figure 2-4 shows the form when it first opens; Figure 2-5 shows what happens if you enter in a string that cannot be parsed.

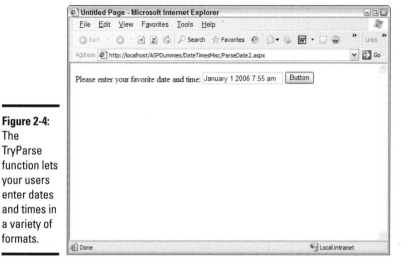

**Book VII
Chapter 2**

Manipulating Dates
and Times

Figure 2-4:
The
TryParse
function lets
your users
enter dates
and times in
a variety of
formats.

Figure 2-5:
If you enter
an invalid
string, you
see an error
message.

Now in terms of usability, I feel obligated to mention that this example does present a slight problem. If I encountered a Web page such as this, I'd be a bit unsure of what I'm supposed to enter — rarely have I seen a Web site where you can enter dates in pretty much any legitimate format you can think of. Also, I'd wonder why there isn't a `Calendar` control available so I can choose a date — and why there's just a text box. Thus, as a designer of the Web page, I'd probably want to add a note to the Web page describing what the user is supposed to enter, and I'd even provide some examples. Or (better yet) I'd use a `Calendar` control to let the user pick a date. (For information about using `Calendar` controls, see Book 2, Chapter 4.)

Chapter 3: Storing Objects in Specialized Collections

In This Chapter

✔ **Looping through a collection**

✔ **Storing data in the ArrayList class**

✔ **Associating data with a Hashtable**

✔ **Stacking and queuing your data**

✔ **Storing collections of strings**

✔ **Sorting associations with an OrderedDictionary**

A collection is a common name for a class that lets you store instances of other classes. Collections vary in design; some let you store only instances of a particular class; others let you store instances of any class. Some collections hold what are called *associations*, where each item in the collection associates groups of two objects, such as cars and colors.

If you're familiar with arrays in .NET programming, then you're already familiar with collections. As with arrays, the collection classes in .NET let you put items in the collection, find out what's in the collection, and iterate through the collection. (The word *iterate* simply means loop through the collection again and again, discovering individual elements one by one.)

One of the limitations of .NET collection classes is that they are not type-specific. In other words, they can hold objects of any class. Version 2.0 of the .NET Framework introduces a new type of collection called a *generic* collection, which can be type-specific. In this chapter, I introduce you to plain-vanilla collections (that is, *non-generic* collections). Then, in Chapter 4 of this mini-book, you'll learn how to use type-specific generic collections.

Iterating Through a Collection

When you loop through all the objects in a collection, the technical term is that you are *iterating* through the collection. The .NET Framework offers various ways to iterate through the different collections:

✦ **For loop with an index:** Using this method, you use a `For` loop with an integer that counts from 0 to one less than the number of items in the list. (Note, however, that this method isn't available for all collections.)

✦ **For each loop:** This is probably the easiest way to iterate through a collection; you use a construct that's built into the C# and VB.NET languages — and specifically designed to iterate through collections.

✦ `IEnumerator` **object:** Each collection includes a separate class that includes the methods defined by an interface called `IEnumerator`, which provides a set of enumeration methods. These `IEnumerator` classes let you step through the elements of collection.

The `For Each` construct makes use of the `IEnumerator` objects. Part of the reason Microsoft gave us the `For Each` construct is so we don't have to directly work with the `Enumerator` object. However, the `IEnumerator` class provides a `Reset` function that lets you back up and start over with the iteration if necessary; it's more flexible than the `For Each` statement.

To demonstrate the three types of iteration, I need to first briefly introduce you to one of the classes I describe in more detail later in this chapter in the section "Using the ArrayList Class." The `ArrayList` class is an extremely easy class to use — it operates much like an array, but provides more flexibility than a simple array.

Listing 3-1 and 3-2 show the code-behind files for the VB.NET and the C# versions of a page that demonstrates the three methods of iterating through a collection. As you can see, both of these files include a `Page_Load` method that creates a collection object and uses various techniques to iterate the collection and write its contents to the page.

All the code listings that are used in this book are available for download at www.dummies.com/go/aspnetaiofd.

Listing 3-1: DemoEnumerator.aspx.vb (VB)

```
Partial Class DemoEnumerator
    Inherits System.Web.UI.Page
    Protected Sub Page_Load(ByVal sender As Object, _
            ByVal e As System.EventArgs) _
            Handles Me.Load
        Dim al As New ArrayList
        al.Add(10)
        al.Add(15)
        al.Add("hello")
        al.Add(20)
        al.Add("goodbye")
        ' Iterate using a for loop
```

```vbnet
        Dim index As Int32
        For index = 0 To al.Count - 1
            Response.Write(al(index))
            Response.Write("<br>")
        Next
        Response.Write("<br>")
        ' Iterate using a for-each loop
        Dim obj As Object
        For Each obj In al
            Response.Write(obj.ToString)
            Response.Write("<br>")
        Next
        Response.Write("<br>")
        ' Iterate using the IEnumerator interface
        Dim en As IEnumerator
        en = al.GetEnumerator
        While en.MoveNext
            obj = en.Current
            Response.Write(obj.ToString)
            Response.Write("<br>")
        End While
    End Sub
End Class
```

Listing 3-2:   DemoEnumeratorCS.aspx (C#)

```csharp
using System;
using System.Collections;
public partial class DemoEnumerator2 : System.Web.UI.Page
{
    protected void Page_Load(object sender, EventArgs e)
    {
        ArrayList al = new ArrayList();
        al.Add(10);
        al.Add(15);
        al.Add("hello");
        al.Add(20);
        al.Add("goodbye");
        // Iterate using a for loop
        Int32 index;
        for (index = 0; index <= al.Count - 1; index++)
        {
            Response.Write(al[index]);
            Response.Write("<br>");
        }
        Response.Write("<br>");
        // Iterate using a for-each loop
        foreach (Object obj in al)
        {
            Response.Write(obj.ToString());
```

(continued)

Listing 3-2: *(continued)*

```
        Response.Write("<br>");
    }
    Response.Write("<br>");
    // Iterate using the IEnumerator interface
    IEnumerator en;
    en = al.GetEnumerator();
    Object o;
    while (en.MoveNext())
    {
        o = en.Current;
        Response.Write(o.ToString());
        Response.Write("<br>");
    }
}
}
```

The `Page_Load` method in both listings 3-1 and 3-2 creates a new `ArrayList` instance and adds several items to the instance.

Next, the code demonstrates how to iterate through the `ArrayList` collection using a `For` loop. You can see how I created an `Int32` variable that serves as the index for the loop. Next is the loop itself. The loop goes from 0 to one less than the number of items in the collection. (Arrays and collections in .NET start with 0 as the index — thus the maximum number is one less than the total number of items in the collection.)

With each iteration of the loop, I write out the item in the loop. To access the item, I use a syntax similar to that of arrays. Here's the VB.NET version:

```
Response.Write(al(index))
```

The individual item is specified with `(al(index))`.

For C#, you use square brackets instead of parentheses:

```
Response.Write(al[index]);
```

In both the VB and C# versions, I then write out a `<br>` tag to start a new line in the Web browser. After finishing the first loop, I begin iterating through the collection, using the `For Each` construct. In the VB.NET version (Listing 3-1), the first thing I do is declare an `Object` instance that gets the value of each item in the collection through each step of the iteration. In the C# version (Listing 3-2), you can't declare the iterator variable used by `foreach` prior to the `foreach` statement. Instead, you declare the iterator variable right inside the `foreach` statement, like so:

```
foreach (Object obj in al)
```

Notice also that if you're using VB.NET, you use two separate, initial-capped words: For Each. If you're using C#, you use a single, lowercased word without a space, foreach. In VB.NET, the For Each construct is incredibly easy to use: After you set up the iteration with the For Each call, the elements of the collection simply get stored in the variable specified in the For Each statement.

Using the ArrayList Class

The ArrayList class is an incredibly useful class that simply stores things; it's a "no-frills" storage class. However, it's more useful than just a regular old array because you can store anything you want in it. It provides methods for adding to the container, and other methods such as those for accessing the items.

Take a look at the following VB code; it demonstrates a basic usage of the ArrayList class.

```
Class SomeClass
    Dim X As Int32
    Dim Y As Int32
    Public Sub New(ByVal AX As Int32, ByVal AY As Int32)
        X = AX
        Y = AY
    End Sub
    Public Overrides Function ToString() As String
        Return String.Format("({0},{1})", X, Y)
    End Function
End Class
Sub ArrayListDemo()
    Dim al As New ArrayList
    al.Add(1)
    al.Add("Hello")
    al.Add(New SomeClass(10, 20))
    Dim obj As Object
    For Each obj In al
        Response.Write(obj.ToString)
        Response.Write("<br>")
    Next
    Response.Write("<br><br>")
    Dim index As Integer
    For index = 0 To al.Count - 1
        obj = al(index)
        Response.Write(obj.ToString)
        Response.Write("<br>")
    Next
End Sub
```

You can see in this example code that I created my own class called `SomeClass`, which does very little other than store a couple members. But I also include a constructor method as well as a `ToString` method that returns a string representation of the class.

In the `ArrayListDemo` function, I show you how to use the `ArrayList` container class. First I create a new instance of `ArrayList`; then the next three lines add data to the collection. You can see the form of the `Add` method; I simply pass the object I'm putting into the collection. The third `Add` line is the most interesting in that I add a new instance of my own `SomeClass` class.

Next I show two ways to iterate through the list, as described in the section "Iterating Through a Collection," earlier in this chapter. The first approach uses the `For Each` construct, while the second approach uses a loop that goes through the indexes of the array.

Inside each loop, I write out the `obj` variable to the Web page. Doing so brings up an interesting point: Can I write just *any* object to the page? The answer is yes. When you write out an object, regardless of type, the .NET Framework simply calls the object's `ToString` method to get back a string representation of the object. `ToString` is a member of the base `Object` class, so you can be assured you'll always get *something* back in string form. However, with your own classes, the default `ToString` method inherited from `Object` simply returns the name of the class. That's pretty boring, so (as you can see in the preceding code) I included a `ToString` method in the `SomeClass` class. The `ToString` method returns a formatted string that shows the members of the `SomeClass` instance.

Sorting a list

If you put a bunch of integers into an array, you can picture in your mind how you would sort the items in the array; one way would be to simply put them in the order of the numbers. If you put these numbers in an array

```
52, 64, 16, 65, 67, 13, 1, 5, 99
```

then the sorted numbers would look like this:

```
1, 5, 13, 16, 52, 64, 65, 67, 99
```

If you put these numbers in an `ArrayList`, you can simply sort the `ArrayList` by using the method called `Sort`, like so:

```
al.Sort()
```

But what if you put objects other than integers in your list? What if you put instances of your own class, SomeClass? In that case, you need to provide the .NET Framework with a way of sorting your instances. The way you do that is by adding a line to your class declaration, stating that your class implements the System.IComparable interface, which is an interface that includes a CompareTo function. Next, you provide the CompareTo that returns an integer value.

But what integer value do you return? When you compare two integers, for example, there are three possible results of the comparison:

+ **Less than:** The first is less than the second.

+ **Equals:** The two numbers are the same.

+ **Greater than:** The first is greater than the second.

In terms of objects, however, you don't just think of a first and second object that you're comparing; instead, you *ask an object to compare itself to another object.* In the world of integers, that means you don't just compare 3 and 7. Instead, you might ask 3 to compare itself to 7, or you might ask 7 to compare itself to 3. If you do the former — ask 3 to compare itself to 7 — then you're asking *Are you less than 7, are you equal to 7, or are you greater than 7?*

To make this comparison concept work, the .NET Framework requires that the object answer the three comparison questions — less than? equal to? greater than? In effect, you're asking a single question of the object you're comparing: *How do you compare to the other object?* Here's how you want the object to answer:

+ **If I am less than the object, then I return a negative number**

+ **If I am equal to the object, then I return 0**

+ **If I am greater than the object, then I return a positive number**

This question is answered by the CompareTo function, which you add to your class; in other words, your CompareTo function returns an integer. As for which negative number and which positive number, it doesn't really matter — although most people usually choose to return –1 for the negative number, and 1 for the positive number.

Take a look at the following VB code; you can see how I included a CompareTo function in my SortableClass class (which is really the same as the Some Class class that I use throughout this chapter):

```
Class SortableClass
    Implements System.IComparable

    Public X As Int32
```

```
        Public Y As Int32
        Public Function CompareTo(ByVal obj As Object) _
        As Integer Implements System.IComparable.CompareTo
            If TypeOf obj Is SortableClass Then
                Dim objSC As SortableClass
                objSC = CType(obj, SortableClass)
                If X = objSC.X Then
                    Return Y.CompareTo(objSC.Y)
                End If
                Return X.CompareTo(objSC.X)
            Else
                Return 0
            End If
        End Function
        Public Sub New(ByVal AX As Int32, ByVal AY As Int32)
            X = AX
            Y = AY
        End Sub
        Public Overrides Function ToString() As String
            Return String.Format("({0},{1})", X, Y)
        End Function
    End Class
    Sub ArrayListDemo2()
        Dim al As New ArrayList
        al.Add(New SortableClass(10, 5))
        al.Add(New SortableClass(5, 6))
        al.Add(New SortableClass(5, 4))
        al.Add(New SortableClass(5, 3))
        al.Add(New SortableClass(15, 4))
        al.Sort()
        Dim index As Integer
        Dim obj As Object
        For index = 0 To al.Count - 1
            obj = al(index)
            Response.Write(obj.ToString)
            Response.Write("<br>")
        Next
    End Sub
```

In the `CompareTo` function, I simply compare the values of the `X` members of the objects. But since those are just integers, I make use of the `Int32` object's own `CompareTo` function, simply returning its value. That saves me the trouble of doing the comparison manually. But if the two `X` members are equal, then I look to the `Y` value and compare it instead.

In the `ArrayListDemo2` method, I then put a bunch of `SortableClass` instances in the `ArrayList` collection, and then call its `Sort` method. Here's the results that appear in the browser when I run the code:

```
(5,3)
(5,4)
```

```
(5,6)
(10,5)
(15,4)
```

The first three items all have a 5 for the X member and so I continue sorting
them by their second value, the Y member. Of course, I could use any algorithm I wanted to do the comparison — but I felt this one was natural. In
your own work, software requirements might demand that you to come up
with a different sorting algorithm.

Comparing different types

If you look at my SortableClass method, you'll notice that it only compares
itself against other SortableClass instances. But that situation begs the
question: What if you put objects of *other* types in the collection? What if you
have SortableClass instances as well as Integers in a single ArrayList —
and you try to sort it?

The answer is you have to write a more general-purpose sorting routine. When
you do so, you put it in a class of your own that implements the IComparer
interface and includes a function called Compare. The Compare function that
you write takes two objects as a parameter — and you use whatever algorithm
you need to compare them. The following VB code is an example:

**Book VII
Chapter 3**

**Storing Objects
in Specialized
Collections**

```
Class SortableClass
    Implements System.IComparable

    Public X As Int32
    Public Y As Int32
    Public Function CompareTo(ByVal obj As Object) _
    As Integer Implements System.IComparable.CompareTo
        If TypeOf obj Is SortableClass Then
            Dim objSC As SortableClass
            objSC = CType(obj, SortableClass)
            If X = objSC.X Then
                Return Y.CompareTo(objSC.Y)
            End If
            Return X.CompareTo(objSC.X)
        ElseIf TypeOf obj Is Int32 Then
            Dim objInt As Int32
            objInt = CType(obj, Int32)
            If X < objInt Then
                Return -1
            Else
                Return 1
            End If
        End If
    End Function
    Public Sub New(ByVal AX As Int32, ByVal AY As Int32)
        X = AX
```

```
            Y = AY
        End Sub
        Public Overrides Function ToString() As String
            Return String.Format("({0},{1})", X, Y)
        End Function
    End Class
    Sub ArrayListDemo2()
        Dim al As New ArrayList
        al.Add(New SortableClass(10, 5))
        al.Add(New SortableClass(5, 6))
        al.Add(New SortableClass(5, 4))
        al.Add(New SortableClass(5, 3))
        al.Add(4)
        al.Add(5)
        al.Add(7)
        al.Add(New SortableClass(15, 4))
        al.Sort(New CustomCompare)
        Dim index As Integer
        Dim obj As Object
        For index = 0 To al.Count - 1
            obj = al(index)
            Response.Write(obj.ToString)
            Response.Write("<br>")
        Next
    End Sub
    Class CustomCompare
        Implements IComparer
        Public Function Compare(ByVal x As Object, _
        ByVal y As Object) As Integer Implements _
        System.Collections.IComparer.Compare

            If TypeOf x Is SortableClass Then
                Return CType(x, SortableClass).CompareTo(y)
            ElseIf TypeOf y Is SortableClass Then
                Return 0 - CType(y, SortableClass).CompareTo(x)
            ElseIf TypeOf x Is Int32 And TypeOf y Is Int32 Then
                Return CType(x, Int32).CompareTo(y)
            Else
                Return 0
            End If
        End Function
    End Class
```

In the `SortableClass` class, I updated the `CompareTo` function to allow it to compare supplied values to an integer (or at least the `Int32` type). To do so, I simply compare the `X` member of the `SortableClass` to the value of the integer. If the `X` value is less than the integer, I return a –1, meaning "less than." Otherwise I return a positive 1. (That means even if the two are equal, I still return a positive 1. That way the integers will always be less than the `SortableClass` instances, meaning the integers will appear first in the sorted list. I didn't have to do it that way; I could do anything I want, but I wanted to add a little mental exercise to this example.)

Now look at the `CustomCompare` class. This is really just a class that includes a single function, `Compare`. The function simply checks the types of the objects coming in. If the object on the left is an instance of `Sortable Class`, the function calls the `SortableClass` object's `CompareTo` function. Otherwise, if the right object is an instance `SortableClass`, I call that object's `CompareTo` function. But notice what I had to do in that case: I had to subtract the result form 0. Why did I do that? Because I'm comparing the objects backwards from what the `Compare` function is supposed to do; I'm calling the `CompareTo` object on the right-hand object — thus the "less-than" and "greater-than" result is reversed from what it should be. To remedy the situation, I flip the sign of the result by subtracting the result from 0.

Finally, if both objects are integers, I call the `CompareTo` function on the first integer, passing the second. Result: I can compare integers, `SortableClass` instances, or any combination thereof.

When you run the code, you see this output:

```
4
5
(5,3)
(5,4)
(5,6)
7
(10,5)
(15,4)
```

Notice that the 5 comes before the three `SortableClass` instances that have 5 in the first element. That happens because I made sure that if an integer had the same value as the X value of a `SortableClass` instance, the integer would always have a less-than value — thus the integer would appear first in the list.

Using the Hashtable Class

The `Hashtable` class is perhaps one of the most useful data structures in the .NET Framework, even if the name is quite unusual. (If you've worked in other languages, you might know a type called `map`. The `Hashtable` in .NET is the same as a `map` in other languages.)

A `Hashtable` instance lets you associate data. For example, if you want to store a list of names and associate a salary with each name, you can use a `Hashtable`. Or, if you want to store a list of vehicle ID numbers — and associate each with the color of the car — you can use a `Hashtable`.

Following is some VB code that demonstrates putting a list of car IDs into a `Hashtable` and associating a color with each:

```
Dim cars As New Hashtable
cars("6789Q345254") = "green"
cars("35T893W2A21") = "red"
cars("T9U3W8OQQ53") = "blue"
cars("T5WQY374833") = "blue"
Response.Write("The car 6789Q345254 is ")
Response.Write(cars("6789Q345254"))
```

The first line of this code creates a new `Hashtable` instance. The next four lines put some data into the `Hashtable` instance. You can see the general format for inserting the data: You type the name of the `Hashtable`, followed by a *key* surrounded by parentheses. In this example, the keys are strings (and are supposed to be vehicle ID numbers, even though I made them shorter than real vehicle ID numbers) — but you can use any type you want for the keys.

Next comes the equal sign, followed by the value you want to associate with the key. Again, in this case, I'm using strings, but you're free to use any type. You can see then that I'm associating the value `"green"` with the ID `"6789Q345254"` using this line:

```
cars("6789Q345254") = "green"
```

Do you notice anything familiar with the `Hashtable`? The `Hashtable` works very much like an array — except instead of having to use only integers for the index, you can use any type you want. (Oh, yes — instead of the term *index*, which is associated with a `Hashtable`, the term is *key*.)

To access the values in the `Hashtable`, you again put your key inside parentheses, just like you would with an array. Here's an example line from the preceding code:

```
Response.Write(cars("6789Q345254"))
```

This code writes out the value for the key `"6789Q345254"` (which you can see is `"green"`).

Each element in a `Hashtable` instance has a unique key. No two elements can share the same key. However, two elements can share the same value. Think of the car example: Two cars won't share the same vehicle ID number, but two cars can have the same color. Knowing that keys are unique, you can probably realize how to change the value in a key: Just reassign it. Suppose you have the following code (notice that the keys are the same in these two lines):

```
cars("T5WQY374833") = "blue"
cars("T5WQY374833") = "red"
```

The first line associates the string `"blue"` with a given car. Then the next line associates the string `"red"` with the very same car. So which one wins out? The most recent one. The second line simply replaced the old color (blue) with the new color (red) — that is, by changing the value to the string `"red"`.

One way to understand the `Hashtable` class — and to recognize when you might need it — is to think of the class as just an array whose indexes are types that don't have to be integers.

The VB code in Listing 3-3 demonstrates that you can use any type, — not just integers — for the keys. The code then shows how to iterate through all the elements in the `Hashtable` instance. (You can put this code in a `Page_Load` event to try it out.)

Listing 3-3:   Iterating through a Hashtable instance (VB)

```
Dim ht As New Hashtable
ht("a") = 1
ht(5) = "hello"
ht("goodbye") = "everybody"
ht("now") = DateTime.Now
ht(DateTime.Now) = "time"
Dim value As Object
value = ht("goodbye")
Response.Write("My entry has value ")
Response.Write(value)
Response.Write("<br><br>")
Dim entry As DictionaryEntry
For Each entry In ht
    Response.Write(entry.Key)
    Response.Write(":")
    Response.Write(entry.Value)
    Response.Write("<br>")
Next
```

The first line creates the `Hashtable` instance. The next line stores a 1 in the table at key `"a"` — which is, of course, a string. The third line does the opposite — it stores a string with a key that's an integer. The fourth line demonstrates storing a string with a key that's also a string. Then the next two lines show that you can even use other types; these two lines, for example, use a `DateTime` structure — first as a value, then as a key.

Next the code demonstrates how to iterate through a `Hashtable`. You can see how this is done: I created an instance of the type `DictionaryEntry`. In a `Hashtable`, you're associating keys with values; together a key and value are stored as a single instance of a class called `DictionaryEntry`.

**Book VII
Chapter 3**

Storing Objects
in Specialized
Collections

To iterate through the entries in the `Hashtable`, use a `For Each` loop in VB.NET, or a `foreach` in C#. Each iteration gives you a `DictionaryEntry` instance. The instance has a `Key` member and a `Value` member, which you use to access (you guessed it) the key and value of the item.

Bear in mind that there's no built-in order to a `Hashtable`, which makes it different from an array. (An array is ordered by its *indexes,* which are integers starting at 0.) Thus you can't rely on any particular order to apply automatically to `Hashtable` entries. In this case, imposing order is a do-it-yourself proposition.

Following are some properties and methods you can use for manipulating `Hashtable` collections.

+ `Count`: As you can probably imagine, this property tells you how many elements are in the `Hashtable` instance.

+ `Add`: This method adds elements to the `Hashtable`. If you have a `Hashtable` instance called `cars` and you want to add an element, you can add an item directly — like so —

  ```
  cars("6789Q345254") = "green"
  ```

  or you can use the `Add` method to accomplish the same thing:

  ```
  cars.Add("6789Q345254", "green ")
  ```

+ `Clear`: Call this method to empty out the `Hashtable`, removing all elements.

+ `Contains`, `ContainsKey`, `ContainsValue`: To find out whether your `Hashtable` instance contains a particular key, you can use either `Contains` or `ContainsKey`. The `Contains` method and `ContainsKey` method are actually the same. For either one, you pass the key you're looking for. Or you can find out whether your `Hashtable` instance contains a particular value. To do so, call `ContainsValue`.

+ `Remove`: Call this to remove an element. Pass the key of the element you want to remove. The following example removes the car with ID `"6789Q345254"` from the list:

  ```
  cars.Remove("6789Q345254")
  ```

If you try to remove an element that doesn't exist by specifying a nonexistent key, nothing will happen. You won't get an error, and you won't get an exception.

Using the Stack Class

A *stack data structure* behaves like a stack of papers sitting on your desk, with the restriction that you can only add one sheet of paper at a time to the top of the stack. Further, to remove paper from the stack, you are only allowed to take a single sheet off the top at a time.

A stack has a huge number of applications in computer science. When you call a function that calls another function that in turn calls yet another function, the computer uses a `Stack` class to keep track of all those functions. When you do a bunch of activities in (for example) Microsoft Word and then choose Edit⇨Undo, the software uses a stack to keep track of the items in the Undo list.

Another way to think about a stack is the concept of *last in, first out* or LIFO (pronounced *life*-oh). A *stack* is simply a list of items that grows each time you add an item — and shrinks each time you remove an item. But when you think about the concept of a stack of paper, when you set one item on the stack and then take an item off, the one you took off is the same one you just put on; the last one on is the first one you take off. Thus comes the concept, "last in, first out." (Yes, "last *on*" would probably make more sense, but then there would be two O's and people like me would get confused.)

The following VB code demonstrates the `Stack` class (you can insert this code into an `.aspx.vb` file and call the `StackDemo` method from your `Form_Load` method):

**Book VII
Chapter 3**

Storing Objects in Specialized Collections

```
Class SomeClass
    Dim X As Int32
    Dim Y As Int32
    Public Sub New(ByVal AX As Int32, ByVal AY As Int32)
        X = AX
        Y = AY
    End Sub
    Public Overrides Function ToString() As String
        Return String.Format("({0},{1})", X, Y)
    End Function
End Class
Sub StackDemo()
    Dim st As New Stack
    Dim obj As Object
    st.Push(1)
    st.Push("Hello")
    st.Push(New SomeClass(1, 2))
    obj = st.Pop
    Response.Write(obj)
    Response.Write("<br>")
    st.Push(15)
    While st.Count > 0
        obj = st.Pop
        Response.Write(obj)
        Response.Write("<br>")
    End While
End Sub
```

The first line of the code creates the new instance of `Stack`. The second line declares an `Object` instance for use later on when the code loops through the stack.

The next three lines put some information onto the stack; you can see that the method in use is called `Push`. Notice that the information in each line is a different type. The first is an integer, the second is a string, and the third is an instance of my own class called `SomeClass`.

The next line blows the top off the stack (although not very dramatically) by calling the `Pop` method — which removes the top item from the stack, and returns the item. You can see in the code that I'm storing the returned item in the `obj` variable.

Notice also the type of variable I'm storing the item in. Since the stack can hold any type of object, I take the safe way out — and just store the item in a variable of type `Object`. (That works because `Object` is the root of all other classes.)

After popping off the top of the stack, I push another item onto the stack. Then I start working my way through the stack. The way I go through the stack is to use a loop that runs as long as there are items in the stack. In each iteration of the loop, I pop the top off and print out what I get.

Here's the output in the final Web page:

```
(1,2)
15
Hello
1
```

Take a look at the order of the output. The first item printed is `(1,2)`, which comes from the `SomeClass` instance that I pushed onto the stack. The first item I popped off the stack was the last item I put on prior to the pop, which was the `SomeClass` instance. (Remember the rule: *Last in, first out.*)

The next item I popped off the stack was the next item I put on it. Again, the last one in is the first one out. Then I didn't add anything else and just proceeded to pop items off the queue.

Using the Queue Class

A *queue data structure* is the logical equivalent of a bunch of people standing in line. Under stress-free situations, the first person in line is the first person to get served. As each new person arrives, he or she goes to the back of the line. As each person at the front of the line is served, that person leaves, and the person behind gets served. One way to look at the queue data structure is as a rule that says, *First in, first out*. If you look at a line of people, the first person in is the first person to get served and get out. (Again, I'm assuming standard operating procedures for lines — no cutting!) Here's a VB example:

```
Dim que As New Queue
Dim obj As Object
que.Enqueue(10)
que.Enqueue("standing in line")
que.Enqueue(20)
obj = que.Dequeue()
Response.Write(obj)
Response.Write("<br>")
que.Enqueue(30)
que.Enqueue("hello")
While que.Count > 0
    obj = que.Dequeue
    Response.Write(obj)
    Response.Write("<br>")
End While
```

The first line creates the Queue instance. The second line creates an Object instance that I later use to iterate through the elements of the queue. In the next three lines I add three items to the queue by using the rather oddly named Enqueue method.

Next, I pull an item out of the queue by calling the (also oddly named) Dequeue method. Since I'm putting different items into the queue, I'm just using a variable of type Object to hold the items I get out of it. The Dequeue method removes an item from the front of the queue and returns the item; I then save the item in the obj variable. Next I print out what I got out of the queue.

Next I add a couple more items to the queue — and begin looping through the queue, using a While loop that runs as long as there are items present in the queue. In each iteration of the loop, I pull the front item off the queue, save it in the obj variable, and then write out the item.

A queue is first-in-first-out structure. Thus, when I added three items and then finally pulled an item out of the queue, the item I got out was the original (first) item I put in.

Collecting Strings

In the next two sections, I cover two different ways of storing collections of strings. One, the StringCollection class, is a general-purpose collection that holds only strings. The second, the StringDictionary class, stores associations between strings.

Using the StringCollection class

The StringCollection class is a handy class for storing strings. It includes methods for adding a single string or a group of strings. It also includes various methods such as those for removing strings and finding strings. The following VB code is a quick demonstration of the StringCollection class.

```
Dim sc As New StringCollection
sc.Add("abc")
sc.Add("ghi")
sc.Add("jkl")
Dim stringarray() As String = {"a", "b", "c"}
sc.AddRange(stringarray)
Dim item As String
For Each item In sc
    Response.Write(item)
    Response.Write("<br>")
Next
```

In this code, the first line creates an instance of StringCollection. The next three lines add some elements to the collection by simply calling the Add method.

The next line creates an array of strings, initializing the array with three strings. Then the following line adds each element of that array to the StringCollection instance. Each element of the array gets added individually to the collection; in this case, since the array has three elements, three elements are added to the StringCollection.

Using the StringDictionary class

The StringDictionary class is a specialized form of an association class that allows strings only for its keys and values. The class works much like the Hashtable class (it even has many of the same methods), except StringDictionary allows strings for *both* keys and values — and only for those. Following is a VB example of the StringDictionary class.

```
Dim sd As New StringDictionary
sd("George") = "Washington"
sd("Abraham") = "Lincoln"
Dim str As String = sd("George")
Response.Write(str)
```

You can see in this example how to add associations. You assign members much like you would an array except you use strings for the keys. Thus in the line

```
sd("Abraham") = "Lincoln"
```

the key is the string Abraham and the value is Lincoln. Next in this code, you can see how I accessed the value associated with the key "George" and saved the value in the String instance str, finally writing out the string.

Ordering Associations with the OrderedDictionary

The OrderedDictionary is much like the Hashtable class, except OrderedDictionary keeps its elements sorted according to the order in which you insert those elements. The following VB code shows how to use the OrderedDictionary class:

```
Dim od As New OrderedDictionary
od.Add("a", "b")
od.Add("abc", "xyz")
od.Add(1, 100)
od.Add("hello", 1000)
od("fivehundred") = 500
Response.Write("od(""abc"") = ")
Response.Write(od("abc"))
Response.Write("<br>od(0) = ")
Response.Write(od(0))
Response.Write("<br>")
Response.Write("All entries in order:<br>")
Dim entry As DictionaryEntry
For Each entry In od
    Response.Write(String.Format("{0} = {1}<br>", entry.Key, entry.Value))
Next
```

After creating an OrderedDictionary instance, the code adds several associations to the dictionary. Notice the code shows two different ways to add associations. The first is through the Add method, like so:

```
od.Add("a", "b")
```

The second's syntax is much like that you find with arrays:

```
od("fivehundred") = 500
```

You can also see, in the calls to Add, that I'm putting various data types in the ordered dictionary.

The `OrderedDictionary` class has some interesting quirks. If you've read the section "Using the Hashtable Class," earlier in this chapter, you're familiar with how you can replace items in the `Hashtable` class simply by setting a new value to an existing key, like so:

```
cars("T5WQY374833") = "blue"
cars("T5WQY374833") = "red"
```

In this example, `cars` is an instance of `Hashtable`. The `OrderedDictionary` performs the same way when you use the array-style syntax as these two lines of code do. However, when you use the `Add` method, the `Add` method always adds to the dictionary and never replaces existing members. Thus, the following two lines create two separate entries in the `OrderedDictionary` instance:

```
od("fivehundred") = 500
od("fivehundred") = 600
```

Since an `OrderedDictionary` instance has an order to it, you can also insert associations into the dictionary. To insert an association into an `OrderedDictionary` instance, use the `Insert` method, passing the index, the key, and the value, like so:

```
od.Insert(3, "goodbye", 10)
```

This sample line inserts the key `"goodbye"` and its value `10` in position 3.

The positions start with 0, which means position 3 is actually the fourth position.

Chapter 4: Building Strongly Typed Collections with Generic Classes

In This Chapter

✔ **Working with the generic List class**

✔ **Employing the generic LinkedList class**

✔ **Using the generic Dictionary class**

✔ **Sorting associations with the SortedDictionary**

✔ **Stacking and queuing typed data**

Starting with .NET 2.0, Microsoft gave us a new type of collection class called a *generic collection*. They call it that, anyway. But as you get acquainted with "generic" collections, you might think the name is a misnomer. After all, the idea behind those collections is to give you a way to create *specialized* containers. (Whoa! That definitely makes "generic" seem like a misnomer of the first degree.)

However, the name makes sense. Microsoft has given us mortals a set of starting points that lets us create collections that hold specific types of data, and only the specific types we tell the collection to hold. These collections are highly specialized — but their starting points are generic; you can use them to create all sorts of specialized classes. Generic starting points make highly specialized results easier to achieve; it makes sense in a warped sort of way.

To make generic collections work, however, Microsoft also had to give us something more. Microsoft has enhanced the C# and VB.NET languages by adding some syntax that goes along with the creation of the generic classes. When you create a specialized collection based on the generic classes, you specify the type of data the collection will hold. With the previous version of VB.NET and C#, no syntax existed to specify the type.

In this chapter, I cover the different generic collection classes available with .NET.

Understanding the Name Game

As you work with the generic collections, you might notice that some of the class names are the same as the collection classes that already exist in .NET, (which I cover in Chapter 3 of this mini-book) — indeed, they are named the same. But that's not a problem; these collections live in a different namespace.

You can approach the namespace difference in two different ways. First, you can use the *fully qualified names* of the classes by specifying the namespace followed by a dot and then the class name, like so:

```
System.Collections.Generic.Dictionary
```

This method works if you're using two different classes that are from different namespaces but have the same name. Otherwise, if you're not using classes that share a name, you can simply use an `Import` or `using` statement. In your `.aspx` file, you would include the following `Import` statement at the top of your file, under the line with the page directive:

```
<%@ Import Namespace="System.Collections.Generic" %>
```

If you're using a `.vb` file, put this line at the top of your file:

```
Imports System.Data.SqlClient
```

Or, if you're using C#, put this line:

```
using System.Collections.Generic;
```

Using the Generic List Class

The generic `List` class is a general-purpose class for storing items of a particular type. This class behaves much like an array — except the class is highly optimized, allowing fast access, search, and sorting of the items.

To use the generic `List` class, you create a new instance of the class, specifying the type of data the class will hold.

The following VB code demonstrates the generic `List` class:

```
Function TestWords(ByVal value As String) As Boolean
    If value(0) = "h" Then
        Return True
    Else
        Return False
    End If
End Function
Sub GenericListDemo()
```

```
        Dim mylist As New List(Of String)
        mylist.Add("hi")
        mylist.Add("goodbye")
        mylist.Add("somewhere")
        mylist.Add("nowhere")
        mylist.Add("hello")
        mylist.Add("hijkl")
        mylist.RemoveAll(New Predicate(Of String)(AddressOf TestWords))
        mylist.Reverse()
        Dim item As String
        For Each item In mylist
            Response.Write(item)
            Response.Write("<br>")
        Next
End Sub
```

The first part of this code is a function I'll talk about shortly when I discuss the `RemoveAll` method. After this function comes a subroutine that demonstrates how to use the `List` class. The first line of this subroutine creates a new instance of `List`. You can see how I use the generic syntax by specifying the words `"Of String"` inside parentheses following the name of the class. That tells the class that I want it to hold only `String` types.

Next, I add several items to the collection by calling the `Add` method. That's easy. Then I demonstrate a really cool feature of the `List` class. The `RemoveAll` function removes all items in the list that match a particular condition. To specify the condition I created a function called `TestWords`. (You can call the function whatever you want.) The function takes a single parameter of the same type as the `List` collection's items. Inside the function, I do my comparison — returning `True` if the string is one I want to remove from the list, and `False` otherwise. In this particular example, I'm testing whether the string starts with the lowercase letter `"h"`. If so, then I return `True`, meaning I want to remove the item.

In the call to `RemoveAll`, I create an instance of a class called `Predicate`, again specifying the type (again, `String`), and then in parentheses I pass the address of the function that does the testing, in this case `TestWords`.

That's all there is to the removal — and when the code runs, it removes all the strings in the list that start with `"h"`. Of course, you can make your removal function do any type of comparison you need; I just created a simple example to demonstrate the capabilities.

Next, just to try out some other features, I reversed the list by calling the `Reverse` method. Then I iterated through the list using the `For Each` syntax, writing out each element of the list, followed by an HTML <br> tag. And here's the output that you see in the browser when you run this example:

```
nowhere
somewhere
goodbye
```

Now here's the same code in C#, since the syntax of the `Predicate` class is a bit different from that of VB.NET:

```
Boolean TestWords(string value)
{
    if (value[0] == 'h')
    {
        return true;
    }
    else
    {
        return false;
    }
}
void GenericListDemo()
{
    List<string> mylist = new List<string>();
    mylist.Add("hi");
    mylist.Add("goodbye");
    mylist.Add("somewhere");
    mylist.Add("nowhere");
    mylist.Add("hello");
    mylist.Add("hijkl");
    mylist.RemoveAll(TestWords);
    foreach (string item in mylist) {
        Response.Write(item);
        Response.Write("<br>");
    }
}
```

In the C# version, everything is pretty much the same as the VB.NET version, except the call to `RemoveAll` is simpler. In C#, you don't have to create a new instance of a `Predicate` class; you just specify the comparison function in your call to `RemoveAll`. C# has a little more knowledge of addresses and pointers, and is therefore able to understand that you're passing the address of the function rather than calling the function.

The output of the C# version of the code is identical to the output of the VB.NET version.

Working with the Generic LinkedList Class

The generic `LinkedList` class is a doubly linked list. It behaves much like the generic `List` class, except each item in the `LinkedList` contains a reference to the previous item and the next item. This linked concept creates an interesting way of storing data. If you think about a simple array, consider what you must do to insert an item into the array. Suppose you have the following numbers in an array:

10 25 64 22 51 90

Now suppose you want to put the number 35 in between the numbers 25 and 64. With an array, you have to move all the numbers — starting with 64 — over one notch to open up space for the 35, like so:

10 25 _ _ 64 22 51 90

Then you can store the 35:

10 25 35 64 22 51 90

If you're dealing with huge amounts of data, this kind of moving can be time-consuming. But with a linked list, you don't need to move anything. Remember, with a linked list, each item contains a reference to the next and the previous item. Or, another way to think of each reference is that the item points to the next item *and* to the previous item, like so:

10 ↔ 25 ↔ 64 ↔ 22 ↔ 51 ↔ 90

To insert the 35 between 25 and 64, here's the drill:

1. You put the 35 somewhere in memory without moving the other items.
2. You remove the 25's pointer to 64.
3. You make the 25 point to the 35 instead, and vice versa.
4. You make the 35 point to the 64, and vice versa, as seen in Figure 7-1.

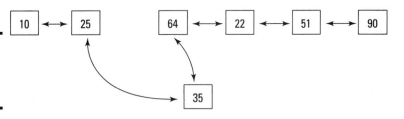

Figure 4-1:
An example
of a
LinkedList.

With the 25 now pointing to and from the 35, and with the 35 now pointing to and from the 64, the 35 is effectively inserted into the list. Even though the 35 doesn't sit in between the 25 and 64 in memory, the 35 is still inserted in the right place. Thus, conceptually, you end up with this:

10 ↔ 25 ↔ 35 ↔ 64 ↔ 22 ↔ 51 ↔ 90

See how easy it is to insert data into a linked list? That's a major advantage over an array — but linked lists come with a downside. What if you want to know what's contained in the fourth position? The only way to know that is to start at the first item, use its pointers to find the second item, and then use the second item's pointers to find the third item. Using the third item's pointers, you can finally find the fourth item. In other words, you have to climb through the list item by item to figure out what's in a particular entry.

Now think about how you would remove an item from a linked list. Suppose you want to take out the 35 that you just put in. How would you remove the 35? No problem — removing is simply the reverse of inserting: You break the pointer between 25 and 35, and the pointer between 35 and 64, and then make the 25 point to the 64, as seen in Figure 4-2.

Figure 4-2:
Removing
an item from
a LinkedList.

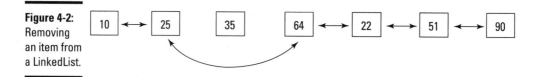

That, of course, leaves the 35 lingering in memory, and so the final step is to remove the 35 from memory.

Of course, if you're using a linked list class such as the LinkedList generic collection, then you don't have to handle all that pointing manually; the LinkedList class takes care of that for you. To insert an item in the list after a particular item, you simply call the AddAfter method, passing the item that will precede your new item, along with your new item. Or, if you prefer, you can call AddBefore — passing the item that comes after the item you're inserting, along with the actual item you want to insert. The AddAfter and AddBefore methods take care of the work of managing the pointers.

To remove an item, you just call the Remove method, passing the item you want to remove. That's pretty easy.

Now I need to mention two more things before I show you some examples. In computer science terminology, the items you put into a linked list are called *nodes*. When you insert an item into the list, you are inserting a new node into the list between two other nodes.

Second, a linked list always has a first and a last item. Usually when you're using an existing class (such as the generic LinkedList class), the class will include members for keeping track of the first and last item. In the case of the generic LinkedList class, you get two properties — First and Last — that let you access the first and last items. These two properties are vital to the linked list; if you want to access the items in the list, you need to know where to start.

Now on to the code for this example. The following VB code demonstrates how to use the LinkedList class:

```
Sub PrintLinkedList(ByVal list As LinkedList(Of Int32))
    If list.Count > 0 Then
        Dim node As LinkedListNode(Of Int32)
        node = list.First
        While Not node Is Nothing
            Response.Write(node.Value)
            Response.Write("<br>")
            node = node.Next
        End While
    End If
End Sub
Sub LinkedListDemo()
    Dim list As New LinkedList(Of Int32)
    Dim node As LinkedListNode(Of Int32)
    Dim savenode As LinkedListNode(Of Int32)
    ' Create the initial list
    node = list.AddFirst(10)
    node = list.AddAfter(node, 25)
    savenode = node
    node = list.AddAfter(node, 64)
    node = list.AddAfter(node, 22)
    node = list.AddAfter(node, 51)
    list.AddAfter(node, 90)
    Response.Write("Initial list:<br>")
    PrintLinkedList(list)
    ' Now insert an item
    list.AddAfter(savenode, 35)
    Response.Write("After insert:<br>")
    PrintLinkedList(list)
End Sub
```

This code includes two subroutines. The first one iterates through the linked list. But look at how the iteration takes place. Instead of using an indexed loop or a For Each construct, I start by grabbing the first node in the list. I print out the node's value, and then move on to the next node. How do I move on? By accessing the node's Next property, like so:

```
node = node.Next
```

The node's `Next` property points to the *next node* (thus demonstrating the linked aspect of the list!). I then loop through the printing and the grabbing of the next node until the node comes back as the value `Nothing`. Then I know I'm done.

Here's the same routine in C#:

```
void PrintLinkedList(LinkedList<Int32> list)
{
    if (list.Count > 0)
    {
        LinkedListNode<Int32> node;
        node = list.First;
        while (node != null)
        {
            Response.Write(node.Value);
            Response.Write("<br>");
            node = node.Next;
        }
    }
}
```

The second subroutine, `LinkedListDemo`, is the main part of the example. This code first creates a new instance of `LinkedList`, specifying that the list will hold integers of the type `Int32`. The next two lines declare (but don't create new instances of) `LinkedListNodes` that hold integers.

Next the code starts adding nodes to the list. Take a look at the special approach I use to add the nodes: I add the first node by calling the `AddFirst` method. This method *inserts* a new node in the first position. (I say *inserts* because if nodes already exist in the list, then the `AddFirst` will insert a new node before any existing nodes.) After adding the node, I save away the result. The result is a new instance of `LinkedListNode`. This resulting node is important! To insert a node into the list, you need to specify which node your new node will *follow* or *precede*. That means you can't lose the node.

I chose to specify which node will precede the new node. Thus, I save away the result of `AddFirst` — and then add a node after this node that I saved away, using the following line:

```
node = list.AddAfter(node, 25)
```

This code inserts the node after the specified node. The call returns the node I just inserted and I save that way again, ready to do the whole insertion process again.

But notice that I also save the node containing 25 and put it aside for later use, tucking it into another variable called `savenode`. That's for later on — when I want to put the 35 in after the 25.

But before inserting the 35, after getting all the numbers into the list, I go ahead and print out the list by calling my PrintLinkedList routine. Then I finally demonstrate inserting a number into the middle of the list:

```
list.AddAfter(savenode, 35)
```

That one line inserts a node into the middle of the list. No shifting is needed. The node goes right in, easily. Then I print out the list again to make sure it worked.

Here's the same LinkedListDemo code in C#:

```
void LinkedListDemo()
{
    LinkedList<Int32> list = new LinkedList<Int32>();
    LinkedListNode<Int32> node;
    LinkedListNode<Int32> savenode;
    node = list.AddFirst(10);
    node = list.AddAfter(node, 25);
    savenode = node;
    node = list.AddAfter(node, 64);
    node = list.AddAfter(node, 22);
    node = list.AddAfter(node, 51);
    list.AddAfter(node, 90);
    Response.Write("Initial list:<br>");
    PrintLinkedList(list);
    list.AddAfter(savenode, 35);
    Response.Write("After insert:<br>");
    PrintLinkedList(list);
}
```

Now here's the output that appears in the browser:

```
Initial list:
10
25
64
22
51
90
After insert:
10
25
35
64
22
51
90
```

To delete a node, call `Remove`, like so:

```
list.Remove(savenode)
```

Or you can specify the value to delete, like this:

```
list.Remove(25)
```

If you have multiple nodes containing the value you're deleting, only the first node will be removed. The `Remove` method returns a `Boolean` value, `True` if an item as removed, and `False` if no items matched the value. Thus, if you want to remove all nodes containing a single value, you can put the call inside the condition of a `While` statement — and leave the loop itself empty. Here's how to do it in VB:

```
While list.Remove(35)
End While
```

And here's the C# version:

```
while (list.Remove(35)) {}
```

Employing the Generic Dictionary Class

The generic `Dictionary` class is a class that lets you store associations. This class works much like the `Hashtable` class described in Chapter 3 of this mini-book, except it's a generic class for creating specialized collections (and it has a more sensible name).

Generic `Dictionary` collections hold pairs (or associations) that consist of a key and a value. The idea is that you store values based on a key. (For more information on this concept, check out Chapter 3 of this mini-book.)

The `Dictionary` class includes methods for adding and removing key/value pairs. The class also includes methods for determining if a key or value is presenting the collection.

To find out the value for a particular key, you can use syntax similar to array syntax. In VB.NET, this syntax looks like this:

```
gd("one")
```

And in C#, the syntax looks like this, using square brackets:

```
gd["one"]
```

If you try to access a key that doesn't exist, youl get a runtime exception that looks like this:

```
The given key was not present in the dictionary.
Exception Details:
System.Collections.Generic.KeyNotFoundException:
The given key was not present in the dictionary.
Source Error:
Line 17:   Dim mystr As String
Line 18:   mystr = gd("abcdef")
Source File: C:\Write\ASPDummies\ASPDummies\
GenericCollections.aspx
Line: 18
```

If you're allowing data entry and can't control whether you try to access a key that already exists, this exception message is certainly not something you'd want to appear in the browser screen. While you could use a `Try/Catch` statement, instead the `Dictionary` class includes a method called `TryGetValue`. This method fills in a variable with the value for the specified key if the key exists, and returns either `true` or `false`, noting whether the key exists. Here's an example in VB.NET:

```
Dim value As String
If gd.TryGetValue("one", value) Then
    Response.Write(value)
End If
```

The first line of this code declares the value variable as type `String`. Then the code calls `TryGetValue`, passing the key, as well as the variable to be filled in. If the call returns a `True`, the code writes out the value obtained. The same code looks like this in C#:

```
string value;
if (gd.TryGetValue("one", out value))
{
    Response.Write(value);
}
```

Now here's a complete VB example that demonstrates the generic `Dictionary` class:

```
Sub GenericDictionaryDemo()
    Dim gd As New Dictionary(Of String, String)
    gd.Add("one", "1")
    gd.Add("two", "2")
    gd("three") = "3"
    Response.Write(gd("one"))
```

```
        Response.Write(gd("three"))
        ' Uncomment this to see an exception
        Dim mystr As String
        mystr = gd("abcdef")
        Dim value As String
        If gd.TryGetValue("one", value) Then
            Response.Write(value)
        End If
End Sub
```

The first line of this sample creates a new `Dictionary` collection, specifying that the collection uses strings for its keys, and strings for its values. Thus it associates strings with strings, and *only* strings with strings.

Next, the code adds some entries to the dictionary. Notice the syntax of the first of these two lines; I'm calling `Add` and passing two strings — the first of these is the key and the second is the value. But the third line demonstrates the more traditional array-style approach for adding items. You're free to use either technique.

Although you can use either `Add` or the array-style syntax to add an item to the dictionary, note that the two differ slightly. The array-style syntax first checks if the key already exists, and if so, replaces the existing key's value with the new value you're adding. The `Add` method, however, never replaces existing keys. Instead, it checks to see whether a key already exists — if so, it throws an exception. (By definition of the `Dictionary` class, you can't have duplicate keys, so the `Add` method won't simply add another key, which would result in two identical keys.)

You can use this difference to your advantage. If you're creating a collection in which you want to overwrite existing data (as when you replace a user's phone number with a new phone number), then you can use array-style syntax without having to handle the situation that a key already exists. But if you want to make sure you're never replacing data that already exists, you can use the `Add` method along with a `Try/Catch` block. Or, if you really want to keep your code solid and robust, don't bother with a `Try/Catch` block; simply check first manually to see whether the key already exists. Here's the code that does the trick:

```
If gd.ContainsKey("one") = False Then
    gd("one") = "1"
Else
    Response.Write("Sorry, we already have that data")
End If
```

Generally speaking, you're better off checking the data manually instead of relying on a `Try/Catch` block; `Try/Catch` blocks tend to be time-consuming. Simply doing a quick check is faster — and makes for better high-performance Web sites.

Using the Generic SortedDictionary Class

The generic `SortedDictionary` class works much like the `Dictionary` class, except `SortedDictionary` keeps its associations sorted by the order specified by the keys. This means, then, that the keys have to be sortable. By default, the basic built-in types (integers and strings) in .NET are sortable. If you use instances of your own class for the keys, then you have to make your class sortable. For a discussion on how to do this, check out Chapter 3 of this mini-book.

The `SortedDictionary` is easy to use when you understand how to use dictionaries. Here's some sample VB code:

```
Sub GenericSortedDictionaryDemo()
    Dim sd As New SortedDictionary(Of Integer, String)
    sd.Add(1, "One")
    sd.Add(5, "Five")
    sd.Add(3, "Three")
    sd.Add(4, "Four")
    Dim pair As KeyValuePair(Of Integer, String)
    For Each pair In sd
        Response.Write(pair)
        Response.Write("<br>")
    Next
End Sub
```

This code creates a new instance of the `SortedDictionary` class, specifying that the instance contains `Integer` types for the keys, and `String` types for the values. Next the code adds four entries to the dictionary, and then iterates through the dictionary. Notice that each item in the dictionary is of type `KeyValuePair`.

Using the Generic Stack Class

The generic `Stack` class is a stack class that holds only data of the type you specify when you create the stack. Here's an example line of VB code in which I create a stack that holds integers of type `Int32`:

```
Dim st As New Stack(Of Int32)
```

After you've created the stack, you can add items to it by using the Push method — passing data of the type you specified when you created the stack. To get an item off the stack, use the Pop method, which removes and returns the top item from the stack. If you want to get the value that's on top of the stack, but not actually remove the value, call Peek.

The following VB code demonstrates how to use the generic Stack.

```
Sub GenericStackDemo()
    Dim st As New Stack(Of Int32)
    st.Push(10)
    st.Push(15)
    Dim x As Int32
    x = st.Pop()
    Response.Write(x)
    x = st.Peek()
    Response.Write("<br>Peeking at top...<br>")
    Response.Write(x)
    Response.Write("<br>")
    Response.Write(st)
    st.Push(1)
    st.Push(2)
    st.Push(3)
    Response.Write("<br>Iterating through the stack...<br>")
    For Each x In st
        Response.Write(x)
        Response.Write("<br>")
    Next
    Response.Write("<br>Does the stack contain 10?<br>")
    If st.Contains(10) Then
        Response.Write("...yes<br>")
    End If
End Sub
```

The first line of this code creates the Stack collection, specifying Int32 as the type. The next two lines push data onto the stack.

Next, I create a variable and pop a value off the stack, storing the value in the variable. I then write out the value just to make sure it worked.

The next few lines demonstrate the Peek method. The first line calls Peek, storing the value in the x variable. Then I print out the value of x.

Next, I push a few more values onto the stack, and then demonstrate iterating through the stack. To iterate, I use the For Each construct, one by one peeking at the values and writing them out. (Iterating through the stack doesn't actually remove anything from the stack.)

Finally, I call the `Contains` method to find out if the stack contains a particular value. The `Contains` method returns a `Boolean` value, either `True` or `False`. In this case, if the stack does contain the value, I print out a friendly message.

Working with the Generic Queue Class

The generic `Queue` class is a collection of types that you specify. The collection keeps your data in a queue structure — you push items into the front, and pull items off the back, one by one; it's much like a queue of people standing in line. (For more details on how queues work, see Chapter 3 of this mini-book.)

With the generic `Queue` class, as with all the generic classes, you specify exactly the type of data that you want to put in the queue. To manipulate the queue, you add items with the `Enqueue` method, and pull items off the end with the `Dequeue` method. If you want to look at the end of the queue without pulling the data out, use the `Peek` method.

The following VB example demonstrates these methods:

```
Sub GenericQueueDemo()
    Dim que As New Queue(Of String)
    que.Enqueue("Jim")
    que.Enqueue("Julie")
    que.Enqueue("Sal")
    que.Enqueue("Pat")
    Dim item As String
    item = que.Dequeue()
    Response.Write("First person to be served is ")
    Response.Write(item)
    que.Enqueue("Angie")
    que.Enqueue("Allison")
    item = que.Dequeue()
    Response.Write("<br>Next person served is ")
    Response.Write(item)
    Response.Write("<br>Remaining people are:<br>")
    For Each item In que
        Response.Write(item)
        Response.Write("<br>")
    Next
End Sub
```

The first line of code inside this subroutine creates a new `Queue` instance, specifying that the queue will hold `String` types. The next four lines add names to the queue. Now remember, the first person in line is the first person served, which is the idea behind a queue. You can see the first name I put in is Jim. When I start pulling names out of the queue, Jim better be the first one served — or else the queue isn't functioning right and we need to get our money back.

The next lines of code declare a `String` variable, and then pull the first name off the queue, finally writing it out. (And yes, in the final output you'll see that the first name out is indeed Jim.)

Next, two more people arrive and their names get added to the queue. I then pull another name off the queue and write it out.

Finally, I iterate through the list just to see who is still waiting. Iterating through doesn't actually remove the items from the list; I'm only looking at the names. In each iteration, I print out the name encountered.

Here's the output from this code:

```
First person to be served is Jim
Next person served is Julie
Remaining people are:Sal
Pat
Angie
Allison
```

Book VIII

Advanced ASP.NET Programming

Contents at a Glance

Chapter 1: Security: Using Login Controls

In This Chapter

✔ **Understanding authentication and authorization**

✔ **Using the Security Administration tool**

✔ **Restricting access**

✔ **Handling logins and lost passwords**

✔ **Managing users and roles programmatically**

Most of us feel uneasy about implementing Web site security, perhaps because it's hard to be 100% sure that you've got it right. Inadvertently allowing the Internet's bad guys to get in could be a Career Limiting Move (CLM) or worse. Therefore, it's comforting to put security in the hands of people who've done it before. Enter Microsoft's ASP.NET team. The team realized that so many of us were reinventing the security wheel (sometimes creating an oval wheel, out of whack) that it made sense to build membership and login capabilities directly into ASP.NET 2.0.

Out of the box, we have all the tools we need to let people log in to the site, view what we allow them to view, and recover their lost passwords. Our goal in this chapter is to implement security while writing as little code as possible. We can do this by leveraging the standard authorization tools and functions in ASP.NET.

As you work with membership terminology, note that *roles* refer to groups or categories of users. In addition, the terms *users* and *members* are interchangeable.

Understanding Authentication and Authorization

Authentication and authorization are easy to confuse. It might help to look at how these concepts work in a restaurant. In our scenario, areas such as the restaurant's entrance, dining room, and kitchen represent Web pages with different access levels.

Anyone off the street can open the restaurant door and stand in the entrance. In that location, a visitor can look around while remaining completely anonymous because no one needs to know who he or she is. There's no need to grant any approval for him or her to be there.

Our restaurant visitor, John Oliver, passes through the entrance. He intends to eat in the restaurant's dining room and has a reservation. He presents himself at the maitre d's stand at the dining room door. Up until now, Mr. Oliver has been anonymous and unchallenged. The "security" context changes at this point. To claim his reserved table Mr. Oliver must lose his anonymity. He identifies himself by telling the maitre d' his name. In this social context, Mr. Oliver's word is sufficient proof for the maitre d' to validate the person in front of him as Mr. Oliver. The maitre d' could have asked for identification, but that would drive Mr. Oliver away. It is, after all, just a restaurant. Mr. Oliver has been *authenticated* at the restaurant because the restaurant employee knows the person with whom he's dealing.

Next, the maitre d' looks for Mr. Oliver's name on the evening's reservation list, which is like a database. The name appears on the list, confirming that the guest may sit at the table set aside for Mr. Oliver. You could say that Mr. Oliver has been *authorized* to enter the dining room and sit at a table.

You can see that authentication and authorization are different issues. *Authentication* establishes who you are; *authorization* establishes what you can do.

Authentication can also establish a pecking order for different groups of people. For example, although Mr. Oliver has been authenticated and authorized to enter the dining room, he has not been authorized to enter the VIP room unless Mr. Oliver's name appears on the VIP list. Nor can he enter the kitchen unless he is a member of the staff.

Implementing Forms Authentication

We're going to walk through the construction of a barebones Web site that uses forms authentication, the normal mode for a password-protected Internet Web site. Forms authentication requires the visitor to submit a valid username and password to gain access to protected pages. If the credentials are valid, the Web server issues a temporary cookie to the browser that acts as a token to allow entry into other protect pages without forcing the user to type the credentials each time.

Before putting a shovel in the ground, it might help to understand the roles of the Web pages in our sample application.

+ `default.aspx`: This is the entrance to our Web site. As with the restaurant, anyone can browse here anonymously.

+ `login.aspx`: This is the page where visitors present their credentials for validation. In the restaurant example in the previous section, the customer identifies himself to the maitre d' to claim a reservation. Behind the scenes, we verify the username and password — just as the maitre d' checks his reservation list.

✦ `reserved.aspx`: Browsers can only view the contents of this page if they have specific permission. In the restaurant scenario, this is the reserved table. Before a customer gets to this place, the maitre d' knows you and specifically grants you access.

✦ `register.aspx`: This is where visitors to our site can request access to private pages. They must provide information about themselves before approval. The comparable step in the restaurant example is giving your name and phone number when making a reservation.

✦ `regular.aspx`: We might allow anonymous browsers to view this page under certain conditions. In a restaurant, this would be an unreserved table in the dining room.

Creating the Web site

The example we are creating in this chapter uses Visual Web Developer Express (VWDE) to create a file-based Web site. We use the Express edition of SQL Server 2005 as the database engine. For maximum simplicity, we use the Visual Basic (VB) language and all the code (both HTML and server-side) goes into the `.aspx`. file. Let's get started!

1. **In Visual Web Developer Express, from the File menu, click New Web Site.**

2. **In the New Web Site dialog box, under Templates, select ASP.NET Web Site.**

3. **In the Location boxes, select File System and enter** `c:\resto` **as the location for the site.**

4. **In the Language box, select Visual Basic.**

5. **Click OK.**

As shown in Figure 1-1, VWDE creates a site that includes three files: `Default.aspx`, `Default.aspx.vb`, `web.config` and a folder, `App_Data`.

**Book VIII
Chapter 1**

**Security: Using
Login Controls**

Figure 1-1:
Solution
Explorer
after
creating
a new
Web site.

6. **Delete** `Default.aspx.`

The default page uses the code-behind model rather than the one-page model that we're using. You build the pages from scratch in the next section.

Adding pages to the resto Web site

Because the chapter is about security rather than design, I won't deal with creative aspects of pages here. Let's just add some plain ASP.NET pages to the site so we have something to configure. To do so:

1. **In Solution Explorer, select the root of the site and right-click it to bring up the context menu.**

2. **Click Add New Item.**

The Add New Item dialog box opens, as shown in Figure 1-2.

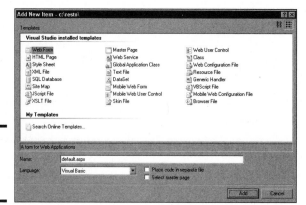

Figure 1-2:
The Add
New Item
dialog box.

1. **From the Visual Studio Installed Templates select Web Form.**

2. **In the Name box, enter the name of the start page,** `default.aspx.`

3. **In the Language box, select Visual Basic.**

4. **Uncheck the check boxes for Place Code In Separate File and Select Master Page.**

5. **Click Add.**

The new ASP.NET page appears in Solution Explorer.

6. **Repeat the preceding steps to add the following pages:** `login.aspx`, `reserved.aspx`, `register.aspx`, **and** `regular.aspx`.

   When you're finished, Solution Explorer should look like Figure 1-3.

Figure 1-3:
Solution
Explorer
after adding
files.

That takes care of creating the raw pages. We add functionality to the pages in subsequent procedures. Before getting to that, however, we have to fix the site's directory structure. We need a directory for the exclusive use of logged in members. Although it's possible to secure individual pages in the `root` folder, ASP.NET's membership features are easiest to apply to whole directories rather than pages. To create the directory, follow these steps:

1. **In Solution Explorer, select the root of the site and right-click it to bring up the context menu.**

2. **Select the New Folder item.**

3. **Name the new folder** `members`.

4. **Drag** `reserved.aspx` **from the** `root` **folder of the Web site and move it into the** `members` **folder.**

We encounter the `members` folder again when we set permissions. First, we have to set up ASP.NET's membership features.

Implementing membership features

Our Web site needs a database to store user information and credentials. When a person logs in, we look up the name and credentials before deciding what pages that person can visit.

You need SQL Server 2005 Express on your workstation for these procedures. (If you haven't installed a copy, now's a good time to do so.)

ASP.NET provides all you need for basic authentication and user management — with little or no code — thanks to the Web Site Administration tool. The hardest part is knowing where to click; the way to get a handle on that is to configure membership for our site. You should still have the `resto` project open. To configure membership for our site, follow these steps:

1. **In the IDE (that's the VWDE development environment), from the Website menu, click ASP.NET Configuration.**

The ASP.NET development server starts up and navigates to the Web Application Administration startup page, as shown in Figure 1-4.

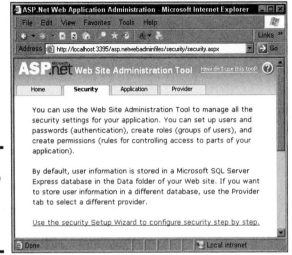

Figure 1-4: Security tab of the Web Site Administration Tool.

2. **Click the Security tab.**

The page may take a few seconds to appear the first time.

3. **Click the link marked Use The Security Setup Wizard to configure security step by step.**

4. **On the Welcome page, click Next.**

5. **On the Select Access Method page, select the radio button for From The Internet and then click Next.**

6. **On the Advanced provider settings page, click Next.**

7. **On the Define Roles page, make sure the check box is cleared and then click Finish.**

The Web Site Administration Tool displays the Security tab. We deal with roles in section "Assigning users to roles," later in this chapter.

Notice that we didn't complete all the wizard steps. That's not a problem because you can restart the wizard at any time to explore its capabilities. There are also other paths to the same functions, such as creating a user.

Before moving on, let's investigate what the wizard has done for us. In your IDE, open Solution Explorer and click the Refresh button. Expand all the nodes and look under the `App_Data` folder — you should see a database file called `ASPNETDB.MDF`, as shown in Figure 1-5.

Figure 1-5: A database file, ASPNETDB. MDF, added to the site.

So far we haven't written any code — but we've managed to create a database that includes numerous tables and stored procedures. You can investigate the database using the Database Explorer. Just go to View⇨Database Explorer. Expand the nodes, as shown in Figure 1-6. (We add data in the section, "Creating users," later in this chapter.)

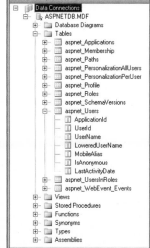

Figure 1-6: Database Explorer shows the membership tables.

Creating users

Our database is now ready for us to add some users, so let's add two user accounts. Once again, we turn to the Web Site Administration tool. To add users, follow these steps:

1. **Navigate to the Security tab (Website⇨ASP.NET Configuration and select the Security tab).**

2. **In the table at the bottom of the page, locate the Users column and click the Create User hyperlink.**

The Create User page appears.

3. **Fill in the user's name, password, e-mail address, security question, and security answer, as shown in Figure 1-7.**

You can make up your own data, but you'll find it easier to follow along later with these values:

- **Username:** JohnOliver

- **Password:** OliverJoh!

- **E-mail:** jo@nowhere.com

- **Security Question:** Your dog's name?

- **Security Answer:** Goldie

ASP.NET requires that your passwords include a combination of upper- and lowercase letters and at least one non-alphanumeric character, such as a punctuation symbol.

Figure 1-7: The Create User page in the Web Site Administration Tool.

```
Create User

        Sign Up for Your New Account
          User Name: JohnOliver
           Password: ••••••••••
   Confirm Password: ••••••••••
             E-mail: jo@nowhere.com
  Security Question: Your dog's name?
    Security Answer: Goldie

                            Create User
```

4. **Click Create User.**

The confirmation message appears.

5. **Click Continue.**

Fixing connection woes

ASP.NET's Web Site Administration Tool does a lot of work behind the scenes. When it creates the membership database, it also builds a database connection string. You can view the string by opening the Database Explorer, selecting ASPNETDB.MDF, and opening the Properties page (that's the F4 key in the default environment).

For example, on my machine the connection string looks like this:

```
"Data
        Source=.\SQLEXPRESS;AttachD
        bFilename=C:\resto\App_Data
        \ASPNETDB.MDF;
Integrated Security=True;
User Instance=True"
```

If you're having trouble connecting to a database that you've created yourself, you might get going again by adapting ASP.NET's membership settings. Also, keep in mind that the IDE recognizes databases more readily when you put the file in the special App_Data folder.

6. **Repeat the preceding steps and create another user with the following values:**

   - **Username:** JillAnon

   - **Password:** AnonJill!

   - **E-mail:** ja@nowhere.com

   - **Security Question:** How high is Up?

   - **Security Answer:** Very

Creating access rules for the pages

Recall that our goal is to allow anyone to browse the default page but permit only specific users to view pages in the members subdirectory. To do this, we have to create some access rules.

Allowing anonymous users access to the root

The first task is to ensure that everyone can reach the pages in the root of the Web, including the home page, default.aspx. To do so, follow these steps:

1. **Navigate to the Security tab (Website⇨ASP.NET Configuration and select the Security tab).**

2. **In the table at the bottom of the page, locate the Access Rules column and click the Create Access Rules hyperlink.**

   The Add New Access Rule page appears.

3. **In the left column, select the root folder (resto).**

4. In the right column, under Rule Applies To, select the Anonymous Users radio button.

5. In the right column, under Permission, select the Allow radio button.

The resulting access rule should look like Figure 1-8.

Figure 1-8:
Allowing access to anonymous users in the root.

Denying access for all users

Our next step is to secure the members subdirectory by keeping everyone out. This exclusion includes anonymous users and users who are logged in. To secure the members subdirectory:

1. In the Web Site Administration Tool, navigate to the Security tab (Website⇨ASP.NET Configuration and select the Security tab).

2. Click Create access rules.

The Add New Access Rule page appears.

3. In the left column, expand the root folder (resto) and select the sub-directory called members.

4. In the right column, under Rule Applies To, select the All Users radio button.

We're creating a rule that applies to everyone.

5. In the right column, under Permission, select the Deny radio button.

The resulting access rule should look like Figure 1-9.

Figure 1-9:
Denying access to all users.

6. Click OK. The Security page reappears.

As of now, nobody can see pages in the `members` folder. We have to add one more rule to make the folder usable by that one special user, `John Oliver`.

Allowing access to one user — John Oliver

Of the two users we created previously, only `John Oliver` is allowed to access the `members` folder, including the `reserved.aspx` page. The following steps provide access to him after he logs in:

1. Navigate to the Security tab (Website⇨ASP.NET Configuration and select the Security tab).

2. Click Create Access Rules.

3. Select the subdirectory called `members`.

4. Select the User radio button.

5. Click the Search for Users link.

The Search for Users page lists the users you added previously. Figure 1-10 shows part of the page with the usernames.

Figure 1-10:
Partial view
of Search
for Users
page.

	User name
☐	JillAnon
☑	JohnOliver

6. Check the check box for JohnOliver and click OK.

The browser returns to the Add New Access Rule page with the username `JohnOliver` in the text box, as shown in Figure 1-11.

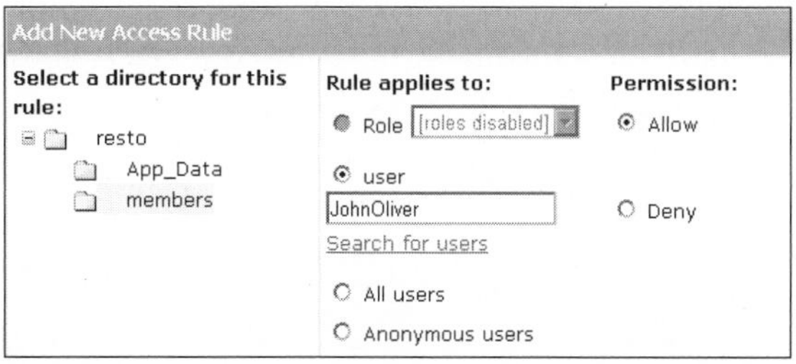

Figure 1-11:
Allowing
access to
John Oliver.

Add New Access Rule

Select a directory for this rule:
- resto
  - App_Data
  - members

Rule applies to:
- ○ Role [roles disabled]
- ⦿ user
  - JohnOliver
  - Search for users
- ○ All users
- ○ Anonymous users

Permission:
- ⦿ Allow
- ○ Deny

**Book VIII
Chapter 1**

**Security: Using
Login Controls**

7. In the Permission area, select the Allow radio button.

8. Click OK.

Reviewing the access rules

You now have two rules in effect for the members subdirectory — *deny all* and *allow John Oliver*. You can (and should) review the rules to confirm that they'll produce the desired result. To review the access rules, follow these steps:

1. Navigate to the ASP.NET Configuration Security tab.

2. Click Manage Access Rules.

The Manage Access Rules page opens, as shown in Figure 1-12.

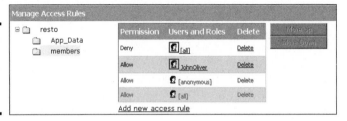

Figure 1-12:
The
Manage
Access
Rules page.

3. Expand the resto **node and click the** members **subdirectory.**

The existing permissions for the subdirectory appear.

It might not be obvious on first viewing, but an analysis of Figure 1-12 shows that we have a problem. John Oliver is denied entry — even though his permission is listed as Allow.

The rule at the top of the list takes precedence over the rules below it. Likewise, the second rule in the list overrides conflicting instructions further down.

Here you can see that Deny All is king of the castle and overshadowing Allow JohnOliver. It may be hard to see in the figure, but the bottom two rules are dimmed (grayed out) because they are inherited from the parent directory.

To fix the hierarchy, move John Oliver's Allow permission higher than the Deny All entry. Here's how:

1. On the Manage Access Rules page, in the Users and Roles column, click the username JohnOliver.

The Move Up button becomes active.

2. **Click Move Up.**

The Allow rule for username JohnOliver moves to the top of the table and overrides the rules below it. Figure 1-13 shows the correct order for the access rules.

3. **Click Done.**

We revisit access rules in the section "Assigning users to roles," later in this chapter, to add a role. However, it's time to put the rules to use and demonstrate how they affect ASP.NET pages.

Using the Login control

When Microsoft's ASP.NET team set out the goals for the 2.0 version, they wanted to reduce the amount of code that developers have to write by 70 percent. The Login control contributes to the code reduction by providing tons of code-free functionality with its default settings.

By the way, have you noticed that we haven't written *any* code yet in this chapter?

Adding the Login control to the page

To allow John Oliver to browse to reserved.aspx in the members subdirectory, you have to provide him with the ASP.NET Login control as a way to present his credentials for authentication.

1. **In Solution Explorer, open** login.aspx **in Design view.**

2. **From the** Login **tab of the toolbox, drag the** Login **control (the one with an icon showing a padlock and a person) and drop it on the design surface.**

Figure 1-14 shows the control and its Smart Tasks menu.

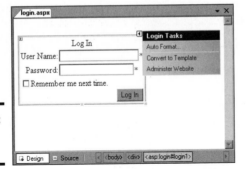

Figure 1-14:
The Login
control.

Script your login

When you test forms authentication, it's highly likely that you'll access pages many times with different usernames and passwords. The `Login` control is a great convenience at design time — but at runtime, you still have to enter the credentials. Copying and pasting the username and password works okay, but even that becomes tedious after a few logins.

You can semi-automate the logins with a little client-side script. I threw together a JavaScript routine to paste into `login.aspx` during development. When you select a username from the drop-down list, the script pushes that username and its password into the appropriate fields in the `Login` control. The sooner you implement this arrangement, the more time you'll save.

In Source view, put the following in the `<head>` of `login.aspx`:

```
<script type="text/javascript">
function autologin()
{
var username =
        document.getElementById("Lo
        gin1_UserName");
var pwd =
        document.getElementById("Lo
        gin1_Password");
```

```
var cntrl =
        document.getElementById("Se
        lect1");
username.value=cntrl.options[cntrl.se
        lectedIndex].text;
pwd.value=cntrl.options[cntrl.selecte
        dIndex].value;
}
</script>
```

Right after the `<body>` tag, insert a drop-down list with the sample usernames and passwords:

```
<select id="Select1"
        onchange="autologin()">
    <option value=""></option>
    <option
        value="OliverJoh!">JohnOliv
        er</option>
    <option
        value="AnonJill!">JillAnon<
        /option>
</select>
```

You might need to adjust the IDs passed to the `getElementById()` function to match the control IDs that ASP.NET generates on the rendered page. The values here assume that your `Login` control's name is `Login1`.

The `Login` control has dozens of properties, including many to customize the text that appears. For example, the `FailureText` property value is a polite string, `"Your login attempt was not successful. Please try again."` You can change the text to wording more appropriate for your site, such as `"Nope, that's not it!"`

Testing the Login control

So far we've generated a user database, added two users to it, added a folder and some ASP.NET pages to our site, configured the permissions, and implemented the login function. Finally, we can test the security by trying to access the restricted page — using three different personas.

The first persona is the anonymous user. We allow this user to browse to pages in the root of the Web site but deny access to the `members` subdirectory. To test this persona:

1. **In Solution Explorer, in the** `members` **folder, right-click** `reserved.aspx`.

2. **From the context menu, click View in Browser.**

The browser opens, but instead of the `reserved.aspx` page, you see `login.aspx`.

This proves that the anonymous user was not allowed to see the page. In fact, ASP.NET's default behavior automatically redirected the browser to the login page. Notice the URL in the browser, repeated in the next line:

```
http://localhost:3235/resto/login.aspx?
ReturnUrl=%2fresto%2fmembers%2freserved.aspx
```

The portion after `ReturnUrl=` is the page the anonymous user tried to reach. The `%2f` parts are escape codes for the forward slash, so the URL translates to:

```
/resto/members/reserved.aspx
```

If the login is successful, `reserved.aspx` is the user's intended destination.

For the next attempt to access the `members` subdirectory, we call on a known user, `JillAnon`. Testing the login for our known user looks like this:

1. **Browse to** `reserved.aspx` **in the** `members` **folder.**

The browser redirects to the login page.

2. **In the User Name box, type** `JillAnon`.

3. **In the Password box, type** AnonJill! **(case-sensitive).**

4. **Click Log In.**

The user failed to access reserved.aspx. The login page reappears.

Actually the login only *appears* to have failed. In the section "Using the LoginName control," later in this chapter, we show that JillAnon did in fact log in — and can navigate to other pages. ASP.NET's default behavior is to bounce browsers to the login page when they're denied access to a page. That can be changed (as detailed in the next section).

Now to test whether the only user who *has* access to reserved.aspx can *get* there. Here goes:

1. **Browse to** reserved.aspx **in the** members **folder.**

The browser redirects to the login page.

2. **In the User Name box, type** JohnOliver.

3. **In the Password box, type** OliverJoh! **(case-sensitive).**

4. **Click Log In.**

The browser navigates to . . . a blank page!

The page is blank because we didn't put anything in it — but look at the address in the browser: It landed on reserved.aspx. You can make the target page more obvious by opening reserved.aspx in Design view and adding identifying text. Browse to the page again and you'll see something like Figure 1-15.

Figure 1-15:
Browsing to
reserved.
aspx.

Using the LoginName control

When we tested the login by JillAnon in the previous section, it *appeared* to have failed. There was nothing obvious to indicate success. You can fix that by adding the LoginName control to a page. If the user is logged in, it displays the name. Here's the fix:

1. **Open** `default.aspx` **in Design view.**

2. **From the** `Login` **tab of the toolbox, drag the** `LoginName` **control to the design surface.**

3. **Browse to** `login.aspx`.

If you browse directly to `default.aspx`, you do so as the anonymous user and won't see a name.

4. **Log in as** `JillAnon` **with the password** `AnonJill!` **(case-sensitive).**

The default page appears with the username, as shown in Figure 1-16.

Figure 1-16:
The
LoginName
control
displays the
username.

The `LoginName` control is handy for personalizing Web pages. People tend to forget themselves when browsing exciting Web pages; this way you can show them who they are at all times while they're logged in.

Using the LoginStatus control

The `LoginStatus` control shows more than whether a user is logged in or out. It detects the user's status and, based on that, creates links to log out or log in.

1. **Open** `regular.aspx` **in Design view.**

2. **From the** `Login` **tab of the toolbox, drag the** `LoginStatus` **control to the design surface.**

3. **Browse to** `regular.aspx` **as an anonymous user**.

The page shows a Login hyperlink.

4. **Click Login.**

The browser navigates to `login.aspx`.

5. **Log in as** `JillAnon` **with the password** `AnonJill!` **(case-sensitive).**

You return to `regular.aspx`, but this time the hyperlink reads Logout.

6. Click Logout.

Behind the scenes, ASP.NET cancels your authentication (that is, logs you out); the `LoginStatus` control reflects this change by displaying the Login hyperlink.

Be sure to provide a way for the user to log out from your secure pages. Often, when people navigate away from secure pages, they think (mistakenly) that they've logged out. If they leave the browser open during a break, a ne'er-do-well could browse back to the secure page while the authentication is valid. Using the Logout link forces the user to re-authenticate.

Using the LoginView control

`LoginView` is a templated control that lets you show completely different content to a user who has logged in and one who has logged out. Templated controls let you go wild with your own customizations. That's because you add your own content rather than just manipulating the properties that Microsoft provides. The templates, `AnonymousTemplate` and `LoggedInTemplate`, act as containers for all kinds of markup, including ASP.NET controls. Here's a short demonstration:

1. Open `regular.aspx` **in Design view.**

2. From the `Login` **tab of the toolbox, drag the** `LoginView` **control to the design surface.**

The control defaults to the `AnonymousTemplate`.

3. Drag an ASP.NET `Label` **control from the toolbox, drop it inside the** `LoginView` **control's outline, and set the label's text to** `"You are not worthy."`

4. Select the `LoginView`, **open its Smart Tasks menu, and select** `LoggedIn Template` **from the drop-down list, as shown in Figure 1-17.**

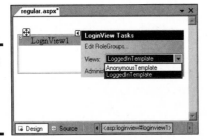

Figure 1-17: Choosing a view in the LoginView control.

5. Drag an ASP.NET `Hyperlink` **control onto the** `LoginView`.

6. **Set the hyperlink's** `Text` **property to** `Members` **and the** `NavigateUrl`
property to `~/members/reserved.aspx`.

7. **Browse to** `regular.aspx` **as an anonymous user.**

The page displays the contents of the label.

8. **Log in at** `login.aspx` **and then browse to** `regular.aspx`.

The page displays the hyperlink.

As you've seen here, you can fill the templates with entirely different content —
such as error messages for logged-in users.

Using the PasswordRecovery control

IT departments know too well that forgotten passwords are among the most
common support tasks that users need (especially after vacations). To save
you the hassle of manually resetting forgotten passwords, ASP.NET offers the
self-service `PasswordRecovery` control. It sends the password to the e-mail
address used at registration, and it works — as long as the person knows his
or her username.

Configuring the SMTP settings

The `PasswordRecovery` control requires access to a Simple Mail Transport
Protocol (SMTP) server to actually send the e-mail containing the password.
Most network operators place restrictions on the use of their SMTP server
to deter spammers. Most mail servers require authentication before sending
e-mail. Some Internet service providers (ISPs) block individual users from
accessing the commonly used ports for SMTP.

It's quite likely that you'll have to check with a system administrator if you
want the exact SMTP settings. For that reason, we can only give you general
instructions on configuring a Web site to use the `PasswordRecovery` control.

We start with the Web Site Administration tool:

1. **Navigate to the Application tab (Website⇨ASP.NET Configuration and
select the Application tab).**

2. **Click Configure SMTP e-mail settings.**

3. **Fill in the settings for your SMTP server.**

You can refer to the following example data:

- **Server Name:** `smtp.mydomain.com`

- **smtp.mydomain.com:** 25

- **E-mail:** `admin@mydomain.com`

- **Sender's username:** pwdrequest@mydomain.com
- **Sender's password:** pwd@#$@%!

4. **Click Save.**

If you don't get the SMTP e-mail settings to work after a few tries, check with your ISP before proceeding. Hitting the mail server with scads of incorrect data could get your e-mail privileges suspended — because you might be mistaken for a hacker.

Adding the PasswordRecovery control to a page

The second phase in setting up password recovery is adding the PasswordRecovery control to a Web page. Here's the drill, using the default configuration:

1. **Open** default.aspx **in Design view.**

2. **From the** Login **tab of the toolbox, drag the** PasswordRecovery **control to the design surface.**

Testing the password recovery feature

To test the functionality of the password recovery feature, follow these steps:

1. **Browse to** default.aspx **as an anonymous user (that is, not logged in).**

   Figure 1-18 shows the default appearance.

Figure 1-18:
The
Password-
Recovery
control.

2. **Type a registered username (for example,** JillAnon**) and then click Submit.**

   The Identity Confirmation page appears with the challenge question, as shown in Figure 1-19.

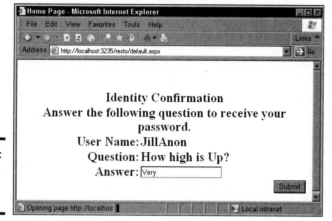

Figure 1-19:
Answer the
challenge
question.

3. Answer the challenge question (`JillAnon`**'s answer is** `Very`**) and click Submit.**

Behind the scenes, ASP.NET sends the password to the e-mail address in the database.

If the SMTP settings and permissions aren't correct, you'll probably see a timeout error message on the Web page.

We used the default settings for the `PasswordRecovery` control, but you can customize the question text, error messages, success messages, and the URL of the page to display after a password recovery.

Use the `MailDefinition` property to define the e-mail message including the e-mail's subject, content, format (plain text or HTML), priority, and sender name. If you're sending the message as HTML, you can include image files such as a background graphic or your site's logo. Add the images in the `EmbeddedObjects` collection editor (MailDefinition⇨EmbeddedObjects).

Using the ChangePassword control

The `PasswordRecovery` control sends the password in unencrypted format, so users should change their password as soon as possible. (Many of us feel that we forget passwords because administrators force us to change them too often, but that's a rant for another time.)

The `ChangePassword` control simplifies the process while enforcing rules (default or custom) about password complexity. Like the other login controls, you can configure the appearance, text, and redirect page. To add a `ChangePassword` control:

**Book VIII
Chapter 1**

**Security: Using
Login Controls**

1. **Add a new ASP.NET page called** `chgpwd.aspx` **to the root of your project.**

2. **From the** `Login` **tab of the toolbox, drag a** `ChangePassword` **control to the design surface.**

3. **In the properties page for the** `ChangePassword` **control, set the** `DisplayUserName` **property to** `true`.

4. **Browse to the page and fill in the text boxes using a registered username (for example,** `JillAnon`**) and password (**`AnonJill!`**), as shown in Figure 1-20.**

Figure 1-20:
The Change
Password
control.

5. **Click Submit.**

The `ChangePassword` function confirms the change.

Wrap the `ChangePassword` control inside a `LoggedInView` template of the `LoginView` control so users who aren't logged in won't see the control.

Assigning users to roles

Previously in the chapter, you created two test users. You gave username `JohnOliver` permission to browse to `reserved.aspx` in the restricted `members` subdirectory. Chances are, a group of users would have access to that resource rather than just one individual user, so it's far more efficient to manage them as a group. Enter ASP.NET roles. By creating a role (such as `EliteMember`), you can assign usernames to the role. If you want to give members of the `EliteMember` role access to a new portion of the site, you set the permissions for the role once — and all the elitists can enter immediately.

You use the Web Site Administration tool to manage roles and add user-names. In our scenario, we create a role, add users to it, and give the role rights to the `members` subdirectory. Here's how we do it:

1. **Navigate to the Security tab (Website⇨ASP.NET Configuration and select the Security tab).**

2. **In the Roles column, click Enable roles.**

   The Create Or Manage Roles link is enabled.

3. **Click Create Or Manage Roles.**

   The Create New Role page appears.

4. **Type a new role name (for example, `EliteMember`) and click Add Role.**

   The new role appears in the list.

5. **Next to the role name, click Manage.**

   The Search for Users page appears.

6. **Search for all users by entering an asterisk (*) in the text box, and then click Find User.**

   The list of usernames appears.

7. **Under the User Is In Role column, select the check box for each user and then click Back.**

   The selected users are added to the `EliteMember` role.

The users are now in a role (group), but the role doesn't have permission to enter the `members` area. That's the task of the next section.

Giving permissions to a role

After you add users to a role, you can manage them as a collection. In this case, we want to give special permissions to the `EliteMember` role.

1. **Navigate to the Security tab by clicking Website⇨ASP.NET Configuration and selecting the Security tab.**

2. **In the Access Rules column, click Create access rules.**

   The Add New Access Rule page opens.

3. **Select the `members` subdirectory.**

4. **Select the Role radio button and from the drop-down list, select `EliteMember`.**

5. Select the Allow permission.

Figure 1-21 shows the resulting settings.

Figure 1-21:
Adding an access rule for a role.

6. Click OK.

Giving the role access to the members folder was easy, but we're not finished yet. You can't be sure that members of the EliteMember group actually have access until you analyze the hierarchy of access rules. Figure 1-22 shows that username JohnOliver is allowed in because his Allow is above everything else. However, the EliteMember role's Allow is trumped by the Deny all above it.

Permission	Users and Roles	Delete
Allow	JohnOliver	Delete
Deny	[all]	Delete
Allow	EliteMember	Delete
Allow	[anonymous]	Delete
Allow	[all]	Delete

Figure 1-22:
Incorrect order of access rules.

A couple of fixes are required at this point: JohnOliver is now a member of EliteMember, so his special permission is unnecessary; the EliteMember role needs to move above the Deny all. To do this fix, follow these steps:

1. Navigate to the Security tab by clicking Website⇨ASP.NET Configuration and selecting the Security tab.

2. Click Manage access rules.

3. Select the members **subdirectory.**

4. Click Delete next to the JohnOliver **username and confirm the deletion.**

5. Click the EliteMember **role and then click Move Up.**

The EliteMember role is now at the top of the rules list, as shown in Figure 1-23.

Permission	Users and Roles	Delete
Allow	EliteMember	Delete
Deny	[all]	Delete
Allow	[anonymous]	Delete
Allow	[all]	Delete

6. Click Done.

You can confirm the access rules by logging in as JillAnon and navigating to reserved.aspx in the members folder. You can see that reserved.aspx is no longer reserved just for JohnOliver.

Without writing a single line of code, we've implemented a very functional membership system. The Web Site Administration tool manages the database and shielded us from the syntax and quirks of web.config files. The ASP.NET login controls ship with default settings that work with little or no configuration.

Peering into the Application Programming Interface (API)

It won't come as a surprise to know that there are APIs for everything we've done so far in this chapter. Microsoft's tools and controls offer a developer-friendly front-end to the extensive Membership, MembershipUser, and Roles classes found in the System.Web.Security namespace. The upshot is that you can work with the classes in code. This section shows how to use some of the capabilities in your own programs.

Using the Membership and MembershipUser classes

The Membership and MembershipUser classes offer functions for creating, deleting, updating, and validating a user. You can use these classes to search for a user, create a list of users, and get the number of logged in users. Some of the examples in this section assume that you're using the membership database with the usernames that we created in the "Creating users" section near the beginning of the chapter.

Adding members programmatically

In the Resto site that we built in the "Creating the Web site" section, the user information includes the username, password, e-mail address, password challenge, and the answer to the challenge. The following VB code re-creates that as it adds a user programmatically. The last parameter of the `CreateUser()` function is a status report.

```
Dim mbrCurrentMember As System.Web.Security.MembershipUser
Dim status As System.Web.Security.MembershipCreateStatus
Try
    mbrCurrentMember =
    System.Web.Security.Membership.CreateUser _
            ("JackieReeve", _
            "ReeveJack!", _
            "rj@nowhere.com", _
            "Your favourite band", _
            "Beatles", _
            True, _
            status)
Catch exc As Exception
    Label2.Text = "Problem: " & exc.Message
End Try
Label2.Text = status.ToString()
```

The first time you run the preceding code, it adds the member and reports `Success`. Run it again without deleting the member. The return code is `DuplicateUserName`, indicating a failure because the username exists.

Deleting members programmatically

Deleting a user account requires less effort than adding one. The `DeleteUser()` function takes the username and a `Boolean` to indicate whether to wipe out all the data related to the user. The method returns `True` if the user was deleted. Here's a VB example:

```
Dim blnRetValue As Boolean
Try
    blnRetValue = System.Web.Security.Membership.DeleteUser _
            ("JackieReeve", _
            True)
Catch exc As Exception
```

```
        Label2.Text = "Problem: " & exc.Message
End Try
Label2.Text = "User deleted?: " & blnRetValue.ToString()
```

Updating members programmatically

To change the stored values for a user, call the Membership's `UpdateUser()` method. It takes a `MembershipUser` object as its value. You can use the `GetUser()` function to return a `MembershipUser` object, change the values, and push the data back to the database. Here's a VB example:

```
Dim mbrCurrentMember As System.Web.Security.MembershipUser
mbrCurrentMember = Membership.GetUser("JackieReeve")
If Not IsNothing(mbrCurrentMember) Then
    mbrCurrentMember.E-mail = "jackie@nowhere.com"
    Try
        Membership.UpdateUser(mbrCurrentMember)
        Label2.Text = "User updated: " & _
            mbrCurrentMember.UserName & ", " & _
            mbrCurrentMember.E-mail
    Catch exc As Exception
        Label2.Text = "Problem: " & exc.Message
    End Try
Else
    Label2.Text = "Problem: Not found"
End If
```

Displaying all members programmatically

You can fetch a list of all members — and all their properties — by using the Membership's `GetAllUsers()` function. The following Visual Basic code dumps all the data into a `DataGrid` control that auto-generates the columns:

```
DataGrid1.DataSource = Membership.GetAllUsers()
DataGrid1.DataBind()
```

Using the Roles class

The `Roles` class lets you manage *roles* (that is, groups of users such as those who are all doing the same type of work or have identical privileges). You can use the functions to add and remove users from roles, find users in a given role, determine whether a user is in a role, and create lists of roles. All the capabilities you find in the graphical Web Site Administration tool are available to your code. (This section assumes that you're using the membership database with the usernames from the "Creating users" section earlier in this chapter.)

Adding a role programmatically

You can pass the name of a role to the `CreateRole()` method to create a role. The code below does just that but calls the `RoleExists()` function to check whether the role is already in use. Here's a VB example:

```
Dim strRoleName As String
strRoleName = "Poobahs"
If Not Roles.RoleExists(strRoleName) Then
    Try
        Roles.CreateRole(strRoleName)
        Label2.Text = "Added Role"
    Catch exc As Exception
        Label2.Text = "Problem: " & exc.Message
    End Try
Else
    Label2.Text = "Role exists. Not added again"
End If
```

Deleting a role programmatically

If you know its name, you can delete a role by passing the name to the `DeleteRole()` function. The following code in Visual Basic does a quick check to make sure the role exists before it tries to remove it.

```
Dim strRoleName As String
strRoleName = "Poobahs"
If Roles.RoleExists(strRoleName) Then
    Try
        Roles.DeleteRole(strRoleName)
        Label2.Text = "Deleted Role"
    Catch exc As Exception
        Label2.Text = "Problem: " & exc.Message
    End Try
Else
    Label2.Text = "Role doesn't exist."
End If
```

Adding users to a role programmatically

The `RemoveUsersFromRole()` method handles the task of adding members to a role. The method takes an array of usernames and the name of the role. It's a good idea to check for the existence of the role by using the `RoleExists()` function. Here's a VB example:

```
Dim arrUsers() As String = {"JackieReeve", "JohnOliver"}
Dim strRoleName As String
strRoleName = "Poobahs"
```

```
If Roles.RoleExists(strRoleName) Then
    Try
        Roles.RemoveUsersFromRole(arrUsers, strRoleName)
        Label2.Text = "User(s) Removed."
    Catch exc As Exception
        Label2.Text = "Problem: " & exc.Message
    End Try
Else
    Label2.Text = "Role " & strRoleName & " doesn't exist."
End If
```

Listing all roles

Fetching the list of roles is as simple as calling the GetAllRoles() function. It returns a string array that can serve as the data for many ASP.NET data controls. The following VB example gets the list of roles and then passes the name of the first role (via the zero index of the array) to the GetUsersIn Role() function. That function then returns the names of all users assigned to the role it specifies.

```
Dim arrRoles() As String
Dim arrMembers() As String
arrRoles = Roles.GetAllRoles()
DataGrid1.DataSource = arrRoles
DataGrid1.DataBind()
arrMembers = Roles.GetUsersInRole(arrRoles(0))
DataGrid2.DataSource = arrMembers
DataGrid2.DataBind()
```

Chapter 2: Using Profiles

In This Chapter

✓ **Enabling anonymous and authenticated profiles**

✓ **Storing and retrieving user preferences**

✓ **Configuring default and custom providers**

✓ **Querying and maintaining the profile database**

*P*eople love to customize their environment. Even where there are rows of look-alike houses, the interiors all look different. Our tastes and preferences lead us to put an individual stamp on whatever we can control. You only have to look at a few Windows desktops to see examples of personalization in the computer world — a vast range of fonts, wallpapers, sounds, and other settings.

We expect our customizations in Windows or on the Web to remain the way we left them until we change the settings. This is *persistence* in geek-speak. When you return to an e-commerce Web site after lunch, you'd like it to recognize the items you put into your shopping cart before you went to eat. Those choices must be stored somewhere.

ASP.NET 2.0 provides a substantial infrastructure that supports tracking data on an individual basis for many scenarios: Visitors to your Web site can customize the appearance of the pages; shoppers don't have to start over if they accidentally close the browser; the site can pre-fill form data such as a shipping address because the user provided it on the last visit. As you see in this chapter, it's remarkably easy to do.

Understanding Profiles

ASP.NET's default profile functions store visitors' information in a SQL Server 2005 database. The great bonus is that you don't have to know anything about database structure, stored procedures, data types, or even SQL syntax. Almost everything you need for keeping individual data is pre-built and waiting for you to switch on and configure.

Here's a look at a typical scenario that shows what goes on behind the scenes when you enable profiles on your site. A visitor browses to one of your pages for the first time as an anonymous user. ASP.NET passes a unique identification cookie to the browser. The cookie expires in about 70 days if the user never returns. If the user does come back, ASP.NET slides the expiration forward so that a frequent visitor never loses his or her settings.

As the user interacts with your ASP.NET pages, your code tells the application what data to save. For example, you might want to capture the user's e-mail address when typed, or do likewise with choices from a list of products, or save a page customization (such as the color scheme from a drop-down list). The `Profile` functions put the information in the database for you, along with details of the identification cookie.

Every time the browser requests a page, ASP.NET checks the content of the identification cookie — and, when required, looks up the corresponding record in its database. Your code uses that data to build a page that reflects the previous settings or re-displays chosen items.

Some people are afraid to let their browser accept cookies and turn that option off. (Most geeks know that a cookie is a very innocuous file, but you can't convince everyone that it's safe.) Even under these less-than-ideal conditions, ASP.NET can recognize the user, at least during the lifetime of the browsing session. Unfortunately, the link to the profile disappears once the user closes the browser. Alas, you have to live with the fact that the cookie-less solution is less than optimal.

As you'll soon see, the techniques for using profiles with anonymous users (that is, users who have not logged in) is a bit different than for authenticated users (users who have logged in). We tackle profiles for anonymous users first, then look at the differences for authenticated users.

Enabling Anonymous User Profiles

Profile support is built in (or "baked in," as they say at Microsoft) to the ASP.NET infrastructure. However, you have to explicitly switch on profile support for anonymous users.

The instructions here assume that you've already created a Web site in Visual Web Developer (or the Express version). If you need help with that aspect, you can refer to the procedures at the beginning of Chapter 1 of this mini-book. The samples are based on a site called `profilesite` written in VB.NET.

To demonstrate the use of profiles, we build a simple Web page after some preparatory steps. For a sneak preview, look at Figure 2-1 to see the product of our efforts.

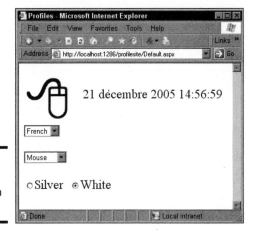

Figure 2-1:
A profile-based Web page.

Deciding what data to store

In ASP.NET profile lingo, each piece of data you store is called a *property*. Before implementing user profiles, it helps to know what properties (user data) you want to track. For our purposes, we're going to track the following properties:

✦ `Language`: A choice of English or French for the date and time

✦ `BGColour`: White or gray background color

✦ `SiteLogo`: The URL of an image that appears on the page

If the user is new to the site, we use default values. You provide the defaults in the following section.

Enabling profiles in the configuration file

In Chapter 1 of this mini-book, we configured membership and roles using the Web Site Administration tool. For some reason, profiles didn't rate the rich graphical treatment where the tool writes the settings. Instead, you need to edit the site's `web.config` file.

If you're working on a live site, make a backup copy of the `web.config` file before you edit it by hand. The syntax in the `web.config` is very finicky and, because elements are case-sensitive, errors are hard to spot. A tiny typo can bring down the whole site until you discover the glitch.

To edit the site's `web.config` file:

1. **Open the site's** `web.config` **file and locate the** `<system.web>` **section.**

2. **Just after the** `<system.web>` **section, add the entry shown below.**

   This element enables anonymous profiles:

   ```
   <!--<system.web> goes here-->
   <anonymousIdentification enabled="true"/>
   ```

3. **Directly after the preceding element, insert the following XML mark-up to define properties:**

   ```
   <profile enabled="true"
       defaultProvider="AspNetSqlProfileProvider">
     <properties>
       <add name="Language" defaultValue="en-CA"
        allowAnonymous="true"/>
       <add name="BGColour"
        defaultValue="background:white"
        allowAnonymous="true"/>
       <add name="SiteLogo" defaultValue="pc.gif"
        allowAnonymous="true"/>
     </properties>
   </profile>
   ```

4. **Look for the** `<authentication />` **element in** `web.config` **and configure the authentication mode to** `None` **so the element looks like the following:**

   ```
   <authentication mode="None"/>
   ```

5. **Save the** `web.config` **file.**

The code in the third step instructs ASP.NET to enable profiles for this site using the built-in provider. Nested inside the `<properties>` tag, you see three `<add>` elements with attributes. The following list shows the most common attributes for properties. We use the first three in the list:

✦ `name`: The name of the property that you want to track. In our example, the values for this attribute are `Language`, `BGColour`, and `SiteLogo`.

✦ `defaultValue`: The initial value of the property. ASP.NET assigns this when it creates the user's profile.

✦ `allowAnonymous`: To allow profiles for unauthenticated (anonymous) users, you must set the value to `true`. The default is `false`, which means there's no record for non-registered visitors.

✦ `type`: This is the variable type for the property. The default value of this attribute is `String`. Because all of our properties are strings, we didn't need to include this type information. The value can be any .NET type such as `System.Int32, System.DateTime, System.Collection.Specialized.StringCollection`, or even a custom type you create in your code.

✦ `serializeAs`: This specifies the serialization formatter for the property. The default is `string`.

Generating the database

At this point, you've defined the properties that you want to track but you don't have anywhere to hold the data once you get it. There's a big empty space inside your site's `App_Data` folder where the data file should be. If you're impatient (like me), you want to see some action — and maybe a little ASP.NET magic.

1. **Add a page called** `create.aspx` **to your project.**

2. **Insert the following code as the handler for the** `Load` **event:**

```
Protected Sub Page_Load _
(ByVal sender As Object, _
ByVal e As System.EventArgs)
    Profile.Language = "en-US"
End Sub
```

3. **Save and run the page.**

4. **In Solution Explorer, refresh the view and look in the** `App_Data` **folder.**

5. **Be amazed to find a new file called** `ASPNETDB.MDF`.

All the preceding code does is assign a value to the `Language` property that we created inside the `web.config` file. ASP.NET determines that we've implemented profiles for our site and therefore generates a database.

While we're sidetracked, let's look closer at the profile database.

Exploring the profile database

So far, we've executed one statement and created a whole database. There's already some data to explore. To do so:

1. **Open Database Explorer (View➪Database Explorer).**

2. **Expand the Data Connections node to show the ASPNETDB.MDF connection.**

3. **Expand the Tables node, as shown in Figure 2-2.**

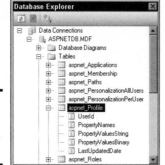

Figure 2-2:
Examining
ASPNETDB.
MDF.

4. **Right-click aspnet_Profile and, from the context menu, click Show Table Data.**

As shown in Figure 2-3, a window opens to reveal a single database record.

Figure 2-3:
A single
database
record.

The record is the profile for the anonymous user who browsed to the `create.aspx` page. Let's analyze the fields and stored values in the `aspnet_Profile` table.

✦ `UserId`: This is a unique identifier for an anonymous user:

`052f8e57-5ffc-42fd-b99f-958cd657d17d`

✦ `PropertyNames`: This is a formatted text string (the data type is `ntext`) such as:

`Language:S:0:5:`

This format stores the name of the property (`Language`), its location (`S` for "values"), its position as an offset (`0`), and length of the data (`5`).

For more detail about the format, search for "Profile Providers (ASP.NET Technical Articles)" on `http://search.msdn.microsoft.com`.

✦ `PropertyValuesString`: This is another formatted text string (`ntext`) with the values referenced by the `PropertyNames` field. An example value is

    en-US

✦ `PropertyValuesBinary`: This is a binary field, not used in our example.

✦ `LastUpdateDate`: A `datetime` data type that holds the time of the last update to the record. Here's an example:

    22/12/2005 3:09:45 AM

If you investigate the `aspnet_Users` table, you'll find other data pertaining to the visit, including a field called `IsAnonymous`, which is `True` for our visitor. The records in these tables ultimately relate to a cookie stored on the user's computer by the browser. Although the cookie data is encrypted, you can read the name: `.ASPXANONYMOUS`.

Building the Profile-Based Web Page

In this section, we build the single ASP.NET page that sets the profile values we defined in the previous sections and retrieves them. The user can customize the page by selecting the logo, background color, and the language of the date and time.

Adding control markup to the page

The controls in the page we're creating (`default.aspx`) serve two roles: The input controls update stored data; the display controls, like the `Image` and `Label` controls, demonstrate the retrieval of property values. Figure 2-4 shows the page under construction in Design view.

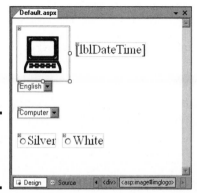

Figure 2-4:
Design view
of default.
aspx.

To create the user interface to set and display profile values:

1. **Add an ASP.NET page to your site. The examples here use** `default.aspx`.

2. **Add an** `Image` **control called** `imgLogo` **to the page as shown in the following code:**

```
<asp:image id="imgLogo" runat="server"
    imagealign="Middle" />
```

3. **Add a** `Label` **control called** `lblDateTime`.

This control displays the server's date and time in the selected language.

```
<asp:label id="lblDateTime" runat="server" />
```

4. **Add a** `DropDownList` **control called** `ddlLanguage` **and configure it as shown in the following code with** `autopostback` **set to** `true` **and with the two list items shown.**

This control lets the user choose the language for the date and time.

```
<asp:dropdownlist id="ddlLanguage" runat="server"
    autopostback="True"
    onselectedindexchanged="ddlLanguage_Chgd">
    <asp:listitem value="en-CA">English</asp:listitem>
    <asp:listitem value="fr-CA">French</asp:listitem>
</asp:dropdownlist><br />
```

5. **Add another** `DropDownList` **control called** `ddlImage`. **Again, set** `autopostback` **to** `true` **and include the three list items, as shown in the following code:**

```
<asp:dropdownlist id="ddlImage" runat="server"
    autopostback="True"
    onselectedindexchanged="ddlImage_Chgd">
    <asp:listitem
    value="pc.gif">Computer</asp:listitem>
    <asp:listitem
    value="mouse.gif">Mouse</asp:listitem>
    <asp:listitem
    value="keyboard.gif">Keyboard</asp:listitem>
</asp:dropdownlist><br />
```

6. **Add two** `RadioButton` **controls called** `rdbtnSilver` **and** `rdbtnWhite`. **Set** `autopostback` **to** `true` **and give them both the** `groupname` **value** `bg`. **Here's the code:**

```
<asp:radiobutton id="rdbtnSilver" runat="server"
    autopostback="True" groupname="bg"
    oncheckedchanged="rdbtn_CheckedChanged"
    text="Silver" /> 
```

```
<asp:radiobutton id="rdbtnWhite" runat="server"
    autopostback="True" groupname="bg"
    oncheckedchanged="rdbtn_CheckedChanged"
    text="White" />
```

7. Make the `<body>` tag accessible to server-side code by giving it an ID (`bdyPage`) and designating it to run on the server, as shown in the following markup:

```
<body id="bdyPage" runat="server">
```

Adding code to retrieve profile values

When the page first loads, you need to fetch the values of the profile properties. If there's a profile for this anonymous user, ASP.NET pulls out the values on demand. If not, it uses the default values that you assigned when declaring the properties in the `web.config` file.

The following code checks the `IsPostBack` property to see whether this is a fresh appearance of the page (that is, not caused by a button click or other event on the page). If not a postback, it sets the drop-down lists to display the value stored in the database for the corresponding property. Likewise, it retrieves the `BGColour` value and uses that to add a style attribute to the `<body>` tag. Depending on the value retrieved, the window background turns silver or white.

```
Protected Sub Page_Load _
 (ByVal sender As Object, _
  ByVal e As System.EventArgs)
    If Not IsPostBack Then
        ddlLanguage.SelectedValue = Profile.Language
        ddlImage.SelectedValue = Profile.SiteLogo
        imgLogo.ImageUrl = Profile.SiteLogo
      bdyPage.Attributes.Add("style", _
            Profile.BGColour)
        lblDateTime.Text = SetDateTime()
    End If
    lblDateTime.Text = SetDateTime()
End Sub
```

Displaying the date and time in the chosen language

`SetDateTime()` is a short function that uses .NET's built-in globalization features to display the date and time according to the language and rules of a given culture. For example, the date and time for French Canada (`fr-CA`) looks like this:

```
21 décembre 2005 21:34:45
```

Where French puts the date before the month, the month comes first when the culture is English Canada (en-CA):

December 21, 2005 9:46:45 PM

The SetDateTime() function creates an instance of the CultureInfo object based on the user's choice of language from the Language property (en-CA or fr-CA). We apply the CultureInfo to the CurrentCulture property of the executing thread. That way, the function returns the date and time based on the culture's rules. We're using the long format for both the date and time.

```
Function SetDateTime() As String
    Dim ci As New System.Globalization.CultureInfo _
        (Profile.Language)
    System.Threading.Thread. _
        CurrentThread.CurrentCulture = ci
    Dim dt As DateTime = Now
    Return dt.ToLongDateString & " " & _
        dt.ToLongTimeString
End Function
```

Storing the language choice in the profile

When the user selects a different language from the drop-down list, the onselectedindexchanged fires. The ddlLanguage_Chgd method handles the event. It assigns the selected value to the Language property which is automatically stored in the profile. Because the language has changed, the date and time display is no longer in the correct language. By calling the SetDateTime() function, we rewrite the text.

```
Protected Sub ddlLanguage_Chgd _
    (ByVal sender As Object, ByVal e As System.EventArgs)
    Profile.Language = ddlLanguage.SelectedValue
    lblDateTime.Text = SetDateTime()
End Sub
```

Storing the image choice in the profile

By choosing a different image from the drop-down list (ddlImage), the user sets off its onselectedindexchanged event. The designated handler, ddlImage_Chgd, stores the name of the selected image in the profile's SiteLogo property. Because the choice of image has changed, we need to reset the image.

```
Protected Sub ddlImage_Chgd _
    (ByVal sender As Object, ByVal e As System.EventArgs)
    Profile.SiteLogo = ddlImage.SelectedValue
    imgLogo.ImageUrl = ddlImage.SelectedValue
End Sub
```

Storing the background color in the profile

This time, we use radio buttons for the selection. The user's options are bewildering and vast: a silver background or a white background. (Tough choice, eh?)

Because the radio buttons share the same `groupname` value, they work together. When the user selects one, its `oncheckedchanged` fires. The buttons share a common handler, `rdbtn_CheckedChanged`, that determines what was checked. The routine stores a style attribute value in the `BGColour` property. Finally, it uses the value while creating a `style` attribute to add to the `<body>` tag.

```
Protected Sub rdbtn_CheckedChanged _
    (ByVal sender As Object, ByVal e As System.EventArgs)
    If rdbtnSilver.Checked Then
        Profile.BGColour = "background:silver"
        bdyPage.Attributes.Add("style", "background:silver")
    Else
        Profile.BGColour = "background:white"
        bdyPage.Attributes.Add("style", "background:white")
    End If
End Sub
```

Testing the profile properties

To confirm that ASP.NET is storing the user's choices and that we're retrieving the property values, you need to browse to the page. Here's a quick test plan:

1. **Browse to the Web page.**

2. **From the upper drop-down list, select French.**

   The date and time appear in French.

3. **From the lower drop-down list, select Keyboard.**

   The keyboard image appears.

4. **Select the radio button for Silver.**

   The background turns gray.

5. **Close all instances of the browser.**

6. **Open the browser again and navigate to the Web page you're testing.**

   The browser displays the logo, language, and background color according to your previous choices, as shown in Figure 2-5.

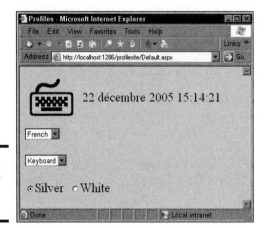

Figure 2-5:
Testing the
profiles
page.

Using Profiles with Authenticated Users

When you configure the site for anonymous users, you do nearly all the work needed to track authenticated users as well. The database, tables, and profile properties are the same. If you want to support profiles only for authenticated users, you can use the same `web.config` file with some minor adjustments.

Recall that we had to explicitly switch on anonymous profiles by adding this to the `web.config` file:

```
<anonymousIdentification enabled="true"/>
```

Likewise, we had to set `allowAnonymous` to `true` for each property:

```
<properties>
  <add name="Language" defaultValue="en-CA"
  allowAnonymous="true"/>
</properties>
```

If you want only authenticated profiles on your site, set `anonymousIdentification` and `allowAnonymous` to `false`. Even easier, you can remove the attributes from the file to force the default values (which are `false` in both cases).

The other change to support profiles for logged-in users is to enable forms authentication. Look for the `<authentication>` section and change the `mode` attribute value to `Forms`, as shown here:

```
<authentication mode="Forms" />
```

Viewing the list of profiles

The Profiles API makes it easy to view and manipulate profile data by exposing several methods in the default provider, SqlProfileProvider. The easiest method for querying the database is GetAllProfiles(). This procedure creates a page that lets you choose whether to view authenticated user profiles, anonymous profiles, or both.

1. **Add an ASP.NET Web form called** viewprofileinfo.aspx **to your project.**

2. **Add a** DropDownList **control called** Ddl1 **to the page and set the** autopostback **to** true. **Add three list items as shown in the following code (which is where the browser chooses the type of users to view):**

```
<asp:dropdownlist id="Ddl1" runat="server"
  autopostback="True"
  onselectedindexchanged="Ddl1_SelectedIndexChanged">
    <asp:listitem value="2">All</asp:listitem>
    <asp:listitem value="1">Authenticated</asp:listitem>
    <asp:listitem value="0">Unauthenticated</asp:listitem>
</asp:dropdownlist><br />
```

3. **Add an ASP.NET** Label **control called** lblRecordCount.

This label displays the number of records returned from the database.

4. **Add an ASP.NET** GridView **control called** GridView1.

Figure 2-6 shows the form in Design view.

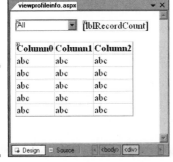

Figure 2-6:
Design view of the form to view profiles.

Book VIII Chapter 2

Using Profiles

5. **Add a subroutine named** ShowProfileData()**, using the following code:**

```
Protected Sub ShowProfileData _
  (ByVal PFO As ProfileAuthenticationOption)
     Dim Provider As SqlProfileProvider
     Dim totalRecords As Integer
```

```
Dim pageIndex As Integer = 0
Dim pageSize As Integer = 100
Provider = Profile.Providers _
    ("AspNetSqlProfileProvider")
GridView1.DataSource = Provider.GetAllProfiles _
    (PFO, pageIndex, pageSize, totalRecords)
GridView1.DataBind()
lblRecordCount.Text = "Records: " & _
    totalRecords.ToString
End Sub
```

6. **In the** Load **event of the form, call** ShowProfileData()**, passing it an** enum **as a parameter.**

The value you pass indicates whether you want authenticated user records, anonymous records, or both:

```
Protected Sub Page_Load _
(ByVal sender As Object, ByVal e As System.EventArgs)
    If Not IsPostBack Then
        ShowProfileData(ProfileAuthenticationOption.All)
    End If
End Sub
```

7. **Add a subroutine called** Ddl1_SelectedIndexChanged **to handle the** SelectedIndexChanged **event of the** DropDownList **control.**

The routine calls the ShowProfileData() method, passing it the user's choice to view profiles of authenticated users, anonymous users, or both. Here's what it looks like:

```
Protected Sub Ddl1_SelectedIndexChanged _
(ByVal sender As Object, ByVal e As System.EventArgs)
    ShowProfileData _
      (CType(Ddl1.SelectedValue, _
      ProfileAuthenticationOption))
End Sub
```

8. **Browse to the page to view the list of profiles.**

Figure 2-7 shows a sample result. Profiles for authenticated users include the username rather than a generated identifier. It may be hard to see in Figure 2-7, but notice that IsAnonymous is false (that is, unchecked) for users who have logged in.

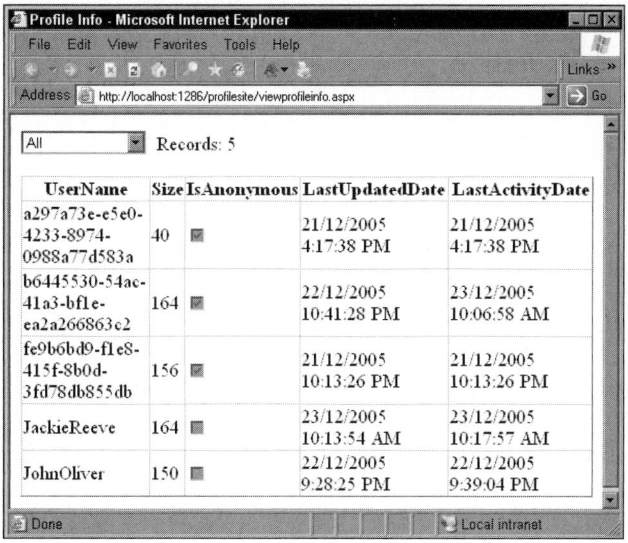

Figure 2-7:
List of all
profiles for
the Web.

There are two key parts to the `ShowProfileData()`. The first gets a reference to the current provider by passing the name of the provider (`AspNet SqlProfileProvider`) to the `Profile` object's `Providers` collection. The `Providers` collection contains all providers registered in the configuration file.

```
Provider = Profile.Providers _
("AspNetSqlProfileProvider")
```

The second key part to the routine is the `GetAllProfiles()` function. Here, you pass an authentication option, page-index and size values, and a reference to an integer variable (`totalRecords`). The function returns a `Profile InfoCollection` that you can consume directly as a `GridView` control's data source. The function fills the variable (which you pass by reference) with the number of records.

```
GridView1.DataSource = Provider.GetAllProfiles _
    (PFO, pageIndex, pageSize, totalRecords)
```

Maintaining the Profiles Database

When you allow anonymous profiles for a busy site, the database can expand rapidly. Many visitors might not return for months — if ever — but their profiles remain. If users delete their cookies, the profile becomes an orphan record. Fortunately, you don't need to be a SQL guru to maintain the profiles database and get rid of inactive profiles.

Deleting inactive profiles

Without reading users' minds, it's hard to know when their profiles become inactive. You can't say whether they intend to come back. It's also a question of degree. If someone hasn't visited your pages in 30 days, does that mean you have to make that profile inactive? The cut-off point amounts to a judgment call.

ASP.NET provides a `DeleteInactiveProfiles()` method that strips unwanted profiles from the database. You have to tell the method which profiles you want to delete — authenticated, anonymous, or all — and set a date before which the system should consider the profile inactive. For demonstration purposes, this section removes anonymous profiles that haven't been used (let's say) in a whole day.

1. **Add an ASP.NET page called** `deleteprofiles.aspx` **to your project.**

2. **Add a** `Label` **control called** `Label1` **and a** `Button` **control called** `Button1` **to the page.**

The markup looks like the following:

```
<asp:label id="Label1" runat="server">
 Click to delete records.
</asp:label>
<br />
<asp:button id="Button1" runat="server"
 onclick="Button1_Click" text="Delete Profiles" />
```

3. **In Design view, double-click the button to create an event handler for the** `Click` **event.**

4. **Add the following code as the event handler:**

```
Protected Sub Button1_Click _
  (ByVal sender As Object, _
    ByVal e As System.EventArgs)
    Dim Provider As SqlProfileProvider
    Dim dtInactiveSince As DateTime
    Dim retValue As Integer
    dtInactiveSince = DateAdd _
        (DateInterval.Day, -1, Now)
    Provider = Profile.Providers _
        ("AspNetSqlProfileProvider")
```

```
retValue = Provider.DeleteInactiveProfiles _
    (ProfileAuthenticationOption.Anonymous, _
     dtInactiveSince)
Label1.Text = "Deleted " & _
    retValue.ToString & " records."
End Sub
```

5. **Browse to** `deleteprofiles.aspx` **and click the button.**

    The routine deletes anonymous profiles that are more than a day old. The label shows the number of records deleted.

The variable `dtInactiveSince` holds a calculated date. In this case, we determine the date using the `DateAdd()` function. The date is one day (-1) before right now (`Now`). Next, we get an instance of the `Provider` object by referencing our registered provider, `AspNetSqlProfileProvider`. The `DeleteInactiveProfiles()` function returns the number of records deleted. We display the returned value in `Label1`.

To delete only authenticated profiles, pass the following:

```
ProfileAuthenticationOption.Authenticated to DeleteInactiveProfiles()
```

Deleting a specific profile

You can remove specific profiles using the `DeleteProfiles()` method. The first version of the method takes a `ProfileInfoCollection` object. That's fine if you're deleting a large number of profiles because it deletes them as a group. However, if you just want to surgically remove one or two profiles, there's a simpler version of the method (an *override* in geek-speak) that works with the username(s) in a string array as a parameter.

1. **Add an ASP.NET page called** `deleteaprofile.aspx` **to your project.**

2. **Add a** `Label` **control called** `Label1` **and a** `Button` **control called** `Button1` **to the page.**

    The code looks like the following:

```
<asp:label id="Label1" runat="server">
 Click to delete records.
</asp:label>
<br />
<asp:button id="Button1" runat="server"
 onclick="Button1_Click" text="Delete a Profile" />
```

3. **In Design view, double-click the button to create an event handler for the** `Click` **event.**

4. **Add the following code as the event handler:**

```
Protected Sub Button1_Click _
(ByVal sender As Object, _
 ByVal e As System.EventArgs)
    Dim strProfileNames() As String = _
        {"JackieReeve", "DoesntExist"}
    Dim Provider As SqlProfileProvider
    Dim retValue As Integer
    Provider = Profile.Providers _
        ("AspNetSqlProfileProvider")
    retValue = Provider.DeleteProfiles _
        (strProfileNames)
    Label1.Text = "Deleted " & _
        retValue.ToString & " records."
End Sub
```

5. **Browse to** `deleteaprofile.aspx` **and click the button**.

The routine deletes `JackieReeve`'s profile and the label shows one deletion.

By declaring a string array in the preceding code, you can add a comma-delimited list of usernames for deletion. In this case, I included a nonexistent username (`DoesntExist`) to show that the `DeleteProfiles()` function doesn't fail or crash if the usernames aren't found. (Of course, in a real application, you probably won't hard-code the usernames as literals.)

Using a Custom Profile Provider

ASP.NET provides the SqlProfileProvider by default. However, there may be situations where you can't use SQL Server. Perhaps your boss only allows Oracle on the site, or your ISP charges too much for SQL Server. It may be that you have an existing database schema and want to remain compatible with legacy systems. (At least one developer I know won't use SQL Server on his site. He sleeps better knowing he's done his part to prevent FoxPro databases from becoming extinct.) Whatever the reason, Microsoft makes it possible to hook profiles up to almost any database, an XML document — or even a lowly text file — as long as someone is willing to write a compatible provider for the data store.

We're not going to write a custom provider here; that's too big a job. However, you can find examples by searching for the Provider Toolkit at `http://msdn.microsoft.com`. Instead of writing a provider, let's look at where to get one for Microsoft Access and how to plug it in to our site.

Obtaining the Access provider

At one point, the ASP.NET team planned to use Access as its default profile database. You might still see references to it in books that were written while ASP.NET 2.0 was still in the beta stage. As we've seen, the release product uses SQL Server 2005 or SQL Server 2005 Express.

In a generous move, Microsoft has made the Access provider's source code available for us to analyze, compile, and use. At the time of writing, the Access provider was featured at

```
http://msdn.microsoft.com/vstudio/downloads/starterkits/
```

Because URLs change, you might want to search the MSDN site for "Sample Access Provider Starter Kit" or try the direct download link:

```
http://download.microsoft.com/download/5/5/b/55bc291f-4316-4fd7-9269-
    dbf9edbaada8/SampleAccessProviders.vsi
```

Building the Access provider

The Sample Access Providers Starter Kit is a C# class library project that includes an empty Access database complete with the required schema. The only glitch is that you need to install a copy of Visual C# Express to compile the source code into a binary file.

You can download (a free download as of this writing) Visual C# Express from

```
http://msdn.microsoft.com/vstudio/express/visualcsharp/
```

Installing the starter kit

After installing VC#, you're ready to install the starter kit. The template kit files come wrapped in a Visual Studio Community Content Installer file (`.vsi`).

1. **Make sure the Visual C# 2005 IDE is not running.**

2. **In Windows Explorer, double-click** `SampleAccessProviders.vsi`**.**

The Visual Studio Content Installer opens.

3. **Click Next. If you get a warning that the file has not been signed, click Yes and continue anyway.**

Not to worry; someone will autograph it later.

4. **Click Finish and then click Close.**

Creating the Visual C# project

Here's how to create a new project based on the ASP.NET Access Providers template.

1. **In Visual C# Express, from the File menu, click New Project.**

The New Project dialog box opens.

2. **Under Project types, expand the Visual C# node and select the Visual Web Developer node (as shown in Figure 2-8).**

3. **Select the ASP.NET Access Providers template.**

4. **In the Name box, replace the default name with** `SampleAccess Providers`**.**

This exact name is important because the configuration file looks for it later on.

5. **Click OK.**

The IDE creates a solution and project called `SampleAccessProviders`.

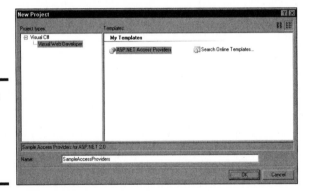

Figure 2-8:
Creating a
C# project
based
on the
template.

Compiling the Dynamic Link Library (DLL)

The sample Access provider comes as a source code project. To use the code as a provider, you need to build the DLL. Here's how you can compile it quickly in Visual C# 2005 Express:

1. **In Solution Explorer, select the project file,** `SampleAccessProviders`**.**

2. **From the Build menu, click Build Solution.**

3. **Make sure the Show All Files button is on, and then expand the project nodes (SampleAccessProviders⇨bin⇨Release).**

Figure 2-9 shows the expansion; use it to confirm that the binary files were created.

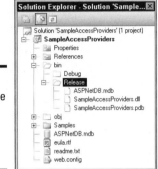

Figure 2-9:
Locating the binary Access provider files.

4. **Exit Visual C# Express.**

Configuring the Web for the Access provider

When you have the Access provider built as a .NET DLL, you can move the required files into the Visual Web Developer Express (VWDE) Web project. Finding the files from the C# project can be tricky. Try looking in

```
C:\Documents and Settings\<user>\My Documents\Visual Studio
     2005\Projects\SampleAccessProviders\SampleAccessProviders\bin\Release
```

where `<user>` is your login name.

1. **With the Web project open (the sample uses** `profilesite`**), create a** `Bin` **folder under the root (Website⇨Add ASP.NET Folder⇨Bin).**

2. **Using Windows Explorer, drag** `SampleAccessProviders.dll` **from the C# project into the Web project's** `Bin` **folder.**

3. **Using Windows Explorer, drag ASPNetDB.mdb from the C# project and drop it into the Web project's** `App_Data` **folder.**

4. **Rename your Web project's** `web.config` **file to** `web.config_sql`.

5. **Using Windows Explorer, drag the** `web.config` **from the C# project and drop it into the root of the Web project.**

   Note that you must use the version of the `web.config` file that comes with the sample Access provider code.

Creating a test page for the Access provider

Your Web project is now set to use the `AccessProfileProvider` rather than the default `AspNetSqlProfileProvider`. The final step is to show that the provider is working. We can do that with a test page, using the following steps:

1. **Add an ASP.NET page called** `Accessprovider.aspx` **to your project.**

2. **Add a** `Button`, `Label`, **and** `GridView` **controls, as shown in the following code:**

```
<asp:button id="Button1" runat="server"
  onclick="Button1_Click" text="Show All" /><br />
<br />
<asp:label id="lblRecordCount" runat="server">
</asp:label><br />
<br />
<asp:gridview id="GridView1" runat="server">
</asp:gridview>
```

3. **Double-click the** `Button` **control to create an event handler, and then substitute the following code:**

```
Protected Sub Button1_Click _
(ByVal sender As Object, _
ByVal e As System.EventArgs)
    ShowProfileData _
    (ProfileAuthenticationOption.All)
End Sub
```

4. **In the page** `Load` **event add the following code:**

This initializes the profile, using the properties defined in the `web.config` file that comes with the Access profile provider sample.

```
Protected Sub Page_Load _
(ByVal sender As Object, _
ByVal e As System.EventArgs)
    Profile.FriendlyName = "Big Charmer"
    Profile.Height = 68
    Profile.Weight = 152
End Sub
```

5. **Add the following** `ShowProfileData()` **subroutine.**

This code is almost the same as what we used in a previous test page, except it references the `AccessProfileProvider`.

```
Protected Sub ShowProfileData _
(ByVal PFO As ProfileAuthenticationOption)
    Dim Provider As _
     Samples.AccessProviders.AccessProfileProvider
    Dim totalRecords As Integer
    Dim pageIndex As Integer = 0
    Dim pageSize As Integer = 100
    Provider = Profile.Providers _
        ("AccessProfileProvider")
```

```
GridView1.DataSource = Provider.GetAllProfiles _
    (PFO, pageIndex, pageSize, totalRecords)
GridView1.DataBind()
lblRecordCount.Text = "Records: " & _
    totalRecords.ToString
End Sub
```

6. **Browse to** `Accessprovider.aspx` **and click the button.**

The grid should display at least one record, as shown in Figure 2-10.

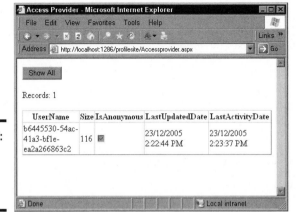

Figure 2-10:
Testing the
Access
provider
page.

A common error that crops up when using Access databases on Internet Information Services goes like this: `The Microsoft Jet database engine cannot open the file.` Try these fixes:

✦ **Make sure the ASPNET user has read and write permissions to the** `App_Data` **folder containing** `ASPNetDB.mdb.`

✦ **Make sure the ASPNET user has both read and write access to the system's TEMP directory.** You can find out the location of the TEMP directory by right-clicking My Computer, going to Properties➪Advanced, and clicking the Environment Variables button.

Chapter 3: Site Navigation

In This Chapter

✔ **Making Web pages easy to navigate with TreeViews, Menus, and breadcrumbs**

✔ **Coding your own navigation controls**

✔ **Knowing where you are with a SiteMap file**

✔ **Sprucing up navigation controls with custom styles**

Disorientation is a very uncomfortable sensation. People need to know where they are, how they got there, and how to get back to where they previously were. This applies not only to physical environments, but also to the virtual space on the Internet. The bigger the Web site, the harder it is to navigate. You can recognize a poorly designed site as you explore it: The only way to get back to a recognizable place is to retype the starting URL.

Navigation tools help visitors build a mental model of the site and categorize huge numbers of pages. The `TreeView` control, with its expandable nodes, helps users deal with hundreds of links in manageable chunks and logical paths. The `Menu` control guides browsers by generating a horizontal or vertical interface that reveals categories and hierarchies as you pass the mouse pointer over an item. *Breadcrumbs*, implemented through the ASP.NET `SiteMapPath` control and its corresponding `Web.sitemap` file, show the user the pathway back up through the site's hierarchy, often with links to each page's parent page.

In this chapter, you learn how to add and configure navigation controls for use on your ASP.NET pages.

Understanding Site Navigation

For a small Web site, you can get away with a list of hyperlinks to content. As the site grows, you need to categorize the pages by building a menu structure with submenus and perhaps a `TreeView` with a few nodes. At a certain point, adding menu items and leaf nodes one at a time becomes unwieldy. Every time a link changes, you've got to open all the files to fix it. That's when you decide that you need a dynamic navigation structure. The controls should build themselves automatically and base themselves on a single data source that you can manage conveniently.

There are three main approaches to constructing navigation controls:

✦ **Use the graphical designer in Visual Web Developer.** This method is fine for static content, or for creating the basic look and feel of a dynamic control.

✦ **Dynamically, using code.** This technique adds nodes, text, and other values programmatically.

✦ **Build the control's structure dynamically by consuming hierarchical data source such as a database or XML file.** This is the best solution for large sites where you add, change, and remove pages frequently.

There's a good chance that you'll have navigation elements on almost every page in the site. Many people create a new page by cloning an existing page, complete with the source page's navigation controls and images. While that works for a while, it creates a potential maintenance nightmare: You have to fix several pages when *anything* changes in the navigation.

The better way is to include your navigation controls in a master page right from the start. When you occasionally need a page that doesn't require navigation (such as a pop-up window), you can make that an exception to the master's rule.

It might be hard to decide whether to use a `TreeView` or a vertical `Menu` control on a site — or both. Both offer style options, but the `Menu` control also offers templates where you can create very sophisticated designs. With a large amount of data, a `TreeView` control loads faster by using the *download-on-demand* option. That's where it fetches data for a node only when the node needs to display it. To let users select multiple items, you might need check boxes. Only the `TreeView` control supports check boxes. To take advantage of on-screen real estate, you can spread `Menu` items horizontally across the page or vertically down the side. A `TreeView` is always vertical (except when the monitor is knocked over).

Using a Web.sitemap File

The `Web.sitemap` file (don't ask me why Microsoft capitalized the first letter of the filename) lets you maintain your site's structure in one place for all to use. `TreeView`, `Menu`, and `SiteMapPath` controls consume its data with very little configuration.

Creating the Web.sitemap file

`Web.sitemap` is a tightly formatted XML document that acts as a simple data store. It defines your site's structure and provides data to the nodes.

Node data includes tooltip text, link text, URLs, and even links to other `sitemap` files.

You add a `Web.sitemap` file to your project by going to Website➪Add New Item➪Site map. Doing so adds a skeleton outline like this:

```
<?xml version="1.0" encoding="utf-8" ?>
<siteMap
xmlns="http://schemas.microsoft.com/AspNet/SiteMap-File-1.0">
    <siteMapNode url="" title=""  description="">
        <siteMapNode url="" title=""  description="" />
        <siteMapNode url="" title=""  description="" />
    </siteMapNode>
</siteMap>
```

The `sitemap` schema defines several elements and attributes that are recognized within a valid `Web.sitemap` file. Here's a quick look at what you can use to create nodes for menus, trees, and breadcrumbs:

✦ `<sitemap>`: The top-level element. You must have one, and only one, of these. Everything else nests inside it. There's one attribute:

- `xmlns`: The value of this attribute identifies the official namespace. This attribute and the long namespace string are not a necessity, but including this shows good form and may help designer tools catch goof-ups.

✦ `<siteMapNode>`: This element creates a node that you can see in the `Menu` or `TreeView`. You must have at least one of these, but chances are you'll have quite a few. To create a hierarchy, you nest `siteMapNode` elements within each other, going deeper and deeper as necessary. For example, the first instance of `siteMapNode` creates a main menu and elements nested within it create submenus. Elements nested within submenus create sub-submenus and so on. Here are the main attributes for a `sitemap` node:

- `url`: This can be a virtual path to a page in your site or a URL path to a page on the other side of the Internet. Use this attribute only if you want the node to be clickable.

- `title`: The value of the `title` attribute is the text that appears on a menu item or tree node. ASP.NET renders the text as a hyperlink if you have the `url` attribute in the same node.

- `description`: This optional text appears as a tooltip when the user hovers the mouse pointer over the menu or tree node. The description text helps people decide if the node contains what they're looking for. It also helps make the site more accessible.

- `siteMapFile`: Lets you link to external site maps by providing the path to the file.

Adding data to the sitemap file

You can add data to the `sitemap` by editing the file in a source code or XML editor. The following VB code shows the nesting of `siteMapNode` elements. For example, you can see that the `siteMapNode` with `title="ASP.NET"` doesn't use a `url` attribute. That's because it only acts as a parent node and container for other nodes. It doesn't link anywhere.

```
<?xml version="1.0" encoding="utf-8" ?>
<siteMap
 xmlns=
"http://schemas.microsoft.com/AspNet/SiteMap-File-1.0">
  <siteMapNode title="Home"
               description="Starting page"
               url="~/default.aspx">
    <siteMapNode title="ASP.NET"
                 description="ASP.NET Resources">
      <siteMapNode title="FAQs"
                   description="Frequently Asked Questions"
                   url="~/faqs.aspx">
        <siteMapNode title ="What's New in 2.0"
                     description="New stuff"
                     url="~/whatsnew.aspx" />
        <siteMapNode title ="Using a TreeView"
                     description="ASP.NET TreeView"
                     url="~/treeview.aspx" />
        <siteMapNode title ="Using a Menu"
                     description="ASP.NET Menu"
                     url="~/menu.aspx" />
      </siteMapNode>
    </siteMapNode>
    <siteMapNode title="Getting Started"
                 description="For beginners"
                 url="~/getstart.aspx" />
    <siteMapNode title="Resume"
                 description="My Curriculum Vitae"
                 url="~/resume.aspx" />
    <siteMapNode title="Contact"
                 description="Ways to contact me">
      <siteMapNode title="E-mail"
                   description="Contact by e-mail"
                   url="~/email.aspx" />
      <siteMapNode title="Phone"
                   description="Reach me by phone"
                   url="phone.aspx"/>
      <siteMapNode title="IM"
                   description="My Messaging IDs"
                   url="~/IM.aspx" />
      <siteMapNode title="Log In"
                   description="Private pages"
```

```
                                url="~/login.aspx" />
          </siteMapNode>
        </siteMapNode>
      </siteMap>
```

TIP

Include the tilde (~) character and a forward slash (/) as part of the URL path for local files. This ensures that pages in subdirectories can always find the root. The tilde is an ASP.NET shortcut for "start at the root of this site."

It's hard to visualize the structure of a site just by staring at the raw XML in a `sitemap` file. Figure 3-1 shows the preceding sitemap data as rendered by a barebones `TreeView` control. It shows the way `siteMapNode` elements nest inside other `siteMapNode` elements. For example, the FAQ, Getting Started, and Resume nodes nest inside the ASP.NET node. Notice that the mouse pointer is hovering over the Phone node that displays the `description` attribute's value as a tool tip.

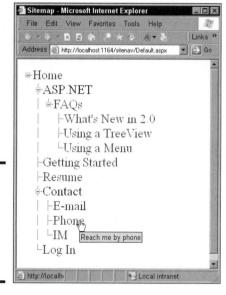

Figure 3-1:
Rendered
sitemap
data using
the
TreeView
control.

Using the SiteMapDataSource control

Out-of-the-box, the `Web.sitemap` file plays very nicely with the `SiteMapPath` (breadcrumb) control. The moment you drop the `SiteMapPath` control on the page, it's ready to render whatever content it finds in `Web.sitemap`. You don't even need to tell it the name of the `sitemap` file.

For other server controls, such as the `TreeView`, `Menu`, and `DropDownList`, you need to call on the `SiteMapDataSource` control. `SiteMapDataSource` (located under the Data tab in the toolbox) fetches the XML from the `Web.sitemap` and makes the data digestible to navigation controls.

This scenario is starting to look like a food chain: the `TreeView` binds to the `SiteMapDataSource` which gets its data from `Web.sitemap` via the `XmlSiteMapProvider`.

If a control isn't getting data from `Web.sitemap`, make sure it has the `SiteMapDataSource` control as a helper.

Now that we have a basic understanding of the `Web.sitemap` file, let's take a more in-depth look at the navigation tools. The following sections examine the `TreeView`, `Menu`, and `SiteMapPath` controls.

Using the TreeView Control

The ASP.NET `TreeView` control displays hierarchical data and hyperlinks to pages on the same site or other Web servers. While often seen as part of a site's navigation tools, the `TreeView` is very useful for representing other hierarchies such as company divisions and departments. Figure 3-2 shows the built-in `XPFileExplorer` style that gives a Web page the look of Windows Explorer.

Figure 3-2:
TreeView
with XPFile
Explorer
image set.

`TreeView` terminology is somewhat upside-down. Here's a summary:

✦ `Root` **node:** Usually found at the top of the tree rather than hidden in the soil at the bottom where real-world roots belong. A `Root` node is an orphan — it has no parents. However, it has at least one child node. A `TreeView` can (but customarily doesn't) have more than one `Root` node.

✦ `Parent` **node:** This node must have a parent node (a node without a parent becomes a root node) and one or more child nodes. You often see parents in a collapsed state, especially if they have many children. (Who says the logical world can't imitate life?)

✦ `Leaf` **node:** These are nodes without child nodes. Unfettered by children, leaves tend to branch out.

Creating a TreeView in Design view

You can build a `TreeView` from scratch using the design tools in Visual Web Developer Express. You can add the nodes, text, links, and styles in the properties pages and collection editors.

The following sections show you how to create a `TreeView` control in Design view and hard-code the nodes in the `.aspx` markup file. Although you may sometimes want to do it this way, you're usually better off using a `Web.sitemap` file to provide the structure displayed by the `TreeView` control. You'll learn how to do that in the section "Creating a TreeView from a sitemap," later in this chapter.

Think twice about hard-coding elaborate styles in Design view. Although you *can* do it, you'll end up wishing you'd spent the time creating a reusable style sheet instead. Go to Book 3, Chapter 4, to see why style sheets are a better idea.

Adding nodes in Design view

You use the `TreeView`'s editor to build the hierarchy of nodes.

1. **From the Navigation tab of the toolbox, drag a** `TreeView` **control to the page.**

The TreeView Node Editor dialog box opens.

2. **As shown in Figure 3-3, click the Add Root button to add a root node. Set the** `Text` **property to** `Newspaper`**.**

**Book VIII
Chapter 3**

Site Navigation

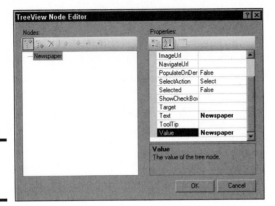

Figure 3-3:
Adding a
root node.

3. With the root node selected, click the Add Child button to add a child node. Set the Text **property to** News Section, **as shown in Figure 3-4.**

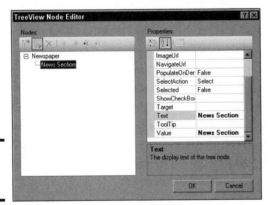

Figure 3-4:
Adding a
child node.

4. With the News Section **node selected, click the Add Child button to add a child node. Set the** NavigateUrl **property to** local.aspx **and the** Text **property to** Local.

If you add a node to the wrong place, click the arrow buttons to adjust the hierarchy.

5. Add a few more parent and child nodes, as shown in Table 3-1.

6. **Click OK when you're done.**

The node editor closes.

7. **In the** `TreeView` **control's property page, set the** `Showlines` **property to** `True`.

Table 3-1	Sample Data for the TreeView Control	
Parent	*Text and Value Property*	*NavigateUrl Property*
News Section	Regional	regional.aspx
News Section	National	national.aspx
News Section	World	world.aspx
News Section	Weird News	weird.aspx
Sports	Hockey	hockey.aspx
Sports	Football	football.aspx
Sports	Tennis	tennis.aspx
Entertainment	Movies	movies.aspx
Entertainment	Television	tv.aspx
Entertainment	Comics	comics.aspx

Figure 3-5 shows the finished `TreeView` in Design view.

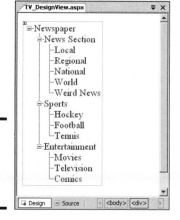

Figure 3-5: TreeView with nodes in Design view.

The designer generated the following code to implement the nodes you added:

```
<asp:treeview id="TreeView1" runat="server" font-size="Large" showlines="True">
  <nodes>
     <asp:treenode text="Newspaper" value="Newspaper">
         <asp:treenode text="News Section" value="News Section">
             <asp:treenode navigateurl="local.aspx" text="Local" value="Local">
             </asp:treenode>
             <asp:treenode navigateurl="regional.aspx" text="Regional"
   value="Regional">
             </asp:treenode>
             <asp:treenode navigateurl="national.aspx" text="National"
   value="National">
             </asp:treenode>
             <asp:treenode navigateurl="world.aspx" text="World" value="World">
             </asp:treenode>
               <asp:treenode text="Weird News" value="Weird News">
               </asp:treenode>
         </asp:treenode>
         <asp:treenode text="Sports" value="Sports">
             <asp:treenode navigateurl="hockey.aspx" text="Hockey"
   value="Hockey">
             </asp:treenode>
             <asp:treenode navigateurl="football.aspx" text="Football"
   value="Football">
             </asp:treenode>
             <asp:treenode navigateurl="tennis.aspx" text="Tennis"
   value="Tennis">
             </asp:treenode>
          </asp:treenode>
         <asp:treenode text="Entertainment" value="Entertainment">
             <asp:treenode navigateurl="movies.aspx" text="Movies"
   value="Movies">
             </asp:treenode>
             <asp:treenode navigateurl="televison.aspx" text="Television"
   value="Television">
             </asp:treenode>
             <asp:treenode navigateurl="comics.aspx" text="Comics"
   value="Comics">
             </asp:treenode>
         </asp:treenode>
     </asp:treenode>
  </nodes>
</asp:treeview>
```

When you mix ASP.NET tags, attributes, and their values in with the HTML markup (as in the preceding code), geeks refer to it as *adding declarative markup.* When you add these in code, you are adding the objects and property values programmatically, or on the fly.

Setting TreeView styles in Design view

You can change almost every aspect of the `TreeView` control, ranging from the fonts, colors, and borders to the images and indentation levels. You have very fine (*granular* in geek-speak) control over individual nodes. Figure 3-6 shows that you can assign different fonts, icons, backgrounds, and colors, depending on the node's place in the hierarchy or on its runtime state (hover or selected).

In addition to the global style property (NodeStyle), you can customize nodes with the HoverNodeStyle, LeafNodeStyle, ParentNodeStyle, RootNodeStyle, and SelectedNodeStyle properties. Figure 3-7 shows changes to the LeafNodeStyle properties.

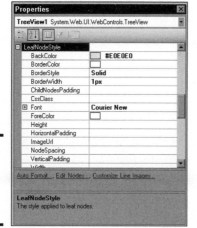

The TreeView designer stores the styles in the markup, just before the closing </asp:treeview> tag, as shown in this sample:

```
<nodestyle font-size="Large" />
<parentnodestyle font-names="Comic Sans MS" />
```

```
<rootnodestyle font-bold="True" font-names="Verdana" />
<leafnodestyle font-names="Courier New" backcolor="#E0E0E0"
    borderstyle="Solid" borderwidth="1px" />
<selectednodestyle font-italic="True" />
<hovernodestyle font-italic="True" />
```

If you're using style sheets (and you should), you can do much of the creative work and testing in Design view — by changing the properties for the node styles. When the nodes look right, re-create the CSS styles, basing them on the attributes and values the designer generates for you. (For more on style sheets, see Book 3, Chapter 4.)

Creating a TreeView programmatically

Almost anything you can do declaratively, you can do in code — including creating a `TreeView` from scratch and making it beautiful. In some cases, you just want to change a few values using code, such as highlighting a node in reaction to the click of a button elsewhere on the page.

Note that I wouldn't recommend creating a `TreeView` control in this way unless you are getting its structure from a database. In most cases, you're better off binding the `TreeView` control to a `sitemap` file, as described in the section "Creating a TreeView from a sitemap," later in this chapter.

Creating a TreeNode

When you assemble a `TreeView` in code, you mainly build `TreeNode` objects and lots of them. Earlier in the chapter, in the section "Using the TreeView Control," various node types (`Root`, `Parent`, and `Leaf`) put in an appearance. The differentiation, however, doesn't mean anything at the creation stage; that's because the type is based on the node's location. For now, a node is a node. (Node types do become significant with styles.)

Creating nodes is a repetitive task that calls for a function. The `BuildNode()` function, shown below, takes two values as parameters and gives back a `TreeNode` object. The first value (`strTextAndValue`) is a string to use as the node's displayed text and value. The second parameter (`strURL`) is optional. It's the URL to which users navigate if they click a `Leaf` node. In the case of a parent node, you sometimes want a URL and sometimes don't. You would include a URL if you have a summary page for the parent node. In this case, the node is solely for drilling down. If you don't provide the `strURL` parameter it's no big deal because the function defaults to an empty string.

```
Private Function BuildNode _
    (ByVal strTextAndValue As String, _
    Optional ByVal strURL As String = "") As TreeNode
' Creates a TreeNode and assigns
' the Text, Value and NavigateUrl
```

```
' values
Dim node As New TreeNode
node.Text = strTextAndValue
node.Value = strTextAndValue
node.NavigateUrl = strURL
Return node
End Function
```

Defining the TreeView

When you know you can generate nodes, it's time to turn to the main routine. You would likely use this code in the handler for the page's `Load` event:

```
Dim tv As New TreeView
tv.ID = "TreeView1"
tv.Font.Size = FontUnit.Large
tv.ShowLines = True
tv.Height = Unit.Pixel(348)
tv.EnableViewState = False
PlaceHolder1.Controls.Add(tv)
```

The code section starts by declaring the variable `tv` that creates an instance of the `TreeView` control object. Set the `ID` of the control and the default size for the tree's font. Turn on the lines that connect nodes to their parent node and make the tree `348` pixels high. By setting `EnableViewState` to `False`, we cut the amount of overhead data and excess markup that the page requires.

The last line in the snippet assumes that you added an ASP.NET `PlaceHolder` control to the page. The line adds the `TreeView` control to the placeholder's `Controls` collection.

Defining the Root node

As in the section "Adding nodes in Design view" (earlier in this chapter), the `TreeView` control must have a `Root` node. The `TreeView` control has a `Nodes` collection that contains all of the top-level (that is, `Root`-level) nodes. The `Nodes` collection's `Add()` method adds the node that the `BuildNode()` function creates. In this case, we pass the name `Newspaper` to `BuildNode()` to create a root to hold the remaining nodes. Notice that the same string, "Newspaper" serves as the `Title` and `Value` properties.

```
tv.Nodes.Add(BuildNode("Newspaper"))
```

Defining the child nodes of the Root node

In this sequence, we add the three nodes that stem from the `Root` node. Figure 3-8 shows these nodes. Every `Parent` node has a `ChildNodes` collection which, remarkably, contains its child nodes.

Figure 3-8:
Nodes that stem from the root node.

We know that the `TreeView`'s `Nodes` collection contains one `Root` node because we just added it in the previous section, "Defining the Root node." The `Root` node has its own `ChildNodes` collection. The `ChildNodes` collection also has an `Add()` method that adds nodes. Knowing this, we can add three child nodes using the following statements:

```
tv.Nodes(0).ChildNodes.Add(BuildNode("News Section"))
tv.Nodes(0).ChildNodes.Add(BuildNode("Sports"))
tv.Nodes(0).ChildNodes.Add(BuildNode("Entertainment"))
```

Geeks call the preceding technique "walking the object model." The idea is to drill down through various objects, properties, collections, and methods to change, add, or remove something.

Adding individual Leaf nodes

We're ready to add some `Leaf` nodes. These are the nodes with no children — such as Local, Regional, National, and World in Figure 3-9. Clicking one of these sends the user to a page in our fictitious Web site.

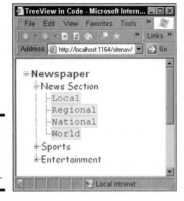

Figure 3-9:
Leaf nodes have no child nodes.

The steps to add the `Leaf` nodes follow the pattern established in the preceding section. The main difference is that we get a reference to the `Parent` node using a variable. We know that the `Root` node has three child nodes. We want to add nodes to the first of those nodes — the one with the text `"News Section"`. In zero-based counting, the first child of the `Root` node is available as `tv.Nodes(0).ChildNodes(0)`. When we call `BuildNode()` this time, we include the URL value to build in the navigation hyperlink.

```
Dim parent As TreeNode
parent = tv.Nodes(0).ChildNodes(0)
parent.ChildNodes.Add(BuildNode("Local", "local.aspx"))
parent.ChildNodes.Add(BuildNode("Regional", "regional.aspx"))
parent.ChildNodes.Add(BuildNode("National", "national.aspx"))
parent.ChildNodes.Add(BuildNode("World", "world.aspx"))
```

The same process happens twice more to add nodes to the `Sports` and `Entertainment Parent` nodes — which can be referenced as `tv.Nodes(0).ChildNodes(1)` and `tv.Nodes(0).ChildNodes(2)`, respectively.

```
parent = tv.Nodes(0).ChildNodes(1)
parent.ChildNodes.Add(BuildNode("Hockey", "hockey.aspx"))
parent.ChildNodes.Add(BuildNode("Football", "football.aspx"))
parent.ChildNodes.Add(BuildNode("Tennis", "tennis.aspx"))
parent = tv.Nodes(0).ChildNodes(2)
parent.ChildNodes.Add(BuildNode("Movies", "movies.aspx"))
parent.ChildNodes.Add(BuildNode("Television", "tv.aspx"))
parent.ChildNodes.Add(BuildNode("Comics", "comics.aspx"))
```

Adding styles to nodes

In an example from the section "Creating a TreeView in Design view," earlier in this chapter, you created different styles for various types of nodes (such as a `Root`, `Leaf`, and `Parent`). The code here duplicates those steps.

For the most part, you design styles in code by altering the style's properties. For example, the following code changes a property in the `TreeView`'s `NodeStyle` object. `NodeStyle` is the overall style that applies until you override it at a more specific level, such as a `LeafNodeStyle`. Let's just set the overall font size to `Large`:

```
tv.NodeStyle.Font.Size = FontUnit.Large
```

Next, we change values in the `TreeView` control's `LeafNodeStyle` object. We set the font to `Courier New`, the background color to `Gray`, and put a solid, 1 pixel border around the text:

```
tv.LeafNodeStyle.Font.Names = New String() {"Courier New"}
tv.LeafNodeStyle.BackColor = Drawing.Color.Gray
```

```
tv.LeafNodeStyle.BorderStyle = BorderStyle.Solid
tv.LeafNodeStyle.BorderWidth = Unit.Pixel(1)
```

Setting the `TreeView`'s `Root` style follows the same pattern: Use the `RootNodeStyle` object and make its font `Verdana` and `Bold`.

```
tv.RootNodeStyle.Font.Bold = True
tv.RootNodeStyle.Font.Names = New String() {"Verdana"}
```

We can make quick work of the `ParentNodeStyle` and `SelectedNodeStyle` by assigning a new font to the former and turning the latter to `Italic` text.

```
tv.ParentNodeStyle.Font.Names=New String() {"Comic Sans MS"}
tv.SelectedNodeStyle.Font.Italic = True
```

`HoverNodeStyle` is the style that determines the appearance of a node when the mouse pointer hovers over it. In this case, we want to have `Italic` text appear while the hovering is going on:

```
tv.HoverNodeStyle.Font.Italic = True
```

If your programming style is to get a reference to an object by declaring a variable, be aware that `HoverNodeStyle` inherits from `Style` rather than from `TreeNodeStyle`. Therefore you need to declare the variable as a `Style` type if you want a reference.

Creating a TreeView from a sitemap

We hook up a `TreeView` control to a `Web.sitemap` file early in this chapter (in a discussion of the `SiteMapDataSource` control). Here we re-create the Newspaper example by putting the data in the `Web.sitemap` file and consuming it.

1. **If your project doesn't include a** `Web.sitemap` **file, add one (Web Site⇨New Item⇨Site Map).**

2. **Replace the existing XML with the content below.**

(This is an abbreviated version with fewer nodes to save space.)

```
<?xml version="1.0" encoding="utf-8" ?>
<siteMap
 xmlns=
"http://schemas.microsoft.com/AspNet/SiteMap-File-1.0">
  <siteMapNode title="Newspaper" description="Newspaper">
    <siteMapNode title="News Section" description="News Section">
      <siteMapNode url="~/local.aspx" title="Local" description="Local">
      </siteMapNode>
      <siteMapNode url="~/regional.aspx" title="Regional"
    description="Regional">
```

```
      </siteMapNode>
      <siteMapNode url="~/national.aspx" title="National"
    description="National">
      </siteMapNode>
      <siteMapNode url="~/world.aspx" title="World" description="World">
      </siteMapNode>
      <siteMapNode url="~/weird.aspx" title="Weird News"
    description="Weird News">
      </siteMapNode>
    </siteMapNode>
    <siteMapNode title="Sports" description="Sports">
      <siteMapNode url="~/hockey.aspx" title="Hockey"
    description="Hockey">
      </siteMapNode>
    </siteMapNode>
  </siteMapNode>
</siteMap>
```

3. **Open an ASP.NET page in Design view.**

4. **From the toolbox, under the Data tab, drag a** `SiteMapDataSource` **control and drop it on the design surface.**

5. **From the toolbox, under the Navigation tab, drag a** `TreeView` **control and drop in on the page.**

6. **As shown in Figure 3-10, use the Smart Tasks menu to set the data source to the** `SiteMapDataSource` **object.**

Figure 3-10:
Setting the
TreeView
data source.

7. **Add styles to the nodes**

   You can use the designer, code the styles, or assign style-sheet classes.

Using the Menu Control

The ASP.NET `Menu` control, shown in Figure 3-11, helps you categorize pages so users can drill down to find the content they seek. In the default configuration, the menu displays the top-level items at all times. The submenus appear dynamically as you hover the mouse pointer over a menu item. The layout of a menu can be horizontal, as shown in Figure 3-11, or vertical. You have a wide range of customization options, including fonts, backgrounds, colors, and even the time a submenu takes to disappear when the mouse pointer moves away from it.

Figure 3-11:
ASP.NET
Menu
control.

Creating a Menu in Design view

You can use the development environment's visual design tools to configure the `Menu`'s appearance and add menu items. A manual approach is acceptable for a very small site, but consider using a `Web.sitemap` file with style sheets for a larger site.

Think twice about hard-coding elaborate styles in Design view. Although you can do it, you might end up wishing you'd spent the time creating a reusable style sheet instead. Go to Book 3, Chapter 4, to see why style sheets are a better idea.

Adding items in Design view

You use the Menu Item collection editor to create the hierarchy. Here's how:

1. **From the Navigation tab of the toolbox, drag a** `Menu` **control to the page.**

2. **Click Edit Menu Items.**

The Menu Item Editor dialog box opens.

3. **Click the** Add a root item **button three times and change the** `Text` **property for the items to** `News Section`, `Sports`, **and** `Hockey` **respectively, as shown in Figure 3-12.**

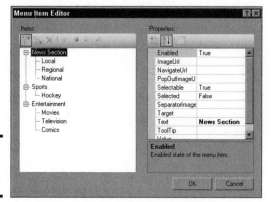

Figure 3-12:
Adding
menu items.

4. **Select a root item and click the Add a Child Item button. Add menu items to each** `Parent`. **Provide a** `Text` **property such as** `Local` **and a** `NavigateUrl` **property such as** `local.aspx`.

   Table 3-2 shows sample data for the menu.

5. **When you're finished, click OK.**

The editor generates markup for you, wrapping the menu items in an `<items>` tag and creating the hierarchy that you see in the following code:

```
<asp:menu id="Menu1" runat="server" orientation="Horizontal">
<items>
    <asp:menuitem text="News Section">
        <asp:menuitem navigateurl="local.aspx"
            text="Local" value="Local"></asp:menuitem>
        <asp:menuitem navigateurl="regional.aspx"
            text="Regional" value="Regional"></asp:menuitem>
        <asp:menuitem navigateurl="national.aspx"
            text="National" value="National"></asp:menuitem>
    </asp:menuitem>
    <asp:menuitem text="Sports" value="Sports">
        <asp:menuitem navigateurl="hockey.aspx"
            text="Hockey" value="Hockey"></asp:menuitem>
    </asp:menuitem>
    <asp:menuitem text="Entertainment" value="Entertainment">
        <asp:menuitem navigateurl="movies.aspx"
            text="Movies" value="Movies"></asp:menuitem>
        <asp:menuitem navigateurl="tv.aspx"
            text="Television"
```

**Book VIII
Chapter 3**

Site Navigation

```
        value="Television"></asp:menuitem>
      <asp:menuitem navigateurl="comics.aspx"
        text="Comics" value="Comics"></asp:menuitem>
    </asp:menuitem>
</items>
</asp:menu>
```

Table 3-2	Sample Data for the Menu Control	
Parent	*Text and Value Property*	*NavigateUrl Property*
News Section	Regional	regional.aspx
News Section	National	national.aspx
News Section	World	world.aspx
News Section	Weird News	weird.aspx
Sports	Hockey	hockey.aspx
Sports	Football	football.aspx
Sports	Tennis	tennis.aspx
Entertainment	Movies	movies.aspx
Entertainment	Television	television.aspx
Entertainment	Comics	comics.aspx

Setting Menu styles in Design view

Menu items commonly look different apart from the obvious text. Top-level items (such as News Section and Sports) are usually *static,* in that they always appear. Submenu items (such as Local and Regional) are usually *dynamic* because they only drop down or fly out when the mouse pointer hovers over their Parent item.

Items also look different depending on what's happening to them. For example, most items take on a contrasting shade when the mouse pointer is over them and still another appearance when you click them.

Menu styles are mostly self-describing; customarily they have names that reflect whether the style attributes belong to static items (for example, StaticMenuStyle) or to dynamic nodes (DynamicMenuItemStyle). Further, the names indicate the *condition* of the static or dynamic style, such as DynamicHoverStyle, which shows only when hovering over a dynamic Menu item.

If you change a style in the designer and the new look doesn't show up, it may be that you're working on a dynamic style instead of the static one, or vice versa.

You could spend years designing a Menu complete with padded borders, shaded backgrounds, custom icons, fancy separators, and dynamic fly-out effects. ASP.NET provides a starting point for your creativity by way of the Auto Format dialog box. To reach Auto Format, right-click the Menu control, and then (from the context menu) click Auto Format.

If you choose the Classic format, the designer inserts a series of style tags just before the closing </asp:menu> tag. The following code shows some sample markup:

```
<staticmenuitemstyle horizontalpadding="5px"
    verticalpadding="2px" />
<dynamichoverstyle backcolor="#284E98" forecolor="White" />
<dynamicmenustyle backcolor="#B5C7DE" />
<staticselectedstyle backcolor="#507CD1" />
<dynamicselectedstyle backcolor="#507CD1" />
<dynamicmenuitemstyle horizontalpadding="5px"
    verticalpadding="2px" />
<statichoverstyle backcolor="#284E98" forecolor="White" />
```

It's hard to design beautiful dynamic Menu items if the designer is showing only the static content. You can make dynamic items visible on the design surface with the help of a Smart Tag item. Here's how:

1. **Select the** Menu **control.**

2. **Click the arrow that points right. It's in the upper-right area of the control.**

3. **On the Smart Tasks menu, locate the Views combo box and select Dynamic, as shown in Figure 3-13.**

The view changes to show a sample of the dynamic content. You can switch back to the static view by selecting Static.

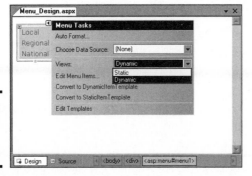

Figure 3-13:
Viewing dynamic menu items.

**Book VIII
Chapter 3**

Site Navigation

This Views feature has its limitations because there's no Hover or Selected option to let you view static or dynamic menu items in those states. For that, there's good old trial-and-error design.

Although you can change attributes by editing the markup, it's faster to use properties pages. Let's change the hover style of the dynamic menu items:

1. **Right-click the** `Menu` **control and from the context menu click Properties.**

2. **Locate the** `DynamicHoverStyle` **property and expand its node.**

3. **Set the properties and values for the style using the data in Table 3-3.**

Table 3-3	DynamicHoverStyle Values
Property	*Value Property*
`BackColor`	`#284E98`
`BorderColor`	`White`
`BorderStyle`	`3px`
`Font @--> Bold`	`True`
`Font @--> Italic`	`True`

Figure 3-14 shows the menu item in the browser as the cursor passes over the `Television` item.

Figure 3-14: The hover menu's border shows its style.

Creating a Menu programmatically

In addition to building and configuring a `Menu` control in markup (that is, declaratively), you can assemble everything in code. Even if you don't want to create every Menu this way, it helps to know how to add or change elements of the control on the fly.

A better way to create a Menu is to bind it to the Web.sitemap file. To learn how to do that, skip ahead to the section "Creating a Menu from a sitemap," later in this chapter.

Creating Menu items

A Menu is mainly items and subitems that are hooked together in a hierarchy. No matter where they appear, all Menu items belong to the same class, Menu Item. The first order of business is to create a function that assembles Menu items for us according to specifications. The BuildItem() function that follows takes the text that appears on the item as a string and an optional URL. The URL isn't required for top-level static items because they might serve only as a gateway to the subitems below them. After assigning the parameters to the appropriate properties, the function returns a MenuItem object that we can insert into the Menu's hierarchy. Here's the BuildItem routine in VB:

```
Private Function BuildItem _
  (ByVal strText As String, _
  Optional ByVal strURL As String = "") As MenuItem
    Dim menuItem As New MenuItem
    menuItem.Text = strText
    menuItem.Value = strText
    menuItem.NavigateUrl = strURL
    Return menuItem
End Function
```

Building the base Menu

To create a Menu from scratch, you need an instance of the ASP.NET Menu class, declared in the following code in the variable mnu:

```
Dim mnu As New Menu
mnu.BackColor = Drawing.Color.FromArgb(181, 199, 222)
mnu.DisappearAfter = 1000
mnu.DynamicHorizontalOffset = 2
mnu.Font.Names = New String() {"Verdana"}
mnu.Font.Size = FontUnit.Large
mnu.ForeColor = Drawing.Color.FromArgb(40, 78, 152)
mnu.ID = "Menu1"
mnu.Orientation = Orientation.Horizontal
mnu.StaticSubMenuIndent = Unit.Pixel(10)
PlaceHolder1.Controls.Add(mnu)
```

The Menu has certain characteristics that it shares with Menu items, such as font sizes, text colors, and backgrounds. Some properties are unique, such as `Orientation` (which can be vertical or horizontal). The `DisappearAfter` property is fun to experiment with. The value (set to `1000` milliseconds here) determines how long a `Menu` takes to disappear after the mouse pointer moves away from it.

The last line of code in this section adds the `Menu` control to the `Controls` collection of a `PlaceHolder` control.

Building the static items

As shown in Figure 3-15, our `Menu` has three static items. These stick-in-the-mud items don't fly about like their children. Their only `Parent` is the `Menu` control as a whole rather than a single `Menu` item.

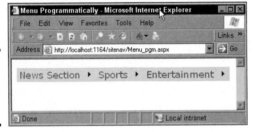

Figure 3-15: Adding static menu items.

Therefore, we need to add the individual `Menu` items to the `Menu`'s `Items` collection. We call on the `BuildItem()` function to create each item and then add it to the collection, as you see in the following lines of code:

```
mnu.Items.Add(BuildItem("News Section"))
mnu.Items.Add(BuildItem("Sports"))
mnu.Items.Add(BuildItem("Entertainment"))
```

Adding child items

Now that the top-level items are in place, we can start adding subitems. This time, we're dealing with a `MenuItem` object as the `Parent` so we declare a variable as such. To get a reference to the `News Section` item, you can refer to it by its index number (`0` in zero-based counting) in the `Menu`'s `Items` collection.

With the reference to the `Parent`, we use the `Add` method of the `ChildItems` collection to add more items to the `News Section`.

```
Dim parent As MenuItem
parent = mnu.Items(0)
```

```
parent.ChildItems.Add(BuildItem("Local", "local.aspx"))
parent.ChildItems.Add(BuildItem("Regional", "regional.aspx"))
parent.ChildItems.Add(BuildItem("National", "national.aspx"))
parent.ChildItems.Add(BuildItem("World", "world.aspx"))
```

There's no need to show the code to add items to the `Sports` and `Entertainment` items because it follows the pattern of the preceding code. The main difference is that you reference each by its index number. For `Sports` it is

```
parent = mnu.Items(1)
```

and for `Entertainment`, it is

```
parent = mnu.Items(2)
```

Configuring item styles

The `Menu` as a whole holds the initial styles of its items, those of its items' items, and so on. (Say *that* out loud three times!) Examples of the styles include the look of a static or dynamic `Menu` item when the mouse pointer is hovering over it — or when an item is selected. Two examples of configuring these in code will give you the idea.

For the first, let's replicate the hover style that we created previously using the designer. The `DynamicHoverStyle` property provides access to the style attributes. For example, we arrange a 3-pixel, solid white border around the item. The text turns white, bold, and italic as the mouse pointer passes over.

```
mnu.DynamicHoverStyle.BackColor = _
    Drawing.Color.FromArgb(40, 78, 152)
mnu.DynamicHoverStyle.BorderColor = Drawing.Color.White
mnu.DynamicHoverStyle.BorderStyle = BorderStyle.Solid
mnu.DynamicHoverStyle.BorderWidth = Unit.Pixel(3)
mnu.DynamicHoverStyle.Font.Bold = True
mnu.DynamicHoverStyle.Font.Italic = True
mnu.DynamicHoverStyle.ForeColor = Drawing.Color.White
```

Recall that the top `Menu` items are static text. The `Menu`'s `StaticMenuItemStyle` property holds the style settings. In the following code, we increase the size of the font and add some padding around the edges:

```
mnu.StaticMenuItemStyle.Font.Size = FontUnit.Large
mnu.StaticMenuItemStyle.HorizontalPadding = Unit.Pixel(5)
mnu.StaticMenuItemStyle.VerticalPadding = Unit.Pixel(2)
```

Creating a Menu from a sitemap

The `Menu` control works with the same `Web.sitemap` as the `TreeView` control. Using a `Web.sitemap` file makes more sense than building `Menu` items by hand because it's far more efficient. When you add or remove an item in a `Web.sitemap`, all `Menu` (and `TreeView`) controls pick up the change immediately with no need to recompile or redeploy the page.

1. **Use the** `Web.sitemap` **file found in the earlier section, "Creating a TreeView from a sitemap."**

2. **In Design view, from the Data tab of the toolbox, drag a** `SiteMapDataSource` **object to the ASP.NET page.**

3. **In the properties page for the** `SiteMapDataSource`, **set the** `ShowStartingNode` **property to** `False`.

   This ensures that the `Menu` doesn't start with the single, top-level item (`Newspaper`) that made sense as a starting point in a `TreeView` control but not in a `Menu`.

4. **From the Navigation tab of the toolbox, drag a** `Menu` **control to the design surface.**

5. **As shown in Figure 3-16, use the menu's Smart Tag to choose the data source, usually** `SiteMapDataSource1`.

Figure 3-16: Setting the menu's data source.

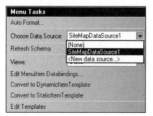

6. **Add styles to the nodes.**

   You can do so by using the designer, hand-coding the styles, or by assigning style-sheet classes.

Using the SiteMapPath Control

The ASP.NET `SiteMapPath`, shown in Figure 3-17, creates a breadcrumb trail that shows Web site surfers the path back through the forest of `Parent` nodes or pages. The control reads directly from the list of pages entered in the `Web.sitemap` file. If the current page doesn't exist in the `sitemap`, the control has no reference to its place in the hierarchy — and therefore displays nothing.

Figure 3-17:
The
SiteMapPath
control.

The `SiteMapPath` sometimes displays the path as plain text without hyperlinks. This happens when the `Parent` node doesn't have an associated page (that is, no `NavigateUrl` value).

Creating a SiteMapPath in Design view

1. **Use the** `Web.sitemap` **file found in the earlier section, "Creating a TreeView from a sitemap."**

2. **Add an ASP.NET page called** `movies.aspx` **to your project.**

`Movies.aspx` exists in the `Web.sitemap` file, and therefore the `SiteMapPath` control is able to build a path to it.

3. **In Design view, from the** `Navigation` **tab of the toolbox, drag a** `SiteMapPath` **control to the ASP.NET page.**

4. **In the control's Properties page, set the properties and values as shown in Table 3-4.**

5. **Save** `movies.aspx` **and browse to the page.**

Figure 3-18 shows the breadcrumb in the browser. The trail leads backward from `Movies`, through `Entertainment`, and finally to `Newspaper` (which is the starting point).

Table 3-4	SiteMapPath Design
Property	*Value Property*
Font	Verdana, Large
NodeStyle @--> ForeColor	Gray

(continued)

Table 3-4 *(continued)*

Property	Value Property
PathSeparator	&gt;
PathSeparatorStyle @--> ForeColor	Black
RootNodeStyle @--> ForeColor	Green
CurrentNodeStyle @--> BackColor	Black
CurrentNodeStyle @--> ForeColor	White

Figure 3-18:
A designer
breadcrumb.

The designer creates the following markup to produce the appearance aspects of the breadcrumb.

```
<asp:sitemappath id="SiteMapPath1" runat="server"
    font-names="Verdana" font-size="Large"
    pathseparator=" > ">
    <pathseparatorstyle font-bold="True" forecolor="Black" />
    <currentnodestyle forecolor="White" backcolor="Black" />
    <nodestyle font-bold="True" forecolor="Gray" />
    <rootnodestyle font-bold="True" forecolor="Green" />
</asp:sitemappath>
```

Notice the use of `" &gt; "` to ensure a nonbreaking HTML space before and after the greater-than (>) symbol.

Creating a SiteMapPath control programmatically

The `SiteMapPath` control exposes its properties so you can build and configure it completely in code. Most of the code in the following sections configures the node styles.

Building the SiteMapPath

Before you can work with the SiteMapPath object, you need to obtain a copy of it (*instantiate* it in geek-speak), using the New keyword. The following code uses the variable smp to represent the control:

```
Dim smp As New SiteMapPath
smp.ID = "SiteMapPath1"
smp.Font.Names = New String() {"Verdana"}
smp.Font.Size = FontUnit.Large
smp.PathSeparator = " > "
PlaceHolder1.Controls.Add(smp)
```

After giving the control an ID value, we set the font to Verdana and super-size it to Large. The PathSeparator property holds the character(s) that appear between the nodes. To replicate the design-mode example, you can use a space, the greater-than sign (>), and another space. The last line of the snippet adds the breadcrumb to the Controls collection of a PlaceHolder control on the design surface.

Adding style to the SiteMapPath

The nodes in the SiteMapPath control have a common style that they share (NodeStyle), plus a more specific style that they acquire depending on their location. The lines that follow make the overall font bold and gray for any style that doesn't have its own specific settings.

```
smp.NodeStyle.Font.Bold = True
smp.NodeStyle.ForeColor = Drawing.Color.Gray
```

The next two lines configure the look of the Root node, which is the starting point. In our example, the Root is the word Newspaper. It appears bold and green (use your imagination). The code looks like this:

```
smp.RootNodeStyle.Font.Bold = True
smp.RootNodeStyle.ForeColor = Drawing.Color.Green
```

Finally, we design the characteristics of the CurrentNode or Leaf. That's the name of the page the user is viewing and the end of the line. We make the text white and the background black so it stands out.

```
smp.CurrentNodeStyle.ForeColor = Drawing.Color.White
smp.CurrentNodeStyle.BackColor = Drawing.Color.Black
```

**Book VIII
Chapter 3**

Site Navigation

Using an image as a path separator

If your Web site has a standard set of icons, you might want to use a custom arrow to separate the paths between breadcrumb nodes. You can do this by implementing a path-separator template.

1. **Add an ASP.NET page named** `weird.aspx` **to your project.**

2. **Add the bitmap that you want to use as the separator to your project.**

For this procedure, the image is a pointing finger called `pointer.gif`.

3. **From the Navigation tab of the toolbox, drag a** `SiteMapPath` **control and drop it onto the design surface.**

4. **Select the control and, from the Smart Tasks menu, click Edit Templates.**

5. **As shown in Figure 3-19, select** `PathSeparatorTemplate` **from the drop-down list.**

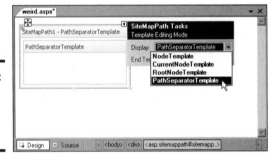

Figure 3-19:
Choosing the Path Separator Template.

6. **From the** `General` **tab of the toolbox, drag an** `Image` **control and drop it in the center area of the** `PathSeparatorTemplate`**.**

7. **Set the** `Image` **control's** `ImageUrl` **property to** `~/pointer.gif`**.**

Figure 3-20 shows the designer with the image inserted.

Figure 3-20:
An image inside the Path Separator Template.

8. On the Smart Tasks menu, click End Template Editing.

The design surface returns to the normal view.

9. Save `weird.aspx` **and open it in the browser.**

The image replaces the default separator, as shown in Figure 3-21.

Figure 3-21:
The image
as the
separator.

Behind the scenes, the designer has inserted the following code to use the pointer image:

```
<pathseparatortemplate>
    <asp:image id="Image1" runat="server"
        imageurl="~/pointer.gif" />
</pathseparatortemplate>
```

**Book VIII
Chapter 3**

Site Navigation

Chapter 4: Working with Themes

In This Chapter

✔ **Creating themes for different audiences**

✔ **Making use of skins, style sheets, and graphics in a theme**

✔ **Deploying themes on one site and on a whole server**

✔ **Finding free sample themes**

Don't underestimate the value of customization to consumers. Just ask anyone who works in the automobile after-market business. Whether it's a chromed die-cast "hang five" accelerator pedal, large dice to dangle from the rearview mirror, or a full-blown flame-effect paint treatment, people spend megabucks to turn a very ordinary car into a personal statement. What they're stating about themselves isn't always clear. Does a mass-produced footprint accelerator say that the driver is a wannabe athletic surfer? By burning up the highway in a car with hot licks, are they saying they're hot too? Maybe it's all just a way to brag that they have a lot of disposable income.

Okay, you're wondering what hot rods and custom car accessories have to do with ASP.NET and themes. Not much, except that ASP.NET helps Web sites appeal to a deep-seated need to customize by letting visitors choose among decorative themes. I'm sure you can attract thousands more hits if your pages include flames in the background, shift knob dice for buttons, and chromed bare feet as menu items.

Understanding Site Themes

If you use Windows XP, you already know about desktop themes. A *theme* provides a unified appearance to visual elements such as windows, buttons, icons, and backgrounds. You can recognize the Windows XP theme by its gradients, rounded buttons, and sculptured borders, as shown in Figure 4-1. When you select a theme, it applies globally to your computer. You don't need to tell the computer to round off the corners on buttons in (for example) Word — it just happens as part of the operating system's function.

Figure 4-1:
Windows
XP theme.

ASP.NET's themes follow a similar pattern to those in Windows. Within the more limited capabilities of HTML, the theme sets the fonts, colors, and borders for various controls on the page such as the `Label`, `GridView`, `Button`, `HyperLink,` and `TextBox` controls. It's very convenient because you define the appearance in one spot and all of the controls of that type pick up the theme's styling automatically.

A theme can apply to every page on a Web site or just to certain pages. Consistency across pages is usually a sign of good design, but it's not a requirement as far as themes go. For example, you could present different themes for different areas of a portal site. The Accountants section would feature plain, monochrome gray tones with a splash of pinstripes. The Lawyers portal would make visitors feel at home by applying shark pictures as the default appearance for `ImageButton` controls.

Each theme sits in its own subdirectory in an ASP.NET site. Within the theme's subdirectory, you find folders for the style sheets, graphics, and skin files that contribute to the theme's appearance. The skin file (using the `.skin` extension) might be new to you. This is where you set the appearance of ASP.NET controls.

Creating an Opening Theme

In this section, we walk through the creation of a theme (component by component) using Visual Web Developer Express (VWDE). This isn't the most elaborate theme you'll encounter but it does illustrate the features. I'll try to make the themes sufficiently obvious so you can see them in black-and-white pages.

Adding the App_Themes folder

ASP.NET expects to find all of a site's themes in the special App_Themes folder. Our theme's name is DullGray, invoking the exciting flair and style of popular accounting manuals. To create the App_Themes folder:

1. **In Solution Explorer, right-click the project name and — from the context menu — click Themes⇨Add ASP.NET Folder⇨Theme, as shown in Figure 4-2.**

   The command creates an App_Themes folder and a default name for the theme.

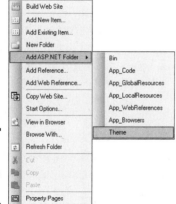

Figure 4-2:
Adding a theme to the project.

2. **Name the theme** DullGray, **as shown in Figure 4-3.**

Figure 4-3:
A folder for DullGray.

Did you notice Microsoft's attempt to trick us (okay, it *could* be just a goof)? In Figure 4-2, you click Theme — but VWDE creates a folder named `App_Themes`. If you click Bin, however, it creates a folder named `Bin`, not `App_Bin`. Likewise, the `App_Code` menu item generates a directory of the same name. The technical term for this inconsistency is WYSISometimesWYG — What You See Is *Sometimes* What You Get.

Adding a .skin file

A skin file (using the extension `.skin`) defines an ASP.NET theme. It describes the appearance and behavior of ASP.NET controls. In some ways, it resembles a Cascading Style Sheet (`.css` file) in that you define fonts, sizes, colors, borders, and other visual properties. However, the format is quite different from a style sheet and more like the content of an ASP.NET page. (For more on style sheets, see Book 3, Chapter 4.)

The first thing is to add a `.skin` file to your theme.

1. **In Solution Explorer, right-click the `DullGray` theme and from the context menu, click Add New Item.**

2. **In the Add New Item dialog box, select the Skin File template and provide the filename, `VeryBland.skin`, as you see in Figure 4-4.**

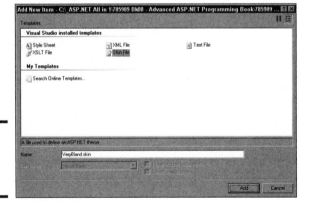

Figure 4-4:
The
VeryBland
skin file.

3. **Click Add.**

The `VeryBland.skin` file appears under the `DullGray` theme folder.

Inside `VeryBland.skin` file, you find two commented-out examples. You see, beneath the skin, it's not much more than a text file with an unusual name. Our task is to define the style properties for all ASP.NET `Button` controls in our site. Figure 4-5 shows the target design for the site's buttons — large, monochrome, with underlined text and a dotted border. Usability tests tell us that accountants favor this style 74.63 percent of the time.

Figure 4-5:
Our target
design for
a button.

Creating rough skin

Notice that when you open a `.skin` file, you do so in a bare-bones editor with no drag-and-drop, no property pages, no IntelliSense support, and no graphical designer. Rather than guessing property names or hand-coding values in a text editor, use the best tool at hand for designing a button — Design view. If we create a regular ASP.NET page as a work area, we can copy the relevant code and paste it into the `.skin` file. To create a style and turn it into a `.skin` file, follow these steps:

1. **Add an ASP.NET page called** `DesignLab.aspx` **to the project.**

2. **From the Standard tab of the toolbox, drag a** `Button` **control and drop it on the page.**

3. **Select the** `Button` **control and set the properties as they appear in the following list:**

- `BackColor`: Gainsboro
- `BorderColor`: DimGray
- `BorderStyle`: Dashed
- `BorderWidth`: 4px
- `Font-Names`: Comic Sans MS
- `Font-Size`: Large
- `Font-Underline`: True
- `ForeColor`: Black
- `Height`: 60px
- `Width`: 150px

4. **Open Source view and check the markup for the** `Button` **control.**

   It should look like the following code:

   ```
   <asp:button id="Button1" runat="server"
   backcolor="Gainsboro" bordercolor="DimGray"
   borderstyle="Dashed" borderwidth="4px"
   font-names="Comic Sans MS" font-size="Large"
   font-underline="True" forecolor="Black" height="60px"
   text="Button1"
    width="150px" />
   ```

5. **Copy the code to the clipboard and paste it into the** `VeryBland.skin` **file, below the commented-out text.**

Refining the skin properties

By pasting in the declarative syntax for the `Button` control, we created a prototype for the `Button` control's skin. However, we gave the `.skin` file too much information. It doesn't need the `id` attribute and we certainly don't want every button the Web site to display the `text` value `"Button1"`. To make the design suitable to use as a skin, follow these steps:

1. **In** `VeryBland.skin`**, delete the** `id` **attribute and its value.**

2. **Delete the** `text` **attribute and its value.**

   What's left is the skin definition for an ASP.NET button and it looks like the following:

   ```
   <asp:button runat="server"
        backcolor="Gainsboro" bordercolor="DimGray"
        borderstyle="Dashed" borderwidth="4px"
        font-names="Comic Sans MS" font-size="Large"
        font-underline="True" forecolor="Black"
        height="60px" width="150px" " />
   ```

Testing the skin

Although we've only created a skin for one control (`Button`), let's verify that it works by creating a test page. To create the test page:

1. **Add a new ASP.NET page called** `blandpage.aspx` **to the project.**

2. **Open the properties page for the** `Document` **object.**

3. **As shown in Figure 4-6, locate the** `StyleSheetTheme` **property and select DullGray from the drop-down list.**

   Visual Web Developer monitors the themes in the special `App_Themes` folder and offers the available theme(s) as choices. The `stylesheet theme` attribute appears in the `@Page` directive, as shown here:

   ```
   <%@ Page Language="VB" stylesheettheme="DullGray" %>
   ```

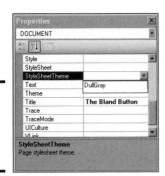

Figure 4-6:
Setting the
StyleSheet
Theme
property.

4. **Drag an ASP.NET** `Button` **control from the toolbox and drop it onto the page.**

   In the designer (shown in Figure 4-7), the button automatically inherits its style from the definition in `VeryBland.skin`.

Figure 4-7:
The Button
control
adopts the
defined
style.

Letting Users Choose a Theme

If you go to the trouble of designing more than one theme, there's a good chance you need a way to let your users choose one of them. In this scenario, our site caters to accountants, lawyers, and the hardy people who work for them. The goal is to offer themes that make people from each profession feel comfortable and at home.

For brevity, we implement only two elements for each theme: the background color and the appearance of a special `Submit` button (using the `ImageButton` control).

Our site has three themes: `Normal`, `Accountant`, and `Lawyer`, as shown in Figure 4-8. There's an image, a style sheet, and a `.skin` file in each. The following sections explain these themes.

**Book VIII
Chapter 4**

**Working with
Themes**

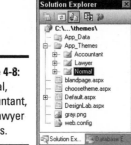

Figure 4-8:
Normal,
Accountant,
and Lawyer
themes.

The Normal theme

The `Normal` theme is the default for the site. It includes a `Normal.skin` file with the following content to define an `ImageButton` control that submits the contents of a form:

```
<asp:imagebutton skinid="okimage" runat="server"
  imageurl="ok.jpg" />
```

The `imageurl` attribute points to `ok.jpg`, the graphic (see Figure 4-9) that appears on the button. A version of `ok.jpg` must be available within each theme.

Figure 4-9:
The Submit
button for
normal
visitors.

The definition for the `ImageButton` control includes a `skinid` attribute. This is required because we don't want every `ImageButton` to use the same image. There'll be different buttons with different text for different themes. (Don't fret if you're like, *Huh?* at this point. It all becomes clearer when we create the selection page in the section "Applying a Theme Programmatically," later in this chapter.)

To set the background color of the page, add a style sheet called `stylesheet.css`. The following line sets the background to white for ordinary visitors:

```
body { background-color:White; }
```

The Accountant theme

For the `Accountant` theme, we can just rename the `DullGray` theme that we created previously in the section "Adding the App_Themes folder." To further accommodate accountants' tastes, we tone down the `ImageButton`. While retaining the name `ok.jpg`, the Submit button for accountants has a more suitable text and a flatter, less-interesting appearance. Figure 4-10 shows the design that our panel of accountants preferred 74.63 percent of the time.

Figure 4-10:
The Submit button for accountants.

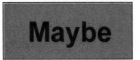

The content of the `skin` file for accountants uses the identical `ImageButton` attributes as the other themes — except, of course, it references the image in its own folder, which isn't in the same place as the others. The following code declares the image to be used:

```
<asp:imagebutton skinid="okimage" runat="server"
  imageurl="ok.jpg" />
```

We found that accountants prefer a subdued environment. We accommodate them in the `stylesheet.css` as follows:

```
body { background-color: Gray}
```

A theme for lawyers

As with the other themes, the `Lawyer` theme features an image (see Figure 4-11) that reflects the flair, dedication, and public image of their profession. The `.skin` file (`Shark.skin`) includes the reference to the `ImageButton` control, as shown in the code below:

```
<asp:imagebutton skinid="okimage" runat="server"
  imageurl="ok.jpg" />
```

Figure 4-11:
The Submit button for lawyers.

**Book VIII
Chapter 4**

Working with Themes

The `Lawyer` theme's style sheet (`stylesheet.css`) doesn't use a background color. Instead, it references a background image, as shown in the following code:

```
body {background-image: url('sharkbg1.gif'); }
```

That completes the theme components. The final task is to create a page in which users can choose a theme and put it to work. This page is known as the selection page, and it is addressed in the next section.

Applying a Theme Programmatically

A *selection page* allows the user to choose a theme and have it applied to the Web page. For the example we've been using in this chapter, the selection page defaults to the `Normal` theme. When users choose their themes from the drop-down list, they see their desired changes happen immediately. Figure 4-12 shows the Web page in action.

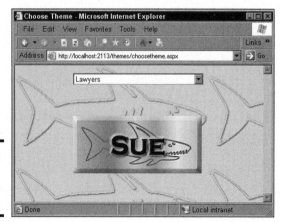

Figure 4-12:
Completed
theme for
lawyers.

To create a selection page, follow these steps:

1. **Add an ASP.NET page named** `choosetheme.aspx` **to the project.**

2. **Add a** `DropDownList` **control to the page. Set the** `AutoPostBack` **property to** `True`.

3. **Add three list items with the names of the themes as shown in the following code:**

```
<asp:dropdownlist id="DropDownList1"
    autopostback="true" runat="server">
    <asp:listitem value="Normal">Normal
```

```
</asp:listitem>
<asp:listitem value="Accountant">Accountant
</asp:listitem>
<asp:listitem value="Lawyer">Lawyers
</asp:listitem>
</asp:dropdownlist>
```

4. **Add an ASP.NET** `ImageButton` **control to the page. Set the** `skinid` **attribute to** `okimage`, **as shown in the following snippet:**

```
<asp:imagebutton id="Image1"
  skinid="okimage" runat="server"/>
```

The preceding doesn't include the `imageurl` property with the location of the image file. That's because we declared the image as part of the definition as `ok.jpg`. ASP.NET inserts the path to the graphic for the selected theme. Note, however, that we used the same name for the graphic in each theme so ASP.NET doesn't get totally confused.

5. **Add a handler for the** `PreInit` **event, as shown in the code in this step.**

This code detects the user's choice of theme and assigns the choice to the `Theme` property:

```
Protected Sub Page_PreInit _
(ByVal sender As Object, _
ByVal e As System.EventArgs)
    Dim strTheme As String = "Normal"
    If (Page.Request.Form.Count > 0) Then
        strTheme = Page.Request("dropdownlist1")
    End If
    Me.Theme = strTheme
End Sub
```

Notice that the preceding code executes on the `PreInit` event rather than the `Load` event. The `Load` event happens too late in the page life cycle for the application of themes. Likewise, we must get the name of the requested theme from the `Page.Request` rather than from the `DropDownList` control. This is because the control's viewstate isn't ready at this point. Fortunately, the user's selection has been posted back by now and therefore is available in the `Request` object.

If you forget the event in which you can safely set the theme, you find out quickly enough. Change the theme in the wrong place and ASP.NET's error message sets you straight pronto:

```
The 'Theme' property can only be set in or before the
'Page_PreInit' event.
```

Storing the Theme in a Profile

If you have a set of themes and a way for users to choose one, it makes sense to store the user's choice. You can store the preference in a cookie — or add it to an individual profile. (To configure your site for profiles, see Chapter 2 of this mini-book.) Once that's ready, here's how to store the theme:

1. **Edit the** `web.config` **file to include** `Theme` **as a value stored in the profile, and then set the** `defaultValue` **to** `Normal`.

   The following code shows how:

   ```
   <!-- system.Web goes here-->
   <authentication mode="Forms" />
   <anonymousIdentification enabled="true"/>
   <profile enabled="true"
           defaultProvider="AspNetSqlProfileProvider">
     <properties>
       <add name="Theme" defaultValue="Normal"
           allowAnonymous="true"/>
     </properties>
   </profile>
   ```

2. **In the** `PreInit` **event, get the user's choice of profile from the** `Request` **object (if it was sent), and store it in the profile.**

3. **Set the theme for the page from the value stored in the profile, like this:**

   ```
   Protected Sub Page_PreInit _
   (ByVal sender As Object, _
   ByVal e As System.EventArgs)
       If (Page.Request.Form.Count > 0) Then
           Profile.Theme = Page.Request("dropdownlist1")
       End If
       Me.Theme = Profile.Theme
   End Sub
   ```

4. **In the** `Load` **event, set the selected value of the** `DropDownList` **control to the theme stored in the profile, as shown in the code that follows:**

   ```
   Protected Sub Page_Load _
   (ByVal sender As Object, ByVal e As System.EventArgs)
       DropDownList1.SelectedValue = Profile.Theme
   End Sub
   ```

5. **Have the code store the name of the selected theme in the profile when the user clicks the** `ImageButton` **control, like this:**

   ```
   Protected Sub Image1_Click _
   (ByVal sender As Object, _
   ByVal e As System.Web.UI.ImageClickEventArgs)
       Profile.Theme = DropDownList1.SelectedValue
   End Sub
   ```

I've got you under my SkinId

If you add a skin to your site but the target controls ignore it, it's probably because of the SkinId property. Check the definition of the control in your .skin file. If there's a SkinId property, that definition is no longer the site's default skin. Only controls that have the matching SkinId will take on the style. For best results, don't add a SkinId anywhere except when you want to give a control a look other than the default design.

Dos and Don'ts for Themes

Here are some guidelines for using ASP.NET themes:

✦ **Do apply only one theme at a time on a page.** Any more and you'll get an error.

✦ **Don't be afraid to put more than one style sheet (.css) in a theme folder.** ASP.NET will generate `<link>` statements for all of the style sheets at runtime.

✦ **Don't use a SkinID property if you want the skin to be the default for the type of control.** See this chapter's sidebar, "I've got you under my SkinId."

✦ **Don't skimp on the number of .skin files.** You can have one .skin file for each type of control (for example, buttons.skin and labels.skin) or put all of the definitions into one .skin file.

✦ **Don't worry if the background syntax checker complains that a control has a SkinID property but its page isn't configured to use a theme.** Everything is fine as long as you intend to set the theme programmatically.

✦ **Don't make fun of lawyers in themes — accountants are safer targets and are less likely to issue writs.** (On the other hand, accountants often don't have a good enough sense of humor to appreciate your subtle jibes — especially around tax time. Kidding. Really.)

Shifting Definitions to Styles

One of the goals in ASP.NET development (some would call it the Holy Grail) is to separate content from presentation. That is, the information that you are offering by way of text and graphics should sit naked and unadorned inside the .aspx file. Then you define presentation elements — such as interesting fonts, coordinated color schemes, and attractive layouts — in a

Book VIII
Chapter 4

Working with Themes

linked style sheet. This way you can swap stylistic elements by changing the `.css` file alone. (For more on style sheets, see Book 3, Chapter 4.)

For example, the code line below shows a Submit button from an ASP.NET page. There's no formatting information in it, not even a reference to the CSS class:

```
<asp:button id="Button1" runat="server"  text="Submit" />
```

The definition in the `.skin` file is even smaller than the button's declarative markup. While dropping the `text` attribute, the definition adds the `cssclass` attribute that points to the style that all buttons on the site must adopt:

```
<asp:button runat="server" cssclass="SubmitButton" />
```

We put the style information in the theme's `.css` file rather than inline on the button's definition. This style sheet includes the appearance characteristics such as the border, font, button color, and width:

```
.SubmitButton
{
border: 1px solid;
width: 100px;
background-color: #cccccc;
font-weight: normal;
}
```

Overriding Themes and Who's the Boss

For the most part, settings in ASP.NET are inherited from the general down the line to the specific item. When you create a global setting at the site level it shows up in the pages and controls. If the same property is specified on a page, the page's version is what the user sees, not the global value. ASP.NET 2.0 themes implement a system of checks and balances where a global property can override the setting on an individual control but a page or a control on the page can veto all themes. This sounds like a system of government, doesn't it?

Theme vs StyleSheetTheme

If you're converting an existing site to use ASP.NET 2.0 themes, you might have existing markup that sets the appearance directly on the control such as this:

```
<asp:button id="Button1"
   backcolor="Red"  runat="server"
   text="Stop!" font-bold="True"
```

```
font-names="Times New Roman"
forecolor="Black" font-size="XX-Large" />
```

The preceding creates a red button in bold Times New Roman font, as you see in Figure 4-13.

Figure 4-13:
Using
locally set
properties.

It would take a lot of work to go into each page of a large site to change the appearance for every control. The boss might decide that themes aren't worth the trouble. Fortunately, you can override all local settings by using the `Theme` property for a page rather than the `StyleSheetTheme` property. The system of overrides can be confusing, so perhaps an example will help.

Let's say your brand new `.skin` file includes a definition for buttons. Henceforth, buttons will have gray text in Arial on a white background:

```
<asp:button
    backcolor="White"
    runat="server"
    font-bold="True"
    font-names="Arial"
    forecolor="Gray"
    font-size="XX-Large" />
```

In the `web.config` file's `<page>` element, designate the theme that overrides all local control styles:

```
<!-- system.web goes here-->
<pages theme="Normal">
```

The definitions in the `Normal` theme now override the red and black on the button creating a gray on white appearance, as you see in Figure 4-14.

**Book VIII
Chapter 4**

**Working with
Themes**

Figure 4-14:
Overriding
the local
settings
properties.

You can also use the `Theme` property in place of `StyleSheetTheme` at the top of an individual page to override local properties, as you see in the following:

```
<%@ page language="VB" theme="Normal" %>
```

Inserting the preceding line in every page on a large site wouldn't make sense because you'd be forced to open each page. That's something you were trying to avoid; you may . . . as well let the computer do the work.

The `Theme` property overrides local settings. The `StyleSheetTheme` property yields to any settings that exist directly on the control in the page.

Implementing a global theme

So far, we've assumed that you're applying ASP.NET themes to just one Web on the server. In some cases, you might have dozens of Webs running on the same server that share the same corporate branding. When the branding changes because the new CEO doesn't like blue, you need to change themes across the board. This calls for global themes.

For the most part the creation of a global theme is the same as a page theme. You assemble the styles, skins, and graphics as before. What's different is the deployment, including where you put the files on Internet Information Services.

1. **On the Web server, locate the folder that is set as the root Web.**

By default, this should be `c:\inetpub\wwwroot\`, but some administrators change it for added security.

2. **Under `wwwroot`, look for the following path that includes the ASP.NET version number (which is 2_0_50727 as of this writing):**

```
\aspnet_client\system_web\2_0_50727
```

3. **Under the version folder (for example,** `2_0_50727`**), create a folder called** `Themes`**.**

   (Don't use `App_Themes` here. That's for individual site themes, not for global themes.)

4. **Under the** `Themes` **folder, create a folder with the theme name (for example,** `Lawyers`**).**

   `system_web\2_0_50727\Themes\`**`Lawyers\`**

5. **Copy the** `.skin`**,** `.css`**, and graphics files into the theme's folder.**

Exempting a page from theming

You could have cases where you don't want a page to use any theme — for example, if you have a pop-up window with a specialized look for entering credit card information. In this case, you can turn off themes by using the `EnableTheming` attribute as part of the `Page` directive:

```
<%@ page language="VB" enabletheming="false" %>
```

Exempting a control from theming

By default, all controls on a page take part in theming and inherit the theme assigned to a page or a site. You probably haven't encountered the `enabletheming` property, even though it's already being applied to your controls. That's because theming is enabled by default if `enabletheming` isn't included in the control.

Sometimes you have a control such as a specialized calendar that you want to exempt from the page's theme. You can switch the `enabletheming` property value to `false` like this:

```
<asp:button enabletheming="false"
  id="Button1"  runat="server"
  backcolor="Red" font-bold="True"
  font-names="Times New Roman"
  font-size="XX-Large"
  forecolor="Black"
  text="You can't touch me!" />
```

Where to Get Themes

Microsoft has created several attractive themes, complete with `.skin` files, style sheets, and images as part of the ASP.NET 2.0 sample applications and starter kits. Figure 4-15 shows the free Corporate template using the Sand theme that comes with it.

Figure 4-15:
A free
corporate-
themed
site from
Microsoft.

Here are the available designs and the included themes:

- ✦ **Commerce:** Includes Jazz, Magnolia, and Snow themes
- ✦ **Corporate:** Has Granite, Paper, and Sand themes
- ✦ **Personal:** Brown, Green, and Red themes
- ✦ **Fun:** Default and Purple themes

You can download these from the Design Templates page at this URL:

`msdn.microsoft.com/asp.net/reference/design/templates/default.aspx`

If they move the page before you can get there, try a search for "Design Templates" or "Starter Kits and XHTML Templates" on `www.msdn.microsoft.com`.

Chapter 5: Building Portals with Web Parts

In This Chapter

✔ Surveying the features of portal sites

✔ Creating Web parts that users can move around the page

✔ Sharing data between Web parts

✔ Displaying Web parts in a catalog

*W*eb portals are hot items in the enterprise, changing the way people do business. They're the concept of one-stop shopping brought to the computer desktop. The same goes for consumer sites where portals are moneymakers because they attract people and increase advertising revenue.

Customization is a big attraction in these browser-based gateways. People like to organize portal pages to suit their style. Preferences include the tools and items they see, where features sit on the page, and the overall appearance of the site. Let's not underestimate the fun part of portals. Just as kids like to play with their food, adults like to tinker with their portal setups.

Web parts are pluggable modules that you drop into a portal page. Microsoft first introduced Web parts in its SharePoint Portal technology. While highly functional for end-users, the first SharePoint Web parts were time-consuming to build because there was no graphical development environment. All that changed with ASP.NET 2.0, where Web parts are no longer exclusive to SharePoint. What's more, Microsoft integrated Web-part development into its mainstream designer tools; anyone can create a Web part.

In this chapter you get an overview of portals and the features that make them attractive to users. Then, we explore the building blocks for the ASP.NET Web part framework. Finally, you build real Web parts that users can drag, drop, hide, and configure on a live Web page.

Understanding Portals

A Web portal is very much like your Windows desktop. It's a workspace or activity center where you have convenient access to the tools you need to get your work done and the software you enjoy for entertainment and recreation. You can customize your Windows desktop by adding shortcuts to favorite programs and hiding items you rarely use. When you log in, the layout and color scheme are as you left them so you can resume your activities without delay.

Web portals work much the same way as a browser-based desktop. Administrators can assemble the links to the tools and information that an information worker needs. The Web pages include the latest company news, alerts, status reports, integrated messaging, schedules, and search engines. Workers can view content from any workstation because the portal is browser-based. Road warriors and home-based workers see the same data as the on-site staff.

While convenient to maintain, it's hard for portal pages to suit the needs of all visitors. Not everyone needs the same tools to do their work. Interests vary widely and one person's lively color scheme is another's psychedelic retro-trip. How do you, as the site owner, decide what to put on the page? The answer is that you *don't* decide. You make all of the information available as modules and let visitors pick what they want and build their own pages. Welcome to Web parts.

An Example Web Portal

Figure 5-1 shows part of my custom page at www.msn.com, co-branded with Sympatico, a nationwide Internet Service Provider (ISP). This portal includes all the features that make portals valuable to users and, in this case, to advertisers as well. As we walk through the features, keep in mind that you can implement everything you see in this portal site using Web parts in ASP.NET 2.0.

Figure 5-1:
Customized portal from msn.com.

Security for your custom page

The Sympatico/MSN portal site uses Microsoft's Passport authentication service, as shown in Figure 5-2. I must sign in before I can reach my custom content. Most Internet Web sites can't afford Passport but get along very well with forms authentication. For more on authentication, see Chapter 1 of this mini-book. Intranets often use Windows authentication for security where employees log on to the network which passes their authentication to any portal that asks for it.

Figure 5-2:
Microsoft
Passport
custom
login page.

Personalization of your page

As they sang in the theme song for the old TV series *Cheers,* "You want to go where everybody knows your name." Once the Sympatico/MSN portal knows who you are, it displays your name in the upper-left area of your page. Figure 5-3 shows some personalization options, and Figure 5-4 shows a window in which you can give the page a new name.

Figure 5-3:
A person-
alized
element in
the portal.

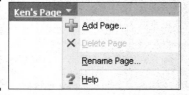

Figure 5-4:
A new title
for the
personal
page.

As we see in the sections that follow, personalization is everywhere in this portal — from the language and color scheme to the content selection and page layout.

Choice of language

As a Canadian portal, Sympatico/MSN operates in both of Canada's official languages. As you can see in Figure 5-5, clicking the français link switches the standard content, including links and the search function, to French. It's often corporate policy — and sometimes the law — to localize portal information. In the Sympatico/MSN site, it's easy to mix English and French content on the same portal page.

Figure 5-5:
Localization
of standard
content in
a portal.

Choice of content

The Sympatico/MSN portal provides a cornucopia of choices from news, sports, entertainment, business, weather, shopping, lotteries, and much more. In many cases, the portal acts as only an aggregator by showing only the headlines and then linking to the Web site of the content owner for details.

The numerous Add Content links on the portal page lead to the Web page dialog box, as shown in Figure 5-6. Users can add or remove content by selecting or unselecting the check boxes. They can also search for information on other Web sites. For example, Figure 5-7 shows the addition of a syndicated news feed (RSS) from a popular ASP.NET bloggers site. The RSS Web part is easy to use: Add the part to the page and point it to the URL of the RSS feed.

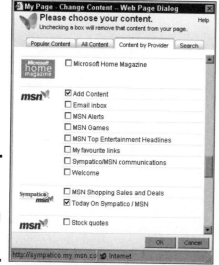

Figure 5-6: Web page dialog box for choosing portal content.

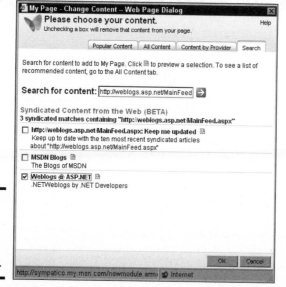

Figure 5-7: Adding an RSS feed to the portal page.

Book VIII
Chapter 5

Building Portals with Web Parts

Custom layout

The Sympatico/MSN portal site organizes information modules into columns. Users can add more columns to the layout and use the mouse to reposition the column. Because each information module is independent, users can drag a module and drop it above or below another module in any column. Figure 5-8 shows a module in motion. The mouse grabs the module using a grip in the module's upper-right corner. Note how the text in the module dims to show the module's transient state. It's moving from the center column to the left column. In the section "Letting the User Move Web Parts Around," later in this chapter, you get to create a Web part that can be moved around like this.

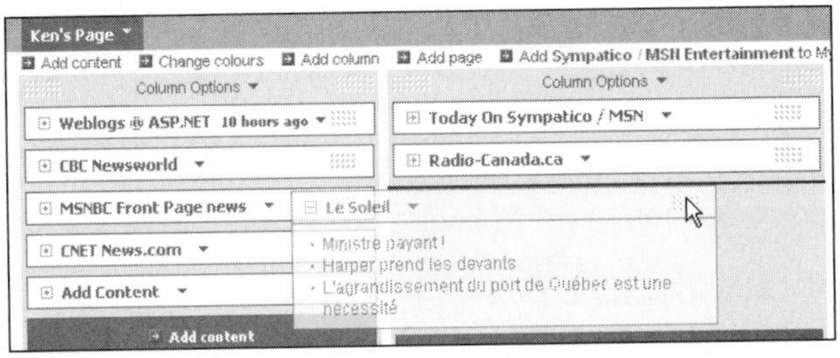

Figure 5-8: Moving a module on the page.

Show and hide content

Just as with the windows in Windows, you can expand and collapse (okay, *restore* and *minimize* in Microsoft-speak) portal modules to save space. Figure 5-9 shows a column with one module expanded for viewing.

Figure 5-9: Expanding and collapsing modules.

Themes

The Sympatico/MSN portal site is fully themed, offering users the choice of seven color decors and 23 graphical themes. The themes range from Windows XP styles to seasonal treatments and holidays, such as Canada Day. For more on creating ASP.NET themes, see Chapter 4 of this mini-book.

Understanding the Parts of Web Parts

Now that we've explored a professional portal and its modular components, let's consider what ASP.NET's Web parts are and how they fit into the portal picture. Web parts mean different things to different users:

✦ **End-user:** To an end-user, a Web part is a window within the Web page, including a title bar and menu options. It has the familiar characteristics of a window — for example, you can close it, minimize it, and restore it.

✦ **Content developer:** To a content developer, a Web part is a container for text, links, images, and dynamic elements such as tooltips.

✦ **HTML developer:** To an HTML developer, Web parts are panels and layers full of HTML and dynamic HTML (DHTML) supported by JavaScript.

✦ **ASP.NET developer:** To an ASP.NET developer, a Web part is a set of configurable ASP.NET server controls that fit into a framework of zones, connect to each other, contain user controls, support personalization, and retain their state during postbacks.

Web parts infrastructure elements

As an end-user portal, the Sympatico/MSN site simplifies its terminology, calling its Web parts modules. When you dig into the guts of it, the supporting infrastructure for Web parts includes several different types of controls that matter to developers but not at all to casual users.

Here are some of the ASP.NET components that make up the Web part framework. We demonstrate each one as we encounter it in roughly the order listed here.

✦ `WebPartManager`: The ASP.NET server-side control that must be added to the page to manage, track, and coordinate the Web parts. End-users don't see this component because it works in the background.

✦ `WebPartZone`: The container for Web parts, providing the layout of regions on the page. You can have zones within zones. Controls must be inside a zone to become Web parts and take part in personalization.

✦ `WebPart`: The user interface that wraps the HTML markup, server-side controls, and programming logic. The result is the windowlike portion of the Web page that users can move and customize.

✦ `ConnectionsZone`: A container for configuring Web part connections.

✦ `CatalogZone`: The container that holds `CatalogPart` controls.

✦ `CatalogPart`: The controls that show users the Web parts that they can add to a page.

+ `EditorZone`: The container that holds the `EditorPart` controls.
+ `EditorPart`: The controls that let users customize a Web part, depending on the properties the part exposes.

Personalization, logins, and Web parts

A portal site that lets users choose and organize content must store the choices as users make them. For example, if the user adds a Web part to her page, the addition of the Web part must be tied to her specific identity — not just to the browser session. A browser session can belong to anyone.

The upshot of this is that a user *must be logged in* before they can modify Web parts. In fact, some Web parts won't display any customization options if the user isn't logged in. Anonymous users see the default Web parts on a page but can't change the UI or save their preferences.

There are two common ways to let a user log in to a Web site:

+ **Use Windows authentication.**
+ **Use forms authentication.**

For Web sites on the Internet, forms authentication is the way to go. Chapter 1 of this mini-book explains how to implement forms authentication. If you haven't already done so, go to Chapter 1 of this mini-book now to set up authentication in preparation for your Web parts pages in the next section.

The procedures here assume that you have SQL Server Express running on your development workstation.

Creating a Simple Web Part

As an introduction to programming Web parts, let's *not* create a `Hello World` Web part. Let's create a sample as complex as the RSS Web part like we saw on Sympatico/MSN — nah, just kidding. We start with a small Web part, but it doesn't say Hello World. We build on the baby steps in subsequent examples.

Faking a login for development purposes

When you think of Web parts, think of logins. That's because a user must be logged in to see the personalization features that Web parts offer. Therefore, you need to create at least one membership account for developing and testing Web parts — someone who can log in.

Membership is covered in Chapter 1 of this mini-book, where you saw how to add usernames and passwords using the ASP.NET Configuration page. However, to save time during development, we take a shortcut (what geeks call a *hack*) by creating a user programmatically and immediately logging him in with code.

Don't use the fake login technique when you deploy the site. All the visitors will share one account if you do.

To create a user programmatically (and log that person in), follow these steps:

1. **Open your project's** web.config **file (add one if necessary).**

2. **Locate the** <authentication> **element and make sure it is using forms authentication as shown below:**

```
<authentication mode="Forms"/>
```

If you find a line that says <authentication mode="Windows"/>, change it to <authentication mode="Forms"/> before you go any further.

3. **Add an ASP.NET page named** login.aspx **to the project. Use the following as the complete code and markup in the** .aspx **page:**

```
<%@ Page Language="VB" %>
<script runat="server">
Protected Sub Button1_Click _
(ByVal sender As Object, ByVal e As System.EventArgs)
    Dim mbrCurrentMember _
        As System.Web.Security.MembershipUser
    Dim status _
        As System.Web.Security.MembershipCreateStatus
    Try
        mbrCurrentMember = _
          System.Web.Security.Membership.CreateUser _
                ("JackieReeve", _
                "ReeveJack!", _
                "rj@nowhere.com", _
                "Your favourite band", _
                "Beatles", _
                 True, _
                 status)
    Catch exc As Exception
        Response.Write("Problem: " & exc.Message)
    End Try
    FormsAuthentication.SetAuthCookie("JackieReeve", _
        True)
    Response.Redirect("starterpart.aspx")
End Sub
```

Book VIII Chapter 5

Building Portals with Web Parts

```
</script>
<html>
<head runat="server">
    <title>Fake Login</title>
</head>
<body>
    <form id="form1" runat="server">
    <div>
      <asp:button id="Button1" runat="server"
       onclick="Button1_Click" text="Do Fake Login" />
    </div>
    </form>
</body>
</html>
```

This page displays a button you can click to create a user named
JackieReeve (if he doesn't already exist) and pass a permanent authorization cookie to log Jackie in.

Note that you can't run this page yet — because it contains a reference to a
page named starterpart.aspx that we haven't yet created. So hold off running the Web site until you complete the next section of the chapter.

Create a page and Web-part zones

Web parts are like factories and housing subdivisions — you can't just plunk
them down anywhere you want. You can only put them in allowed zones
according to the rules.

Web-part zones designate regions of the page that can hold Web parts. The
zones offer a little support to the parts as well. They render some of the User
Interface (UI), such as titles, borders, headers and footers, and special buttons (more on that in the section "Creating a data consumer Web part," later
in this chapter). For our Hello-World free demonstration, we use two zones.
The page uses an HTML table to separate the zones and a couple of login
controls to track who we are.

To create the infrastructure to hold Web parts in an ASP.NET page:

1. **Add an ASP.NET page called** starterpart.aspx **to your project.**

2. **In Design view, from the Login tab of the toolbox, drag and drop a**
   LoginName **control onto the page.**

   This lets you confirm that you are logged in as a user.

3. **From the toolbox, drag and drop a** LoginStatus **control onto the page.**

   This provides a link to login.aspx if you're not logged in.

4. **In Design view, from the WebParts tab of the toolbox, drag a** `WebPartManager` **control and drop it on the page.**

You must have a `WebPartManager` control on every Web part page and the manager's markup must come before the markup of any Web parts. ASP.NET's compiler will alert you to this requirement if you forget.

5. **Add an HTML table to the page (Layout⇨Insert Table) with two columns and two rows, as shown in Figure 5-10.**

Figure 5-10: WebPart Manager and an HTML table.

6. **From the toolbox, drag the** `WebPartZone` **control and drop it into the upper-left cell of the table.**

7. **Using the** `WebPartZone` **control's Properties page, set the** `Width` **to** 275px.

8. **From the toolbox, drag a second** `WebPartZone` **control and drop it into the lower-left cell of the table.**

9. **Using the second** `WebPartZone` **control's properties page, set the** `Width` **to** 275px.

You now have the basic infrastructure in place, including the `WebPart Manager` and two zones, but no content. The declarative markup looks like the following:

```
<asp:loginname id="LoginName1" runat="server" />
<asp:loginstatus id="LoginStatus1" runat="server" />
<asp:webpartmanager id="WebPartManager1" runat="server">
</asp:webpartmanager>
<table>
    <tr>
        <td style="width: 100px">
            <asp:webpartzone id="WebPartZone1"
```

```
        runat="server" width="275px">
        </asp:webpartzone>
    </td>
    <td style="width: 100px">
    </td>
</tr>
<tr>
    <td style="width: 100px">
        <asp:webpartzone id="WebPartZone2"
        runat="server" width="275px">
        </asp:webpartzone>
    </td>
    <td style="width: 100px">
    </td>
</tr>
</table>
```

Add some Web-part content

If you're impatient and ran `starterpart.aspx` already, you no doubt found the experience is underwhelming. There's nothing to see except the login stuff — but we fix that with the addition of ASP.NET server controls. By slotting them into the right places, you make them into magical Web parts.

To add some ASP.NET server controls, follow these steps:

1. **In Design view of** `starterpart.aspx`, **drag a** `Label` **control and drop it inside** `WebPartZone1`.

2. **Switch to Source view, and locate the** `Label` **control that you just added. Configure the markup to look like this:**

```
<!--Inside a zonetemplate -->
<asp:label id="Label1" runat="server"
title="The Time Zone">
<h3><%=Now.ToLongTimeString%></h3>
</asp:label>
```

The Visual Web Developer syntax checker complains that

```
Attribute 'title' is not a valid attribute of element
'label'.
```

Don't worry about it. The validator doesn't realize that the `Label` control has ascended to the status of a Web part and therefore has additional properties.

3. In Design view, drag an ASP.NET `Calendar` **control from the toolbox and drop it inside** `WebPartZone2`.

4. In Source view, add a title attribute to the `Calendar` **control so it looks like the following:**

```
<!-- Inside a zonetemplate-->
<asp:calendar id="Calendar1"
title="The Date Zone"
runat="server"></asp:calendar>
```

Figure 5-11 shows the completed page in Design view, with the `Label` control in the upper zone and the `Calendar` control in the lower zone. We're ready to play with, er, *execute* formal testing on the Web-part page.

Figure 5-11: Here's a starter Web-part page with zones and controls.

Test the Web-part page

The test phase includes logging in and exploring the Web parts on the page. These are pretty bare bones, but they are quite instructive. Don't be alarmed if some pages take longer than expected to execute the first time. ASP.NET is setting up some databases and generally building the infrastructure to support Web parts and personalization.

To test the Web-part page, follow these steps:

1. **Open** `starterpart.aspx` **in the browser.**

The time appears in the Time zone and the calendar appears in the Date zone, as shown in Figure 5-12. If you think this is rather ordinary, you're right. Why? Because there's no logged-in user.

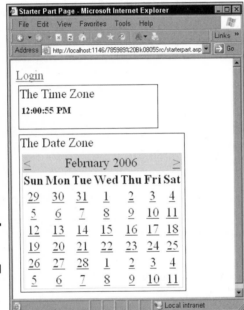

Figure 5-12:
A WebPart
Zone control
with a
label inside.

2. **Click the** Login **link.**

The Login page appears.

3. **Click the Do Fake Login button.**

The `starterpart.aspx` page reappears, but, as you see in Figure 5-13, this time it recognizes that username `JackieReeve` is logged in, and displays his ID and the Login link button.

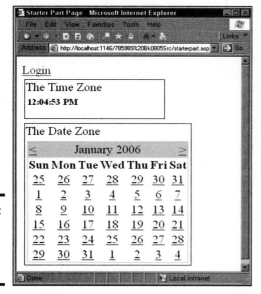

Figure 5-13:
A WebPart
Zone page
with a user
logged in.

4. Click the tiny down arrow in the upper-right corner of the Time zone.

As you see in Figure 5-14, a menu appears, showing Minimize and Close options. These items are known as *Verbs* in ASP.NET lingo.

Figure 5-14:
The
Minimize
and Close
verbs in the
Web part.

For better visibility on the printed page, I increased the font size of the menu items. You can do the same by going to `WebPartZone1`⇨ `MenuVerbStyle`⇨Font⇨Size⇨ Large.

5. **Click Minimize.**

The Time zone collapses.

6. **Click the tiny arrow again.**

The `Restore` verb appears.

7. **Using the menus, collapse both Web parts and then close the browser.**

8. **Reopen the browser on** `starterpart.aspx`.

The Web parts appear the way you left them.

If you click the <u>Logout</u> link, you discover that the menu items on the Web parts don't show up. ASP.NET personalization is unavailable to anonymous users.

This is just a quick demonstration of Web parts. There's far more you can do, including making the parts more attractive, letting users move them around, and connecting two Web parts together.

Oops, I closed the Web part and it's gone!

While testing the Web parts, you might have clicked the Close button. The Web part disappeared and you can't get it back, right? Been there, done that. We don't have a catalog to add Web parts back in yet, so the quick fix is to reset the state of all users.

Here's how to return the Web parts to their default state for all members of the site. It uses the `PersonalizationAdministration` object.

To return the Web parts to their default state for all members of the site:

1. **Add an ASP.NET page called** `reset.aspx` **to your project.**

2. **Replace the existing content of** `reset.aspx` **with the following:**

```
<%@ Page Language="VB" %>
<script runat="server">
Protected Sub Button1_Click _
(ByVal sender As Object, _
ByVal e As System.EventArgs)
    Dim intCount As Integer
    intCount = _
     PersonalizationAdministration.ResetAllState _
     (PersonalizationScope.User)
    Response.Redirect("starterpart.aspx")
End Sub
```

```
</script>
<html>
<head runat="server">
    <title>Reset Page</title>
</head>
<body>
    <form id="form1" runat="server">
    <div>
        <asp:button id="Button1" runat="server"
        onclick="Button1_Click" text="Reset" />
    </div>
    </form>
</body>
</html>
```

3. **Run the page and click the Reset button.**

This wipes out the personal settings of all users of the site. The preferences are gone forever.

Letting the User Move Web Parts Around

In the preceding sections, you created a page in which users could minimize,
restore, and close a Web part. We saw in the discussion of portals that another
desirable feature is the ability to redesign the page by moving modules
around. Implementing Design mode takes a little bit of code in ASP.NET, but
it isn't difficult.

Adding code to support Web-part Design mode

The trick to making Web parts movable is to put the Web-parts page into
Design mode. The WebPartManager control knows how to do that and
much more.

1. **Open** starterpart.aspx **in Design view.**

2. **From the toolbox, drag an ASP.NET** DropDownList **control and drop it
on the design surface below the** WebPartManager **control but above
the table.**

Using code, we're going to fill the DropDownList control with the available modes for the Web parts.

3. **Drag an ASP.NET** Button **control from the toolbox and drop it next to
the drop-down list, as shown in Figure 5-15.**

Figure 5-15:
A DropDown
List and a
Button
control for
selecting
a mode.

4. **In Source view, add the subroutine** GetDisplayModeItems() **by using the following code:**

```
Protected Sub GetDisplayModeItems()
    DropDownList1.Items.Clear()
    DropDownList1.Items.Add("--Select--")
    For Each wpdm As WebPartDisplayMode In _
      WebPartManager1.SupportedDisplayModes
        DropDownList1.Items.Add(wpdm.Name)
    Next
End Sub
```

The GetDisplayModeItems() routine adds items to the DropDownList control. The items are the available display modes for the page's Web parts. For now, there are only two modes, Design and Browse. Rather than hard-coding the names, we loop through the WebPartManager control's SupportedDisplayModes to get the list and then add each mode's name to the DropDownList control.

5. **Double-click the** Button **control to create a skeleton handler.**

6. **In Source view, add the following code to handle the button's** Click **event:**

```
Protected Sub Button1_Click1 _
(ByVal sender As Object, ByVal e As System.EventArgs)
    If DropDownList1.SelectedItem.Text <> _
        "--Select--" Then
        WebPartManager1.DisplayMode = _
            WebPartManager1.SupportedDisplayModes _
            (DropDownList1.SelectedItem.Text)
    End If
End Sub
```

The dangers of Web parts

The `WebPartManager` looks innocuous on the page, but Microsoft's lawyers have added more warning text than you'd see on a can of pesticide. If you look at the control's Properties page, you'll see this text, among other deathless prose:

`"This Web Part Page has been personalized. As a result, one or more Web Part properties may contain confidential information. Make sure the properties` `contain information that is safe for others to read. After exporting this Web Part, view properties in the Web Part description file (.WebPart) by using a text editor such as Microsoft Notepad."`

It's a wonder they don't make you sign an agreement not to sue them if you faint at the sight of shocking accounting data, and bruise your lip on the keyboard's spacebar.

When the user clicks the button, the preceding code checks the `DropDown List` control to find out which item the user selected. If it's not the instructional `"--Select--"` item, the routine gets the selected item's text — and uses that to look up the index of the `SupportedDisplayModes` collection. When it has the Display mode (for example, Design), it instructs the `WebPartManager` to put the Web parts into the selected mode.

7. Add the following code to handle the page's `Load` event.

```
Protected Sub Page_Load _
(ByVal sender As Object, _
ByVal e As System.EventArgs)
    If Not User.Identity.IsAuthenticated Then
        DropDownList1.Visible = False
        Button1.Visible = False
    End If
    If Not IsPostBack Then
        GetDisplayModeItems()
    End If
End Sub
```

The preceding code checks that the current user is authenticated. If not authenticated, it hides the `DropDownList` control and the `Button` control. There's no point even showing the user the choice of modes because she can't use them until she logs in.

Playing with Web-part Design mode

Finally, you're set to play runtime designer with the controls on the page. To do so:

1. **Browse to** `starterpart.aspx` **and log in (if that's required).**

2. **From the** `DropDownList` **control, select Design and then click OK.**

3. **Hover the mouse pointer over the text** `The Time Zone`.

The cursor changes to the Move style.

4. **Drag the Time Zone Web part from** `WebPartZone1` **(shown in Figure 5-16) and drop it into** `WebPartZone2`.

Web-part zones feel uncomfortable when empty, and plead for attention with the following message: `Add a Web Part to this zone by dropping it here.`

Figure 5-16:
A Web part being moved from one zone to another.

5. **From the** `DropDownList` **control, select Browse and then click OK.**

Notice that you can't move the Web parts in Browse mode.

We've allowed a logged-in user to redesign the page by changing the order of the Web parts.

If the drop-down list is empty, check the `<Page>` directive in the `starter part.aspx` page. It should contain the attribute `AutoEventWireup="True"`. If it specifies `AutoEventWireup="False"`, change it to `"True"`.

Connecting Web Parts Together

Perhaps the most powerful aspect of Web parts is the way they connect to data and pass information among themselves. In this section, we build an example that connects two parts. The page generates an interface in which the user can manipulate and reconnect compatible Web parts. Figure 5-17 gives you a preview of the many elements that go into the example.

Figure 5-17: A connectable Web-part page.

Before we can connect anything, we need to create some building blocks. This includes three user controls to consume and provide data. We create these in the following sections.

Book VIII Chapter 5

Building Portals with Web Parts

Creating a data consumer Web part

The Web parts in this section are ASP.NET user controls. You can use custom server controls instead, but that's more work than we want to take on here.

The first component, `display.ascx`, builds a `TextBox` Web part that consumes (and displays) data from a provider. To create this component, follow these steps:

1. **Add an ASP.NET Web user control called** `display.ascx` **to your project, making sure to use Visual Basic (VB) as the language and placing the code in a separate file.**

2. **In Design view, add an ASP.NET** `TextBox` **control named** `txtChosen` **to the user control.**

3. **In the code-behind file (**`display.ascx.vb`**), insert the following code after the** `Inherits` **statement:**

```
' Place after Inherits System.Web.UI.UserControl
Private _selectedDate As IDate
Private _selectedColour As IColour
```

The preceding declares variables to hold objects we create later. Don't worry about the editor's complaints that `IDate` and `IColour` aren't defined. We'll fix that in a moment.

4. **Immediately after the preceding code, add the following subroutines:**

```
<ConnectionConsumerAttribute _
 ("Selected Date", "SelectedDate")> _
 Sub setDateText(ByVal SearchText As IDate)
   Me._selectedDate = SearchText
End Sub

<ConnectionConsumerAttribute _
 ("Selected Colour", "SelectedColour")> _
 Sub setColorText(ByVal ColourText As IColour)
    Me._selectedColour = ColourText
End Sub
```

The preceding ungainly looking subroutines start with extra data (enclosed in angle brackets) that the Web part framework requires. In geek-speak, the subroutines have been *decorated.* These additional attributes make them potential data consumers (`ConnectionConsumer` `Attribute`), give them a friendly screen name (`Selected Colour`), and provide them with an ID (`SelectedColour`) so other controls or code can look them up.

5. **Add the following handler routine that runs when the page's** `PreRender` **event fires:**

```
Protected Sub Page_PreRender _
(ByVal sender As Object, _
ByVal e As System.EventArgs) _
Handles Me.PreRender
    If _selectedDate IsNot Nothing Then
        txtChosen.Text = _
        _selectedDate.SelectedDate.ToShortDateString
    End If
    If _selectedColour IsNot Nothing Then
```

```
            txtChosen.ForeColor = _
            Drawing.ColorTranslator.FromHtml _
            (_selectedColour.SelectedColour)
        End If
    End Sub
```

The preceding code lets this control consume data passed from other Web parts. The first `If` statement inserts the text part of the data. The second changes the color of the text based on another piece of data.

You now have a somewhat useless-looking user control that has special attributes to let it serve as a functional data-consuming Web part.

Creating a data provider Web part

The `display.ascx` user control that we created in the previous section gets its data from other controls on the page. A control that supplies data must be identified as a *provider*. In this case, we use a `Calendar` control to contribute the selected date as data.

1. **Add an ASP.NET Web user control called** `cal.ascx` **to your project, making sure to use VB as the language and placing the code in a separate file.**

2. **In Design view, add an ASP.NET** `Calendar` **control named** `Calendar1` **to the surface.**

3. **In the code-behind file (**`cal.ascx.vb`**), add the following code after the** `Inherits` **statement:**

   ```
   Implements IDate
   Public ReadOnly Property SelectedDate() _
     As Date Implements IDate.SelectedDate
       Get
           Return Calendar1.SelectedDate.Date
       End Get
   End Property
   ```

   The preceding indicates that we intend to use the `IDate` object (which we haven't created yet) and its `SelectedDate` property to convey the date the user has chosen from the calendar.

4. **After the preceding code, add the** `GetSelectedDate()` **function with the following code:**

   ```
   <ConnectionProviderAttribute _
     ("Selected Date", "SelectedDate")> _
   Public Function GetSelectedDate() As IDate
       Return Me
   End Function
   ```

As mentioned previously, this function is specially equipped for use in data exchange. This time, the added attribute is `ConnectionProvider Attribute` — which, you probably guessed, allows it to connect to another Web part as a data provider. Figure 5-18 shows the user control in Design view. It doesn't look like much now, but it will be quite powerful by the time we've finished with it.

Figure 5-18:
A user
control
calendar
ready to
connect

Creating a connectable data provider

Our third user control is also a data provider. It's a `DropDownList` control that lets the user choose one of three colors. (Additional colors, as they say, are left as an exercise for the reader.)

1. **Add an ASP.NET Web user control called** `ColourSel.ascx` **to your project, making sure to use VB as the language and placing the code in a separate file.**

2. **From the toolbox, drop a** `DropDownList` **control named** `DropDownList1` **on the page. Add three items to the list so the markup looks like the following:**

```
<asp:dropdownlist id="DropDownList1"
runat="server"
autopostback="True"
onselectedindexchanged=
"DropDownList1_SelectedIndexChanged"
    title="Select Colour">
    <asp:listitem>Red</asp:listitem>
    <asp:listitem>Green</asp:listitem>
    <asp:listitem>Blue</asp:listitem>
</asp:dropdownlist>
```

Note that `autopostback` is set to `True` and `onselectedindexchanged` references a subroutine to handle the event.

3. **In the code behind file (**`ColourSel.ascx.vb`**), add the following code after the** `Inherits` **line:**

```
Implements IColour
Public ReadOnly Property SelectedColour() As String _
    Implements IColour.SelectedColour
        Get
            Return DropDownList1.SelectedValue
        End Get
End Property
```

The preceding indicates that we are implementing the `IColour` class (not created yet) and its `SelectedColour()` property. This is part of the conduit that provides the selected color value to another Web part on the page.

4. **Add the** `GetSelectedColour()` **function to pass along the color name by inserting the following code:**

```
<ConnectionProvider _
("Selected Colour", "SelectedColour")> _
Public Function GetSelectedColour() As IColour
    Return Me
End Function
```

As in the previous user control, this function is decked out to be a data provider when connected.

5. **Add the following handler routine to run when the user makes a new selection from the** `DropDownList` **control:**

```
Protected Sub DropDownList1_SelectedIndexChanged _
(ByVal sender As Object, ByVal e As System.EventArgs) _
Handles DropDownList1.SelectedIndexChanged
    GetSelectedColour()
End Sub
```

This code executes the previous function, `GetSelectedColour()`.

That's it for the user controls. We still need to do some work on an ASP.NET page to turn the user controls into full-fledged Web parts. First, there's some unfinished plumbing.

Creating a data exchange interface

Web parts are fussy about how they communicate. In the normal Web page scenario, you can just tell a `Label` control to display the value typed into a `TextBox` control. Web parts are like quarreling spouses who only talk to each other through intermediaries.

The *intermediaries* in this case are two homegrown interfaces called IDate and IColour. They each expose one property: SelectedDate() and SelectedColour() respectively. You saw these being implemented in each of the user controls that handles data.

To create the interfaces and properties for the Web parts:

1. **Add a class file called** IData.vb **to the** App_Code **folder in your project. (Add the folder if required using Add ASP.NET Folder⇨App_Code.)**

2. **Remove the existing content of the file and replace it with the following code:**

```
Imports Microsoft.VisualBasic
Public Interface IDate
    ReadOnly Property _
        SelectedDate() As Date
End Interface
Public Interface IColour
    ReadOnly Property _
        SelectedColour() As String
End Interface
```

The preceding creates the interfaces and one property for each. SelectedDate is a Date type and SelectedColour is a String type. With the addition of this code, the background compiler should stop whining about missing members.

You can check if you've missed a step by selecting Build Web Site from the Build menu. The ASP.NET compiler fills the Error List pane with details of anything that doesn't compute. Don't worry about complaints regarding the Title attribute. The compiler issues warnings because it isn't sufficiently aware of what attributes Web parts can use.

Getting Web parts on the same page

We now have three user controls that we designed to talk to each other. They must, as they say, all be on the same page — which means adding an ASP.NET page and configuring it for the Web-part framework.

Setting up the page

The first item of business is adding the page and placing a table to create a layout for parts to come. To do so:

1. **Add an ASP.NET page called** connwebparts.aspx **to your project using Visual Basic and no separate code file.**

2. **In Design view, from the WebParts tab of the toolbox, drag a** `WebPartManager` **control and drop it on the design surface.**

A Web-part page must have a `WebPartManager` control and it must precede all other Web-part controls on the page.

3. **In Source view, locate the** `WebPartManager` **control and replace the existing markup with the following:**

```
<asp:webpartmanager id="WebPartManager1"
    runat="server">
    <staticconnections>
        <asp:webpartconnection
            id="Connection"
            consumerid="Display1"
            providerid="Cal1"
            consumerconnectionpointid="SelectedDate"
            providerconnectionpointid="SelectedDate"
            />
    </staticconnections>
    <personalization enabled="true" />
</asp:webpartmanager>
```

4. **In Design view, add an HTML table (Layout⇨Insert Table) with one row and three columns.**

These cells hold components that you add in subsequent procedures.

5. **Configure the table cells so the** `valign` **property is set to** `top`.

This is just for cosmetics, so the controls don't wander up and down in the cell.

6. **In the page** `Load` **event, add the following code to prevent use of the page unless the user is logged in:**

```
Protected Sub Page_Load _
  (ByVal sender As Object, _
   ByVal e As System.EventArgs)
    If Not User.Identity.IsAuthenticated Then
        Response.Write("Please log in first.")
        Response.End()
    End If
End Sub
```

Because we're using personalization, the Web parts need a known user. The code given here stops cold at the first sign of an unauthenticated user.

Adding Web-part zones to the page

Recall that Web parts need to sit inside zones. One zone would be sufficient, but to keep the page tidy and demonstrate some features, we splurge and use two zones. We add them both to the same table cell. Here's the drill:

Book VIII Chapter 5

Building Portals with Web Parts

1. In Design view, drag a `WebPartZone` **control from the toolbox and drop it in the left-hand cell. Set the** `HeaderText` **property for** `WebPartZone1` **to Top Zone.**

2. **Insert a plain old horizontal rule (**`<hr />`**) below the** `WebPartZone` **control.**

3. **Drag another** `WebPartZone` **control and drop it below the horizontal rule, still in the left-hand cell. Set the** `HeaderText` **property to** `Bottom Zone`**.**

   The design surface looks like Figure 5-19.

Figure 5-19:
The Web-
part zones.

Adding Web parts to the zones

With the zones ready, we can start adding the user controls and turning them into genuine Web parts. To do this:

1. **From Solution Explorer, drag** `display.ascx` **and drop it into the open rectangle area of the Top Zone.**

2. **Drag** `Cal.ascx` **and drop it onto the open area of Bottom Zone.**

3. **Drag the** `ColourSel.ascx` **user control and drop it into the open rectangle area of Bottom Zone.**

   The generated code for the zones looks like the following:

```
<asp:webpartzone id="WebPartZone1" runat="server"
  headertext="Top Zone">
 <zonetemplate>
   <uc1:display id="Display1" runat="server" />
 </zonetemplate>
</asp:webpartzone>
<hr />
<asp:webpartzone id="WebPartZone2" runat="server"
```

```
    headertext="Bottom Zone">
  <zonetemplate>
    <uc3:cal id="Cal1" runat="server" />
    <uc2:coursel id="ColourSel1" runat="server" />
  </zonetemplate>
</asp:webpartzone>
```

Figure 5-20 shows the appearance of the design surface with the Web parts in place.

Figure 5-20:
The Web parts in their zones.

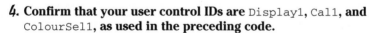

4. **Confirm that your user control IDs are** `Display1`, `Cal1`, **and** `ColourSel1`, **as used in the preceding code.**

We use these IDs in the static connection in the next section and they need to be exact. It's possible that the IDE could generate slightly different IDs as you drag and drop.

Adding a static connection

Two of the Web parts, `display.ascx` and `cal.ascx`, will have a *static connection*. That means the connection is in place the moment the page fires up.

The user doesn't have to do anything to set them working together. Static connections live inside the `WebPartManager` control. We can configure the connection using markup (*declarative code* in geek-speak). Here's how:

1. **In Source view, locate** `WebPartManager1`.

2. **Replace the existing markup for the** `WebPartManager` **control with the following:**

```
<asp:webpartmanager id="WebPartManager1"
    runat="server">
  <staticconnections>
      <asp:webpartconnection
          id="Connection"
          consumerid="Display1"
          providerid="Cal1"
          consumerconnectionpointid="SelectedDate"
          providerconnectionpointid="SelectedDate"
          />
  </staticconnections>
  <personalization enabled="true" />
</asp:webpartmanager>
```

The preceding inserts two sections into the manager. The first, `<staticconnections>`, holds a Web-part connection between the consumer (`Display1`) and the provider (`Cal1`). The connection point IDs happen to use the same name, `SelectedDate`. The second section, `<personalization>` ensures that ASP.NET stores each user's configuration of the Web part in the personalization database.

You're no doubt asking where this `SelectedDate` thingy originates. If you open `display.ascx.vb` and look at the `ConnectionConsumer Attribute`, you find that the second parameter is `SelectedDate`. That's where we declared it as "decoration" to the `setDateText()` method. Likewise, if you open `Cal.ascx.vb`, you find code that turns the `GetSelectedDate()` function into a connection provider attribute, as seen in the following code:

```
<ConnectionProviderAttribute _
("Selected Date", "SelectedDate")> _
Public Function GetSelectedDate() As IDate
    Return Me
End Function
```

Adding visual appeal to the Web part

The connected Web parts are just about ready to go. You might have noticed in Figure 5-20 that the page looks ugly and bare. Let's get rid of the "Untitled" labels and improve the overall appearance. To get started with the makeover, follow these steps:

1. **Open** `connwebparts.aspx` **in Source view and locate the user control with the ID** `display1`.

2. **Add a** `title` **attribute with the value Display so the markup looks like the following:**

```
<uc1:display id="display1" runat="server"
title="Display" />
```

3. **Add** `title` **attributes to the two other user controls,** `Cal1` **and** `ColourSel1` **with the values** `Calendar` **and** `Colour Choice`, **respectively.**

4. **In Design view, select** `WebPartZone1` **and click the right arrow to open the Smart Tasks menu.**

5. **Click AutoFormat and, in the Auto Format dialog box, select Professional (as shown in Figure 5-21) and click OK.**

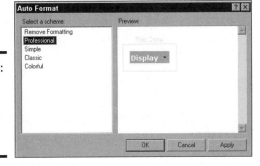

Figure 5-21: A professional theme for the Web part.

6. **Select** `WebPartZone2` **and use Auto Format to apply the Professional theme.**

Testing the connection

The moment you've been working toward has arrived: testing the connection between two of the Web parts. Recall that the `Calendar` Web part is the provider and the `Display` Web part is the consumer. To test the connection:

1. **Make sure your site is configured for personalization.**

2. **Make sure you are logged in to the site.**

3. **Browse to** `connwebparts.aspx.`

   The `Display` part shows the default date, which is sometime before you were born.

4. **Select a date in the Calendar Web part.**

   The Display part shows the selected date, as you see in Figure 5-22.

Figure 5-22: The completed connection between two Web parts.

We now have Web parts that send and receive data. In a more advanced scenario, you can imagine a `DataView` Web part that you fill with data from a database. When the user selects a row, a second Web part receives a parameter and uses that to look up and display related records.

Connecting Web Parts Dynamically

The previous Web part connection was *static,* meaning the two parts connect as soon as the page loads. The great thing about Web parts is that once you configure them to send and receive data, end-users can add and change the connections themselves.

Web parts à la mode

Web-part pages have different modes that affect what you can do with them. In the earliest example, you saw how to put the page into Design mode (`DesignDisplayMode`) so users could drag a Web part from one zone and put it into another. Here are the display mode values you'll use most often:

✦ `BrowseDisplayMode`: This is the mode for interacting with the page in a normal browserish way. When you clicked a date in the previous example, the Web parts interacted in Browse mode.

✦ `DesignDisplayMode`: Design mode lets you move Web parts around. The header area appears and shows the Move cursor to indicate you can start dragging.

✦ `CatalogDisplayMode`: This is where you list Web parts that users can add to the page. The Web-part framework generates a dialog box that handles the plumbing for you.

✦ `EditDisplayMode`: When a page is in Edit mode, an extra menu item appears on each Web part. As you see in the later section "Using the Editor Controls," this display mode lets users edit details of the Web part such as the title.

✦ `ConnectDisplayMode`: This is the mode that lets user connect, disconnect, and rearrange data connections. The Web-part framework creates the user interface automatically. When a page is in this mode, a Connect menu item appears on connectable parts.

There are several ways to put a page into one of the display modes or to cancel a mode and go back to browsing. Often you select an item from a Web-part's menu to change modes. You can alter the mode programmatically in response to a button click or other event. We encounter the Web-part editor controls later on in the section "Using the Editor Controls." These controls change modes based on user clicks.

Creating a mode selector

We play with modes quite a lot in the rest of the chapter, so it's worthwhile to take a minute to assemble a control that makes it easy to change modes on the page. We use a `RadioButtonList` control and a bit of programming code. To add a mode selector:

1. **Open** `connwebparts.aspx` **in Design view.**

2. **From the toolbox, fetch an ASP.NET** `RadioButtonList` **control and drop it into the middle column of the table.**

3. **Set the** `Name` **property to** `rblDispMode`.

4. Switch to Source view, and configure the properties and list items as shown in the following markup:

```
<asp:radiobuttonlist id="rblDispMode" runat="server"
    autopostback="True" width="100%"
    backcolor="Black" bordercolor="White"
    borderstyle="Double" borderwidth="1px"
    forecolor="White">
    <asp:listitem>Browse</asp:listitem>
    <asp:listitem>Design</asp:listitem>
    <asp:listitem>Catalog</asp:listitem>
    <asp:listitem>Edit</asp:listitem>
    <asp:listitem>Connect</asp:listitem>
</asp:radiobuttonlist>
```

Figure 5-23 shows the display mode controller in Design view.

Figure 5-23: The display mode controller.

5. Add the following handler for the `RadioButtonList` **control's** `SelectedIndexChanged` **event.**

```
Protected Sub rblDispMode_SelectedIndexChanged _
(ByVal sender As Object, _
 ByVal e As System.EventArgs) _
 Handles rblDispMode.SelectedIndexChanged
    Select Case rblDispMode.SelectedIndex
        Case 0 : WebPartManager1.DisplayMode = _
                    WebPartManager.BrowseDisplayMode
        Case 1 : WebPartManager1.DisplayMode = _
                    WebPartManager.DesignDisplayMode
        Case 2 : WebPartManager1.DisplayMode = _
```

```
                        WebPartManager.CatalogDisplayMode
        Case 3 : WebPartManager1.DisplayMode = _
                 WebPartManager.EditDisplayMode
        Case 4 : WebPartManager1.DisplayMode = _
                 WebPartManager.ConnectDisplayMode
    End Select
End Sub
```

The preceding executes when a user clicks a radio button. The logic sets the `WebPartManager` control's `DisplayMode` property to the corresponding value for the selected mode.

If you run the page and click the buttons at this point, you get error messages for some modes. We haven't yet added the corresponding zones and controls to support all the modes.

Adding a ConnectionsZone interface

By selecting the Connection radio button, you can put the page into Connect mode. However, there's no graphical interface in the page to arrange a manual connection. For that, we need to add a zone; the following steps do the trick:

1. **In Design view, from the WebParts tab of the toolbox, drag a** `ConnectionsZone` **control and drop it into the column on the right.**

2. **Use the Smart Tasks menu to apply the Professional format to the** `ConnectionsZone` **control.**

   Figure 5-24 shows the control in Design view.

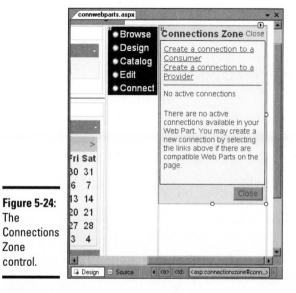

Figure 5-24:
The Connections Zone control.

Book VIII
Chapter 5

Building Portals
with Web Parts

As soon as you add the `ConnectionsZone` control, it's ready to help users connect and disconnect any Web parts that are configured to share data.

Making connections

The `ConnectionsZone` control may surprise you when you view the page. At first, it doesn't seem to be doing much — but it's hard at work behind the scenes.

In this procedure, we connect the Colour Choice Web part using the interface:

1. **Browse to** `connwebparts.aspx`.

2. **From the** `RadioButtonList` **control, click Connect.**

The labels for the Top Zone and Bottom Zone appear. The form is now in Connect mode.

3. **In the bottom part of the page, locate the Colour Choice Web part and click the down arrow to make the menu appear.**

Surprise! The menu includes a new Connect item, as shown in Figure 5-25.

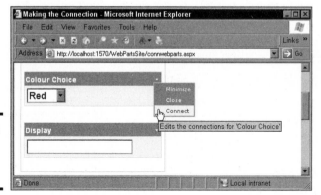

Figure 5-25:
The
Connect
menu item.

4. **Click the Connect item.**

The Connections Zone pane appears, indicating there are no active connections for the Colour Choice Web part.

5. **Click the Create a Connection to a Consumer link in the Connections Zone pane.**

The pane displays a drop-down list that includes one available consumer Web part which is Display (Selected Colour), as shown in Figure 5-26. This means you can send a value from the Colour Choice drop-down list to the Display Web part.

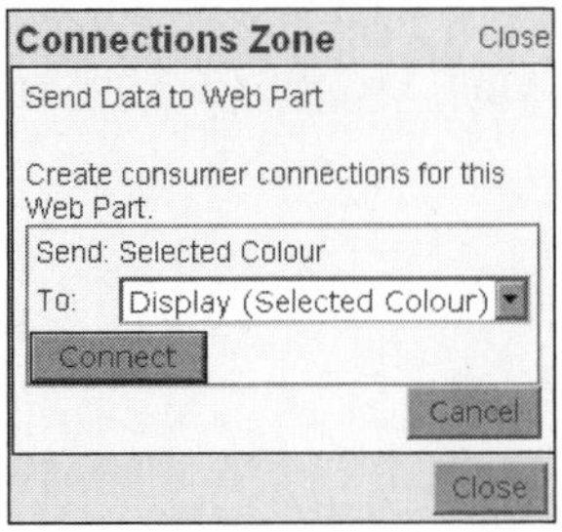

Figure 5-26:
Selecting
a data
consumer.

6. **Select the item and click Connect.**

   The Connections Zone lists the action.

7. **Look at the** `TextBox` **control in the Display Web part.**

   The textbox now renders the date text in the selected color as indicated in the Colour Choice area at the bottom of the page.

8. **Select Green and Blue from the drop-down list.**

   The Display text changes color according to the choice. Meanwhile, the Connections Zone (as shown in Figure 5-27) lists the connection status plus a Disconnect button.

Figure 5-27:
Selecting
a data
consumer.

Somehow, a choice in one Web part changed the color of the text in another. We built this capability into both the Display and the Colour Choice Web parts when they were still user controls. Colour Choice became a connection provider with this code:

```
<ConnectionProvider _
    ("Selected Colour", "SelectedColour")> _
    Public Function GetSelectedColour() As IColour
        Return Me
    End Function
```

The Display Web part was able to consume the color value thanks to this routine:

```
<ConnectionConsumerAttribute _
  ("Selected Colour", "SelectedColour")> _
  Sub setColorText(ByVal ColourText As IColour)
      Me._selectedColour = ColourText
  End Sub
```

When the Web part has received the value that's being passed, it applies the color name to the `TextBox` control's `ForeColor` property.

```
txtChosen.ForeColor = _
 Drawing.ColorTranslator.FromHtml _
 (_selectedColour.SelectedColour)
```

This technique shows that you can pass all kinds of data between controls — not just dates and numbers.

Breaking connections

Users can break static and dynamic connections using the Connections Zone panel. To break a connection:

1. **Browse to** `connwebparts.aspx` **and click the Connect radio button.**

2. **In the Display Web part, click the arrow to bring up the drop-down list.**

3. **Click Connect.**

The Connections Zone pane appears.

4. **Locate the connection for Selected Date and Calendar and then click Disconnect.**

5. **Click the Browse radio button and select a date in the Calendar Web part.**

Notice that the date in the *Display date* area no longer changes. If you close and reopen the browser, the connection remains closed because these settings are part of the logged in user's personal profile.

Some controls might display error messages when you break their static connection. Test them to see what they look like when they have no data.

Using the Editor Controls

Once you give users a taste of freedom, they'll want to change even more aspects of their portal page. We saw, for example, that the Sympatico/MSN portal page allows users to change the greeting that defaulted to Ken's Page.

The `EditorZone` control has specialized functions and a graphical interface to make changes to elements of a page. However, like contestants on *Who Wants to be a Millionaire?*, they need a little help.

Adding EditorZone and AppearanceEditorPart controls

The `EditorZone` control works as a container for other editor controls. For the most part, it supplies OK, Cancel, Apply, and Close buttons. In this procedure, we introduce the `AppearanceEditorPart` control:

1. **Open** `connwebparts.aspx` **in Design view.**

2. **From the toolbox, drag an** `EditorZone` **control and drop it in the upper area of the right-hand column.**

Figure 5-28 shows the `EditorZone` control on the page.

Figure 5-28:
The
EditorZone
control.

3. **From the toolbox, drag an** `AppearanceEditorPart` **and drop it on the** `EditorZone` **control, just above the buttons.**

4. **Use Auto Format to apply the Professional format to the Editor Zone.**

   Figure 5-29 shows the two controls together in Design view.

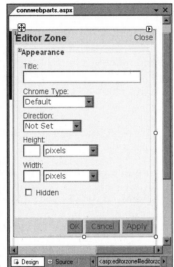

Figure 5-29:
The
embedded
Appearance
EditorPart
control.

Changing a Web part's appearance

The `AppearanceEditorPart` lets users change several features of a Web part, including the text. To allow the user to change the Web part's appearance:

1. **Browse to** `connwebparts.aspx` **and click the Edit radio button.**

2. **On the Calendar Web part, click the down arrow to display its menu.**

3. **Select the** `Edit` **item.**

   The `Edit` item is available because we're in Edit mode. The Editor Zone pane appears.

4. **In the Editor Zone's Title box, change the text to** `Ken's Own Calendar`**, as shown in Figure 5-30.**

   (Technically speaking, you *could* use your own name instead of mine. That would be highly risky and certainly detract from the attractiveness of the part. But do it if you must.)

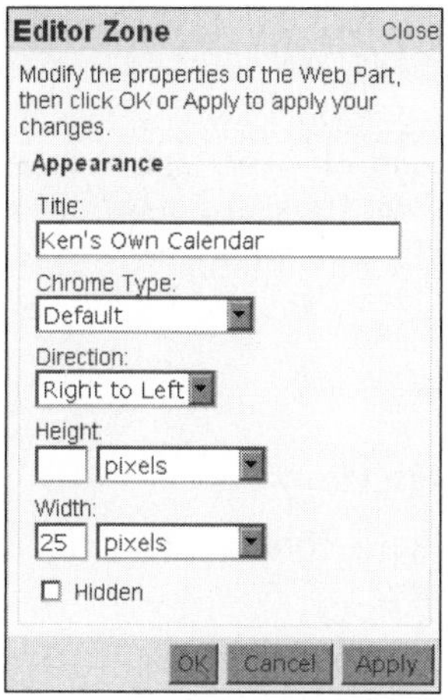

Figure 5-30: Editing a Web-part title.

5. Click the OK button.

You've customized the title for the Calendar Web part. You can play with the other editing options if or when you have time. Be aware that in our case, the height and width settings don't have any effect because the controls are constrained by column settings and the size of their containers.

Using other editor parts

You can add these other editor parts to the Editor Zone:

✦ LayoutEditorPart: Lets the user change the selected Web part's borders (known as Chrome in Microsoft land) and zone.

✦ PropertyGridEditorPart: Lets users edit custom properties that a Web part allows to be changed.

✦ BehaviorEditorPart: Lets users edit many parts of the user interface including links, icons, and modes such as editing and connections.

Letting Users Select Their Web Parts

If your page is like the Sympatico/MSN portal shown at the start of this chapter, users probably want to pick topics that appeal to them. In a corporate setting, you might have Web parts that create graphs, display tables of data, and communicate with other employees — but which aren't used all the time. Users may want to remove them and bring them back as required.

Adding CatalogZone and DeclarativeCatalogPart controls

The `CatalogZone` control acts as the container and middle manager for other Web parts. Like a greeter in a big box store, it puts a face on the page to direct Web parts to the right place. The `DeclarativeCatalogPart` lets users select from controls that you've made available for them.

To create a catalog to hold Web parts:

1. **Open** `connwebparts.aspx` **in Design view.**

2. **From the toolbox, drag a** `CatalogZone` **control and drop it in the upper area of the right-hand column.**

3. **Drag a** `DeclarativeCatalogPart` **control from the toolbox and drop it in the open area inside the** `CatalogZone` **control.**

4. **Select the** `DeclarativeCatalogPart` **and from the Smart Tasks menu, click Edit Templates.**

The interface changes, as shown in Figure 5-31.

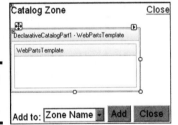

Figure 5-31:
Adding to
the catalog.

5. **From Solution Explorer, drag** `display.ascx` **and drop it into the WebParts Template area.**

6. **From the** `DeclarativeCatalogPart`**'s Smart Tasks menu, click End Template Editing.**

7. **In Source view, locate the markup for** `Display2` **and add a** `title` **attribute with the value Chosen Data.**

The markup for the zone and catalog part should look like the following:

```
<asp:catalogzone id="CatalogZone1"
  runat="server"
  width="250px">
    <zonetemplate>
        <asp:declarativecatalogpart
        id="DeclarativeCatalogPart1" runat="server">
            <webpartstemplate>
```

```
<uc1:display id="display2"
    runat="server" title="Chosen Data" />
</webpartstemplate>
</asp:declarativecatalogpart>
</zonetemplate>
</asp:catalogzone>
```

The preceding code makes the Display Web part available in the catalog; you can add the other Web parts if you want. Be sure to add the `title` attribute to each one. Otherwise you'll have a bunch of no-name parts.

Selecting a part from the catalog

Our Chosen Data Web part is ripe for the picking. We just need to go into the proper mode to get it. To select the calendar from the catalog, follow these steps:

1. **Browse to** `connwebparts.aspx` **and click the Catalog radio button.**

The Catalog Zone pane opens, including Declarative Catalog (as shown in Figure 5-32).

Figure 5-32:
The Declarative Catalog in action.

Book VIII
Chapter 5

Building Portals
with Web Parts

2. **Check the Chosen Data Web part.**

3. **From the drop-down list, select Bottom Zone and click Add.**

The Web part appears in the selected zone.

4. **Click the Connect radio button.**

5. **In the Chosen Data Web part, from the menu, select Connect.**

The Connections Zone appears.

6. **Click Create a Connection to a Provider.**

7. **From the upper drop-down list, select the item (for example, Ken's Own Calendar, as you see in Figure 5-33) and click Connect.**

Figure 5-33:
The
Declarative
Catalog in
action.

8. **From the lower drop-down list, select the item and click Connect.**

9. **Select a date from the Calendar Web part and a color from the Colour Choice Web part.**

The Chosen Data Web part displays the selected date in the chosen color.

When you select a connectable part from the catalog, all its connection properties are available.

Chapter 6: Creating and Consuming Web Services

In This Chapter

- ✓ Looking under the hood of a typical Web service
- ✓ Creating a simple Web service to return a value
- ✓ Using different programs to consume a Web service
- ✓ Building a Web service that finds Elvis Presley

A few years ago, the public-relations departments of the big software companies touted Web services as *The Next Big Thing* in the computer world. The hype faded as people realized that the standardization of data exchange protocols was just an addition to the technology toolbox, not the answer to all distributed computing issues.

Web services are primarily a platform- and language-independent protocol for sending and receiving data over the Internet. The services let computer programs talk to other computer programs in a text format that people can read and understand. The data can be an inquiry such as the availability of a product or for a list of clients. A Windows server can request data through a company firewall without needing to know that the answer is coming from a Unix machine on the other side of the globe.

What *is* remarkable is the effort that Microsoft put into its development tools to make Web services easy to create and consume in the .NET platform.

In this chapter, you learn about Web services and then create some of your own. You put the Web services to work in sample applications — not all of which require the .NET platform.

All the code listings that are used in this book are available for download at www.dummies.com/go/aspnetaiofd.

Understanding Web Services

Web services aren't complicated. When you cut through the hype, the concepts are quite simple. True, there's a lot of technology behind the scenes, but the tools hide that part as well.

Let's walk through a very typical scenario involving a homeowner and his supercomputer. (If you don't have a supercomputer at home, don't worry. You can still follow along.)

A supercomputer scenario

The supercomputer in the basement of your home performs calculations and data manipulation faster than any other computer on earth. You haven't told anyone, but the prime reason you bought such power is to feed your impatient passion for computerized chess. Oh, and you use it as a word processor.

When you don't need the machine for your chess games, you're willing to sell some of the processing time to offset the huge electricity bill. Here are some of the criteria for your sideline business service:

+ **The service must not jeopardize the security of existing operations or interrupt a game.**

+ **Customers of the service should not know what kind of computer you have or any of its technical specifications.**

+ **The service must be totally automated so you can sell excess computing capacity at any time without breaking your concentration.**

+ **The service should be widely available to anyone who has the money to pay for it.**

+ **You don't want to waste time away from the chess board to hook up customers or teach them how to submit processing requests.**

A super solution

To your great surprise, the solution I'm proposing for you is an XML Web service. You'll need a Web server, a firewall, and some programming to get started.

Here's how we get data into and out of the service:

1. **A client (more precisely, the client's computer program) wraps the data to be processed in an electronic envelope made up of XML tags.**

The computer connects to your Web server over the Internet and submits the data it wants processed.

2. **Your Web server receives the data packet, ensures that it meets the established standard, and unwraps it to get at the payload — the requested computation.**

3. **If the pre-computation data is safe and acceptable, the Web server passes it through the firewall via a secure connection to the supercomputer.**

4. **The supercomputer reads the data, produces an answer, and hands the answer back through the firewall to the Web server.**

5. **The Web server bundles the answer in a standardized, XML-based return envelope and sends it as a response to the client's request.**

6. **The client's system unwraps the package and uses the answer in its own processes.**

What you've just seen is a Web service transaction, or software as a service. The envelopes that wrap the data adhere to a standard known as the Simple Object Access Protocol, or SOAP. SOAP uses self-describing XML markup as a container for the data. Because XML is text-based, people and programs can read it to see what it contains.

The black box

The client in this scenario knows nothing about you or that you have a supercomputer. She may be curious as to how your system can come back with answers in seconds that take her machine almost a day. But what she cares most about is that the answer is correct and fast.

Your system is acting as a *black box*. How you produce the result remains a mystery to her. For all clients know, you could be a conglomerate with a nationwide distributed grid computing system rather than a simple chess fanatic. Nobody sees the computer or the algorithm you use. Users just see the Internet URL, their request, and the result. Your chess game goes on uninterrupted.

Exposing an API

To the client, you're publishing an application programming interface (API) for her consumption. The client can run the same calculation on a machine in-house and get the same result — if she wants to wait for a day. If you're busy on the supercomputer and not allowing it to handle jobs for others, the client may well start the processing internally. To her, the main difference is that your API is located somewhere across the Internet and produces the result a heck of a lot faster.

The API is a type of contract. You might tweak the algorithms to make the program run faster and even offer some alternative versions with different syntax, but no matter how you tweak it, the published API always accepts the same type of data and produces the expected result.

Not just HTTP

Your Web service operates over the Internet using the common HTTP protocol. However, it could travel in several other ways. For example, if you had an FTP server, the client could drop requests there and pick up the answers. Your software could accept e-mail messages from clients with SOAP packages included as attachments. The software would pull out the bundled request, and submit it for processing. An e-mail server that supports the Simple Mail Transport Protocol (SMTP) would e-mail back the answer automatically.

If the expanding supercomputation business threatened to steal too many cycles from your chess program, you could put requests in a queue. When the chess program is waiting for your move, the supercomputer could pick a couple of items out of the queue and crunch away on them. When finished, it would return the answers to a pickup directory for forwarding. Maybe you'd charge less for delayed results, or perhaps the system could offer a secondary Web service that clients could poll for the estimated wait time.

Expanding demands

Sometimes sidelines and hobbies become a person's main business. Some of the clients are getting more demanding. They want you to offer enhanced privacy for their messages, encryption, a guarantee that requests and responses will be delivered, and a way to route a request to somewhere else if your system can't process the computation right away.

It can be done

You can build everything that you've read in the preceding scenarios with existing tools and technologies. Some aspects, like security, require add-ons to the basic SOAP protocol. You'd certainly need more servers and software, but it can be done without a lot of grief. Given that you already have the supercomputer to crunch the data — lucky you! — the rest is relatively cheap.

Now that you understand what a Web service is or can be, we can launch into building one with Visual Web Developer Express (VWDE). No, we won't be hooking it up to the supercomputer — our computation needs aren't that extreme.

Creating a Web Service

Creating a Web service using Visual Web Developer Express is easier than creating a Web page because there's only half as much to do. Unlike a Web page, a Web service has no user interface. There are no buttons or boxes to design.

(Actually, that's not quite true because ASP.NET automatically builds some user interface elements for testing the Web service. We dig into that in the section "Providing information to clients," later in this chapter.

Add a Web service to your project

Our first Web service is a converter from Arabic numbers to Roman numerals. There's strong demand for this service in Hollywood where the artists who create the credits for films use Roman numerals for the copyright date.

To get started, you should have an ASP.NET Web project open. We're coding the Web services in Visual Basic (VB).

1. **In Solution Explorer, right-click the project name and, from the context menu, click Add New Item.**

The Add New Item dialog box opens.

2. **In the Templates area, select the Web Service item and name the file** `romannumerals.asmx`, **as shown in Figure 6-1.**

Hey, did you notice the new extension, `.asmx` there? Microsoft reserves the extension `.asmx` for Web services. The `.asmx` extension ensures that the Web server produces XML output rather than HTML (or XHTML). A regular `.aspx` page is intended for browsing while a `.asmx` file is for data exchange.

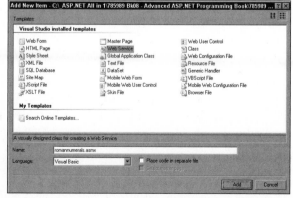

Figure 6-1:
Adding a
Web service
to a project.

3. **Select Visual Basic as the language, clear the Place Code in Separate File check box, and click Add.**

Visual Web Developer adds two files to your project: an `.asmx` file and a `.vb` file. Then, it opens the `.vb` file in the editor, as shown in Figure 6-2.

Figure 6-2:
Skeleton
Web service
in Code
view.

At this point, you have a somewhat usable `"Hello World"` Web service because Microsoft inserts the skeleton code as an example.

Analyze this!

Notice that there's no Design mode choice for a Web service. As previously mentioned, a Web service is all code, all the time. Here's the complete starter code for the Web service:

```
<%@ WebService Language="VB" Class="romannumerals" %>
Imports System.Web
Imports System.Web.Services
Imports System.Web.Services.Protocols
<WebService(Namespace := "http://tempuri.org/")> _
<WebServiceBinding(ConformsTo:=WsiProfiles.BasicProfile1_1)>_
Public Class romannumerals
    Inherits System.Web.Services.WebService
    <WebMethod()> _
    Public Function HelloWorld() As String
        Return "Hello World"
    End Function
End Class
```

Let's look at what goes into the default code before we start changing it to implement our own service.

The opening line

```
<%@ WebService Language="VB" Class="romannumerals" %>
```

is the directive that tells ASP.NET and the compiler to treat this code as a Web service using Visual Basic. The `Class` attribute defines the name of the class the page uses. The next three lines,

```
Imports System.Web
Imports System.Web.Services
Imports System.Web.Services.Protocols
```

import three main namespaces so we don't need to refer to objects by their complete, fully qualified names.

We start getting into the meat of the Web service with this line:

```
<WebService(Namespace := "http://tempuri.org/")> _
```

The `WebService` attribute sets the namespace for the Web service class. A *namespace* distinguishes the methods and properties in our Web service from any others. Stay tuned because in the next section we change the namespace from the default (`http://tempuri.org/`).

Next is the `WebServiceBinding` attribute for the class:

```
<WebServiceBinding(ConformsTo:=WsiProfiles.BasicProfile1_1)>
```

The *binding* defines the message format and protocol details for a Web service. It's somewhat like a dialect in the English language. This one indicates that the Web service conforms to a specification called WSI Basic Profile version 1.1 put out by the Web Services Interoperability Organization (`www.ws-i.org`).

The `Class` and `Inherits` keywords in the following lines are standard fare for .NET applications:

```
Public Class romannumerals
    Inherits System.Web.Services.WebService
```

It's the `WebMethod` attribute on the `HelloWorld()` function that makes the function available to serve remote Web clients. Without the attribute (*decoration* in geek-speak), the function isn't exposed to the outside world.

```
<WebMethod()> _
Public Function HelloWorld() As String
  Return "Hello World"
End Function
```

What's this tempuri.org?

When you first encounter the default namespace in Microsoft's Web services, you naturally wonder what `http://tempuri.org/` is all about. Is *tempuri* really an organization with its own Web site? The answer is no and yes.

Namespaces are a way of assigning a unique name to your modules so consumers can distinguish *your* `GetValue()` method from the millions of others out there on the Web. Namespaces look like Internet addresses, which is why people often mistake them for URLs. Yes, they can point to a real address and Web page, but they don't have to do so.

When your Web service is ready for production use, you should replace the default namespace with your own permanent version. For example, I use `http://kencox.ca/webservices/` as my namespace.

In the case of `http://tempuri.org/`, Microsoft created the namespace as the default for its programming tools. As it happens, Microsoft also registered the `tempuri.org` domain and put up a Web page there. If you go to the Web site, you get an explanation and links to more information on namespaces.

The `HelloWorld()` function's only purpose is to return a string of text. We remove the default function and create our own in the next section.

Replace the default namespace

The default namespace in the previous section (`http://tempuri.org/`) is okay to use for development and testing, but a production Web service should have a unique and permanent namespace. It's easier to set this up from the start rather than going back in afterward to make changes or risk forgetting it until someone asks about it.

For this example, I'm using my own unique namespace, `http://kencox.ca/webservices/`, because the domain name belongs to me and is under my control. Thus, my namespace is declared as follows:

```
<WebService(Namespace:="http://kencox.ca/webservices/")> _
```

Once you have set the namespace, don't change anything about it, including the case and the forward slash at the end. Web service clients can be extremely picky about the namespace, so you don't want any confusion with multiple versions — however slight the difference — hanging around.

Add the RomanNumerals function

Our Web service converts Arabic numbers to Roman numerals. After you've created the `romannumeral.vb` file, delete the `HelloWorld` function and add the function shown in Listing 6-1.

Listing 6-1:   The RomanNumerals function (VB)

```
<WebMethod()> _                                             →1
Public Function RomanNumerals _                             →2
  (ByVal strVal As String) As String
    Dim strErr As String = "Error: No conversion"
    Dim intVal As Integer
Try                                                         →3
    intVal = CInt(strVal)
Catch ex As Exception
    RomanNumerals = strErr
    Exit Function
End Try
If (intVal < 1) Or (intVal > 4999) Then                     →4
    RomanNumerals = strErr
Else
    Dim intCounter As Integer = 0                           →5
    Dim strOut As String = ""
    Dim ar() As Integer = _                                 →6
    {1000, 900, 500, 400, 100, 90, 50, _
    40, 10, 9, 5, 4, 1}
    Dim ro() As String = _                                  →7
    {"M", "CM", "D", _
    "CD", "C", "XC", "L", "XL", "X", "IX", _
    "V", "IV", "I"}
     While intVal                                           →8
        While intVal >= ar(intCounter)                      →9
            intVal = intVal - ar(intCounter)
            strOut = strOut & ro(intCounter)
        End While
        intCounter = intCounter + 1
    End While
    RomanNumerals = strOut                                  →10
End If
End Function
```

The following paragraphs describe the key points of this listing:

+ **→1:** The first lines declare the function name (`RomanNumerals`). This function accepts a parameter named `strVal` and returns a `String` value.

+ **→2:** The `RomanNumerals` function uses two local variables: `strErr`, which holds the error message string, and `intVal`, the integer version of the value that's passed in via the `strVal` parameter.

♦ →**3:** We wrap the next portion of the code in a `Try...Catch` block because it must deal with unknown, unvalidated, and potentially malicious data. If there's something bizarre about the incoming string that throws an exception, we'd rather catch the exception and send back a generic error message than show the results of a crash.

Security experts hammer away at one theme in particular: *All user input is evil until proven otherwise.* That is, never trust data until you've checked it for yourself. It's not as paranoid as it sounds; many of the worst security vulnerabilities stem from too much trust on the part of programmers. They trust that users will not send a value so ridiculously large that it crashes the module. Worse, when the module crashes, the malicious payload executes code to take over the computer.

To validate and cleanse the incoming data, we use the VB `CInt()` function to turn a string into an integer. If the user sends a string that can't be converted into an integer, such as `ddfdfdfdfd`, then `CInt()` throws an exception that our `Try...Catch` block catches. `CInt()` rounds the fractional part in case the input indicates a fraction, such as "10.1." If there's an error, the `Catch` portion sets the return value to an error message (`Error: No conversion`) and bails out of the function.

♦ →**4:** The final purity check is for the size of the number. We can only realistically convert numbers from 1 to 4999 into Roman numerals. Anything outside that range returns the error message rather than a result.

♦ →**5:** The code from this point on is executed only if the data has passed our validity checks. We start by declaring more variables and setting up two arrays that will help with the conversion to Roman numerals.

♦ →**6:** The first array, `ar()`, holds Arabic numbers.

♦ →**7:** The second array, `ro()`, holds the corresponding constructions for Roman numerals.

♦ →**8:** Next comes a series of `While` loops. This one watches the incoming value and continues as long as it is greater than zero.

♦ →**9:** This `While` loop, nested within the one at line 8, does the heavy lifting. It checks that the current value is greater than or equal to the current Arabic value. If so, it subtracts the value contained in the array and builds `strOut` that holds the Roman numeral during construction.

During each iteration, the loop tests whether the current array value fits into what remains of the original value. By the end, the function has reduced the original value to zero and inserted Roman numerals into the final array.

♦ →**10:** The last step assigns the string to the function's name (`RomanNumerals`) so it can return the value.

A quick test of the Web service

The `RomanNumerals` Web service created in the previous section is now ready to deploy and test. ASP.NET offers a handy interface for testing and debugging a Web service on the development machine. In effect, it builds a client Web page on the fly.

1. **In Solution Explorer, right-click** `romannumerals.asmx` **and then click View in Browser.**

A Web page appears with the supported operation, as shown in Figure 6-3.

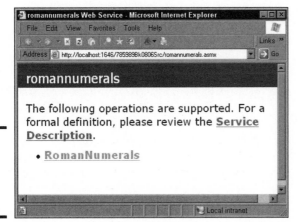

Figure 6-3:
The supported operations Web page.

2. **Click the** RomanNumerals **link, which is the name of the only operation we have so far.**

A test page for the `RomanNumerals` Web service appears.

3. **In the text box, type** `1947` **(as shown in Figure 6-4) and then click Invoke.**

As you see in Figure 6-5, a new browser instance opens with the XML that the Web service returned.

Let's look at what the service returned. The code starts with the XML declaration and then a single `<string>` tag marked with the namespace `http://kencox.ca/webservices/`, as seen in the following code:

```
<?xml version="1.0" encoding="utf-8"?>
<string
    xmlns="http://kencox.ca/webservices/">MCMXLVII</string>
```

Embedded in the `<string>` tag is the answer to our query. In Roman numerals, 1947 is MCMXLVII.

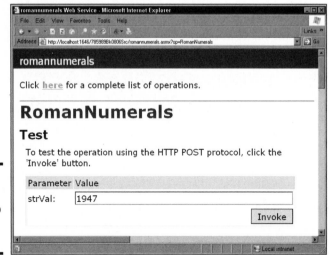

Figure 6-4:
Providing a
test value to
the Web
service.

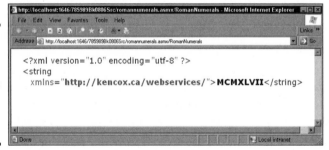

Figure 6-5:
The XML
that the
Web service
returns
includes the
answer.

Other valuable information

When you test the service on the local machine, the page displays valuable
information for anyone who wants to consume the Web service. For example, Figure 6-6 shows the syntax for requesting a conversion using the HTTP
Post method with the SOAP 1.1 standard.

The first part of the documentation (that's the code following this paragraph) tells developers what needs to be in the HTTP header information,
including the `Content-Type` and `Content-Length` items. In the section
"Using the service from VBScript," later in this chapter, I show how to construct a query using the header details.

```
POST /785989Bk0806Src/romannumerals.asmx HTTP/1.1
Host: localhost
```

```
Content-Type: text/xml; charset=utf-8
Content-Length: length
SOAPAction: "http://kencox.ca/webservices/RomanNumerals"
```

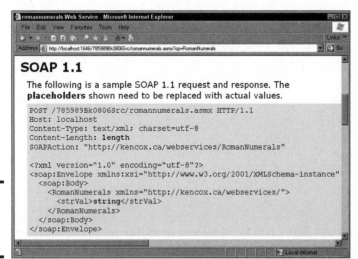

Figure 6-6:
Information
for
consumers.

The remaining instructions constitute the XML content to submit to the
Web service. You can see in the code that follows that the first tag is
`<soap:Envelope>`, the overall container for the message. The attributes
provide details as to the namespaces to which the format belongs.

```
<?xml version="1.0" encoding="utf-8"?>
<soap:Envelope
    xmlns:xsi="http://www.w3.org/2001/XMLSchema-instance"
    xmlns:xsd="http://www.w3.org/2001/XMLSchema"
    xmlns:soap="http://schemas.xmlsoap.org/soap/envelope/">
```

Inside the envelope, you find the `<soap:Body>` tag. It holds the key content
including the function that we want to call (`<RomanNumerals>`, the namespace to which it belongs (`http://kencox.ca/webservices/`), and the
parameter to send `<strVal>`. In the following code, the word *string* is
only a placeholder that will be replaced with a value such as 1947, as in
`<strVal>1947</strVal>`.

```
  <soap:Body>
    <RomanNumerals xmlns="http://kencox.ca/webservices/">
      <strVal>string</strVal>
    </RomanNumerals>
  </soap:Body>
</soap:Envelope>
```

**Book VIII
Chapter 6**

**Creating and
Consuming
Web Services**

On a production server, normally the display of test content for a Web service is turned off by default because IT people feared (with good reason) that putting that stuff out in the open could help hackers mess with your service. If you want to switch the test on, just after `<system.web>`, add this markup to your `web.config` file:

```
<!--system.web goes here-->
    <webServices>
     <protocols>
       <add name="HttpPost" />
       <add name="HttpGet" />
       <add name="Documentation" />
     </protocols>
    </webServices>
```

Providing information to clients

To help developers who are writing consumers of your Web service, you can add descriptive text to the `WebService` and `WebMethod` attributes. For example, the text below replaces the default description for the class, even using some HTML markup for emphasis. It also replaces the default version of the Web service name to display upper- and lowercase on the help page:

```
<WebService _
  (Description:="<b><i>Providing Web services to friends," & _
              " Romans, and countrymen.</i></b>", _
  Name:="RomanNumerals", _
  Namespace:="http://kencox.ca/webservices/" _
  )> _
```

In the same way, you can add help text for the exposed function by using the `Description` parameter, like this:

```
<WebMethod(Description:="This method converts an " & _
"integer between 1 and 4999 (<b>passed as a string</b>) " & _
"to a Roman numeral.")>
```

Figure 6-7 shows the result of adding the preceding descriptions.

Consuming a Web Service

With our Web service up and running, we can create some clients for it. The first client is an ASP.NET page. After that we'll venture further — outside of the .NET Framework.

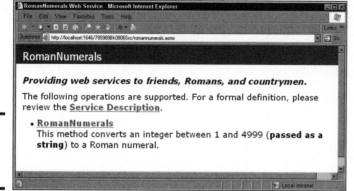

Figure 6-7:
Adding
descriptive
help text.

Using the service in a Web page and project

"A professional makes it look easy," my friend John used to say. If he was right about that, Visual Studio 2005 and Visual Web Developer Express are highly professional products for hooking up to Web services. The tools do a superb job of generating — but hiding — all the complicated plumbing that makes consuming a Web service possible.

Setting up the Web page

To consume the Web service, we need a simple graphical interface to send a conversion request and display the results. Here's how to create the graphical interface:

1. **Add an ASP.NET Web form called** `rnconsumer.aspx` **to your project using VB as the language and with no separate code file.**

2. **In Design view, from the Standard tab of the toolbox, drag and drop an ASP.NET** `TextBox` **control on the page. Change the control's** `ID` **to** `txtInteger`.

3. **Also from the toolbox, drag and drop a** `Button` **control onto the page, and then change the control's** `ID` **property to** `btnSubmit`.

4. **Add a** `Label` **control named** `lblResult` **to the page, making the default text an empty string.**

   Figure 6-8 shows the completed Web form.

With the user-interface (UI) work out of the way, we can move on to wiring up to the Web service.

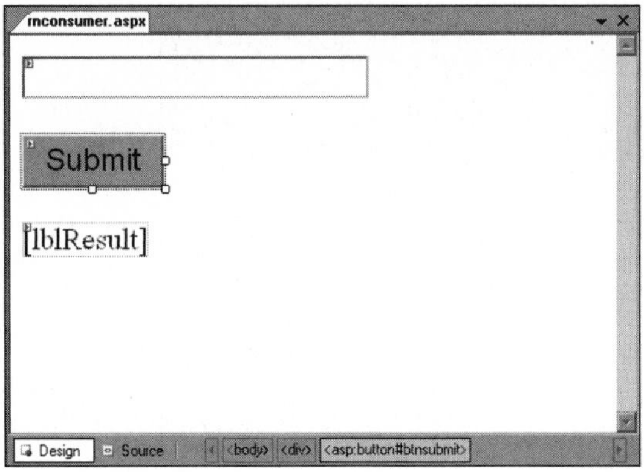

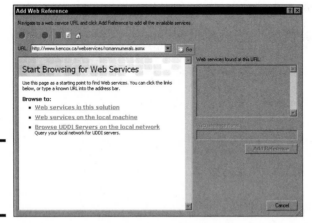

Figure 6-8:
Web form
to request a
conversion.

Adding the Web reference

You won't be surprised to learn that a program needs to know where to look for the Web service. Visual Web Developer Express provides an easy tool for adding the URL and associated code to your project. To add the Web reference, follow these steps:

1. In Solution Explorer, right-click the project name and, from the context menu, click Add Web Reference.

The Add Web Reference dialog box opens (as shown in Figure 6-9).

Figure 6-9:
Add Web
Reference
dialog box.

2. If you're testing the Web service on your local machine, click the link marked Web services on the local machine. When the Services page appears (as shown in Figure 6-10), click romannumerals.

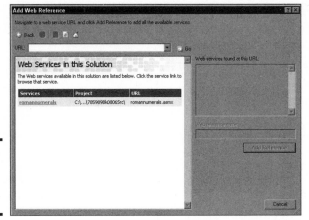

Figure 6-10:
Testing a
local Web
service.

3. **If you're connected to the Internet and testing a Web service on a remote Web site, enter the URL in the URL box and click the Go button.**

You can use a full URL such as

```
http://www.kencox.ca/webservices/romannumerals.asmx
```

The dialog box displays the help page of the Web service, as shown in Figure 6-11.

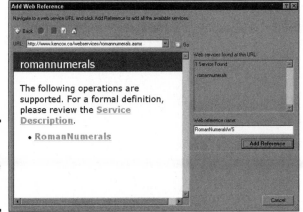

Figure 6-11:
Testing a
Web service
on the
Internet.

Book VIII
Chapter 6

Creating and
Consuming
Web Services

4. **In the Add Web Reference dialog box, change the default Web reference name to** `RomanNumeralsWS` **and then click Add Reference.**

The Visual Web Developer Express integrated development environment (IDE) makes a number of changes to your project. For example, there's a new section inside the `web.config` file that looks like this:

```
<appSettings>
<add key="RomanNumeralsWS.romannumerals"
value="http://www.kencox.ca/webservices/romannumerals.asmx"/>
</appSettings>
```

In Solution Explorer, you find an `App_WebReferences` folder with a subdirectory called `RomanNumeralsWS`. Inside the subdirectory are some filenames that recall a popular type of music from the '70s: `romannumerals.disco`, `romannumerals.discomap`, and `romannumerals.wsdl`. If you boogie on down and open `romannumerals.wsdl`, you get to see the glitzy innards that Microsoft hides from you. It's the official XML and SOAP description of what the Web service accepts and what it gives back. That stuff is best left to the machines to read — or people who are developing with less sophisticated tools.

Connecting the Web reference to the page

With the Web reference and the UI in place, we can connect them and give the service a whirl. Did you notice that we haven't had to write any code so far? It's time to write a few lines. Here we go:

1. **In Design view, double-click the button to create a default handler for the `Click` event.**

2. **In Source view, replace the existing code with the following:**

```
Protected Sub btnSubmit_Click _
(ByVal sender As Object, ByVal e As System.EventArgs)
    Dim strRN As String
    Dim strVal As String = txtInteger.Text
    Dim wsRN As New RomanNumeralsWS.romannumerals
    strRN = wsRN.RomanNumerals(strVal)
    lblResult.Text = strVal & "=" & strRN
End Sub
```

The preceding code declares two string variables, `strRN` and `strVal`. We store the text value from the `TextBox` control in `strVal`. When declaring the variable `wsRN`, we also create an instance of the Roman numerals Web service object.

The heart of the action is in `wsRN.RomanNumerals(strVal)`, which passes the Arabic number (as a string) to the `RomanNumerals()` function of the Web service. We store the returned result (a string) in `strRN`. The last line builds the text to display on the label.

Trying the Web service from the page

It's time to test the page to see if it calls the Web service and gets an answer. To run the test, follow these steps:

1. **Browse to** rnconsumer.aspx.

2. **In the** TextBox **control, type** 2006 **and then click Submit.**

The page refreshes. It could take a short while the first time as ASP.NET compiles the page and the Web service.

The response comes back as shown in Figure 6-12. You can see that 2006 is MMVI in Roman numerals.

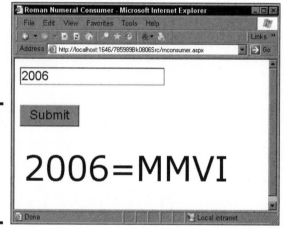

Figure 6-12:
Testing the ASP.NET page against the Web service.

Testing isn't complete until you've tried invalid data. For example, if you type Fifty instead of 50 you should get the following message:

```
Fifty=Error: No conversion
```

Even if you use extensive validation on the Web page to prevent it from submitting bogus or malicious data to the Web service, the Web service must still handle its own validation. You can't rely on validation from another source. As described in the section "Using the service from VBScript," later in this chapter, there are ways of submitting data without going through the page you created.

All user input is evil until proven otherwise.

Using the service from Windows Forms

If you have Visual Basic (VB) or C# Express, you can build a Windows Forms application to consume the Web service. Figure 6-13 shows a small application that uses the Roman numerals Web service.

Figure 6-13: A Windows application consuming the Web service.

The steps to add the Web reference are identical to the ASP.NET version. You can see for yourself that the code to access the Web service is remarkably similar to the Web form:

```
Public Class WSform
    Private Sub btnSubmit_Click _
    (ByVal sender As System.Object, _
    ByVal e As System.EventArgs) _
    Handles btnSubmit.Click
        Dim strRN As String
        Dim strVal As String = txtInteger.Text
        Dim wsRN As New RomanNumeralsWS.romannumerals
        strRN = wsRN.RomanNumerals(strVal)
        lblResult.Text = strRN
    End Sub
End Class
```

Another minor difference between the platforms is that the Windows form stores the Web reference information in the `app.config` file, part of which appears as follows:

```
<applicationSettings>
  <wsconsumer.My.MySettings>
   <setting name="wsconsumer_RomanNumeralsWS_romannumerals"
   serializeAs="String">
   <value>http://www.kencox.ca/webservices/romannumerals.asmx
   </value>
```

```
    </setting>
   </wsconsumer.My.MySettings>
</applicationSettings>
<!-- Closing /configuration tag goes here-->
```

Using the service from VBScript

Although Web services became popular (and easier to use) with the arrival of the .NET Framework, they're definitely not limited to the *technologie du jour*. Here's an example of a script that consumes the Web service. Written in VBScript, it uses using the `Wscript.exe` command-line utility found in Windows.

1. **Create a text file named** `ws.vbs` **with the code in Listing 6-2 as the complete contents of the file.**

2. **In the script, replace the first section of bold text with the URL of your Roman numerals Web service.**

3. **Also in the script, replace the namespace (the second section of bold, after the** `SOAPAction` **header with your namespace).**

4. **Open a Command prompt (Start⇨Run⇨cmd⇨OK).**

5. **Change to the directory where you created** `ws.vbs`**.**

6. **From the command line, type the following command and press Enter:**

```
wscript  ws.vbs
```

At this point, you may get a security warning about the safety of the script. You can acknowledge that it's safe to run.

Figure 6-14 shows an input box with `2006` as the default value for the Web service to convert.

Figure 6-14: Input prompt from a command-line script.

Book VIII Chapter 6

Creating and Consuming Web Services

7. **Click OK to send the integer value to the Web service.**

A message box appears with a large amount of XML text, as shown in Figure 6-15.

Figure 6-15:
Message
box with
returned
XML.

Listing 6-2: ws.vbs, a VBScript script that consumes the Roman numerals Web service

```
' ** Command line usage:
' **       wscript ws.vbs
Dim mhttp
Dim s
dim innum
innum=InputBox("Number (1-4999) to convert?", _
    "Roman Numerals", "2006")
Set mhttp = CreateObject("MSXML2.XMLHTTP")
mhttp.Open _
"POST", _
"http://www.kencox.ca/webservices/romannumerals.asmx", _
    False, "", ""
mhttp.setRequestHeader "SOAPAction", _
"http://kencox.ca/webservices/RomanNumerals"
mhttp.setRequestHeader "Content-Type", "text/xml"
s = s & "<?xml version=""1.0"" encoding=""UTF-8""?>"
s = s & "<soap:Envelope "
s = s & "xmlns:xsi=""http://www.w3.org/"
s = s & "2001/XMLSchema-instance"" "
s = s & "xmlns:xsd=""http://www.w3.org/2001/XMLSchema"" "
s = s & "xmlns:soap=""http://schemas.xmlsoap.org/"
s = s & "soap/envelope/"">"
s = s & "<soap:Body>"
s = s & "<RomanNumerals xmlns=""http://kencox.ca/"
s = s & "webservices/"">"
s = s & "<strVal>" & cstr(innum) & "</strVal>"
s = s & "</RomanNumerals>"
s = s & "</soap:Body>"
s = s & "</soap:Envelope>"
mhttp.send s
msgbox mhttp.responseText, 0 ,"Roman numerals response"
```

The `ws.vbs` script uses the `MSXML2.XMLHTTP` object to send and receive the SOAP packets. Most of the script is taken up with building the XML string that the Web service expects to see. The code below shows what the `mhttp.send` method posts to the Web service. The payload (2006) is in bold text.

```
<?xml version="1.0" encoding="UTF-8"?>
<soap:Envelope
```

```
xmlns:xsi="http://www.w3.org/2001/XMLSchema-instance"
xmlns:xsd="http://www.w3.org/2001/XMLSchema"
xmlns:soap="http://schemas.xmlsoap.org/soap/envelope/">
    <soap:Body>
        <RomanNumerals xmlns="http://kencox.ca/webservices/">
            <strVal>2006</strVal>
        </RomanNumerals>
    </soap:Body>
</soap:Envelope>
```

If you wonder how I knew what XML to generate to get the result, recall that the Web service generates a documentation page that shows the request and response markup for SOAP exchanges.

If you look closely at Figure 6-15, you can see that the Web service returned the Roman numeral as requested. There's a lot of overhead in the SOAP wrapper that makes the tiny payload difficult to find. To save you from eye-strain, here's the returned XML (formatted for readability) with the payload in bold text.

```
<?xml version="1.0" encoding="utf-8"?>
<soap:Envelope
xmlns:soap="http://schemas.xmlsoap.org/soap/envelope/"
xmlns:xsi="http://www.w3.org/2001/XMLSchema-instance"
xmlns:xsd="http://www.w3.org/2001/XMLSchema">
    <soap:Body>
        <RomanNumeralsResponse
         xmlns="http://kencox.ca/webservices/">
            <RomanNumeralsResult>MMVI</RomanNumeralsResult>
        </RomanNumeralsResponse>
    </soap:Body>
</soap:Envelope>
```

Pick a platform

More and more software packages support Web services. For example, you can import data from a Web service into a Microsoft Excel spreadsheet. If you want to use Web services in Excel, be sure to search the Microsoft Web site (http://www.microsoft.com/) for Microsoft Office 2003 Web Services Toolkit. The free download includes a dialog box (shown in Figure 6-16) that generates most of the code you need.

Although the examples here use the Windows platform, you can see that nothing in XML — or, for that matter, in SOAP packets — is exclusive to Microsoft. When you get down to it, it's just text. With a little knowledge of HTTP protocols, you could generate and transmit the same markup from a Java program on a Mac or Linux machine. You'd get the same XML response that you can parse with whatever tools you have available.

**Book VIII
Chapter 6**

**Creating and
Consuming
Web Services**

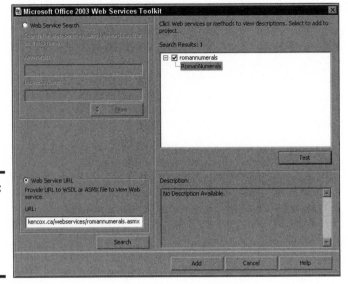

Figure 6-16:
The Office
2003 Web
Services
Toolkit in
action.

Serving a Larger Helping of Data

Let's face it — our Roman numerals Web service is pretty skimpy with the data. There's a good chance that you'll need to send the contents of at least one database record, if not many rows of information. A Web service handles that just as easily, which the following sections illustrate.

Preparing the RockHits Web service

This time, our Web service returns an ADO.NET `DataSet` containing a list of rock 'n' roll hits based on a user query. Although the samples only return two or three rows, you can apply the solution to a huge database.

Creating some data

For convenience, we're using a small XML file as the database. The advantage is that you can read the data easily in this book and type it in if you can't get your hands on the source code. Normally data would come from a relational database, such as SQL Server 2005 or Access.

1. **In your project's** `App_Data` **folder, add an XML file called** `hits.xml`.

2. **Add the XML markup in Listing 6-3 below to** `hits.xml`.

This creates five records for the XML database.

Listing 6-3: An XML database for the RockHits Web service

```xml
<?xml version="1.0" encoding="UTF-8"?>
<hits>
  <Table>
    <id>1</id>
    <title>Love Me Tender</title>
    <artist>Elvis Presley</artist>
  </Table>
  <Table>
    <id>2</id>
    <title>A Thousand Miles Away</title>
    <artist>The Heartbeats</artist>
  </Table>
  <Table>
    <id>3</id>
    <title>Come Go With Me</title>
    <artist>The Dell-Vikings</artist>
  </Table>
  <Table>
    <id>4</id>
    <title>All Shook Up</title>
    <artist>Elvis Presley</artist>
  </Table>
  <Table>
    <id>5</id>
    <title>Bye Bye Love</title>
    <artist>The Everly Brothers</artist>
  </Table>
</hits>
```

Making a Web service

The Web service reads the XML file from the previous section and then filters the data according to the query passed in from the client.

1. **Add a Web service named** `rockhits.asmx` **to your project.**

2. **Add the following code to** `rockhits.asmx` **to create the**
   `GetDataView()` **function.**

```vb
<WebMethod _
(Description:="Gets a subset of records." & _
"Try ""artist='Elvis Presley'""")> _
Public Function GetDataView _
  (ByVal strFilter As String) As Data.DataSet
    Dim ds As New Data.DataSet
    Dim ds2 As New Data.DataSet
    ds.ReadXml(Server.MapPath("~/App_Data/hits.xml"))
    Dim dv As New Data.DataView(ds.Tables(0))
```

```
      dv.RowFilter = strFilter
      dv.AllowNew = False
      dv.AllowEdit = False
      dv.AllowDelete = False
      ds2.Tables.Add(dv.ToTable)
      Return ds2
   End Function
```

3. **Browse to** `rockhits.asmx` **and click the** `GetDataView` **link.**

4. **In the test page, type** `artist='Elvis Presley'` **(including the single quotes), as shown in Figure 6-17, and then click Invoke.**

The browser displays the contents of a serialized `DataSet` (see Figure 6-18) that includes details of hit records by Elvis Presley.

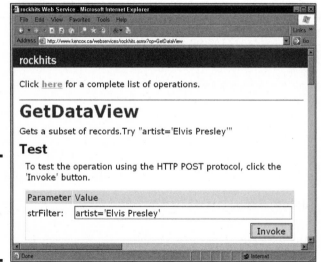

Figure 6-17:
Testing a
query in the
RockHits
Web
service.

The `GetDataView()` function creates two `DataSet` objects. It uses one to read in the XML markup from the `hits.xml` file. The `DataView` object (`dv`) filters the contents of the `DataSet` based on the query that is passed to the function. The `DataView` results are converted to a `DataTable` with the `ToTable()` method and that table is added to the second `DataSet` (`ds2`). The function returns the second `DataSet` to the caller.

A `DataSet` object is especially easy to create and consume when you need to return multiple rows from a Web service. We *consume* the data (feed it to a hungry application) in the next section.

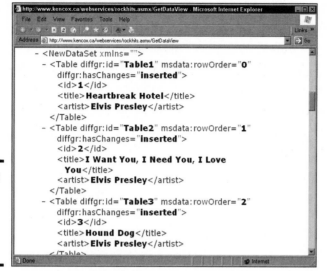

Figure 6-18:
Results of
the query
for artist=
'Elvis
Presley'.

Consuming the DataSet

This final procedure shows how to fetch the records that the preceding section's Web service returns. I won't go into all the detail here because you can refer back to the section "Creating a Web Service" near the beginning of this chapter if you need help. To consume the `DataSet`, follow these steps:

1. **Add a Web reference called** `hitsws` **to your project that points to the RockHits Web service.**

2. **Add an ASP.NET Web form called** `hitlist.aspx` **to your project.**

3. **In Design view, drag a** `GridView` **object from the toolbox and drop it on the page.**

4. **Double-click in an empty area of the page to create a handler for the** `Load` **event and replace it with the following code:**

```
Protected Sub Page_Load _
(ByVal sender As Object, _
ByVal e As System.EventArgs)
    Dim ws As New hitsws.rockhits
    Dim ds As Data.DataSet
    ds = ws.GetDataView("artist='Elvis Presley'")
    GridView1.DataSource = ds
    GridView1.DataBind()
End Sub
```

5. **Browse to** `hitlist.aspx`.

The `GridView` control displays the hit records by Elvis Presley, as shown in Figure 6-19.

Figure 6-19:
The
returned
rows in the
GridView.

You can see that a Web service that returns rows of data is almost identical to a query that you create on your local machine.

Securing a Web Service

Security isn't a big issue for the little Web service we created here because we don't want to keep anyone out. However, you probably want to restrict access to data in a business-to-business exchange. Here are some ways to secure a Web service:

✦ **Use SSL:** The Secure Sockets Layer (SSL) using client certificates ensures that sensitive exchanges over HTTPs are encrypted. A packet sniffer can still see the data go by — but it won't make any sense.

✦ **Use HTTP authentication:** By requiring a Web service client to "log on" to the Web site with a username and password, you control who can send and receive data. There's a wide range of authentication and authorization options, including role-based security, as discussed in Chapter 2 of this mini-book.

✦ **Accept requests from specific IP addresses:** In Internet Information Services, you can specify the IP addresses of business partners' servers, or a range of addresses that can access the site where the Web service is offered. The door slams in everyone else's faces.

✦ **Use the Web Services Enhancements (WSE) 3.0 technology from Microsoft:** WSE 3.0 includes add-on assemblies and helper classes that secure messages with encryption and digital signatures. Look for WSE at `http://msdn.microsoft.com/webservices/`.

Index

E

F

Q

S

USINESS, CAREERS & PERSONAL FINANCE

0-7645-5307-0

0-7645-5331-3 *†

Also available:

Accounting For Dummies †
0-7645-5314-3

Business Plans Kit For Dummies †
0-7645-5365-8

Cover Letters For Dummies
0-7645-5224-4

Frugal Living For Dummies
0-7645-5403-4

Leadership For Dummies
0-7645-5176-0

Managing For Dummies
0-7645-1771-6

Marketing For Dummies
0-7645-5600-2

Personal Finance For Dummies *
0-7645-2590-5

Project Management For Dummies
0-7645-5283-X

Resumes For Dummies †
0-7645-5471-9

Selling For Dummies
0-7645-5363-1

Small Business Kit For Dummies *†
0-7645-5093-4

IOME & BUSINESS COMPUTER BASICS

0-7645-4074-2

0-7645-3758-X

Also available:

ACT! 6 For Dummies
0-7645-2645-6

iLife '04 All-in-One Desk Reference
For Dummies
0-7645-7347-0

iPAQ For Dummies
0-7645-6769-1

Mac OS X Panther Timesaving
Techniques For Dummies
0-7645-5812-9

Macs For Dummies
0-7645-5656-8

Microsoft Money 2004 For Dummies
0-7645-4195-1

Office 2003 All-in-One Desk Reference
For Dummies
0-7645-3883-7

Outlook 2003 For Dummies
0-7645-3759-8

PCs For Dummies
0-7645-4074-2

TiVo For Dummies
0-7645-6923-6

Upgrading and Fixing PCs For Dummies
0-7645-1665-5

Windows XP Timesaving Techniques
For Dummies
0-7645-3748-2

OOD, HOME, GARDEN, HOBBIES, MUSIC & PETS

0-7645-5295-3

0-7645-5232-5

Also available:

Bass Guitar For Dummies
0-7645-2487-9

Diabetes Cookbook For Dummies
0-7645-5230-9

Gardening For Dummies *
0-7645-5130-2

Guitar For Dummies
0-7645-5106-X

Holiday Decorating For Dummies
0-7645-2570-0

Home Improvement All-in-One
For Dummies
0-7645-5680-0

Knitting For Dummies
0-7645-5395-X

Piano For Dummies
0-7645-5105-1

Puppies For Dummies
0-7645-5255-4

Scrapbooking For Dummies
0-7645-7208-3

Senior Dogs For Dummies
0-7645-5818-8

Singing For Dummies
0-7645-2475-5

30-Minute Meals For Dummies
0-7645-2589-1

NTERNET & DIGITAL MEDIA

0-7645-1664-7

0-7645-6924-4

Also available:

2005 Online Shopping Directory
For Dummies
0-7645-7495-7

CD & DVD Recording For Dummies
0-7645-5956-7

eBay For Dummies
0-7645-5654-1

Fighting Spam For Dummies
0-7645-5965-6

Genealogy Online For Dummies
0-7645-5964-8

Google For Dummies
0-7645-4420-9

Home Recording For Musicians
For Dummies
0-7645-1634-5

The Internet For Dummies
0-7645-4173-0

iPod & iTunes For Dummies
0-7645-7772-7

Preventing Identity Theft For Dumm
0-7645-7336-5

Pro Tools All-in-One Desk Referen
For Dummies
0-7645-5714-9

Roxio Easy Media Creator For D
0-7645-7131-1

Separate Canadian edition also available
Separate U.K. edition also available

vailable wherever books are sold. For more information or to order direct: U.S. customers visit www.dummies.com or call 1-877-762-2974.
K. customers visit www.wileyeurope.com or call 0800 243407. Canadian customers visit www.wiley.ca or call 1-800-567-4797.

SPORTS, FITNESS, PARENTING, RELIGION & SPIRITUALITY

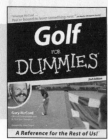

0-7645-5146-9

0-7645-5418-2

Also available:

- Adoption For Dummies
  0-7645-5488-3
- Basketball For Dummies
  0-7645-5248-1
- The Bible For Dummies
  0-7645-5296-1
- Buddhism For Dummies
  0-7645-5359-3
- Catholicism For Dummies
  0-7645-5391-7
- Hockey For Dummies
  0-7645-5228-7

- Judaism For Dummies
  0-7645-5299-6
- Martial Arts For Dummies
  0-7645-5358-5
- Pilates For Dummies
  0-7645-5397-6
- Religion For Dummies
  0-7645-5264-3
- Teaching Kids to Read For Dummies
  0-7645-4043-2
- Weight Training For Dummies
  0-7645-5168-X
- Yoga For Dummies
  0-7645-5117-5

TRAVEL

0-7645-5438-7

0-7645-5453-0

Also available:

- Alaska For Dummies
  0-7645-1761-9
- Arizona For Dummies
  0-7645-6938-4
- Cancún and the Yucatán For Dummies
  0-7645-2437-2
- Cruise Vacations For Dummies
  0-7645-6941-4
- Europe For Dummies
  0-7645-5456-5
- Ireland For Dummies
  0-7645-5455-7

- Las Vegas For Dummies
  0-7645-5448-4
- London For Dummies
  0-7645-4277-X
- New York City For Dummies
  0-7645-6945-7
- Paris For Dummies
  0-7645-5494-8
- RV Vacations For Dummies
  0-7645-5443-3
- Walt Disney World & Orlando For Dummie
  0-7645-6943-0

GRAPHICS, DESIGN & WEB DEVELOPMENT

0-7645-4345-8

0-7645-5589-8

Also available:

- Adobe Acrobat 6 PDF For Dummies
  0-7645-3760-1
- Building a Web Site For Dummies
  0-7645-7144-3
- Dreamweaver MX 2004 For Dummies
  0-7645-4342-3
- FrontPage 2003 For Dummies
  0-7645-3882-9
- HTML 4 For Dummies
  0-7645-1995-6
- Illustrator CS For Dummies
  0-7645-4084-X

- Macromedia Flash MX 2004 For Dummie
  0-7645-4358-X
- Photoshop 7 All-in-One Desk
  Reference For Dummies
  0-7645-1667-1
- Photoshop CS Timesaving Techniques
  For Dummies
  0-7645-6782-9
- PHP 5 For Dummies
  0-7645-4166-8
- PowerPoint 2003 For Dummies
  0-7645-3908-6
- QuarkXPress 6 For Dummies
  0-7645-2593-X

ETWORKING, SECURITY, PROGRAMMING & DATABASES

0-7645-5784-X

Also available:

- A+ Certification For Dummies
  0-7645-4187-0
- Access 2003 All-in-One Desk
  Reference For Dummies
  0-7645-3988-4
- Beginning Programming For Dummies
  0-7645-4997-9
- C For Dummies
  0-7645-7068-4
- Firewalls For Dummies
  0-7645-4048-3
- Home Networking For Dummies
  0-7645-42796

- Network Security For Dummies
  0-7645-1679-5
- Networking For Dummies
  0-7645-1677-9
- TCP/IP For Dummies
  0-7645-1760-0
- VBA For Dummies
  0-7645-3989-2
- Wireless All In-One Desk Reference
  For Dummies
  0-7645-7496-5
- Wireless Home Networking For Dummie
  0-7645-3910-8